Learning from Violent Extremist Attacks: Behavioural Sciences Insights for Practitioners and Policymakers is a significant piece of work written with the security practitioner and policy-maker in mind. It is a collection of thoughtful contributions by a community of social scientists, led by Dr. Majeed Khader and his fellow editors, applying their training, scholarship, and experience to try and unpack various facets of the complex phenomenon of violent extremism we are faced with today.

The project is ambitious and formidable in its comprehensiveness — tackling a full range of issues and questions on the subject — from the individual and social psychology of extremists, the strength and limits of different assessment tools, and of approaches to rehabilitation, to societal resilience, crisis planning, and consequence management in a public engagement terrain permeated by social media. And, for good measure, it even raises the potential boon for policing and counter-terrorism agencies that can accrue from tapping smart technology in a smart city like Singapore.

Notwithstanding its very broad range, stretched and covered in more than 600 pages, the reader will be pleased to find that its individual chapter-pieces are typically written in a succinct, balanced, and pointed manner, making them reader-friendly and very accessible. More importantly, the reader will also find that many of these pieces consistently succeed in drawing out practical lessons, raising crucial questions including prevailing knowledge deficits (which researchers can follow up on), and frequently offer valuable insights, which can only better inform and inspire policy and practice.

Dr. Majeed and his team are to be congratulated for this very commendable collaborative work. It reflects a healthy and growing community of social scientists in Singapore and the region who are focused and engaged in a subject of real and urgent importance to the well-being of our various societies. And it has produced this book which I would strongly recommend as an essential read for all who want to know more and to better understand this complex subject we are still grappling with today.

Mr. Benny Lim
Permanent Secretary, Ministry of Home Affairs (2005–2011), and Permanent Secretary, National Security and Intelligence Coordination (2011–2016)

This book is an essential read for those kept awake at night wondering how they can stop the next attack and what to do the day after. Majeed Khader and his team of behavioural scientists have provided lessons that inform both policy-making and operational tactics. For the academic researcher, the book also offers a rare Asian perspective on a global scourge.

Mr. Ali Soufan
CEO of The Soufan Group, author of The Black Banners & Anatomy of Terror, and former FBI Supervisory Special Agent

This is both an important and timely publication. The rich and textured offerings within go some considerable way to bridging the gap between academia and practitioners in the field of countering violent extremism and radicalisation studies. The sheer wealth of insights will repay close reading on the part of the expert, practitioner, or diligent layman.

Dr. Shashi Jayakumar
Senior Fellow, and Head, Centre of Excellence for National Security, RSIS, and Executive Coordinator, Future Issues and Technology

Learning from Violent Extremist Attacks

Behavioural Sciences Insights for Practitioners and Policymakers

Learning from Violent Extremist Attacks

Behavioural Sciences Insights for Practitioners and Policymakers

editors

Majeed Khader
Ministry of Home Affairs, Singapore &
Nanyang Technological University (NTU), Singapore

Neo Loo Seng
Jethro Tan
Ministry of Home Affairs, Singapore

Damien D Cheong
S. Rajaratnam School of International Studies (RSIS), NTU, Singapore

Jeffery Chin
Ministry of Home Affairs, Singapore

World Scientific

EW JERSEY • LONDON • SINGAPORE • BEIJING • SHANGHAI • HONG KONG • TAIPEI • CHENNAI • TOKYO

Published by

World Scientific Publishing Co. Pte. Ltd.
5 Toh Tuck Link, Singapore 596224
USA office: 27 Warren Street, Suite 401-402, Hackensack, NJ 07601
UK office: 57 Shelton Street, Covent Garden, London WC2H 9HE

British Library Cataloguing-in-Publication Data
A catalogue record for this book is available from the British Library.

LEARNING FROM VIOLENT EXTREMIST ATTACKS
Behavioural Sciences Insights for Practitioners and Policymakers

ISBN 978-981-3275-43-0

For any available supplementary material, please visit
https://www.worldscientific.com/worldscibooks/10.1142/11134#t=suppl

Desk Editor: Karimah Samsudin

Typeset by Stallion Press
Email: enquiries@stallionpress.com

Contents

Acknowledgements

This book is a testimonial to the valued relationships and collaborations that the editors have developed with subject matter experts over the years. Thus, we would like to acknowledge the generous help and support that we have received from all the remarkable people involved in this book. Without their support, this book would not have become a reality.

We would like to take this opportunity to thank World Scientific Publishing, the publisher of this book, and in particular, Ms. Karimah Samsudin, the editor who has supported us tirelessly throughout this book project.

Next, we are profoundly grateful to the authors who are gracious enough to contribute their expertise and for their faith in the project.

A number of the Home Team Behavioural Sciences Centre (HTBSC) colleagues gave generously of their time, insights, and administrative support. We would like to acknowledge Ms. Pamela Goh, Ms. Verity Er, and Ms. Vaishnavi Honnavalli for providing valuable assistance and reviews that greatly improved the coherence and readability of the book. Ms. Ruth Gan and Ms. Rae Yi Yap also provided extremely valuable formatting input during the final edit of the book. They have been superb.

This project is not an official government endeavour and has not received government funding in any way. The views expressed here represent the views of the authors mainly and the editors. They do not represent the official views of the Government of Singapore in anyway. Despite this, we have received encouragement. For this, we are grateful to Mr. Pang Kin Keong, Mr. Leo Yip, Mr. Lai Chung Han, Mr. Loh Ngai Seng, Ms. Goh Soon Poh, Mr. Puah Kok Keong, Mr. T. Raja Kumar, Mr. Hoong Wee Teck, Mr. Desmond Chin, Mr. Eric Yap Wee Teck, Mr. Clarence Yeo, and Mr. Teo Tze Fang for their support and guidance which have greatly contributed to the rigour of this book project. We are also thankful for the support from Mr. Abdul Jalil, Mr. S. Krishnan, Dr. Rosleenda Mohamad Ali, and Ms. Bridget Roberts. In addition, we would like to express our most sincere gratitude to Ms. Chua Lee Hoong for her valuable support. We would also like to express our appreciation to the support provided by our valued-partners from Ministry of Home Affairs [Joint Training Centre (JTC), Heritage Development Unit (HDU), Centre for Protective Security Studies (CPSS)], Naval Criminal Investigative Service (NCIS) Singapore Field Office, Universitas Indonesia (UI), The Japanese Embassy of Singapore, and Southeast Asia Regional Centre for Counter Terrorism (SEARCCT). At Nanyang Technological University (NTU), our thanks go to Associate Professor Joyce Pang, Associate Professor Ringo Ho, and Associate Professor Kumar Ramakrishna for their support, guidance, and help with this project.

Furthermore, we wish to convey our heartfelt appreciation to our colleagues at HTBSC and National Security Studies Programme for their personal and professional support. Their moral support and dedicated involvement were our motivational force for this project.

Finally, the editors would like to take this opportunity to thank the members of our families. Majeed is deeply thankful to Leong Tscheng Yee, Tasneem and Raouf, and his mum Hawa for their unconditional love and support. Loo Seng is deeply indebted to his wife, Onpapha, and his three children, Xi Zhen, An Qi, and An Ping, for their love and support. Jethro could not have completed this book without the support of his loving wife, Peiwei. Damien would like to thank V, M, and C for their unwavering dedication, and K, NSSP, and RSIS colleagues for their continued support. Jeffery is grateful to his wife, Mol, for her love, understanding, and unwavering support.

About the Contributors

Ahmad Naufalul UMAM is Psychology Lecturer at Mercu Buana University Indonesia, and has been working with Indonesia's National Counter-Terrorism Agency (Badan Nasional Penanggulangan Teroris, or BNPT) as in-prison facilitator and observer since 2016. Umam completed his Master degree in Science of Social Psychology at Universitas Indonesia and his undergraduate degree at Universitas Indonesia and University of Queensland. His research interests are the expression of religious ideology in daily activities and the interaction between media use and cognition. Several works that have been presented include *Challenge of Multiculturalism: Islam in Indonesia from Psychological Point of View* at UIN Jakarta 2015 International Conference of Southeast Asian Islam; *Hijab Fashion Interpretation among Fashion Professionals and General Public in Indonesia* at Biennial Seminar of Semiotic, Pragmatic and Culture 2016 Conference in Faculty of Cultural Studies UI; *The Need for Cognitive Closure and Belief in Conspiracy Theories: An Exploration of the Role of Religious Fundamentalism in Cognition* at Asia-Pacific Research in Social Sciences and Humanities 2016 Conference in Depok, Indonesia; and *The Threatened Thought: Cognition and Conspiracy Theory* at Asian Association of Social Psychology 2017 Conference in Massey University, New Zealand.

Bilveer SINGH is a Singapore citizen. He received his basic education at the then University of Singapore and graduated with Honours in Political Science from the National University of Singapore. He received his MA and PhD in International Relations from the Australian National University (ANU). He is currently an Associate Professor at the National University of Singapore (NUS) and an Adjunct Senior Fellow at the Centre of Excellence for National Security (CENS), S. Rajaratnam School of International Studies (RSIS), Nanyang Technological University (NTU), Singapore. He specialises in regional security issues with a focus on Indonesia. He has published widely on issues relating to great power relations in Southeast Asia, Indonesian politics and security issues, as well as on Singapore's politics and foreign policy. Two of his recent publications include *Quest for Political Power: Communist Subversion and Militancy in Singapore,* (Singapore: Marshall Cavendish, 2015), and *Understanding Singapore Politics*, (Singapore: World Scientific, 2017). He has also authored a Working Paper for Chiangrai University titled *The Threat of Terrorism in ASEAN: Focus on Indonesia* (2017).

Bridget ROBERT is Head Psychologist of a Counter-Terrorism Operations Division within the Ministry of Home Affairs (MHA), Singapore. She works with a team of psychologists undertaking psychological assessments and intervention in the rehabilitation of detainees and those released under supervision. The team also leads in the development and undertaking of psychological research of direct application to the field of counter-terrorism.

Damien D. CHEONG is a Research Fellow at the National Security Studies Programme (NSSP), S. Rajaratnam School of International Studies (RSIS), Nanyang Technological University (NTU), Singapore. Prior to this, he was Research Fellow and Coordinator of the Homeland Defence Programme at the Centre of Excellence for National Security (CENS) at RSIS from 2011 to 2017. He has researched and written on various topics related to homeland security, strategic communication, and political violence. His current research focuses on small state security.

Dashalini KATNA is currently a Ph.D. candidate in psychology at the School of Social Sciences, NTU. Her research is focused on intra- and intergroup dynamics that motivate and mobilise individuals in the context of countering threats of extremist violence and crime convergence, and how emergent trends arising from these interactions may inform and enhance homeland and global security practices.

Eunice TAN is Senior Psychologist and Assistant Director of the Operations and Leadership Psychology (OLP) Branch, Home Team Behavioural Sciences Centre (HTBSC), Ministry of Home Affairs (MHA), Singapore. As a pioneering member of the centre, she played an integral role in the development and setup of the research and training centre, particularly in the area of leadership assessment, selection, development, and training. Her early forays into behavioural sciences research at HTBSC involved understanding the radicalisation processes of terrorists. Her presentation and work on a radicalisation model of terrorists, based on the Singapore experience with terrorism in 2002, won the Chris Hatcher Award for Best Vision during the 34th Annual Conference of the Society for Police and Criminal Psychology (SPCP) in 2007. Eunice's main research interests include understanding offending behaviour, radicalisation processes of extremists, the assessment and selection of high potentials, issues in critical incident command, crisis leadership, and command leadership in the public safety and security context. As part of her secondary duties, Eunice has been a team psychologist with the Crisis Negotiation Unit of the Singapore Police Force (SPF) since 2007. In addition, she is also part of the Critical Incident Stress Intervention and Support team led by the Singapore Police Psychological Services Division. Eunice holds an MSc in Investigative and Forensic Psychology from the University of Liverpool (U.K.). She is also a member of the Society of Police and Criminal Psychology (SPCP), USA.

Gabriel ONG is Deputy Director with the Psychological and Correctional Rehabilitation Division (PCRD) of the Singapore Prison Service (SPS). Concurrently, he is a Senior Assistant Director with the Resilience and Safety Psychology Branch (RSP) of the Home Team Behavioural Sciences Centre (HTBSC). Both PCRD and

HTBSC are psychology units in the Ministry of Home Affairs (MHA), Singapore. His primary roles at SPS include overseeing the evaluation of rehabilitation programmes and regimes. Prior to this, he was involved in forensic risk assessment and offender rehabilitation, specifically in the area of sexual and violent offending. His primary roles at the HTBSC include overseeing research on issues such as violent extremism and resilience. He holds a Doctor of Psychology (Clinical) from the James Cook University (Singapore). He has been with the Ministry of Home Affairs (MHA), Singapore, since 2001.

Jane QUEK is Psychologist with the Resilience, Safety and Security Psychology branch in the Home Team Behavioural Sciences Centre (HTSBC). Her early forays into behavioural sciences research studying the peer influence on radicalisation, and assessment centres, and leadership selection. She was also part of a team of psychologists that pioneered an Assessment Centre for potential Home Team Uniform Public Service Leaders. Other areas of her work include studying the psychological motivations of xenophobia and related social conflicts. She is also holding concurrent appointment as a psychologist supporting the Crisis Negotiation Unit and Critical Stress Incident Management in the Singapore Police Force. She is trained in counselling, suicide intervention, and victim care. She holds a BA in Psychology from the Nanyang Technological University (NTU), Singapore.

Jasminder SINGH is Senior Analyst at the International Centre for Political Violence and Terrorism Research (ICPVTR) at the S. Rajaratnam School of International Studies (RSIS), Nanyang Technological University (NTU), Singapore. Jasminder has a Masters in Strategic Studies from RSIS. He was previously a Research Associate with Strategic Nexus Consultancy. He has written extensively on terrorism in Southeast Asia, with a focus on Indonesia and the Philippines. His research focus is on the sources of extremism and terrorism in Southeast Asia and on what needs to be done to counter the threat. Jasminder speaks Bahasa Indonesia and has done extensive field research in Indonesia.

Jeffery CHIN is Senior Psychologist at the Home Team Behavioural Sciences Centre (HTSBC), and Senior Psychologist with the Police Psychological Services Division. Key areas of his work at the centre include applied research in violent extremism, investigative interviewing, deception, and leadership during critical incidents. As a concurrent appointment, Jeffery also supports the operations of the Crisis Negotiation Unit, Singapore Police Force as a psychologist. Jeffery holds a Master's degree in Investigative and Forensic Psychology from the University of Liverpool (U.K.). His Master's dissertation topic was on critical incident leadership.

Jessie Janny THENARIANTO is a student at School of Psychology, Universitas Ciputra Surabaya. She is actively involved in Mental Health, Educational, and Developmental Psychology (MED-PSY) Research Center at Universitas Ciputra. Having a growing interest in the field of forensic and criminal psychology, she recently took part in the 8th Indonesian Association of Forensic Psychology (APSIFOR) National Scientific Meeting. Her works include topics related to the adolescence and young adulthood context, such as burnout, motivation, shame, self-leadership, and organizational behaviour.

Jethro TAN is Senior Researcher with the Home Team Behavioural Sciences Centre (HTBSC). His research focuses on whole-of-society resilience in the aftermath of crisis. He studies a variety of security related issues pertaining to the day after terror scenarios, such as crisis communications, online falsehoods, and psychological trauma. Jethro is currently pursuing a Master of Social Science (Psychology) from the National University of Singapore (NUS).

Jony Eko YULIANTO teaches Social Psychology at Universitas Ciputra Surabaya. He is an active member of Indonesian Psychologist Association, Indonesian Social Psychologist Association, and has written more than 30 op-ed articles in national newspapers in Indonesia. He holds a Bachelor of Psychology from Universitas Airlangga Surabaya and a Master of Arts in Social Psychology from Universitas Gadjah Mada Yogyakarta. Some of his works related to criminal, forensic, law, and political psychology spread from the topic of women inmates, hoax information, and forgiveness issue in law context. The interest of studying Internet and human behaviour began when he received a prestigious grant from Directorate of Research and Higher Education in Indonesia for the project titled *Consumer trust on e-commerce business in Indonesia: An explorative study* (Grant Number: 022/UC-LPP/ST/II/2016).

Joseph FRANCO specialises in countering violent extremism (CVE), counter-insurgency, and counter-terrorism. As Research Fellow with the Centre of Excellence for National Security (CENS) at S. Rajaratnam School of International Studies (RSIS), Joseph examines terrorist networks in maritime Southeast Asia and best practices in countering violent extremism (CVE). He obtained his MSc in International Relations at RSIS through an ASEAN Graduate Scholarship. Joseph previously worked for the Chief of Staff, Armed Forces of the Philippines (AFP), and the J3, AFP; researching extensively on internal conflict, peacekeeping operations, defence procurement, Asia-Pacific security, and special operations forces. Joseph was also the lead writer of the AFP Peace and Development Team Manual — a novel, community-based approach to insurgency. He is a frequent resource person for international media such as *Time*, *Channel NewsAsia*, and *Deutsche Welle*.

Joshua D. FREILICH is a member of the Criminal Justice Department at John Jay College. He is Creator and co-Director of the U.S. Extremist Crime Database (ECDB). Freilich's research focuses on the causes of and responses to terrorism, measurement issues, and criminology theory, especially environmental criminology and crime prevention.

Joyce S. PANG received her undergraduate training in psychology from Smith College, MA, U.S., and her PhD in personality psychology from University of Michigan, MI, U.S. As a personality psychologist, she is interested in the assessment of individual differences and in making finer distinctions between personality dimensions in order to increase theoretical understanding of how personality affects behaviour. In all her research, Joyce adopts a "person *x* situation" perspective to understand how individual differences predict different reactions within different social contexts, which in turn lead to important personal and social outcomes. Joyce S. Pang is the current Associate Professor and Head of Psychology at Nanyang Technological University (NTU), Singapore.

Ken CHEN XINGYU is Behavioural Sciences Research Analyst at the Home Team Behavioural Sciences Centre (HTBSC). Chen's research is in the areas of resilience, safety, and security psychology which is supplemented by his background in communications. He has researched the psychological factors driving the spread of information during situations of high uncertainty such as scares and conflicts. As a Behavioural Sciences Research Analyst, Chen has presented to Home Team officers, community leaders, and Home Team psychologists on a variety of topics such as fake news and resilience to terror attacks. He has also presented about resilience on the day after terror incidents at Safety, Security Watch Group (SSWG) seminars to institutes of higher learning as well as industry partners. His current research interests include online misinformation, social resilience, individual crisis preparedness, and sentiment analysis.

Kumar RAMAKRISHNA is a tenured Associate Professor and Head Policy Studies, as well as Coordinator of the National Security Studies Programme (NSSP), in the Office of the Executive Deputy Chairman, S. Rajaratnam School of International Studies (RSIS), in Nanyang Technological University (NTU), Singapore. He was previously the Head of the Centre of Excellence for National Security (CENS) at RSIS from 2006 to 2015. A historian by background, Associate Professor Ramakrishna has been a frequent speaker on counter-terrorism before local and international audiences, a regular media commentator on counter-terrorism, and an established author in numerous internationally refereed journals. His first book, *Emergency Propaganda: The Winning of Malayan Hearts and Minds*

1948–1958 (2002) was described by the International History Review as "required reading for historians of Malaya, and for those whose task is to counter insurgents, guerrillas, and terrorists". His second major book, *Radical Pathways: Understanding Muslim Radicalisation in Indonesia* (2009) was featured as one of the top 150 books on terrorism and counter-terrorism in the respected journal *Perspectives on Terrorism*, which identified Associate Professor Ramakrishna as "one of Southeast Asia's leading counterterrorism experts". His most recent books are *Islamist Terrorism and Militancy in Indonesia: The Power of the Manichean Mindset* (2015), *Original Sin? Revising the Revisionist Critique of the 1963 Operation Coldstore in Singapore* (2015), and *Singapore Chronicles: Emergency* (2016).

Leevia DILLON is a Doctoral student at John Jay College of Criminal Justice. She is a Research Assistant for Dr. Freilich on the federally funded project, the Extremist Crime Database (ECDB). Her research interests include violent extremism, online radicalization, threat assessment, and cybercrimes.

Loo Seng NEO is Principal Behavioural Sciences Research Analyst with the Home Team Behavioural Sciences Centre (HTBSC) at the Ministry of Home Affairs (MHA), Singapore. For the past 12 years, Loo Seng has been specialising in the area of violent extremism, particularly in the fields of online radicalisation, online threat assessment, pre-attack warning signs, and psychology of violent extremism. He works with a team of research analysts undertaking behavioural sciences research on violent extremism, resilience, and intergroup conflict. He has presented at many international conferences, trained law enforcement officers, and published many government research reports and peer-reviewed journals and book chapters on the topic of violent extremism. He has also co-edited a book titled *Combating Violent Extremism and Radicalisation in the Digital Era* (2016), and a four-volume compendium titled *A Behavioural Sciences Approach to Understanding Terrorism* (2017). Loo Seng is currently pursuing his PhD in psychology, researching on the personality profile of violent extremists at Nanyang Technological University (NTU), Singapore.

Majeed KHADER is Director of the Home Team Behavioural Sciences Centre (HTBSC) under the Ministry of Home Affairs (MHA), and Chief Police Psychologist. Dr. Majeed is also the Chief Psychologist of the Ministry of Home Affairs (MHA). A trained hostage negotiator, his previous operational duties include being the Deputy Commander of the Crisis Negotiation Unit and a trainer with the negotiation unit. He teaches criminal psychology as an Assistant Professor (Adjunct) at the School of Social Sciences at Nanyang Technology University (NTU), Singapore. For the past 25 years, Dr. Majeed has overseen the development of psychological services in the areas of stress, resilience, employee selection, deception psychology, leadership, crisis negotiations, crime profiling, and crisis psychology. For his work, he was awarded the National Day Public Administration Award (Bronze) in 2006 by the President of Singapore and, once again, the Public Administration Award Silver in 2014. A pioneer forensic psychologist, Dr. Majeed holds a Master's degree (with Distinction) in Forensic Psychology from the University of Leicester (U.K.) and a PhD in Psychology (specialising in personality and crisis leadership) from the University of Aberdeen, Scotland. Dr. Majeed has been invited as a speaker to organisations in Indonesia, Malaysia, Japan, Canada, Hong Kong, the U.K., and the U.S. to share on crime psychology, terrorism, and leadership. He has also presented at the FBI, NCIS, and the RCMP. He has been the Chairman of the Asian Conference of Criminal and Operations Psychology thrice. He is the Asian Director of the U.S.-based Society of Police and Criminal Psychology (SPCP), and a member of the Asia Pacific Association of Threat Assessment Professionals. He is a Registered Psychologist with the Singapore Psychological Society, and a member of the British and American Psychological Societies. He has contributed to several book chapters and published widely in peer-reviewed journals such as *Journal of Research in Personality*, *Journal of Occupational Health Psychology*, *Psychology & Health*, *Cognition and Emotion*, *International Journal of Psychophysiology*,

Personality and Individual Differences, *International Journal of Police Science & Management*, *Journal of Police and Criminal Psychology*, and *Security Journal*.

Mirra Noor MILLA is currently a Social Psychologist and Lecturer at Faculty of Psychology, Universitas Indonesia. Her research experience on the topic of terrorism and radicalism and the deradicalisation intervention programme in cooperation with Indonesia's National Counter-Terrorism Agency. Milla completed her doctoral degree in Science of Social Psychology at Universitas Gadjah Mada, 2009, with a dissertation titled *Dinamika Psikologis Pelaku Teror; Studi tentang Identitas dan Pengambilan Keputusan Jihad di Luar Wilayah Konflik pada Terpidana Kasus Bom Bali*. Some of her other writings related to terrorism include *Mengapa Memilih Jalan Teror; Analisis Psikologis Pelaku Teror* (2010), "The impact of leader–follower interaction on the radicalisation of terrorist's minds: A study on the convicted Bali Bombers" in the *Asian Journal of Social Psychology*, "An introduction to radicalism of civil society movement in Indonesia: Intersection and shifting ideology between Socialist and Jihadist" in *Social Science Research Network* (2015), and *Radikalisasi online pada Kelompok Teroris di Indonesia*, a book chapter in *Psikologi dan Teknologi Informasi* (2016). Milla has actively presented her research on terrorism and radicalism at various international scientific forums.

Muhammad Faizal Bin ABDUL RAHMAN is Research Fellow with the Centre of Excellence for National Security (CENS) at the S. Rajaratnam School of International Studies (RSIS). Faizal previously served with the Ministry of Home Affairs (MHA), Singapore, where he was a Deputy Director and had facilitated international engagements with foreign security counterparts. He also had postings in the Singapore Police Force where he supervised and performed intelligence analysis, achieving several commendation awards including the Minister for Home Affairs National Day Award (2009) for operational and analysis efficiency; and in the National Security Research Centre (NSRC) at the National Security

Coordination Secretariat (NSCS), where he led a team to research emergent trends in domestic security and monitor terrorism-related developments. Faizal also has certifications in Counter-Terrorism, Crime Prevention, and Business Continuity Planning. His research interests are Counter-Terrorism, Strategic Foresight and Intelligence, and Implications of Global Trends on Homeland Security.

Nur Aisyah ABDUL RAHMAN is a Behavioural Sciences Research Analyst with the Home Team Behavioural Sciences Centre (HTBSC). Her main area of research revolves around maintaining social cohesion. Aisyah has done some research on prejudice, hate incidents, maintain racial and religious cohesion in a multicultural organization, Islamophobia, and right-wing extremism. She has done seminars and trainings for police officers, religious leaders, and community leaders. Aisyah graduated summa cum laude from the University at Buffalo, with a bachelor's degree in in Psychology. She has been a trained volunteer Victim Care Officer (VCO) with the Singapore Police Force since 2014, where she provides support to victims of sexual crimes. She believes in tolerance and respect, as well as in having a robust collection of sunglasses.

Nur Elissa Ruzzi'eanne Bte RAFI'EE is a Behavioural Sciences Research Analyst with the Home Team Behavioural Sciences Centre (HTBSC) at the Ministry of Home Affairs (MHA), Singapore. Ruzzie has been specialising in the area of Islamophobia, particularly in the areas of countering Islamophobia in communities. Ruzzie is a graduate from University at Buffalo, New York State University, U.S.

Omer Ali SAIFUDEEN is Senior Assistant Director at the National Security Research Centre, National Security Coordination Secretariat, Prime Minister's Office, Singapore.

Pamela GOH is a Behavioural Sciences Research Analyst with the Home Team Behavioural Sciences Centre (HTBSC). As a research analyst, her individual research portfolio is encapsulated by the resilience theme, and it includes crowd psychology and cyber hygiene.

In essence, she is interested in understanding what contributes to the individual, community, and national's resilience in the event of a crisis from these perspectives. A key research area that Pamela looks into is the role of non-governmental organisations (NGOs) in the event of a violent extremist attack, and how civil societies in general can contribute to and complement Singapore's governmental efforts. Together with her team in HTBSC, the other areas that she has looked into are Singaporeans' perceptions to national resilience, cyber resilience, and fake news. Apart from resilience, Pamela is also interested in and has helped to write research papers that are terrorism-related. In addition to research, she also conducts seminars and trainings for government stakeholders, community leaders, and private companies. Pamela also holds other appointments in HTBSC, including being an internship manager for HTBSC's internship programme, as well as a Victim Care Officer (VCO) under the Singapore Police Force.

Raymond LEE is a trained fire officer and para counsellor with the Singapore Civil Defence Force (SCDF). He is currently holding the appointment of Senior Critical Incident Management Officer with EBSC, the psychology unit of SCDF. Captain Raymond provides psychological support for SCDF operations, manages critical incidents and also enhances the operation psychology resilience of SCDF frontliners through conducting relevant lessons.

Sheryl CHUA is Psychologist with the Ministry of Home Affairs (MHA), Singapore. In the Home Team Behavioural Sciences Centre (HTBSC), she is part of the Operations and Leadership Psychology (OLP) Branch. Her work involves developing the Assessment Centre exercises for the selection and assessment of scholars and high-potential officers. Her research in HTBSC is in the areas of crisis and command leadership and she conducts training in these topics for Home Team leaders. Sheryl is also the Internship Manager in HTBSC, and her work involves selection and supervision of interns. She is a certified para-counsellor and is trained in critical incident stress management (CISM), suicide first aid, and psychological first aid. Sheryl completed her Ph.D. in Psychology with Nanyang Technological University (NTU), Singapore in 2017. Her thesis employed the use of qualitative ethnographic interviews, scale development methodology, and quantitative analyses to examine the influence of fear of failure and *kiasuism* on entrepreneurial intention. Her research interests include crisis and command leadership, critical incident management, crisis ready mindset, entrepreneurship, and *kiasuism*.

Shi Hui TEE is Behavioural Sciences Research Analyst with the Home Team Behavioural Sciences Centre (HTBSC) at the Ministry of Home Affairs (MHA), Singapore. Shi Hui specialises in research on violent extremism. Her research areas include the motivations and personality of lone wolf violent extremists in both terrorist organisations as well as right-wing organisations. She also looks into the development of trust relationships between violent extremists in the online community. She has also held seminars and conducted trainings for officers and relevant stakeholders on the topic of violent extremism. She is a member of the Online Radicalisation Research Community of Practice (ORRCOP) that comprises Singaporean practitioners and subject matter experts involved in research related to online radicalisation. Shi Hui has published several research reports on violent extremism and related topics.

Shuktika BOSE completed her BPsySc. from Griffith University, Australia, and both her BSocSc (Psych) (Hons) and MPsych (Clin) from Bond University, Australia. As a Clinical Psychology Registrar, Shuktika provides psychological services in youth mental health and corrective services. She was the 13th International Visiting Researcher with the Singaporean Ministry of Home Affairs, completing an eight-week research project in 2017, addressing *Psychological First Aid: Models, Cultural Differences, and Implications for Implementation in Singapore*. Shuktika is also a Bond University Lecturer in the criminology field, and tutor in the Psychology and Core Curriculum fields. Her research areas include psychological first aid, community perceptions of crime, and perceptions of domestic and family violence.

Siew Maan DIONG is currently Principal Psychologist with the Singapore Civil Defence Force (SCDF). She oversees the psychological resilience and crisis management programmes for firefighters and paramedic officers in the SCDF. Together with her team of psychologists and counsellors, she has developed and enhanced the counselling and crisis management framework as well as peer support programmes in SCDF. Recently, the team has also completed a series of psychological preparation training to help firefighters and paramedics deal with terror-related incidents. Concurrently, Siew Maan is also the Deputy Director of the Home Team Behavioural Sciences Centre (HTBSC). She was involved in the development of assessment framework to select high potential uniformed officers for the Ministry. She has also trained uniformed officers in crisis and command leadership. Prior to her current appointment, Siew Maan has accumulated more than 10 years of experience as a psychologist with the Singapore Police Force. Siew Maan has helped to coordinate several psychological operations to monitor and assess the police officers' morale during major operations, and was also involved in supporting an overseas police humanitarian operation during the Asian Tsunami in 2006.

Stephanie NEUBRONNER is Research Fellow in the National Security Studies Programme (NSSP) at the S. Rajaratnam School of International Studies (RSIS), Nanyang Technological University (NTU), Singapore. Her research interests include sociocultural identity, governance and social relations, and the influence of new media. Prior to joining RSIS, Stephanie was a researcher at the Institute of Policy Studies (IPS), Lee Kuan Yew School of Public Policy (LKYSPP), National University of Singapore (NUS).

Steven M. CHERMAK is Professor in the School of Criminal Justice at the Michigan State University, U.S. He studies domestic terrorism, media coverage of crime and justice issues, and the effectiveness of specific policing strategies. Chermak's publications have appeared in *Justice Quarterly*, *Terrorism and Political Violence*, *Crime and Delinquency*, and the *Journal of Quantitative Criminology*.

Thomas Koruth SAMUEL is, at present, Director of the Digital Strategic Communications Division (DSCD) with the Southeast Asia Regional Centre for Counter-Terrorism (SEARCCT), which is under the purview of the Ministry of Foreign Affairs, Malaysia. He started off as a volunteer Health Officer for World Vision East Timor in 2003, and then moved to the Research and Publications division in SEARCCT in 2004. He served as the division's director from 2010 to 2016 before assuming his current position with the DSCD. He has an honours degree in Biomedical Technology (2000) and a Master's degree in Strategic and Defence Studies (2005) from the University of Malaya, Malaysia. He is currently pursuing his PhD in the area of youth radicalisation. His main areas of research include the narratives of the terrorists and the subsequent counter-narratives, the radicalisation process, strategic communications, and youth involvement in terrorism. He is also very interested in mediation, conflict resolution, and "spoiler management" during times of conflict. He lectures frequently on counter-terrorism and international security and has delivered lectures in numerous countries. He has also represented Malaysia and led delegations as an officer for the Ministry of Foreign Affairs. He has written several articles, papers, and monographs, and has been interviewed on radio. He is, at present, Senior Fellow with the International Centre of Excellence for Countering Violent Extremism (Hedayah Centre) based in Abu Dhabi, United Arab Emirates.

Vaishnavi HONNAVALLI has an undergraduate degree in Psychology and a master's each in Criminology and Forensic Psychology from the U.K. As a postgraduate student, her core area of research included rehabilitative studies and perspective studies on criminal behaviour. Currently, she is Behavioural Sciences Research Analyst at the Home Team Behavioural Sciences Centre (HTBSC), Ministry of Home Affairs (MHA), Singapore. She has been with the research and training outfit for close to two years, conducting research in the area of online radicalisation, leadership in violent extremist groups, and the psychology of violent extremism. She is part of a core team that regularly conducts trainings and workshops for law enforcement officers as well as organisations in the private sector on these topics. She has published many research reports on the topic of violent extremism, as well as contributed to books written on violent extremism and child abuse. She enjoys sharing her research findings with practitioners, policymakers, and experts at various platforms, and is enthusiastic about the dynamic and evolving research on violent extremism. She has also co-edited a four-volume compendium titled *A Behavioural Sciences Approach to Understanding Terrorism*. She is a member of the British Psychological Society (BPS).

Verity ER is Behavioural Sciences Research Analyst at the Home Team Behavioural Sciences Centre (HTBSC) under the Ministry of Home Affairs (MHA), Singapore. Together with a team of researchers, Verity explores how crises, such as violent extremist attacks, can adversely impact race and religion, as well as *vice versa* — one of which is the phenomenon of religious fundamentalism. Beside looking at religious fundamentalism in secular states, Verity has also previously studied such inclinations in Aceh, a Muslim-majority area. She has also delved into other areas of research on youth extremism, Islamophobia, and the psychological motivations behind hate incidents, particularly focusing on how community cohesion would be implicated. She is also a trainer for Home Team officers on how to handle race and religious issues in the workplace. Verity graduated with a Bachelor of Arts in Psychology from the University at Buffalo–Singapore Institute of Management program.

Wahyu CAHYONO is Researcher and practitioner in the field of radicalism and violent extremism in the Laboratory of Political Psychology under the Faculty of Psychology, Universitas Indonesia (UI). She completed her Master's Degree in Psychology of Social Intervention at UI in 2005. In recent years, Wahyu got involved in identification and deradicalisation activities together with BNPT. Some related researches of Wahyu are *Measuring Radicalism Using Impilicit Attitude Test* (2016) and *Use of Internet in Radicalization: Social Network Analysis on Stage Radicalization* (ongoing). In addition, Wahyu also actively became a consultant for the ministry of social wellness and ministry of education in the issue of mental health and psychosocial support for their program.

Wei Jie TAN is Psychologist with the Emergency Behavioural Sciences and CARE Unit (Singapore Civil Defence Force), and had a stint with the Police Psychological Services Division in 2013. Wei

Jie's duties as a psychologist involves supporting the operations of emergency responders which includes psychological preparation for deployment for overseas operations, management of critical incidents, and assessment of morale for local operations. Wei Jie's research interests include various areas within Organisational Psychology and Psychometrics. In addition, Wei Jie is also interested in the area of enhancing public safety officer performance (e.g., through training or psychophysiological methods). Wei Jie obtained his Bachelor of Social Sciences in Psychology with Honours from the National University of Singapore (NUS), and has a Master of Science in Health Psychology from University College London.

Whinda YUSTISIA is Lecturer in Faculty of Psycholgy Universitas Indonesia (UI), and Researcher in Lab of Political Psychology, UI. She completed her master's degree in Social and Organizational Program from University of Exeter, U.K. She has involved in some of deradicalisation programs managed by BNPT (identification and rehabilitation programs). Her major research interests are on intergroup relationship, terrorism, political ideology, religious fundamentalism, and intergroup contact.

Whistine CHAI is Senior Psychologist from the Crime, Investigation, and Forensic Psychology Branch of the Home Team Behavioural Sciences Centre (HTBSC). Key areas of her work at the centre include applied research in risk assessment, threat assessment, criminal and crime behaviours, and drug profiling. As a concurrent appointment, Whistine also supports the operations of the Crisis Negotiation Unit and Critical Stress Incident Management, Singapore Police Force as a psychologist. An Honours Graduate from the National University of Singapore, Whistine also holds a Master's degree (with Distinction) in Clinical Forensic Psychology from the world-renowned Institute of Psychiatry, Psychology and Neuroscience, King's College London, U.K. For her Master's degree, she was awarded two awards by King's College London; namely, The John Gunn Prize for the Highest Overall Mark, as well as The Sheilagh Hodgins Prize for the Highest Dissertation Mark on the programme.

Learning from Violent Extremist Attacks: An Introduction

MAJEED KHADER*, LOO SENG NEO*, JETHRO TAN*, DAMIEN CHEONG†, and JEFFERY CHIN*

**Home Team Behavioural Sciences Centre, Ministry of Home Affairs, Singapore*
†National Security Studies Programme, S. Rajaratnam School of International Studies, Nanyang Technological University, Singapore

> As we observed in recent times, terrorists have started to use common tools — knives, vehicles — for their attacks, and we have to be prepared to respond to such attacks in Singapore. We look at what overseas forces do in response to attacks in their country — in London, in New York, in Paris. We *learn* from them, we *adapt* our tactics, our training and our response protocols to deal with some of these attacks of concern.
>
> — Law and Home Affairs Minister, K. Shanmugam (2017)

Introduction

The violent extremist threat is a clear and present one. The increasing number of attacks all over the world coupled with the emergence of groups like the Islamic State of Iraq and Syria (ISIS) underscore the unpredictability of such threats, and more importantly, how fast the violent extremism threat landscape has changed. The last few years, in particular, have witnessed enormous changes in how violent extremists have learned and evolved.

For example, the increased connectedness gifted by the advent of the Internet and social media has redefined the manifestation of violent extremism (which has affected societies for centuries), and blurred the geographical boundaries of violent extremism and the distinction between international and domestic security concerns. Serving as an effective conduit for communication, the Internet has been exploited by violent extremists, regardless of affiliations, for recruitment, propaganda creation and dissemination, sharing of vital information, and data mining purposes (Neo *et al.*, 2016), facilitating their capability to act and provide more opportunities for individuals to be radicalised online. At the same time, access to radical content that was previously ceded to physical interactions at clandestine locations, has gradually become the purview of the online milieu. These developments have inevitably led to the notable rise of more assertive, adaptive, and intelligent adversaries capable of perpetuating heinous acts of terror such as the London 7/7 attacks, the November 2015 Paris attacks, or the establishment of a physical caliphate in Syria and Iraq. The perpetrators (e.g., Al-Qaeda, ISIS) have defied conventional knowledge and assumptions that law enforcement had about violent extremism, and demonstrated how violent extremists are able to circumvent counter violent extremism measures and stay one step ahead of law enforcement.

Another uniqueness of modern violent extremism is that violent extremists also learn from each other and from the experiences of other groups whom they often seek to establish relationships and networks with (Rapoport, 2006). Members of the Jemaah Islamiyah (JI) have attended Al-Qaeda's training camp in Afghanistan during the 1990s, displaying some form of knowledge transfer relationship with Al-Qaeda. Non-jihadi groups, such as the Irish Republican Army (IRA), have also sought training and material support from like-minded international groups such as the Euskadi Ta Askatasuna

(ETA) in Spain. Such exchanges of skills and knowledge among the radical enclaves have created more opportunities for violent extremist groups to employ inventive tactics to spread their radical ideas and recruit new members. More importantly, such "learning" endeavours swaddle an added layer of complexity to the threat of violent extremism, and drive home the point that it is still on an ascendant trajectory which is unlikely to abate any time soon. In recent times, despite efforts by the U.S.-led coalition forces to reduce its presence on the ground (i.e., loss of physical territory, death of key leaders), ISIS has successfully exploited the Internet to maintain relevance amongst its supporters, coordinate and carry out attacks, and inspire lone wolf attacks in countries such as Australia, Canada, France, Germany, and Spain. The fact that these lone wolf attackers utilised non-conventional and readily available items (e.g., trucks, knives) further contributes to the unpredictable threat of violent extremism.

While most of the expression of violent extremism has its epicentre in the Middle East region, the myriad of studies by researchers have also warned and emphasised how Southeast Asia is not immune to the threat. This recent threat comes in the form of increased attacks in the region, as well as the influx of returning foreign fighters into Southeast Asia, be it to return to their home country or to join violent extremist groups in the region. These returning fighters have received training in ISIS's training camps and are hardened with war experience, both of which provides them with the skill set required to successfully carry out a deadly attack (Byman, 2017). In fact, such security concerns were thrust back into the limelight with the 2017 Marawi City siege in the Philippines, as well as the attacks on churches in Surabaya, Indonesia in 2018. These trends inevitably foster a keen sense of vulnerability one may have towards violent extremism and suggest that the threat has become uncomfortably close to home.

The Role of Behavioural Sciences and Psychology

Faced with the quandary, challenges, and responsibilities of ensuring the safety of the society, practitioners and policymakers have therefore come to realise the grim reality about the changing nature of the threat and how static planning, preparations, and assumptions would never be enough to counter it. This failure to understand the learning capabilities of violent extremists and to stay ahead of "the curve" may have led us to underestimate the threat and, hence, adversely impact law enforcement's capability to implement effective counter measures. Extant measures (e.g., tell-tale indicators) may also be rendered obsolete, and this directly affects the way law enforcement agencies pre-empt potential attacks.

While many have taken decisive steps to respond and mitigate the impact of an attack, the daunting task of countering violent extremism is still plagued by the lack of basic understanding of the phenomenon despite its prevalence, accentuating fears that violent extremism is an inevitable threat to every country. Thus, how can law enforcement learn to better deal with violent extremists? What can we learn from past attacks to ensure that the society is prepared to respond to an attack?

As such, this book titled *Learning from Violent Extremist Attacks: Behavioural Sciences Insights for Practitioners and Policymakers* attempts to fill a gap in the extant literature by offering a behavioural sciences approach to integrate our understanding of the threat of violent extremism, with knowledge drawn from diverse fields such as psychology, sociology, history, political science, technology, and communications, to identify the lessons learned and provide scientifically defensible interventions and approaches for both the practitioners and policymakers. And there is a good reason for doing so.

Human behaviour is directly relevant to the business of countering violent extremism; it is not only about understanding the mind and behaviour of the violent extremists, but also about predicting and managing behaviours effectively. As Khader (2011, pp. 5–6) opines, "behavioural sciences have much to say that should inform strategies for counterterrorism and counter-intelligence...officers need to be constantly ahead of these behavioural trends by understanding through research the psyche of individuals, groups and trends". Thus, the appreciation of how the field of behavioural sciences can act as force multipliers to understand violent extremists' behaviours and cognitions will give us greater confidence on the steps that are required to examine and recognise how violent extremists have "changed", so as to learn and stay on top of these developments. This is in line with what the Law and Home Affairs Minister K. Shanmugam mentioned, "we look at what overseas forces do in response to attacks in their country...we learn from them, we adapt our tactics, our training and our response protocols to deal with some of these attacks of concern" (Loke, 2017).

Understanding the Threat of Violent Extremism in Singapore

Singapore, like all countries in the world, faces the threat of violent extremism. Despite being a small nation-state, Singapore has successfully dealt with and neutralised the threat posed by violent extremists, from incidents such as the SQ117 hijack by four members of the Pakistan People's Party in 1991, the 2001 and 2002 arrests of Jemaah Islamiyah (JI) members under the country's Internal Security Act (ISA) for planning to launch a series of bomb attacks in Singapore, the threat of self-radicalised individuals such as Abdul Basher who are influenced by radical propaganda online, and more recently, to the threat posed by ISIS and its regional affiliates. The fact that these attacks did not happen, and were aptly and timely detected and contained by the Internal Security Department (ISD), the Ministry of Home Affairs (MHA), as well as the Ministry of Defence (MINDEF) suggests that a major part of this "success story" can be attributed to the security approach and apparatus that were implemented in Singapore. In fact, since 2002, close to 80 Singaporeans have been detained under the ISA for violent extremism-related activities (Loke, 2017).

Singapore's Approach to Countering Violent Extremism

Singapore's counter violent extremism strategy has been primarily led by the ISD and augmented by other agencies and community partners (e.g., Religious Rehabilitation Group (RRG) and the Muslim community) to achieve a whole-of-society approach. Besides just apprehending and detaining violent extremists to neutralise the threat posed, ISD has been "running a holistic rehabilitation programme in partnership with various Muslim organisations to ensure those detained for terrorist activity do not re-engage in such activity upon their release" (Counter-Terrorism Operations Division, 2014, p. 53). The programme provides three types of rehabilitation to the detainees (Counter-Terrorism Operations Division, 2014):

- *Psychological rehabilitation*: Psychological counselling and assessments are conducted by psychologists to assess the detainees' ability to "cope with the mental stressors of detention as well as their psychological reasoning to establish their propensity for hatred and violence, and vulnerability to radical influence...assess behavioural and cognitive aspects of the detainees' progress in rehabilitation" (p. 53).
- *Social rehabilitation*: Social support is provided to the detainees and their families to ensure that the detainees can re-integrate smoothly into society and that the family unit remains functional. Financial support, education for the children, and academic and vocational training for the detainees are some of the assistance provided by ISD to help the detainees and their families.
- *Religious rehabilitation*: Given that radical ideology plays an important role in the detainees' radicalisation process, this rehabilitation aspect of the programme focuses on educating them and their families about the proper teachings and interpretations of Islam. Conducted by volunteer religious teachers and scholars from the RRG,[1] regular counselling sessions are held to wean the detainees away from the radical ideology they had imbibed previously.

[1]The website of RRG is as follows: https://www.rrg.sg/.

Thus, the focus of the Singapore programme is to prevent those with a commitment to radical ideology from engaging in violent extremist-related activities and inoculate their families against radical beliefs.

Besides rehabilitation, anti-terrorism legislations such as the ISA have been used to complement the efforts by law enforcement agencies. In recent times, new legislations such as the Infrastructure Protection Bill and the amended Public Order Act have been enacted to reinforce security in iconic buildings and those that house essential services, and beef up security measures (e.g., deploying armed security officers) at events with large crowds respectively (Mokhtar, 2017).

It is also essential to recognise the role of MINDEF in working in tandem with the Home Team to fight against the threat of violent extremism and strengthen homeland security. As demonstrated in the SQ117 hijack in 1991 and the Laju Incident in 1974, the military played a significant role in neutralising the violent extremists and protecting the lives of Singaporeans. To step up their involvement, the Singapore Parliament amended the Singapore Armed Forces (SAF) Act in May 2007 to:

> Give the SAF additional powers against potential terror suspects, the setting-up of the Special Operations Task Force in 2009 equipped with the capabilities and equipment for peacetime contingencies, and the strengthening of interoperability between multiple agencies such as the Singapore Police Force through the NorthStar series of exercises (Lim, 2016, p. 39).

Over the years, the military has established specialist groups to deal with potential chemical, biological, radiological, and explosive threats posed by violent extremists (Lim, 2012). Furthermore, the military has strengthened its contributions towards the global fight against violent extremism, such as participating in the U.S.-led coalition against ISIS.

Efforts to counter violent extremism do not reside solely within the purview of law enforcement agencies. It is a concerted effort that requires the involvement of every citizen, regardless of race and religion. As the Security Education Command (2013, p. 39) emphasised:

> Countering the ideas thus requires more than just rehabilitating the terrorists. The battle has to be fought upstream, through a structured engagement programme to raise community awareness of the threat the militant ideas pose. The efforts are aimed at ensuring that militant ideas are marginalised, that they do not gain a foothold in the psyche of the mainstream and a consensus is forged with the community to counter terrorism.

In order to inoculate the community against radical ideology, there is therefore a need to forge "good" partnerships with the various community groups, and "reassure the various communities here that calls for violence by the Al-Qaeda and JI terrorists did not resonate with the local Muslim community" (Security Education Command, 2013, p. 35). More importantly, given the high likelihood of an attack, there is an urgent need to prepare the community for the "day after" scenario; prepare the community to build trust, strengthen bonds, and maintain and expand our common space with one another, so that in the aftermath of an attack, Singaporeans can stand together and provide a strong community response against violent extremism.

To sensitise, train, and mobilise the community in the fight against violent extremism, the national level SGSecure movement[2] was launched in September 2016 (Lam, 2017). It aims to equip the community with the knowledge on how to prevent and deal with an attack, and safeguard Singapore's way of life. There are three components to the movement: (1) stay alert — where Singaporeans are advised to keep a look out and report any security threat, thereby maintaining community vigilance; (2) stay united — where Singaporeans are advised to build stronger community ties and safeguard Singapore's racial and religious harmony, thereby maintaining community cohesion; and (3) stay strong — where Singaporeans are advised to learn how to protect ourselves and those

[2]The website of SGSecure is as follows: https://www.sgsecure.sg/.

around us if caught in an attack, thereby building community resilience. To date, the authorities have reached out to many Singaporeans about the SGSecure movement through initiatives such as Emergency Preparedness Days (Loke, 2017).

Not if But When

Despite these initiatives, the terror threat to Singapore is at its highest levels in recent years due to regional security developments. Multiple attacks targeting Singapore's neighbours (e.g., Jakarta attack in 2016, Puchong grenade attack in 2016, Marawi siege in 2017) as well as attempts to target Singapore (i.e., plans to attack Marina Bay with rockets from Batam in 2016), coupled with the increased number of individuals who are radicalised by ISIS's online propaganda, are indications of the dire threat facing Singapore. The release of the ISIS propaganda video featuring Singaporean, Megat Shahdan Abdul Samad, in September 2017 further attests to these security concerns.

Thus, there is the likelihood that these security developments in the region and their associated negative consequences (e.g., intercommunal tensions) would reverberate here. In addition, the "blowback effect" arising from the increased flow of returning foreign fighters from Syria and Iraq to Southeast Asia may inject "new life" into the regional radical enclaves and threaten the security of regional countries, including Singapore — i.e., these fighters are likely to be more skilled in attack tactics, more ideologically motivated, and able to access wider terror networks and links formed in Syria and Iraq. As Prime Minister Lee Hsien Loong mentioned during his National Day Rally speech, "In Singapore, we are taking this absolutely seriously. It is not just an external threat around us, it can also be, and it is, a domestic issue because Singaporeans are not uniquely immune to jihadist propaganda" (Prime Minister's Office, 2016).

In light of the increasingly complex threats of violent extremism, Singapore needs to remain vigilant, and step up its efforts to counter threats that would have catastrophic consequences and unravel Singapore's social fabric (Security Education Command, 2013).

In fact, eight key takeaways have been highlighted from the inaugural "Singapore Terrorism Threat Assessment Report 2017" by the Ministry of Home Affairs (Lam, 2017). They are:

(1) ISIS posed the biggest terror threat to Singapore, while the threat of Al-Qaeda and JI still remain.
(2) Singapore is being targeted by ISIS and other violent extremist groups for its involvement in international coalitions against violent extremism.
(3) There are concerns that individuals who are radicalised by the online propaganda of ISIS and other violent extremist groups may heed the call of these groups to carry out lone wolf attacks in Singapore.
(4) Singapore faces threat posed by some radicalised foreigners (e.g., Bangladeshi foreign workers, Indonesian domestic helpers) who are living and working in Singapore.
(5) ISIS also posed the most significant threat to the region for the last few years through its links to several regional attacks as well as connections to regional violent extremist groups.
(6) Regional authorities have uncovered many plots and arrested many violent extremists as part of their initiative to fight the threat of violent extremism.
(7) While there is no credible indication of imminent attack on Singapore, Singapore's security agencies remain on high alert.
(8) The community plays a critical role in the fight against violent extremism and there is a need to sensitise, train, and mobilise the community in the fight against terror (i.e., SGSecure movement).

In this regard, as the threat of violent extremism facing Singapore is set to "evolve" in relation to external influences (i.e., from regional or online) and persist in the years ahead, it is essential that law enforcement scrutinise these security trends and identify learning lessons to counter future attacks. Moreover, it is important not to discount the role of the community in supporting the herculean task of countering violent extremism as every Singaporean has a role to play in creating the "ideal of a harmonious and tolerant multi-ethnic and multireligious society, in order to prevent dangerous, radical ideas from taking root in Singapore" (Ministry of Home Affairs, 2003, p. 1).

It is Important not to be Complacent

> In an ideal world, everyone will be trained and ready today. But is that realistic? Given the number of companies, establishments, and given that we are and have been a very safe place, the first and most difficult task is getting people to understand that this is real and this is serious ... And given that we've been talking about it now for a few years, yes — people might start thinking 'well yes, it is high' — (but) it's not that they don't believe us, they might accept that it is high — but routine sets in. We just have to keep ploughing on, we just have to keep sending out the message, we just have to keep training people. You don't want the alternate situation — a lot of people get sensitised very quickly to the risk if there is an attack and people die.
>
> — Law and Home Affairs Minister K. Shanmugam (2017)

The persistence of the threat of violent extremism means that Singaporeans cannot remain complacent about the threat. However, the absence of attacks in Singapore has been interpreted by many that Singapore is a "very safe place". A retreat into this superficial sense of security may make us feel better in the short term, but this could be a grave mistake in the long run, as it is merely a form of false comfort. In particular, individuals may dismiss the slew of security-related messaging from the government as something that does not apply to them; worse, they may be overwhelmed by the glut of announcements or initiatives that does not really capture the imagination of the people, leading to messaging fatigue. Thus, as Law and Home Affairs Minister K. Shanmugam shared, "the first and most difficult task is getting people to understand that this is real and this is serious" (Loke, 2017).

Further concern is warranted because complacency may arise from the fact that the community believes the role of securing

Singapore resides solely under the government's purview. Research suggests people tend to perceive that the government should be responsible for crisis recovery (e.g., after an attack), and turn to them for guidance in times of such crisis (Sheppard, 2009).

While the government has taken necessary measures and precautions to counter the threat of violent extremism, it is important to be cognisant that there are no foolproof approaches that can insulate any country completely from the threat of violent extremism today. With the finite resources that law enforcement agencies have on what to emphasise on and prioritise their attention to, the daunting task of countering violent extremism takes on a whole new dimension, moving beyond simply providing the physical security apparatus and interventions, but also managing the expectations of the community at large, as well as ensuring the well-being of the law enforcement officers.

Know your Enemy, Know His Sword

Beyond simply reacting to any mere threat of an attack, strategies to deter and disrupt violent extremism could be designed to focus on eliminating the threat before it has a chance to appear. To do so, there needs to be an understanding of how law enforcement derives learning lessons from past experience of dealing with violent extremists, and more importantly, how violent extremist groups adapt over time into more effective entities and increasingly dangerous threats.

Nevertheless, many security observers have failed to comprehend the need for such basic understanding, and attempt to focus on the former and develop strategies without recognising the fact that violent extremist groups learn and adapt. Extant research has been more than forthcoming in identifying instances where the authorities have failed to detect and mitigate acts of terror, attributing them to a myriad of reasons ranging from intelligence failure (i.e., inability to discern vital warning signs), collection failure (i.e., inability to obtain relevant and timely information), to analytical failure (i.e., inability to connect various disparate information into actionable intelligence).

There were also instances highlighted where despite accurate and timely warnings, the inadequate response by law enforcement to disrupt violent extremists' capabilities may have led to the culmination of an attack.

The onus is therefore on law enforcement to be able to move beyond the myopic emphasis that "learning from past failures" is sufficient, and redirect efforts to be constantly ahead of trends that can be derived through research on the psyche of individuals and groups involved in violent extremism. When a violent extremist group exhibits the capacity to learn, it can purposefully adapt to measures implemented by law enforcement, and act systematically to enhance its capabilities and advance its strategic agenda. If law enforcement lacks the ability to learn about the adaption of violent extremists, its effectiveness in devising measures to reduce the threat will largely be determined by chance. The chance that violent extremists have not changed their *modus operandi* (i.e., from improvised explosive device (IED) to easily available items like knives and vehicles) and/or dissemination strategies for their propaganda materials (i.e., from hard copies distribution to the use of social media like Facebook and Twitter). Even more importantly, the chance that its current strategies are still effective in neutralising violent extremists' operations and support activities. As violent extremism expert, Paul Wilkinson, remarked, "Fighting terrorism is like being a goalkeeper. You can make a hundred brilliant saves but the only shot that people remember is the one that gets past you" (cited in Taylor, 2008, p. 57). With high stakes involved, the demands placed on law enforcement to keep the community safe are therefore substantial.

Thus, until law enforcement agencies appreciate the potential contribution of deciphering learning lessons (i.e., understand the mechanisms through which those changes occur and factors that influence group learning ability) from the behaviours of individual groups and how they have learnt and adapted, agencies would lack the ability to anticipate how groups are evolving over time and the actual level of threat they pose. In fact, Jackson and colleagues (2005) argued that the learning capabilities of violent extremist groups can serve as a primary determinant to understand and gauge the level of threat.

With sufficient knowledge about violent extremist groups' learning processes, insights can be derived to affect the nature of such learning capabilities and limit the options they have available to overcome and thwart law enforcement's tactics and security measures. The knowledge to discern what it means in terms of violent extremists' adaptive behaviours could also potentially assist in developing metrics to assess the level of preparation in relation to whether, when, where, and how violent extremists will strike. In a way, it would allow law enforcement to anticipate how a violent extremist group may operate in the future. More importantly, appreciating, understanding, and staying on top of violent extremist groups' learning processes will provide valuable insights to design and develop better policies and tactics for law enforcement, and deny violent extremists the element of surprise in their tactics and operations. Thus, focusing on the learning capabilities of violent extremists rather than adopting a reactive stance towards any new developments may allow practitioners, policymakers, and academics to better appreciate their complex and evolving nature, leading to a more successful outcome in addressing the threat.

Learning from Violent Extremist Attacks: Behavioural Sciences Insights for Practitioners and Policymakers

By better understanding what constitutes *Learning from Violent Extremist Attacks*, this book engages with the concept of deriving insights from violent extremist group learning processes and extant measures implemented by law enforcement, and contributes to the debate among practitioners and policymakers on how best to counter this emerging threat. In the contemporary battle against violent extremism, it is not identifying the relevant concepts associated with learning from attacks *per se* that are of vital interest, but rather the specific implications and follow-up questions surrounding the learning process that may improve security strategies and policies.

In this book, a range of chapters which explores two general themes relevant in the context of violent extremism, i.e., (1) learn to deal with violent extremists, and (2) learn to respond to violent extremist attacks, will be introduced. For the former, the chapters concentrate on how law enforcement can learn to: (1) understand regional violent extremism developments, (2) better identify violent extremists, (3) introduce relevant community level interventions, and (4) deal with at-risk population. For the latter, the chapters focus on how law enforcement can learn and identify strategies to: (1) foster resilience among the population, (2) build cyber psychological resilience against online threats, (3) enhance emergency preparedness in terms of government's response towards consequent societal reactions, and (4) maintain communal harmony in the aftermath of an attack. Every single chapter in this book is premised on the view that insights from these research areas have something to contribute to the overall learning from violent extremist attacks.

There are three ways in which this book adds unique value to the extant literature on violent extremism. Firstly, the book recognises the complexity undermining the pressing problem of violent extremism, and aims to provide a multidisciplinary approach to the issue at hand. Of particular value is the confluence of perspectives from psychologists, historians, political scientists, criminologists, sociologists, communication experts, and researchers in behavioural sciences. This will provide readers with greater confidence on the steps that need to be taken to resolve this problem. Secondly, this book encapsulates an endeavour to solicit and harness the insights of practitioners, policymakers, and subject matter experts in the field of violent extremism. Slated for practitioners and policymakers, the contributors share their perspectives and wealth of experience that could enrich and act as a critical and timely resource to educate prevention and intervention efforts. As much of the literature on this is written in an academic tone (i.e., may not address the operational issues pertaining to countering violent extremism), this endeavour seeks to address this gap and provide unique insights into learning from violent extremist attacks. Lastly, this book aims to present insights from an Asian perspective in order to ensure that the information presented is relevant to local practitioners and policymakers. To this end, the editors (from the Home Team Behavioural Sciences Centre at the Ministry of Home Affairs, Singapore, together with the National Security Studies Programme at the S. Rajaratnam School of International Studies) have invited local and regional partners to contribute chapters to the topic of violent extremism, where much of the scholarship has largely originated from the Western perspective.

These three points underscore the *raison d'être* behind this book, and to tailor the content further for the targeted audience of practitioners and policymakers, the chapters are designed to be short and succinct so as to provide a clear and manageable elaboration of the insights put forth by the contributors. More importantly, the editors attempt to convey a spirit of openness whereby the contributors are strongly encouraged to share any useful insight that has not been heard of before or which runs against prevailing conventional views. Rather than echoing conventional views, this approach acknowledges the rich and varied range of disparate questions and issues associated with violent extremism, and serves as a starting point for readers to reflect and envision new areas of research. For the purpose of this book, a working definition of violent extremism would be "a willingness to use or support the use of violence to further particular beliefs, including those of a political, social or ideological nature. This may include acts of terrorism."[3] (Nasser-Eddine *et al.*, 2011, p. 9), and for purpose of clarity, the terms "terrorism" and "violent extremism" are used interchangeably in this book.

---

[3] According to Schmid (2011), the revised academic consensus definition of terrorism is: "Terrorism refers on the one hand to a doctrine about the presumed effectiveness of a special form or tactic of fear-generating, coercive political violence and, on the other hand, to a conspiratorial practice of calculated, demonstrative, direct violent action without legal or moral restraints, targeting mainly civilians and non-combatants, performed for its propagandistic and psychological effects on various audiences and conflict parties" (p. 86).

Part 1: Learning to Deal with Violent Extremists

To facilitate the understanding of issues pertaining to learning to deal with violent extremists, the chapters in this part have been organised broadly in the following themes, demarcated by sections. These sections are:

- Section 1: Insights from regional violent extremism developments (Chapters 1–3)
- Section 2: Insights for the identification of violent extremists (Chapters 4–8)
- Section 3: Insights for community level interventions (Chapters 9–12)
- Section 4: Insights for dealing with at-risk population (Chapters 13–15)

Insights from Regional Violent Extremism Developments

The three chapters under Section 1 of the book discuss key recent violent extremism developments in the Southeast Asia region. Each chapter is associated with identifying learning lessons that practitioners and policymakers should be cognisant of in pre-empting and preventing similar attacks from transpiring. Bilveer Singh's opening chapter, "Terrorist Attacks in Indonesia: Insights for Practitioners and Policymakers" (Chapter 1), examines the long history of violent extremism in Indonesia. He discusses how the nexus between local violent extremist groups with transnational groups such as Al-Qaeda and ISIS has changed the threat landscape, and how law enforcement should adapt their approaches and strategies to counter the emerging threat posed. The next two chapters analyse the game changing Marawi siege by ISIS-linked jihadists in the southern part of the Philippines. The five-month siege dominated discussion of violent extremism and represents a new danger for the Philippines and even Southeast Asia. Joseph Franco, in his chapter "Confronting the Threat of an ISIS Province in Mindanao" (Chapter 2), focuses on the challenges of inhibiting the emergence of an ISIS province in Mindanao, from the pre-violent conflict up to the aftermath of widespread violence. On a related note, Jasminder Singh, in his chapter "Insights for Practitioners and Policymakers from the Marawi Siege, May–October 2017" (Chapter 3), highlights the factors that led to the Marawi siege, as well as how the Philippine Government eventually defeated and retook the city from the ISIS-linked jihadists.

Insights for the Identification of Violent Extremists

While countries are grappling with the increasing threat of violent extremism, law enforcement agencies are faced with the daunting task of identifying and preventing the next attack. Bearing this in mind, the second section of the book moves on to a group of chapters which focuses on strategies to enhance the identification of violent extremists. Whistine Chai, in her chapter "Threat Assessment of Violent Extremism: Considerations and Applications" (Chapter 4), discusses the major challenges of identifying violent extremists, especially the lone wolf operatives, and how threat assessment can be used to overcome these issues. She introduces the key principles of threat assessment which emphasises the need to conduct an in-depth evaluation of an individual's background, characteristics, lifestyle, and observable behaviours. Muhammad Faizal focuses on the use of smart technologies (e.g., artificial intelligence) in his chapter "Leveraging Smart Technology for Better Counter-Terrorism Intelligence" (Chapter 5), and discusses how it can support the various steps in the intelligence cycle by augmenting the surveillance of the physical space of cities in order to produce actionable intelligence to prevent violent extremist threats among other crime and security issues. He emphasises that the use of smart technologies would be particularly relevant for global cities such as Singapore that have embarked on smart cities initiatives. Next, Omer Saifudeen, in his chapter "A Common Framework for Pre-Radicalisation Indicators" (Chapter 6), highlights another interesting angle to mitigate potential threats, i.e., the idea of pre-emptively intervening to prevent an individual "predisposed" to radicalisation from spiralling further towards violent extremism. He uses a seven-factor pre-radicalisation indicator framework to expound real and relevant implications surrounding efforts to identify "early-warning" pathway models and associated indicators. Adding to the theme of identifying violent extremists, Vaishnavi Honnavalli, in her chapter "Five Things to Know About Assessment Tools for Violent Extremism" (Chapter 7), discusses the increasing utilisation of assessment tools by practitioners in the context of violent extremism. Through this, she argues that assessing risk for violent extremism is different from the assessment of risk for general violence; practitioners and policymakers have to be mindful of these differences when applying these tools in the practical setting for violent extremism. In the final chapter of this section, Shi Hui Tee, in her chapter "Lone Wolf Violent Extremism and Mental Illness: Learning Lessons from an Asian Perspective" (Chapter 8), looks specifically at the embodied relationship between lone wolf violent extremism and mental illness. She argues that the increased media portrayal of lone wolf violent extremists as mentally ill individuals has provided practitioners and policymakers with a "powerful" lens to identify and assess the threat posed. In that context, she discusses the need for research to shed light on the possibility of a connection between the two constructs.

Insights for Community Level Interventions

Safeguarding against the threat of violent extremism is everyone's responsibility. Thus, the central question underlying the third section of the book revolves around how community level interventions, which involve the cooperation between the government and the public, can be enhanced based on insights from past case studies and new findings from the behavioural sciences perspective. Kumar Ramakrishna, in his chapter on "The 4 'M' Strategy of Combating Violent Extremism: An Analysis" (Chapter 9), introduces a model aimed to understand how violent extremists have created and disseminated their propaganda to shape the hearts and minds of their target audience. Through the use of case examples, he showcases how this 4 'M' (i.e., ***m***essenger, ***m***essage, ***m***echanism, and ***m***arket receptivity) model has the potential to guide policy interventions to undermine the overall reach and appeal of radical propaganda. In the chapter on "Bystander Intervention to Prevent Radicalisation" (Chapter 10), Loo Seng Neo, Joyce Pang, and Jeffery Chin seek to answer the question of how the community can be encouraged not to "stand by and do nothing" (i.e., be bystanders), and report more. Recognising that the literature is replete with striking cases of individuals who have witnessed signs of radicalisation to violence in others but failed to report or intervene, the authors critique the extant studies and consider findings from their own study on bystander effect in violent extremism reporting, suggesting five key points that may support practitioners and policymakers in encouraging community reporting of potential radicalised individuals. Next, Dashalini Katna, in her chapter "The Inseparable Brothers-in-Arms: Understanding the Instrumentality of Violent Extremism in Strengthening Intergroup Conflict" (Chapter 11), examines the intricacies within the intergroup conflict–violent extremism connection. In it, she describes how every intergroup conflict primarily revolves around incompatible perspectives between the opposing parties, and identifies approaches aimed at reducing incompatibility of intergroup perceptions and restraining the pursuit of violence. Finally, Thomas Koruth Samuel, in his chapter "Engaging Youths in Counter Violent Extremism (CVE) Initiatives" (Chapter 12), looks at how youths have been exploited and manipulated by violent extremists. He underscores the urgent need to both develop youth-based CVE material as well as equip the young people with the skill set to develop their own CVE content to appeal to their peers. In particular, he shares valuable learning lessons derived from the experience of organising the "Student Leaders Against Youth Extremism and Radicalisation" workshops in Malaysia.

Insights for Dealing with At-Risk Population

In the final section of Part 1, the hands-on experiences that the contributors gained in dealing with at-risk population were chronicled in three chapters. Of note is the central idea, that to understand how to manage and mitigate the threat posed by returning fighters from Syria and Iraq, and detainees incarcerated for violent extremism-related offences, it is important to situate this within the larger frame of the personality and psycho-social factors that influence the individual, which in turn lead to important personal and social outcomes. Bridget Robert, in her chapter "At-Risk and Radicalised Singaporean Youths: Themes Observed and Considerations for a Youth-Centric Rehabilitation Framework" (Chapter 13), provides insights about the key issues of youth radicalisation in the Singaporean context. She identifies a sample of themes observed in at-risk and radicalised Singaporean youths who had been attracted to ISIS's online propaganda, and suggests five rehabilitation principles that practitioners and policymakers can consider in developing a youth-centric rehabilitation framework. Mirra Noor Milla and Ahmad Naufalul Uman, in their chapter "Understanding Intergroup Contact on Terrorist Prisoners in Indonesia" (Chapter 14), describe their experiences in engaging more than 150 terrorists in 53 prisons in Indonesia. They share how introducing positive intergroup contact in the de-radicalisation programmes can play an important role in breaking the barrier of an "us-versus-them" mentality, and increasing acceptance for alternative social identity. Leading on from this, Whinda Yustisia and Wahyu Cahyono, in their chapter "In the Search of Home: Tackling Support for ISIS Ideology Among Ordinary People" (Chapter 15), explore strategies to prevent people from joining violent extremist groups such as ISIS. Utilising information gathered from interviewing an ISIS supporter and his family members after they returned to Indonesia from Syria, the authors share how radical ideology can appeal to ordinary people, and suggest strategies to tackle ISIS's appeal.

Part 2: Learning to Respond to Violent Extremist Attacks

To facilitate the understanding of issues pertaining to learning to respond to violent extremist attacks, the chapters in this second part have been organised broadly in the following themes, demarcated by sections. These sections are as follows:

- Section 5: Strategies to build resilience (Chapters 16–19)
- Section 6: Strategies to build cyber psychological resilience (Chapters 20–23)

- Section 7: Strategies to build emergency preparedness (Chapters 24–27)
- Section 8: Strategies to build communal harmony (Chapters 28–30)

Strategies to Build Resilience

Section 5 of the book contains four chapters on contemporary issues in building resilience among the population in the "day after" scenario. Recognising the detrimental psychological impact of violent extremism on individuals' wellbeing, these chapters seek to identify strategies to facilitate recovery and resilience building efforts, and minimise potential long-term negative effects on the society. Jethro Tan, Jane Quek, and Gabriel Ong, in their chapter "Preparing for the Day After Terror: Five Things to Do to Build National Resilience" (Chapter 16), focus on building national resilience as a macro-level approach to deal with the threat of violent extremism. They underscore the need to first understand what may potentially happen in the aftermath of an attack, and then develop strategies that can be undertaken to address these consequences. Five guiding principles to supplement preparatory efforts after an attack were then identified. By doing so, the authors discuss how instilling these principles would prepare the nation to cope and recover from the consequences caused by violent extremism and eventually thrive post-crisis (i.e., being resilient). Complementing the previous chapter, Shuktika Bose, in her chapter "Psychological First Aid: Addressing Worldwide Challenges for Implementation in an Asian Context" (Chapter 17), outlines how psychological interventions is essential in the day after scenario. She proposes the use of psychological first aid, as it can play a significant role in alleviating the psychological stress and promoting resilience of those in need, and highlights challenges associated with community training of psychological first aid. Next, Shi Hui Tee, in her chapter "Responding to a Violent Extremist Attack: Insights from the 2016 Orlando Shooting Incident" (Chapter 18), adopts a case study approach to identify how the Orlando community reacted during and in the aftermath of the Pulse nightclub shooting. She showcases how an adequately facilitated community response can help to mitigate post-crisis damage and recover from the attack. Finally, Pamela Goh, in her chapter "Against the Norm: The Act of Helping During Violent Extremist Attacks" (Chapter 19), describes the peculiar phenomenon of helping others in times of an attack. Although it is counter-intuitive to act beyond one's personal safety and wellbeing, such pro-social behaviours have emerged naturally and at considerable levels. She outlines the need to understand these pro-social behaviours, and more importantly, for law enforcement agencies to account for them in their emergency planning.

Strategies to Build Cyber Psychological Resilience

The four chapters under Section 6 examines the role of the Internet and social media in shaping public views and reactions towards violent extremism. The focal point is the repertories of strategies put forth by the contributors that elucidate the relevance and importance of the behavioural sciences perspective in building cyber psychological resilience. Stephanie Neubronner, in her chapter "Managing Social Media in an Event of a Terror Attack" (Chapter 20), discusses the role of social media in mediating response and recovery strategies before, during, and after an attack. She highlights how government initiatives such as SGSecure and the Total Defence Campaign have adopted the use of social media, and stresses the need for authorities to mitigate the potential issues brought about by the use of social media in order to ensure that the community responds appropriately and bounces back should an attack occur. On a related note, Leevia Dillon, Joshua Freilich, and Steven Chermak, in their chapter on "Media Effects within the Context of Violent Extremism in the Post-9/11 Era" (Chapter 21), explore the effects of media coverage on violent extremism by highlighting the importance of media framing and its potential to shape public support and inform policies targeted towards countering violent extremism. They also highlight the unintended role played by media in sensationalising and magnifying the reach of violent extremists. Next, Jony Eko Yulianto and Jessie Janny Thenarianto, in their chapter "Social Media Response after an

Attack: Perspectives from the Jakarta Bombings" (Chapter 22), examine the use of social media, especially Twitter, after the 2016 and 2017 Jakarta bombings. Using these two attacks as reference, they observe similar online behavioural patterns among the Indonesian netizens after the attacks, and then highlight the challenges and opportunities that practitioners and policymakers should be mindful of. Finally, Ken Chen, in his chapter "Fake News After a Terror Attack: Psychological Vulnerabilities Exploited by Fake News Creators" (Chapter 23), looks at the spread of fake news after an attack and the ensuing real-world repercussions such as communal discord within the society. On the basis of the most recent literature, he identifies five psychological vulnerabilities that have been exploited by fake news creators to advance their agendas, and discusses ways to inoculate the public against the negative effects of fake news.

Strategies to Build Emergency Preparedness

Section 7 explores specific strategies and preparations that contributes to an understanding of the degree of emergency preparedness on the government's ability to react to violent extremist attacks. Starting from this premise, the four chapters in this section attempt to shed insights on how governments can focus their efforts on preparing their countries for any potential terror incidents. Siew Maan Diong, Wei Jie Tan, and Raymond Lee, in their chapter "Emergency Preparedness Towards Terror Attacks in Singapore" (Chapter 24), provide a thoughtful account of the challenges that may affect emergency preparedness at various levels of the society, and suggest tangible strategies on how practitioners and policymakers can react constructively to violent extremism threats in a manner that minimises the negative consequences on the safety and health of individuals, as well as to promote resilience after an attack. Next, Sheryl Chua, Majeed Khader, and Eunice Tan, in their chapter "The Looming, the Creeping and the Black Swan: Modern Crises and Recommendations for Building Resilience" (Chapter 25), critically review and summarise the literature on "modern crisis" (e.g., violent extremism; more complex, dynamic, transboundary, and have cascading effects), and explain how it is distinct from conventional crisis. This, as the authors argue, reflects the new characteristic of threats the world is facing, and underlines the need to adopt new practices and strategies to anticipate and mitigate the uncertain, unimaginable, and unforeseeable modern crises. Focusing on the need to treat target hardening as a pre-emptive rather than reactive approach, Damien Cheong, in his chapter "Striking the Right Balance in Relation to Target Hardening" (Chapter 26), identifies the challenges that practitioners and policymakers may face in the implementation of such measures, and suggests approaches to mitigate these challenges. In particular, he reasons that target hardening involves more than simply erecting protective measures around buildings or public venues, and entails taking steps to deter, and in the wake of the attack, help post-incident investigation. In his second chapter, "Risk and Crisis Management during a Major Terror Attack: Singapore's Approach" (Chapter 27), Damien Cheong discusses five key challenges *vis-à-vis* crisis and risk management during a major terror attack, as well as five potential mitigating responses. He opines that the pre-emptive and holistic approach, as adopted by Singapore, may be the most effective way to deal with the evolving threat of violent extremism.

Strategies to Build Communal Harmony

The last section of the book is dedicated to overcoming the potential segregations within the community in the aftermath of violent extremism-related incidents. As race and religious issues are, by nature, highly sensitive, the next three chapters explore strategies that may foster communal harmony and enable communities to cope better in the wake of an attack. Verity Er, in her chapter "The Effects of Religious Fundamentalism on Communal Harmony" (Chapter 28), sheds light on five key aspects of religious fundamentalism, a phenomenon often misunderstood as merely devoutness towards one's faith. She discusses the potential impacts religious fundamentalism can have on social cohesion, showing how the underpinnings of a religious fundamentalist mindset have to be taken into account in order to explore ways to prevent it from escalating into violent extremism. Next, Nur Aisyah, in her chapter "How Can Right-Wing Extremism Exacerbate Islamophobia After a Jihadi Attack? Insights from Europe" (Chapter 29), examines the recent expression of right-wing extremism in Europe (i.e., intolerance of immigrants and Islam), and discusses how such themes of intolerance towards other cultures and religions may manifest in Singapore and split the multicultural social fabric apart. Utilising various case study examples, she then proposes strategies to mitigate the effects of right-wing extremism and Islamophobia. Leading on from this, Nur Elissa Ruzzi'eanne, in her chapter "Islamophobia and its Aftermath: Strategies to Manage Islamophobia" (Chapter 30), describes the manifestation of Islamophobia in light of its "close" association with instances of jihadi terror attacks, and discusses how such attitudes may create divisions between non-Muslims and Muslims and prevent Muslims from integrating into mainstream communities. Given that the spotlight has been cast on how governments would respond to such threats, she explores key points about Islamophobia and identifies five strategies to manage it.

Conclusion: Key Takeaways for Practitioners and Policymakers

In conclusion, the editors would like to remind readers about the central premise of this book, which is to examine the pressing problem of violent extremism from a multidisciplinary behavioural sciences perspective. To address the unique needs of practitioners and policymakers, this book seeks to elucidate behavioural sciences insights based on the ways law enforcement has dealt with violent extremists in the past, as well as, how violent extremist groups have adapted over time into more effective entities and increasingly dangerous threats. The consequent positive societal reactions, reduction in attacks and/or threats faced, as well as enhancement in the ability of communities to cope in the wake of an attack are some key areas that could be gleaned from a resilient society which has successfully learnt from violent extremist attacks.

It is also essential to advocate the appreciation of the "human" dimension behind the entire counter-violent extremism strategy, and explore this dimension in the context of the psyche of individuals, groups, and trends, so as to be constantly ahead of violent extremists. Bearing this in mind, the various chapters can be seen as attempts to advance the topic and contribute to the endeavour of developing better policy and operational interventions. Hopefully, this book may serve as a starting point for greater discussions and continued study of this topic, and pave the way for many more outputs that can further shed valuable insights for practitioners and policymakers.

Practitioners and Policymakers Guide to Utilising the Book

This final section highlights several guidelines on how the readers can utilise the key takeaways found in this book. First of all, this book will be of value to practitioners (e.g., police officers, intelligence officers, analysts), policymakers, academics, students, and general readers who have an interest in violent extremism. In addition, social scientists such as psychologists, sociologists, or political scientists may also find this book useful. Second, readers have to look beyond the key takeaways highlighted in each chapter and use them as a starting point to envision new areas of exploration. Any intention to use the key takeaways directly in an operational or legal context should be cautioned, as this book is not intended for this purpose; the editors are candid enough to acknowledge the crucial need to operationalise the information to fit one's needs and there is no "one-size-fits-all" solution. Readers are therefore advised to consult the relevant authorities or experts if they plan to apply the information in an operational or legal context. Lastly, in keeping with the tagline for "behavioural sciences insights for practitioners and policymakers", the editors put together a repository of potential research questions that practitioners and policymakers may have and the associated relevant chapters. Based on insights derived from a behavioural sciences angle, the research questions and relevant chapters are summarised in the following table (Table 0.1).

Table 0.1: Research Questions and the Corresponding Relevant Chapters.

Research Question	Chapter(s)
How can we better assess the risk/threat for violent extremism posed by a person-of-interest?	4, 6, 7
How can we better prepare law enforcement officers for the day after scenario?	24, 25, 27
How can we better understand the threat of violent extremism in Singapore?	13, 24, 26, 27
How can we better understand the threat of violent extremism in Indonesia?	1, 14, 15, 22
How can we better understand the threat of violent extremism in the Philippines?	2, 3
How can we better understand the threat of violent extremism in in Malaysia?	12
How can we better understand the threat posed by lone wolf violent extremism?	6, 8, 18
How can we better understand youth and violent extremism?	12, 13
How can we ensure that communal harmony is maintained in the day after scenario?	28, 29, 30
How can we increase reporting rates of violent extremism within the community?	10
How can we improve crisis management in the day after scenario?	2, 24, 25, 27
How can we inoculate the community against the spread of fake news in the day after scenario?	20, 21, 23
How can we manage the negative effects associated with the use of social media in the day after scenario?	19, 20, 21, 22, 23
How can we manage the threat posed by violent extremist groups?	9, 10, 11, 12
How can we minimise the reach and influence of violent extremist's ideology?	9, 15
How can we reduce the psychological trauma faced by the community in the day after scenario?	16, 17
How can we use technology to abet extant counter violent extremism measures?	5
How can we use to enhance the resilience of the community in the day after scenario?	16, 17, 18, 19, 20, 24

In closing, the editors cite Josephine Teo, Second Minister for Home Affairs, who said that: "Our preparedness must go beyond the Home Team. Every Singaporean has a role to play, and the community must be ready, which is why we have SGSecure." (Ng, 2018). These comments greatly echo the sentiment of the editors of this book, who are psychologists and behavioural scientists by training. To safeguard our society and social harmony, everyone has to work together and stay alert, stay united, and stay strong so that we *learn* and *adapt* to the ever-changing threat of violent extremism.

References

Byman, D. (2017). Frustrated foreign fighters. *Lawfare*. Retrieved from https://lawfareblog.com/frustrated-foreign-fighters.

Counter-Terrorism Operations Division (2014). The stages of change in the rehabilitation of terrorist operatives: The Singapore experience. *Home Team Journal*, *5*, 53–58.

Jackson, B., Baker, J., Cragin, K., Parachini, J., Trujillo, H., & Chalk, P. (2005). *Organisational Learning in Terrorist Groups and its Implications for Combating Terrorism*. Santa Monica, CA: RAND Corporation.

Khader, M. (2011). Behavioural sciences in Home Team operations: 'Mindware' to complement our hardware. *Home Team Journal*, *3*, 4–9.

Lam, L. (2017). Singapore under highest terror threat in recent years: 8 key points from MHA's terror report. *The Straits Times*. Retrieved from https://www.straitstimes.com/singapore/singapore-under-highest-terror-threat-in-recent-years-8-key-points-from-mhas-terror-report.

Lim, G.H. (2012). A ready SAF: A strategy for tomorrow. *Pointer*, *38*(1), 41–49.

Lim, G.G.N. (2016). The future of the Singapore Armed Forces amidst the transforming strategic, geopolitical and domestic environment. *Pointer*, *42*(3), 38–48.

Loke, K.F. (2017). Anti-terror efforts to continue as threats remain at 'a high level': Shanmugam. *Channel NewsAsia*. Retrieved from https://www.channelnewsasia.com/news/singapore/anti-terror-efforts-to-continue-as-threats-remain-at-a-high-9504264.

Ministry of Home Affairs (2003). *White Paper: The Jemaah Islamiyah Arrests and the Threat of Terrorism*. Singapore: Author.

Mokhtar, F. (2017, December 20). Looking ahead to 2018: Even as IS weakens, evolving terror threat looms for S'pore. *Today*. Retrieved from https://www.todayonline.com/singapore/looking-ahead-2018-even-isis-weakens-evolving-terror-threat-looms-spore.

Nasser-Eddine, M., Garnham, B., Agostino, K., & Caluya, G. (2011). *Countering Violent Extremism (CVE) Literature Review*. Edinburgh, Australia: Australian Government, Department of Defence, Command and Control Division, Defence Science and Technology Organisation (DSTO).

Neo, L.S., Dillon, L., Shi, P., Tan, J., Wang, Y., & Gomes, D. (2016). Understanding the psychology of persuasive violent extremist online platforms. In M. Khader, L. S. Neo, G. Ong, E. Tan, & J. Chin (Eds.), *Combating Violent Extremism and Radicalisation in the Digital Era* (pp. 1–15). Hershey, PA: IGI Global.

Ng, J.S. (2018). Parliament: Home affairs ministry budget to expand by more than 10%, largely to boost fight against terror. *The Straits Time*. Retrieved from https://www.straitstimes.com/politics/parliament-home-affairs-ministry-budget-to-expand-by-more-than-10-per-cent-largely-to-boost.

Prime Minister's Office (2016). National day rally 2016. Retrieved from http://www.pmo.gov.sg/national-day-rally-2016.

Rapoport, D.C. (Ed.) (2006). *Terrorism: Critical Concepts in Political Science*. New York: Routledge.

Schmid, A.P. (Ed.) (2011). *The Routledge Handbook of Terrorism Research*. New York: Routledge.

Security Education Command (2013). Community outreach & partnership: The ISD story. *Home Team Journal*, 4, 34–42.

Sheppard, B. (2009). *The Psychology of Strategic Terrorism: Public and Government Responses to Attack*. New York: Routledge.

Taylor, J.L. (2008). Government: Target, protector, aggressor. In R.J. Burke, & C.L. Cooper (Eds.), *International Threats and Terrorism to Security: Managerial and Organisational Challenges* (pp. 57–80). Cheltenham, U.K.: Edward Elgar.

LEARNING TO DEAL WITH VIOLENT EXTREMISTS

Section 1

Insights from Regional Violent Extremism Developments

The threat of terrorism, the skills of terrorists, the networks, have gone from wholesale to retail and that is why we are seeing more lone wolf attacks and small cells.

DR NG ENG HEN
MINISTER FOR DEFENCE

CHAPTER 1

Terrorist Attacks in Indonesia: Insights for Practitioners and Policymakers

BILVEER SINGH

Department of Political Science,
National University of Singapore, Singapore

Introduction

Indonesia has a long history of "black flags" — Islamist religious extremism and terrorism — threatening its national security in one way or another. While Indonesia suffered terrorist attacks from Islamist radical groups such as the Darul Islam (DI) in the 1940s right through to the mid-1960s, and through groups such as Komando Jihad in the 1970s, it was only since the 1980s that the character of the threat changed fundamentally. This was mainly due to the nexus between the various local terrorist and extremist groups with international and transnational terrorist organisations such as the Al-Qaeda (AQ) and the Islamic State (IS), also known as Daesh.

Against this backdrop, this chapter will attempt to provide what can be considered as learning points from terrorist attacks in Indonesia. This will be undertaken by first listing the key terrorist attacks that have taken place in Indonesia since the late 1990s. This will be followed by a discussion of the key points and challenges that policymakers and practitioners need to be aware of regarding the threat of Islamist extremist and terrorist groups. Following this, the key tangible approaches adopted by strategic practitioners to address the threat posed by Islamist extremists and terrorists will be looked at.

Key Terrorist Attacks in Indonesia Since the Late 1990s

Since the 1990s, for instance, Indonesia has suffered almost continuous terrorist attacks, as shown in Table 1.1. Table 1.1 clearly shows that in the last 20 years or so, Indonesia has had a litany of attacks from both religious and non-religious terrorist groups. This was also true from the period from the late 1940s through to the 1970s (Soebardi, 1983). For the purpose of this chapter, the focus will be on Islamist-based extremist and terrorist groups. This is particularly important as Indonesia is the largest Muslim nation in the world with almost 90% of its 265 million people (in 2017) belonging to the Islamic faith.[1] Historically, Indonesia has experienced separatist movements that are both Islamist and non-Islamist in character, with the DI often described as the source of almost all key extremist and terrorist groups in Indonesia since the 1970s to this day (Mbai, 2014). There is also a clear nexus and linkage between extremism and terrorism, with Ansyaad Mbai, the former Head of Indonesia's counter-terrorist agency, describing extremism as the "mother" of terrorism (Mbai, personal communication, January 6, 2018).

[1]For more information, please refer to http://www.worldometers.info/world-population/Indonesia-population/.

Table 1.1. List of Terrorist Attacks in Indonesia, 1997–2018.

Date/Year	Incident	Casualties
13 Sep 1997	Bomb explodes in Demak, Central Java, planted by East Timor pro-independence fighters.	No fatalities
18 Jan 1998	Bomb explodes in Central Jakarta. No one claims responsibility.	No fatalities
11 Dec 1998	Bomb explodes in Atrium Plaza Senen Shopping Centre, Jakarta. Perpetrated believed to be Jemaah Islamiyah (JI).	No fatalities
19 Apr 1999	Bomb explodes in Istiqlal Mosque, Jakarta, the largest mosque in the capital. Perpetrator — JI.	4 injured
1 Aug 2000	Bomb explodes outside the residence of the Philippines Ambassador to Indonesia. Perpetrator — JI.	2 killed and 21 injured
14 Sep 2000	Bomb explodes at basement of Jakarta Stock Exchange. Perpetrator — JI.	15 killed and 27 injured
24 Dec 2000	Multiple church bombings in Indonesia by JI.	18 killed and 48 injured
12 Oct 2002	First Bali bombing. Perpetrator — JI.	202 killed and 240 injured
5 Aug 2003	Hotel JW Marriott bombing in Jakarta by JI.	12 killed and 150 injured
31 Dec 2003	A bombing at a night market in Aceh by the Free Aceh Movement.	10 killed and 45 injured
9 Sep 2004	JI bombing outside the Australian Embassy in Jakarta.	9 killed and 150 injured
13 Nov 2004	Bomb explodes in a bus in Poso, Sulawesi. Perpetrator — JI.	6 killed and 3 injured
28 May 2005	JI-linked groups bomb morning market in Tentena, Sulawesi.	22 killed and 40 injured
1 Oct 2005	Second Bali bombing by JI.	20 killed and 100 injured
31 Dec 2005	JI-led bomb explodes in market in Palu, Sulawesi.	8 killed and 53 injured

(*Continued*)

Table 1.1. (*Continued*)

Date/Year	Incident	Casualties
17 Jul 2007	Hotel JW Marriott and Ritz-Carlton bombed in Jakarta by JI.	7 killed and 50 injured
15 Apr 2011	JI-led suicide bombing in a Cirebon mosque, Java.	1 killed and 28 injured
25 Sep 2011	JI linked suicide bombing at Church in Solo, Java.	1 killed and 14 injured
8 Apr 2012	Plane shot down by Papuan separatists at Puncak Jaya, Papua.	1 killed
17 Aug 2012	JI-linked group shoots policemen in Solo, Java.	2 injured
17 Aug 2012	Policemen murdered by a JI-linked group.	2 killed
27 Nov 2012	Policemen killed by Papuan separatists in Jayawijaya, Papua.	3 killed
14 Jan 2016	IS-linked terrorists attack police post in Jakarta.	7 killed
24 May 2017	IS-linked suicide bombing in a bus terminal in Jakarta.	5 killed and 10 injured
25 Jun 2017	IS-linked militants killed policemen in Medan, Sumatra.	3 killed
30 Jun 2017	IS-linked militants attack two police officers in Jakarta.	2 injured
9 May 2018	Pro-IS terrorist inmates riot in a police prison in Jakarta.	5 killed
13 May 2018	3 churches bombed by suicide bombers in Surabaya by pro-IS militants.	18 killed and 40 injured
14 May 2018	Suicide bombing outside a police station in Surabaya by pro-IS militants.	4 killed and 10 injured
16 May 2018	Pro-IS militants attack a police station in Pekanbaru, Sumatra.	5 killed

Source: Compiled by author from media sources.

Some of the key extremist and terrorist groups in Indonesia would include the following:

a) Darul Islam (DI),
b) Komando Jihad (KJ),
c) Jemaah Islamiyyah (JI),

d) Laskar Jundullah (LJ),
e) Komite Penanggulangan Krisis (KOMPAK),
f) Mujahidin Indonesia Timor (MIT),
g) Mujahidin Indonesia Barat (MIB),
h) Jamaah Ansharut Tauhid (JAT),
i) Jamaah Ansharut Daulah (JAD),
j) Abu Umar Group,
k) Abu Roban Group,
l) Islamic State (IS) (in Indonesia), and
m) Katibah Nusantara (Indonesians-led pro-IS group in Syria and Iraq).

Key Points That Practitioners and Policymakers Need to be Aware of Regarding Religious-based Extremism and Terrorism in Indonesia

In view of the relatively long history of the threat of terrorism in Indonesia and the existence of manifold terrorist and extremist groups committed to the use of violence to achieve their political goals, there are a number of key points that practitioners and policymakers would need to be aware of regarding religious-based extremism and terrorism in Indonesia.

(1) *Key Drivers of Extremism and Terrorism*

The first relates to the manifold factors that can influence individuals to become susceptible to radical ideologies. In this regard, much research has been undertaken to explain why there is a segment of the Indonesian population that is attracted to religious extremism and terrorism as an approach to achieve their individual or group goals, especially through the use of violence to establish an Islamic State. For instance, a survey carried out by Alvara, a Jakarta-based pollster, reported that while the majority of 4,200 Muslim students surveyed in the top schools and universities in Java disagreed with the establishment of an Islamic Caliphate and the use of violence, some 20% stated that they were prepared to wage jihad to achieve a Caliphate ("One in five Indonesia students support Islamic Caliphate: Survey", 2017).

Why then are some Indonesians attracted to the radical and extremist route to achieve their political goals? In this regard, researchers have pointed out to the importance of both domestic and international factors as being the key primers for radicalism in Indonesia. Some of the key drivers for radicalism and terrorism in Indonesia, from the domestic perspective, would include the following:

a) Existence of repressive regimes in Indonesia, especially from the Sukarno to the Suharto era, which often saw Muslims and their political aspirations being repressed. This has included the rejection of the 1945 Jakarta Charter, which included reference to Indonesia as an Islamic State, the violent repression of Muslims during the DI rebellion and the regional revolts in the 1950s, the banning of *Masjumi*, a leading Muslim political organisation during the Sukarno era, the Tanjung Priok massacre in Jakarta in 1984 that led to the killing of between 400 and 700 Muslims by security forces.
b) The belief that national politicians, mostly of secular orientations, were prepared to accommodate to the West's political and economic interests in the country.
c) The objection by many Muslims of Indonesia's adoption of the West's political, economic, and social systems such as democracy, secularism, pluralism, and the free market, which were seen to be detrimental to Muslim interests in the country, benefitting only the Chinese minority and foreign interests.
d) The unhappiness with the national moderate Muslim political parties and elites who were seen to be extremely crisis-prone, split, and only interested in their parochial personal interests, leads to the attraction of the radicals and their ideologies who often justify the use of violence to undertake political change.
e) In view of the disappointment with the Indonesia State and its policies since independence, many Muslim groups have espoused the radical path to exploit the existence of pervasive political, economic, and social-cultural grievances, the political space provided by democratisation since 1998, the ease with which the radical narratives, discourses, and ideas have been spread and

permeated nationally, and the increasing belief that Islamist radical ideologues and ideologies provide a powerful tool to explain past and present ills as well as provide a useful path for the bright future ahead.

The litany of domestic factors and drivers are further buttressed by various external imperatives that provide a powerful case in support of the radicals and their approaches. Some of the key external factors include:

a) The continued existence of the West's hegemony in the political–economic–social–cultural arena, especially since colonialism and presently symbolised by the United States, which is blamed for most of the ills that have fallen upon Muslims and Muslim states.
b) The clear dominance of the West over Muslim states, especially politically, economically, and militarily, including in the Middle East, which have led many to blame the West's dominance as a cause of Muslims' backwardness, divisions, and troubles.
c) Directly related to the above is the clear enmity and aggression of the West against Muslim states in the last 20 years or so, best evident in the invasion of Afghanistan, Iraq, and the aggressive policies towards Iran, Syria, Libya, Yemen, Sudan, and Somalia.
d) There is also the belief that the West practices double standards when it comes to assisting Muslim states and their people, best evident in the late responses to crises in Palestine, Bosnia, Yemen, Libya, Ambon, etc., including the West near-blind support for Israel's repression and persecution of the Palestinians in the last five to six decades, and the recent Washington's policy of recognising Jerusalem as Israel's capital. This means that there are powerful and pervasive anti-Islamist reference points in the world that can easily be used by radical ideologues to mobilise Muslims against the West and their interests, including their friends and allies in Muslim majority states who are seen as "lackeys" or "agents" of the infidel West.
e) There is also the powerful role of transnational Islamist movements and groups such as AQ, IS, and even Hizbut Tahrir that have been preaching the development of an alternative state system to the

existing Westphalian one, mainly through the establishment of an Islamic Caliphate. This has been strongly facilitated by the easy access to radical ideology through cyberspace and personal interactions due to easy international travel.

(2) *Ease of Spreading Radical Narratives and Ideologies*

The ease of spreading radical narratives that justify the use of violence by terror groups is evident in the continuous efforts by radical ideologues and their supporters in undertaking upstream, middle-stream, and lower-stream radicalisation measures targeted at the vulnerable population.

(3) *Radicalisation Efforts in Educational and Religious Institutions, and Prisons*

In Indonesia's case, a particular concern is the concerted efforts to spread radical ideology nationally through the hijacking of educational and religious institutions as well as through prisons. This means that the conveyor belt is almost unending as radical ideologues are always able to find adherents to support their causes, usually couched in religious terms and often included the use of violence.

(4) *Role of the Social Media*

As Indonesia is one of the most cyberspace-penetrated states in the world, the use of the new media, including social media, has been particularly effective in spreading radical ideologies and narratives, which often means that the State apparatus is always trying to play catch up with the radicals, all the more, in an increasingly democratic atmosphere that is opposed to the rise of an autocratic or authoritarian state.

(5) *Links with Transnational Terror Groups*

The success of radicals in Indonesia is also, in a large measure, due to their links with international terror groups, such as transnational movements that includes AQ, IS, and Hizbut Tahrir. While policing the world's largest archipelagic state is difficult, Indonesia's problems and challenges are doubly enhanced due to the international drivers that have facilitated the spread of radical ideology in the republic, especially, the largest Muslim state and one that believed Muslims were systematically repressed by the state since 1945.

In summary, while many factors stand out, some of the more important ones accounting for the spread of radicalism in Indonesia include:

a) The long history in Indonesia of individuals and groups wanting to establish an Islamic State based in *Syariat Islam* as Indonesia is the largest Muslim nation.
b) Since the fall of Suharto in 1998, there is the freedom of expression guaranteed by law to spread Islamic teaching in schools and religious institutions that have allowed the "Islamist narratives" to percolate throughout the society without hindrance.
c) The ease with which to influence people in Indonesia, allowing easy access to support and recruits in the country for Islamist-related causes even if it entails the use of violence.
d) The high and intense feeling of solidarity of most Indonesians with Islamist-oriented causes, both at home and abroad.
e) The existence of external factors that compel Indonesians to support causes in view of the belief that Muslims worldwide and Islam as a whole are under attack from the West which aims to continue the practice of colonialism through old and new ways in order to maintain the West's political, economic, military and social-cultural dominance, and hegemony at the expense of Muslims.

Key Approaches and Strategies Adopted to Counter the Threat Posed by Islamist Radicalism and Terrorism in Indonesia

(1) *Institutional and Legal Measures*

Indonesia's counter-terrorism efforts were largely a monopoly of the military in the past. Detachment 81 was a unit within the Special

Forces Command or KOPASSUS of the Indonesian military that was tasked with counter-terrorism duties. This changed fundamentally following the police being separated from the military command in 1999 and with the rise of the threat of terrorism in Indonesia, counter-terrorism increasingly became a prerogative of the Indonesian Police. An important consideration for the shift from the military to the police was also the belief that the military tends to rely on excessive force and violence and its success tends to be only temporary in nature, with radical groups becoming even more militant eventually (Mbai, 2014). As terrorism was seen as a political and not a military struggle, a more creative approach was needed, dubbed the "soft approach", in which the police, adept in law and order maintenance, was believed to be more adept (Mbai, 2014).

In countering terrorism, following the 12 October 2002 Bali bombings, Indonesia has enacted a number of institutional and legal reforms to respond to the threat of terrorism and extremism. Following the 2002 Bali bombings, the Indonesian Police established the Counter-Terrorism Task Force (*Satgas Bom*) to get to the root of the Bali attack. This was to eventually result in the establishment of the Special Detachment 88 (Densus 88) of the Indonesian Police that has been in the forefront of neutralising terror threats in Indonesia. At a broader political level, the Megawati Government quickly established the Counter-Terrorism Co-ordination Desk within the Co-ordinating Ministry of Politics and Security in 2002. Following the bombing outside the Australian Embassy in 2004, the Indonesian government established the Anti-Terrorism Task Force under BIN, the National Intelligence Agency, mainly to coordinate intelligence activities among various ministries to track terrorists nationwide. However, in view of the Indonesian military prior expertise on counter-terrorism and the continued spate of terror attacks, there were criticisms from within and outside of Indonesia that the Indonesia Police-centric approach to counter-terrorism was counter-productive and a more broad-based approach should be adopted, including bringing the military into the fold. Partly due to this and in order to bring all counter-terrorism efforts under "one roof", in 2010, Indonesia established the National Counter-Terrorism

Agency (Badan Nasional Penanggulangan Terrorisme) or BNPT to coordinate activities against extremists and terrorists in the country.

As was argued by Ansyaad Mbai (2014, p. 136), Indonesia first Head of the BNPT, the pre-BNPT approach to counter-terrorism was based on four legs:

a) Making the war on terrorism Indonesia's own matter.
b) Enlisting former terrorists as anti-terrorism campaigners.
c) Letting elite police forces rather than the military lead the counter-terrorism operations.
d) Try the terrorists judiciously and transparently in court.

Adopting a whole-of-government approach, that included police and military personnel, the BNPT, reporting to the President, was tasked with formulating policies on counter-terrorism, coordination, operational tasks covering prevention and enforcement, and international cooperation (Mbai, 2014).

Indonesia has enacted a number of counter-terrorism laws even though most observers believe that these need to be strengthened. Following the October 2002 Bali bombings, the Megawati Government rapidly passed its first counter-terrorism law, Law No. 15, 2003 on Countering Terrorism. In 2013, Law No. 9 on the Prevention and the Suppression of the Financing of Terrorism was also enacted. Indonesia has also enacted other counter-terrorism laws, in sync with the international community, including the Joint Regulation on Listing of Identity of Persons and Corporations in the List of Suspected Terrorists and Terrorist Organisations, and Freezing, Without Delay, Funds Owned by a Persons or Corporations Listed in the List of Suspected Terrorists and Terrorist Organisations (Combating Transnational Crime, 2016).

However, due to the continued spate of attacks and the threat of terrorism in Indonesia, there have been growing pressures to amend the existing laws. The major impetus was the rise of the IS threat where many Indonesians were involved as foreign fighters and where local groups supported the IS. There were also heightened fears of the threat that could be posed by returning fighters to Indonesia's national security. Following the January 2016 terrorist attack in Jakarta, pressure mounted on the Jokowi Government to amend the existing counter-terrorism laws that were deemed to be ineffective. Among others, this called for the following (see Singh, 2016):

a) The widening of the definition of radicalism and terrorism.
b) Granting the security apparatus powers to hold a suspect longer than a week without a criminal charge to allow the police more time to gather sufficient evidence to charge an individual.
c) Permitting the police to detain an individual for 180 days rather than the current 120 days so that a strong case can be made against suspects. Widening the definition of radicalism and terrorism will allow this in cases of incipient acts of terrorism.
d) Permitting communication, financial transactions, and intelligence reports to be used as evidence in courts to charge suspects for terrorism.
e) Giving intelligence officers the right to arrest terrorist suspects.
f) The revocation of citizenship for Indonesians who join a foreign terrorist group or participate in wars in a foreign country.
g) That acts of insulting the Indonesian State be criminalised, including viewing an Indonesian as a traitor if he/she fights for or pledges loyalty to other groups such as IS.
h) There were also calls for a more effective de-radicalisation and counter-radicalisation measures including strengthening the prison system, currently seen as the epicentre for terrorist recruitment in Indonesia, and the setting up of a special high security prison for leading jihadists and ideologues.

However, due to Indonesia's past negative experience with State-based authoritarianism, there remain embedded fears that the authorities may abuse their powers, especially the police and military. This also included concerted opposition from the main secular and Islamist political parties as well as civil society groups, fearing that the new laws could be abused and used against political dissenters rather than terrorists and to trample on human rights. This has been worsened by the concerted criticisms from the international community, especially scholars and civil society groups (Hwang, 2017). Thus, when the Indonesian Government decided to ban Hizbut Tahrir Indonesia on grounds that "it's vision of establishing an Islamic caliphate contradicted the value of Pancasila, which values diversity and pluralism", there was widespread criticism of the move. President Jokowi signed a regulation in lieu of law (Perpu) banning Hizbut Tahrir in July 2017 (Batu, 2017; Erlangga & Bilianzia, 2017). On 25 May 2018, following a spate of terrorist attacks in the country, Indonesia passed a new anti-terrorist law that empowered the military and police to more robustly counter the threat.

(2) *Indonesia's Hard Measures*

The establishment of Densus-88 proved critical in neutralising the threat posed by JI. Between 2002 and 2017, more than 1,300 Indonesian terrorists and extremists have been detained with more than 100 others killed in counter-terrorist operations. Despite criticisms from various human rights groups, the preparedness of the Indonesia State to criminalise and deal with an iron-fist those bent on the use of violence to achieve their political goals has been effective in denting the threat posed by jihadism thus far.

(3) *Indonesia's Soft Measures*

Together with the hard approach, various soft measures have also been instituted to adopt a balance and well-calibrated strategy to neutralise what essentially is a political threat to the state of Indonesia. Among others, these measures include:

a) Engaging former radicals and terrorists to show that the old cause was an error and this is often undertaken through the publication of books, lectures, and talk shows.
b) Partnering with the larger Muslim community, especially Nahdatul Ulama and Muhammadiyah, the two largest social-religious organisations in the country, to delegitimise the appeal of radicals and counter them by supporting the call for pluralism, diversity,

and tolerance, especially as enshrined in the country's state ideology of Pancasila.

c) Public campaigns through the mass media of the dangers of radicalism and terrorism.
d) Inter-agency cooperation, especially police, military, and intelligence agencies as well as mobilising every relevant ministry that aims to eradicate poverty, enhance knowledge, and promote pride and health of the Indonesian State and nation.
e) Academic and scholarly writings aimed at delegitimising the discourses of the extremists and the ideologies that they spread.
f) Partnering with religious leaders, especially respected Islamic scholars and religious figures, to provide deeper understanding of Islamic teachings and prevent its hijacking by radical discourses.
g) Prison monitoring to prevent radicalisation of the inmates by radicals.

(4) *Strengthening Intelligence Cooperation and Effectiveness*

This is mainly aimed at monitoring and reconnaissance of radical leaders and movements at home. As Indonesia is an archipelago consisting of 17,520 islands, the need for effective intelligence is one of the keys to neutralising the threat posed by extremism and terrorism, and this requires not just the mechanics of effective intelligence gathering and analysis but also, first and foremost, cooperation among the various military, police, and civilian intelligence agencies in the country. This has been taking place albeit at a slow pace due to inter-agency fighting over "turfs" and competition among the different agencies.

(5) *International Cooperation*

As no one state can counter the threat of terrorism today, the importance of international cooperation cannot be underestimated. In this regard, Indonesia has strongly emphasised the centrality of cooperation at the bilateral and multilateral levels. This is best evident through the Jakarta Centre for Law Enforcement Cooperation based in Semarang. Indonesia is also a signatory of various bilateral and multilateral agreements at the regional and international levels on counter-terrorism. According to the Indonesian Foreign Ministry, the country has engaged in various cooperation with the United Nations Counter Terrorism Implementation Task Force, the Terrorism Prevention Branch — United Nations Office for Drugs and Crime and the United Nations Counter-Terrorism Executive Directorate (Combating Transnational Crime, 2016). Indonesia has also ratified eight international conventions on counter-terrorism which strengthens its national legal framework to deal with the threat of extremism and terrorism (Combating Transnational Crime, 2016).

Conclusion

Indonesia provides a tried-and-tested laboratory of what practitioners and policymakers can learn from on what to do and what not to do in countering violent extremism in a state. Since the first Bali bombings in October 2002, much has been done to neutralise the threat posed by JI. This resulted in the police action that led to more than 120 terrorists being killed and more than 1,300 extremists and terrorists being jailed after being charged in courts for terrorism-related offence from 2003 to the present period. While leading terrorists such as Noordin M. Top, Dr. Azahari, and Dulmatin have been killed, leading ideologues such as Abu Bakar Bashyir, Aman Abdurrahman, and Abdullah Sunata are still languishing in prison.

While there is much success to talk of, at the same time, the threat of extremism and terrorism remains. Indonesians are among the leading supporters of the IS and actually provide the largest support in terms of manpower for its fighting unit in the Middle East called Katibah Nusantara that was led by a leading Indonesian radical, Bahrumsyah, who was killed in April 2018. Another Indonesian, Abu Jandal, who also played a key role in the unit, was killed in 2016.

In view of these developments, the case of Indonesia provides much that can be learnt as far as countering extremism and terrorism is concerned. Yet, as the threat continues, it is in part due to the fact that Indonesia is not only the largest Muslim nation in the world but also one where the constitution provides all kinds of freedoms that often constrain law makers from taking action against extremists. In this regard, one of Indonesia's most difficult challenges is to come out with effective counter-narratives to weaken, challenge, and neutralise the ideology that is being spread nationally through the mainstream and social media, through publications, in various educational and religious institutions, and even in prisons. If policymakers and practitioners are mindful of these "dos" and "don'ts", then there is much that can be learnt to make a state's counter-terrorism programme much more effective.

References

Batu, S. L. (2017). Jokowi signs regulation banning Hizbut Tahrir. *The Jakarta Post*. Retrieved from http://www.thejakartapost.com/news/2017/07/11/jokowi-signs-regulation-banning-hizbut-tahrir.html.

Combating transnational crimes (2016). Ministry of Foreign Affairs, Republic of Indonesia. Retrieved from https://www.kemlu.go.id/en/kebijakan/isu-khusus/Pages/Combating-Transnational-Crimes.aspx.

Erlangga, A. M., & Dilianzia, Y. (2017). Has Indonesia gone too far with its Hizbut Tahrir Ban? *Vice News*. Retrieved from https://www.vice.com/en_id/article/8qwx4x/has-indonesia-gone-too-far-with-its-hizbut-tahrir-ban.

Hwang, J. C. (2017). The unintended consequences of amending Indonesia's anti-terrorism law. *Lawfare*. Retrieved from https://www.lawfareblog.com/unintended-consequences-amending-indonesias-anti-terrorism-law.

Mbai, A. (2014). *The New Dynamics of Terror Networks in Indonesia*. Jakarta: AS Production Indonesia Publishing.

One in five Indonesia students support Islamic Caliphate: Survey (2017). *Reuters*. Retrieved from https://www.reuters.com/article/us-indonesia-islam-radicalism/one-in-five-indonesian-students-support-islamic-caliphate-survey-idUSKBN1D20KW.

Singh, B. (2016). Revising Indonesia's Anti-Terrorism Law. *RSIS Commentary*. Singapore: S. Rajaratnam School of International Studies.

Soebardi, S. (1983). Kartosuwiryo and the Darul Islam rebellion in Indonesia. *Journal of Southeast Asian Studies*, *14*(1), 109–133.

CHAPTER 2

Confronting the Threat of an ISIS Province in Mindanao

JOSEPH FRANCO

S. Rajaratnam School of International Studies, Nanyang Technological University, Singapore

Introduction

For five months, the Battle for Marawi dominated the discussion of violent extremism in the Philippines and even Southeast Asia. There were valid concerns that the siege was the harbinger of a revitalised Islamic State (IS) caliphate, this time centred on Southeast Asia. The ability of the IS-linked Maute Group (MG) and its allies, both Filipino and foreign fighters, to withstand government forces for an extended period only stoked such grim assessments. For the IS leadership in Syria and Iraq, the battle was a welcome respite. Images of intense fighting streaming in from Marawi provided propaganda fodder for IS supporters and sympathisers. It allowed IS to construct a narrative that offset the loss of the physical caliphate in the Middle East.

For the Philippines, the battle was the largest urban warfare scenario that the security services faced; drawing comparisons to the

World War Two-era Battle of Manila. More than a thousand were killed, mostly militants, when the end to major combat operations was declared on 23 October 2017 (Ng & Mogato, 2017). The fighting exhausted the already-stretched-thin Philippine military. Marawi, known as the centre of Islamic education and economic activity in central Mindanao was severely damaged. Reconstruction of the city would cost nearly SGD 2.3 billion (Salaverria, 2017), an amount exceeding the entire annual budget of Philippine government agencies.

The fighting may have ended and the commercial heart of Marawi may have been retaken, but the Battle for Marawi was not won. Less than three months after the liberation of Marawi, there is already unsettling news of the possibility of another similar attack in the future. In January 2018, the Intelligence Service of the Armed Forces of the Philippines warned that 50 foreign violent extremists remain in Mindanao, rebuilding a 400-strong force "almost the same strength that initially turned (*sic*) Marawi" (Torres-Tupas, 2018). It is clear that the gaps exposed by the Battle for Marawi need to be resolved lest a similar crisis unfolds in the near-term.

This chapter will look into the challenges of inhibiting the emergence of an IS province or *wilayah* in Mindanao. This includes challenges faced by stakeholders in detecting "weak" pre-attack signals, and ensuring both crisis and post-crisis communications. After identifying such challenges, this chapter shall attempt to provide policy prescriptions that seek to integrate lessons learned that could be surmised from the Battle for Marawi.

Challenges to Inhibiting the Emergence of a "Wilayah Mindanao"

The Battle for Marawi started when the Philippine military launched an *in extremis* operation to capture Isnilon Hapilon, the leader or *emir* of IS-pledged extremists in Mindanao. Expecting only a few dozen gunmen, the military forces were surprised when hundreds of MG fighters emerged from pre-established fighting positions. The tactical surprise the MG had over the security forces is hardly unexpected. Marawi is witness to frequent and sporadic episodes of violence. Any sudden appearance of armed fighters in the city was often met by residents in a dismissive fashion. The implicit expectation was that an open display of arms, should it develop into a skirmish, would cause minimal disruption and damage.

This heightened threshold for violence made it difficult to spot the early warning indicators of the impending violence. On a more strategic level, there were indications that everything was not "business-as-usual". As early as 2016, the MG had publicly threatened to "go down from the mountains to burn Marawi", only to solicit an angry response from Philippine President Rodrigo Duterte: "Go ahead, be my guest" (Macas, 2016). Rather than being blasé, the MG threat should not have been dismissed as mere bluster. Duterte's rhetoric only served to reinforce the complacent mindset in some segments of the security services.

(1) *Detecting Upstream Indicators such as Increased Recruitment*

Sans the Duterte's rambling policy pronouncements, it is apparent that the Philippine security services had a daunting task ahead of them. The MG, and the wider Maute clan, is just one of the many threat groups active in Mindanao. Decades of combat experience with different armed threat groups led to the creation of internal security doctrine, training, and practices more suited to addressing rural-based violent extremist groups. Prior to the Battle for Marawi, the MG followed this rural template, featuring in three major campaigns against the Philippine Army in rural Lanao del Sur, south of Marawi (Franco *et al.*, 2017).

What was missed by the military was the growing sophistication of the MG, specifically in conducting and documenting its urban operations. Telegram was the messaging app of choice by the MG and its sympathisers for disseminating images and video of attacks on military intelligence personnel based in Marawi (Franco, 2017a). Not only were the MG able to kill intelligence operatives, they were also able to identify and film sensitive installations around Marawi.

It was clear that the MG was drawing its membership not just from the rural population. What was emerging was an extremist group with a tech-savvy membership. The MG took advantage of the presence of Mindanao State University (MSU) in Marawi City in its recruitment campaign. Through Telegram, the MG and other IS-linked personalities were able to entice vulnerable youth to join violent extremist groups (Institute for Policy Analysis of Conflict (IPAC), 2017). Compared to other forms of digital messaging, encrypted apps were far beyond the reach of security services. Though such medium of communication, the MG was able to quietly amass its followers and lay the groundwork for the Maute siege.

(2) *Crafting a Responsive and Non-partisan CVE Campaign*

The use of encrypted messaging apps by the MG shrouded from view their actual strength and capabilities. However, even prior to the emergence of such technologies, the use of discreet communications by extremists has always existed. For security stakeholders, the most visible point of interaction for violent extremists to would-be recruits is their efforts at broadcasting and disseminating propaganda. As alluded to earlier, the MG was able to indigenise pre-existing jihadist content from the IS core and tweak it for their domestic audience (Franco *et al.*, 2017).

While the dynamics of online radicalisation remain contested, what is more readily apparent is the glaring lack of a comprehensive countering violent extremism (CVE) or preventing violent extremism (PVE) campaign by Manila. Decades into fighting the various violent extremist groups in Mindanao, the Philippines has yet to launch a cohesive CVE policy that would address the ideological appeal of jihadist belief in the Philippines. There is even lesser, or more correctly, no focus on the distinctiveness of online extremist propaganda.

At the very least, the national political leadership could have taken a consistent stance whenever the issue of violent extremism is brought up in the public space. Even Duterte's contrived tough-guy macho image curiously appeared ambivalent when it comes to violent extremist groups in Mindanao. On one occasion, Duterte defended the Abu Sayyaf Group (ASG) as "guys driven to desperation" (Parco, 2016). A year later, he repeatedly threatened the ASG that he will literally eat the liver of its members with "salt and vinegar" (Agence France Presse, 2017).

(3) *Detecting Imminent Pre-attack Indicators*

Given the stated goals of the MG to bring the fight to one of Mindanao's major urban centres, it would be fair to assume that there would be greater efforts to detect pre-attack indicators. Arguably, the raid to arrest Hapilon could be viewed as the culmination of an intelligence coup. But as the military itself admitted, it "underestimated" (Maitem & Umel, 2017) the strength of the MG or as the President himself put it, a "failure of intelligence" (Macas, 2017). Specifically, there were questions raised about how the MG were able to bring nearly a thousand militants into the city, nearly four times the initial estimates by the military.

Failure to detect the entry of violent extremists into the city cannot be solely attributed to the neutralisation of military intelligence operatives. It was symptomatic of pervasive insecurity in the city, which made it a conducive arena for violent extremist groups. When the fighting began, the MG and its other allies were able to take advantage of Marawi's built environment. Bunkers and shelters built by families to protect themselves during clan conflicts were turned by the MG into fighting positions. The proliferation of illicit firearms in the city was also exploited by the MG, providing them with a virtually inexhaustible supply of weapons and ammunition.

However, it was not only resources and preparations *in situ* that was missed by authorities. As the Battle for Marawi raged, it was belatedly discovered that the MG received financial aid from the IS leadership. More than S$2 million was transferred to the MG, according to the Philippine military ("IS provided more than S$2 million to support Marawi siege: Philippines military chief", 2017).

This discovery was contrary to prior operational methodologies of violent extremists in central Mindanao, which largely acquired their resources through self-sustaining criminal activity.

(4) *Developing Decisive Kinetic Military Capabilities*

Once a violent extremist group launches an attack, its swift defeat is necessary to deny it a propaganda opportunity. The MG's intent is to use the Marawi siege as a signal that it is ready to transit into a full-fledged *wilayah* in Southeast Asia. By holding the city, it would be able to mimic how IS captured the cities of Raqqa in Syria and Mosul in Iraq.

Had they successfully entrenched their presence, the MG would probably seek to present an image of Marawi as an idyllic and picturesque *hijrah* or migration destination for IS fighters and their families. Instead, the narrative of the MG shifted immediately. Propaganda videos as seen in the "Inside the Khilafah" series revealed the utter devastation of the Maute-held parts of the city. Rather than builders of a caliphate, the MG spun their actions as defenders — attributing the damage to the "crusaders" besieging their city (Franco, 2017b).

In reality, the Armed Forces of the Philippines (AFP) was ill-equipped for sustained urban conflict. Compared to other Philippine cities, Marawi's residences and commercial establishments were largely built with reinforced concrete as a hedge to aforementioned clan conflicts. This meant that the AFP had to resort to field expedient measures to maximise its firepower. Artillery was used as direct fire weapons, while lightly armoured vehicles were reinforced with wooden armour. Close air support from Air Force attack planes proved inadequate to destroy MG fortifications, necessitating repeated sorties.

Improvisation, while sufficing to dislodge the enemy, largely contributed to the scale of the destruction. Urban conflict is inherently destructive. However, had the AFP possessed more precision guided weapons, it would have mitigated the degree of collateral damage to the infrastructure of the city. It should also be stressed that combat in built-up areas would have been easier for the

AFP, had it possessed more robust communication equipment and ISR (intelligence, surveillance, and reconnaissance) assets.

(5) *Ensuring Accurate Crisis Communications*

The Battle for Marawi also showed the necessity of effective crisis communications, both in managing the immediate effects of the conflict and its aftermath. When the skirmishes first erupted, Manila was caught flat-footed with most of the law enforcement and military leadership overseas. When the Duterte Administration declared martial law over Mindanao, it referenced events that would be immediately disproven to not have occurred — such as the alleged beheading of the police chief in Marawi ("A police chief Duterte claimed was beheaded in Marawi siege says he's safe", 2017). This error highlights the necessity of attaining adequate situational awareness even in the face of crisis. In the Marawi case, the intent to promptly rationalise a political decision — the martial law declaration, only perpetuated erroneous information.

The hyperbolic claims made in the midst of the Marawi siege can be attributed to the penchant of Duterte to exaggerate events, only to backtrack when called out for the error. However, this is also indicative of the multiplicity of public affairs and communications offices linked to the Presidency. National, regional, and provincial offices, all maintain their respective press operations. This is on top of the various civil relations, civil military operations, and psychological operations units comprising the AFP. In short, the structural incoherence and stovepipes in various segments of the government may confuse the public.

Fortunately, it prevailed upon the Duterte Administration to streamline the communications flow regarding the Battle for Marawi. A week into the fighting, a "Mindanao Hour" was instituted as thrice-weekly "program to update the public on developments regarding the armed conflict in Mindanao" (Cabuenas, 2017). The Mindanao Hour designated only two individuals to be the public face of the government's crisis response: the presidential spokesperson and the AFP spokesperson.

Winning the Battle(s) after Marawi

The wide array of challenges facing stakeholders to prevent another Marawi siege requires employing a comprehensive approach. Violent extremism could not be resolved simply by kinetic measures to bring an end to an armed uprising. Simply countering the ideology of committed violent extremists is also self-limiting and freezes counterterrorism stakeholders into reacting to their adversaries' initiatives. The following prescriptions try to cover complementary approaches that cover the entire spectrum from pre-violent conflict up to the aftermath of widespread violence.

(1) *Identify Youth Leaders to Champion PVE and CVE*

Without the benefit of hindsight, it is difficult to fully grasp the upstream drivers of recruitment into violent extremist groups. There is no single profile that could be considered a stand-in as *the* type of individual vulnerable to recruitment. Rather than allocating disproportionate resources to finding out what kind of personality gets radicalised and recruited, it may be more productive to look instead at factors, which keep individuals away from violence. Taking this a step further, it may be useful to instead identify individuals or groups that could champion moderation, and channel radical mindsets into positive political action.

In the case of Marawi, a more engaged youth and student sector could have inoculated the mass base from which the MG recruited its fighting force. The student sector in the Philippines, especially in tertiary institutions, has a long, storied history of political activism. In Mindanao, the opposition to the dictatorial Marco regime crystallised competing student protest movements into a national-level movement in the 1970s. Fast forward to the present, MSU's student body continued this tradition albeit with a less adversarial relationship with the various post-Marcos regimes.

Youth leadership programmes could act as a way to channel student movements' exuberance and desire to affect political change. Admittedly, Manila would have to keep a light touch with such an effort, and prevent any impression that the capital is re-establishing dominance over the minority Filipino Muslim population. Civil society organisations (CSOs) and non-government organisations (NGOs) can act as surrogates for a deft national government policy, taking advantage of the pre-existing network of peace advocacy groups found in Mindanao. The skill sets necessary for effective peacebuilding and post-conflict reconstruction are fungible to the requirements of PVE and CVE. The presence of CSOs and NGOs in Mindanao constitute a virtuous network to counter-balance the illicit networks built by groups such as the MG.

(2) *Data-driven PVE and CVE*

Given the proliferation of various CSOs and NGOs, it is just a matter of collecting the relevant information to build up a common picture of the challenge posed by violent extremism. Various entities working on peace in Mindanao hold quantitative and qualitative data, which can be useful to build a nuanced picture of violent extremism. Conflict data as maintained by International Alert-Philippines and other initiatives funded by multilateral donors such as the World Bank, provide publicly-available data at the most granular level. *Barangay*, or village-level data, could provide insights to which areas may be vulnerable to the illicit activities of violent extremist groups.

Instead of simply rebranding strategies used to dismantle the secular Communist insurgency for Muslim Mindanao, Manila should start from scratch using information gathered in a scientific and systematic manner. By doing so, a new strategy would gain legitimacy. First, by anchoring a strategy on correct information, any malicious accusations of CVE or PVE solely targeting a religion is discredited. Second, a data-driven strategy would foster a greater sense of ownership for everyone involved as it would allow for crowdsourcing solutions.

(3) *Fused Offline and Online Intelligence*

Complementing the data-driven approach to PVE and CVE is the push for better intelligence gathering to guide kinetic operations.

Violent extremists' use of information and communications technology inevitably leave digital "breadcrumbs" for security agencies to follow. Open source intelligence (OSINT) techniques that are used widely in the private sector remain largely untapped by the Philippine security services. It must be stressed that opportunities abound for security services to scoop up publicly-accessible social media content produced by violent extremist groups. These can serve as leads for more technical means of intelligence gathering.

Encryption, as mentioned earlier, denies security services easy access to extremists' correspondence. Digital tools are bound by the limits of mathematics and physics that underlie encryption. However, what is online can be broken into by offline means. Encrypted chat applications, at its very core, remain tools used by individual humans. Tradecraft and investigation, social engineering, agent-handler networks may sound like relics of the Cold War, but are very much relevant in the post-9/11 era. Extremists could be targeted by subterfuge, ensnared by honeypots, and/or duped by operatives in digital disguise. Extremists do not hold the monopoly in digital duplicity and should thus be considered as fair game for "ungentlemanly" tactics.

(4) *Constant Monitoring of Adversary Capabilities*

The capabilities of violent extremist groups should also be monitored instead of fixating solely on their intent. Pronouncements made by the MG should not be taken at face value; given the faster news cycle and shorter attention spans, propaganda by violent extremist groups is often taken at face value. Eager to debunk extremist claims, counter-propaganda by stakeholders ends up legitimising the extremist discourse by inadvertently elevating ridiculous claims as binary equals.

For the CVE and counter-terrorist practitioner, it would be more practical to assess the capability of extremist groups to contextualise the threats made. By refraining from echoing extremist propaganda, the tendency of the populace to panic is minimised, curtailing its reach. At the same time, it would allow security services tasked with kinetic responses longer lead time to prepare responses and counter-measures.

For instance, it had been previously known that the MG and/or its allies had been experimenting with rudimentary fixed wing drones two years prior to the Battle for Marawi (Franco *et al.*, 2017). There was no discernible effort by the AFP to deny the MG opportunities to improve their tactics. By the time the Battle for Marawi erupted, the military was in for a surprise. The ability of the MG to monitor AFP movements in real-time was unprecedented — it took several debacles and deadly ambuscades before the counter-drone tactics were employed.

(5) *Cohesive Crisis and Strategic Communications*

The confusion that reigned during the opening salvoes of the Battle for Marawi could have been mitigated by communication plans put in place prior to the crisis. The so-called fog of war is pervasive in any form of conflict even between state and non-state actors. Confusion over the minutiae of how many were killed in a pitched urban conflict in Marawi is understandable, if any mistakes are rectified immediately and in a transparent manner. Obviously, attempts at transparency are complicated if national-level leaders have a penchant to share lurid and inaccurate details, ostensibly to galvanise public support. Chicanery may appear useful in the midst of the crisis, but it lays the foundation for public mistrust for any future crisis communication campaign.

The Mindanao Hour initiative is an example of an *ad hoc* arrangement formalised as the fighting continued unabated. Its longevity could not be attributed solely to its streamlined approach, but perhaps due to the protracted nature of the conflict. The critical lesson here: it does not suffice to have just unity of command in combat. Unity of communications is as important, especially if an adversary considers combat as a source of propaganda and not just as a fight between two armed parties.

It must also be stressed that the day-to-day of crisis communications should not impede the development and continuity of longer term strategic messaging campaigns. Notwithstanding the damage wrought to Marawi, the AFP came out of the fighting with a very favourable public perception. The sticky message and hashtag-friendly slogan of #SupportOurTroops became the shorthand for the themes of valour, integrity, and duty that were embedded into the AFP's social media presence throughout the Marawi siege. The flexibility of #SupportOurTroops makes it a viable slogan for a more enduring strategic communications theme.

Conclusion

End of fighting in Marawi has not terminated the threat posed by violent extremist groups. As IS reverts its influence back into the online space, its leadership is expected to seek out areas to open new fronts. The ability of the MG and its allies to hold a major urban centre and receive foreign fighters underscores the vulnerability of Mindanao to foreign jihadists' incursion. The challenges faced by stakeholders to prevent the permanent presence of an IS unit in Mindanao require a comprehensive approach. Only the combination of kinetic and non-kinetic initiatives, spanning the pre- and post-conflict periods could deny violent extremist groups another opportunity to launch another Marawi siege. Otherwise, Marawi siege could take its place as a model for jihadist expeditionary strategy not just in Southeast Asia but in other ungoverned spaces.

References

A police chief Duterte claimed was beheaded in Marawi siege says he's safe (2017). *The Philippine Star*. Retrieved from http://beta.philstar.com/headlines/2017/05/26/1703813/police-chief-duterte-claimed-was-beheaded-marawi-siege-says-hes-safe#IQePAeeD7uoF1zqu.99.

Agence France Presse (2017). 'I will eat your liver. I will eat it in front of you,' Duterte tells Islamist militants behind kidnappings. *South China Morning Post*. Retrieved from http://www.scmp.com/news/asia/southeast-asia/article/2101529/i-will-eat-your-liver-i-will-eat-it-front-you-philippines.

Cabuenas, J. V. D. (2017). Malacañang to launch 'Mindanao Hour' to update public on Marawi operations. *GMA News Online*. Retrieved from http://www.gmanetwork.com/news/news/nation/612424/malacanang-to-launch-mindanao-hour-to-update-public-on-marawi-operations/story/.

Franco, J. (2017a). Assessing the feasibility of a 'Wilayah Mindanao'. *Perspectives on Terrorism*, *11*(4), 29–38.

Franco, J. (2017b). Marawi: Winning the war after the battle. *International Centre for Counter-Terrorism*. Retrieved from https://icct.nl/publication/marawi-winning-the-war-after-the-battle/?lipi=urn%3Ali%3Apage%3Ad_flagship3_profile_view_base%3Bp9DEcoMRQ8OyGDI9kF9eZg%3D%3D.

Franco, J., Domingo, F., & Tolosa, K. (2017). Maute Group: What you need to know. *Security Reform Initiative* [Frequently Asked Questions]. Retrieved from http://www.securityreforminitiative.org/wp-content/uploads/2017/06/SRI-FAQs-Maute-Group-What-We-Need-To-Know-1.pdf.

Institute for Policy Analysis of Conflict (IPAC) (2017). Marawi, the "East Asia Wilayah" and Indonesia. *IPAC Report*, *38*. Retrieved from http://file.understandingconflict.org/file/2017/07/IPAC_Report_38.pdf.

IS provided more than S$2 million to support Marawi siege: Philippines military chief (2017). *TODAY Online*. Retrieved from http://www.todayonline.com/world/asia/provided-more-s2-million-support-marawi-siege-philippines-military-chief.

Macas, T. (2016). Duterte rebuffs Maute Group on threat to burn Marawi if AFP attacks won't stop. *GMA News Online*. Retrieved from http://www.gmanetwork.com/news/news/nation/592213/duterte-rebuffs-maute-group-on-threat-to-burn-marawi-if-afp-attacks-won-t-stop/story/.

Macas, T. (2017). Duterte admits failure of intelligence in Marawi City. *GMA News Online*. Retrieved from http://www.gmanetwork.com/news/news/nation/619295/duterte-admits-failure-of-intelligence-in-marawi-city/story/?tag=sona2017.

Maitem, J., & Umel, R. (2017). DND Chief admits underestimating Maute strength. *Inquirer.net*. Retrieved from http://newsinfo.inquirer.net/911735/dnd-chief-admits-underestimating-maute-strength.

Ng, R., & Mogato, M. (2017). Philippines declares battle with Islamist rebels over in Marawi City. *Reuters*. Retrieved from https://www.reuters.com/article/us-philippines-militants/philippines-declares-battle-with-islamist-rebels-over-in-marawi-city-idUSKBN1CS0F5.

Parco, B. (2016). Duterte says ASG not criminals; gunmen were 'driven to desperation'. *GMA News Online*. Retrieved from http://www.gmanetwork.com/news/news/nation/572986/duterte-says-asg-not-criminals-gunmen-were-driven-to-desperation/story/.

Salaverria, L. B. (2017). Marawi rebuilding to cost about P90B. *Inquirer.net*. Retrieved from http://newsinfo.inquirer.net/947478/philippine-news-updates-marawi-marawi-rehabilitation-majul-gandamra.

Torres-Tupas, T. (2018). About 50 foreign terrorists now operating in Mindanao — military official. *Inquirer*. Retrieved from http://newsinfo.inquirer.net/961159/about-50-foreign-terrorists-now-operating-in-mindanao-military-official?utm_campaign=Echobox&utm_medium=Social&utm_source=Facebook#link_time=1516169038.

CHAPTER 3

Insights for Practitioners and Policymakers from the Marawi Siege, May–October 2017

JASMINDER SINGH

S. Rajaratnam School of International Studies, Nanyang Technological University, Singapore

Introduction

The Marawi Siege or Incident from May to October 2017 was, in its simplest form, an attempt to replicate and transplant the self-proclaimed Islamic State's model of territorial control in Syria and Iraq into southern Philippines (Institute for Policy Analysis of Conflict (IPAC), 2016, 2017a, 2017b). It was to establish an Islamic State in Southeast Asia *à la* the Islamic State in Syria and Iraq (ISIS). Even though it failed, the fact that the terrorists could control large parts of the city for five months was a totally new experience and model of operation for jihadists in the Southeast Asian region. Today, with the terrorists often dubbed as some of the "best learning organisations" in the world, the question is, where is the next Marawi in Southeast Asia? Also, what led to the Marawi Incident, and how did the Philippine Government eventually succeeded in defeating the jihadists? Finally, what lessons can be learnt from the Marawi Incident for practitioners and policymakers in the region?

The Marawi Siege

From May to October 2017, the city of nearly 200,000 inhabitants, known as the Islamic city of peace in Mindanao, was partially occupied by jihadists. The Marawi Siege is best understood by being informed of the key actions and activities that took place from May to October, as listed in Table 3.1.

Five Factors that Led to the Marawi Siege

In a way, what transpired in Marawi from May to October 2017 was the culmination of a simmering jihadi conflict that had afflicted south Philippines for many decades (Coronel-Ferrer, 2017; Quimpo, 2016). However, more specifically, it was the result of changing alignments and alliances from pro-Al Qaeda to the ISIS that had been taking place since 2014 and, in particular, since 2016. In fact, in June 2016, ISIS released a video that recognised the pledges of allegiance from various militant groups in Mindanao with the Abu Sayyaf Group (ASG) leader, Isnilon Hapilon, recognised as the *Emir* of ISIS Philippines. The *Amaaq News* Agency, an ISIS's mouthpiece, acknowledged the presence of 10 such groups in six locations throughout Mindanao, including ASG, the Maute Group (MG), and *Katibah al-Muhajir*, a cell consisting of migrants from Malaysia and Indonesia (Singh & Jani, 2017a). ISIS's mouthpiece *Rumiyah* also began to refer to Philippines terrorists as being part of the "khilafah in East Asia". ISIS began describing Mindanao as a "Land of Hijrah and Jihad". From mid-2016 onwards, ISIS's sympathisers began popularising the terms "Wilayah al-Filibin" and "Wilayah Asia Timur" (or the East Asia Province in Malay), using them interchangeably. Many ISIS news reports on the region also began

Table 3.1. Timeline of the Marawi incident from May to October 2017.

Date	Incident
23 May	Marawi City, considered as a religious centre in Mindanao, was overrun by pro-Islamic State jihadists under the leadership of Isnilon Hapilon (the Emir of the Southeast Asia Wilayah and the Abu Sayyaf Group (ASG) leader), with the support of the Maute brothers, especially Abdullah and Omarkhayam.
24 May	President Rodrigo Duterte placed Mindanao under martial law with government officials claiming that an international band of fighters from the Middle East and Southeast Asia were supporting the jihadi takeover of the city.
31 May	The Moro National Liberation Front (MNLF) positioned fighters around Marawi City in support of the government's military operation.
1 Jun	In its bid to retake Marawi, 10 Filipino soldiers were killed in friendly fire.
8 Jun	The communist New People's Army deployed fighters in Marawi to support the government's forces.
10 Jun	13 Filipino Marines were killed.
13 Jun	The government announced that it was aware of the ISIS plot to seize Marawi.
29 Jul	Security forces scored a major victory in capturing key installations in the city.
5 Sep	The U.S. pledged U.S.$15 million for relief, recovery, and rehabilitation of Marawi City.
23 Sep	Security forces captured Marawi's third strategic bridge.
14 Oct	The government spokesperson claimed that 161 soldiers and 47 civilians had died with 817 militants killed. More than 360,000 people have also been displaced.
15 Oct	After many failed deadlines, the military announced its target to end the crisis.
16 Oct	The Philippines' Defence Chief, Delfin Lorenzana, announced that Hapilon and Omarkhayam are killed.
17 Oct	Duterte announced the liberation of Marawi City from the terrorists with a total of 163 government troops, 47 civilians, and 847 Maute fighters killed.
19 Oct	Duterte confirmed the death of Malaysian jihadi, Dr Mahmud Ahmad, who was allied with the Abu Sayyaf and Islamic State, as well as funded the Marawi operations.
21 Oct	The U.S. FBI confirmed Hapilon's death through DNA testing.
23 Oct	Delfin announced the termination of all combat operations in Marawi City.

Source: Compiled by author from public sources.

talking of al-Filibin as constituting the locus of ISIS's operations in *Sharq Asiya* (East Asia) (Singh & Jani, 2017a).

Also, in June 2016, *An-Naba*, ISIS's official weekly newsletter, began reporting news of skirmishes and attacks, and the taking over of militant camps by the Armed Forces of the Philippines (AFP), as if pro-ISIS fighters were engaged in regular warfare. On 24 November 2016, in an attempt at securing territory, MG planted an ISIS flag in front of the municipal hall of Butig, Lanao del Sur, in a siege that displaced close to three quarters of the population of the town. It took six days for the AFP to push MG back into the hills (Singh & Jani, 2017a). In hindsight, the Butig attack was a precursor of what was to transpire in Marawi City six months later. While ISIS did not consider *qital tamkin,* or conquering of territories, as its primary *modus operandi* of terrorism in the Philippines, there appears to be changes taking place that is in line with what had transpired in the Middle East, even though by this time ISIS was beginning to lose key territories in Iraq and Syria (Singh & Jani, 2017a).

Also, in line with the ISIS "business model" in the Middle East, Filipino jihadists in Mindanao began to accept the idea of accommodating foreign fighters in their ranks, as was done by Jemaah Islamiyah in the past or by ISIS in the Middle East. For instance, on 6 April 2017, the *Jama'at al Muhajirin wa al-Ansar bi al-Filibin* (JMAF) was formed — pledging allegiance to Abu Bakar al-Baghdadi — and operated in Maguindanao, Cotabato, and Davao, and led by Esmail Abdulmalik alias Abu Turaifie (Franco, 2017). This was also in line with Mindanao being a "Land of Hijrah and Jihad" or *ard al-hijrah wa al-jihad* (Singh & Jani, 2017a). In view of the deteriorating situation for ISIS in the Middle East, the call for jihadists to travel to Mindanao was consistent with the ISIS narrative, where Mindanao was viewed as an important node in the global caliphate (Singh & Jani, 2017d). Hence, if a foreign fighter was unable or unwilling to travel to the Middle East, ISIS was telling prospective jihadists from Indonesia, Malaysia, Singapore, Pakistan, Saudi Arabia, Yemen, India, Morocco, Turkey, China, and Chechnya to join the ISIS franchise in the Philippines.

These changing alignments and establishment of coalitions in support of ISIS were a consequence of a number of developments. First, it was in response to the AFP's commitment to neutralise the terror threat in Mindanao. Second, many jihadi groups were pledging loyalty to ISIS due to their sense of disillusionment with the failure of the peace deal negotiations. Many in areas controlled by the Moro Islamic Liberation Front (MILF) had invested hope in the peace deal, but its abortion following the 2015 Mamapasano Incident forced them to believe that a diplomatic solution was never possible. This made terrorism an attractive option rather than face the wrath of the AFP and corrupt politicians. Third, there was also the possibility that Mindanao could become a global village of "migrant fighters" from as near as Malaysia and Indonesia to as far as Morocco. To prevent a *déjà vu* scenario of the Afghan returnees in the 1980s, many states in the region began sharing intelligence on returning militants but it appeared to be a little too little and too late (Singh & Jani, 2017a).

Yet, in reality, the Marawi Siege, an urban war between pro-ISIS fighters and government forces, was also accidental. The 23 May 2017 military clash with armed fighters of Abu Sayyaf and the Mautes is believed to have been triggered by the AFP's attempt to arrest Philippines ISIS's leader, Hapilon (Fonbuena, 2017). This prompted the pro-ISIS fighters to fight back by declaring Marawi City as a new caliphate of ISIS in the Philippines. There is much support to the notion that what eventuated as a five-month siege of Marawi City was triggered by a botched attempt by the AFP to capture ISIS leaders in the city. This was because the Philippine Government is believed to have learnt that ISIS leaders were in Marawi City and that they planned to occupy the Islamic city of Marawi. According to Philippines Solicitor General, Jose Calida:

> ...the Philippine Government received intelligence information at least five days before the Militants prematurely launched their bloody assault on Marawi City on May 23 after Government forces raided the hideout of militant leaders led by Isnilon Hapilon. The rebel plan was to launch the attack on May 26 or 27, the start of the Muslim holy month of Ramadhan in the country's south. The said attack would have served as the precursor for other rebel groups to stage their own uprisings across Mindanao in a bid to simultaneously establish a *wilayah* in the region ("Philippines says it learned of city siege plans in advance", 2017).

This leads one to conclude that there are five factors that practitioners and policymakers should be aware of about what led to the Marawi Siege. These are:

a) The Marawi Siege was not a standalone event but a culmination of ongoing jihadi struggle in the Philippines since the 1960s, first being led by the MNLF, then by the MILF, followed by a whole litany of groups such as the Abu Sayyaf and others which were aligned with the Al Qaeda at first and later to ISIS, and which joined forces in a mega coalition in an attempt to capture Marawi City along the lines of what ISIS had achieved in parts of Iraq and Syria.
b) It also stemmed from the failure of government forces to anticipate that the jihadists, which have been operating in areas such as Jolo and Basilan would target Marawi City. In a way, it was a major failure on the part of the intelligence agencies to detect the plan by pro-ISIS elements to capture Marawi even though later this was denied by Manila. If it was really true that the Philippine Government had prior knowledge of the plot, it is unlikely that a relatively small military force would have been deployed in Marawi City and top political and military leaders would still have accompanied President Duterte to Moscow. Philippines Defence Secretary, Delfin Lorenzana admitted that "there are a lot of talks coming around that there was a failure of intelligence, in a way it was" (Mangosing, 2017).
c) It was also a result of the failure of the Philippine counter-terrorist agencies to take seriously the narratives that were being put out by ISIS and its propaganda machinery about Mindanao and the Philippines in ISIS game plan. With ISIS speaking of Mindanao as a "Land of Hijrah and Jihad" and especially after the Butiq attack, the Philippine Government should have anticipated that something "big" was likely to happen, something that analysts were already predicting following ISIS's slow defeat in the Middle East and its attempts to divert attention elsewhere, especially after the Philippines was declared as part of ISIS's *wilayah*.

d) The failure of the Philippines security and intelligence apparatus is also apparent from the fact that Marawi City was not simply an operation conducted by Filipino jihadists but also by many foreign fighters. There were serious lapses in security, especially in the south of the country that so many outsiders could congregate in Marawi City in support of an ISIS operation from May to October 2017.
e) The Marawi Siege, though eventually defeated, was also the result of the success of the jihadists in diverting and splitting the deployments of Philippine security forces in various parts of Mindanao, that allowed the jihadists to attack almost at will and occupy the urban centre of Marawi City for nearly 150 days.

Identifying the Key Approaches that Led to the End of the Marawi Siege

The Marawi Siege proved costly for the Philippines and dented the reputation of its counter-terrorist agencies that needed five months to silence the guns of the jihadists and regain lost territories, especially since terrorists are not noted for holding territories compared to launching deadly attacks (Singh, 2017b). With more than a thousand lives lost and more than 360,000 people displaced, not to mention the millions of dollars of damage done to the city centre, it will take a long time and hundreds of millions of dollars to restore the city to normalcy.

Still, eventually, the Philippines succeeded in retaking Marawi City from the jihadists. This was the result of a number of strategies, even though they would prove costly in the short to medium term. The success in retaking Marawi was due to the following factors:

a) The determination of Duterte Government, especially the security apparatus to isolate Marawi City and, hence, the jihadists in a particular locality of the city and where they could, through attrition, defeat them physically.
b) The systematic efforts by the government to win domestic and international support in its operations against the jihadists, even

though it costs the loss of many lives and massive damage to property.

c) The "bullet for bullet" approach of the security forces that ended the siege and where the jihadists were prepared to fight to the last. However, once their key leaders were killed, the siege dissipated and ended with a victory for the Philippines Government.
d) Just as the ISIS-led terrorists operated on the model of "whole-of-terrorist" network, part of the reason for the success of the Duterte government in ending the Marawi Siege was also the concept of "whole-of-government-society" approach to isolate the ISIS-led terrorists in Marawi City. This was done by garnering the support of the Communist New People's Army (NPA) and Islamists from the MNLF and MILF to fight against the Hapilon-led forces.
e) A major reason for the success of the Philippine Government in Marawi City was the inability and prevention of the Hapilon-led forces from diverting their offensive operations elsewhere outside Marawi City. This greatly benefitted the AFP and the counter-terrorist forces as they could concentrate on isolating and exterminating the jihadists who were holed up in a particular part of Marawi City, even though it took five months to end the siege as this was an urban warfare where the forward movement is slow and highly dangerous.

Lessons for Practitioners and Policymakers from the Marawi Siege

Even though the Philippine Government eventually succeeded in seizing control of the city from the jihadists and killing the country's top Islamist militants, Hapilon and Omarkhayam Maute, it was nevertheless achieved at great costs in terms of lives and property, as well as the embarrassment that it was the first successful capture by jihadists of a government territory *à la* ISIS in the Middle East. It also ended for good the much-debated discussion about whether there were ISIS and pro-ISIS operatives in the Philippines (Singh, 2017b).

The game-changing Marawi incident where, for the first time, pro-ISIS jihadists were able to practice the concept of *qital tamkin,* namely, of undertaking armed struggle aimed at seizing territories wherein Islamic law is applied in an urban environment in Southeast Asia, represents a new danger that offers many lessons and meanings for counter-terrorism in the region (Singh & Jani, 2017c). Some of these are explained in the following.

(1) *Rise of the Concept and Practice of Whole-of-terrorist Network*

With ISIS seeing its supporters as "soldiers of the Khilafah", a whole-of-terrorist network became the *modus operandi* for the Marawi Siege. The network included terrorists of various nationalities, including from the Philippines, Indonesia, Malaysia, Myanmar, Singapore, and possibly Chinese Uighurs, Myanmar Rohingyas, as well as Arabs and Africans. This network demonstrates close cooperation between jihadists from Southeast Asia, including the revival of old networks, such as that of the Jemaah Islamiyah. It also highlights the extreme vulnerability of the tri-border region of southern Philippines, East Malaysia, and eastern Indonesia to terrorism in the region.

(2) *ISIS's Regional Offensive*

The ISIS-sanctioned and -supported Marawi city attack shows that the region is important strategically for ISIS, and this is partly due to the majority of its Muslim adherents being Sunni Muslims. Indonesia has the largest Muslim population in the world and the country's military leaders have noted that ISIS cells exist in nearly all the provinces. This becomes all the more important at a time when ISIS is decentralising its operations in the face of its apparent defeat in the Middle East, and it having lost its cities and territories in Mosul and Raqqa. The ISIS-style jihadism in the Philippines is an attempt at the regionalisation of Islamic State in Southeast Asia. The danger of the Marawi attack is that it may motivate other groups to adopt the ISIS "business model" of attacking government forces and occupying cities in the region. Such attacks are likely to prove very costly to the region, causing, among others, increase in instability, increase in sectarianism, negatively affecting economic growth, and creating a negative image for the region. For the terrorists, however, this is a positive zero-sum game to win more recruits, publicity, resources, and possibly territory.

(3) *Need for Effective Counter-measures*

After many decades of attempting to make the region's ground infertile for extremism and terrorism, the Marawi Incident clearly signposted that much more needs to be done. As the siege was permitted to play out for five months, it gave the jihadist ideologues an opportunity to frame religious arguments in their favour, in turn, providing the potential for a long-term threat to the region. While deradicalisation and counter-ideology measures are important long-term measures, the short-term measures are vitally important in neutralising the terrorist threat. In this regard, in addition to preventing bomb attacks and assassinations, and the capture of cities and territories by terrorists, a whole-of-government and a whole-of-society approach becomes even more imperative. States would have to move beyond the rhetoric of counter-terrorism and undertake more decisive actions. In the case of Indonesia, for instance, through *Operation Tinombala*, it was demonstrated that it was possible to neutralise terrorist networks through close cooperation between military, police, and intelligence agencies, rather than quarrelling about who should dominate the "turf" of counter-terrorism. Even more important as terrorists have mastered the art of urban warfare, there is a need for counter-terrorist agencies to acquire urban warfare tactics. Beyond collaboration, there is a need for the police and military to cross-train so as to completely acquire and master the tradecraft and skills of urban warfare in its various dimensions.

(4) *Danger of ISIS Returnees from the Middle East and Marawi*

For Southeast Asia, while there is much concern about ISIS returnees from Iraq and Syria, with the Marawi attack, there is also the need to be concerned with returnees from the southern Philippines who have experienced a new type of jihad. As many non-Philippines Southeast Asian jihadists were involved in the Marawi attack, greater regional cooperation would be imperative to defeat the threat of terrorism in the region. The announcement on 13 June 2017 that joint patrols in the Sulu Sea will be operationalised, displays the seriousness with which governments are approaching the issue and is "two-cheers" for joint counter-terrorism efforts in the region.

(5) *Danger of Post-Hapilon Jihadism in the Philippines and Southeast Asia*

Even though the deaths of Hapilon and Omarkhayam are significant, there are still many other key jihadi leaders in Mindanao, including Abu Abdillah al Muhajir, the purported leader of the East Asia Wilayah. The deaths of Hapilon and Omarkhayam is likely to dent the morale of the jihadi fighters, but with both seen as syahids or martyrs dying for the jihadi cause, this is also likely to boost new recruits into the jihadi movement. Just as the deaths of many previous commanders and leaders of various jihadi and militant groups — like Mohammad Jaafar Maguid of the Ansarul Khilafah Philippines and Khaddafy Janjalani of the ASG — did not terminate the jihadi movement, the same can be expected of the situation in the Philippines. ISIS has continued to call on its supporters to view the Philippines as the "Land of Hijrah and Jihad", best epitomised by an ISIS video involving Singaporean jihadi that was released on 30 December 2017. In fact, in addition to the Middle East ISIS narrative, there is also the Marawi narrative which aims to exhort its supporters and recruits to continue the struggle and launch attacks against the "enemies" wherever and whenever possible.

In view of the Marawi experience, jihadists in Southeast Asia are already talking of training the next generation of mujahidins in the region. As a pro-ISIS posting warned, "Marawi is just the beginning" and "new cubs and soldiers" will be trained to fight the "crusader forces". The Marawi experience is seen as part of the jihadists' laboratory to enhance their coming struggle. From this perspective, the survivors of the Marawi siege are likely to continue the struggle in the Philippines and in all probability, the scale of violence may increase markedly.

(6) *ISIS's Tactics in the Philippines*

For pro-ISIS jihadists such as Hapilon and the Maute brothers, they had a different conception of victory as compared to professional militaries. For a western commander, they usually measure success in terms of enemy casualties, dwindling enemy resistance, troop advancements, and territories that are recaptured. For ISIS's strategists behind the Marawi attack, they viewed success from a different angle. This was seen from the perspective of:

a. Turning the residents of Marawi against the military, the government, and countrymen, exposing the state's inability to protect its citizens, and slowly weakening the state's resolve to secure its peripheral territories. To achieve these objectives, the Islamic State in the Philippines strived to ensnare the military in a prolonged battle and create a humanitarian crisis with evacuations and displacement of people.
b. Drawing the military into urban warfare by fighting in an urban environment which they had prepared for in advance. Even though the jihadists eventually lost the battle, forcing the military into bombing houses to clear sniping positions and tunnelled strongholds have also resulted in huge casualties on all sides. The aim was to eventually blame the state security apparatus for the resultant destruction, especially since much of the historical city of Marawi has been devastated, and this fallout will transpire when the evacuees return.
c. In the military struggle for Marawi City, the jihadists resorted to game-changing suicide attacks, charging out into clusters of soldiers in order to lob grenades, even if they may lose their lives. These suicide attacks or *istishhad* (martyrdom operations) have been viewed as heroic acts to gain another narrative advantage against a powerful enemy. The person who carries out such an

act will be celebrated by terrorists and their supporters as *shahid* or a martyr. Istishhad also encompasses suicide bombing, which was suspected to have happened on 13 August 2017 in Marawi city. If confirmed, it would be the first known suicide attack in the Philippines. Continued suicide bombings in Marawi and elsewhere would demoralise the troops, terrorise the population, create further instability in the state, and delegitimise the political leaders. For ISIS's strategists, these human "smart bombs" are cheap, use low-technology, require little training, and are difficult to stop. Such bombs can also reach their targets with ease. They also easily compensate for the asymmetry of a powerful enemy, and can have the desired negative and disastrous psychological impact on the enemy and its population.

(7) *Rise of Post-Hapilon pro-ISIS Leadership in the Philippines*

Even though Hapilon may be dead, this does not lead to the crumbling of the jihadi movement or struggle in the Philippines. If anything, new leaders will emerge, as has been the pattern of jihadi regeneration in the past, be it in the Philippines or rest of Southeast Asia. In the context of South Philippines, where clan and tribal ties are extremely critical in leadership selection and leading of any jihadi movement, three key leaders are worth watching. First is Abu Dar, a Maranao. Originating from Lanao del Sur, he is a member of the Maute Group (MG) and believed to be the spiritual adviser of the MG. He has also been identified by the Philippines military as the current leader of the MG, being the sole survivor of the Marawi siege. Also important is Abu Turaifie who leads the breakaway faction of the Bangsamoro Islamic Freedom Fighters. The new group is known as Jamaatul Muhaajireen Wal Ansar and is based in the Maguindanao region of south Philippines. Third in importance is Furuji Indama, of Yakan ethnicity, based in Basilan, who is from the ASG, the key group that led the Marawi siege under the leadership of Hapilon. Clearly, in the post-Hapilon era, there are established jihadi leaders in the Philippines and whoever is helming the jihadi struggle, the Southeast Asian region has to be vigilant, as the threat remains an urgent one.

Conclusion

In some ways, the Marawi City incident or siege is not only a turning point and watershed for counter-terrorism operations in the Philippines but also for the whole of Southeast Asia. This is based on the fact that the Marawi Siege was part of ISIS's offensive in Southeast Asia, undertaken in the name of the East Asian Wilayah and under its Emir, Hapilon, and also involved many terrorists from Southeast Asian states such as Indonesia, Malaysia, and Myanmar. It was also for the first time that terrorist groups have succeeded in holding a territory for almost five months while in the past, its attacks tended to be assassinations or bomb attacks on strategic or symbolic installations such as airports, police stations, or hotels. It is in view of these factors that there is much to learn from the Marawi Siege, especially on why terrorists may be tempted to capture territories, what went into their planning (that was almost undetected), and how eventually the security forces succeeded in defeating the terrorists in Marawi City. Now, the key question is: what should be expected after the Marawi City incident, especially in view of the fact that many of its leaders are still alive such as Abu Turaifie and Abu Dar (Singh, 2017c).

References

Coronel-Ferrer, M. (2017). Jihadists rise in Mindanao. *Inquirer.net*. Retrieved from http://newsinfo.inquirer.net/903518/jihadists-rise-in-mindanao.

Fonbuena, C. (2017). Where the Marawi war began: The safe house in Basak Malutlut. *Rappler*. Retrieved from https://www.rappler.com/newsbreak/in-depth/184915-marawi-war-began-safe-house-basak-malutlut.

Franco, J. (2017). Assessing the feasibility of a 'Wilayah Mindanao'. *Perspectives on Terrorism*, *11*(4), 29–38.

Institute for Policy Analysis of Conflict (IPAC) (2016). *Pro-ISIS groups in Mindanao and their links to Indonesia and Malaysia* (Report No. 38).

Retrieved from http://file.understandingconflict.org/file/2018/04/IPAC_Report_33_Edit.pdf.

Institute for Policy Analysis of Conflict (IPAC) (2017a). *Marawi, the 'East Asia Wilayah' and Indonesia* (Report No. 33). Retrieved from http://file.understandingconflict.org/file/2017/07/IPAC_Report_38.pdf.

Institute for Policy Analysis of Conflict (IPAC) (2017b). *Post-Marawi lessons from detained extremists in the Philippines* (Report No. 41). Retrieved from http://file.understandingconflict.org/file/2017/11/IPAC_Report_41_Davao.pdf.

Mangosing, F. (2017). Marawi crisis was a lesson for us — Lorenzana. *Inquirer.net*. Retrieved from http://newsinfo.inquirer.net/917448/marawi-crisis-was-a-lesson-for-u.

Philippines says it learned of city siege plans in advance. (2017). *Bloomberg*. Retrieved from https://www.bloomberg.com/news/articles/2017-06-14/philippines-says-it-learned-of-city-siege-plans-in-advance.

Quimpo, N. G. (2016). Mindanao: Nationalism, Jihadism and frustrated peace. *Journal of Asian Security and International Affairs*, *3*(1), 1–26.

Singh, J. (2017a). The 2017 Marawi Attacks: Implications for regional security. *RSIS Commentaries*. Singapore: S. Rajaratnam School of International Studies. Retrieved from URL: https://www.rsis.edu.sg/rsis-publication/icpvtr/co17120-the-2017-marawi-attacks-implications-for-regional-security/#.W4oNb_ZuJPY

Singh, J. (2017b). "Liberation" of Marawi: Implications for Southeast Asia. *RSIS Commentaries*. Singapore: S. Rajaratnam School of International Studies. Retrieved from URL: https://www.rsis.edu.sg/rsis-publication/icpvtr/co17197-liberation-of-marawi-implications-for-southeast-asia/#.W4oNl_ZuJPY.

Singh, J. (2017c). ISIS' Amin Baco: Tri-border Emir in Southeast Asia. *RSIS Commentaries*. Singapore: S. Rajaratnam School of International Studies. Retrieved from URL: https://www.rsis.edu.sg/rsis-publication/icpvtr/co17223-isis-amin-baco-tri-border-emir-in-southeast-asia/#.W4oNrfZuJPY

Singh, J., & Jani, M. H. (2017a). ISIS in East Asia: Strategic shifts and security implications. *RSIS Commentaries*. Singapore: S. Rajaratnam School of International Studies. Retrieved from URL: https://www.rsis.edu.sg/rsis-publication/icpvtr/co17090-isis-in-east-asia-strategic-shifts-and-security-implications/#.W4oNxvZuJPY

Singh, J., & Jani, M. H. (2017b). IS-inspired militancy in Mindanao is far from over. *Today Online*. Retrieved from http://www.todayonline.com/commentary/inspired-militancy-mindanao-far-over.

Singh, J., & Jani, M. H. (2017c). The siege of Marawi city: Some lessons. *RSIS Commentaries*. Singapore: S. Rajaratnam School of International Studies. Retrieved from URL: https://www.rsis.edu.sg/rsis-publication/icpvtr/co17153-the-siege-of-marawi-city-some-lessons/#.W4oN-fZuJPY

Singh, J., & Jani, M. H. (2017d). The Marawi narrative: "Inside the Caliphate". *RSIS Commentaries*. Singapore: S. Rajaratnam School of International Studies. Retrieved from URL: https://www.rsis.edu.sg/rsis-publication/icpvtr/co17169-the-marawi-narrative-inside-the-caliphate/#.W4oOEvZuJPY

Section 2

Insights for the Identification of Violent Extremists

If you have a lone wolf... mounting something and people do not know about it, it is very difficult to pre-empt and prevent... If you have a group, then there will be signs... we may pick something up, and we have a better chance of breaking it up beforehand. But even then, it is not certain.

MR LEE HSIEN LOONG
PRIME MINISTER

CHAPTER 4

Threat Assessment of Violent Extremism: Considerations and Applications

WHISTINE CHAI

Home Team Behavioural Sciences Centre, Ministry of Home Affairs, Singapore

Introduction

As the world witnesses an upward trend of violent extremist attacks in the last decade, actively preventing attacks via identifying threats and implementing appropriate interventions would be imperative. Often, studies reveal that violent extremism emerges from a heterogeneous population, and identifying individuals at risk of radicalisation is challenging (Christmann, 2012). The profile of violent extremists diverges in various areas including socioeconomic status, education, and family background (Christmann, 2012). In the past, violent extremists were perceived as individuals who would be affiliated to known violent extremist networks or trained in weapons or paramilitary training. As lone wolf attacks such as the 2014 Sydney siege and the 2016 Orlando shooting have shown, the perpetrators did not exhibit any of the aforementioned characteristics, and these attacks defy expectations of who a violent extremist should be (Chew & Chai, 2016).

How can these lone wolf operatives who claim to act on behalf of violent extremist groups, but are not directly supported or instructed by them, be identified? Can attacks by these individuals be intervened and prevented? These questions can be potentially addressed by the notion of threat assessment. Threat assessment has been proven to be integral in the management and prevention of targeted violence (Meloy & Hoffman, 2013), and this chapter will discuss how threat assessment can be applied to violent extremism.

Threat Assessment as a Fact-Based Evaluation Approach

Developed and fine-tuned by the United States Secret Service, threat assessment is adopted to identify the level of threat posed by an individual to a known group or individual at a particular time. Specifically, threat assessment is a fact-based evaluation approach designed to identify, assess, and manage targeted violence, and it can be applied in various domains such as domestic violence and even violent extremism (Borum *et al.*, 1999).

Instead of relying on descriptive or demographic variables to create a profile of attackers, threat assessment recognises that low frequency of targeted violence requires an approach that is versatile yet specific enough to minimise wrongful identification (be it a threat or non-threat) due to extrapolation from insufficient profiles. Threat assessment utilises the Structured Professional Judgment (SPJ) approach that is highly contextualised. As this approach is individualised and time-specific, threat assessment should be conducted at regular intervals to determine the changing levels of threat posed by the same subject (Meloy & Hoffman, 2013).

Threat Assessment as an Effective Approach in Assessing Violent Extremism

Compared to traditional violent extremist assessment approaches, the threat assessment approach may be more effective in identifying and preventing lone wolf threats, which tend to be more fluid, isolated, and volatile than previous violent extremist threats (Christmann, 2012). Lone wolves usually operate alone, and their modus operandi is self-directed (Honnavalli *et al.*, 2017). Past incidents suggest that lone wolves tend to operate under the radar of traditional violent extremist assessment approaches which may be merely sensitive to the *intent*, *commitment*, and *capability* of the attacker (Böckler *et al.*, 2015; Chew & Chai, 2016; O'Brien, 2014). The following discusses why traditional violent extremist assessment approaches may not be apt for predicting and identifying lone wolf attacks.

Traditional violent extremist assessment approaches predominantly focus on the intent, commitment, and capability of an attacker. Intent can be identified when the attacker communicates the plans or intentions to launch an attack. Commitment is shown through the attacker's affiliation with the violent extremist groups, and capability can be measured in the amount of weapons or paramilitary training that the attacker had undergone (Böckler *et al.*, 2015; Chew & Chai, 2016; O'Brien, 2014). However, recent high-profile lone wolf attacks, such as the 2011 Frankfurt airport attack, the 2014 Sydney siege, and the 2016 Orlando shooting, have shown that lone wolf attackers may not have communicated any intention or had direct affiliation with any violent extremist groups. Further investigation also revealed that these perpetrators did not have adequate training for the attacks. In all three cases, one man with a gun was all it took (Böckler *et al.*, 2015; Chew & Chai, 2016; O'Brien, 2014).

Many traditional violent extremist assessment procedures are designed for the detection of affiliated violent extremists, and these assessment items and criteria may not characterise lone wolf attackers. For example, Leson (2005) lists the following as characteristics to evaluate the threat of violent extremists who are affiliated with groups:

a) *Existence*: Presence of a violent extremist group, and the group is able to gain access to a particular district or location.

b) *Capability*: Capacity or ability of a violent extremist group to conduct a successful attack.
c) *Intent*: Indication of a violent extremist group activity — projected or conducted.
d) *History*: Presence of violent extremist activity/movement in the past.
e) *Targeting*: Presence of activity or credible information that signals any preparations for a violent extremist operation.
f) *Security environment*: Nature of political and security environment, and how it may impact the ability of a violent extremist group to carry out the attack.

The aforementioned characteristics would work well for identifying affiliated violent extremists, but may prove otherwise for lone wolves as they may not be affiliated to any existing violent extremist groups, nor have demonstrated any violent extremist activity in the past. Given that threat assessment is an approach that is versatile yet specific enough to identify unique cases, this chapter proposes the use of threat assessment to determine the nature and the degree of risk a given individual may pose. How does threat assessment fit into violent extremism? Literature review suggests that the three guiding principles of threat assessment correspond with the main findings in the research on violent extremism.

Threat Assessment Principle 1: There are Pathways to Violent Extremism

Importantly, threat assessment is governed by three fundamental principles (Fein & Vossekuil, 1998). The first principle states that there is always a pathway to targeted violence, with a series of perceptible thoughts and actions (see Figure 4.1 for an example of an escalation pathway of targeted violence). Threat assessment assumes that targeted violence is not spontaneous but usually requires a plan which fulfils the motives of the perpetrator. Henceforth, the violent extremists would undergo a path where he gradually becomes radicalised and sees violence as the way to

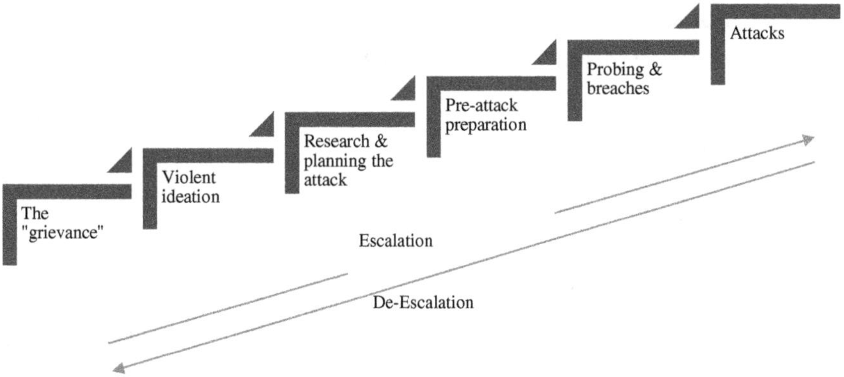

Figure 4.1. Escalation Pathway of Targeted Violence (Calhoun & Weston, 2003).

achieve his/her goals. Specifically, personal grievance plants the seed for violent ideation. Violent ideation then leads to the conducting of research and making preparation for the attack. Similarly, convergent findings from the violent extremism literature highlight that the process of radicalisation is a gradual one, via a pathway or series of phases before plotting the actual attack (Honnavalli *et al.*, 2017; Prech, 2007). By and large, violent extremists would go through a cycle of probing and breaches before the actual attacks. Given this pathway of targeted violence, there will be signs of preparation for an attack in order to achieve these goals (Borum *et al.*, 1999).

Various pathways (e.g., Staircase to Terrorism, RECRO Model) have been proposed to understand one's gradual embrace of radical ideologies and consequential implementation of violent action (e.g., Gill, 2007; Moghaddam, 2005; Neo, 2016; Neo & Dillon, 2016; Sageman, 2007; Taarnby, 2005; Wiktorowicz, 2004). Dean (2014) provides a comprehensive review of the proposed models of pathways to violent extremism. While different proposed models may emphasise on different factors such as social environment or online environment in the path of radicalisation and violent extremism, all models have a common characteristic: they acknowledge that radicalisation is a process that has a unique combination of precipitating characteristics.

Threat Assessment Principle 2: Violent Intent and Behaviours Stem from a Combination of Precipitating Factors

The second principle of threat assessment argues that violence is a result of an interaction between the subject, past adversities, and current circumstances. The perpetrator of an attack may exhibit unique characteristics or risk factors that increase the risk of one's degree of violence. For example, endorsing an ideology that justifies the use of violence has been shown to be a risk factor that may increase an individual's risk of violent extremism (Pressman, 2009). Significant events in the perpetrator's history may lead to grievances and violent intent, and current circumstances may provide an opportunity for him or her to commit the actual attack. The resultant violent action therefore precipitates from an interaction between the three factors and should not be derived solely from one.

Violent extremism is determined and driven by multiple factors and motivations, such that different individuals go through individualised pathways of radicalisation, and some may move on to commit violent action. Each individual ascribes meaning to their actions based on the interactions of different factors. For example, Borum (2015) suggests eight clusters of risk and protective factors that elevate or reduce an individual's risk of violent extremism: emotion, behaviours, cognitive style, beliefs/ideology, attitudes, social factors, identities, and capacities/abilities. These eight factors can be further categorised into factors relating to subject, past adversities, or current circumstances, supporting the idea that an individual may be predisposed to violent extremism given his attributes and past and present conditions.

Threat Assessment Principle 3: There are Warning Signs that Signal an Impending Terror Attack

Finally, the third principle highlights the importance of identifying warning signs in detecting and mitigating threats. Warning behaviours are changes in behaviours that indicate an enhanced risk of violence that requires an operational response (Meloy *et al.*, 2012). Warning behaviours constitute dynamic variables that grant accuracy to acute violence risk assessment. However, warning behaviours can only serve as signals if they are observed in the first place. Threat assessment would not be feasible if warning behaviours are absent prior to an attack (Unsgaard & Meloy, 2011). Therefore, intelligence and information gathering are crucial in detecting warning behaviours.

Past research has successfully identified some warning behaviours specific to different types of targeted violence (Meloy *et al.*, 2012). For instance, among adolescent mass murderers or school shooters, suicide ideation and indirect communication of malicious intents to family tend to signal an imminent threat. More than half the adolescent mass murderers or school shooters made threats to third parties prior to committing the transgression (Chia & Chai, 2015; Meloy *et al.*, 2001). As there is a pathway of attack, threat assessment principles assume that one will make preparations at an opportune time for attack. Likewise, in order to launch a successful attack, the violent extremist will need to make preparations which may require months to years. Inevitably, during the preparations phase, there would be signs of pre-attack behaviours that are accessible to the investigator for assessment. Recognising these warning behaviours will enable the law enforcement officers and professionals to detect and prevent immediate threats of terror attacks (Chia & Chai, 2015).

Threat Assessment Consists of Five Key Steps

With a better understanding of the three guiding principles, threat assessment consisting of five key steps could be conducted. Threat assessment entails an in-depth evaluation of an individual's background, characteristics, lifestyle, and observable behaviours which vary from non-threatening to malicious (O'Toole & Smith, 2013). While conducting threat assessment, the investigator is involved in a dynamic process, from the analysis of fact patterns of the case to the interpretation of observable behaviours displayed by the perpetrator (O'Toole & Smith, 2013). In threat assessment, each case will be treated differently and objectively. The approach adopted will make allowances for variation in behaviours, and different types and degrees of preventive and intervention strategies (Chia & Chai, 2015; O'Toole, 2000).

Ideally, the investigators should seek information from a wide array of sources when conducting threat assessment. For instance, information can be gathered from material possessions of the subject, his/her social network, and past records. Corroboration of evidence originating from multiple sources will allow investigators to be more confident in the data they have collected. As shown in Figure 4.2, essential information should be drawn from at least five different areas: facts that bring the perpetrator to attention, information about the perpetrator, warning behaviours, motives, and target selection (Fein *et al.*, 1995).

Step 1: Gathering Facts about the Threat/Case of Concern

An investigator should start with gathering more facts, followed by a preliminary analysis of the situation that first qualifies a subject as a threat or concern. For instance, if there is any report of complaints about this individual, what are the reasons for

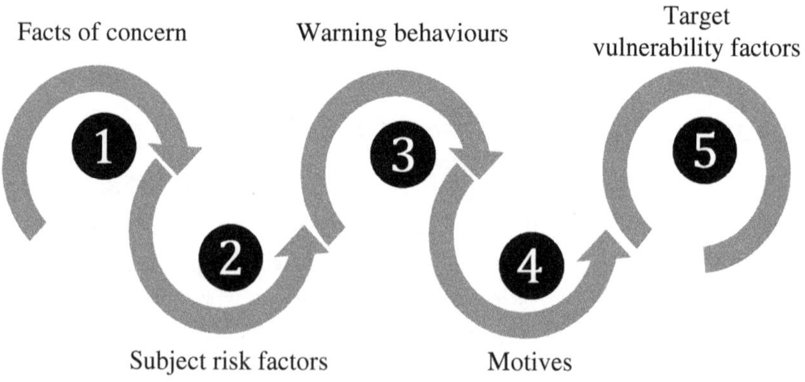

Figure 4.2. Five Steps of Threat Assessment.

reporting? Has anyone observed any dangerous or inappropriate online/offline activities by this person? Initial attention conferred on this person can stem from third-party reporting instead of direct observation by the investigator; the investigator has to be critical about the informant's reliability. Sometimes, others may possibly communicate misleading and erroneous information as a way of retaliation or as a distraction to mask their own violent endeavours (Borum *et al.*, 1999; Meloy *et al.*, 2012).

Step 2: Assessing Risk Factors of the Subject

Moving to the second step, the threat assessment approach states that more information about the person should be gathered in terms of the following three aspects (Meloy *et al.*, 2012):

a) Identification information (e.g., name).
b) Background information (e.g., criminal records).
c) Current life information (e.g., quality of life, nature and quality of relationships, recent crises or losses).

Assessing risk factors is critical in identifying which individuals are likely to commit future acts of terror attacks. Specific to violent extremists, apart from psychological, behavioural, and social factors, contextual factors such as religious beliefs, political viewpoints, and ideological doctrine should be considered as well (Bakker, 2006; Pressman, 2009). This information allows us to assess the presence of one's characteristics or attributes that may elevate one's level of violence. This is critical in aiding us to identify individuals at risk of orchestrating a terror attack.

In the past, professionals used to rely on their own experience and criteria to assess the risk of violence in individuals (Hart, 2008). This decision-making approach solely based on the clinician's intuition and experience has been heavily criticised as subjective, unprofessional, and ambiguous (Pedersen *et al.*, 2010). With the proliferation of the range of risk assessment methods available in the mental health and criminal justice system, risk assessment of violence in different contexts (workplace, school, stalking, etc.) have been developed (Andrews *et al.*, 2006; Fazel *et al.*, 2012; Guy, 2008; Harris *et al.*, 2004). Similarly, there have been several risk assessment tools established in the field of violent extremism to assist professionals and officers to assess individuals at risk of violent extremism. For example, risk assessment tools such as the Violent Extremism Risk Assessment 2 (VERA 2) (Pressman & Flockton, 2014), Extremism Risk Guidance 22+ (ERG 22+) (Silke, 2014), Online Violent Extremism Screening Tool (OVEST) (Neo & Dillon, 2016), and Terrorist Radicalisation Assessment Protocol (TRAP-18) (Meloy & Gill, 2016) have been found to be useful. Table 4.1 lists some examples of risk factors listed in VERA 2 that the investigator can consider when assessing an individual's level of risk in the context of violent extremism.

Table 4.1. Risk Factors of Violent Extremism.

S/N	Domain	Risk Factors
1	Beliefs and attitudes	• Commitment to ideology justifying violence • Victims of injustice and grievances • De-humanisation/demonisation of identified targets of injustice • Rejection of democratic society and values • Feelings of hate, frustration, persecution, alienation • Hostility to national collective identity • Lack of empathy, understanding outside own group
2	Context and intent	• Seeker, consumer, developer of violent extremist materials • Identification of target (person, place, group) in response to perceived injustice • Personal contact with violent extremists • Anger and expressed intent to act violently • Expressed desire to die for cause or martyrdom • Expressed intent to plan, prepare violent action • Susceptible to influence, authority, indoctrination

(*Continued*)

Table 4.1. (*Continued*)

S/N	Domain	Risk Factors
3	History and capability	• Early exposure to pro-violence militant ideology • Network (family, friends) involved in violent action • Prior criminal history of violence • Tactical, paramilitary, explosives training • Extremist ideological training • Access to funds, resources, organisational skills
4	Commitment and motivation	• Glorification of violent action • Driven by criminal opportunism • Commitment to group, group ideology • Driven by moral imperative, moral superiority • Driven by excitement, adventure

Source: From VERA 2 (Pressman & Flockton, 2014).

Step 3: Identifying Warning Behaviours Exhibited by Subject

After assessing the person's level of risk, the next step involves assessing the person's behaviours to determine the likelihood of an impending attack. Generally, there are eight red flags that signal change and an imminent threat, as highlighted in Table 4.2 (Meloy *et al.*, 2012).

Threat assessment assumes that targeted violence is premeditated, and therefore warning behaviours which indicate planning and preparation could be observed. Preparatory behaviours include enhanced concern and attention towards instances of targeted violence, indication of intentions to carry out attacks, and disclosure of such intents directly to the target or indirectly to the subject's social network (Borum *et al.*, 1999). For example, Germaine Lindsay, one of the four violent extremists who detonated bombs on three trains on London Underground on July 7, 2005, displayed several warning signs prior to the bomb attack. After his conversion to Islam, he had changed drastically in terms of his lifestyle and religious practice, and was observed to be fixated on Jihad. In the weeks leading to the attack, Lindsay shared his plans to carry out an attack with others. These were clear red flags that were observable; and his plans could have been mitigated (Neo *et al.*, 2017).

Table 4.2. Warning Behaviours of Impending Attacks.

S/N	Warning Behaviour(s)	Description	Examples
1	Pathway	Indication of research, planning, and preparation of an attack.	Subject acquired weapons or conducted research on how to make bombs.
2	Fixation	Increasing preoccupation with person or cause. It may be due to obsessive drive for violence to redress or remediate the injustice. Individuals may also suddenly change their lifestyles in response to their preoccupation with the cause.	Subject spent time surfing websites that host radical materials.
3	Identification	Identify with law enforcement, military paraphernalia, attackers or assassin.	Subject expressed interest in becoming a martyr.
4	Novel aggression	Act of violence committed (unrelated to target) for the first time. The individual may also want to prove his/her "worth". This may manifest itself in the readiness to inflict pain on others. as it is perceived as the route to honour and social acceptance within the radical community.	Subject assaulted others as an attempt of "testing out".
5	Energy burst	Increase in frequency/variety of behaviours related to target.	Subject visited the potential site of attack several times a week.
6	Leakage	Communication to a third party of one's intention to do harm to the target. The individuals may release statements online that justify the use of violence on the enemies. The individuals may also disseminate propaganda materials within their family and peer networks to garner their support.	Subject posted hate messages online.

(*Continued*)

Table 4.2. (*Continued*)

S/N	Warning Behaviour(s)	Description	Examples
7	Last resort	Behavioural or verbal evidence of increasing desperation and distress.	Subject threatened suicide.
8	Directly communicated	Communication of a direct threat to target/law enforcement.	Subject informed others of his/her plans to carry out a terror attack.

Sources: From Neo *et al.* (2017) and Meloy *et al.* (2012).

Similarly, an in-depth case study analysis of the Sydney Siege incident revealed that the tragedy could have been possibly prevented or intervened (Chew & Chai, 2016). The perpetrator, Man Haron Monis, was described as secretive, capable of manipulation and narcissism, had a sense of grandiosity, and a desire to be in the limelight. Risk assessment conducted retrospectively disclosed that Monis had a long history of violence and exhibited several warning behaviours which indicated that he was plotting a terror attack. His pledge of allegiance to the Islamic State of Iraq and Syria (ISIS) coincided with the strengthening ISIS influence, and his attack was conducted in response to ISIS' call for action a few months before the actual attack (Chew & Chai, 2016; O'Brien, 2014; Thawley & Comley, 2015).

Step 4: Evaluating Motives of Subject

The fourth step of threat assessment pertains to the subject's motives. It is important to note that violent extremists seldom spontaneously carry out attacks for no apparent reason (Neo *et al.*, 2011). Given that motives are closely tied to target selection, identifying the subject's motives provides clues on who and where the subject may attack. Contrary to popular belief, a subject's motivation to attack is rarely due to hatred or hostility towards his/her intended target. For instance, assassination attempts on political leaders are seldom propelled by differences in political outlook (Fein & Vossekuil, 1999). This pinpoints the importance of evaluating the subject's motives comprehensively.

Studies have shown that violent extremists may be driven by different motives such as to satisfy curiosity (during earlier phase), need for identity or belonging, to right a perceived injustice, or for thrill and excitement (Borum, 2011; Honnavalli *et al.*, 2017). For instance, the Sydney Siege perpetrator Man Haron Monis was driven and motivated by criminal opportunism, in an effort to gain political attention to himself. On the other hand, the "underwear bomber", Umar Farouk Abdulmutallab, who attempted to detonate explosives hidden in his underwear while onboard a plane to U.S., was motivated by the mere sense of belonging that he had received in radical forums (Walton *et al.*, 2012). The sense of affiliation and belonging received from the radical forums increased his inclination to support violent extremist groups and causes.

Examining the motives is critical as it may explain how violent extremists are involved and the routes they may take subsequently, so that timely and appropriate intervention can be carried out. This also sheds light on some questions that we may have regarding our individuals of interest: whether they will continue to be involved, digress their paths, or reject violent extremism eventually (Borum, 2011).

Step 5: Evaluating Subject's Target Selection

The last step in threat assessment considers the management and protection of the target with the aim to thwart any attack plans. Specific to violent extremism, Neo and colleagues opined that target selection by violent extremists may be influenced by numerous factors. If the intention is to intimidate and undermine the opponent, locations and targets with significant meaning to the opponent would be selected (Neo *et al.*, 2011). Past cases indicated that terror attacks are commonly launched at places with a high volume of human traffic in order to incite the most fear. A subject may start with a consideration of multiple targets and then finally narrow it down to one target. Additionally, a subject may change targets over time. Threat assessment would have to recognise that target selection is dynamic and can change over time, hence allowing law enforcement officials to anticipate the subject's reaction to increased security in an original target. By understanding the subject's initial reasons and considerations for a specific target and his subsequent change of target, prevention of an attack can be done by "managing" both the perpetrator and target (Borum *et al.*, 1999; Chew & Chai, 2016).

The threat assessment approach allows investigators to evaluate and identify Monis as a high-risk individual. Further assessment may also possibly pinpoint his target and chosen location of attack. Monis has had an extensive history of holding one-man protests in Martin Place, a signal that he may choose this location as it is a familiar target. Lindt Chocolate Café at Martin Place was subsequently selected as the location of attack as it was strategically located opposite Channel 7 news studios. This was not surprising as he had always desired media attention. A siege at Lindt Chocolate Café would have fulfilled his quest for a full media coverage of his plot (Chew & Chai, 2016; O'Brien, 2014). This case study sets forth a key notion to all. Should threat assessment be integrated as part of law enforcement's assessment framework, it can be a preventive strategy to pre-empt and mitigate any potential violent extremist attack plans.

Conclusion

Threat assessment is a process of gathering information to determine the level of threat of targeted violence posed by an individual or a group (Meloy & Hoffmann, 2013). Often, threat assessments of perpetrators reveal a range of psychological, behavioural, and contextual factors, as well as warning signals that increase their risk of violence and likelihood of an attack. Since the concept was introduced, threat assessment has been proven relevant and crucial in the prevention and management of targeted violence (Meloy & Hoffmann, 2013).

This chapter discusses the role of threat assessment in identifying, assessing, and managing violent extremist threats. Given the increasing pervasiveness of radical materials via the internet, individuals can now explore radical ideas in isolation, contact like-minded individuals, and be predisposed to ideologies prescribed by members of violent extremist groups. The online platform offers a breeding ground for radicalised lone wolves to explore plans of attack without receiving any direct support or instruction from violent extremist groups. Anyone can be potentially radicalised to become a violent extremist. As there is no one pattern or profile that holds for all violent extremists, instead of "profiling" a potential case of violent extremism, threat assessment emphasises the analysis of prominent pathways of ideas and actions that perpetuate violent tendencies (Borum, 2015; Borum *et al.*, 1999). In summary, the key principles of threat assessment have been highlighted, and how it can be applied in the context of violent extremism has been presented.

Acknowledgement

The views expressed in this chapter are the author's own and do not represent the official position or view of the Ministry of Home Affairs, Singapore.

Editors' Note

Readers are advised to contact the ISD Counter-Terrorism Centre Hotline (1800-2626473) if they are in doubt about the potential threat posed by an individual of interest. Alternatively, they can contact the Religious Rehabilitation Group (RRG) Helpline (1800-7747747).

References

Andrews, D. A., Bonta, J., & Wormith, J. S. (2006). The Recent Past and Near Future of Risk and/or Need Assessment. *Crime & Delinquency*, 52(1), 7–27.

Bakker, E. (2006). *Jihadi Terrorists in Europe: Their Characteristics and the Circumstances in which they joined the Jihad — An Exploratory Study.*

Netherlands: Netherlands Institute of International Relations Clingendael.

Böckler, N., Hoffman, J., & Zick, A. (2015). The Frankfurt airport attack: A case study on the radicalisation of a lone-actor terrorist. *Journal of Threat Assessment and Management*, *2*(3–4), 153–163.

Borum, R. (2011). Radicalisation into violent extremism: A review of conceptual models and empirical research. *Journal of Strategic Security*, *4*(4), 7–36.

Borum, R. (2015). Assessing Risk for Terrorism Involvement. *Journal of Threat Assessment and Management*, *2*(2), 63–87.

Borum, R., Fein, R., Vossekuil, B., & Berglund, J. (1999). Threat assessment: Defining an approach to evaluating risk of targeted violence. *Behavioural Sciences and the Law*, *17*(3), 323–337.

Calhoun, T., & Weston, S. (2003). *Contemporary Threat Management*. San Diego, CA: Specialized Training Services.

Chew, C. M. A., & Chai, X. T. W. (2016). *Lessons from the Sydney Siege: Applying the Threat Assessment Framework to Terrorism*. Singapore: Home Team Behavioural Sciences Centre.

Chia, X., & Chai, X. T. W. (2015). *Threat Assessment: Preventing Violence before Perpetrator Strikes*. Singapore: Home Team Behavioural Sciences Centre.

Christmann, K. (2012). *Preventing Religious Radicalisation and Violent Extremism: A Systematic Review of the Research Evidence*. London: Youth Justice Board.

Dean, G. (2014). *Neurocognitive Risk Assessment for the Early Detection of Violent Extremists*. New York: Springer.

Fazel, S., Singh, J. P., Doll, H., & Grann, M. (2012). Use of risk assessment instruments to predict violence and antisocial behaviour in 73 samples involving 24 827 people: Systematic review and meta-analysis. *BMJ*, *345*. Retrieved from https://www.bmj.com/content/345/bmj.e4692.

Fein, R. A., & Vossekuil, B. (1998). *Protective Intelligence and Threat Assessment Investigations: A Guide for State and Local Law Enforcement Officials*. Washington, DC: US Department of Justice.

Fein, R. A., & Vossekuil, B. (1999). Assassination in the United States: An operational study of recent assassins, attackers, and near-lethal approachers. *Journal of Forensic Sciences*, *44*(2), 321–333.

Gill, P. (2007). A multi-dimensional approach to suicide bombing. *International Journal of Conflict and Violence*, *1*(2), 142–159.

Guy, L. S. (2008). Performance indicators of the structured professional judgment approach to assessing risk for violence to others: A meta-analytic survey. Unpublished Doctoral Dissertation. Vancouver, BC: Simon Fraser University.

Hart, S. D. (2008). Preventing violence: The role of risk assessment and management. In A. C. Baldry, & F. W. Winkel (Eds.), *Intimate Partner Violence Prevention and Intervention: The Risk Assessment and Management Approach* (pp. 7–18). Hauppauge, NY: Nova Science Publishers.

Harris, G. T., Rice, M. E., & Camilleri, J. A. (2004). Applying a forensic actuarial assessment (the Violence Risk Appraisal Guide) to non-forensic patients. *Journal of Interpersonal Violence, 19*(9), 1063–1074.

Honnavalli, V., Neo, L. S., & Khader, M. (2017). *The ABCs of Violent Extremism: What Home Team Officers Need to Know About Violent Extremism*. Singapore: Home Team Behavioural Sciences Centre.

Leson, J. (2005). New Realities — Law enforcement in the post 9/11 era: Assessing and managing the terrorism threat. Retrieved from https://www.ncjrs.gov/pdffiles1/bja/210680.pdf.

Meloy, J. R., & Hoffman, J. (2013). *International Handbook of Threat Assessment*. New York: Oxford University Press.

Meloy, J. R. & Gill, P. (2016). The Lone-Actor Terrorist and the TRAP-18. *Journal of Threat Assessment and Management, 3*(1), 37–52.

Meloy, J. R., Hoffman, J., Guldiman, A., & James, D. (2012). The role of warning behaviours in threat assessment: An exploration and suggested typology. *Behavioural Sciences and the Law, 30*(3), 256–279.

Meloy, J. R., Hempel, A., Mohandie, K. Shiva, A., & Gray, T. (2001). Offender and offense characteristics of a non-random sample of adolescent mass murderers. *Journal of the American Academy of Child and Adolescent Psychiatry, 40*(6), 719–728.

Moghaddam, F. M. (2005). The staircase to terrorism: A psychological exploration. *American Psychologist, 60*(2), 161–169.

Neo, L. S. (2016). An Internet-Mediated Pathway for Online Radicalisation: RECRO. In M. Khader, L. S. Neo, G. Ong, E. M. Tan, & J. Chin (Eds.), *Combating Violent Extremism and Radicalization in the Digital Era* (pp. 197–224). Hershey, PA: IGI Global.

Neo, L.S., & Dillon, L. (2016). *Online Violent Extremism Screening Tool.* Singapore: Home Team Behavioural Sciences Centre.

Neo, L. S., Khader, M., & Ang, J. (2011). Identifying terrorism behavioural clues: Can pre-attack terrorism related behaviours be identified?

A psychological and behavioural based analysis of 30 terror attack. *Volume I: Terrorism Behavioural Clues (Research Report: 02/2011)*. Singapore: Home Team Behavioural Sciences Centre.

Neo, L. S., Khader, M., Ang, J., Ong, G., & Tan, E. (2017). Developing an early screening guide for jihadi terrorism: A behavioural analysis of 30 terror attacks. *Security Journal*, *30*(1), 227–246.

O'Brien, N. (2014, December 31). Why Islamic State glorified the Sydney siege. *ABCNews*. Retrieved from http://www.abc.net.au/news/2014-12-31/obrien-why-islamic-state-glorified-the-sydney-siege/5993830.

O'Toole, M. E. (2000). *The School Shooter: A Threat Assessment Perspective*. Washington, DC: Federal Bureau of Investigation, U.S. Department of Justice.

O'Toole, M. E., & Smith, S. S. (2013). Fundamentals of threat assessment for beginners. In J. R., Meloy, & J. Hoffmann (Eds.), *International Handbook of Threat Assessment*. New York: Oxford University Press.

Pedersen, L., Rasmussen, K., & Elsass, P. (2010). Risk assessment: The value of structured professional judgments. *International Journal of Forensic Mental Health*, *9*(2), 74–81.

Prech, T. (2007). Home grown terrorism and Islamist radicalization in Europe: From conversion to terrorism. Retrieved from http://justitsministeriet.dk/sites/default/files/media/Arbejdsomraader/Forskning/Forskningspuljen/2011/2007/Home_grown_terrorism_and_Islamist_radicalisation_in_Europe_-_an_assessment_of_influencing_factors__2_.pdf.

Pressman, E. (2009). *Risk Assessment Decisions for Violent Political Extremism*. Canada: Public Safety Canada.

Pressman, E., & Flockton, J. (2014). Violent extremist risk assessment: Development of the VERA 2 and applications in the high security correctional setting. In A., Silke (Ed.), *Prisons, Terrorism and Extremism: Critical Issues in Management, Radicalization and Reform* (pp. 122–143). London: Routledge.

Sageman, M. (2007). Radicalization of global Islamist terrorists. US: United States Senate Committee on Homeland Security and Governmental Affairs. Retrieved from https://www.hsgac.senate.gov/imo/media/doc/062707Sageman.pdf.

Silke, A. (2014). Risk assessment of terrorists and extremist prisoners. In A. Silke (Ed.), *Prisons, Terrorism and Extremism* (pp. 108–121). London: Routledge.

Taarnby, M. (2005). Recruitment of Islamist terrorists in Europe: Trends and perspectives. Retrieved from https://www.investigativeproject.org/documents/testimony/58.pdf.

Thawley, M., & Comley, B. (2015). Martin Place siege: Joint Commonwealth — New South Wales review. Retrieved from https://www.pmc.gov.au/sites/default/files/publications/170215_Martin_Place_Siege_Review_1.pdf.

Unsgaard, E., & Meloy, J. R. (2011). The assassination of the Swedish Minister for Foreign Affairs. *Journal of Forensic Sciences*, *56*(2), 555–559.

Walton, G. M., Cohen, G. L., Cwir, D., & Spencer, S. J. (2012). Mere belonging: The power of social connections. *Journal of Personality and Social Psychology*, *102*(3), 513–532.

Wiktorowicz, Q. (2004). Joining the cause: Al-Muhajiroun and radical Islam. Memphis, TN: Rhodes College,. Retrieved from http://insct.syr.edu/wp-content/uploads/2013/03/Wiktorowicz.Joining-the-Cause.pdf.

CHAPTER 5

Leveraging Smart Technology for Better Counter-Terrorism Intelligence

MUHAMMAD FAIZAL BIN ABDUL RAHMAN

S. Rajaratnam School of International Studies, Nanyang Technological University, Singapore

> ...surveillance technology are going to improve. But as important is the use of analytics, to look at a large amount of data and pull out of that meaningful evidence that someone might be planning a terrorist attack. That's going to be increasingly useful for police and counter-terrorism officials.
>
> Michael Chertoff
> Former U.S. Secretary of Homeland Security

Introduction

Terrorism is a perennial scourge to the human civilisation and can affect any society regardless of political systems, creed, and geography. Jihadi terrorism in particular is the security preoccupation of many countries and communities given its global tentacles, persistence, and potentially detrimental implications to key foundations of national security including peace and order, social cohesion, trust and confidence in government institutions, and economic stability. The detrimental implications of terrorism would peak upon the occurrence of physical attacks that are committed using various tactics that result in casualties. This creates an atmosphere of public fear and wide media coverage that maximises the propaganda effect, and puts pressure on governments to take a certain course of action or/and policy change (Boltz *et al.*, 2002).

Homeland security (including law enforcement, border security, and domestic intelligence) agencies are hence exploring new technological solutions to prevent terrorist threats among other crime and security issues both at the domestic and international spheres (INTERPOL, 2017). The fourth industrial revolution, which is characterised by a range of smart technologies that is changing the way people live and work (World Economic Forum, n.d.), can be envisioned to have a dramatic impact on the way that terrorists may operate as well as how countries and communities can protect themselves against attacks. The way that homeland security agencies perform intelligence work — which is an essential element of counter-terrorism (CT) — can potentially transform with the use of smart technologies.

This chapter first discusses the contemporary problem of jihadi terrorism to global cities and follows up with how smart technologies — which refer to the fusion of artificial intelligence (AI), Internet of Things (IoT) sensors and data analytics — enable augmented surveillance of the physical space of cities in order to produce actionable intelligence for countering jihadi terrorism. Examples of smart technologies include Smart CCTVs, body-worn police cameras, aerial drones, patrol robots, and remote patrolling systems that homeland security agencies are increasingly deploying for protecting public spaces and by private security companies for guarding their clients' assets and premises. Global cities refer to urban areas (including city-states) which are important population and economic centres of nations, hubs within the global economic system (Charnock, n.d.), and located in non-conflict zones.

Persistence of Jihadi Terrorism

Jihadi terrorism creates persistent and widespread alarm that put the strain on the resources of governments, cities, and communities worldwide striving to counter it while simultaneously managing other domestic and cross-border crime and security issues. Homeland security agencies, even in relatively safer countries, are therefore compelled to transform the way they function and engage with the communities that they seek to protect. For example, the Global Terrorism Index (GTI) report by the Institute for Economics and Peace consistently ranks Singapore as one of the safest countries in the world (Mahzam & Abdul Rahman, 2016). Nonetheless, the Singapore government is making more investments in homeland security technology as a force multiplier given the challenges associated with human limitations such as changing demographics and greater operational demands that emanate from threats that are constantly evolving especially terrorism (Ministry of Home Affairs, 2015). Moreover, Singapore, since 2016, has shifted the narrative of terrorism used in community engagements. Terrorism is no longer a probable threat but an actual one; the Minister for Law and Home Affairs had stressed that "it is no longer a question of whether an attack will take place, but really, when is an attack going to take place in Singapore, and we have to be prepared for that" (Cheong, 2016, para. 10).

The confluence of several factors facilitated by technology contributes to the persistence of terrorism. Key among these factors are five overarching ones: (a) unkillable ideology, (b) timeless threat, (c) capacity to evolve, (d) elusive followers, and (e) decentralised strategy.

Unkillable Ideology

The jihadi ideology espouses the eschatological narrative of a celestial battle between good and evil; it will continue to live on as long as discrimination and injustice — actual or perceived — exist. This jihadi ideology essentially colours the worldview and fuels the motivation of jihadi terrorists especially those in conflict zones. Other individuals — in non-conflict zones such as global cities — may adopt the same jihadi ideology to justify the use of illegal violence to address their grievances that may stem from a variety of socioeconomic, political, personal, and behavioural issues (Gul, 2017).

The Global Terrorism Index (GTI) 2017 report found multiple paths to radicalisation where ideology can intersect with myriad socioeconomic and political issues that constitute actual and perceived discrimination and injustice, or even certain criminal backgrounds that may make some individuals more susceptible to violence (Institute of Economics & Peace, 2017). One noteworthy Singapore case study involved the individual known as Wang Yuandongyi. Wang had no direct connection with the conflict in Syria and Iraq, but was motivated to join the Kurdish militia and take up arms in order to help people whom the Islamic State of Iraq and Syria (ISIS) is oppressing (Jayakumar, 2016). In the December 2017 case of an attempted bombing attack in New York by Bangladeshi immigrant Akayed Ullah, Ullah said that ISIS's propaganda and American actions in the Middle East inspired him to commit the attack ("New York Port Authority attack: Akayed Ullah 'inspired by IS'", 2017). To Ullah, these reasons seemed enough for him to commit an act of violence against his adopted city, despite it providing him with the socioeconomic opportunities (e.g., job, personal safety) which his country of origin lacks. For these cases, technology, specifically social media and Internet plays a facilitative role in the radicalisation process.

Timeless Threat

Ideology essentially makes jihadi terrorism a threat that is timeless such that it has resurrected itself in similar forms over the decades; it makes the threat both strategic and tactical in nature such that solely kinetic means — military campaigns and enforcement actions — cannot vanquish the threat. In Islam, mainstream Muslim scholars including those in Singapore have labelled jihadi terrorists as the "Khawarij", who are a category of deviants whose rise was foretold as a threat by Prophet *Muhammad* more than a millennium ago (PERGAS, 2014).

Indeed, the threat has surfaced itself on many notable episodes in the modern era. The 1970s witnessed the dramatic siege of the Grand Mosque of Mecca in 1979 that was committed by the jihadi movement known as the "Ikhwan", and led by charismatic Wahhabi cleric *Juhayman al Uteybi* who was disillusioned with modernity and the Saudi government (Magolan, 2014). The late 1980s saw the formation of Al-Qaeda by Osama Bin Laden (OBL) who led the movement in committing the shocking September 11 attacks in 2001; the threat level of the movement had since fluctuated but terrorism analysts fear that one of OBL's sons — Hamza Bin Laden — may one day revive the group's dominance (Moore, 2017). In 2013, the international community was alarmed by the rise of ISIS that emerged from a diminished Al-Qaeda affiliate (Al-Qaeda in Iraq), following the declaration of a caliphate by Abu Bakr Al-Baghdadi, and exploited social media technology with great finesse in order to galvanise foreign fighters and supporters across the globe at an unprecedented scale (Hashim, 2014).

Capacity to Evolve

Islamic eschatology and historical trends of jihadi terrorism present a crucial lesson for practitioners and policymakers in the field of counter-terrorism: the threat will not end and will outlast Al-Qaeda and ISIS. Despite ISIS facing military setbacks and territorial losses in Syria and Iraq, jihadi terrorism is likely to remain an enduring threat that will persist for decades to come. This is possible given the propensity of jihadi terrorists and their supporters to evolve their tactics by adapting to new challenges and opportunities; two important examples that involve technology substantiate this point. First, ISIS demonstrated great proficiency in the use of social media to promote its brand, recruit, and mobilise fighters and supporters across borders, and promulgate terror tactics. Hence, ISIS has successfully achieved the objective of "crowdsourced terrorism" which security agencies and the affected communities are struggling to counter (Hui, 2017). Second, ISIS demonstrated its ability to leverage commercially available and affordable new technologies to adapt its tactics according to terrain and current operational efforts by security forces. The urban conflict in the city of Marawi, Southern Philippines had seen this ability in ISIS-inspired militants — Maute Group — who had gathered intelligence on the Philippines security forces by using aerial drones acquired from dealers in Hong Kong (Franco, 2017).

Counter-terrorism efforts, especially in global cities, is set to be a more demanding race as jihadi terrorists will expectedly continue to ride the wave of globalisation, urbanisation, and new technologies to strengthen their nexus and outsmart homeland security agencies (Abdul Rahman, 2017a). According to the GTI 2017 report, analysis of terrorism trends since 2014 revealed an increase in ISIS-related foiled and successful attacks in Organisation for Economic Co-operation and Development (OECD) countries since 2014. These attacks were notably characterised by changes in tactics and targets that were widely promoted by ISIS and Al-Qaeda over social media and the Internet in order to maximise the impact on public fear and lessen the risk of interception by security forces. Looking ahead, there is a serious concern over the risk of terror attacks to global cities as urbanisation — leading to higher density population and more socio-economic activities — would make cities more awash with soft targets. Homeland security agencies will find it more challenging to engage the communities to build social cohesion and vigilance, and to detect and monitor clandestine activities that may be indicative of possible terrorist threats. As cities develop into smart cities (or smart nation) in the backdrop of the fourth industrial revolution, terrorists would expectedly seek new vulnerabilities and exploit new technologies for purposes of recruitment, channelling resources, planning, and execution of attacks (Institute of Economics & Peace, 2017).

Given these imminent challenges, it is paramount that homeland security agencies anticipate how terrorists may combine both unsophisticated tactics and new technologies to evade interception and launch successful attacks in cities. Indeed, the use of vehicular attacks (as an unsophisticated but effective tactic) and the use of more advanced but affordable and accessible means (new technology including drone swarms) are among the emergent trends highlighted in a report on "Jihadist Terrorism 16 Years after 9/11" (New America, 2017). In addition, the predilection of jihadist terrorists to misuse religious texts — Quranic and Hadiths — suggests that there is value for homeland security agencies to consult religious scholars in anticipating how terrorists may adapt or distort religious texts to justify the use of new tactics. For example, it is plausible for jihadi terrorists to promote the use of aerial drones by distorting the Quranic story of the "People of the Elephant and the Army of Ababeel". The story revolves around flocks of birds (known as Ababeel) which were carrying fiery stones and sent by *God* to bombard an advancing and superior foreign army that attempted to attack the *Kaaba* in Islam's holy city of Mecca (Ghafour, 2014).

Elusive Followers

The rise of ISIS in 2013 had aggravated three challenges for homeland security agencies striving to prevent jihadi terrorists from launching attacks in global cities. First, it is difficult to detect and prevent attacks by lone wolves who are often elusive as they can be "clean-skins" — people with no criminal records and not known to security agencies — and are likely to commit acts of violence after being radicalised online. This is a serious problem for cities such as Singapore, which are essentially highly digitised societies with strong anti-terrorism laws (Mahzam & Abdul Rahman, 2016). Furthermore, their unsophisticated attack tactics (such as knife attacks and vehicular attacks) can be discreet yet deadly, and are difficult to stop even upon detection (Abdul Rahman, 2017c). Aside from its elusiveness and shocking impact, unsophisticated attack tactics may have some basis in Islamic history. For example, the *Rumiyah* magazine by ISIS featured stories of medieval era conflicts where the knife or sword was the primary weapon of early generations of pious *mujahideen* who vanquished their adversaries to defend Islam. Hence, lone wolves and their unsophisticated attack tactics in a way is an asymmetric response to sophisticated counter-terrorism measures used by homeland security agencies in global cities (Abdul Rahman, 2016a).

Second, the cosmopolitan character of global cities implies that such cities can be susceptible to terror plots by foreign individuals (e.g., migrant workers, students) who were either radicalised online or clandestinely linked to regional militant networks (Mahzam & Abdul Rahman, 2016). As foreigners, these individuals may elude the attention of homeland security agencies, as there may be no available records to flag their predilection for crime and terrorism. These individuals can be either lone wolves or part of a more organised group, and may choose to attack their city of residence or neighbouring cities instead of their country of origin. For example, one of the individuals (Leonardus Hutajulu) linked to the pro-ISIS Batam (Indonesia) cell *Katibah Gonggong Rebus* (KGR) that plotted to attack Singapore's Marina Bay area had reportedly tried to seek employment in Singapore. The possible intent of seeking employment was reportedly to help facilitate lawful travel for KGR members into Singapore (Chan, 2016).

Third, ISIS had galvanised foreign fighters at an unprecedented scale and this will continue to be a problem even after the collapse of the so-called caliphate in Syria and Iraq. Their sheer numbers and obscure travel patterns may help them elude security agencies seeking to apprehend and rehabilitate them. These fighters, especially if battle-hardened and radicalised further while abroad, may serve not only tactically as attackers but also strategically as purveyors of terrorist ideology and terror tactics in the regions that they migrate to after fleeing Syria and Iraq (Jerard, 2017). Relatively safe cities such as Singapore may still be susceptible to threats from foreign fighters operating in other places in the region due to reasons such as limited de-radicalisation and rehabilitation efforts, limited enforcement, and operational constraints faced by security agencies in other countries. There is the possibility of some fighters linking up with criminal groups to travel across borders and into global cities using illegal means in order to elude the intelligence radar of homeland security agencies (Abdul Rahman, 2016b). Moreover, individuals who are radicalised online and aspire to become foreign fighters but found it difficult to travel to conflict zones to wage Jihad, may choose to become lone wolves and target their home cities.

Decentralised Strategy

Across the aforementioned three challenges, the threat from lone wolves is perhaps the most pronounced; it constitutes the strategy of decentralising terrorism. Al-Qaeda promoted the strategy after realising how effective counter-terrorism efforts are in crippling organised terrorist groups; ISIS implemented the strategy with greater success (Mendelsohn, 2016). For example, research on terrorist attacks affecting cities in the West over the past decade indicates that lone wolf attacks have seen an upward trend since 2013 (Dongen, 2017); this coincides with the appearance of ISIS.

In the context of global cities, lone wolves may be either citizens (including naturalised citizens) or foreigners who target the cities that they live and work in. The low predictability of lone wolf attacks can threaten to engulf the surveillance gaze and resources of homeland security agencies that are simultaneously guarding against foreign fighters and terrorist groups, as well as other crime and public order issues (Abdul Rahman, 2016b). Research on past terrorist attacks suggests that it is more difficult to detect, monitor, and prevent lone wolves as compared to individuals and known suspects linked to organised terrorist groups. While potential lone wolves may express their views and intent on social media and Internet, it is unrealistic and not possible for intelligence analysts in homeland security agencies to trawl the entire universe of social media and Internet, and detect all potential threats even with the aid of automation — AI and machine learning (ML) (Kaati & Pontus, 2011). Furthermore, the online detection of possible or articulated intent may not necessarily unveil useful information on where, when, and how the lone wolf will strike.

Faint Signals in Unpredictability

Incidences of self-directed attacks affecting cities in non-conflict zones were committed by individuals with no apparent connections with terrorist groups, especially since 2014, have cast much spotlight on the unpredictability and predominance of threat from lone wolves. For example, a CNN report has described ISIS as having "mastered the art of creating lone wolves" (Willingham, 2017). Governments and terrorism experts often explained that unlike terrorist fighters and members or supporters of terrorist groups who are known (or convicted), traditional methods of intelligence collection have limitations in detecting and stopping lone wolves before they can act. Moreover, the time taken for a lone wolf to progress from the radicalisation phase to the operational phase may be shorter compared to other terrorists, hence leaving security agencies with less time to act (Ang *et al.*, 2017).

While potential lone wolves were more likely to leave digital traces of their views and intent on social media and Internet forums, they may grow more circumspect and be less vocal in online space in order to evade detection by homeland security agencies as well as members of the community. They may also turn to encrypted communications channels to consume terrorist propaganda and learn the various terror tactics. Their preference for unsophisticated attack tactics (e.g., knife attacks, vehicle ramming) as compared to improvised explosive devices (IEDs) suggest that their suspicious pre-attack activities are less detectable during the process of weapons and materials acquisition. It is either the lone wolves' limitations in terms of lack of technical expertise and resources, or the calculated decision to evade detection by homeland security agencies that drove them to this preference (Dongen, 2017). The activity of acquiring explosive precursors for bombs is more likely to raise suspicion as compared to purchasing knives from the supermarket or renting a vehicle. The activity of purchasing increasingly affordable and publicly available technology — such as consumer drones — for the purpose of weaponisation would also be less likely to raise suspicion.

Potential lone wolves may however leave certain faint signals — that are indicative of their intent and likely tactics — in the physical space. These signals may also be used as clues for intelligence analysts when conducting intelligence probes that were initiated due to information — of possibly radicalised individuals — that were received through online sources or/and traditional methods (e.g., HUMINT, community policing, intelligence liaisons, communications intercepts). Despite efforts to make their intent and actions clandestine, lone wolves would still need to carry out certain pre-attack activities in the physical space, as this is where the (soft) targets exist and where the attacks would occur. Two ISIS-inspired terrorist cases demonstrate this point. Mohamed Lahouaeij-Boublel who committed the 2016 Bastille Day attack (vehicle ramming) in the city of Nice, France in ISIS's name was reportedly never on the watch-list of homeland security agencies for signs of radicalisation. However, he had driven his rented truck to survey the targeted location (Promenade des Anglais) twice in the days leading to the attack ("Attack on Nice: Who was Mohamed Lahouaiej-Bouhlel?", 2016). The Federal Bureau of Investigations (FBI) had earlier investigated Omar Mateen after he made pro-ISIS comments to his colleagues before he committed the 2016 Orlando nightclub shooting. The FBI closed the investigations, as there was no information to substantiate him as a threat. However, he had surveyed the targeted and other potential locations (Pulse Nightclub and Disney World) in the weeks leading to the attack (Perez *et al.*, 2016).

Smart Technology: Scanning Beyond the Obvious

Smart technology — for augmented surveillance of the physical space to predict possible or imminent threats, profile and track persons (and objects) of interest — is important as it can support efforts to prevent lone wolf attacks (and other forms of terrorist attacks) by complementing online (social media and Internet) surveillance and traditional methods of intelligence collection (e.g., HUMINT, communications intercepts). Given that ideology, adaptability, and nature of attackers make jihadi terrorism a persistent threat, global cities need to capitalise on the potential of smart technologies — which can improve over time with AI and ML, and deployed in an agile way — as a countervailing force to develop better actionable intelligence for counter-terrorism. Essentially, augmented surveillance should be one of the key deliverables for global cities especially those which have embarked on smart city initiatives — projects that rely heavily on data, autonomous and sensor technology — to improve the way people work, live, and play.

Cities that aspire to become smart cities should intrinsically be safe cities.

The idea of leveraging smart technologies to detect faint signals is premised on the concept of protective intelligence which stipulates that terrorist attacks generally follow a discernible pattern of activities (terrorist attack cycle) that begin with pre-operational surveillance and analysis of potential targets (persons and places) (McCullar, 2010). The hostile surveillance activities constitute the stage in the terrorist attack cycle that would be most susceptible to detection by homeland security agencies (Stratfor, 2009). Lone wolves may be more susceptible to detection as compared to terrorist groups as these individuals would have to conduct each stage of the terrorist attack cycle by themselves (Stewart, 2017). Furthermore, lone wolves may lack the operational knowledge to conduct proper surveillance activities, as they may be unable to draw on the expertise of trained jihadi terrorists and hence face a higher risk of detection for behaving in an irregular manner. The use of smart technologies to detect terrorist surveillance activities — in the form of suspicious persons, behaviour, and objects — in urban settings would be comparable to the use of military drones (Unmanned Aerial Vehicles) in conflict zones to complement HUMINT and manual patrol operations in uncovering possible threats on the ground (Axe, 2011; iHLS, 2017). Some research reports have described the complementary role of smart technologies in urban and civilian settings. An example is as follows (Elizabeth, 2015, p. 15):

> On the street, a police officer uses his body-worn camera to scan a crowd; the feed is sent in real time back to the department where facial recognition and movement analysis software alerts the patrol officer as to whether furtive movements or people on watch lists have been identified. Police follow up on these alerts to identify people who should be immediately investigated. Other people are dismissed as not posing an immediate threat but are logged on watch lists for future reference.

Smart technologies hence can serve as powerful tools to help intelligence analysts enrich and narrow any gaps in information collected from other sources, enhance the ability to conduct surveillance and analyses of targets (persons, objects, and places of interest), and produce threat assessments to support operational decisions. When used on suspected lone wolves, smart technologies can potentially help intelligence analysts gain an early and more comprehensive appreciation of an individual's threat level — such as his intent, capabilities, and attack plans — in order for pre-emptive actions to be taken before the threat can materialise (Augenstein, 2017).

The effectiveness of smart technologies however would require more than just its physical implementation to support current operational practices and overcome human limitations. Three important approaches should buttress its implementation, and these are: (a) reimagining operational practices, (b) integration of smart technology systems with private security companies, and (c) interoperability with other mission-critical systems in homeland security.

Reimagining Operational Practices

There should be the reimagining of operational practices in order to stay resilient in the face of constantly evolving threats and to avoid intelligence failures (Kruys, 2006). These practices would include: (a) updating training curriculum to equip officers with new skillsets so that smart technology systems can be well-harnessed, (b) updating the tradecraft of collating and analysing different types of structured and unstructured data and ambiguous information gathered from smart technology systems, and (c) enhancing protocols for information-sharing and interface between intelligence officers and frontline patrol and investigation officers to ensure an efficient flow from the phase of developing intelligence on threats to the phase of taking action to prevent them.

Underpinning these practices is a strategic level appreciation of the various types of potential threats (e.g., mindsets and likely behaviour may differ for different types of terrorists and criminals) which would help in determining the types of data and information that are most useful for developing intelligence and the optimal course of action to prevent the threats from materialising. Furthermore, while security agencies and suppliers often hail smart technologies as a force multiplier for physical security, there has to be critical analysis of how it in practice can support the various steps in the intelligence cycle (planning, collection, processing, analysis, and dissemination), and ameliorate the known causes of intelligence gaps.

Integration of Smart Technology Systems with Private Security Companies

There should be more integration of smart technology systems — but at an appropriate and safe level — used by homeland security agencies (e.g., police) and the private security companies. Integration of systems would enable homeland security agencies to attain wider real-time access to private security systems; this potentially enhances the capacity of homeland security agencies and private security companies to share information of possible terrorist pre-operational surveillance activities promptly for timely intelligence analyses, hence reducing any blind spots in surveillance and gaps in information sharing (Abdul Rahman, 2017c). The use of AI and ML in the systems would not only help to process voluminous information more efficiently but can potentially distil different insights. This is possible over time as the systems are "thinking" machines that may "see" data and patterns differently from humans, and hence generate a diversity of assessments which can be useful to intelligence analysts who in practice should exercise some levels of scepticism and explore alternative hypotheses (Richards, 1999). The integration of smart technology systems used by homeland security agencies and the private security companies however must come with certain data-protection safeguards in order to embed trust. Internally, both sides would need well-defined roles and responsibilities with regard to technical, cost sharing, operational, and policy issues that may underlie the integration of systems. Externally, the public may have different expectations for government (homeland security agencies) and private security companies with regard to issues of privacy and civil liberties.

Interoperability with Other Mission-critical Systems in Homeland Security

There should be interoperability — but at an appropriate and safe level — between smart technology systems and other mission-critical systems in homeland security. Mission-critical systems include: (a) criminal intelligence databases; (b) command, control, and communications systems; (c) border and immigration databases; (d) robotic patrol systems such as police robots and drones; (e) international law enforcement databases such as INTERPOL's, EUROPOL's, and ASEANAPOL's databases; and (f) databases of external partners — both public and private (e.g., vehicle rental companies). Interoperability of systems would increase the utility of smart technology systems in supporting real-time intelligence analyses of possible or imminent threats and help inform operational decisions on the ground (Abdul Rahman, 2016c). For example, the detection of a possible lone wolf by Smart CCTVs can be followed up with the immediate dispatch of police drones or robots in the vicinity either as: (a) a form of visible deterrence and to warn the public if the threat is ongoing or (b) to neutralise the threat quickly so as to reduce casualties. This operating procedure is conceivable for cities where robotic systems (autonomous or semi-autonomous) complement human police and security officers on the ground, and especially during life-threatening situations where quick response is necessary (Ackerman, 2014). At present, the market has been developing law enforcement robots that are not only equipped with surveillance features but also non-lethal weaponry such as tasers and acoustic devices to subdue dangerous and non-compliant suspects (Elizabeth, 2016). More importantly, homeland security agencies would have to address the various barriers (such as technical compatibility of existing systems and the ways data are codified, cost-sharing issues, legal issues on data exchange, and differences in culture, policies, and procedures across agencies) that may make complete interoperability difficult to achieve (Benson & Grieve, 2016).

From Intelligence to Action: The Hunt and Defence

The use of smart technologies for augmented surveillance should incorporate intelligence techniques and procedures that are agile and adaptable to ensure applicability across a range of terrorist and criminal threats. Techniques and procedures for information gathering and analysis of more elusive threats — such as lone wolves — are likely to be useful against other forms of threats. For intelligence to be actionable, intelligence analysts should use smart technologies with four important considerations in mind and these are: (a) cognisance of technology's potential capabilities and limitations, (b) AI ethics, (c) asking the right questions, and (d) intelligence scenarios and long-term efforts.

Cognisance of Technology's Potential Capabilities and Limitations

Intelligence analysts have to be cognisant of the potential capabilities and limitations of smart technologies while being mindful of the need for intelligence to be actionable in order to facilitate pre-emptive efforts. Depending on the nature of terrorist threat and intelligence analysis of it, pre-emptive efforts may take the forms of preventive detentions, tapping on HUMINT sources to gather additional information, more police patrols and community engagements on the ground, target-hardening measures, and public advisories. Hence, intelligence analysts should not be over-reliant on smart technologies but regard it as tools that complement existing methods of online surveillance and traditional intelligence collection (Abdul Rahman, 2017b).

AI Ethics

Intelligence analysts have to appreciate the ethical issues that accompany the use of smart technologies, which are essentially machines that think and inform decisions that would affect security operations as well as the people that homeland security agencies seek to protect. Several ethical issues exist but among these, the risks of algorithmic bias and "black box" effect would be more concerning to the security field (Abdul Rahman, 2017c).

The negative outcomes of algorithmic bias — due to AI algorithms inadvertently coded with the biases of its human programmers — include: (a) false positives or false alerts leading to wrongful profiling and arrest and (b) false negatives leading to the failure to identify threats that consequently infiltrate defences. Furthermore, data may inadvertently contain human biases along the lines of race, religion, and neighbourhood, hence leading to automated discrimination against certain communities and ex-criminals (although reformed). For example, there were concerns that the use of predictive policing systems (e.g., "Beware") such as the one used by Chicago Police would lead to racial discrimination towards non-white people (Stroud, 2016). The negative outcomes of the black box effect stem from machines becoming smarter without human inputs due to advances in ML. The machines' thought processes become increasingly incomprehensible to the users, hence giving rise to concerns over fairness and accountability in decision-making especially when errors occur. For example, there were concerns that the use of recidivism assessment systems (e.g., Compas) such as the one used in Wisconsin, the U.S., have led to criminals being served excessively harsh and unfair sentences, but the users do not understand how the algorithm in the system works (Israni, 2017).

As the use of smart technologies grows, agencies would need to discern what the acceptable equilibrium is between: (a) facing the negative outcomes resulting from the risks and (b) making lives better for people by mitigating security threats (Bossman, 2016). From the operational perspective, the negative outcomes may compel homeland security agencies to expend more resources due to pursuing the wrong leads and make reparation to the people affected by the risks. From the strategic perspective, the negative outcomes may beg the question: is there a difference between what the homeland security agencies and people understand as acceptable equilibrium? This question can have implications on the relationship — trust and confidence — between homeland security agencies and people. A situation that must be avoided is the one in which people fear homeland security agencies more than criminals and terrorists.

Asking the Right Questions

Intelligence analysts have to ask the right questions to ensure that they use smart technologies with the right techniques and procedures in order to shed light on the terrorists' plans. Essentially, the detection of terrorist surveillance activities through the use of smart technologies should lead to intelligence analysis that results in uncovering the identities and backgrounds of possible attackers and their network of supporters, possible targets, mode and patterns of travel, concealment and escape methods, surveillance and attack tactics, mode of communications, etc. As there can be multiple pathways for radicalisation and different roles (attacker, supporter, sympathiser), a well-defined analysis framework which includes individualised approaches can help in systematically assessing the risk levels for suspicious individuals flagged by smart technology systems.

A well-defined analysis framework is necessary given the potential for information overload to occur especially when intelligence analysts have to manage the volume, variety, and velocity of data that may come from smart technology systems while concurrently reviewing information from online and traditional sources. While AI and ML would be helpful to great extent in sieving out suspicious individuals, intelligence analysts still need to gather further information and conduct deeper analysis of these individuals. This includes the critical step of determining the stage of the terror attack cycle that the suspicious individual is currently going through. An individualised approach is important especially for lone wolf situations in order to determine necessary considerations that inform operational decisions. These include whether: (a) these individuals have certain grievances — no matter how remote or unlikely — that may motivate them to consider acts of violence under the guise of ideology and (b) there are issues or incidents that may be inconsequential or resolved to the public but may trigger the individuals to commit acts of violence (Boltz *et al.*, 2002).

Intelligence Scenarios and Long-term Efforts

At the operational level, intelligence analysts should leverage smart technologies and adapt the associated techniques and procedures for various intelligence scenarios. These scenarios include: (a) ongoing or prolonged intelligence probes on suspicious individuals; (b) information on imminent threats that are received on short notice, hence requiring an urgent response; (c) intelligence support for an ongoing terror-related event or post-event investigations (e.g., to track terrorists in order to prevent further attacks); and (d) intelligence support for security response to unusual or unexpected situations (Lawrenson, n.d.).

At the strategic level, intelligence analysis supported by the use of smart technologies should contribute to risk assessments that inform longer term counter-terrorism efforts. These efforts include: (a) planning physical measures and policies to better protect potential targets that may be soft, strategic, or iconic in nature; (b) training public and private security officers in order to keep pace with evolving terrorist tactics; (c) sharing information with other public and private partners in order to jointly prevent threats; (d) identifying new avenues for enhancing existing counter-ideology programmes; and (e) advising policymakers and decision makers in the national security establishment.

Conclusion

This chapter discussed why jihadi terrorism in particular is a perennial security problem for global cities given the confluence of several factors that is facilitated by technology such as an unkillable jihadi ideology, the propensity of jihadi terrorists and their supporters to evolve their tactics, and the recruitment of elusive operatives and followers especially lone wolves. Amid these, growing urbanisation — leading to higher density population and more socio-economic activities — would make global cities more awash with soft targets, and hence, more challenging to protect. With ISIS facing military setbacks and territorial losses in the Middle East, jihadi terrorists would attempt to sustain their brand and influence by shifting more attention to other regions including cities in non-conflict zones.

Smart technologies — for augmented surveillance of the physical space to predict possible or imminent threats and profile persons of interest — is important as it can support efforts to prevent terrorist attacks by complementing online surveillance and traditional methods of intelligence collection. This point is particularly relevant for global cities that have embarked on smart cities initiatives. The terrorists' pre-operational surveillance and analysis of potential targets constitute the stage in the terror attack cycle that would be most susceptible to detection by homeland security. Lone wolves may be more susceptible to detection as compared to terrorist groups as these individuals would have to conduct each stage of the terror attack cycle by themselves, hence leaving faint signals that may be detectable by smart technology systems.

The effectiveness of smart technologies would require more than just its physical implementation to support current operational practices. Security agencies should reimagine these practices in order to stay resilient in the face of constantly evolving threats and to avoid intelligence failures. There should be more integration of smart technology systems used by homeland security agencies and the private security companies to reduce any blind spots in surveillance and gaps in information sharing. The smart technology systems used by homeland security agencies should have interoperability with other mission-critical systems to support real-time intelligence analyses of possible or imminent threats, and help inform operational decisions on the ground.

Most importantly, there has to be critical analysis of how smart technologies in practice can support the various steps in the intelligence cycle besides functioning as a force multiplier for physical security. The use of smart technologies should be premised on intelligence analysis techniques and procedures that are applicable for various terrorist and criminal threats, and should help shed light on the terrorists' plans so that pre-emptive efforts can be taken. There has to be an appreciation of the ethical issues that accompany the use of smart technologies. Smart technologies when well harnessed can enhance counter-terrorism intelligence both at the operational and strategic levels.

References

Abdul Ghafour, P. K. (2014, October 9). Saudis retrace route of Abraha's army that came to destroy Kaaba. *Arab News*. Retrieved from http://www.arabnews.com/saudi-arabia/news/641556

Abdul Rahman, M. F. (2016a, October 13). Sharpening defences against the blade of terrorism. *Eurasia Review*. Retrieved from https://www.eurasiareview.com/13102016-sharpening-defenses-against-the-blade-of-terrorism-analysis/.

Abdul Rahman, M. F. (2016b, October 25). Bracing communities for returning foreign fighters. *Eurasia Review*. Retrieved from http://www.eurasiareview.com/25102016-bracing-communities-for-returning-foreign-fighters-analysis/.

Abdul Rahman, M. F. (2016c, December 13). Smart CCTVs: Third Eye of Secure Cities. *RSIS Commentary*. Retrieved from https://www.rsis.edu.sg/rsis-publication/cens/co16300-smart-cctvs-third-eye-of-secure-cities/#.WkMG1HtlLIU.

Abdul Rahman, M. F. (2017a, July 24). Law Enforcement: Security Challenges Ahead. *RSIS Commentary*. Retrieved from https://www.rsis.edu.sg/rsis-publication/cens/co17139-law-enforcement-security-challenges-ahead/#.WjHRnXtlLIU.

Abdul Rahman, M. F. (2017b, June 1). Artificial Intelligence: Why It won't Displace Police Analysts. *RSIS Commentary*. Retrieved from https://www.rsis.edu.sg/rsis-publication/nts/co1709-artificial-intelligence-why-it-wont-displace-police-analysts/#.WnvqY_lubIU.

Abdul Rahman, M. F. (2017c, December 14). Smart Security: Balancing Effectiveness and Ethics. *RSIS Commentary*. Retrieved from http://www.rsis.edu.sg/wp-content/uploads/2017/12/CO17235.pdf.

Ackerman, E. (2014). Emergency response teams combine mobile robots, drones, and dogs. *IEEE Spectrum*. Retrieved from https://spectrum.ieee.org/automaton/robotics/military-robots/emergency-response-teams-combine-mobile-robots-drones-and-dogs.

Ang, B., Cheong, D. D., & Vasu, N. (2017). Session 2: Innovation in terrorism and counter-terrorism. *11th Asia-Pacific Programmes for Senior National Security Officers: Innovation and National Security*. RSIS Event Report.

Attack on Nice: Who was Mohamed Lahouaiej-Bouhlel? (2016). *BBC*. Retrieved from http://www.bbc.com/news/world-europe-36801763.

Augenstein, S. (2017). NYC truck terror attack: New 'lone wolf' study may help analysis. *PoliceOne.com News*. Retrieved from https://www.policeone.com/investigations/articles/455533006-NYC-truck-terror-attack-New-lone-wolf-study-may-help-analysis/.

Axe, D. (2011). With drone and satellites, US zeroed in on Bin Laden. *Wired*. Retrieved from https://www.wired.com/2011/05/with-drones-and-satellites-u-s-zeroed-in-on-bin-laden/.

Benson, T., & Grieve, G. (2016). *Principles of Health Interoperability*. London: Springer International Publishing.

Boltz, F., Dudonis, K., & Schultz, D. (2002). *The Counterterrorism Handbook: Tactics, Procedures and Techniques*. U.S.: CRC Press LLC.

Bossman, J. (2016). Top nine ethical issues in artificial intelligence. *World Economic Forum*. Retrieved from https://www.weforum.org/agenda/2016/10/top-10-ethical-issues-in-artificial-intelligence/.

Chan, F. (2016). Suspect in foiled Marina Bay rocket attack planned to get job on Sentosa. *The Straits Times*. Retrieved from http://www.straitstimes.com/asia/se-asia/suspect-planned-to-get-job-on-sentosa.

Charnock, G. (n.d.). Global City. *Encyclopedia Britannica*. Retrieved from https://www.britannica.com/topic/global-city.

Cheong, D. D. (2016). Terror strike in Singapore 'only a matter of time'. *The Straits Times*. Retrieved from http://www.asiaone.com/terror-strike-singapore-only-matter-time.

Dongen, T. V. (2017). The fate of the perpetrator in the jihadist modus operandi: Suicide attacks and non-suicide attacks in the west, 2004–2017. *ICCT Research Paper*. Retrieved from https://icct.nl/publication/the-fate-of-the-perpetrator-in-the-jihadist-modus-operandi-suicide-attacks-and-non-suicide-attacks-in-the-west-2004-2017/.

Elizabeth. E. J. (2015). The new surveillance discretion: Automated suspicion, big data, and policing. *Harvard Law & Policy Review, Vol. 10*. Retrieved from https://pdfs.semanticscholar.org/e422/85d1f5edfd77f7061c76cf239ce54da574d2.pdf.

Elizabeth, E. J. (2016). Policing police robots. *UCLA Law Review*. Retrieved from https://www.uclalawreview.org/policing-police-robots/.

Franco, J. (2017). The battle for Marawi: Urban warfare lessons for the AFP. *Security Reform Initiative*. Retrieved from http://www.securityreforminitiative.org/2017/10/04/battle-marawi-urban-warfare-lessons-afp/.

Ghafour, P. K. A. (2014). Saudis retrace route of Abraha's army that came to destroy Kaaba. *Arab News*. Retrieved from http://www.arabnews.com/saudi-arabia/news/641556.

Gul, Z. (2017). Smart policies to end extremism and violent ideology. *Inside Sources*. Retrieved from http://www.insidesources.com/smart-policies-end-extremism-violent-ideology/.

Hashim, A. S. (2014). From Al-Qaida affiliate to the rise of the Islamic Caliphate: The evolution of the Islamic State of Iraq and Syria (ISIS). *RSIS Policy Report*. Retrieved from https://www.rsis.edu.sg/wp-content/uploads/2014/12/PR141212_The_Evolution_of_ISIS.pdf.

Hui, J. Y. (2017). Crowdsourcing terrorism: Utopia, martyrdom and citizenship reimagined. *Journal of Asian Security and International Affairs*, *4*(3), 337–352.

iHLS. (2017). Algorithms to Save Intelligence Analysts' Time. *Israel's Homeland Security News*. Retrieved from https://i-hls.com/archives/80418.

Institute of Economics & Peace (2017). *Global Terrorism Index 2017: Measuring and Understanding the Impact of Terrorism*. Retrieved from http://economicsandpeace.org/reports/.

INTERPOL (2017). *INTERPOL World 2017 to Showcase the Latest Innovations for Future Security Challenges*. Retrieved from https://www.interpol-world.com/sites/live.interpolworld2017.site.gsi.sg/files/%5BPress%20Release%5D%20INTERPOL%20World%202017%20to%20Showcase%20the%20Latest%20Innovations.pdf.

Israni, E. T. (2017). When an algorithm helps send you to prison. *The New York Times*. Retrieved from https://www.nytimes.com/2017/10/26/opinion/algorithm-compas-sentencing-bias.html.

Jayakumar, S. (2016). The curious case of Wang Yuandongyi: Why do some want to fight with anti-ISIS groups? *RSIS Commentary*. Retrieved from https://www.rsis.edu.sg/rsis-publication/cens/co16074-the-curious-case-of-wang-yuandongyi-why-do-some-want-to-fight-with-anti-isis-groups/#.WjCUgntlLIU.

Jerard, J. (2017). Commentary: Are lone wolves or regional terrorist networks more dangerous to Singapore? *Channel News Asia*. Retrieved from https://www.channelnewsasia.com/news/singapore/commentary-are-lone-wolves-or-regional-terrorist-networks-more-8907484.

Kaati, L., & Pontus, S. (2011). Analysis of competing hypothesis for investigating lone wolf terrorists. *European Intelligence and Security Informatics Conference (EISIC)*. Retrieved from http://ieeexplore.ieee.org/document/6061221/?reload=true.

Kruys, G. P. H. (2006). Intelligence failures: Causes and contemporary case studies. South Africa: Institute for Strategic Studies, University of Pretoria. Retrieved from https://repository.up.ac.za/handle/2263/3078.

Lawrenson, S. LLC. (n.d.). How to hunt "Criminals and Terrorists: The Actionable Intelligence Workshop". *National White Collar Crime Centre & New York Police Department*. Retrieved from https://www.nw3c.org/docs/Courses/course-description — hunt.pdf?sfvrsn=2.

Magolan, M. (2014). Book review: The siege of Mecca by Yaroslav Trofimov. *Homeland Security Affairs*. Retrieved from https://www.hsaj.org/articles/265.

Mahzam, R., & Abdul Rahman, M.F. (2016, December 19). Singapore's threat outlook 2017: The terrorist challenge ahead. *RSIS Commentary*. Retrieved from https://www.rsis.edu.sg/rsis-publication/cens/co16306-singapores-threat-outlook-2017-the-terrorist-challenge-ahead/#.Wi-OUntlLIU.

McCullar, M. (2010). How to look for trouble — A Stratfor guide to protective intelligence. *Stratfor Global Intelligence*. Austin, TX: Stratfor.

Mendelsohn, B. (2016). ISIS's lone-wolf strategy. *Foreign Policy Research Institute*. Retrieved from https://www.fpri.org/article/2016/08/isis-lone-wolf-strategy/.

Ministry of Home Affairs (2015). *Executive Summary of the Ministry of Home Affairs' Committee of Supply (COS) Debate 2015*. Retrieved from https://www.mha.gov.sg/Newsroom/speeches/Pages/Executive-Summary-of-the-Ministry-of-Home-Affairs%E2%80%99-Committee-of-Supply-(COS)-Debate-2015.aspx.

Moore, J. (2017). The chosen one? Al-Qaeda's next leader could be Osama bin Laden's son Hamza. *The Soufan Group*. Retrieved from http://www.soufangroup.com/ali-soufan-cited-in-newsweek-the-chosen-one-al-qaedas-next-leader-could-be-osama-bin-ladens-son-hamza/.

New America (2017). Jihadist terrorism 16 years after 9/11: A threat assessment. Retrieved from https://www.newamerica.org/international-security/policy-papers/jihadist-terrorism-16-years-after-911-threat-assessment/.

New York Port Authority attack: Akayed Ullah 'inspired by IS' (2017). *BBC*. Retrieved from http://www.bbc.com/news/world-us-canada-42320366.

Perez, E., Prokupecz, S., & Yan, H. (2016). Omar Mateen scouted Disney complex, Pulse, official says. *CNN*. Retrieved from http://edition.cnn.com/2016/06/14/us/orlando-shooter-omar-mateen/index.html.

PERGAS (2014). Media statement on "Religious Guidance on Acts of Violence and Extremism". *Singapore Islamic Scholars & Religious Teachers Association (PERGAS)*. Retrieved from http://www.pergas.org.sg/media/MediaStatement/Media-Statement-IS-English-Final.pdf.

Richards, J. H. Jr. (1999). Psychology of intelligence analysis. *Centre for the Study of Intelligence, Central Intelligence Agency*. Retrieved from https://www.cia.gov/library/center-for-the-study-of-intelligence/csi-publications/books-and-monographs/psychology-of-intelligence-analysis/PsychofIntelNew.pdf.

Stewart, S. (2017). The terrorist attack cycle remains unbroken. *Stratfor Worldview*. Retrieved from https://worldview.stratfor.com/article/terrorist-attack-cycle-remains-unbroken.

Stratfor (2009). The terrorist attack cycle. *Stratfor Global Information Services*. Austin, TX: Stratfor.

Stroud, M. (2016). The minority report: Chicago's new police computer predicts crimes, but is it racist? *The Verge*. Retrieved from https://www.theverge.com/2014/2/19/5419854/the-minority-report-this-computer-predicts-crime-but-is-it-racist.

Willingham, A. J. (2017). ISIS has mastered the art of creating lone wolves. *CNN*. Retrieved from http://edition.cnn.com/2017/03/23/world/isis-lone-wolf-social-media-trnd/index.html.

World Economic Forum (n.d.). *The Fourth Industrial Revolution, by Klaus Schwab*. Retrieved from https://www.weforum.org/about/the-fourth-industrial-revolution-by-klaus-schwab.

CHAPTER 6

A Common Framework for Pre-Radicalisation Indicators

OMER ALI SAIFUDEEN

National Security Coordination Secretariat, Prime Minister's Office, Singapore

Introduction

The idea of pre-emptively intervening to prevent an individual "predisposed" to radicalisation from spiralling further towards extremism is an attractive idea that has resulted in a whole array of "early-warning" pathway models and associated indicators. However, the indicators that exist further "upstream" or "pre-radicalisation" indicators, as they will be addressed in this chapter tend to be highly subjective. Furthermore, the line between what is a pre-radicalisation indicator and what is indicative of someone already radicalised can be blurred and subject to operational definitions determined by the parties requiring the assessment.

For the purposes of this chapter, pre-radicalisation refers to the *cognitive non-violent* stage in which the individual harbours, nurtures, and supports the views of extremists while in the process of *exploring* these ideas. There might exist some structural or intrinsic *propensities* or *vulnerabilities* contributing to this process as

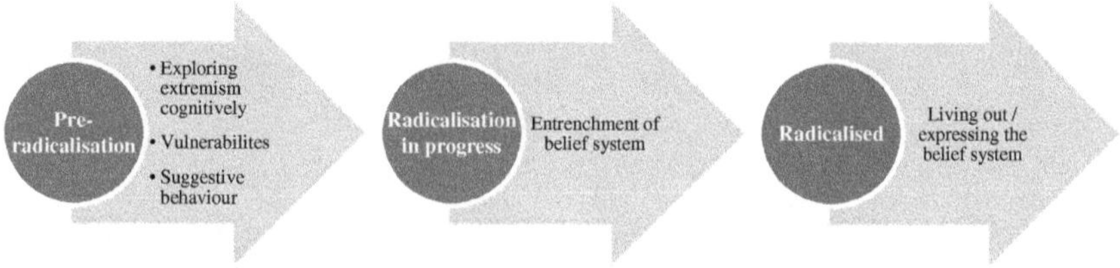

Figure 6.1. Defining and Situating the Pre-radicalisation Stage.

well. At this stage, one would see behaviour that is only suggestive of the individual's worldview that is in a state of flux and has yet to crystallise into a belief system. This is where we draw the line between pre-radicalisation and radicalisation. What happens after this point is the rest of the radicalisation process, namely, entrenchment of the belief system that advocates violence, followed by living out or expressing the belief system. At this last stage, all that remains is planning for the act of violence and the right opportunity to carry it out (see Figure 6.1).

Challenges Facing Practitioners

To reduce false positives at the pre-radicalisation stage requires taking a highly nuanced perspective according to the experiential/situational context (i.e., in which contexts do indicators appear). Furthermore, many indicators do not occur in a vacuum and require an understanding of the "milieu" (e.g., peer networks), as well as the structural environment surrounding the individual (Bouhana *et al.*, 2014).[1]

Currently, individual extremism/radicalisation risk assessment tools adopt the Structured Professional Judgments (SPJ) model — e.g., VERA 2, Extremism Risk Guidelines (ERG 22+), and Radicx[2] (Spee & Reitsma, 2017). Such assessments require practitioners such

[1]Schmid (2013) stresses that radicalisation studies have predominantly favoured analysis at the micro level, but a holistic examination should integrate the meso (community/milieu) and macro (structural) influences as well.

[2]A framework used by the Dutch to provide an insight into potential radicalisation and youth extremism. Only available in the Dutch language.

as counsellors rating an individual according to a set of indicators and background factors. However, these assessment tools may not be well suited for pre-radicalisation cases in which a lot of pre-defined triggers and enablers *have yet to manifest*, and would only appear during episodes with specific actors the individual associates with.

Another challenge lies in determining the propensities or vulnerabilities to radicalisation. Scholarly works on propensity have generally taken an empirical approach that focuses on the frequency in which that characteristic is observed. An example of this is the Risk Propensity Scale (RPS) that requires an individual to complete a questionnaire (Meertens & Lion, 2008). A complete assessment would need to take into account the inputs of significant individuals and peers in the individual's life. These personalities need to be identified by examining the social structures surrounding the individual in question. This input from an individual's milieu is especially relevant for pre-radicalisation assessment as friends/close peers are often the first to observe signs of vulnerability or propensity to radicalisation (Bouhana *et al.*, 2014; Lam, 2017). Friends, particularly, are more likely than family to observe these signs. However, their close identification with the potential radical prevents them from connecting these signs to extremism. Even if they do, they do not talk about these signs to avoid damaging their relationships with the potential radical. Many also do not come forth to report due to fear of repercussions for themselves and the individual as a result of reporting (Williams *et al.*, 2016). Another challenge arising from turning to peer networks as an early warning alert for radicalisation is that in a number of cases, friends/close peers, and family were in fact the influence behind the individual's radicalisation in the first place (Burke, 2015; Stankov, 2018). Having a network of family or friends who were involved in violent action or supportive of it constitutes one of the domains (i.e., History and Capability) that demonstrates vulnerability to extremism in the VERA and VERA 2 risk assessment frameworks (Pressman, 2009; Pressman & Flockton, 2012).

Milieus and social structures are especially important at the pre-radicalisation stage. A theoretical framework that supports this statement is the Situational Action Theory (SAT) (Wikström & Treiber, 2015), that explains why people engage in rule-breaking/crime. SAT is ideal for explaining the pre-radicalisation stage as it examines the development of criminal propensities that can be adapted to explain the development of radical propensities. SAT also explains how a pathway to action (in this context engaging in radical/terrorist activities) is a product not purely of the environment or individual's proclivities, but rather the individual's perception and response based on interactions between both of these factors (Wright, 2012). The key question here is how the choice towards engaging in actual terrorist action is made. Motivation alone is not sufficient for engaging in terrorism (Bouhana *et al.*, 2014). Bouhana and colleagues (2014) explain that one can choose other alternatives or venting/coping mechanisms for their grievances. To engage in terrorism, one first needs to see it as a viable alternative. However, even those who see terrorism as a viable alternative may choose to still not engage in it for a whole variety of practical reasons such as restrictions or lack of opportunities. Hence, other factors cited by Bouhana *et al.* (2014) such as individual propensity, moral context, available choices, and perception also influence the early stages of radicalisation, and can determine the translation of motivation into actual terrorist action. This chapter will adapt the criminological focus of SAT to illustrate vulnerabilities that specifically influence pre-radicalisation.

This will culminate towards a discussion of cognitive and behavioural indicators that are suggestive of a pre-radicalised individual. Using these suggestive indicators as an initial guide, the chapter will deconstruct the various radicalisation pathway models, risk assessment frameworks, and information fact sheets produced for practitioners, to look for other pre-radicalisation indicators. Fortunately, many of these instruments explicitly list out indicators existing at the early stages of radicalisation. This amalgamated collation of indicators for pre-radicalisation will then be ranked by frequency of their mention in an instrument. Finally, by means of a case study, there will be an illustration of how this synthesised and ranked list of pre-radicalisation indicators might manifest in actual cases of radicalisation.

Situational Action Theory

Pre-radicalisation indicators anecdotally would be almost synonymous with the notion of propensities. In the Situational Action Theory (SAT), propensity is a person's tendency to perceive and choose a particular action when motivated to act. An individual's propensity is developed by how one perceives and deals with multiple environmental settings (i.e., activity field) they have to face on a long-term basis (Bouhana *et al.*, 2014). Propensity development is also the product of both cognitive nurturing and moral education one receives (Treiber, 2017).

Cognitive nurturing is an experiential process that is a product of one's inherent neurological makeup and experiences that creates new neural pathways and influences one's neurocognitive functions. These functions are associated with higher-order thinking such as choosing between alternatives when you have conflicting rules, abstract thinking, problem solving, exercising cognitive flexibility, and most importantly showing restrain and limiting impulsive or habitual/reactionary behaviour (Treiber, 2017). This aspect of showing restrain and forbearance is best nurtured during childhood in activities or tasks that teach patience or require control of one's emotions. Through these activities, the neural pathways that control this function are strengthened (Wikström & Treiber, 2017).

Moral education refers to value-based rules of conduct in particular circumstances and moral filters that one learns from their experiences and influences (Treiber, 2017). An individual's moral education is the product of instructions one receives, observing the consequences of certain behaviours or by trial and error through experience (Wikström & Treiber, 2017). The adaption of SAT to examine radicalisation pathways is not unprecedented. SAT had previously been used to create a systematic review of empirical observations associated with Al-Qaeda-influenced radicalisation (Bouhana *et al.*, 2014).

There are a number of situational factors and structural conditions adapted from the SAT that relate to the pre-radicalisation stage, as explained next.

Lifestyle Changes (e.g., migration, incarceration or going to university, life changes due to death of family member)

Such events confront individuals with unprecedented and challenging situations requiring flexibility and adaption. Such situations become aggravated if there is no social support to assist and offer guidance. Those who are not mentally equipped to deal with such cognitive demands, and those who repeatedly face such challenging circumstances that exhaust their mental capacities may seek relief in categorical rule guidance as it alleviates the burden of decision-making. They may also gravitate to easy explanations to their predicament that pin the blame on particular groups or the authority. This includes simplistic solutions that advocate attacking the supposed source of their problems (Bouhana *et al.*, 2014).

Selection

Certain people find themselves in particular situations or interactions that lead to radicalisation. Why an individual chooses or ends up in a certain environmental setting is a result of social selection and self-selection. Social selection of an environment stems from the peers and social networks one frequents. It sets the stage for self-selection that leads to preference formation. Self-selection is a result of one's personal preferences/interests in a particular subject (e.g., martial arts) resulting in them being in that environment and meeting people with similar interests (e.g., martial arts convention) (Bouhana *et al.*, 2014). In the same vein, someone who is discriminated against might gravitate towards homogeneous settings where one finds only those from the same identity group. This individual might prefer to spend more time in such a setting. Through this exposure, the chances of meeting radicalising agents who have gone through similar experiences and individuals who convey extremist reasons to explain their injustices increases (Bouhana *et al.*, 2014).

Social Emergence

There are systemic factors that can contribute to the social emergence of radicalising environments. These include segregation resulting in polarised milieus; the effectiveness of support and direction provided by communities, schools, and families; formal and informal mechanisms of social control; and the extent to which radical influencers are able to move freely within the population. Such meso-level factors which exist between macro (e.g., civil war in the country) and microlevel influences (e.g., individual propensities) create radicalising milieus (Bouhana *et al.*, 2014).

Suggestive Indicators of Radicalisation by Centre for the Study of Democracy

A 2017 study done by the Centre for the Study of Democracy (CSD) provided a framework for early warning indicators. These indicators were divided into behavioural and cognitive indicators suggestive of radicalisation. Behavioural indicators are those that include changes in practices, actions, and appearance. Cognitive indicators are those dealing with expression of opinions, beliefs, and attitudes at verbal level. Cognitive and behavioural indicators in CSD's framework were labelled as suggestive, red flags, or high risk. High risk indicators are those that show imminence of further escalation into violence. Red flags are stronger indicators than suggestive indicators of risk-relevant behaviours and attitudes (CSD Policy Brief, 2017). The suggestive indicators in CSD's framework can relate to the pre-radicalisation stage being discussed in this chapter.

Individual indicators across any level should not be viewed in isolation. They need to be considered in combination with other indicators, the context of the individual's local environment and circumstances, before making the decision to send out an alert (CSD Policy Brief, 2017). The decision to escalate a case and send out an alert will become a pedantic exercise if the assessment is based solely on prescriptive rules. Rather, this decision should be the outcome of consultations with various community institutions (e.g., social services, youth workers, police, town councils/resident committees, schools) that the individual has had a deep-seated history with. Such institutional staff are in a position to give highly relevant insights on the individual's frame of mind and current situation based on their experience with the said individual.

This doctrine is embedded in the "Info-house" approach used in Aarhus, Denmark, to make consultative assessments about the radicalisation of an individual. Info-house essentially represents a framework for local cooperation between the police and municipal social service administrations that result in information sharing, alerts, and joint assessments regarding an individual at risk of radicalisation. If the case is deemed to be due to non-extremism related issues such as poor welfare/social support, gang influence, etc., then it is referred to other initiatives offered by departments in the info-house. As much as possible, the case will be assigned to someone the individual already knows and trusts. This can be a trusted person from the meso-level milieu of the individual at risk such as a youth community worker, football/sports coach, or teacher that the individual trusts. To reduce the impression of an enforced order, participation in sessions with these mentors from the programme is optional (Danish Institute for International Studies, 2015).

Cognitive Pre-Radicalisation Indicators

Monitoring an individual's hate speech provides an avenue to gauge the extent to which radical ideas have been entrenched at the cognitive level. Hate speech would often encompass the following suggestive cognitive indicators that reflect the individual's thought (CSD Policy Brief, 2017).

Openly voicing grievances

The individual has little inhibitions expressing his views and, in many cases, relishes the need to be heard. This could be the result of a psychological process known as deindividuation. According to this theory, when individuals feel they are not given attention or respected as individuals, they lose their self-awareness, inhibitions, and restraints (Borum, 2004). Borum (2004) explains that factors such as anonymity, physical arousal due to aggressive actions, or the confidence arising from mob/group behaviour only strengthen the "deindividuated state" of the individual. However, CSD cautioned that in countries facing economic difficulties and much grievances against the state, this indicator is a rather common expression of general discontent by the masses, and not an indicator of radicalisation per se (CSD Policy Brief, 2017).

Expressing a dichotomous worldview

This is commonly referred to as the absolutist black and white thinking or "us-versus-them" thinking. However, if the injustice frame commonly used by extremists was deconstructed, we would observe dichotomous thinking manifesting in four levels namely, political, ideological, cultural/social, and personal (Dean, 2014). At the political level, it is often framed as the injustice arising from the "haves and have-nots" based on real or imagined grievances. At the ideological level, it segregates between those who are with the cause or against it. At the cultural/social level, it can refer to those who have been left behind, or loners who by virtue of being in the out-group and not part of any preferential in-group, get bullied, face discrimination, and/or ridicule. Finally, dichotomous thinking at the individual level can manifest in how one's everyday focus is consumed in coming up with plans for revenge (Dean, 2014).

Expressing disrespect of or rejecting the legitimacy of (secular) authorities

There are two kinds of narratives expressing this theme that are appealing to potential radicals. One is the notion of political resistance. Jihadi ideologues have over time escalated the adoption of class war and anti-capitalist rhetoric to expand the scope of their cause beyond the confines of religious grievances (Kabbani, 2006). The French riots of 2005 by second and third generation immigrants consisting mostly of North African Arabs, were devoid of religious narratives. The riots were instead driven by a sense of hopelessness due to poverty and lack of opportunities (Smith, 2005). Yet, these are the very reasons that make these rioters ripe for jihadi recruitment. Similarly, the Islamist group, Hizb-ut-Tahrir (HUT) has also capitalised on resistance narratives stemming from poverty and disenfranchisement that was prevalent in immigrant communities. In a leaflet dated 9 June 2005, HUT portrayed the conflict between the United States and the Islamic world in classic Marxist terms (Kabbani, 2006). Religious narratives that pitch the struggle in terms of an existential attack against the religion or any other identity/group that potential radicals hail from, constitute the other kind of appealing narrative. This narrative rides on self-legitimisation that the radical group successfully touts using attractive media pitches or rhetoric (Pearce, 2014).

Behavioural Pre-Radicalisation Indicators

Behavioural indicators are reflective of a person's interactions. Suggestive behavioural indicators, according to CSD's framework, are explained below (CSD Policy Brief, 2017).

Having contacts with or being under the influence of a radical ideologue/role model

There will be occasions in which the individual might directly or indirectly speak with reverence about these ideologues/role models. The extent of this influence becomes apparent when the individual is no longer willing to consider the perspectives of others (CSD Policy Brief, 2017). It is especially pronounced when the individual visibly or aggressively reacts to any criticism about the said ideologue/role model. Individuals who innately revere such influential personalities have a low threshold for criticisms directed at these ideologues/role models. This is because a threat to the ideologue/role model becomes a threat to their cherished beliefs stemming from these influences, that have become a part of their ego/sense of self. This process is known as self-identification and it explains why followers of charismatic leaders will aggressively defend their leaders as they are in effect defending an ideal version of themselves they are struggling to become, that is modelled on these leaders (Ricketts & Ricketts, 2011). Hence, during casual conversations with such individuals, it might be possible to get them to manifest this behaviour by simply injecting any form of criticism about their ideologues/role models.

Group isolation and encapsulation

An individual confining a greater part or all of one's interactions within a chosen group is not a sign of radicalisation per se. However, it is one of the precursors that increases one's vulnerability to radicalisation especially if the said group advocates an insular approach to shield themselves from outside perspectives that threaten their beliefs, and also vilifies other groups in the process. This situation is exacerbated by group-think[3] (Psychologists for Social Responsibility, n.d.).

Noticeable change in religious and other everyday routines

In particular, this indicator is referring to the kind of drastic and visible personal changes that an individual undertakes to the point they become a central part of one's life (CSD Policy Brief, 2017). While the incidence of individuals making drastic lifestyle changes are pretty common, as with other fluid indicators, the need for attention increases considerably if this indicator appears in conjunction with other pre-radicalisation warning signs.

Cutting ties with family and friends, and becomes socially withdrawn

While such behaviour might be indicative of other issues such as family problems, drug addiction etc., increasing isolation has been often cited as a noticeable indicator of an individual's vulnerability to radicalisation (Subedi, 2017). If this escalates to an actual unaccounted disappearance, it needs to be accorded attention, investigated diligently, and not simply dismissed as being a phase endemic of any troubled youth. The mother of the Gulshan Café attackers from Bangladesh alleged that she had informed law enforcement about her missing son, but the authorities had not taken

---

[3]This term was created by social psychologist Janis (1972). It is a process in which faulty decisions are made due to group pressures. Alternate perspectives are not considered and other groups are dehumanised. Groups which shield themselves against outside opinions are therefore vulnerable to group-think.

the matter seriously. She strongly voiced the need for a separate platform for lodging complaints over missing youths, that could also disseminate information to all relevant law enforcement agencies ("Inmates exposed to radicalisation", 2018).

Early Warning Tools for Front-Line Practitioners

The people best positioned to recognise early signs of vulnerability are often public sector and community workers that frequently encounter people at risk. They may interact with them on a variety of issues that are unrelated to radicalisation (e.g., housing, town council issues, welfare). This is opportunistic as it places them in an ideal position to gain a keen appreciation of the individual's social milieu (i.e., peer networks) and vulnerabilities. The frequency of interactions such practitioners have with vulnerable individuals, creates greater opportunities for spotting indicators that have yet to manifest and only appear during sporadic episodes in the individual's life. Recognition that this group is ideal for sending out radicalisation alerts has given rise to a number of risk/vulnerability assessment tools and training manuals specifically designed for practitioners. Besides, the suggestive indicators of radicalisation created by CSD, other vulnerability markers and early warning indicators of radicalisation used in some of the more prominent tools are explained below.

TerRa[4] Toolkit for Teachers and Youth Workers

This initiative by the European Commission and its Director General for Migration and Home Affairs, illustrates some characteristics of what vulnerability to radicalisation might entail (de Wolf, 2014). Namely,

a) A lack of belonging to any particular identity.
b) Connection to a radical group via familial (e.g., sibling, parent) or close peer relationships.

---

[4]According to de Wolf (2014), "TerRa is a two year, Europe wide, network-based prevention and learning project, funded by the European Commission, DG Home Affairs. It is carried out by Impact Knowledge and Advice Centre, Amsterdam, and AV11M, Madrid. Its toolkit is aimed at professionals Europe wide and addresses the full spectrum of the commonest forms of radicalisation currently in Europe."

c) Experiencing discrimination — real or perceived.
d) Social isolation as a result of being a victim of bullying.

Vulnerability Assessment Framework

The Channel programme in the U.K. uses a multiagency panel consisting of local authorities (e.g., police, social services, schools, NGOs) to conduct risk assessment for identifying vulnerable individuals at the early stage of radicalisation and provide support for them. Local partnerships that run the Channel programme use the vulnerability assessment framework (VAF) to carry out such assessments that are used to complement their professional judgement. For pre-radicalisation indicators, we are interested in the "engagement factors" which are at times cited as "psychological hooks" that create the needs, susceptibilities, motivations, and contextual influences needed to push individuals onto the pathway to extremism (Channel Vulnerability Assessment, 2012). They are listed as follows:

a) Feelings of grievance and injustice.
b) Feeling under threat.
c) A need for identity, meaning, and belonging.
d) A desire for status.
e) A desire for excitement and adventure.
f) A need to dominate and control others.
g) Susceptibility to indoctrination — lacking access to moral role models or balanced arguments via education that can build up their resilience against extremist thinking ("Let's talk about it", n.d.).[5]
h) A desire for political or moral change.
i) Opportunistic involvement.
j) Family or friends involved in extremism.
k) Being at a transitional time of life.

[5]The "Let's Talk About It" public education website (www.ltai.info) in the U.K. is an initiative consisting of government and civil society agencies that provides practical help and guidance about radicalisation to the public.

l) Being influenced or controlled by a group to the point of adopting their behaviours (e.g., causes, symbols) and loss of other interests. Possessing their ideological materials and moving onto recruiting others (Dzhekova *et al.*, 2017).
m) Relevant mental health issues.

U.K. School Advisories Based on U.K. Crown Prosecution Service and PREVENT

Schools in the U.K. have a statutory duty under The Counter-Terrorism and Security Act 2015 to report on indicators of radicalisation in their students. Many U.K. schools disseminate the guidance on list of indicators of "vulnerability"[6] to radicalisation (Thomas Clarkson Academy, n.d.), which is given by the U.K. Crown Prosecution Service and PREVENT (i.e., The U.K.'s Counter-Terrorism strategy):

a) Identity crisis — distanced from their cultural/religious heritage and discomfort about their place in society.
b) Personal crisis — family tensions, isolation, low self-esteem, dissociated from existing friendships and involvement with new, questioning identity, faith and belonging.
c) Personal circumstances — migration, local community tensions and events in originating country, personal experience of racism/discrimination, perception of being victimised by unfair Government policies.
d) Unmet aspirations — perceptions of injustice, failure, and societal rejection.
e) Experiences of criminality — risk taking behaviour through associations with criminal groups, prison experience, or due to poor resettlement/reintegration processes.
f) Special educational needs — difficulties with social interaction, empathy, understanding consequences of actions and motivations of others.

---

[6] Adapted from Thomas Clarkson Academy (n.d.).

Community Policing Preventing Radicalisation & Terrorism Manual

Community Policing Preventing Radicalisation & Terrorism (CoPPRA) was developed by the Belgian Federal Police in cooperation with police agencies from 11 EU member states for training and awareness raising among EU community police officers (Dzhekova *et al.*, 2017). In particular, it mentions indicators that hint at the radicalisation process being underway, namely:

a) Social isolation and a changing attitude towards others. Partaking in minor crimes.
b) Notable change in physical appearance or names one uses to address himself/herself.
c) Glorification of extremist themes and violence, being outspoken and demonstrative of extremist worldviews.
d) Contact with extremist groups and possesses extremist materials, change in religious practices, and observed to take part in secret meetings.

The key attribute in many of these indicators is when the change is drastic enough to become noteworthy — e.g., a notable change in appearance or religious practice and openly supporting extremist worldviews. These noteworthy changes should, at the very least, prompt the need for intervention providers to check in on the said individual and find out the reasons behind such notable behavioural changes.

Canadian Centre for the Prevention of Radicalisation into Violence (CPRLV) Behavioural Barometer

This "Barometer" has four categories ranked in increasing order of seriousness, namely — insignificant behaviour, troubling behaviour, worrisome behaviour, and alarming behaviour. Insignificant behaviour indicators help distinguish between behaviours that commonly get associated with radicalisation, but are actually benign. This includes taking a keen interest in national or international

Table 6.1. Key Attributes of Troubling and Worrisome Behaviour.

Category	Key Attributes
Troubling behaviour	a) Polarising and absolutist views, cannot tolerate or consider differing viewpoints and reconsider their own stance. Rejecting institutional rules based on their ideology or beliefs or refusing to participate in group activities because of the nature of the other group. b) Preaching their intolerant views. c) Expressing the need to dominate and control others. d) Sense of victimisation, rejection. e) Ascribing to conspiracy theories. f) Increasing isolation and moving away from family and peers. g) Behaviours leading to rupture in family. h) Sudden changes in habits.
Worrisome behaviour	a) Cuts off family ties and moves closer to alternate social group. Hides evidence of new lifestyle but displays symbols of support for violent extremist groups. b) Disinterested in professional or school activities. c) Becomes obsessed with religious eschatology and messianic views. d) Legitimises the use of violence to defend cause/ideology. Expresses hatred of other groups/individuals.

Source: Centre for the Prevention of Radicalisation Leading to Violence (CPRLV) (2016).

events, speaking up against social injustices or becoming more religious (Centre for the Prevention of Radicalisation into Violence [CPRLV], 2016). Troubling and worrisome behaviour relate more to the pre-radicalisation indicators. Troubling behaviour describes signs that are indicative of personal conflicts that lead one to ascribe to a particular cause or ideology. Worrisome behaviour is an escalation of the pre-radicalisation stage and the beginnings of a radicalisation pathway. It is marked by a mistrust of mainstream society and the world, and supporting violent solutions (CPRLV, 2016). An amalgamation of the key attributes from these two behaviours are given in Table 6.1.

A Synthesised Pre-Radicalisation Framework for Practitioners

Table 6.2 presents a grouping of pre-radicalisation/vulnerability indicators from the various instruments described earlier according

Table 6.2. Synthesised Compilation of Pre-radicalisation Indicators.

Theme	CSD/EU	CHANNEL VAF	CoPPRA	TERRA	UK Schools Advisories	CPRLV
Isolation, rejecting mainstream life/ groups (Frequency: 7)	Social withdrawal and isolation Group isolation	—	Social isolation, attitude change to others	Social isolation via bullying	—	Social isolation Reject rules on ideological grounds Reject mainstream group activities due to differences in identity
Personal crisis/ circumstances, behavioural/ mental issues (Frequency: 7)		Personal circumstances — mental health, crisis, *etc.*			Personal crisis Personal circumstances Unmet aspirations Special education needs	Behaviour causing conflict/ rupture with family Need to dominate others
Extremist contacts/ connections/ acts of criminality (Frequency: 6)	Contacts/ connections to extremists	Extremist connections — family and peers	Extremist contacts/ connections Minor crimes	Contacts/ connections to extremists via family/ peers	Criminality experience	
Expressing, glorifying and justifying extremism or extremist groups (Frequency: 5)	No inhibitions expressing extremist views Reject or disrespect of secular authority		Extremist justifications/ glorifications			Legitimises and expresses specific/ targeted hatred and use of violence Preaches these intolerant views

(*Continued*)

Table 6.2. (*Continued*)

Theme	CSD/EU	CHANNEL VAF	CoPPRA	TERRA	UK Schools Advisories	CPRLV
Injustice frame/ perceived or real victimisation/ discrimination (Frequency: 4)		Injustice and siege mentality		Discrimination		Obsession with religious eschatology/ messianic views/ conspiracy theories — leading to siege or victim mindset Sense of victimisation and rejection
Identity crisis (Frequency: 3)		Identity, purpose, personal wants and control		Identity confusion	Identity crisis	
Notable behaviour change/habits/ appearance changes — risk taking (Frequency: 3)	Notable behaviours change/habits/ appearance changes — risk taking		Notable changes — appearance, names			Drastic behaviours changes/habits/ appearance changes — risk-taking
Dichotomous, polarising/ absolutist/ inflexible views (Frequency: 3)	Dichotomous views					Polarising/absolutist views Dichotomous and inflexible views

to overarching themes. Within instruments such as the VAF when many engagement factors are listed, they are grouped into larger collectives (e.g., personal circumstances include mental health issues/mental characteristics (need to dominate others) or personal crisis). The overarching themes stemming from grouping together various indicators can be seen in the left-hand column of Table 6.2.

The "frequency" in the left-hand column reflects the extent to which indicators coming under these overarching themes appear. Since all these instruments are the product of analysing real-world data and case examples, a plausible inference is that indicators with a higher frequency of mention are more commonly observed in cases of pre-radicalisation. Hence, we are able to rank the various overarching pre-radicalisation categories that can be seen in Table 6.2. We have further condensed and rephrased the pre-radicalisation indicators from the above table into the following seven factors:

a) Isolation and societal withdrawal.
b) Past and present psychological trauma/crisis/circumstances.
c) Sustained associations with negative influencers/groups (e.g., criminality).
d) Expressing radical sentiments/actions with little or no inhibitions.
e) Siege mentality and victim mindset.
f) Identity crisis/notable behaviour change/risk taking[7] (Reynolds *et al.*, 2015).
g) Absolutism.

Illustrating the Seven Factor Pre-Radicalisation Indicator Framework

Momin Khawaja was a 39-year-old Canadian who was convicted for a fertilizer bomb plot in the U.K. in 2004. The Momin case study by

[7]An identity crisis is closely correlated with corresponding behavioural change — in the form of seeking identity, breaking social norms towards in-group norms, having explicit demonstrations of new in-group identity through behaviour change/appearance, and taking risks to fulfil realisation of this newfound identity. Hence, these two indicators have been combined into a consolidated category (see Reynolds *et al.*, 2015).

the National Consortium for the Study of Terrorism and Responses to Terrorism (START) (2016), offers a comprehensive illustration of the early stages of radicalisation, and how the seven factor pre-radicalisation indicators manifest during an individual's development. This is because this case study taps on Momin's court trial documents which include hundreds of pages of his emails and blog posts that describe noteworthy comments and description of significant moments from his childhood, schooling and work experiences. In addition, the case study taps on his own writing that provides a detailed account of his shift from radical thought to action. However, this case study is not meant to be representative of what happens in all instances of pre-radicalisation. Neither are all cases of pre-radicalisation bound to manifest all seven factors. What the case study of Momin offers instead is a closer look at how each of the seven factors can originate, manifest in the actions and words of the individual, and eventually progress towards the decision to undertake action. The point in which the individual decides to undertake action is one of the lines we draw between pre-radicalisation and radicalisation. The other demarcation to distinguish between these two stages would be when the individual becomes fixated and absolute with worldviews that advocate violence as the solution.

Signs of Momin's political awakening actually became evident only around September 2000 when he was about 21 years old. Momin was born to parents born in Kashmir and the family then moved to Pakistan. During his trial, Momin had mentioned how the political problems in Kashmir had always been a big issue in his family (START, 2016). It seemed his co-conspirators in the 2004 bomb plot also shared this similar grievance over Kashmir (START, 2016). Eventually, they moved from Pakistan to Canada. In his early years, Momin's father was teaching and studying at the University of Toronto when Momin began his elementary schooling. At some point, as part of his father's employment as school administrator, he took the family to Libya, Pakistan, and Saudi Arabia. His family spent about two years in Libya and when the U.S. air-strikes happened in 1986, they left a lasting impact with Momin who was seven-year-old at that time. There might have been some *latent residual trauma*[8] from these experiences, as years later, in his emails he described how Americans were indiscriminately victimising Muslims: "I guess the weasels at the white house were bored one day, and decided to test out their latest fire-power by dropping bombs on innocent Muslims" (START, 2016, p. 8). However, Momin was a regular child who enjoyed watching Western TV and grew up reading popular English children's books. His experience in Pakistan and Saudi Arabia did not seem to have any effect on his political views nor was there any indication of him being exposed to Wahhabi views or radical individuals. Furthermore, when he was back in Canada growing up, he did not feel discriminated against or at a disadvantage. His father being in the academic field, allowed his family to live a comfortable middle-class life. Neither did Momin get involved in criminal or gang-related activities. However, his brother had a criminal record for stealing a car (National Consortium for the Study of Terrorism and Responses to Terrorism (START), 2016).

One significant factor that facilitated his path to radicalisation was the kind of music he listened to. Music apparently played a big role in Momin's life before and after his radicalisation. Much of his preferred music seemed to be "gangsta" rap with aggressive lyrics. Later on, this progressed towards *Nasheeds* (Islamic songs) with lyrics that spoke about Muslims being victimised. In fact, Momin gravitated to any kind of music that was politically inspiring. In particular, he liked to listen to the World War Two Russian "Katyusha Song" about a Russian girl missing her lover who was fighting with the Red Army (START, 2016). In some ways, this was the beginning of Momin connecting deeply with those whom he saw as victims of political oppression. This "humiliation by proxy" or perceived humiliation happens when an individual transposes the victimisation of other individuals to his/her own lives. Very often, it is the product of what the media one ascribes to portray (Khosrokhavar, 2010). The individual in this case might not be going through any victimisation per se via these issues portrayed by the media. However, they feel

[8]Pre-radicalisation indicator 2: Past and present psychological trauma/crisis/ circumstances.

deeply for others going through it as they identify with them due to some shared cause or identity. Hence, such individuals feel outrage when hearing about the suffering of those they identify with as if it were happening to them. This was the beginning of Momin's *identity crisis*,[9] and all the experiences that led up to this point entrenched in him a *siege mentality* and *victim mindset*.[10]

When he was attending Algonquin college, Momin who was around 18 at this time, developed the view that individual behaviour is determined by the circle of friends one keeps, and behaviour can be changed by changing one's circle of friends:

> If you spend all day in a perfume shop, you'll smell amazing, but if you're having problem with girls, smoking, and just bad behaviour, change your circle of friends. Don't spend time with people who are like that. I remember when I left high school I did change as a person, partly because I no longer chilled with the same people anymore... (START, 2016, p. 12).

At some point here, he might have felt that to be a person with better morals, he needed a set of friends that espoused such virtues. One of the "circle of friends" he hung out with was a group of students known as Pakistanis With Attitude (PWA). PWA was insular, discouraged mixing with others, and had a reputation for being standoffish (START, 2016). This was the beginning of Momin's increasing *isolation*[11] to a particular clique and *withdrawal*[12] from his mainstream circle of friends. This increasing isolation was promoted by *sustained associations*[13] with the PWA that advocated such negative exclusivist attitudes.

A semblance of early radical influence in fact also came from his parents. Momin had a close and positive relationship with his parents. His father propagated the view that the Muslim world is

---

[9]Pre-radicalisation indicator 6: Identity crisis.

[10]Pre-radicalisation indicator 5: Siege mentality and victim mind-set.

[11]Pre-radicalisation indicator 1: Isolation.

[12]Pre-radicalisation indicator 1: Societal withdrawal.

[13]Pre-radicalisation indicator 3: Sustained associations with negative influencers/groups.

being victimised by the West. However, this was a view that was common to many Muslims who felt victimised by the West and that the war on terror is a war on Islam. Hence, it was natural for his son to take on similar sentiments. The only crucial difference was that for Momin, this worldview has escalated into advocating terrorism (START, 2016). Momin's mother doted on him. When he was young, she read stories from Islamic history that inspired him. One story in particular had a marked impact on him to the point that he called this story his favourite in an email to a friend:

> ...I always wanted to be a soldier, cuz when I waz like 5 yrs old: me mum and I would read story about Alio radiAllahuAnhu and how he chopped off the head of Marhab the kafir and about jihad and stuff. Lolz, I loved it even then and wud repeat that story of Ali radiAllahuAnhu over and over again... (START, 2016, p. 18).

His mother denied ever knowing about his "jihadist-type thinking", but had overheard his plans to travel to distant destinations (START, 2016). His sense of altruism peaked in 2000 and was brought about by a number of events. In 1998/1999, when his grades began to slip, he gave up a partying lifestyle and began to focus on his studies. In 2000, he became a regular visitor and volunteer teacher on Islamic studies for the boys at Bilal Mosque. He enjoyed teaching these boys and watching them progress. His focus at this point according to his brother was on "school, work, and marriage" (START, 2016, p. 19).

His political views around this time were predisposed to lean towards more radical worldviews. He confided to his prospective fiancée about how he felt different from others as he questioned much about the Muslim situation due to global events such as the Palestinian Intifada. He felt that from being "normal" and perhaps apathetic to such events, his life changed as he began to focus on what was happening to Muslims around the world. In an email to his prospective fiancée, he hinted at the apathy of Muslims who are caught up in their own lives and not paying any attention to the suffering of others as the reason for Islam's predicaments:

> But once i grew up i felt that something was wrong, terribly wrong. Right around the age of 21 i realized that all the fun pastime

> activities that everyone was into were a waste of time and did not benefit Islam and the Muslims in any way. so i left everything. When the Palestinian intifada happened i started looking into my own life and questioning myself as to why our situation was so bad? [*sic*] (START, 2016, pp. 19–20).

Global events that followed such as the Second Palestinian Intifada, the 9/11 attacks, and the U.S. invasion of Afghanistan only entrenched this belief. These beliefs developed into an absolute conviction that someone needs to do something. Momin felt if nobody was going to do anything about the victimisation of Muslims, then it is up to him. If he was going to take some form of action, he felt this required him making changes to his life, namely sacrifices and preparation to be in a position of strength from which effective reprisals can be made. The following quote from him illustrates how he saw preparation as a necessary condition for resisting effectively from a position of strength:

> America is at war with Islam, Israelis at war with Islam, so we do not treat Ariel Sharon and George Bush with compassion, do we? They have slaughtered tens of thousands of our brothers and sisters. The blood of the Ummah has been spilt... This is the precise reason for the Jihad, the training, warfare, weaponry, and war-like mentality against those who commit acts of aggression... This is why the preparation and equipment is needed, so that its presence emanates a prowess that deters any who might harbour ill intentions, like the example of a 300 pound football player who does not need to tell people about his strength, since his sight alone will intimidate any (START, 2016, p. 22).

At this point, Momin had not quite decided to undertake violent action. His idea of "preparation" had an almost deterrent ring to it. Nonetheless, Momin already had a highly *absolutist*[14] worldview that puts the blame for many issues facing Muslims squarely on a fixed reason, namely, that there was a war on Islam waged by the West and her allies. By this stage, his absolutist views were also easy

[14] Pre-radicalisation indicator 7: Absolutism.

to observe as he had *little or no inhibitions in expressing radical sentiments or actions.*[15] However, according to CPRLV's behaviour barometer, the need to do something about social injustice would still be in the realm of "insignificant behaviour" as this can be a positive virtue if channelled in the right way. Hence, absolutist worldviews and the lack of inhibitions in the expression of radical sentiments can be better indicators of pre-radicalisation rather than the overarching desire to do something about injustice *per se*.

It was the Second Palestinian Intifada that started shifting Momin from simply sympathising with Muslims in such situations to advocating violent means to address these issues. After the Afghan invasion, he made the decision to travel to Afghanistan to fight. This was demonstrated by an oath of allegiance he made to a group known as the "Ansaar Youth Organisation" in which he said that he intends to be a "Mujahid" (one who undertakes jihad). At this point, when the decision to commit a violent act happened, according to the parameters set in this chapter, his pre-radicalisation stage has effectively ended. The following quotation from him following these global events illustrates how his thought patterns became increasingly geared towards deciding that he should act:

> I realized that 'I' must change myself first, must be willing to make a difference. Everyone assumes SOMEONE else is probably doing something to help, so why should "I" bother. Its not true, No one does anything. lf I want change I have to do something about it. Change requires hardship, trials. Sacrifice, pain, suffering, loss of life, loss of wealth. Do the Muslims think that Jannah is so cheap? (START, 2016, p. 21).

These themes of altruism and noble sacrifices are powerful ideas that are commonly used in jihadi recruitment narratives, and this is reflected in artwork promoting militant jihadism that is easily found on the internet. In particular, such artwork celebrates the few that are willing to undertake such sacrifices and emphasises how these individuals are special and among the noble chosen few. If one were to

---

[15] Pre-radicalisation indicator 4: Expressing radical sentiments/actions with little or no inhibitions.

do an image search on Google with the keyword "Mujahid", multiple jihadi imagery glorifying militant jihad and alluding to the idea of the "Noble few" can be found.

Monin's entrenchment of the view that violence works, can be seen in the comments he made around the end of his pre-radicalisation stage. In 2003, when he was about 24, Momin posted an extensive message on his blog in which he reminisced threatening an oppressive religious instructor at a local Islamic madrasah (religious school) when he was about five years old, and how this stopped the instructor's bullying behaviour.

> I looked at him, and threw his stick back at him and said to him, "I'm going to go to my house and I'm getting MY stick, and MY stick is bigger than YOUR stick, and I'm going to bring it here, and I'm going to beat YOU with it! Do you understand??. It worked! He didnt say a damn thing to me. He didnt hit me. He just told me to go back and sit ... After that incident, some of the older kids at the madressa worked up the courage to stand up to him as well... Remember, it only takes one person to start a revolution, to bring about change. The molvi WAS eventually canned, but not before causing his share of trouble ... What's my point in this? well, its just a reminder that sometimes actions that would normally be NOT allowed, become necessary and even praiseworthy due to the special circumstances surrounding them. If you have no other way of achieving a sincere and righteous objective, except through questionable means, then thats what you have to do. [*sic*] (START, 2016, pp. 33–35).

Conclusion

Insights for Policymakers and Practitioners: When Do You Raise the Alarm?

Given their broad coverage, these seven pre-radicalisation indicators can naturally manifest in other forms of deviance and/or mental health issues besides extremism[16]:

[16]More information about how these indicators can manifest in some of these mental health disorders can be found in the Diagnostic and Statistical Manual of Mental Disorders, 4th Edition, Text Revision (DSM-IV-TR).

1. Isolation and societal withdrawal — depression, schizoid, or other related personality disorders (Baek, 2014).
2. Past and present psychological trauma/crisis/circumstances — post-traumatic stress disorders (PTSD).
3. Sustained associations with negative influencers/groups — gang/criminal associations, substance abuse and related disorders, etc.
4. Expressing radical sentiments/actions with little or no inhibitions — sociopathy (Peterson, 2015).
5. Siege mentality and victim mindset — paranoid personality disorder (Bressert, 2017).
6. Identity crisis/notable behaviour change/risk-taking — criminality, dissociative identity, and borderline personality disorders, (Salters-Pedneault, 2018).
7. Absolutism — anxiety disorders, depression, suicidal ideations (Al-Mosaiwi & Johnstone, 2018), dehumanising targeted person/groups.

Hence, a comprehensive approach in dealing with pre-radicalisation would benefit from involving those who are outside of the traditional domains of security, but nonetheless have a much keener appreciation of the social issues and radicalisation enabling environments surrounding a vulnerable individual. In particular, this is referring to mental health professionals, counsellors (educational, welfare or medical), educators, and youth workers who often come across individuals who may be vulnerable to radical influences during periods of crisis. By addressing any of the seven pre-radicalisation indicators in such vulnerable individuals, one is also able to prevent other potential "deviant" trajectories (e.g., via criminality, mental disorders) that could make someone susceptible to radical thinking.

When to raise the alarm should not be seen as a fixed point of reference as intervention should instead be an ongoing process — to be applied even if only one of these indicators were to manifest. Even insignificant behaviour such as the desire for social justice should not be ignored completely, but rather extra attention and effort need to be put in to ensure these energies are channelled towards positive outcomes. Any form of *light intervention* or simply *attention*, when pre-radicalisation indicators are observed or even when insignificant behaviour is observed, is better than no action.

Finally, an appreciation of the sources of negative influence inherent in the individual's local environment and triangulation with other sources of information such as one's peers, community, and local authorities should also be taken into consideration when assessing such individuals.

Editors' Note

Readers are advised to contact the ISD Counter-Terrorism Centre Hotline (1800-2626473) if they are in doubt about the potential threat posed by an individual of interest. Alternatively, they can also contact the Religious Rehabilitation Group [RRG] Helpline (1800-7747747).

References

Al-Mosaiwi, M., & Johnstone, T. (2018). In an absolute state: Elevated use of absolutist words is a marker specific to anxiety, depression, and suicidal ideation. *Clinical Psychological Science*. doi: 10.1177/2167702617747074.

Baek, S. (2014). Psychopathology of social isolation. Retrieved from https://www.ncbi.nlm.nih.gov/pmc/articles/PMC4106767/.

Borum, R. (2004). *Psychology of Terrorism*. Tampa: University of South Florida.

Bouhana, N., Thornton, A., Corner, E., Malthaner, S., Lindekilde, L., Schuurman, B., & Perry, G. (2014). D3.1 Risk analysis framework v2 public — PRIME FP7. Retrieved from http://www.fp7-prime.eu/deliverables/PRIME_D3.1_Risk_Analysis_Framework_Public.pdf.

Bressert, S. (2017). Paranoid personality disorder. Retrieved from https://psychcentral.com/disorders/paranoid-personality-disorder/.

Burke, J. (2015). 'Jihad by family': Why are terrorist cells often made up of brothers? *The Guardian*. Retrieved from https://www.theguardian.com/world/2015/nov/17/jihad-by-family-terrorism-relatives-isis-al-qaeda.

Centre for the Prevention of Radicalisation Leading to Violence (CPRLV) (2016). The behaviour barometer: An education and awareness tool.

Retrieved from https://info-radical.org/wp-content/uploads/2016/08/BAROMETRE_EN_CPRLV_2016-1.pdf.

Channel Vulnerability Assessment (2012). Retrieved from https://www.gov.uk/government/publications/channel-vulnerability-assessment.

CSD Policy Brief (2017). Monitoring radicalisation and extremism — Center for Study of European Democracy (CSD). Retrieved from http://www.csd.bg/fileSrc.php?id=23150.

Danish Institute for International Studies. (2015). An introduction to the Danish approach to countering and preventing extremism and radicalisation. Retrieved from http://www.ft.dk/samling/20151/almdel/reu/bilag/248/1617692.pdf.

de Wolf, A. (2014). TerRa toolkit — Teachers & youth workers. Retrieved from http://terratoolkit.eu/wp-content/uploads/2014/09/TERRATOOLKIT_FULL_PRINT_web_27.pdf.

Dean, G. (2014). *Neurocognitive Risk Assessment for the Early Detection of Violent Extremists*. Cham: Springer International Publishing.

Dzhekova, R., Mancheva, M., Stoynova, N., & Anagnostou, D. (2017). Monitoring radicalisation: A framework for risk indicators. Retrieved from http://www.csd.bg/artShow.php?id=17916.

Inmates exposed to radicalisation. (2018). *The Daily Star*. Retrieved from http://www.thedailystar.net/frontpage/keep-watch-your-children-1522810.

Janis, I. L. (1972). *Victims of Groupthink: A Psychological Study of Foreign Policy Decisions and Fiascoes*. Boston, MA: Houghton Mifflin.

Kabbani, S. (2006). The globalization of Jihad: From Islamist resistance to war against the west. Retrieved from http://www.islamicsupremecouncil.org/understanding-islam/anti-extremism/56-the-globalization-of-jihad-from-islamist-resistance-to-war-against-the-west.html?showall=1.

Khosrokhavar, F. (2010). The psychology of global jihadists. In C. B. Strozier, D. M. Terman, J. W. Jones, & K. Boyd (Eds.), *The Fundamentalist Mindset Psychological Perspectives on Religion, Violence, and History* (pp. 145–146). Oxford: Oxford University Press.

Lam, L. (2017). Singapore under highest terror threat in recent years: 8 key points from MHA's terror report. *The Straits Times*. Retrieved from http://www.straitstimes.com/singapore/singapore-under-highest-terror-threat-in-recent-years-8-key-points-from-mhas-terror-report.

Let's talk about it (n.d.). Spotting the signs. Retrieved from http://www.ltai.info/spotting-the-signs/.

Meertens, R. M., & Lion, R. (2008). Measuring an individual's tendency to take risks: The risk propensity scale. *Journal of Applied Social Psychology*, *38*(6), 1,506–1,520.

Mujahid (n.d.). Retrieved from https://jihadprincess.deviantart.com/art/Mujahid-183059308.

National Consortium for the Study of Terrorism and Responses to Terrorism (START). (2016). *Momin Khawaja: Mechanisms of Radicalization*. Retrieved from https://www.start.umd.edu/pubs/START_CSTAB_2.5_MominKhawajaMechanismsofRadicalization_Aug2016.pdf.

Pearce, C. (2014). IS: Resistance and extremism. Retrieved from https://www.thegazelle.org/issue/51/features/isis-and-islam.

Peterson, T. (2015). Signs of a sociopath are big-time scary. Retrieved from https://www.healthyplace.com/personality-disorders/sociopath/signs-of-a-sociopath-are-big-time-scary.

Pressman, D. E. (2009). *Risk Assessment Decisions for Violent Political Extremism*. Ottawa: Public Safety Canada.

Pressman, D. E., & Flockton, J. (2012). Calibrating risk for violent political extremists and terrorists: The VERA 2 structured assessment. *The British Journal of Forensic Practice*, *14*(4), 237–251.

Psychologists for Social Responsibility (n.d.). *What is Groupthink?* Retrieved from http://www.psysr.org/about/pubs_resources/groupthink%20overview.htm.

Reynolds, K., Subasic, E., & Tindall, K. (2015). The problem of behaviour change: From social norms to an ingroup focus. *Social and Personality Psychology Compass*, *9*(1), 45–56.

Ricketts, C., & Ricketts, J. C. (2011). *Leadership: Personal Growth and Career Success* (3rd edn.). Clifton Park, NY: Rhoades.

Salters-Pedneault, K. (2018). What identity problems do BPD sufferers endure? Retrieved from https://www.verywellmind.com/borderline-personality-disorder-identity-issues-425488.

Schmid, A. P. (2013). *Radicalisation, De-radicalisation, Counter-radicalisation: A Conceptual Discussion and Literature Review*. The Netherlands: The International Centre for Counter-Terrorism — The Hague.

Smith, C. S. (2005). Immigrant rioting flares in France for ninth night. *New York Times*. Retrieved from http://www.nytimes.com/2005/11/05/world/europe/immigrant-rioting-flares-in-france-for-ninth-night.html.

Spee, I., & Reitsma, M. (2017). *RADICX — Instrument to Detect the 'state of radicalisation' from Youth*. The Netherlands: VET Contra.

Stankov, L. (2018). Brussels attacks: Why do family members commit terrorism together? *The Conversation*. Retrieved from http://theconversation.com/brussels-attacks-why-do-family-members-commit-terrorism-together-56800.

Subedi, D. (2017). Early warning and response for preventing radicalization and violent extremism. *Peace Review*, *29*(2), 135–143.

Thomas Clarkson Academy (n.d.). *Prevent and Radicalisation*. Retrieved from https://www.thomasclarksonacademy.org/page/?pid=112.

Treiber, K. (2017). Situational action theory and PADS. In A. Blokland, & V. van der Geest (Eds.), *The Routledge International Handbook of Life-Course Criminology* (Chapter 5). London and New York: Taylor & Francis.

Wikström, P., & Treiber, K. (2015). Situational theory. In A. R. Piquero (Ed.), *The Handbook of Criminological Theory* (pp. 415–444). New York: John Wiley & Sons.

Wikström, P., & Treiber, K. (2017). Beyond risk factors: An analytical approach to crime prevention. In B. Teasdale, & M. S. Bradley (Eds.), *Preventing Crime and Violence*. Switzerland: Springer.

Williams, M. J., Hogan, J. G., & Evans, W. P. (2016). The critical role of friends in networks for countering violent extremism: Toward a theory of vicarious help-seeking. *Behavioral Sciences of Terrorism and Political Aggression*, *8*(1), 45–65.

Wright, J. (2012). Situational action theory. Retrieved from http://criminology.wikia.com/wiki/Situational_Action_Theory.

CHAPTER 7

Five Things to know about Assessment Tools for Violent Extremism

VAISHNAVI HONNAVALLI

Home Team Behavioural Sciences Centre, Ministry of Home Affairs, Singapore

Introduction

Violent extremist attacks have become more frequent in the recent years with changes in political climates and foreign policies. While societies are grappling with the increasing number of casualties of violent extremist attacks, law enforcement agencies are working to identify and prevent the next violent extremist attack. Historically, the role that practitioners in law enforcement played in countering violent extremism have been reactive rather than preventive (Borum *et al.*, 1999). However, under the current security climate, such practices have to change. In particular, assessment tools are being increasingly utilised to identify the level of risk/threat posed by individuals detained for involvement in violent extremism. This chapter will highlight five basic aspects of assessment tools that practitioners, academics, and policymakers need to be cognisant of in the context of violent extremism.

What Type of Assessment Tools Are There?

Assessment tools can be categorised into two groups: tools for (1) threat assessment and (2) risk assessment.

Threat assessment is concerned almost entirely with the risk of targeted violence by a subject of concern and has a behavioural and observational policing focus (Meloy *et al.*, 2012), aimed at preventing a violent extremist attack (Borum, 2015b). Primarily, it is administered during the investigation of a person of interest, prior to arrest, to determine the nature and level of threat management — i.e., whether the individual should be monitored further, given an official warning by authorities or there are sufficient grounds for an arrest.

Risk assessment is defined as a projection of the likelihood that a hazardous behaviour or event will occur (Kraemer *et al.*, 1997; Roberts & Horgan, 2008), relying more on historical and dispositional variables (Meloy *et al.*, 2012), while predicting future risk as well as formulating strategies to manage this risk (Llyod & Dean, 2015). Risk assessments are conducted under two conditions: (1) to determine risk management and rehabilitation strategies while the offender is in custody or (2) to determine likelihood of re-offending and inform suitability for early release.

Implication

However, user needs to be mindful of the limitations associated with the assessment tools when using them due to an array of challenges. Firstly, the inability of academic researchers to have access to individuals in custody who are considered violent extremists due to national security protection (Monahan, 2012), when developing a tool. Thus, the tool might not accurately measure behaviours exhibited by a violent extremist. Secondly, due to the low-base rate of the occurrence of violent extremist attacks, the predictive capacity of the tool for targeted violence risk will continue to be poor (Meloy *et al.*, 2015). Moreover, unlike the knowledge base of general violence, the literature bank on violent extremism pales in comparison, hence the same level of understanding of risk of involvement in violent extremism does not exist yet (Borum, 2015a). Finally, risk assessment tools potentially have been misused as screening tools to identify individuals who display vulnerability towards violent extremism (Reed, 2016), which increases the propensity for wrongful arrests and mistrust in authority. Despite so, assessment tools are integral in counter-violent extremism efforts as it aids in decision-making regarding a person of interest. There are excellent early efforts in developing assessment tools for violent extremism, which lay down the platform on which further research is required.

What Are Some Commonly Used Assessment Tools?

There are multiple assessment tools designed to assess the level of risk of violent extremists, but for the purpose of this chapter, three tools have been selected for discussion as there is existing literature that reviews them.

Extremism Risk Guidance 22+ (ERG 22+)

ERG 22+ is a risk assessment tool developed by the National Offender Management Service (NOMS)[1] (U.K.), as part of the *Prevent*[2] strategy (Silke, 2014). It is used by practitioners to identify pathways and motivations of those convicted of engaging in violent extremist activities to better inform interventions for disengagement and desistance (Dean, 2014). Therefore, it is administered on convicted extremist offenders in custody and community to measure

[1]NOMS is now known as Her Majesty's Prison and Probation Service, which is responsible for the rehabilitation management of individuals detained for engaging in violent extremism.

[2]Prevent is part of the U.K.'s counter-terrorism strategy. It is aimed at stopping individuals from supporting or becoming violent extremists.

changes in risk over time, playing a central role in key decision-making in sentence management — i.e., security re-classification, release on parole, types of intervention approaches (National Offender Management Service, 2014).

ERG 22+ (see Table 7.1) has 22 factors that are categorised under three main dimensions: (1) engagement, (2) intent, and (3) capability. Engagement refers to factors or circumstances which may motivate someone to engage with a violent extremist group or ideology. Intent focuses on circumstances or factors which may enable the individual to be prepared to offend on behalf of the group, cause, or ideology. Finally, capability refers to circumstances that enable someone to

Table 7.1. Factors for ERG 22+

Domains	Factors
Engagement	1. Need to redress justice and express grievances.
	2. Need to defend against threat.
	3. Need for identity, meaning, and belonging.
	4. Need for status.
	5. Need for excitement, comradeship, or adventure.
	6. Need for dominance.
	7. Susceptibility to indoctrination.
	8. Political/moral motivation.
	9. Opportunistic involvement.
	10. Family or friends support extremist offending.
	11. Transitional periods.
	12. Group influence and control.
	13. Mental health.
Intent	1. Over-identification with a group or cause.
	1. Us and them thinking.
	2. Dehumanisation of the enemy.
	3. Attitudes that justify offending.
	4. Harmful means to an end.
	5. Harmful end objectives.
Capability	1. Individual knowledge, skills, and competencies.
	1. Access to networks, funding, and equipment.
	2. Criminal history.
	+ Any other factor.

Source: Llyod & Dean (2015).

actually commit a particular offence. The "+" suffix accommodates any other factors that appear relevant (Dean, 2014). However, Llyod and Dean (2015, p. 51) also voice concern that:

> There remain important questions to be explored, most notably around reliability and validity, but in the meantime the ERG provides a systematic, transparent, and accessible framework for engaging, assessing, and managing extremist offenders and those vulnerable to engagement in prison and the community.

Violent Extremism Risk Assessment 2 (VERA 2)

VERA 2 was developed as a risk assessment tool by Pressman and Flockton in 2010 for correctional settings to evaluate individuals convicted of violent extremism related offences, and to assess their risk of re-offending and determine the nature of interventions required in custody (Pressman & Flockton, 2014). It constitutes 31 risk and protective factors (see Table 7.2), which are segregated into five conceptual domains: (1) beliefs and attitudes, (2) content and intent, (3) history and capability, (4) commitment and motivation, and (5) protective.

The beliefs and attitudes domain refers to factors that relate to the individual's world view and goals (consistent with an individual's accepted ideology) and may provide a foundation for extremism. Content and intent domain encompasses factors that are pertinent to the conscious "intention" to act with unlawful violence to support an ideology, and examines contextual influences on intention. History and capability entails factors that indicate the capability of an individual to plan and carry out a violent extremist attack. The commitment and motivation domain includes factors that are potential drivers of an individual's commitment to violent extremism. Lastly, factors under the protective domain indicate circumstances or instances that mitigate influences towards violent extremist action (Pressman & Flockton, 2014).

VERA 2 is not intended to serve as a definitive predictive instrument for those who have not offended, but rather to provide indication of the likelihood of danger that the individual poses to

Table 7.2. Factors for VERA 2

Domains	Factors
Beliefs and attitudes	1. Commitment to ideology justifying violence. 2. Victims of injustice and grievances. 3. Dehumanisation/demonization of identified targets of injustice. 4. Rejection of democratic society and values. 5. Feelings of hate, frustration, persecution, alienation. 6. Hostility to national collective identity. 7. Lack of empathy, understanding outside own group.
Context and intent	1. Seeker, consumer, developer of violent extremist materials. 2. Identification of target (person, place, group) in response to perceived injustice. 3. Personal contact with violent extremists. 4. Anger and expressed intent to act violently. 5. Expressed desire to die for cause or martyrdom. 6. Expressed intent to plan, prepare violent action. 7. Susceptible to influence, authority, indoctrination.
History and capability	1. Early exposure to pro-violence militant ideology. 2. Network (family, friends) involved in violent action. 3. Prior criminal history of violence. 4. Tactical, paramilitary, explosives training. 5. Extremist ideological training. 6. Access to funds, resources, organizational skills.
Commitment and motivation	1. Glorification of violent action. 2. Driven by criminal opportunism. 3. Commitment to group, group ideology. 4. Driven by moral imperative, moral superiority. 5. Driven by excitement, adventure.
Protective	1. Reinterpretation of ideology as less rigid, absolute. 2. Rejection of violence to obtain goals. 3. Change of vision of enemy. 4. Involvement with non-violent, deradicalisation, offence-related programs. 5. Community support for non-violence. 6. Family support for non-violence.

Source: Pressman & Flockton (2014).

themselves and others around them post arrest (Pressman & Flockton, 2014). Therefore, it cannot be used as a tool for threat assessment.

It is to be used with convicted violent extremists to assist with security and case management decisions for these offenders (Pressman & Flockton, 2014). The reliability and validity of the VERA approach is supported by independent research conducted on the VERA protocol (Beardsley & Beech, 2013). The authors found that majority of the VERA factors were easily mapped to five case studies of violent extremists who had different motivations and roles, regardless of whether they worked alone or as part of a group. However, the authors also highlighted that:

> [O]nly a small sample of terrorists were studied, all of whom were male domestic terrorists who had carried out the most extreme terrorist offences, leading to a large number of fatalities. Therefore, any conclusions drawn on the applicability of the VERA may not accurately represent terrorists outside this group (Beardsley & Beech, 2013, p. 11).

Currently, VERA 2 has been revised to VERA 2-revised (Radicalisation Awareness Network, 2017).

Terrorist Radicalisation Assessment Protocol (TRAP-18)

Meloy and colleagues (2012) developed a typology of eight warning behaviours for assessing the threat of intended violence. They examined previous research on risk factors associated with intended violence.[3] Meloy *et al.* (2015) improved on the initial typology of eight warning behaviours and incorporated 10 distal characteristics, drawing from empirical studies and the authors' case experience with lone wolves, to develop the TRAP-18, a threat assessment tool (see Table 7.3). These distal characteristics elucidate the psychopathology or "mindset" of

[3]Meloy *et al.* (2012) examined research on public targets, psychiatric patients, adolescent and adult mass murders, school shooters, spousal homicide perpetrators, workplace violence attackers, figure assassination, corporate celebrity stalking, and both domestic and foreign acts of terrorism.

Table 7.3. Factors for TRAP-18 (Meloy *et al.*, 2015).

Domains	Factors
Warning behaviours	1. Pathway warning behaviour.
	2. Fixation.
	3. Identification.
	4. Novel aggression.
	5. Energy burst.
	6. Leakage.
	7. Last resort.
	8. Directly communicated threat.
Distal characteristics	1. Personal grievance and moral outrage.
	2. Framed by an ideology.
	3. Failure to affiliate with an extremist group.
	4. Dependence on the virtual community.
	5. Thwarting of occupational goals.
	6. Changes in thinking and emotion.
	7. Failure of sexual-intimate pair bonding.
	8. Mental disorder.
	9. Creativity and innovation.
	10. Criminal violence by history.

violent extremists, focusing on the dimensional aspects of the individual's mental structure and cognitive functioning (Meloy *et al.*, 2015). In other words, the justification for the use of violence towards others and self is provided by the presence of these factors. TRAP-18 consists of 18 coded behavioural patterns focusing only on targeted violence — acts which are intended and purposeful — rather than general violence. The 18 behavioural factors are divided into two sets of eight warning behaviours (proximal and dynamic patterns indicative of accelerating risk for targeted violence), and 10 distal characteristics (aspects of the lone actor that may prompt further intelligence gathering and monitoring without requiring actual risk assessment unless warning behaviour is present) (Meloy & Gill, 2016).

The authors propose for TRAP-18 to be used as investigative template for operational purposes (Meloy *et al.*, 2015), and designed it for use by intelligence agencies to conduct investigations on persons of interest in order to aid in the prioritisation of cases (Meloy & Gill, 2016). When the tool was applied to a small sample ($N = 22$) of violent extremists in Europe (lone actors and members of autonomous cells), it demonstrated good-to-excellent interrater reliability and content validity; researchers were able to identify majority of the factors being present for each case example (Meloy *et al.*, 2015). The authors contend that "the sample in this study was quite small, and all findings should be treated as preliminary ... Further research by independent groups is warranted to confirm or disconfirm its merit" (p. 149).

Implication

Efforts to administer risk assessment tools in the context of violent extremism is still under-researched and lacks demonstrative validity. All the three tools discussed in this chapter have a common limitation — i.e., the tools lack validity. There is also insufficient evidence to suggest a direct link between some of the factors found in these tools and participation in violent extremism. Although the ERG 22+ was developed a few years ago and has been used within the correctional setting in the U.K., it lacks substantial amount of studies that can support the validity of the tool. This is a similar limitation for the VERA 2 protocol. While there are several studies that can attest to the credibility and usability of the tool, the sample sizes of these empirical research studies are not significant enough. As for TRAP-18, it is a new threat assessment protocol and understandably lacks demonstrative validity as a psychometric measure of the risk of violent extremism (Meloy *et al.*, 2015).

How Different is Violent Extremism from General Violence in Terms of Assessment?

Violent extremists are diverse in their motivation and ideology (Hart *et al.*, 2017; Silke, 2014). Assessment tools currently used for the assessment of general violence have not been validated on ideologically motivated violent offenders, and these offenders are known to differ significantly in motivation, background, and other characteristics from non-ideological violent offenders (Pressman & Flockton, 2014). Hence, the factors to assess risk of violent extremism will be different from the factors of existing instruments that address general violence (Monahan, 2012). Less than one-third of the indicators of the HCR-20,[4] which is used in forensic settings to assess common violence risk, was found to have little relevance to violent extremists (Pressman, 2008). This is because the majority of the risk factors pertains to history of violence and background information of the person of interest (i.e., psychopathy, substance use, employment problems). However, research has not found all violent extremists to experience early patterns of violence, past offence, education failure or other socio-economic depravation (Bakker, 2006; Silber & Bhatt, 2007). Mullins (2011) suggests that there is nothing unique about the backgrounds of violent extremists that makes them stand out from the rest of the population. A study looking at assessing the risk of violent extremism using VERA-2 and HCR-20 V3 found that violent extremist offenders were rated as significantly lower in risk than the general violent offenders on the HCR-20 V3 but significantly higher in risk according to VERA-2 (Pressman & Flockton, 2014). This was due to the violent extremists scoring low in the historical

---

[4]The HCR-20 was developed by Webster and his colleagues to help make structured decisions about violence risk. Since the publication of Version 1 in 1995 and Version 2 in 1997, it has become the most widely used and validated violence risk assessment instrument (Webster *et al.*, 1997). It consists of 20 risk factors divided into three scales — (1) historical, (2) clinical, and (3) risk management. The historical scale consists of risk factors that focus primarily on past behaviours, features of mental disorder, and life challenges that have been demonstrated in the literature to elevate the risk for violence. The clinical scale consists of five risk factors dealing with the recent past (up to 12 months) that focus primarily on an individual's emotional, cognitive, and behavioural functioning, as well as compliance with and responsivity to intervention and risk reduction strategies. Finally, the risk management scale pertains to functioning in the future (up to the next 12 months), which determines the individual's continued living within an institution (i.e., prison, hospital), for community discharge planning or for continuing community supervision (Douglas, 2014). HCR-20 V3 is commonly used within U.S. forensic systems for conditional release planning, as well as for institutional risk assessment and management (Douglas, 2014).

scale of the HCR-20 V3 (which accounts for one third of the assessment), as those risk factors were not present for the violent extremists. Therefore, getting a low overall rating of risk, and an inaccurate representation of the level of risk.

Implication

Academics recommend for VERA-2 to be used in conjunction with other tools (e.g., HCR-20 V3) that assess general violence, for a comprehensive risk assessment (Hart *et al.*, 2017). Although the risk factors for general violence and violent extremism are different, the HCR-20 V3 provides valuable information concerning the individual's risk for general violence, which can be incorporated into any violent extremism risk assessment tool (Meloy & Gill, 2016). A person who is suspected of violent extremism can also be at risk for other forms of violence. Thus, a combination of tools can be utilised on one individual, but the judgement on the level of risk needs to be analysed carefully. VERA-2 is essential for the detailed assessment of extremist desires, belief, and attitudes, that are assessed only in general terms in HCR-20 V3 (Hart *et al.*, 2017). It is beneficial to gather information on the background of the individual to guide the overall assessment process, but the focus should not be exclusively on one's history of violence. Rather, there is a need to identify factors that are indicative of actions, or changes in behaviour patterns which could be evidence of planning or preparing to carry out an attack (i.e., the warning behaviours and distal characteristics of TRAP-18).

Can an Assessment Tool be Used for Multiple Purposes?

Assessment tools are designed for specific purposes and over-extending their use to other purposes have consequences. This can be seen with the ERG 22+. As part of the Prevent programme in 2012, the government developed an Extremism Risk Screen (ERS) to guide decisions about identifying a potential violent extremist, their vulnerability to being drawn into terrorism as a consequence of radicalisation, and the kind of support that they need (HM Government, 2015). The ERS's function was to serve as a threat assessment tool, and the factors were adopted from the ERG 22+. However, the ERS did not function adequately as a threat assessment tool as there were disproportionate numbers of false positives reported to the authorities; it was a legal requirement for public sector workers to report individuals who they deemed as "at-risk" based on the ERS (Reed, 2016). Thus, disproportionate number of Muslims within hospitals, schools, and higher education bodies were reported to authorities as vulnerable individuals, resulting in erosion of trust between the service providers and the community (Open Society Justice Initiative, 2016; Reed, 2016). The reporting made British Muslims feel discriminated against (Open Society Justice Initiative, 2016). It also resulted in the community viewing public sector workers as government spies, corrupting the trust between the community and security agencies (Open Society Justice Initiative, 2016).

Implication

There is a need to identify the objective of the assessment tool and not misuse it beyond its original purpose. Although risk factors underlying assessment and screening tools may be similar, the manifestations of the indicators to look out for differ. For example, ERG 22+ was developed through interviews with Al-Qaeda detainees but:

> [M]any of the Vulnerability Assessment Framework (VAF) factors — for example, the need for identity, meaning and belonging; a desire for status; and desire for excitement and adventure — are so widely prevalent so as to capture virtually every young person within the net of 'vulnerability' (Open Society Justice Initiative, 2016, p. 39).

Therefore, using an assessment tool for the purpose of identifying vulnerable individuals in society can be very misleading. One of the biggest challenges of violent extremism risk assessment is the low base rates against which the factors can be mapped. Besides the fact that not everyone follows a similar pathway of radicalisation (Borum, 2015a), there is also the need to acknowledge the difference between extremist thoughts and willingness to act on those thoughts (Monahan, 2012). Risk assessment tools thus far have not been able to accurately predict who will commit an act and who will not (Sarma, 2017). Hence, it is presumptuous to suggest that everyone follows a similar pathway to radicalisation and that risk factors can be generalised for violent extremism, especially since there are different types of violent extremism. In addition, it might be ambitious to expect one assessment tool to be able to differentiate (whether someone only has adopted the ideology or is willing to take action as well), predict (whether this person is willing to carry out an attack if released back into society), prevent (further inclinations to carry out a violent extremist attack), and manage (gathering insights about the level of risk in order to design appropriate measures to reduce reoffending).

Do Assessment Tools Account for the Diversity of Activities that Violent Extremists Get Involved in?

Participation in violent extremism can be varied, which impacts the level of threat or risk posed by the individual. Individuals do not necessarily have to participate in the main execution of the attack; they could provide intelligence, finance, logistic, or even training support. An American Think Tank, New America, found that many homegrown violent extremists in United States were arrested for financing and providing resources for terror plots, rather than actively attempting to carry out the attack (Bergen, 2017). The warning signs and motivations of someone financing violent extremism are likely to be different from someone training to carrying out an attack (Monahan, 2012), and that in turn impacts their level of risk. Borum (2015b) also suggests that people can be involved in violent extremism in a variety of ways, and these modes of involvement can change over time and across roles. For example, individuals in their teens and 20s, may be more actively engaged in the planning or execution phase of violent extremist attacks, but as they grow older, they may opt for more ideological or leadership roles (Silke, 2014). Horgan (2008) is of the belief that certain risk factors may open up the opportunity for radicalisation into violent extremism, while other factors might come into play only when the individual moves further along the pathway of becoming a violent extremist. Therefore, it is necessary to identify the risk outcome that is to be assessed by any type of assessment tool (risk or threat), which may be dependent on the type of involvement of the individual in violent extremism.

Implication

Considering that different individuals may pose different levels of risk for different roles at different points in time, the focus of risk assessment should vary not only across different individuals but also account for the different roles they play in the group (Silke, 2014). Assessment tools should be able to account for the diversity of involvement in violent extremism and its associated factors. Professionals designing these tools should ensure that the tool is comprehensive to cover for this wide spectrum of demands and be able to (if possible) demarcate the level of threat or risk involved accordingly. Efficacy of assessment tools can be increased by demonstrating how the presence of a factor has led individuals to engage in violent extremism (Borum, 2015a). There is currently insufficient evidence to link the indicators to the occurrence of a violent extremist attack (Schuurman & Eijkman, 2015). Hence, further research is necessary to prove that the indicators of an assessment tool are themselves sufficient to identify the intent or capability to commit a violent extremist attack.

Conclusion

There is a gamut of assessment tools available for practitioners to assess risk of violence. However, assessing risk of violent extremism is more specific. It is challenging to identify individual risk factors due to a small sample size to draw information from. Furthermore, culture and context play a significant role in determining the usability of a tool for a society. Most of these tools are developed in the West and based on western samples. There is a need to localise tools and take into account localised issues or cultural nuances, which might be different from the western context. Multiple studies are of the opinion that the predictive validity of tools improve when the demographic characteristics of the tested sample are closer to the original validation sample of the tool (Sarma, 2017; Singh *et al.*, 2011). Singh and his colleagues (2011) also found that for tools to accurately detect an individual's risk of future offending, it should be designed for more specific populations. Thus, there is a need for each country to develop their own tool or be able to adapt the western tools while paying attention to the cultural idiosyncrasies.

Acknowledgement

The views expressed in this chapter are the author's only and do not represent the official position or view of the Ministry of Home Affairs, Singapore.

Editors' Note

Readers are advised to familiarise themselves with the conceptual and theoretical issues associated with each tool before using them. This can be achieved, for example, by attending training workshops on the use of these tools.

References

Bakker, E. (2006). *Jihadi Terrorists in Europe their Characteristics and the Circumstances in Which They Joined the Jihad: An Exploratory Study.* The Hague: Netherlands Institute of International Relations.

Beardsley, L. N., & Beech, R. A. (2013). Applying the violent extremist risk assessment (VERA) to a sample of terrorist case studies. *Journal of Aggression, Conflict and Peace Research*, *5*(1), 4–15.

Bergen, P. (2017). *United States of Jihad. Who are America's Homegrown Terrorists and How Do We Stop Them?* New York: Broadway Books.

Borum, R. (2015a). Assessing risk for terrorism involvement. *Journal of Threat Assessment and Management*, 2(2), 63–87.

Borum, R. (2015b). Operationally relevant research and practice in terrorism threat assessments. *Journal of Threat Assessment and Management*, 2(3-4), 192–194.

Borum, R., Fein, R., Vossekuil, B., & Berglund, J. (1999). Threat assessment: Defining an approach for evaluating risk of targeted violence. *Behavioural Sciences and the Law*, *17*, 323–337.

Dean, C. (2014). The healthy identity intervention: the UK's development of a psychologically informed intervention to address extremist offending. In A. Silke (Ed.), *Prisons, Terrorism and Extremism* (pp. 89–107). London: Routledge.

Douglas, K. S. (2014). Version 3 of the historical-clinical-risk management-20 (HCR-20V3): Relevance to violence risk assessment and management in forensic conditional release contexts. *Behavioural Science and Law*, *32*, 557–576.

Hart, S. D., Cook, N. A., Pressman, E., Strang, S., & Lim, L. Y. (2017). A Concurrent Evaluation of Threat Assessment Tools for the Individual Assessment of Terrorism. Report submitted to the Canadian Network for Research on Terrorism, Security and Society. Retrieved from https://www.tsas.ca/working-papers/a-concurrent-evaluation-of-threat-assessment-tools-for-the-individual-assessment-of-terrorism/

HM Government (2015). Channel duty guidance. *Protecting Vulnerable People from being Drawn into Terrorism*. U.K.: Author.

Horgan, J. (2008). From profiles to *pathways* and roots to *routes*: Perspectives from psychology on radicalisation into terrorism. *Annals of the American Association of Political and Social Sciences*, *618*, 80–94.

Kraemer, H., Kazdin, A., Offord, D., Kessler, R., Jensen, P., & Kupfer, D. (1997). Coming to terms with the terms of risk. *Archives of General Psychiatry*, *54*, 337–343.

Lloyd, M., & Dean, C. (2015). The development of structured guidelines for assessing risk in extremist offenders. *Journal of Threat Assessment and Management*, 2(1), 40–52.

Meloy, J. R., & Gill, P. (2016). The lone-actor terrorist and the TRAP-18. *Journal of Threat Assessment and Management*, *3*(1), 37–52.

Meloy, J. R., Hoffmann, J., Guldimann, A., & James, D. (2012). The role of warning behaviors in threat assessment: An exploration and suggested typology. *Behavioral Sciences and the Law*, *30*, 256–279.

Meloy, J. R., Roshdi, K., Glaz-Ocik, J., & Hoffman, J. (2015). Investigating the individual terrorist in Europe. *Journal of Threat Assessment and Management*, *2*(3-4), 140–152.

Monahan, J. (2012). The individual risk assessment of terrorism. *Psychology, Public Policy, and Law*, *18*(2), 167–205.

Mullins, S. (2011). Australian jihad: Radicalisation and counter-terrorism — Analysis. *Eurasia Review*. Retrieved from http://www.eurasiareview.com/19102011- australian-jihad-radialisation-and-countre-terrorism-analysis/.

National Offender Management Service (2014). *Extremism Risk Guidance 22+ & Extremism Risk Screen*. HM Government.

Open Society Justice Initiative (2016). Eroding Trust. The UK's PREVENT Counter-Extremism Strategy in Health and Education. Retrieved from http://opensocietyfoundations.org/reports/eroding-trust-uk-s-prevent-counter-extremism-strategy-health-and-education.

Pressman, D. E. (2008). Exploring the sources of radicalization and violent radicalization: Transatlantic perspectives. *Journal of Security Issues, 2*, 1–20.

Pressman, D. E., & Flockton, J. (2014). Violent extremist risk assessment: Issues and applications of the VERA 2 to the high security prison setting. In A. Silke (Ed.), *Prisons, Terrorism and Extremism: Critical Issues in Management, Radicalisation and Reform* (pp. 122–143). New York: Routledge.

Radicalisation Awareness Network (2017). Preventing radicalisation to terrorism and violent extremism. Prison and probation interventions. Retrieved from https://www.dbh-online.de/sites/default/files/prison-and-probation-interventions_en.pdf.

Reed, S. (2016). The prevent programme: An ethical dilemma for teachers as well as psychiatrists. *BJ Psych Bulletin*, *40*, 85–86.

Roberts, K., & Horgan, J. (2008). Risk assessment and the terrorist. *Perspectives on Terrorism*, *2*(6), 3–9.

Sarma, M. K. (2017). Risk assessment and the prevention of radicalisation from nonviolence into terrorism. *American Psychologist*, *72*(3), 278–288.

Schuurman, B., & Eijkman, Q. (2015). Indicators of terrorist intent and capability: Tools for threat assessment. *Dynamics of Asymmetric Conflict*, *8*(3), 215–231.

Silber, M. D., & Bhatt, A. (2007). *Radicalisation in the West: The Homegrown Threat*. New York: New York City Police Department.

Silke, A. (2014). Risk assessment of terrorists and extremist prisoners. In A. Silke (Ed.), *Prisons, Terrorism and Extremism* (pp. 108–121). London: Routledge.

Singh, P. J., Grann, M., & Fazel, S. (2011). A comparative study of violence risk assessment tools: A systematic review and metaregression analysis of 68 studies involving 25,980 participants. *Clinical Psychology Review*, *31*, 499–513.

Webster, C. D., Douglas, K. S., Eaves, D., & Hart, S. D. (1997). HCR-20: Assessing risk for violence (Version 2). British Columbia, Canada: Simon Fraser University.

CHAPTER 8

Lone Wolf Violent Extremism and Mental Illness: Learning Lessons from an Asian Perspective

SHI HUI TEE

Home Team Behavioural Sciences Centre, Ministry of Home Affairs, Singapore

Introduction

Lone wolf attacks in the Western countries have been steadily on the rise over the years. There has been an increase in the number of successful lone wolf attacks being carried out, from 15 in the 1990s to 35 in the 2010s (Worth, 2016). The attacks have also been getting deadlier over the decades, with approximately a total of 30 deaths in the 1990s, to 115 deaths in the 2010s (Worth, 2016). Some notable recent lone wolf violent extremist attacks include the 2016 Orlando nightclub shooting killing 49 and the 2017 Las Vegas shooting killing 58. As the Islamic State in Iraq and Syria lose their physical territory in the Middle East and shift towards encouraging lone wolf attacks, the threat of lone wolf violent extremism increases in Southeast Asia, where countries such as Singapore, Indonesia, and the Philippines are increasingly worried about the threat of lone wolf violent extremist attacks (Chan, 2016; Guzman, 2017; Ng, 2017). The high psychological impact as a result of lone wolf violent extremism attacks are also a cause for concern (Byman, 2017), as the community suffers a hit and sees the onset of mental health issues such as post-traumatic stress disorder (PTSD), depression, and anxiety after an attack (Razik *et al.*, 2013; Whalley & Brewin, 2007).

Against that backdrop, more researchers have been looking into the issue of lone wolf violent extremism, focusing on different aspects of the topic. Adapting from the lone wolves typology of Pantucci (2011)[1] and the lone-actor terrorist classification from Gill *et al.* (2014),[2] this chapter defines lone wolf violent extremists as individuals independent of violent extremist groups who engage in violence based on their own internalised radical views. These individuals can either act alone or in pairs.[3] Given the increased media reporting on lone wolf violent extremism and mental illness, with many media reports portraying lone wolf violent extremists as mentally ill individuals, researchers have looked into the relationship between lone wolf violent extremism and mental illness in the Western countries over the years (Corner & Gill, 2015; Gill *et al.*, 2014).

Why is There a Need to Look at Lone Wolf Violent Extremism and Mental Illness?

"Lone wolf violent extremism" and "mental illness" are the first two constructs that media reporters think of following a possible violent

[1]Pantucci (2011) has four categories of the lone wolf violent extremists: (i) individual terrorist, (ii) individual: (i) loner, (ii) lone wolf, (iii) lone wolf pack, and (iv) lone attacker.
[2]Gill *et al.* (2014, p. 426) have three categories of the lone wolf violent extremist: (i) individual terrorist, (ii) individual terrorist with command and control, and (iii) isolated dyads.
[3]This definition excludes "lone attackers" by Pantucci (2011) and "individual terrorist with command and control" by Gill *et al.* (2014) as individuals in the above two categories are not independent of violent extremist groups.

extremism event, which would lead to the "risk of conflating religious devotion with mental illness ... and of simplifying and demonizing both" (Gore, 2016, para. 11). In that context, researchers have hoped to shed light on the possibility of a connection between the two constructs. For example, when lone wolf violent extremists were compared with group-based violent extremists and the general population, it was found that some mental illnesses, such as schizophrenia, delusional disorders, and autism spectrum disorders, were more commonly prevalent in lone wolf violent extremists (Corner *et al.*, 2016). However, current research has not been conclusive, and more needs to be examined in the area of lone wolf violent extremism and mental illness.

Five Things to Know About Lone Wolf Violent Extremism and Mental Illness

To understand the connection between lone wolf violent extremism and mental illness, there are five key things that policymakers and practitioners in Asian countries need to take note of. This section highlights the five main points on lone wolf violent extremism and mental health.

Firstly, research on lone wolf violent extremists in Western countries have found that while not all lone wolf violent extremists have a mental illness, lone wolf violent extremists have a higher likelihood of being mentally ill as compared to group-based violent extremists and the general population (Seifert, 2015). A study on right-wing violent extremism found that loners have a significantly higher likelihood of having a mental illness prior to carrying out an attack (Gruenewald *et al.*, 2013). Gill and colleagues (2014) found that 31.9% of the lone actors in their sample had been diagnosed with mental illnesses, while a further study by Corner and Gill (2015) confirmed that lone wolf violent extremists were 13.49 times more likely to have a mental illness as compared to group-based violent extremists. On the flipside, there are cases where lone wolf violent extremists were not mentally ill, and were highly successful and functioning individuals. An example would be the Boston bomber, Dzhokhar Tsarnaev, who was fully functional, well-behaved, smart, and popular in school, but eventually perpetrated the Boston bombing attack that killed three (Ghose, 2015).

Secondly, the presence of mental health issues may make some individuals vulnerable to the risk of getting involved in violent extremism. Corner and Gill (2015) found that the lone wolf violent extremists in their sample "who had a spouse or partner who was involved in a wider movement were 18.07 times more likely to be mentally ill" (p. 28). These results may be attributed to the possibility that these mentally ill individuals may have a higher vulnerability to be radicalised by the violent extremist ideologies of their spouses. The Royal College of Psychiatrists (RCP) (2016) highlighted that mental illnesses may predispose one to negative influence, where individuals may be exploited by violent extremists with radical ideologies and hence be recruited or groomed to carry out violent extremist attacks. In the case of Nicky Reilly, a failed suicide bomber, learning difficulties and Asperger's syndrome made him vulnerable to violent extremism, where he was obsessed with violence and was radicalised and groomed to carry out a suicide bombing attack (Morris, 2008). This shows that while not all mentally ill individuals are lone wolf violent extremists, the presence of mental health issues could make one vulnerable to being radicalised.

Thirdly, the mental illnesses that mentally ill lone wolf violent extremists suffer from may go undiagnosed and unmonitored for a variety of reasons. There have been many cases where individuals have used mental health issues as an argument for a lighter sentence in court.[4] An example of a violent extremist whose mental state was analysed in court is Theodore "Ted" Kaczynski, the Unabomber, who killed three and injured 23 others through a series of parcel bombs over 17 years (McPadden, 2017). Psychologists and psychiatrists who have examined Kaczynski and his profile over the years before his arrests, as well as after his arrest, have not been able to agree with a single diagnosis; he was suspected to have various forms of mental

[4]The defendant may plead for the insanity defense in court, if he/she were to be legally "insane" (i.e., no control or consciousness of their actions) at the time of committing the crime that they are being tried for (see Insanity defense (n.d.)).

illnesses ranging from personality disorders, paranoia, schizophrenia, insomnia, anxiety, to issues with gender identity and relationship issues with women (Chase, 2000; Diamond, 2008; Kaczynski, 2012). However, monetary and legal concerns may have impeded Kaczynski from receiving the help and assistance he required, where his mental health issues, while detected, were not properly diagnosed and hence were untreated (Kaczynski, 2012; Kaczynski's Schizophrenia, 1998). It may not have been possible for these signs to be recognised by others earlier, as mental health issues were not actively discussed in the past (Bright, 2006; Marmion, 1998).

Fourthly, symptoms of mental health issues can become a trigger for an attack. While the prevalence of depression was found to be lower in lone wolf violent extremists when compared to the general population, depression was found to be a possible trigger for violence (Corner & Gill, 2015). Other specific psychotic symptoms such as delusions and hallucinations were also found to be able to trigger and result in violent psychotic actions (Junginger, 1996). This was further supported by Heer (2014), who raised examples of how delusions and hallucinations could be a cause for violence in mentally ill individuals. In the case of Michael Zehaf-Bibeau, the perpetrator of the Canadian Parliament Hill attack, hallucinations and delusions that were in line with his radical Islamic ideology led him to believe that God was speaking to him prior to his attack, hence possibly driving him to engage in violent actions (Friscolanti, 2014).

Finally, lone wolf violent extremists who are mentally ill exhibit pre-attack warning signs which can be picked up by bystanders. In comparing political group actors with mentally disordered lone wolf attackers, James *et al.* (2007) found mentally ill attackers "evince warning behaviours" that were mostly deluded and "actively psychotic" when carrying out the attacks (p. 343). Michael Zehaf-Bibeau told others prior to his attack that the devil was after him, and that they should pray as the world was ending (Ahmed & Botelho, 2014; Beeby, 2014). For Nicky Reilly, his extreme level of religiosity, obsession with the September 11 Twin Towers attack and the suicide note that he had written were clear warning signs of his radicalisation (Gardham *et al.*, 2008; Williams, 2009).

Furthermore, his friends and family members were able to observe drastic changes in his personality, where Reilly changed from a gentle, polite man, to a withdrawn, aggressive man (Morris, 2008). These case examples show that even while undiagnosed, mentally ill individuals do exhibit symptoms that are in line with their mental health issues and their radical ideologies.

Five Learning Lessons for Policymakers and Practitioners in Asian Cultures

After understanding the connection between lone wolf violent extremism and mental illness, there are five learning lessons distilled for policymakers and practitioners in Asian cultures. This section places an emphasis on the differences between the Western and Asian cultures, and highlights five key learning lessons.

Firstly, when looking at mental illness and lone wolf violent extremism in Asian cultures, it is important for policymakers and practitioners to note that most of the research has been carried out in Western countries, and hence little is known about the relationship between mental illness and lone wolf violent extremism in Asian countries. However, there remains a distinct difference, where even in recent years, research has found that there still exists a much stronger stigma against individuals with mental health issues in the Asian cultures as opposed to the Western cultures (Chan, 2017; Elias, 2015; Li & Browne, 2000; Philomin, 2015). This leads to an increased difficulty for policymakers and practitioners to understand the connection between mental illness and lone wolf violent extremism in Asian cultures, as the cultural issue would first have to be addressed. As such, further research should be carried out to understand the role of mental health in lone wolf violent extremism (i.e., causal, correlational, mediating, moderating) in Asian cultures. However, to do so, policymakers and practitioners should tackle the prerequisite of raising awareness on mental illness, so as to instil a deeper level of knowledge and understanding on mental illness within the Asian cultures. This would reduce the stigma attached to mental illness, facilitating research in mental illness and lone wolf violent extremism.

Secondly, the stigma attached to mental health issues in Asian cultures may cause more mental illnesses to be under-diagnosed or even undiagnosed as compared to their Western counterparts (Martin, 2017). Other factors such as poverty and the lack of mental health service providers may also contribute to an under-diagnosis of mental illnesses in Asian countries (Kaczynski, 2012). This sheds light on the importance of not being over fixated on a mental health diagnosis of a lone wolf violent extremist, or totally ignoring the role of mental health in lone wolf violent extremism. An example would be the case of Ted Kaczynski, who was only diagnosed with a mental disorder by the court upon his arrest. Hence, when looking at lone wolf violent extremism in Asian countries, policymakers and practitioners would therefore need to take extra care to weigh and consider, among other factors, the role of mental health issues in lone wolf violent extremism. For example, mental health issues could also be incorporated as an aspect of violence risk assessments, which would help organisations to identify at-risk individuals so as to monitor these at-risk individuals for signs of violent extremism. If required, these at-risk individuals may be directed to mental health service providers for further help.

Thirdly, as Asian countries adopt the psychiatric diagnosis guide developed in Western countries, there is a higher risk of misdiagnosis as cultural differences would not be accurately identified and considered in Western diagnosis guides. While the latest edition of the Diagnostic and Statistical Manual of Mental Disorders (DSM-5) takes into consideration the symptoms in mental illnesses observed across the globe, it still may not be able to fully capture the nuances of the many cultural differences between the Western and Asian cultures (Norbury & Sparks, 2013). Language mastery and differences may pose an issue as well, where diagnosis pointers may be lost in translation. Furthermore, similar to Western cultures, an individual's diagnosis could vary between different mental health professionals, which would pose as a difficulty to the examination of the role of mental health issues in lone wolf violent extremism. Hence, in the study of the role of mental illness in lone wolf violent extremism, instead of focusing on the presence of a fixed mental illness diagnosis, it would be prudent for researchers, practitioners, and policymakers to focus on the common symptoms of mental illnesses associated with lone wolf violent extremism instead, and delve deeper into the connection between the observed symptoms and the role these symptoms play in lone wolf violent extremism. It is therefore important for policymakers and practitioners to work closely with mental health professionals in monitoring the mental health of the population, correctly identifying and better understanding the symptoms that may be associated with lone wolf violent extremism.

Fourthly, according to the Royal College of Psychiatrists (RCP) (2016), earlier intervention and treatment may minimise the risk of violence of mentally ill individuals who may be more vulnerable to the radical ideologies of others. However, in doing so, there is an urgent need to consider the cultural differences in the acceptability of methods used by the policymakers in addressing the issue. As Asian cultures tend to be more collectivistic in nature, one of the recommendations is for policymakers and practitioners to consider a communal approach to the issues. Awareness on the warning signs of the relevant mental illnesses that are more commonly associated with lone wolf violent extremism (i.e., schizophrenia, delusional disorders, autism spectrum disorders) can be raised. Family members could also be encouraged to be more accepting of these mental health issues and the associated lone wolf violent extremism risks. This may in turn lead to a higher level of utilisation of mental health services, which allows these vulnerable individuals to seek help, minimising their risk of being radicalised by others. In addition, an accurate understanding of the lone wolf violent extremism risks in mentally ill individuals could encourage family members and the community to be more likely to and less fearful of reporting the warning signs of these individuals. In the Asian context, families could be educated on ways for them to seek help on a safe platform (e.g., anonymous, private, and confidential) regarding mental health issues and lone wolf violent extremism when needed. This may indirectly help to reduce the number of lone wolf violent extremism attacks.

Finally, there is a need for Asian countries to develop their own lone wolf typology, and look at the issue of mentally ill lone wolf violent extremists from multiple angles (e.g., psychological, cultural, legal, political, economic, environmental) instead of adopting typologies developed based on Western samples. The new typology should take into consideration the interaction between the mental health symptoms, personality of the individual, and the environment, and more, and be able to put the issues into context, possibly helping to accurately predict operational outcomes pertaining to an individual, such as the risk level, possible mode of operation, target choice, and more. In the long run, this typology would be able to help researchers, policymakers, and practitioners differentiate the mentally sound lone wolf violent extremists from the mentally ill lone wolf violent extremists, and provide deeper insights on the preventive, de-radicalisation, and disengagement measures that can be employed to reduce lone wolf violent extremism in Asian countries.

Acknowledgement

The views expressed in this chapter are the author's only and do not represent the official position or view of the Ministry of Home Affairs, Singapore.

Editors' Note

It is essential to note that mental illness is not a cause *per se*, and is not the only and sole factor associated with lone wolf violent extremism. More research is required to examine this phenomenon and its relationship with mental illness especially in an Asian context.

References

Ahmed, S., & Botelho, G. (2014). Who is Michael Zehaf-Bibeau, the man behind the deadly Ottawa attack? *CNN*. Retrieved from http://edition.cnn.com/2014/10/22/world/canada-shooter/index.html.

Beeby, D. (2014). Ottawa shooting: Michael Zehaf-Bibeau not among 90 being probed, RCMP say. *CBC News*. Retrieved from http://www.cbc.

ca/news/politics/ottawa-shooting-michael-zehaf-bibeau-not-among-90-being-probed-rcmp-say-1.2810113.

Bright, C. (2006). Ted Kaczynski: A story of mental illness, brother says. *Independent Record*. Retrieved from http://helenair.com/news/local/ted-kaczynski-a-story-of-mental-illness-brother-says/article_7fbcb98b-6d0a-5f3b-9ea5-f834fb47c729.html.

Byman, D. L. (2017). How to hunt a lone wolf: Countering terrorists who act on their own. *Brookings*. Retrieved from https://www.brookings.edu/opinions/how-to-hunt-a-lone-wolf-countering-terrorists-who-act-on-their-own/.

Chan, F. (2016). Indonesia sees more lone-wolf terror attacks. *The Straits Times*. Retrieved from http://www.straitstimes.com/asia/se-asia/indonesia-sees-more-lone-wolf-terror-attacks.

Chan, R. (2017). Asian Americans are undergoing a silent mental health crisis. *Tonic*. Retrieved from https://tonic.vice.com/en_us/article/xwgg4d/asian-americans-are-undergoing-a-silent-mental-health-crisis.

Chase, A. (2000). Harvard and the making of the Unabomber. *The Atlantic, June 2000 Issue*. Retrieved from https://www.theatlantic.com/magazine/archive/2000/06/harvard-and-the-making-of-the-unabomber/378239/.

Corner, E., & Gill, P. (2015). A false dichotomy? Mental illness and lone-actor terrorism. *Law and Human Behaviour*, *19*(1), 23–34.

Corner, E., Gill, P., & Mason, O. (2016). Mental health disorders and the terrorist: A research note probing selection effects and disorder prevalence. *Studies in Conflict & Terrorism*, *39*(6), 560–568.

Diamond, S. A. (2008). Terrorism, resentment and the Unabomber. *Psychology Today*. Retrieved from https://www.psychologytoday.com/blog/evil-deeds/200804/terrorism-resentment-and-the-unabomber.

Elias, P. (2015). The silence about mental health in South Asian culture is dangerous. *New Republic*. Retrieved from https://newrepublic.com/article/122892/silence-mental-health-south-asian-culture-dangerous.

Friscolanti, M. (2014). Uncovering a killer: Addict, drifter, walking contradiction. *Macleans*. Retrieved from http://www.macleans.ca/news/canada/michael-zehaf-bibeau-addict-drifter-walking-contradiction/.

Gardham, D., Allen, N., Savill, R., & Edwards, R. (2008). Exeter explosion: Autistic bomb suspect 'radicalised by gang'. *The Telegraph*. Retrieved from www.telegraph.co.uk/news/uknews/2016420/Exeter-explosion-Autistic-bomb-suspect-radicalised-by-gang.html.

Ghose, D. (2015). Boston bomber was a bright student — Teachers. *Morning News USA*. Retrieved from https://www.morningnewsusa.com/boston-bomber-was-a-bright-student-teachers-2318544.html.

Gill, P., Horgan, J., & Deckert, P. (2014). Bombing alone: Tracing the motivations and antecedent behaviors of lone-actor terrorists. *Journal of Forensic Sciences*, *59*(2), 425–435.

Gore, W. (2016). Mental illness has become a convenient scapegoat for terrorism — but the causes of terror are rarely so simple. *Independent*. Retrieved from http://www.independent.co.uk/voices/german-terror-attacks-mental-illness-religion-isis-terrorism-scapegoats-a7155366.html.

Gruenewald, J., Chermak, S., & Freilich, J. D. (2013). Distinguishing "loner" attacks from other domestic extremist violence. *Criminology & Public Policy*, *12*(1), 65–91.

Guzman, C. (2017). Duterte fears terrorists will resort to 'lone wolf' attacks. *CNN Philippines*. Retrieved from http://cnnphilippines.com/news/2017/10/27/rodrigo-duterte-terrorist-lone-wolf-attack.html.

Heer, J. (2014). The link between terrorism and mental illness. *The New Yorker*. Retrieved from https://www.newyorker.com/news/news-desk/line-terrorism-mental-illness.

Insanity defense. (n.d.). *Find Law*. Retrieved from http://criminal.findlaw.com/criminal-procedure/insanity-defense.html.

James, D. V., Mullen, P. E., Meloy, J. R., Pathé, M. T., Farnham, F. R., Preston, L., & Darnley, B. (2007). The role of mental disorder in attacks on European politicians 1990–2004. *Acta Psychiatr Scand*, 116, 334–344.

Junginger, J. (1996). Psychosis and violence: The case for a content analysis of psychotic experience. *Schizophrenia Bulletin*, *22*(1), 91–103.

Kaczynski, D. (2012). Unabomber's brother on violence and treating mental health. *Chron*. Retrieved from http://www.chron.com/news/article/Unabomber-s-brother-on-violence-and-treating-3760714.php%20.

Kaczynski's Schizophrenia (1998). *Los Angeles Times*. Retrieved from http://articles.latimes.com/1998/jan/31/local/me-14026.

Li, H. Z., & Browne, A. J. (2000). Defining mental illness and accessing mental health service: Perspectives of Asian Canadians. *Canadian Journal of Community Mental Health*, *19*(1), 143–160.

Marmion, S. (1998). Unabomber's psychiatric profile reveals gender-identity struggle. *Chicago Tribune*. Retrieved from http://articles.chicagotribune.com/1998-09-12/news/9809120119_1_unabomber-theodore-kaczynski-dr-sally-johnson-paranoid-schizophrenia.

Martin, H. (2017). Depression under-diagnosed in Maori, Pacific and Asian communities: Study. *Stuff*. Retrieved from https://www.stuff.co.nz/national/health/91943291/depression-underdiagnosed-in-maori-pacific-and-asian-communities-study.

McPadden, M. (2017). Crime History: "Unabomber" Ted Kaczynski pleads guilty, gets 8 life sentences. *Crime Feed.* Retrieved from http://crimefeed.com/2017/01/crime-history-unabomber-ted-kaczynski-pleads-guilty-gets-life-8-times/.

Morris, S. (2008). Nicky Reilly: From BFG to failed suicide bomber. *The Guardian.* Retrieved from https://www.theguardian.com/uk/2008/oct/15/uksecurity1.

Ng, K. (2017). Lone wolves most worrisome in Singapore's fight against terror. *Today Online.* Retrieved from http://www.todayonline.com/singapore/lone-wolves-most-worrisome-singapores-fight-against-terror-pm-lee.

Norbury, C. F., & Sparks, A. (2013). Difference or disorder? Cultural issues in understanding neurodevelopmental disorders. *Developmental Psychology, 49*(1), 45–58.

Pantucci, R. (2011). *A* typology of lone wolves: Preliminary analysis of lone Islamist terrorists. The International Centre for the Study of Radicalisation. Retrieved from http://icsr.info/wp-content/uploads/2012/10/1302002992ICSRPaper_ATypologyofLoneWolves_Pantucci.pdf.

Philomin, L. E. (2015). Considerable stigma against mental illness: Study. *Today.* Retrieved from http://www.todayonline.com/singapore/considerable-stigma-towards-mentally-ill-imh-study.

Razik, S., Ehring, T., & Emmelkamp. P. M. G. (2013). Psychological consequences of terrorist attacks: Prevalence and predictors of mental health problems in Pakistani emergency responders. *Psychiatry Research*, 207, 80–85.

Royal College of Psychiatrists (RCP). (2016). Counter-terrorism and Psychiatry. *Position Statement PS04/16.* Retrieved from https://www.rcpsych.ac.uk/pdf/PS04_16.pdf.

Seifert, K. (2015). Lone-wolf terrorists and mental illness. *Psychology Today.* Retrieved from https://www.psychologytoday.com/blog/stop-the-cycle/201501/lone-wolf-terrorists-and-mental-illness.

Whalley, M. G., & Brewin, C. R. (2007). Mental health following terrorist attacks. *British Journal of Psychiatry*, 190, 94–96.

Williams, R. (2009). Hunt continues for extremists who encouraged jailed Exeter bomber. *The Guardian.* Retrieved from https://www.theguardian.com/uk/2009/jan/30/giraffe-attempted-bombing-jail-sentence.

Worth, K. (2016). Lone wolf attacks are becoming more common — and more deadly. *Frontline.* Retrieved from http://www.pbs.org/wgbh/frontline/article/lone-wolf-attacks-are-becoming-more-common-and-more-deadly/.

Section 3

Insights for Community Level Interventions

Our preparedness must go beyond the Home Team. Every Singaporean has a role to play, and the community must be ready, which is why We have SGSecure.

MRS JOSEPHINE TEO
MINISTER FOR MANPOWER AND
SECOND MINISTER FOR HOME AFFAIRS

CHAPTER 9

The 4M Strategy of Combating Violent Extremism: An Analysis

KUMAR RAMAKRISHNA

S. Rajaratnam School of International Studies, Nanyang Technological University, Singapore

Introduction

On 29 December 2017, a video surfaced on a website known to be associated with the notorious Islamic State of Iraq and Syria or ISIS, called *Khayr Wilayah Media*. Eight minutes long, the clip — in Arabic and English — featured among other things an interview in English with a suicide bomber about to embark on a car bomb attack, footage of ISIS attacks in France, Middle Eastern conflict zones, as well as festive celebrations in Western capitals such as Sydney and New York City. In particular, the video included a segment in which the known Singaporean ISIS militant Megat Shahdan Abdul Samad — who had first surfaced on social media in September 2017 — and also known by the moniker Abu Uqayl, led two other Southeast Asian-looking ISIS fighters, most likely wanted Malaysian militants, in executing three kneeling Arab-looking prisoners, via gunshots at close range. Before carrying out the cold-blooded murders, Abu Uqayl addressed the camera in English. He urged ISIS supporters to "slay the enemies of Allah wherever you can find them", insisted that "the fighting has just begun" and "we will never stop cutting off the heads of every *kuffar* and *murtadin* until we cleanse the land of Islam from East Asia to the West of Africa". The shocking video clip garnered massive attention on social media, prompting the Islamic Religious Council of Singapore (MUIS) to roundly condemn the clip, charging that it represented a "desperate attack" by ISIS to drive a wedge between Muslim and non-Muslim Singaporeans. As Singaporean terrorism analyst Bilveer Singh pointed out, the video clip "reinforces the need to be vigilant as the Islamic State remains an existential threat", and that the "video is a daring challenge to states and it is up to Southeast Asian governments to respond to ensure that the terrorists do not succeed even once" (Singh, 2018).

The Five Key Challenges in the Counter-Narrative Policy Space

This brings us to the five key challenges that practitioners and policymakers need to address in dealing with the ongoing and rapidly evolving threat of violent Islamist extremism of the type that animates ISIS and its ideological bedfellows in Southeast Asia and elsewhere.

- Our overall strategic objective must be to ensure that our *Narrative* is fundamentally more attractive to the target audience than the competing vision of the violent extremists.
- The *Memes* that constitute our narrative in the social media space or elsewhere must be "stickier" than those of the violent extremists.
- Our choice of *Messenger* must enjoy greater personal credibility with the target audience than that of the extremist ideologues.
- The *Mechanisms* that we employ to impart our messages to the target audience must be more effective that those employed by the violent extremists.

- Policymakers need to ensure that the *Market Receptivity* of the target audience is promoted, by coordinating whole-of-government policies such that activities within the counter-narrative space are supported and not inadvertently undercut by policy and military missteps in the wider operational space.

To meet the abovementioned five key challenges, this chapter proposes the adoption of what may be called the "4M" strategy for countering violent extremism (CVE) of the type that animates ISIS and its affiliates. This 4M strategy will now be teased out as part of the "Five Responses" section below.

Response One: The Strategic Objective — The Need for *Memes* that are "Stickier" than those of the ISIS Extremists

During the recently concluded presidential hustings in Singapore, President Halimah Yacob attracted much attention with an arresting slogan for her campaign: "Do good, do together". Responding to public criticism of the technically ungrammatical phrasing, she explained that she chose the phrase as "it's catchy, it's easy to understand, easy for everyone to relate" (Koh, 2017). She was absolutely spot on and made a profound point about slogans in general that have wider implications actually. At one level, the advertising world has long understood the principle that the best slogans, or to use the more technical term — memes — need not be grammatically correct, just *memorable*. Journalist Malcolm Gladwell — author of the classic study *The Tipping Point* — recounts that in 1954, when the American tobacco company Winston introduced filter-tip cigarettes, it marketed them via the ungrammatical slogan "Winston tastes good *like* a cigarette should", rather than "Winston tastes good *as* a cigarette should". He notes that within months, "on the strength of that catchy phrase", Winston outsold its major rivals and ultimately became the top cigarette brand in the country. Thus, an effective meme must be colloquial and memorable to work — not necessarily grammatical (Gladwell, 2002).

This bears further analysis. In our modern, Internet-saturated world, there is a surfeit of news — true and "fake" — competing for our attention via multiple channels; it is no longer just television, radio, and print but increasingly online via Facebook, Twitter, YouTube, WhatsApp, Telegram, and a myriad other social media applications on our increasingly inexpensive and permanently wired-up smartphones and laptops. Gladwell (2002) hence argues that whatever we are urged "to read and watch, we simply don't remember". This is precisely why modern actors — whether advertisers, political parties, governments, and even terrorist and insurgent groups — must fight hard to achieve information dominance over a target audience. This is because only through such control can the actor attain the ultimate goal of all such quests: capturing the hearts and minds of the constituency in question. Hence the various memes that comprise a wider overall narrative simply must be "catchy, easy to understand, easy for everyone to relate". It is suggested here that the four Ms help us grasp how an actor can employ such memes and the wider narratives they ultimately constitute to attain the information dominance needed to decisively shape the hearts and minds of a target audience: the Message, the Messenger, the Mechanism, and Market Receptivity. The four Ms are certainly relevant to the domain of CVE.

Response Two: The Message[1]

The first element of the 4M strategy is that the essential *Message* encoded in the meme and wider narrative must be "sticky". That is, it should be simple to grasp, attention-grabbing, and memorable, or as Gladwell puts it, the "presentation and structuring of information" can "make a big difference in how much of an impact" is made (Gladwell, 2002, p. 25). Researchers Chip and Dan Heath (2008, pp. 14–18) have identified several factors that make a message and its constituent memes sticky: first, *simplicity* — the content of the

[1]This section is adapted from Ramakrishna (2015). The 4M strategy seeks to improve upon and refine the author's earlier counter-ideological response (CIR) Model, discussed in Ramakrishna (2016b).

message must be both simple but profound, so that it can be easily recalled. Think of the Nike slogan "Just Do It", for example. Second, *unexpectedness* — the message must contain counter-intuitive elements that snare attention. Third, *concreteness* — "naturally sticky ideas", the Heaths observe, are also "full of concrete images — ice-filled bathtubs, apples with razors — because our brains are wired to remember concrete data". Fourth, *credibility* — "sticky ideas", the authors aver, need to be culturally authentic and believable to the target audience. Fifth, *emotions* — the message must appeal viscerally to the audience. On this respect, Indonesian CVE activist and researcher Noor Huda Ismail's documentaries that explore the impact of violent extremist ideology on families that have been involved in the ISIS conflict in Syria are powerful, precisely because they show the emotional cost of engagement with such extremist causes (Topsfield, 2016). Sixth, and finally, *stories* — the Heaths argue that target audiences are better able to recall messages embedded in memorable stories.

To be sure, there are many moderate Muslim clerics in Southeast Asia who are capable of spinning sticky messages that may be capable of competing effectively against the ideological appeals of ISIS extremists. In village communities in West Java, for example, some preachers are popular as their sticky messages, rather than engaging with cumbersome "broader social questions", focus instead on "allegories and narrative accounts created out of daily experience". One observer (Millie, 2008, pp. 82, 91–92) recounts in this regard the impact of one itinerant cleric, Kiai Al-Jauhari:

> I have often seen audiences transfixed by Al-Jauhari's allegories and narrative accounts. He transforms Islamic messages into narrations made up of highly recognisable material, with no shortage of humour added to the mix. People are engrossed as he unfolds his creations. I have frequently asked village and mosque officials why they engage Al-Jauhari ... The most common answer is that he is able to hold people's attention for long periods of time.

It may be argued further, that in the age of the social media sound bite, it would be important for attractive speakers like Kiai Al-Jauhari to be able to translate his entertaining homilies into forms that would become readily digestible "snackable content" for busy, "bored at work" consumers who prefer material that is "fast and fun, geared to spread via Facebook" (Foer, 2017, p. 140). In short, the intrinsic attractiveness of the message sticks in the minds of the audience long after the messenger leaves.

Response Three: The Messenger

The *Messenger* that purveys the message is also important. He or she must enjoy significant personal credibility with the target audience. This commodity, the leading Allied propagandist in World War Two and former Labour Government Minister in the 1960s, Richard Crossman observed, was all-important (Ramakrishna, 2002). Selecting credible interlocutors is very audience-specific, moreover. Some Southeast Asian counter-terrorism officials, for instance, concede that globally famous progressive Muslim scholars are often dismissed by violent Islamist militants as working for the government. Hence, while such scholars may be effective in communicating with the wider community, former radicals may have relatively greater traction with the militant constituency. For instance, in Malaysia, the former Jemaah Islamiyah (JI) financier Wan Min Wan Mat has proven to be an effective interlocutor in the wider counter-extremism efforts of the Police Special Branch (Ramakrishna, 2016a), while in Indonesia, former JI senior operational leaders, such as Nasir Abbas, have played similar roles (Ramakrishna, 2009). This is not a new idea either. During the 1950s, at the height of the British colonial counter-insurgency campaign against the Communist Party of Malaya (CPM), while Government Information Services churned out publicity material to educate the public, surrendered Chinese guerrillas were often employed to reach out to their former comrades in the Malayan jungles to entice them to surrender as well, with considerable success. A good example of this was the former CPM leader Lam Swee, whose Government Information Services' booklet *My Accusation* — provided an insider's account of the contradictions between CPM rhetoric and the harsh reality on the ground — caused much havoc within the Communist ranks (Ramakrishna, 2002). For current CVE efforts therefore, it would appear that a judicious mix of moderate religious scholars and carefully selected former radicals may be needed. The messenger conveying the meme, in short, matters too.

Response Four: The Mechanism

To be sure, the relative merits of CVE communication platforms such as face-to-face, print, broadcast, and online media have received scrutiny. Many views abound. For instance, in Indonesia, Twitter has been exploited by "Net-savvy radicals" to "lobby for their causes" (Nazeer, 2011). The *Jemaah Ansharut Tauhid* network, implicated in terrorism-related cases in the country, has also used various "internet and social networking sites" and YouTube to put out content (International Crisis Group, 2010, p. 5). More than a quarter of the Indonesia's 240 million people are on Facebook, "thanks in large part to cheap and fast Internet-capable phones", and young people are unsurprisingly being targeted for terrorist recruitment via social media (Karmini, 2013). In any case, the current Indonesian police chief, General Tito Karnavian, iterated that in his view, face-to-face contact is more important than the Internet in socialising individuals into violent Islamist ideology, and that the "final touch is the personal touch" (Ramakrishna, 2015, pp. 231–232). The respected terrorism analyst Sidney Jones of the Institute of Policy Analysis of Conflict in Jakarta agreed, opining that "although terrorists groups' Internet use is growing, they still do most of their recruiting face-to-face at traditional places such as prayer meetings" (cited in Karmini, 2013). Additionally, print media such as the 137-page comic *I Found the Meaning of Jihad*, chronicling the well-known life story of Nasir Abbas ("Captain Jihad: Ex-terrorist is comic book hero", 2011), and well-received locally-produced documentaries such as *Prison and Paradise* — about the children of the JI perpetrators of the October 2002 Bali bombings as well as their victims — have also proven to be quite impactful (Nurhayati, 2011).

Taking a few steps back analytically, comparatively little attention has been placed on the underlying principles that should guide their employment. Two principles from the comparatively sophisticated and successful British psychological warfare effort in World War Two stand out in this regard. First, the art of propaganda is to conceal that you are actually engaging in it (Nirmala, 2013). Hence, whether using online or offline communication platforms, one's narrative must not come across to the audience as blatantly as "propaganda". National campaigns calling on the public to stand firm against violent extremism are needed, but the same memes should also be conveyed by "softer", indirect, non-governmental means as well, such as blogs, podcasts, commentary and talk shows involving famous sports, media, and entertainment personalities. A second principle was captured in the saying: "Entertainment is a valuable narcotic for dulling the sensibilities of a propaganda-conscious mind" (Crossman cited in Ramakrishna, 2002, p. 19). This is why the British in 1950s Malaya invested in a strong Malayan Film Unit and Radio Malaya's Community Listening Service featuring the legendary Lee Dai Soh, to enthral rural and urban audiences with anti-Communist memes integrated with music, drama, humorous sketches, and short films about the new lives of reformed guerrillas (Ramakrishna, 2002). It is thus telling that modern CVE analysts, like the Dutch-Somali commentator Ayaan Hirsi Ali, similarly call for the use of humour and satire to undercut violent extremist appeals today (Whitworth, 2017). The satirical and funny British film *Four Lions* is one example of entertainment as a way to promote the anti-extremist meme amongst vulnerable but wary audiences (Morris, 2010).

Response Five: Market Receptivity

Finally, the effective absorption by an audience of memes and narratives is also influenced by situational context; put another way, are the "consumers" in the target market receptive to your "products"? In September 1949, British High Commissioner Henry Gurney's amnesty for Malayan Communists failed, but by August 1957, Malayan Prime Minister Tunku Abdul Rahman's Merdeka Amnesty succeeded spectacularly in collapsing the CPM's morale. Why? One of the key factors was that in 1949 the public knew the government was not winning, but by Tunku's time, it was patently obvious that the Communists were utterly on the back foot. In other words, by late 1957, the *Market* in question, the demoralised, rapidly dwindling numbers of Communist guerrillas in the Malayan jungle, starved of food and medicines and severely harassed by the Security Forces, were ready to lay down arms and were actively looking for a way out (Ramakrishna, 1999).

Similarly, in today's CVE context, as long as the objective political and socioeconomic grievances that underpin Muslim separatism in the southern Philippines continue to be relatively unaddressed, we shall likely see more sieges such as the standoff between ISIS-linked militants and the Philippines military in Marawi City in Mindanao that lasted for five months from May to October 2017, resulting in more than a thousand people being killed ("Army Says battle for Marawi to end soon, 1,000 dead", 2017). It has long been recognised that in the Mindanao context, sheer military force is not enough to resolve the issue of violent extremist ideology. Instead, "poverty, illiteracy, bad governance, wide availability of loose firearms, and non-enforcement of the rule of law in southern Philippines created a fertile ground for radicalisation to take root" (Quilala & Dino, 2015, p. 1). In this respect, there is a consensus that the proposed Bangsamoro Basic Law (BBL) "which provides a regional governance system, addresses both major political and economic redistribution issues, and important religious and cultural identity needs and grievances of contemporary Moros", represented an "important step in insuring [the Philippines] from the threat of ISIS" (Quilala, & Dino, 2015, p. 2). Failure to deal with such underlying problems would only "fuel the recruitment drives" of pro-ISIS militant groups in Mindanao (Jopson, 2016). In terms of our analysis in this chapter, the Marawi episode suggests that no number of counter-extremist memes and narratives are likely to resolve the situation in and of themselves. Memes and the wider narratives they constitute are not magic bullets — they can only work if the market is *receptive*.

Conclusion

The Marawi example also reinforces the point that Southeast Asia, including Singapore today, is being assailed by a concerted ISIS social media onslaught seeking to split our respective multicultural social fabrics apart. This point is clearly driven home by the December 2017 Abu Uqayl video mentioned at the start of this chapter. Hence, preserving national unity in globalised, multicultural, multireligious Singapore in an increasingly inclement strategic environment — witness the SGSecure meme "Not if, but When"[2] — should be a no-brainer. Now more than ever, therefore, positive national narratives and their constituent memes — no matter how ungrammatical as long as they are sticky — are in fact very much needed to maintain social and psychological resilience. Countering the violent extremist threat posed by ISIS and its affiliates requires nothing less.

References

Army says battle for Marawi to end soon, 1000 dead (2017). *AFP*. Retrieved from http://news.abs-cbn.com/news/10/16/17/army-says-battle-for-marawi-to-end-soon-1000-dead.

Captain Jihad: Ex-terrorist is comic book hero (2011). *CBS News*. Retrieved from https://www.cbsnews.com/news/captain-jihad-ex-terrorist-is-comic-book-hero/.

Foer, F. (2017). *World Without Mind: The Existential Threat of Big Tech*. London: Penguin Press.

Gladwell, M. (2002). *The Tipping Point: How Little Things can make a Big Difference*. US: Back Bay Books.

Heath, C., & Heath, D. (2008). *Made to Stick: Why Some Ideas take Hold and Others Come Unstuck*. London: Arrow.

International Crisis Group (2010). *Indonesia: The Dark Side of Jama'ah Ansharut Tauhid* (Asia Briefing 107). Jakarta/Brussels: Author.

Jopson, T. (2016). Making peace with the Bangsamoro basic law. *East Asia Forum*. Retrieved from http://www.eastasiaforum.org/2016/05/11/making-peace-with-the-bangsamoro-basic-law/.

Karmini, N. (2013). AP Exclusive: Facebook broke Indonesia terror case. *The Jakarta Post*. Retrieved from http://www.thejakartapost.com/news/2013/06/21/ap-exclusive-facebook-broke-indonesia-terror-case.html.

Koh, V. (2017). 'Do good do together' catchy, easy to understand: Halimah. *Today*. Retrieved from http://www.todayonline.com/singapore/halimah-defends-ungrammatical-campaign-slogan-calls-it-catchy.

[2]Refer to https://www.sgsecure.sg/resources/pages/default.aspx?tabID=3&pgNo=4.

Millie, J. (2008). 'Spiritual meal' or ongoing project? The dilemma of Dakwah Oratory. In G. Fealy, & S. White (Eds.), *Expressing Islam: Religious Life and Politics in Indonesia* (pp. 80–94). Singapore: Institute of Southeast Asian Studies.

Morris, C. (Director) (2010). *Four Lions* [Motion Picture]. UK: Film4 Productions, Wild Bunch, Warp Films.

Nazeer, Z. (2011). Indonesia faces rising intolerance. *The Straits Times.*

Nirmala, M. (2013). Waging propaganda war against terrorists. *The Straits Times.* Retrieved from http://www.straitstimes.com/singapore/waging-propaganda-war-against-terrorists.

Nurhayati, D. (2011). 'Prison and paradise' gives a voice to terrorism survivors. *The Jakarta Post.* Retrieved from http://www.thejakartapost.com/news/2011/10/12/prison-and-paradise-gives-a-voice-terrorism-survivors.html.

Quilala, D., & Dino, L. M. (2015). *Radicalization in East Asia: Addressing the Challenges of the Expanding ISIS Influence.* Philippines: University of the Philippines, Center for Integrative and Development Studies and the U.P. Press.

Ramakrishna, K. (1999). Content, credibility and context: Propaganda, government surrender policy and the Malayan communist terrorist mass surrenders of 1958. *Intelligence and National Security*, *14*(4), 242–266.

Ramakrishna, K. (2002). *Emergency Propaganda: The Winning of Malayan Hearts and Minds 1948–1958.* Richmond, Surrey: Curzon.

Ramakrishna, K. (2009). *Radical Pathways: Understanding Muslim Radicalization in Indonesia.* London and Westport: Praeger Security International.

Ramakrishna, K. (2015). *Islamist Terrorism and Militancy in Indonesia: The Power of the Manichean Mindset.* Singapore: Springer.

Ramakrishna, K. (2016a). Reflections of a reformed Jihadist: The story of Wan Min Wan Mat. *Contemporary Southeast Asia*, *38*(3), 495–522.

Ramakrishna, K. (2016b). Towards a comprehensive approach to combating violent extremist ideology in the digital space: The Counter-Ideological Response (CIR) Model. In M. Khader, L. S. Neo, G. Ong, E. Tan, & J. Chin (Eds.), *Combating Violent Extremism and Radicalization in the Digital Era* (pp. 260–282). Hershey, PA: IGI Global.

Singh, B. (2018). Singapore's Islamic State Jihadi. *The Diplomat.* Retrieved from https://thediplomat.com/2018/01/singapores-islamic-state-jihadi/.

Topsfield, J. (2016, July 22). Jihad selfie: The story of how Indonesian teenagers are recruited to Islamic State. *The Sydney Morning Herald.*

Retrieved from https://www.smh.com.au/world/jihad-selfie-the-story-of-how-indonesian-teenagers-are-recruited-to-islamic-state-20160722-gqb8gy.html.

Whitworth, D. (2017). We've had life of Brian, now we need life of Muhammad. *The Times*. Retrieved from https://www.thetimes.co.uk/article/weve-had-life-of-brian-now-we-need-life-of-muhammad-09dkqxmjm.

CHAPTER 10

Bystander Intervention to Prevent Radicalisation

LOO SENG NEO*, JOYCE S. PANG†, and JEFFERY CHIN*

*Home Team Behavioural Sciences Centre, Ministry of Home Affairs, Singapore
†School of Social Sciences, Nanyang Technological University, Singapore

Introduction

The literature is replete with striking cases of individuals who have witnessed signs of radicalisation to violence but failed to report or intervene. A review of literature reveals cases of such bystander behaviour such as the 2009 Fort Hood attack, where Nidal Hassan's colleagues noticed a drastic change in his worldview (McKinley & Dao, 2009), and the 2016 Orlando Pulse nightclub shooting where the wife of Omar Mateen knew about her husband's intention to commit the attack (Tacopino, 2018). In both cases, reports suggest that the individuals in question failed to intervene. The drastic consequences and the nature of the bystanders' non-reporting behaviours have continued to perplex authorities and raised new security concerns as these individuals, such as Hassan's colleagues or Mateen's wife, were in an ideal position to guide individuals in need of help to the relevant authorities. It could be argued that these individuals may have exhibited the bystander effect (Latané & Darley, 1970), with regard to their lack of participation in reporting suspicious cases. In this context, bystander intervention in radicalisation incidents fall under the category of prosocial and helping behaviour — i.e., preventing the person of interest from harming themselves and others by reporting them in advance. Thus, Staub (2013) opines that bystanders play a determining role in the trajectory of future threats based on their degree of involvement.

Nonetheless, there also have been a few cases where signs of radicalisation came to the attention of authorities, and potential attacks were thwarted. For example, the attempt to target soldiers from Fort Dix in 2007 was pre-empted due to timely information provided by a member of public (Russakoff & Eggen, 2007). However, there is a discrepancy in terms of the number of cases reported versus those that were not. Thus, insights into the (perceived or otherwise) obstacles that prevent these individuals from reporting and/or intervening, and suggestions for overcoming these barriers have clear practical significance.

The field of bystander effect and related intervention research has been the subject matter of a number of domains, including sexual violence (e.g., McMahon, 2015), bullying (e.g., Pozzoli *et al.*, 2012), cyberbullying (e.g., Machackova *et al.*, 2015), whistle-blowing in organisation (e.g., Dozier & Miceli, 1985), workplace bullying (e.g., Hellemans *et al.*, 2017), and dating aggression (e.g., Edwards *et al.*, 2015). In the domain of radicalisation, however, the topic of bystander effect and relevant interventions has been understudied (Schillinger, 2014; Williams *et al.*, 2016).

Given the current difficulties in countering radicalisation (e.g., limited manpower, difficulty in identifying and tracking person of interest by authorities), community reporting of suspected radicalisation to violence is an utmost necessity. This would facilitate the early identification of radicalised individuals, which involves procedures to ascertain whether the person of interest is in the nascent stages of radicalisation, and if one would further gravitate towards violent extremism. Thus, this chapter is an attempt to contribute to this growing and important area of bystander intervention. It identifies five key points, based on insights derived from a behavioural sciences angle, that law enforcement practitioners, policymakers, and academics need to be aware of.

There are Warning Signs that Bystanders Can Observe

While there is no standard violent extremist profile in terms of their socio-economic and educational backgrounds, there are tell-tale signs in terms of behaviours and beliefs, exhibited by individuals who are radicalised or are in the process of being radicalised[1] (Clutterbuck & Warnes, 2011; Neo *et al.*, 2017b). Individuals may show an observable range of warning signs that can be gleaned by others (Meloy *et al.*, 2015). For example, in the time leading up to an attack, Gill *et al.* (2014) found that people were aware of the grievances that caused the violence, the perpetrator's commitment to a specific radical ideology, and the perpetrator's intent to commit attacks. In fact, former assistant to the U.S. President for Homeland Security and Counter-terrorism, Lisa Monaco, had underscored the urgency to educate members of the public about the need to recognise and report suspicious activities:

> In more than 80 percent of cases involving home-grown violent extremists, people in the community — whether peers or family members or authority figures or even strangers — had observed warning signs a person was becoming radicalised to violence. But more than half of those community members downplayed or dismissed their observations without intervening (Monaco, 2014).

The significance of community reporting as a way of thwarting potential attacks is further summed up by Pantucci *et al.* (2016, p. 15), who stated that "the logic underlying a societal response is

[1]Research suggests that there is a pathway of radicalisation into violent extremism and individuals do not become violent extremists "overnight". See Borum (2011) for more information.

that actors within that community such as doctors, social workers, librarians or even a neighbour may interact with potential lone actors and detect unusual behaviour".

There are two implications arising from the finding that there are warning signs that bystanders can observe in most cases. Firstly, there is a need to identify and determine who these bystanders in question are. Based on interviews conducted with the law enforcement and Muslim communities in the U.S., Williams *et al.* (2016) have identified close friends (more so than school counsellors, religious leaders, or family members) to be in the best position to notice early signs of radicalisation. Similar results were also seen in the Singapore context. Results from a survey of 254 participants[2] revealed that close friends and family members were deemed most likely to notice early signs of individuals becoming radicalised (see Figure 10.1; Neo, 2016). Understandably, there is therefore a need to target interventions at

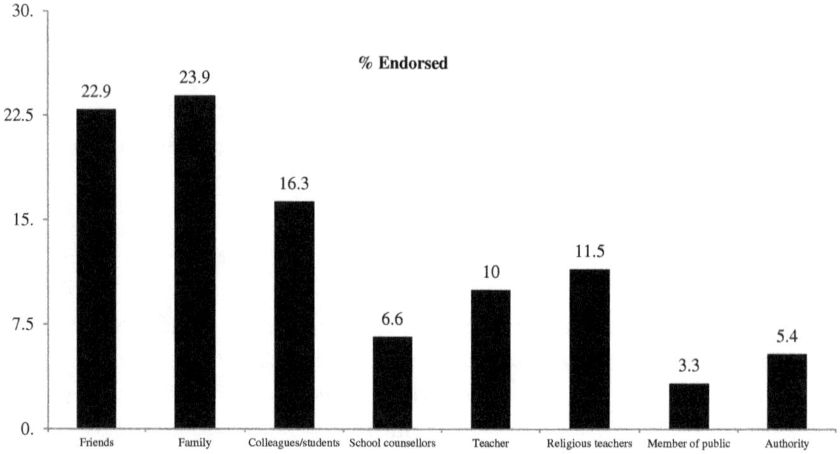

Figure 10.1. Views on Which Group is in the Best Position to Notice Early Signs of Radicalisation (Neo, 2016).

[2]The participants were all Singaporeans who were administered the survey using Google Forms. Participation is voluntary and the participants range from 18 to 73 years old. In terms of gender, 123 participants are male and 131 are female. At the time of writing, more studies are being conducted by the authors to gather more data and validate the current findings.

these two groups of interest such as providing them with information on what to look out for.

Secondly, it is important to recognise the varied responses that bystanders can have. Not every bystander is willing to report the person of interest to the relevant authorities (i.e., indirect intervention). The variety of bystander responses includes inaction (e.g., ignoring what is happening), joining in (e.g., encouraging the person to pursue radical cause), or direct intervention (e.g., attempting to contain the situation). Given that bystander effect studies (e.g., McMahon & Banyard, 2012; Hawkins *et al.*, 2001) in other domains suggested that the responses of bystanders have an impact on the person of interest, bystanders can condone and embolden the actions of the person by not reporting, or directly hinder the radicalisation trajectory by reporting.

Furthermore, unlike conventional bystander effect studies, where there is a clear demarcation of who the victim and the perpetrator are, it may not be the case in the context of radicalisation (Fox *et al.*, 2016). To begin with, is the individual viewed as a victim of radicalisation or a potential perpetrator of violence? These are essential questions because an individual's likelihood of intervention is influenced by how he/she perceives the person of interest. For example, if people perceive the radicalised individual to be a "victim" who is in need of help and misguided (whom they may be inclined towards protecting from punishment) rather than as a "perpetrator", they are more likely to report the individual to the relevant authorities. However, there are certain situational barriers that the bystanders have to surmount first before they can do so.

There are Barriers that Bystanders have to Overcome before Reporting

The term "bystander effect" was first coined by social psychologists Latané and Darley (1970) in the wake of the Genovese case. In 1964, Kitty Genovese was brutally murdered outside her apartment as 38 neighbours — i.e., bystanders — witnessed but did not come to her assistance (Lurigio, 2015). In an attempt to understand why individuals do not intervene in emergency situations such as the Genovese case, Latané and Darley (1970) conducted seminal work to identify the barriers and psychological processes that influence a bystander's decision to take action, and proposed a five-step bystander intervention model: (i) notice an event, (ii) interpret the event as an emergency, (iii) assume responsibility for intervening, (iv) know how to intervene, and (v) intervene. The successful completion of all five steps can potentially lead an individual to perform helping behaviour (for review, see Dovidio *et al.*, 2006).

In contrast, situational factors such as the presence of other individuals may interfere with the successful completion of these steps, and contribute to errors in decision-making at each step (Anker & Feeley, 2011). For example, the bystander effect emerges when bystanders fail to notice the event, do not interpret the event as an emergency, do not accept the responsibility to help, and have little knowledge of how to help. In fact, results from a meta-analysis conducted by Fischer *et al.* (2011) corroborated these findings and identified several other factors that may be related to the decreased likelihood of helping behaviour. For instance, the likelihood of helping decreases when bystanders fear that their helping behaviours may be evaluated negatively by non-intervening bystanders — e.g., running the risk of embarrassment and ridicule for misinterpreting the event as one that requires assistance (van den Bos *et al.*, 2009), facing potential retaliation from perpetrator (Madfis, 2014), and getting themselves or the victim in trouble (Zhong, 2010). This may lead the bystander to "diffuse" and shift his/her responsibility for intervention to other bystanders, which in turn inhibits helping.

However, it is important to distinguish radicalisation from conventional types of domains studied (e.g., sexual violence, bullying) in the bystander effect literature, including its frequent occurrence behind closed doors, and how it may not be perceived as an emergency due to the long period of time it takes for someone to become radicalised (Fox *et al.*, 2016).

Nevertheless, many of the barriers of bystander action in radicalisation are found to be similar to barriers documented in the general bystander effect literature (Neo, 2016; Williams *et al.*,

2016). Given that the potential bystanders are likely to be close friends and family members of the person of interest (as highlighted earlier), they may be the least willing to report their suspicions due to fear of: (i) damaging their relationship with the individual, (ii) putting the individual in danger from policing officials, and (iii) putting themselves in danger from policing officials (Williams *et al.*, 2016). Similarly, in his research on bystander effect in violent extremism in Singapore, Neo (2016) found that the top four most endorsed reasons for not taking positive action after witnessing signs of radicalisation were all associated to some sort of fear (see Figure 10.2).

Taken as a whole, these findings suggested that the authorities should not expect this group of bystanders (i.e., close friends and family members with whom relationships are primarily built upon genuine and mutual concern) to overcome these fears and report the person of interest easily (Williams *et al.*, 2016). The act of reporting entails the risk of harming treasured personal relationships. Furthermore, it is logical to assume that this group of bystanders is less likely to correctly recognise signs of radicalisation. For example, they may not believe that their friend/family member is serious about

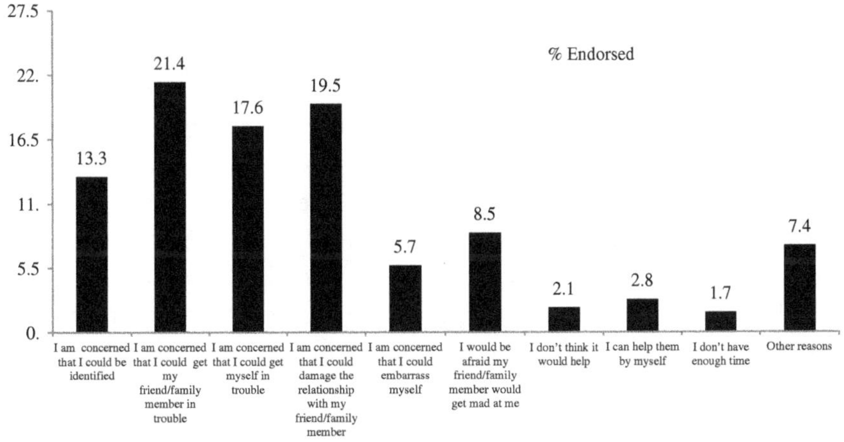

Figure 10.2. Views on What Would Prevent you from Speaking with the Police about Your Concerns (Neo, 2016).

his/her intent to commit violence. This may be attributed to what Williams *et al.* (2016, p. 58) described:

> [I]nsofar as violent extremism carries a stigma, the degree to which associate-gatekeepers [bystanders] identify with someone, whom they observe engaging in behaviours potentially indicative of violent extremism, the more that such gatekeepers might 'turn a blind eye' toward, or otherwise excuse, those behaviours.

It therefore suggests that the fear of mislabelling and stigmatising one's friend/family member as a potential violent extremist may lead the bystander to discount the severity or presence of the warning signs, thereby decreasing his/her likelihood to report.

Thus, with respect to overcoming bystanders' reluctance to intervene, there is a need to first circumvent the element of fear associated with reporting and offer them a safe platform to do so (Neo, 2016). Firstly, given the sensitivities involved (e.g., fear of getting it wrong and damaging relationship with individual), it is reasonable to assume that members of public may find it challenging to cooperate (i.e., reporting) with authorities. Therefore, there is a need for the relevant authorities to reach out and provide reassurances to the public that investigations concerning radicalisation will be carried out professionally. For example, bystanders who report must be assured that they are reporting for the benefit and safety of the individual and the wider community, and that they are not condemning a friend/family member to life in prison (Ramalingam, 2014). In addition, individuals would not be penalised for reporting false positives as long as the intention to report is not frivolous — i.e., with regard to the fear of being identified and getting it wrong. Exit and rehabilitation programs for radicalised individuals must also be communicated to the public so that the bystanders would know that by reporting, the person of interest would receive the help that he/she requires. Akin to the Yellow Ribbon Project for ex-offenders in Singapore (see Abdullah, 2017), authorities could also share success stories of rehabilitated violent extremists turning their lives around and making meaningful contributions to the society.

Secondly, the utilisation of anonymous reporting channels[3] may help to mitigate the perceived risk of being identified; similar efforts in the whistle-blowing literature have also been found to be effective in overcoming the negative consequences of the bystander effect (e.g., Gao *et al.*, 2015). Furthermore, such channels of reporting should be made easily accessible to the public, with the platforms being simple for the community to use. In Singapore, the SGSecure mobile app was introduced in September 2016 for Singaporeans to submit information on any incident(s) relating to violent extremism (Chew, 2016). Besides serving as an easily accessible platform for users to upload photo, video, or text descriptions about suspicious incidents or objects, it also provides useful guidelines (e.g., what suspicious behaviours to look out for, what to do if you are caught in an attack, making it easier for bystander to take notice of a crisis/ emergency and help) for Singaporeans, and updates about the latest situation in the event of major emergencies.

Although each of these respective suggestions may enhance the likelihood of intervention, it is important for authorities not to overuse responsibility messages to hold members of public responsible for their friends'/family members' behaviour, thereby instilling a sense of guilt if they fail to do so.

The Approach of Guilt-tripping the Bystanders Will not Work

There are many situations in which reporting is perceived as a form of ethical action (e.g., Fredricks *et al.*, 2011). While it is easy to hold someone accountable and responsible for their friends'/family members' actions, it may not be perceived as "fair" in the eyes of these individuals as they may have also been deeply affected by their friends'/family members' behaviours (e.g., the loss of a child after he/ she travelled to the Middle East to join the Islamic State in Iraq and Syria (ISIS), Muslims feeling stigmatised by the rest of the community).

[3]Alternatively, the act of reporting can be kept confidential with the promise of non-identification. This may assist in further investigation by the authorities if more information is required, or if the information provided is unclear.

In their engagements with the Muslim community in the U.K., Awan and Guru (2017) observed that many parents were presented with such a dilemma. These parents faced the possibility of alienating their own children by providing the authorities with information about their children. McVeigh (2014) also highlighted a similar case where a parent, at the behest of police to engage the authorities if they observed warning signs, regretted reporting her son to the police when he returned from Syria as her son subsequently received a 12-year jail sentence. Even in the non-radicalisation setting, Gao *et al.* (2015) found that whistle-blowing intentions of executives and upper management, as compared to lower-level employees, are hindered by their sense of responsibility to not disclose fraud occurrences in order to protect the reputation of the company.

To understand this relationship better, Neo (2016) utilised the first four steps of the bystander intervention model by Latané and Darley (1970) to understand the perceptions that Singaporeans may have about reporting those who exhibit signs of radicalisation to the appropriate authorities. Based on the findings[4] collected from 254 participants, there was a surprising positive relationship between Step 1 (noticing an event) and Step 4 (know how to help). Further statistical analysis using structural equation modelling (SEM) was performed to parse out the relationships between the four steps (see Figure 10.3). Results suggested that there is a strong relationship between Step 1 (noticing an event) and Step 4 (know how to help), and a weak relationship between Step 3 (assume responsibility for intervening) and Step 4 (know how to help). This suggests the possibility that (i) the intention to perform helping behaviour (i.e., reporting) in the radicalisation context may not follow the usual sequential fashion of the bystander intervention model and (ii) the weak relationship between Steps 3 and 4 may be attributed to the presence of other factors such as the dilemmas the bystander experienced between wanting to help the potentially radicalised individual and reporting the individual to the authorities.

[4]A 14-item survey was developed based on insights from the bystander intervention model, extant survey studies on bystander intervention, and the Home Team Behavioural Sciences Centre's (HTBSC) research on the bystander effect.

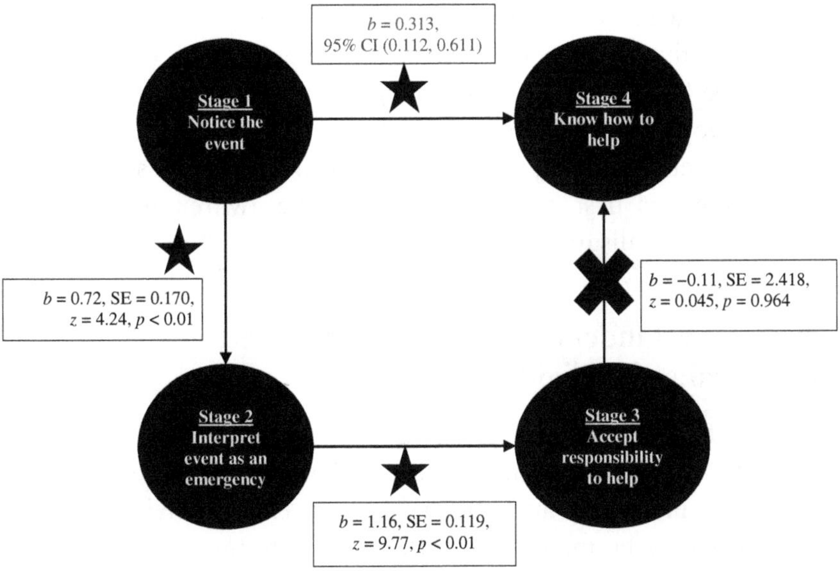

Figure 10.3. Relationships Between the Four Steps of the Bystander Intervention Model (Neo, 2016).

More importantly, the findings presented herein points specifically to the importance of not "guilt-tripping" the bystanders by holding them responsible for their friends'/family members' behaviour — i.e., based on the weak relationship between Step 3 (assume responsibility for intervening) and Step 4 (know how to help). The findings advance the idea that outreach efforts should focus on providing opportunities for bystanders to report if they witness signs of radicalisation (i.e., based on the strong relationship between Step 1 (noticing an event) and Step 4 (know how to help)), and providing reassurances to them that they are reporting for the benefit and safety of the person of interest and the wider community. In other words, the individuals' likelihood to report increases if they are simply asked to do so whenever they witness signs of radicalisation. Anker and Feeley (2011) found similar results. By simply providing students with the opportunity to register as organ donors, students' intentions to donate in the future were increased.

Additionally, to overcome the bystander intervention inertia, outreach efforts have to provide information that is simple and easy to relate, as well as specific instructions on how to respond if they witness something suspicious. Prominent examples include the campaign "If You See Something, Say Something", which was implemented by the U.S. Department of Homeland Security. However, in order to elicit the intention to report once the bystanders witnessed signs of interest, there is first a need to raise public awareness about the threat that radicalisation poses.

Educate Bystanders That the Threat Posed by Radicalised Individuals is Severe

A major concern about reporting signs of radicalisation is the ambiguity of the phenomenon itself. There is a wide range of behaviours involved, and depending on each individual, these behaviours may be manifested differently in terms of their severity and violence. On the one hand, there are behaviours that would generally be considered as obvious "red flags" or high-risk situations, including the expressions to kill and the desire for martyrdom (Kebbell & Porter, 2012). These behaviours are recognised as credible warning signs that radicalised individuals may espouse before they perpetuate an attack. It is therefore reasonable to fathom that the bystanders would classify the presence of these signs as an emergency. On the other hand, there are behaviours that contribute to the nascent stages of radicalisation (low-risk situations) including the expression of intolerance towards a particular group, the use of the Internet to search for radical propaganda, etc. (Neo *et al.*, 2017a). The behaviours at this end of the spectrum are less obvious, and therefore their connection to radicalisation may not be recognised nor judged as an emergency. As a result, radicalisation can be more difficult for the bystanders to notice than an overt emergency situation (e.g., murder) like the one highlighted in Latané and Darley's (1970) model. This notion is best exemplified by how Muslim parents in Britain felt: "Parents don't know if their children are going to Syria. So how can we report them? I am not sure what to look for? What are the signs? This just looks like spying" (Awan & Guru, 2017, p. 35). In other words, individuals (i.e., friends/family members) who are in an ideal position to witness signs of radicalisation may not understand the severity of the behaviours as well as what to look out for.

Hence, there is a need to educate the bystanders that the threat posed by radicalised individuals is severe (i.e., one is one too many) and that it is a form of emergency. Indeed, bystander effect research on alcohol overdose in college students (Blavos *et al.*, 2014) and sexual harassment (Fischer *et al.*, 2006) have shown that bystanders are motivated by the perceived severity of the situation (e.g., the victim may die) to render assistance. As explained by Fischer *et al.* (2006, p. 269):

> [W]e assume that dangerous emergencies are recognised as real emergencies more clearly and thus increase the costs for not helping the victim. As a consequence, the bystander's empathic arousal increases, which finally leads to more helping — independently of whether the bystander is alone or accompanied by other bystanders.

Similarly, the extent to which bystanders' behaviour may be moderated by the severity of the situation is also seen in the survey study by Neo (2016). It was revealed that the scenario where one observes an individual mentioning his/her "intention to commit violence" (i.e., high-risk situation) would trigger more participants to report, as compared to another scenario in which the individual only exhibits early signs of radicalisation (i.e., low-risk situation). Interestingly, participants expressed less concern about getting their friends/family members in trouble, as well as damaging their relationship with them in the high-risk situation. In both high- and low-risk situations, however, the participants are still equally concerned about getting themselves into trouble (see Figure 10.4). It could be that these participants in the high-risk situation have appreciated the severity of the situation, which resulted in their increased intentions to report, despite the potential of getting themselves into trouble.

Based on these insights, several implications for law enforcement practitioners, policymakers, and academics have been identified.

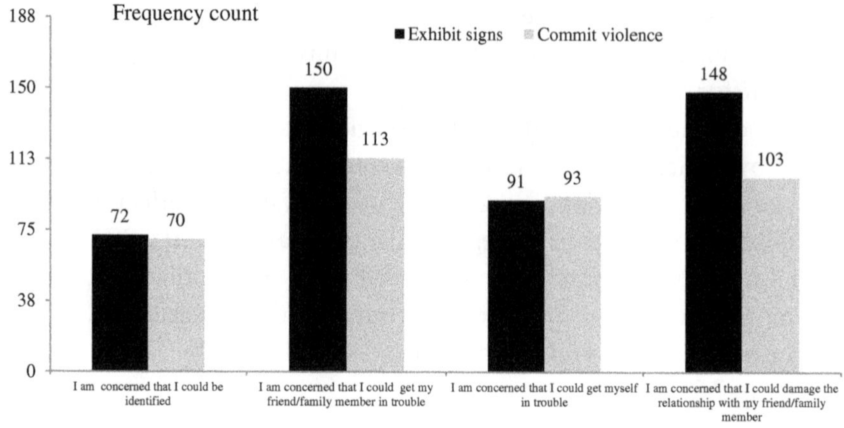

Figure 10.4. Impact of the Severity of the Situation on the Bystander Effect (Neo, 2016).

Firstly, it provides guidance on how outreach efforts should be tailored in ways that articulates what are clear warning signs of radicalisation (i.e., associated with high-risk situation) where the bystanders can intervene upon recognition. There is also the need to impress upon the bystanders to interpret situations, where such signs of radicalisation are salient, as emergencies that require their actions. This in turn may increase the opportunities for individuals to become "positive" bystanders that help guide the person of interest away from becoming radicalised. For example, in the Press Release by the Ministry of Home Affairs on 12 June 2017, it was mentioned that:

> The heightened terrorism threat worldwide and in Singapore makes it imperative for family members and friends to raise to the authorities anyone they suspect of being radicalised or planning terror activities. Singapore can be made safer if family members and friends do this. The time between radicalisation and committing violence can be very short in some cases. Recent terror attacks around the world have shown how terrorists can use easily available objects like vehicles and knives to commit violence. Such an act would drive a wedge between Muslims and non-Muslims and divide our communities, which is precisely what the terrorist groups want (Ministry of Home Affairs, 2017, para. 5).

Secondly, there is a need to establish outreach programs that consider the level of general knowledge that the public may have about the topic of radicalisation; in fact, there are many examples where members of public did not understand basic concepts associated with radicalisation (Awan & Guru, 2017). For instance, they may misconstrue a practising Muslim as a potential violent extremist. This may alienate the affected community and negatively affect social cohesion. Thus, programs should (i) address the roles of a positive bystander, (ii) challenge myths and misconceptions about radicalisation, (iii) share signs of radicalisation, and (iv) recognise and reinterpret bystander intervention for radicalisation as events that affect the community. This would also shape public perceptions towards radicalisation and generate greater awareness about the threat it poses. However, there is a need to first create a safe and conducive culture which encourages reporting, in order for such outreach programs to work.

Create A Culture Where Reporting is the Norm

Safeguarding against the threat of radicalisation is everyone's responsibility. Indeed, a key counter-radicalisation initiative adopted by many countries is to foster and enhance the cooperation between the government and the public (Dunn *et al.*, 2016; Spalek, 2014). Such community engagements may have a positive influence on eliciting bystander actions if there is an established level of confidence and trust between the two entities; members of public would be more willing to share information about any potential radicalisation activities. For example, Pantucci *et al.* (2016, p. 16) highlighted the success story of the case of Andrew Ibrahim in the U.K.:

> In April 2008, members of a Bristol mosque noticed burn marks on Ibrahim's hands and arms; already concerned by his radical views, they contacted their community police officer. When police subsequently raided Ibrahim's flat, they discovered explosives, a suicide vest and evidence that he had been planning to attack a local shopping centre. Strong relationships between the police and

the community had created an environment in which Ibrahim's suspicious behaviour could be detected and his plans disrupted.

However, if members of public perceive the authorities to be unjust and untrustworthy (e.g., due to racial prejudice), they will demonstrate an unwillingness to come forward with important but potentially incriminating information (Awan, 2012; Weitzer & Tuch, 2004). In such circumstances where the authorities are viewed with suspicion, members of public would likely react in a similar manner as what Uzma Hussain did: "I would not call them because the police might just come knocking on my door and arrest my other children. Hard to trust them" (Awan & Guru, 2017, p. 34). These examples therefore underscore the importance of building a culture that embraces the cooperation and trust between the government and the public, which in turn may encourage bystanders to intervene in a positive manner.

Besides building trust, recent studies have identified other factors that may facilitate the creation of a positive culture for bystander actions. For example, studies have found that social norms and perception of cohesiveness have a strong influence on bystander intervention. Cantillon's (2006) analysis of youth delinquency found that members of the neighbourhood are more likely to offer assistance when they feel a greater sense of social and emotional connection to their neighbours. Group membership is also a contributing factor, where people are more likely to intervene when those who require assistance are perceived to be an in-group member (Levine & Manning, 2013). Similarly, Rutkowski *et al.* (1983) shared how a program was able to stimulate bystander responsiveness in New York City by fostering the sense of community cohesiveness. Thus, the notion of a shared common identity may translate into cultural norms about how each individual should react in bystander situations.

This conclusion supports the potential use of a collective identity, which members of public can relate to, in outreach programs. For example, by engaging all Singaporeans, including the authorities and those who may become radicalised in outreach programmes, people can be reminded of their shared membership as members of the

Singapore community. In addition, outreach programs should reiterate that acts of radicalisation are not only wrong, immoral, and illegal, but antithetical to the Singaporean national identity shared by all citizens. An example would be the "Stand United" messaging that was shared as part of the national SGSecure movement (Seow, 2017). Besides emphasising the need for Singaporeans to build strong ties with their neighbours and the community, it also underscores an equally essential message for Singaporeans to maintain the ties and look out for one another especially after an attack. However, implementing such programs is challenging as trust[5] between the government and members of public must be engendered (as highlighted earlier), and steps taken to ensure the public can accurately identify concerning behaviour.

Other bystander effect studies (e.g., Abbate *et al.*, 2013; Garcia *et al.*, 2002) have determined that pre-emptive approaches such as the priming of individuals with helping-related words would increase their likelihood to engage in bystander action. This approach is based on the premise that the willingness to provide help for the sake of others can be activated at the subconscious level (White & Malkowski, 2014). In other words, authorities would be well advised to prime the public to act on the needs and well-being of other members of their community. In light of these findings, outreach programs can incorporate the use of priming to emphasise the importance of helping (e.g., "by reporting (the person of interest), you are helping him/her receive the assistance that he/she requires"). This positive framing may also reinforce the assertions identified earlier: (i) individuals' likelihood to report increases if they are simply asked to do so whenever they witness signs of radicalisation and (ii) individuals are more willing to help others who share the same group membership. These suggestions have the potential to

[5]Besides building trust between the authorities and members of public, it is also important to build trust within a segment of the community. For example, there is a need to build trust among the followers of the different branches and schools in Islam. Failing to do so may present a daunting task for the Muslim community to build trust with other communities (e.g., non-Muslims).

play a critical role in creating a culture where reporting is the norm; all members are willing and able to intervene and become active in reporting signs of radicalisation.

Conclusion

The current state of violent extremism makes community reporting of suspected radicalisation to violence absolutely essential. This chapter, therefore, seeks to answer the question of how to encourage the community not to "stand by" (i.e., be bystanders) and report more. Based on the insights derived from a behavioural sciences angle, five key points and their associated implications for law enforcement practitioners, policymakers, and academics have been identified.

Acknowledgement

The views expressed in this chapter are the authors' only, and do not represent the official position or view of the Ministry of Home Affairs, Singapore.

Editors' Note

It is essential to recognise the difficulties (i.e., barriers) that bystanders may face whilst reporting their family members, friends, or colleagues whom they suspected to be radicalised. More research is required to examine this phenomenon (which the authors are embarking on to gather more data) in an Asian context.

References

Abbate, C. S., Ruggieri, S., & Boca, S. (2013). Current problems and resolutions: The effect of prosocial priming in the presence of bystanders. *The Journal of Social Psychology*, *153*(5), 619–622.

Abdullah, Z. (2017). Yellow ribbon Prison Run: Ex-gangster knows how to help at-risk teens. *The Straits Times*. Retrieved from http://www.

straitstimes.com/singapore/ex-gangster-knows-how-to-help-at-risk-teens.

Anker, A. E., & Feeley, T. H. (2011). Are nonparticipants in prosocial behavior merely innocent bystanders? *Health Communication*, 26, 13–24.

Awan, I. (2012). The impact of policing British Muslims: A qualitative exploration. *Journal of Policing, Intelligence and Counter-Terrorism*, 7(1), 22–35.

Awan, I., & Guru, S. (2017). Parents of foreign "terrorist" fighters in Syria — Will they report their young? *Ethnic and Racial Studies*, *40*(1), 24–42.

Blavos, A. A., Glassman, T., Sheu, J., Diehr, A., & Deakins, B. (2014). Using the health belief model to predict bystander behavior among college students. *Journal of Student Affairs Research and Practice*, *51*(4), 420–432.

Borum, R. (2011). Radicalization into violent extremism II: A review of conceptual models and empirical research. *Journal of Strategic Security*, *4*(4), 37–62.

Cantillon, D. (2006). Community social organization, parents, and peers as mediators of perceived neighborhood block characteristics on delinquent and prosocial activities. *American Journal of Community Psychology*, *37*(1–2), 111–127.

Chew, H. M. (2016). First look at SGSecure app: How to use it? *The Straits Times*. Retrieved from http://www.straitstimes.com/singapore/first-look-at-sgsecure-app-how-to-use-it.

Clutterbuck, L., & Warnes, R. (2011). *Exploring Patterns of Behaviour in Violent Jihadist Terrorists*. Santa Monica, CA: RAND Corporation.

Dovidio, J. F., Piliavin, J. A., Schroeder, D. A., & Penner, L. A. (2006). *The Social Psychology of Prosocial Behavior*. Mahwah, NJ: Lawrence Erlbaum Associates.

Dozier, J. B., & Miceli, M. P. (1985). Potential predictors of whistleblowing: A prosocial behavior perspective. *Academy of Management Review*, *10*(4), 823–836.

Dunn, K. M., Atie, R., Kennedy, M., Ali, J. A., O'Reilly, J., & Rogerson, L. (2016). Can you use community policing for counter terrorism? Evidence from NSW, Australia. *Police Practice and Research*, *17*(3), 196–211.

Edwards, K. M., Rodenhizer-Stämpfli, K. A., & Eckstein, R. P. (2015). Bystander action in situations of dating and sexual aggression: A mixed methodological study of high school youth. *Journal of Youth Adolsecence*, *44*, 2,321–2,336.

Fischer, P., Greitemeyer, T., Pollozek, F., & Frey, D. (2006). The unresponsive bystander: Are bystanders more responsive in dangerous emergencies? *European Journal of Social Psychology*, *36*, 267–278.

Fischer, P., Kruger, J. I., Greitemeyer, T., Vogrincic, C., Kastenmmuller, A., Frey, D., & Kainbacher, M. (2011). The bystander-effect: A meta-analytic review on bystander intervention in dangerous and non-dangerous emergencies. *Psychological Bulletin*, *137*(4), 517–537.

Fox, J., Neo, L. S., & Khader, M. (2016). Overcoming the Bystander Effect: Increasing community reporting of suspected violent extremism. Research Report No. 08/2016. Singapore: Home Team Behavioural Sciences Centre.

Fredricks, S., Ramsey, M., & Hornett, A. (2011). Kinship and bystander effect: The role of others in ethical decisions. *Journal of Religion and Business Ethics*, *2*(1), 1–22.

Gao, J., Greenberg, R., & Wong-On-Wing, B. (2015). Whistleblowing intentions of lower-level employees: The effect of reporting channel, bystanders, and wrongdoer power status. *Journal of Business Ethics*, *126*, 85–99.

Garcia, S. M., Weaver, K., Moskowitz, G. B., & Darley, J. M. (2002). Crowded minds: The implicit bystander effect. *Journal of Personality and Social Psychology*, *83*(4), 843–853.

Gill, P., Horgan, J., & Deckert, P. (2014). Bombing alone: Tracing the motivations and antecedent behaviours of lone-actor terrorists. *Journal of Forensic Sciences, 59*(2), 425–435.

Hawkins, D. L., Pepler, D., & Craig, W. (2001). Peer interventions in playground bullying. *Social Development*, *10*, 512–527.

Hellemans, C., Dal Cason, D., & Casini, A. (2017). Bystander helping behavior in response to workplace bullying. *Swiss Journal of Psychology*, *76*(4), 135–144.

Kebbell, R. M., & Porter, L. (2012). An intelligence assessment framework for identifying individuals at risk of committing acts of violent extremism against the West. *Security Journal*, *25*(3), 212–228.

Latané, B., & Darley, J. M. (1970). *The Unresponsive Bystander: Why Doesn't He Help?* Englewood Cliffs, NJ: Prentice Hall.

Levine, M., & Manning, R. (2013). Social identity, group processes, and helping in emergencies. *European Review of Social Psychology*, *24*(1), 225–251.

Lurigio, A. J. (2015). Crime narratives, dramatizations, and the legacy of the Kitty Genovese murder: A half century of half truths. *Criminal Justice and Behavior*, *42*(7), 782–789.

Machackova, H., Dedkova, L., & Mezulanikova, K. (2015). Brief report: The bystander effect in cyberbullying incidents. *Journal of Adolescence*, *43*, 96–9.

Madfis, E. (2014). Averting school rampage: Student intervention amid a persistent code of silence. *Youth Violence and Juvenile Justice*, *12*(3), 229–249.

McKinley, J. C., & Dao, J. (2009, November 8). Fort hood gunman gave signals before his rampage. *The New York Times*. Retrieved from https://mobile.nytimes.com/2009/11/09/us/09reconstruct.html?referer=https://www.google.com.sg/.

McMahon, S. (2015). Call for research on bystander intervention to prevent sexual violence: The role of campus environments. *American Journal of Community Psychology*, 55, 472–489.

McMahon, S., & Banyard, V. L. (2012). When can I help? A conceptual framework for the prevention of sexual violence through bystander intervention. *Trauma, Violence, & Abuse*, *13*(1), 3–14.

McVeigh, T. (2014). 'Police betrayed me', says mother of imprisoned British jihadi. *The Guardian*. Retrieved from http://www.theguardian.com/world/2014/dec/06/yusuf-sarwar-mother-british-jihadist-police-betray-syria.

Meloy, J. R., Roshdi, K., Glaz-Ocik, J., & Hoffmann, J. (2015). Investigating the individual terrorist in Europe. *Journal of Threat Assessment and Management*, 2(3-4), 140–152.

Ministry of Home Affairs (2017, June 12). Detention of a radicalised Singaporean under the Internal Security Act (Press release). Retrieved from https://www.mha.gov.sg/newsroom/press-releases/newsroom-detail-page?news=detention-of-a-radicalised-singaporean-under-the-internal-security-act.

Monaco, L. O. (2014). Countering violent extremism and the power of community. Remarks by Assistant to the President for Homeland Security and Counterterrorism Lisa O. Monaco. Massachusetts: Harvard Kennedy School forum.

Neo, L. S. (2016). Understanding the bystander effect in the context of violent extremism: An exploratory study. *Paper Presented at the 3rd Asian Conference of Criminal and Operations Psychology (ACCOP), Singapore.*

Neo, L. S., Dillon, L., & Khader, M. (2017a). Identifying individuals at risk of being radicalised via the internet. *Security Journal*, *30*, 1112–1133.

Neo, L. S., Khader, M., Ang, J., Ong, G., & Tan, E. (2017b). Developing an early screening guide for jihadi terrorism: A behavioural analysis of 30 terror attacks. *Security Journal*, *30*, 227–246.

Pantucci, R., Ellis, C., & Chaplais, L. (2016). *Lone-Actor Terrorism: Literature Review*. United Kingdom: Royal United Services Institute.

Pozzoli, T., Ang, R. P., & Gini, G. (2012). Bystanders' reactions to bullying: A cross-cultural analysis of personal correlates among Italian and Singaporean students. *Social Development*, *21*(4), 686–703.

Ramalingam, V. (2014). *On the Front Line: A Guide to Countering Far-Right Extremism*. UK: Institute for Strategic Dialogue.

Russakoff, D., & Eggen, D. (2007). Six charged in plot to attack Fort Dix. *The Washington Post*. Retrieved from http://www.washingtonpost.com/wp-dyn/content/article/2007/05/08/AR2007050800465.html.

Rutkowski, G. K., Gruder, C. L., & Romer, D. (1983). Group cohesiveness, social norms, and bystander intervention. *Journal of Personality and Social Psychology*, *44*(3), 545–553.

Schillinger, T. (2014). *Bystander Effect and Religious Group Affiliation: Terrorism and the Diffusion of Responsibility*. Walden University: Walden Dissertations and Doctorial Studies.

Seow, J. (2017). SGSecure pledge urges citizens to stay alert, united. *The Straits Times*. Retrieved from http://www.straitstimes.com/singapore/sgsecure-pledge-urges-citizens-to-stay-alert-united.

Spalek, B. (2014). Community engagement for counterterrorism in Britain: An exploration of the role of "connectors" in countering takfiri jihadist terrorism. *Studies in Conflict & Terrorism*, *37*, 825–841.

Staub, E. (2013). Building a peaceful society origins, prevention, and reconciliation after genocide and other group violence. *American Psychologist*, *68*(7), 576–589.

Tacopino, J. (2018). Pulse nightclub shooter's wife was aware of plot — and did nothing. *New York Post*. Retrieved from https://nypost.com/2018/01/05/pulse-nightclub-shooters-wife-was-aware-of-plot-and-did-nothing/.

van den Bos, K., Müller, P. A., & van Bussel, A. A. L. (2009). Helping to overcome intervention inertia in bystander's dilemmas: Behavioral disinhibition can improve the greater good. *Journal of Experimental Social Psychology*, *45*, 873–878.

Weitzer, R., & Tuch, S. A. (2004). Race and perceptions of police misconduct. *Social Problems*, *51*, 305–325.

White, C. H., & Malkowski, J. (2014). Communicative challenges of bystander intervention: Impact of goals and message design logic on strategies college students use to intervene in drinking situations. *Health Communication*, *29*, 93–104.

Williams, M. J., Horgan, J. G., & Evans, W. P. (2016). The critical role of friends in networks for countering violent extremism: Toward a theory of vicarious help-seeking. *Behavioral Sciences of Terrorism and Political Aggression*, *8*(1), 45–65.

Zhong, L. Y. (2010). Bystander intervention and fear of crime: Evidence from two Chinese communities. *International Journal of Offender Therapy and Comparative Criminology*, *54*(2), 250–263.

CHAPTER 11

The Inseparable Brothers-in-Arms: Understanding the Instrumentality of Violent Extremism in Strengthening Intergroup Conflict

DASHALINI KATNA

School of Social Sciences,
Nanyang Technological University, Singapore

Introduction

Like fingerprints, no two intergroup conflicts[1] emerge and evolve alike (Salomon, 2004). Intergroup conflicts that follow destructive trajectories and outcomes, rather than its constructive counterpart,

[1] An intergroup conflict is defined as the perceived incompatibility of goals or values between two or more individuals, in which these individuals classify themselves as members belonging to different social group memberships (in-group and out-group) (Böhm *et al.*, 2018).

weaponise the spectre of violent extremism.[2] Identified as a persistent security threat that has not spared any nation of its impact, violent extremism may stealthily enculturate, hybridise, and cement itself into a necessary way of societal life that crosses borders. Interviews with the Islamic State of Iraq and Syria (ISIS) informants and defectors revealed that cadres of combat-trained foreign operatives are rerouted quickly by the *Emni* (intelligence and external operations arm of ISIS) to their home countries or a third country to recruit and conduct attacks (Callimachi, 2016; Speckhard & Yayla, 2017). Immune to containment and eradication strategies by military and intelligence capabilities, current research and policy surrounding violent extremism and its interdependency with intergroup conflicts remain inadequate and stymied by ambiguities (Alimi *et al.*, 2015).

A common complexity entrenched in almost every intergroup conflict primarily revolves around incompatible perspectives between the opposing parties (Al-Krenawi, 2017; Christie & Louis, 2012). Analysing perspective divergences between a group and its rival group(s) could offer greater granularity on why and how members become motivated to espouse and readily demonstrate violent extremism. In addition, an extensive scrutiny into the sources of hostilities between rivalling groups could deploy the realist evaluation framework that specifies what would work, for whom, under which conditions, and how (Gielen, 2017). The awareness gained from explaining and predicting specific intents, decisions, and behaviours to endorse and engage in violent extremism could be leveraged to develop evidence-guided research and policy for security agencies to delineate and prepare for possible future scenarios of different intergroup conflict theatres. Attaining a comprehensive understanding of the intricacies within the intergroup conflict–violent extremism connection is thus critical, for the global community of security practitioners and policymakers to formulate responses that effectively detect, disrupt, defeat, and deter the eventualities of this threat.

[2]The definition of violent extremism — as a willingness to support the use of and conduct violence to further political, social, or ideological beliefs — was adopted from Horgan *et al.* (2017).

This chapter calls attention to five issues which influence the incompatibility of intergroup perceptions and fuel acts of violent extremism. Approaches aimed at restraining the pursuit of violence and its room for manoeuvre are discussed: (1) delivering emotive communications, (2) interdicting intragroup processes within clandestine groups, (3) synthesising predictive drivers and assessments, (4) interpreting and responding to costly signalling, and (5) influencing competitive terrorist relationships.

Issues in Sight

Issue 1: The Need for Communications in Managing Public Overreactions that May Intensify Social Polarisation in the (Immediate) Aftermath of a Terror Incident

In his statement after his arrest, Faisal Shahzad, who had a failed attempt to detonate a car bomb in Times Square in 2010, was reported to have felt enraged about the post-9/11 treatment of Muslims in the United States and the West, and about the U.S. military intervention in Iraq under the alleged search for weapons of mass destruction (Lyons-Padilla *et al.*, 2015). A number of survey studies that examined individuals who experienced harsh anti-Muslim discrimination evidenced justification and support for terror attacks in Muslim diaspora populations (Cherney & Murphy, 2017; Victoroff *et al.*, 2012). Post-attack public responses, particularly exclusivist sentiments, may indirectly harden radical mindsets and aggressive behaviours of potential perpetrators over time, leaving violent extremists resistant to change (Hanes & Machin, 2014; Kaakinen *et al.*, 2017). Playing into the hands of violent extremist groups like ISIS that aspire to destroy the "grey zone" or the harmony between Muslims and non-Muslims across societies, the rise in public fear and Islamophobic assaults engender fertile conditions that could motivate at-risk and radicalised individuals, who may harbour strong desire for revenge or to retaliate (Neo *et al.*, 2017).

In the conflict between the state and violent extremist groups, the escalation of hostility could be strongly contingent on the ensuing reactions of the government which may sway public apprehension (McCauley, 2017; Sageman, 2016). Public opinion polls indicated that support for government agencies' capabilities to provide security and cope with crises declined significantly after the 22 July terror attacks in Norway (Christensen & Aars, 2017) and 2015 attacks in Paris (Bryant, 2016). Different types, intensity, and interplay(s) of reactions like perceptions of fear and instability of the government elicited by national and international audiences, leaders in political-religious-social spheres, and civilian-users on traditional (Glad *et al.*, 2017) and social media platforms (Lin *et al.*, 2017) could galvanise potential extremists. Helping to win "more than half of the battle" as quoted by Ayman al-Zawahiri (as cited in Smith & Walsh, 2013), intense media attention, and sensationalist reporting of terror attacks were found to encourage negative portrayals of Muslims (Ahmed & Matthes, 2016), and more attacks in the future (Grinnell, 2017; Jetter, 2017).

Issue 2: The Need to Identify Entry Points that can Undermine Intragroup Dynamics Among Clandestine (Online and Offline) Violent Extremist Networks

Territorial losses from battlefield failures (Tyner, 2016), state pressure, and tighter security environments continue to encourage diffusion and decentralisation of extremist groups (Hafez, 2016). While enabling evasion from security surveillance, this restructuring strategy can yield smaller, homegrown, underground, and informal units (Knoke, 2015; Reedy *et al.*, 2013). According to interrogation records documented by European intelligence agencies, combatants who were assigned to conduct attacks had been organised into small-scale, discrete groups based on nationality and language, and usually touched base with each other on the eve of their departure to their designated locations (Callimachi, 2016). Rather than a top-down process, member recruitment often begins with more of a bottom-up process, as radicalised enthusiasts actively seek contact and volunteer with various facilitators through the Internet (Aly, 2017). Describing the Italian Islamist network as a fragmented milieu and led by single persons or tight-knit clusters that may challenge monitoring, Marone

(2017) utilised case studies to highlight how *muhajirun* aspirants may find extremist contacts through familial connections as well as indoctrinate, and engage kin and kith as co-conspirators.

Moreover, radicalised individuals may identify vicariously with and be inspired by "small-world-networks", like al-Muhajiroun, that maintain firm and covert lines of connections with active leaders, evoking a sense of camaraderie and interaction (Kenney *et al.*, 2017). The growth of small cells and lone actors distributed, far and wide, warrants scrutinising in-group dynamics and processes on a finer scale to uncover how types of peer-to-group interactions underlying the efficiency of the constellations of secretive cells and larger network structures could be compartmentalised, penetrated, and limited. Weak "bridges" between clusters and their directionalities can be exploited to identify highly contributory actors who may bring primary to rudimentary capital (i.e., logistics, communications, financial, social resources) to the group for its longevity, resilience, and lethality (Baaken & Schlegel, 2017; Decker & Pyrooz, 2015; Koehler-Derrick & Milton, 2017).

Issue 3: The Need for Monitoring Threat Appraisals of Returnees (Committed to Re-unite, Proselytise, and Attack) and their Associates

The timely processing, analysing, triaging, and follow-ups of vast volumes of data on the unprecedented scope and inflow of returnees and their activities continues to be a ubiquitous challenge for intelligence agencies (Byman, 2016; Speckhard *et al.*, 2017). Extant research on violent extremism has unveiled a large array of proximal and distal drivers (Neo *et al.*, 2017) and elaborate pathways[3] (Khalil, 2017; Malthaner, 2017; McGilloway *et al.*, 2015) that focus on multiple tiers such as the disillusioned individual, within the group, and between affiliated or opposing groups. Classified as antecedents,

[3]These determinants can be further categorised as values, needs, emotions, ideologies, and mechanisms which may vary at exogeneous and endogenous levels (Monahan, 2015; Stern, 2016).

catalysts, intermediate by-products, inhibitors, or consequences, these risk factors, independently and conjointly, capture distinct mechanisms which may differ in importance, causality, and sequence across conflict theatres with varying intensity. Through indispensable, round-the-clock surveillance and tracking of "red flags", which may substantially predict online and offline movements of returnees, amateurs, and lone actors, this can be exceptionally intensive for intelligence services which are already stretched thin on resources (Byman, 2016).

However, the focus on how the trajectories of risk indicators may interact, complement, and give rise to actual planning, preparation, and execution of violent extremist behaviours has been under-emphasised (Wikström & Bouhana, 2016). Examinations on attack modes of lone actors by Lindekilde *et al.* (2017) and Schuurman *et al.* (2017), for instance, demonstrated that certain radicalisation patterns, like lone actors with a volatile or autonomous nature, could differentiate specific pre-attack behavioural preferences such as the level of involvement in planning and preparing groundwork, types of target and weapon, and engaging in leakage behaviours about their motives and capabilities. Unlike the conveyor belt progression, tracking and predicting the volatile nature of violent extremism can be more complicated than the straightforward process of enumerating necessary and sufficient tipping points at specific junctures (Borum, 2015; McCauley & Moskalenko, 2017). Charting out temporal and causative linkages of warning signs into interconnected systems could holistically illustrate and prioritise the heterogeneity, density, and trends among violent extremists (like ideological and geographical variations), which may elucidate their violent intent and acts to ongoing and potential threats, risks, and opportunities.

Issue 4: The Need to Interpret Costly Signals Displayed by Violent Extremists

"Each terrorism attempt — successful or not — serves as a reinforcer, generating waves of excitement" (quote by Steven Stalinsky, as cited in Warrick, 2018). For the defending group, any amount of damage inflicted on the adversarial group(s) is marked as a small, victorious step that contributes to the collective annihilation of the enemy

(Kydd & Walter, 2006). The motivation of members to launch costly signals that destabilise and eliminate is greater when they view their group as being in a defensive than offensive posture (Böhm *et al.*, 2018). Signals from violent extremists can vary in terms of cost, effectiveness, and target audience. Reading costly signals from the opponent(s) can result in a multitude of either flawed or sound interpretations (Kearns *et al.*, 2014). After the downfall of bin Laden and the elimination of key lieutenants, former Director of National Intelligence James Clapper reported that a rebranded and resurrected Al-Qaeda (AQ) could be "positioned to make gains" (Hoffman, 2016). Likewise, ISIS which had been initially viewed as being disinterested in global terrorist operations, has thus far orchestrated major international attacks (Hoffman, 2016). Such (mis)calculations raise concerns that the global security community may overlook signals and form misleading assumptions of violent extremist groups.

The adept application of costly signals by violent extremists is not a skill that is inherent or instantly acquired. Instead, these signals are often learnt from various avenues like the media, knowledge exchanges between terrorist organisations, and historical conflicts (Kettle & Mumford, 2017). Knowing how members in violent extremist groups learn and innovate may advance the understanding about why, what, and how they choose to signal, which cautions against generalisations that may oversimplify distinct threats (Novenario, 2016; Singh, 2017). Such information could be channelled towards deciphering a group's capabilities which can aid intelligence and information-gathering, as well as averting signal interpretation mistakes by the receiver. Defensive measures such as target hardening of key infrastructure could be seen as provocation by violent extremist groups and increase the appeal of signalling attacks, which may necessitate adaptive and robust counter-strategies (Hastings & Chan, 2013; Hsu & McDowall, 2017).

Issue 5: The Need to Anticipate How Rivalries Affect the Evolution of Intergroup Conflicts and Violent Extremism

Conventional wisdom held that fierce disagreements over ascendancy between ISIS and AQ would exacerbate and portend the demise of both organisations, but emergent competitive currents continue to boost greater intergroup violence (Hamming, 2017; Hoffman, 2016). Splintering and outbidding have been associated with increases in the total number of terrorist recruits, cells, franchises, attacks, and casualties (Cohen *et al.*, 2018; Zech & Kelly, 2017). Biberman and Zahid (2016) suggested that outbidding behaviours may incline towards brutal attacks against highly vulnerable and shocking targets like students who were attacked in the Berlin and Peshawar school massacres. The outbidding strategy enables vying terrorist groups to exhibit their credible commitment to the group's cause, gain legitimacy, coerce or inspire public sympathy and support, and compel opponents to respond with their attacks, to avoid the risk of becoming redundant (Choi, 2018; Young & Dugan, 2014). Competition may foster innovation of adaptive tactics, which can extend group survivability and escalate intergroup conflict (Phillips, 2015). Decentralised cells, new off-shoots, as well as desperate and fractured groups of violent extremists could be determined to stand out from the crowd and win the "hearts and minds" competition through dramatic displays of operational strength (Conrad & Greene, 2015; Nemeth, 2014). In this competitive ecosystem, the entry of more peripheral upstarts and spin-off movements that may be more violent, unpredictable, strategic, and risk-taking, could employ greater lethality to outdo one another (Decker & Pyrooz, 2015; Glazzard *et al.*, 2017; Winter & Clarke, 2017).

By performing surprise and spectacular attacks, such entrants establish credentials and catch the attention of larger organisations like ISIS and, simultaneously, win over disenchanted supporters who opine such strikes as acts of empowerment rather than savagery. Challenges that arise from outbidding could be compounded by the triangulation of intergroup conflicts, illicit networks of organised crime, and variants of violent extremist organisations (Carrapico *et al.*, 2014; Clarke, 2016). Small-scale, violent extremist projects could be microfinanced by narcotics peddlers who may provide operatives with financial flexibility for travelling and procuring necessary resources for planning a terrorist attack like weapons, vehicles, and burner phones (Ranstorp, 2016).

Approaches

Approach 1: Framing and Delivering Emotive Communications

Government, religious, and community grassroots leaders could utilise emotion-based, positive strategic communications to modulate and to potentially avert public anxiety in the aftermath of a terror incident (Ćosić *et al.*, 2018). Following the 7/7 London attacks, the U.K. government's official statement, which was viewed as trustworthy, competent, and coherent, was able to create a sense of control amongst its populace (Crijns *et al.*, 2017). During the four-day Westgate siege in Nairobi, al-Shabaab militants constantly published live tweets containing threatening graphic images and ideological content that targeted its sympathisers and the Kenyan population, while the Kenyan government was more focused on preparing its operations amid the confusion and panic (Mair, 2016). Rather than a one-size-fits-all message, broader messages followed by targeted, narrower messages that resonate with key audiences such as civilians, potential radicals, and associate gatekeepers, could be disseminated. For example, messages for civilians could emphasise about allaying, resisting, and prolonging a climate of fear, anger, and distrust towards (suspect) communities, whilst messages directed at potential radicals could seek to dissuade their extremist beliefs that exhort violence and discourage their interest to join a terrorist group or execute a lone attack.

Opposed to stressing on criminality and danger, the tone and content of such public messaging practice could underscore "safeguarding" and "health promotion", which may encourage reporting from associate gatekeepers, or kin and kith of extremists. These strategic messages could be crafted using face-to-face video communications compared to tweets, phrased in cognitively simplistic terms, and could be modelled after Hollywood-inspired narratives that portray acts of courage and commend the government's determination (Speckhard & Shajkovci, 2018). In line with whole-of-community initiatives, a multiagency approach that incorporates the co-development, production, and distribution of messages could be utilised (Parker *et al.*, 2017). In the wake of a terror incident, the messages from this broad range of (security- and non-security-based) actors could convey that the logical remedy to the current situation would be unity, resilience, and civic-mindedness. Firm communication and action from public (and private) sector entities may facilitate the population to adapt more confidently to the volatile situation and to avoid overreactions which can feed into violent extremism. New threats like deliberate online falsehoods and digitally altered media may jeopardise the positive effects of these emotive communications.

Approach 2: Interdicting Intragroup Processes within Clandestine Groups

The present degradation of ISIS areas has not diminished its continuing efforts to stay relevant, engage, and incite digital natives in its virtual Caliphate to conduct attacks like "bombmaking to the poisoning of food supplies" (Warrick, 2018, para. 25). This migration to the cybersphere entails closer attention to be channelled towards covert, online communities within much larger networks which may influence small cells and lone actors (Freeman *et al.*, 2017). These small-group, communication exchanges rely on multilingual, social networking platforms that can serve as a rich ground to examine and disrupt virtual, intragroup dynamics, and processes (Dovidio, 2013). The advent of big data surveillant technologies comprising open-source and social media network analysis could distinguish and prioritise "hubs-and-brokers", mobs, key agents like opinion leaders and groomers within terrorist networks, disseminator accounts that provide inspiration and information on ground, and "throwaway accounts" which distribute intergroup conflict propaganda that lingers online for a limited duration (Gupta *et al.*, 2015; Conway *et al.*, 2017). A dilemma that authorities face is to either permit the presence of such hidden cells and networks to gather information and track members, or to instantly shut down the accounts. Frameworks and criterions that define and evaluate conditions and thresholds based on short- and long-term objectives and consequences could be developed in order to gauge the risks involved.

In addition to the focus on different radicalisation processes and locales such as prison, school, or place of worship, analysts may stratify small-cell radicalisation sources into discrete groups that attract individuals with different predispositions and skills "such as foreign fighters vs. homegrown fighters, bomb-makers vs. bomb-planters, and group-actors vs. lone-actors" (Gill *et al.*, 2017, p. 100). These categorisations may draw on the complementarity between online and offline interactions which could help to populate, (re)-distribute, and reinforce extremist narratives and behaviours, as well as attack plans and preparations (Corner *et al.*, 2016). Utilising observations from social network analyses of intragroup and intergroup dynamics, leaders in political, social, and religious spheres could build and maintain affiliation and trust with at-risk individuals, which may avert potential attacks (Goh, 2018). Law enforcement agencies may partner with established and start-up app designers (messaging, wallet, and networking apps) to identify opportunities for product exploitation, manipulation, and improvement, and develop pre-emptive solutions to alert, monitor, and regulate functions like private channels and secret terminology that enable violent extremist groups to operate unsuspectingly.

Approach 3: Synthesising Predictive Drivers and Assessments of High-risk Returnees and Violent Extremists

A pressing challenge in effectively triaging foreign terrorist fighters who return to their homelands, is the paucity of specifically developed risk assessment instruments (Radicalisation Awareness Network — Centre of Excellence (RAN CoE), 2017), while established and adaptive tools like CYBER-VERA (Pressman & Ivan, 2016) and SAVE (Dean & Pettet, 2017) assess the risk of would-be violent extremists. In contrast, the RAN CoE Returnee 45 (Lynch, 2017; Radicalisation Awareness Network — Centre of Excellence RAN CoE, 2017 is an investigative tool that is specialised for operational planning and intervention management, and measures the overall risk of a returnee who might still be preoccupied with violent extremist ideologies and domestic attack plans or has truly denounced from the group. These risk assessments could be integrated with computational methods like digital forensics intelligence and social media intelligence, where trends on discussions, opinions, and behavioural patterns could be collected for data mining analyses to track offenders in real time. Through this multidisciplinary and component process, vulnerability (and protective) markers as well as socio-demographic variations could be harvested and mapped onto sequential and temporal processes that vary for sympathisers, lone actors, returnees susceptible to recidivism, and propaganda disseminators (Gill *et al.*, 2017). In addition to interventions, these trajectories could be translated into machine learning-enabled forensic technologies that could aid greater analytical power and timely decision-making for intelligence services.

The Online Violent Extremism Screening Tool, for example, is an on-going initiative undertaken by the Home Team Behavioural Sciences Centre (HTBSC) in Singapore, to detect individuals who might be involved in online violent extremism and to prioritise suitable interventions ("Tool to help police spot suspects engaging in extremism being developed", 2016). Similarly, Camacho *et al.* (2016) developed the RiskTrack software tool that utilises behavioural sciences and computational informatics methods to trace individuals with high risk of being radicalised and committed to violence by measuring "signs and characteristics" from their interactions in online social networks. Obtaining promising initial results, the tool, which is currently a prototype, aims to encompass a more comprehensive set of person- and group-based risk indicators, which could identify how nonlinear dynamics in online violent extremist communities may support pre-attack actions (Gilpérez-López *et al.*, 2017). Focused on media-sharing social networks, the U.K. Home Office and ASI Data Science jointly created an AI-based algorithmic system which is able to filter ISIS propaganda material on the web, based on typical features like logos and soundtracks, for removal (Lee, 2018). Efforts to strengthen the tool include sharing the tool with smaller and upcoming social media platforms that may have inadequate resources, extending its detection functions beyond ISIS to other violent extremist groups, identifying individuals who consistently re-upload deleted content, and detecting changes in language and style of violent extremist groups.

Approach 4: Interpreting and Responding to Costly Signalling from Violent Extremist Groups

In an interview with the Washington Post news agency in 2014, the former U.S. Director of National Intelligence James Clapper reported that "[w]e underestimated ISIL [ISIS] ... which is an imponderable" (Payne, 2014). Likewise, Lahoud and Collins (2016) proposed that the misjudgements of viewing ISIS through the lens of AQ and aggregating regional terrorist groups as affiliated with AQ instead of discerning their differences on a microlevel so as to formulate appropriate counter-approaches may have led to oversights in anticipating ISIS's global rise. In the same way, the heavy and unforeseen reliance on encrypted messaging apps like Skype and Telegram (Al-Rawi, 2016; Bloom *et al.*, 2016) demonstrates the tactical innovation of terrorist groups to constantly search for means to conceal their communications and readily change platforms as virtual environments become more hostile. Interpretations and responses to costly signals like attacks and threats from violent extremists thus could be developed appropriately through reduced dependency on the use of past knowledge of terrorist organisations and assumptions about the continuity of current events, to understand emergent developments. Conversely, understanding how different classes of costly signals and countermeasures by security agencies may reinforce intent, attitudes, and behaviours of militancy like deliberate provocation, vehicular attacks, and hostage-takings. Simulations based on past intergroup conflicts could be created to understand how signals are exchanged between security agencies, types of violent extremist groups, and other actors (i.e., civilians and media) related to attack planning and preparations, target and weapon selection, lethality of *modus operandi*, shifts in the rules of engagement from low-intensity intergroup conflicts which may be predictive of future attacks.

Approach 5: Influencing Competitive Terrorist Relationships Among Opposing Groups

Accentuating the dissension and accusations that rival violent extremist groups level amongst themselves could generate unease and hesitations for fence-sitting radicals, which may render radicalisation and violent extremism as less attractive (Novenario, 2016). Besides underlining the outbidding between groups, counter-messaging approaches could create awareness by highlighting defections of senior ideologues like Abu Bakar Ba'asyir who once praised AQ's activities, but defected to ISIS and had later rejected the group's brutal methods (Soeriaatmadja, 2016). Religious leaders may call attention to flawed theological reasonings adopted by violent extremist groups, to subvert their legitimacy and authority more credibly. Headed by Speckhard and her colleagues, the "ISIS Defectors Interviews Project 2016" is a compilation of life experiences shared by young and old ISIS members who renounced the group (Speckhard & Yayla, 2016).

Highly revealing about the life of an ISIS member, these textual memes of defectors could include more movie-like appeal and certain narrative content such as "[b]edtime was 10 p.m. We had to wake up for morning prayers and shower in cold water. A lot of people cried..." that may appeal to individuals who pursue disciplined and routine lifestyles, but might not effectively repel the group's governance, ways of life, and ideologies (Speckhard & Yayla, 2016). Fostering mutual knowledge, these narratives could be shared with non-Muslims communities and converts who could be vulnerable to misinformation. Disrupting outbidding attacks by violent extremist groups would require timely and accurate, information-sharing and shared situational awareness on national and international levels, which may involve long-term, multi stakeholder participation. However, historical instances of strange bedfellows and unholy alliances have often illustrated how shared hatred towards common foe(s) may override intergroup rivalry. Mergers may enable terrorist groups to share resources, spread information, and access new technological capabilities, which may lead to more lethality and longer survivability (Phillips, 2018).

References

Ahmed, S., & Matthes, J. (2017). Media representation of Muslims and Islam from 2000 to 2015: A meta-analysis. *International Communication Gazette*, *79*(3), 219–244.

Alimi, E. Y., Bosi, L., & Demetriou, C. (2015). *The Dynamics of Radicalization: A Relational and Comparative Perspective*. New York: Oxford University Press.

Al-Krenawi, A. (2017). *Building Peace through Knowledge*. Cham, Switzerland: Springer International Publishing AG.

Al-Rawi, A. (2016). Video games, terrorism, and ISIS's Jihad 3.0. *Terrorism and Political Violence*, 1–21.

Aly, A. (2017). Brothers, believers, brave mujahideen: Focusing attention on the audience of violent jihadist preachers. *Studies in Conflict & Terrorism*, *40*(1), 62–76.

Baaken, T., & Schlegel, L. (2017). Fishermen or swarm dynamics? Should we understand jihadist online-radicalization as a top-down or bottom-up process? *Journal for Deradicalization*, *13*, 178–212.

Biberman, Y., & Zahid, F. (2016). Why terrorists target children: Outbidding, desperation, and extremism in the Peshawar and Beslan school massacres. *Terrorism and Political Violence*, 1–16.

Bloom, M., Tiflati, H., & Horgan, J. (2017). Navigating ISIS's preferred platform: Telegram1. *Terrorism and Political Violence*, 1–13.

Böhm, R., Rusch, H., & Baron, J. (2018). The psychology of intergroup conflict: A review of theories and measures. *Journal of Economic Behavior & Organization*. In Press. Advance Online Publication: https://doi.org/10.1016/j.jebo.2018.01.020.

Borum, R. (2015). Assessing risk for terrorism involvement. *Journal of Threat Assessment and Management*, *2*(2), 63–87.

Bryant, E. (2016). Hollande under fire after Nice attack. *Deutsche Welle*. Retrieved from http://www.dw.com/en/hollande-under-fire-after-nice-attack/a-19409689.

Byman, D. (2016). The jihadist returnee threat: Just how dangerous? *Political Science Quarterly*, *131*(1), 69–99.

Callimachi, R. (2016). How ISIS built the machinery of terror under Europe's gaze. *The New York Times*. Retrieved from http://www.nytimes.com/2016/03/29/world/europe/isis-attacks-paris-brussels.html?_r=0.

Camacho, D., Gilpérez-López, I., Gonzalez-Pardo, A., Ortigosa, A., & Urruela, C. (2016). *CEUR Workshop Proceedings*. Retrieved from http://ceur-ws.org/Vol-1794/afcai16-paper5.pdf.

Carrapico, H., Irrera, D., & Tupman, D. (2014). Transnational organized crime and terrorism: Different peas, same pod? *Global Crime*, *3*(4), 213–218.

Cherney, A., & Murphy, K. (2017). Police and community cooperation in counterterrorism: Evidence and insights from Australia. *Studies in Conflict & Terrorism*, *40*(12), 1,023–1,037.

Choi, S. W. (2018). *Emerging Security Challenges: American Jihad, Terrorism, Civil War, and Human Rights*. Santa Barbara: Praeger.

Christensen, D. A., & Aars, J. (2017). The 22 July terrorist attacks in Norway: Impact on public attitudes towards counterterrorist authorities. *Scandinavian Political Studies*, *40*(3), 312–329.

Christie, D. J., & Louis, W. R. (2012). Peace interventions tailored to phases within a cycle of intergroup violence. In L. Tropp (Ed.), *The Oxford Handbook of Intergroup Conflict* (pp. 252–272). New York: Oxford University Press.

Clarke, C. P. (2016). Drugs & thugs: Funding terrorism through narcotics trafficking. *Journal of Strategic Security*, *9*(3), 1–17.

Cohen, S. J., Kruglanski, A., Gelfand, M. J., Webber, D., & Gunaratna, R. (2016). Al-Qaeda's propaganda decoded: A psycholinguistic system for detecting variations in terrorism ideology. *Terrorism and Political Violence*, *30*(1), 142–171.

Conrad, J., & Greene, K. (2015). Competition, differentiation, and the severity of terrorist attacks. *The Journal of Politics*, *77*(2), 546–561.

Conway, M., Khawaja, M., Lakhani, S., Reffin, J., Robertson, A., & Weir, D. (2017). Disrupting Daesh: Measuring takedown of online terrorist material and it's impacts. *VOX-Pol Network of Excellence* (pp. 1–47). Retrieved from http://www.voxpol.eu/download/vox-pol_publication/DCUJ5528-Disrupting-DAESH-1706-WEB-v2.pdf.

Corner, E., Gill, P., & Mason, O. (2016). Mental health disorders and the terrorist: A research note probing selection effects and disorder prevalence. *Studies in Conflict & Terrorism*, *39*(6), 560–568.

Ćosić, K., Srbljinović, A., & Popović, S. (2018). Emotionally based strategic communications in the process of societal deradicalization. *International Journal of Strategic Communication*, *12*(2), 196–214.

Crijns, H., Cauberghe, V., & Hudders, L. (2017). Terrorism threat in Belgium: The resilience of Belgian citizens and the protection of governmental reputation by means of communication. *Public Relations Review*, *43*(1), 219–234.

Dean, G., & Pettet, G. (2017). The 3 R's of risk assessment for violent extremism. *Journal of Forensic Practice*, *19*(2), 91–101.

Decker, S. H., & Pyrooz, D. C. (2015). "I'm down for a Jihad": How 100 years of gang research can inform the study of terrorism, radicalization and extremism. *Perspectives on Terrorism*, *9*(1), 1–9.

Dovidio, J. F. (2013). Bridging intragroup processes and intergroup relations: Needing the twain to meet. *British Journal of Social Psychology*, *52*(1), 1–24.

Freeman, L., Schroeder, R., & Everton, S. F. (2017). Social media exploitation by covert networks: A case study of ISIS. *Communications of the Association for Information Systems*, *41*(1), 97–120.

Gielen, A. J. (2017). Countering violent extremism: A realist review for assessing what works, for whom, in what circumstances, and how? *Terrorism and Political Violence*, 1–19.

Gill, P., Corner, E., Conway, M., Thornton, A., Bloom, M., & Horgan, J. (2017). Terrorist use of the internet by the numbers: Quantifying behaviors, patterns and processes. *Criminology & Public Policy*, *16*(1), 99–117.

Gilpérez-López, I., Torregrosa, J., Barhamgi, M., & Camacho, D. (2017). An initial study on radicalization risk factors: Towards an assessment software tool. *Paper Presented at 28th International Workshop on Database and Expert Systems Applications (DEXA), Lyon, France.*

Glad, K. A., Thoresen, S., Hafstad, G. S., & Dyb, G. (2017). Survivors report back: Young people reflect on their media experiences after a terrorist attack. *Journalism Studies*, 1–17.

Glazzard, A., Jesperson, S., Maguire, T., & Winterbotham, E. (2017). *Conflict, Violent Extremism and Development: New Challenges, New Responses*. Cham: Springer.

Goh, C. (2018). Religious leaders must understand how followers interpret what they teach: Masagos. *Channel NewsAsia*. Retrieved from https://www.channelnewsasia.com/news/asiapacific/religious-leaders-must-understand-followers-interpret-masagos-9949726.

Grinnell, D. (2017). Interpreting public reactions to terrorist events using open source network analysis. In M. Conway *et al.* (Eds.), *Terrorists' use of the Internet: Assessment and Response* (pp. 290–304). Amsterdam, NL: IOS Press.

Gupta, D. K., Spitzberg, B., Tsou, M. H., An, L., & Gawron, J. M. (2015). Ideas and violence. In L. Fenstermacher (Ed.), *Countering Violent*

Extremism: Scientific Methods and Strategies (pp. 44–55). Dayton, OH: Air University Press.

Hafez, M. (2016). The ties that bind: How terrorists exploit family bonds. *CTC Sentinel*, *9*(2), 15–17.

Hamming, T. R. (2017). The Al Qaeda–Islamic State Rivalry: Competition yes, but no competitive escalation. *Terrorism and Political Violence*, 1–18.

Hanes, E., & Machin, S. (2014). Hate crime in the wake of terror attacks: Evidence from 7/7 and 9/11. *Journal of Contemporary Criminal Justice*, *30*(3), 247–267.

Hastings, J. V., & Chan, R. J. (2013). Target hardening and terrorist signaling: The case of aviation security. *Terrorism and Political Violence*, *25*(5), 777–797.

Hoffman, B. (2016). The coming ISIS–Al Qaeda merger: It's time to take the threat seriously. *Foreign Affairs*. Retrieved from https://www.foreignaffairs.com/articles/2016-03-29/coming-isis-al-qaeda-merger.

Horgan, J., Altier, M. B., Shortland, N., & Taylor, M. (2017). Walking away: The disengagement and de-radicalization of a violent right-wing extremist. *Behavioral Sciences of Terrorism and Political Aggression*, *9*(2), 63–77.

Hsu, H. Y., & McDowall, D. (2017). Does target-hardening result in deadlier terrorist attacks against protected targets? An examination of unintended harmful consequences. *Journal of Research in Crime and Delinquency*, *54*(6), 930–957.

Jetter, M. (2017). The effect of media attention on terrorism. *Journal of Public Economics*, *153*, 32–48.

Kaakinen, M., Oksanen, A., & Räsänen, P. (2018). Did the risk of exposure to online hate increase after the November 2015 Paris attacks? A group relations approach. *Computers in Human Behavior*, *78*, 90–97.

Kearns, E. M., Conlon, B., & Young, J. K. (2014). Lying about terrorism. *Studies in Conflict & Terrorism*, *37*(5), 422–439.

Kenney, M., Coulthart, S., & Wright, D. (2017). Structure and performance in a violent extremist network: The small-world solution. *Journal of Conflict Resolution*, *61*(10), 2,208–2,234.

Kettle, L., & Mumford, A. (2017). Terrorist learning: A new analytical framework. *Studies in Conflict & Terrorism*, *40*(7), 523–538.

Khalil, J. (2017). The three pathways (3P) model of violent extremism: A framework to guide policymakers to the right questions about their preventive countermeasures. *The RUSI Journal*, *162*(4), 40–48.

Knoke, D. (2015). Emerging trends in social network analysis of terrorism and counterterrorism. In R. Scott, & S. Kosslyn (Eds.), *Emerging Trends in the Social and Behavioral Sciences: An interdisciplinary, Searchable, and Linkable Resource* (pp. 1–15). New York: John Wiley & Sons Inc.

Koehler-Derrick, G., & Milton, D. J. (2017). Choose your weapon: The impact of strategic considerations and resource constraints on terrorist group weapon selection. *Terrorism and Political Violence*, 1–20.

Kydd, A. H., & Walter, B. F. (2006). The strategies of terrorism. *International Security*, *31*(1), 49–80.

Lahoud, N., & Collins, L. (2016). How the CT community failed to anticipate the Islamic State. *Democracy and Security*, *12*(3), 199–210.

Lee, D. (2018). U. K. unveils extremism blocking tool. *BBC News*. Retrieved from http://www.bbc.com/news/technology-43037899.

Lin, Y. R., Margolin, D., & Wen, X. (2017). Tracking and analyzing individual distress following terrorist attacks using social media streams. *Risk Analysis*, *37*(8), 1,580–1,605.

Lindekilde, L., O'Connor, F., & Schuurman, B. (2017). Radicalization patterns and modes of attack planning and preparation among lone-actor terrorists: An exploratory analysis. *Behavioral Sciences of Terrorism and Political Aggression*, 1–21.

Lynch, O. (2017). Understanding radicalisation: Implications for criminal justice practitioners. *Irish Probation Journal*, *14*, 78–91.

Lyons-Padilla, S., Gelfand, M. J., Mirahmadi, H., Farooq, M., & van Egmond, M. (2015). Belonging nowhere: Marginalization & radicalization risk among Muslim immigrants. *Behavioral Science & Policy*, *1*(2), 1–12.

Mair, D. (2016). #Westgate: A case study: How al-Shabaab used Twitter during an ongoing attack. *Studies in Conflict & Terrorism*, *40*(1), 24–43.

Malthaner, S. (2017). Processes of political violence and the dynamics of situational interaction. *International Journal of Conflict and Violence, 11*, 1–10.

Marone, F. (2017). Ties that bind: Dynamics of group radicalisation in Italy's jihadists headed for Syria and Iraq. *The International Spectator*, *52*(3), 48–63.

McCauley, C. (2017). Misunderstanding terrorism (Book review). *Dynamics of Asymmetric Conflict: Pathways Toward Terrorism and Genocide*, *10*(1), 74–77.

McCauley, C., & Moskalenko, S. (2017). Understanding political radicalization: The two-pyramids model. *American Psychologist*, *72*(3), 205–216.

McGilloway, A., Ghosh, P., & Bhui, K. (2015). A systematic review of pathways to and processes associated with radicalization and extremism amongst Muslims in Western societies. *International Review of Psychiatry*, *27*(1), 39–50.

Monahan, J. (2012). The individual risk assessment of terrorism. *Psychology, Public Policy & the Law*, 18, 167–205.

Nemeth, S. (2014). The effect of competition on terrorist group operations. *Journal of Conflict Resolution*, *58*(2), 336–362.

Neo, L. S., Khader, M., Ang, J., Ong, G., & Tan, E. (2017). Developing an early screening guide for jihadi terrorism: A behavioural analysis of 30 terror attacks. *Security Journal*, *30*(1), 227–246.

Novenario, C. M. I. (2016). Differentiating Al Qaeda and the Islamic State through strategies publicized in jihadist magazines. *Studies in Conflict & Terrorism*, *39*(11), 953–967.

Parker, D., Pearce, J. M., Lindekilde, L., & Rogers, M. B. (2017). Challenges for effective counterterrorism communication: Practitioner insights and policy implications for preventing radicalization, disrupting attack planning, and mitigating terrorist attacks. *Studies in Conflict & Terrorism*, 1–28.

Payne, S. (2014). Obama: U.S. misjudged the rise of the Islamic State, ability of Iraqi army. *The Washington Post*. Retrieved from https://www.washingtonpost.com/world/national-security/obama-us-underestimated-the-rise-of-the-islamic-state-ability-of-iraqi-army/2014/09/28/9417ab26-4737-11e4-891d-713f052086a0_story.html?utm_term=.3742786e9122.

Phillips, B. J. (2015). Enemies with benefits? Violent rivalry and terrorist group longevity. *Journal of Peace Research*, *52*(1), 62–75.

Phillips, B. J. (2018). Terrorist group rivalries and alliances: Testing competing explanations. *Studies in Conflict & Terrorism*, 1–23.

Pressman, D. E., & Ivan, C. (2016). Internet use and violent extremism: A cyber-VERA risk assessment protocol. In M. Khader, L. S. Neo, G. Ong, E. Tan, & J. Chin (Eds.), *Combating Violent Extremism and Radicalization in the Digital Era* (pp. 391–409). US: IGI Global.

Radicalisation Awareness Network — Centre of Excellence (RAN CoE). (2017, July). *RAN Manual: Responses to Returnees: Foreign Terrorist Fighters and their Families*. Retrieved from https://ec.europa.eu/home-affairs/sites/homeaffairs/files/ran_br_a4_m10_en.pdf.

Ranstorp, M. (2016). Microfinancing the Caliphate: How the Islamic State is unlocking the assets of European recruits, *CTC Sentinel*, *9*(5), 11–15.

Reedy, J., Gastil, J., & Gabbay, M. (2013). Terrorism and small groups: An analytical framework for group disruption. *Small Group Research*, *44*(6), 599–626.

Sageman, M. (2016). *Misunderstanding Terrorism*. Philadelphia: University of Pennsylvania Press.

Salomon, G. (2004). Does peace education make a difference in the context of an intractable conflict? *Peace and Conflict*, *10*(3), 257–274.

Schuurman, B., Bakker, E., Gill, P., & Bouhana, N. (2017). Lone actor terrorist attack planning and preparation: A data-driven analysis. *Journal of Forensic Sciences*, 1–10.

Singh, R. (2017). A preliminary typology mapping pathways of learning and innovation by modern jihadist groups. *Studies in Conflict & Terrorism*, *40*(7), 624–644.

Smith, M., & Walsh, J. I. (2013). Do drone strikes degrade Al Qaeda? Evidence from propaganda output. *Terrorism and Political Violence*, *25*, 311–327.

Soeriaatmadja, W. (2016). Bashir withdraws support for ISIS. *The Straits Times*. Retrieved from: http://www.straitstimes.com/asia/bashir-withdraws-support-for-isis.

Speckhard, A., & Shajkovci, A. (2018). How can Hollywood help fight ISIS and similar terrorist groups? *ICSVE Brief Reports*. Retrieved from http://www.icsve.org/brief-reports/how-can-hollywoo...terrorist-groups.

Speckhard, A., & Yayla, A. S. (2016). *ISIS Defectors: Inside Stories of the Terrorist Caliphate*. McLean, VA: Advances Press, LLC.

Speckhard, A., & Yayla, A. S. (2017). The ISIS Emni: The origins and inner workings of ISIS's intelligence apparatus. *Perspectives on Terrorism*, *11*(1), 1–15.

Speckhard, A., Shajkovci, A., & Yayla, A. (2017). Following a military defeat of ISIS in Syria and Iraq: What happens next after the military victory and the return of foreign fighters? *Journal of Terrorism Research*, *8*(1), 81–89.

Stern, J. (2016). Radicalization to extremism and mobilization to violence: What have we learned and what can we do about it? *The ANNALS of the American Academy of Political and Social Science*, *668*(1), 102–117.

Tool to help police spot suspects engaging in extremism being developed. (2016, July 13) *Channel NewsAsia*. Retrieved from https://www.channelnewsasia.com/news/singapore/tool-to-help-police-spot-suspects-engaging-in-extremism-being-de-7912602.

Tyner, E. (2016). Do territorial control and the loss of territory determine the use of indiscriminate violence by incumbent actors? An examination of the Syrian civil war in Aleppo over 45 weeks. *Journal of Terrorism Research*, 7(1), 52–66.

Victoroff, J., Adelman, J. R., & Matthews, M. (2012). Psychological factors associated with support for suicide bombing in the Muslim diaspora. *Political Psychology*, *33*(6), 791–809.

Warrick, J. (2018). '*We are in your home*': After losses, ISIS steps up campaign to inspire attacks. *The Washington Post*. Retrieved from https://www.washingtonpost.com/world/national-security/we-are-in-your-home-after-losses-isis-steps-up-campaign-to-inspire-attacks/2018/01/22/421678a4-f7d6-11e7-a9e3-ab18ce41436a_story.html?utm_term=.e8846912c4ac.

Wikström, P. O. H., & Bouhana, N. (2016). Analyzing radicalization and terrorism: A situational action theory. In G. LaFree, & J. D. Freilich (Eds.), *The Handbook of the Criminology of Terrorism* (pp. 175–186). MA: John Wiley & Sons Inc.

Winter, C., & Clarke, C. P. (2017). Is ISIS breaking apart?: What its media operations suggest. *Foreign Affairs*. Retrieved from https://www.foreignaffairs.com/articles/2017-01-31/isis-breaking-apart.

Young, J. K., & Dugan, L. (2014). Survival of the fittest: Why terrorist groups endure. *Perspectives on Terrorism*, *8*(2), 2–23.

Zech, S., & Kelly, Z. (2015). Off with their heads: The Islamic State and civilian beheadings. *Journal of Terrorism Research*, 6(2), 1–11.

CHAPTER 12

Engaging Youths in Counter-Violent Extremism (CVE) Initiatives

THOMAS KORUTH SAMUEL

Southeast Asia Regional Centre for Counter-Terrorism (SEARCCT), Ministry of Foreign Affairs, Malaysia

Introduction

On 26 May 2014, Ahmad Tarmimi Maliki had the "dubious honour" of being the first Malaysian suicide bomber linked to *Daesh* when he blew up 25 elite Iraqi soldiers at Iraq's SWAT headquarters in the al-Anbar province. Reports indicated that he drove a "military SUV which was filled with tonnes of explosives" into the SWAT headquarters, killing himself in the process. Tarmimi's actions together with his photograph was subsequently reported in *Daesh*'s official website with the heading, *Mujahidin Malaysia Syahid Dalam Operasi Martyrdom* describing Tarmimi as Malaysia's first suicide bomber. He was 27 years old when he died ("ISIS and the first Malaysian suicide bomber", 2014).

Muhammad Wanndy Mohamed Jedi, also known as Abu Hamzah Al Fateh, left for Raqqa, Syria with his wife in 2014 and was reportedly killed on 26 April 2017 in a drone attack there. He caught the attention of the Malaysian public when he appeared in a video that showed the beheading of a Syrian man. He also developed the skills and networking for both fundraising and recruiting and was linked to at "least a third of the more than 250 people arrested for ISIL-linked activities in Malaysia between 2013 and 2016" ("Top Malaysian ISIL operative killed in Syria", 2017). Significantly, he was credited to be the mastermind behind the Movida-Puchong attack which injured eight people in June 2016, and which thus far remains the sole *Daesh*-inspired attack in Malaysia. Given these developments, Wanndy was named "Specially Designated Global Terrorist" making him a "high-profile target for law enforcement agencies worldwide" ("Top Malaysian ISIL operative killed in Syria", 2017). He was 26 years old when he died.

The capacity and capability of terrorists to identify, indoctrinate, and recruit young people is something that has grown in scale, threat, and impact. This chapter attempts to have a better understanding on this phenomenon by delineating the issues and challenges and subsequently proposing some ideas and recommendations. For purposes of clarity, the terms "terrorism" and "violent extremism" are used interchangeably in this chapter.

Youth and Violence

Peter Singer in his book, "Children at War", gave a glimpse of the extent of the problem. 300,000 boys and girls under the age of 18 are combatants fighting in almost 75% of the world's conflicts (Singer, 2005). Eighty percent of these conflicts where children are present include fighters under the age of 15, and approximately 40% of the armed organisations in the world (157 of 366) use child soldiers (Singer, 2005).

Militants often times target youth, ranging in age from early teens to young adults (J. Liow, personal communication, March 10, 2011), while males between the ages of 18 and 35 have always been the focus of terrorist organisations such as the Japanese Red Army and the Red Brigade based in Italy (K. Ramakrishna, personal communication, March 9, 2011). In Indonesia, terrorist organisations such as *Darul Islam* have targeted people as young as 16 to 17 years old (N.H. Ismail, personal communication, April 5, 2011).

The Mumbai attacks that took place in November 2008 which left 165 individuals dead were a series of 10 coordinated attacks orchestrated by 10 individuals. The common denominator between the 10 perpetrators? They were all young. Besides the eldest terrorist, Nazir (Abu Umer) who was 28 years old, the average age of the other nine terrorists was only 23 years old. The leader, Ismail Khan, was just 25 years old (Samuel, 2012).

Abdurajak Janjalani, the founder of the *Abu Sayyaf Group* (ASG), was in his 20s when he showed interest in terrorist activities, and only 26 when he formed the ASG. When he died in 1998, his 22-year-old younger brother, Khadaffy Janjalani, took over as the new *emir*, or leader, of the ASG. In 2009, the ASG was led by Yasser Igasan who was only 21 years old when he joined the movement (Banlaoi, 2009).

The link between youths and terrorist organisations was further highlighted when the U.K.'s MI5 Chief, Mr. Jonathan Evans, went on record to state that "extremists were methodically and intentionally targeting young people and children in the U.K.", and that groups like Al-Qaeda were recruiting children as young as 15 to wage "a deliberate campaign of terror" in Britain (Johnston, 2007). He further reiterated that terrorists were "radicalising, indoctrinating and grooming young, vulnerable people to carry out acts of terrorism" and that urgent action was required on the part of the U.K. Government "to protect its children from exploitation by violent extremists" (Johnston, 2007).

Perhaps the reality of the involvement of young people in terrorism was best seen in the Guantanamo Bay detention facilities, when the authorities had to set up Camp Iguana, a detention facility dedicated to juvenile detainees aged between 13 and 15 years ("Guantanamo bay-Camp delta", 2011), while those between the ages of 16 and 18 were held at the adult facility, Camp X-Ray (Singer, 2005).

What are the challenges that we face and subsequently how then could we possibly proceed?

Challenges

The Lack of Data

Copernicus was once said to have remarked, "to know that we know what we know, and to know that we do not know what we do not know, that is true knowledge" (Big Think Editors, 2014).

With regard to the relationship between youth and radicalisation, there is precious little that we know and there is a lot that we do not know. That has ironically not stopped us from forming policy, developing guidelines, and carrying out programmes.

A dangerous cocktail of ignorance, a misplaced sense that doing something must be better than doing nothing and arrogance.

This has to stop.

A good place to start is to make an inventory of the precious little that we do know and more importantly what we need to know.

Understanding the terrorist message

Terrorism can be understood in the context of "communication and propaganda" and is often times seen as a "combination of both violence and propaganda" to "advertise" (Schmid & Graaf, 1982), and convince others on the groups' potential to cause "harm and to destroy" (Schmid, 2005). This propaganda forms the basis of the terrorist narrative. Steven R. Corman points out that "narratives are powerful resources for influencing target audiences; they offer an alternative form of rationality deeply rooted in culture, which can be used to interpret and frame local events and to strategically encourage particular kinds of personal action" (Corman, 2011).

Given this, analysis needs to be conducted on understanding the message and narrative of the terrorists that are targeting the youth with the view that such understanding would then better equip us to design both a counter-narrative and an alternative narrative for the youth. Only once we have understood the message and appeal of their narrative, could we begin to decipher the reasons, logic and rationale behind the decision of the youth to either support or sympathise with the terrorists.

Identifying the messenger

There is also the need to seek out the characteristics of the *terrorist* messenger who is bringing forth their message to the youth. Under whose guidance is the terrorist propaganda being crafted and disseminated to the youth?

Is it the terrorist ideologues from places such as Syria or Iraq who are developing the terrorist message and call to the youths?

Or is it home-grown terrorists, who are the voice radicalising and recruiting potential youths in the region?

Could it be returning foreign terrorist fighters, who having tasted battle now have the "street credentials" and therefore are able to appeal to the youth?

Or is it influential YouTubers or cyber troopers, who have never seen combat but are nevertheless looked up and idolised by their young followers over cyberspace?

Given that the characteristics of the terrorist messengers described above differ, it would most likely follow that their skill set, talent, influence, and target audience could also vary. Therefore, a more nuanced understanding on such messengers would certainly be very useful in either countering their message or blunting their appeal among the youth.

Isolating the specific target audience

While we are focused on the youth, the demographic is nevertheless extremely large and diverse. Among the subcategories of the youth would include youths from religious schools and institutions seeking to uphold their religious beliefs, youths seeking to atone for their past perceived failures, youths looking for adventure and thrills, youths undergoing a personal crisis, youths from broken homes, youths from difficult social-economic positions, youths who were recently converted and have a new-found misguided religious fervour, idealistic youths wanting to make a difference, angry youths wanting to seek revenge, youths wanting to defend the "oppressed", youths who were misinformed, youths seeking love/relationships, youths undergoing an identity crisis, and youths wanting something new in life.[1]

To better understand these subcategories, it would be useful to tap into experts and "gatekeepers". Gatekeepers could be defined as individuals or organisations that have access to those specific subgroups, and this could include parents, teachers, lecturers, religious leaders and workers, counsellors, youth workers, siblings, YouTubers, and online personalities. Due to their close proximity and access to these specific subcategories, these gatekeepers have the potential to understand both the thinking and behavioural patterns of the youth, and could provide valuable information and insight into subtle shifts in the thought process and actions of the youths in their spheres.

The Lack of Passion

Terrorism is often times cited as a classic example of "asymmetric warfare". However, many a times, there is also an asymmetry of passion displayed between the terrorists, and particularly between the policymakers involved in counter-terrorism. This imbalance is frequently picked up by the youth who place a great deal of emphasis on passion and idealism. The perceived bureaucratic and patronising manner in which policymakers deal with the issue of the youth and their involvement in terrorism is often times compared to the seemingly "passionate" call of the terrorists to the youth to join "a cause worthy of their potential". There is little doubt on who stands the better chance to draw the youths.

Hence, we need to attract the "right" people who would be infectious with their drive and able to inspire the young people to

---

[1]This is not an exhaustive list.

discover the truths about the terrorists. As I mentioned in my earlier writings:

> We need to hire passionate people in counter-terrorism who will literally shake us from our slumber. We need to get victims of terrorism and former rehabilitated terrorists and institutionalise them in our counter-terrorism intervention programmes; from the planning to the implementation stage. We need to find officials, academics and policymakers who have fire in their bellies and like the terrorists, want to be in no other place, but in the thick of the battle. In short, we need to have a shake-up in the system and redesign it in such a way that will allow the entry of such passionate people in the field of counter terrorism (Samuel, 2016).

The Lack of Creativity

One cannot compartmentalise youth, counter-terrorism, and creativity. Indeed, Navarro and Villaverde speak on the need, among others for, "loads of imagination" and "creative foresight" (Navarro & Villaverde, 2014). Often times, counter-terrorism programmes that focus on the youth use the same template, style, and setting that is used for every other programme. We are comfortable using the message, messenger, and medium on a target audience that thinks, feels, operates, and reacts in a completely different manner. Dominic Contreras in his article, *Terrorist Threat Demands Creative Intelligence*, quoted Rolf Mowatt-Larsses, a former Central Intelligence Agency (CIA) officer who observed that there was "a deficit in creative thinking regarding counter-terrorism ..." (Dominic, 2011–2012).

Hence, it is imperative that we redesign our programmes for the youth to cater for unorthodox and unconventional ways to reach out and impact them. While we must not abandon ideas and strategies that we have used with the youth that have and are working, we need new, creative, and innovative youth-based counter-terrorism strategies that will, God-willing, turn the tide. There is therefore an urgent need to get people with such creative and imaginative ideas on board to look at and redesign our youth-based programmes. It must be stressed that such people, whom might not necessarily be at the moment, part of our existing system or even part of the Government, as rightly observed by Navarro and Villaverde (2014) that "imagination is not common in bureaucracies". This needs to change, especially when we are targeting the youth.

The Possible Way Forward

Equipping the Youth

For too long, we have based our premise that youths are the target audience for our counter-violent extremism (CVE) work and that the authorities need to develop, facilitate, and conduct programmes and activities for them. The relationship has been that of a service-provider and client.

Perhaps, it is time to engage the youth to reach out to the youth. Given that young people are already familiar to their lingo, are themselves part of the target audience, and are already immersed in the medium, they would have a distinctive advantage over the authorities, who have to learn the "language" of the youth, understand their aspirations and desires, attempt to "break-into" their following, bridge the possible generational-divide, and most importantly, earn the trust (Samuel, 2018).

While the authorities should not completely step out of this field, they might perhaps take a backseat role and instead could collaborate, share, facilitate, and work with youth leaders, influencers, and change-agents among the youth. Hence, the new role of the authorities would be to seek out young people and facilitate *them* to reach out to their fellow peers.

In Malaysia, the Southeast Asia Regional Centre for Counter-Terrorism (SEARCCT), under the Ministry of Foreign Affairs, Malaysia, together with funding support from our international partner, decided to "walk the talk" and facilitated the "Student Leaders Against Youth Extremism and Radicalisation" (SLAYER) Workshop.

The workshops (we conducted two of these workshops in five days) brought 100 university undergraduate leaders from various races, religions, and cultures from all over Malaysia over a period of two-and-a-half days in April 2017 (Samuel, 2018). Each workshop was divided into four components. Firstly, we found young Malaysians such as Paralympians and celebrities, who could connect with youths and inspire them to realise the tremendous creativity, potential, and talents they possess. These speakers shared their triumphs and failures and showed the young people that heroes do not necessarily have to carry guns and lob grenades before they can make a difference.

Secondly, we brought in counter-terrorism experts to share with the young people the deceptive myths propagated by the terrorists. These experts, psychologists, and even former terrorists then went on to build mental and emotional "firewalls" in the hearts and minds of the young people.

Thirdly, we brought in our social media experts to show and teach the young people specific skills such as creating online digital banners and posters through readily available free software.

Lastly, we organised a hackathon, to give the young participants the platform not only to put theory into practise but more importantly to recognise and allow them the space to actively participate in countering violent extremism. Specifically, the youth designed digital end products to counter terrorists' claims.

Not only did we develop tremendous content, but the hackathon was organised in such a way that the young people were judged not only on the quality of their digital end products but also on the quantitative reach of their dissemination (i.e., how many likes the end products received). Hence, we not only developed content but were able to "push" that content to the people who needed to see it the most; the youth.

What did we achieve from this paradigm-shift of partnering the youth?

Qualitatively, we were able to train 100 young leaders in producing and disseminating digital CVE products. It did not end there. These young leaders then went back to their respective campuses and, on their own, initiated workshops and sessions for their fellow peers. They also became our strong advocates and started, *on their own*, to stress the importance of building "mental firewalls" in the hearts and minds of their peers.

In terms of quantitative results; we were amazed. With the assistance of the young people, SEARCCT's ability to produce digital content doubled and then tripled. Most significantly, in the five days that we had the two SLAYER workshops, our reach on social media increased[2] by a staggering 20,000%.[3]

Partnering with the youth paid off handsomely.

Developing Youth-based CVE Material

We are in dire need of youth-based CVE resources that would act as "mental firewalls" to prevent or, if necessary, deal with terrorist rhetoric and ideology. Among the specific tools that could be developed for the youth include animation, songs, modules, games, music videos, digital comic books, and guides, for focus group discussions, both online and offline, that would focus on both the counter and alternative narratives.

While countering the terrorist's narratives that are being disseminated among the youth are essential, it also means that the authorities are constantly reacting to the agenda set by the terrorist groups and are, most of the times, one step behind. Hence, there is an urgent need to develop an alternative narrative for the youth that tells or "retells" the story in a way that is positive, proactive, and creative. For example, presenting to the youth the idea that non-violence is a credible and viable model to address grievances would be a significant move. Given that terrorists advocate indiscriminate violence as a crude way to address all their grievances, there is therefore the urgent need for debunking the idea that violence is

[2]Due to the sensitivity of the nature of our work, I will not be publishing our account names on social media, but would welcome anyone who would like to know more to contact us directly.

[3]According to our Facebook analytics during that period of time.

effective in bringing about positive change and subsequently to propose models of non-violence as a possible alternative approach in addressing issues and challenges. To do this, we need to develop a more nuanced and robust concept of non-violence for the youth, which can subsequently be marketed as a contender to terrorism as a way to resolve grievances and resolve conflict.

In this regard, our past experiences with the youth has shown that they are drawn, not so much to academic arguments or theoretical models, but rather to real-life case studies. For example, the campaign against the slave trade by William Wilberforce, the movement for female suffrage by Susan B. Anthony, Carrie Chapman Catt, and numerous others, the Gandhian philosophy of *satyagraha* (devotion to truth), Nelson Mandela's struggle to overcome apartheid in South Africa, and Martin Luther King Jr.'s part in the American Civil Rights movement (Williams & Head, 2007) are excellent materials that would be well accepted by the youth. In this regard, it would even be better to showcase local and contextualised examples which would resonate even more with the young people.

Creating these products and tools for the youth would be a cross-cutting multidisciplinary endeavour that should involve psychologists, communications specialists, marketers, advertisers, content developers, editors, youth workers, and other relevant experts. In this regard, the role of advertisers and marketers must be thoroughly explored in developing intervention programmes to counter terrorism for the youth. These people are gifted with the ability to modify thinking, influence choices, and alter behaviour. Their expertise, knowledge, and experience particularly into the youth psyche as well as in campaigns to change their thinking, behaviour, and action would make them a potentially powerful ally in the efforts to win over the "hearts and minds" of the youth.

Identifying and Training Messengers

The efficacy of the message would greatly hinge upon the ability of the messenger to connect, engage, and be accepted by the youths. Potential messengers for the youth would include victims of terrorism, former terrorists who have been rehabilitated, television personalities, entertainment and sports celebrities and influential bloggers, "thought shapers", "opinion makers", and "influencers" over the Internet.

Former terrorists who have been rehabilitated and victims of terrorism offer a powerful story that could be harnessed in countering the terrorist narrative among the youth. For example, Indonesia's Nasir Abbas's (a former rehabilitated leader of *Jemaah Islamiyah*) compelling story and his understanding on the nuances of terrorism in Indonesia has made him a powerful tool in countering the terrorist narratives, particularly among school and university students.

Victims are also another source of powerful narratives that could provide a "powerful emotional narrative" that has the potential to "reinforce dissatisfaction" over the method and the approach taken by the terrorists (Williams & Head, 2007). Their story also has the potential to counter the often times evocative premise that the terrorists are representing and fighting for a victimised group of people. As highlighted by Schmid, "victim and survivor voices need not only be heard, but ought to be amplified" (Schmid, 2014).

Enhancing Dissemination

Having developed the content, identified, and trained the messengers, it is then vital that we disseminate the narrative to the youths. Among the possible ways that we could use to spread the message to the youth include public awareness talks, group discussions, lectures, and focus group discussions both on and offline.

Social media platforms, universities, high schools, faith-based and civil organisations play a significant role in the lives of the young people and have the potential to reach and impact the youth in a practical and sustainable manner and in ways that the authorities by themselves will never be able to replicate or duplicate. As mentioned in my earlier writings,

> Given their existing presence on the ground, coupled with the possible relationship already established with the people, perhaps

> the time has come for the counter-terrorism authorities to reach out to these conduits and train them instead of the status quo, which is to reach out to the people directly. For this to happen, the authorities need to grasp with the premise that the top-down hierarchical approach generally used in the past, might no longer be as effective and should instead consider using a partnership model, based on empowering certain segments of the community to reach out to the end user (Samuel, 2016).

Conclusion

Terrorists are targeting the youth. They see young people as the lynchpin that will determine their success. They are catering messages that directly appeal to the youth. These messages emphasise that they are fighting on behalf of a defenceless group of victims against a "godless" adversary, that indiscriminate violence is the only way as there is no other alternative, that their actions are legitimate, and that while there might be losses, victory will certainly be theirs in the near future.

The mediums that the terrorists are using are channels and platforms that the youths are already present and active in, thereby enabling the terrorists an unprecedented access and reach. The terrorists' ability to exploit social media through platforms such as Facebook, YouTube, Telegram, and Instagram has been both fascinating to study from a researcher's point of view and chilling to observe from the security standpoint.

The messengers that the terrorists have specifically used to develop, disseminate, and perpetuate their message have proven to be excellent in understanding the psyche of the youth as well as their innate desire for significance. Through sound bites such as YODO ["You Only Die Once — Make It Count"] (Underwood, 2016), and "sometimes people with the worst pasts create the best futures" (Gaub & Lisiecka, 2017), these terrorists have not only given meaning and significance to those who might be struggling with issues or personal crises, but also channels for these youths to express their devotion, sincerity, sense of sacrifice, courage, and desire to make a difference.

In the face of all these, while there have been exceptions, the stark reality is that we have little data to support any of our work in this particular area, limited creativity, and a dearth of passion. Our efforts to engage and get the youth on board CVE activities remain dismal, and the dissemination of relevant materials remain uncoordinated and disjointed.

Hence, there is a desperate need to both develop youth-based CVE material as well as equip the young people with the skill set to develop their own CVE content to appeal to their peers. There is a dire need to identify and train "messengers" that would be in the best position to identify, connect, and engage with the youth on matters pertaining to terrorism. Lastly, there is an urgent need to ensure that the message reaches the intended target group of youths. Until and unless these fundamental issues are addressed, youths will continue to be exploited and manipulated by terrorists.

References

Banlaoi, R. C. (2009). Youth as victims and perpetrators of terrorism: The Philippine case. *Paper presented at International Conference on Youth and Terrorism, Malaysia, 2014, February 26.*

Big Think Editors (2014). Copernicus on true knowledge. *Big Think.* Retrieved from http://bigthink.com/words-of-wisdom/copernicus-on-true-knowledge.

Corman, S. C. (2011). Understanding the role of narrative in extremist strategic communication. In L. Fenstermacher, & T. Leventhal (Eds.), *Countering Violent Extremism: Scientific Methods and Strategies* (pp. 35–43). Washington, DC: NSI Inc.

Dominic, C. (2011–2012). Terrorist threat demands creative intelligence. *Belfer Centre for Science and International Affairs.* Retrieved from https://www.belfercenter.org/publication/terrorist-threat-demands-creative-intelligence.

Gaub, F., & Lisiecka, J. (2017). The Crime-Terrorism Nexus. *European Union Institute for Security Studies (EUISS), 10.* Retrieved from https://www.iss.europa.eu/sites/default/files/EUISSFiles/Brief_10_Terrorism_and_crime.pdf.

Guantanamo bay-Camp delta (2011). *Global Security.* Retrieved from http://www.globalsecurity.org/military/facility/guantanamo-bay_delta.htm.

ISIS and the first Malaysian suicide bomber (2014). *The Star*. Retrieved from https://www.thestar.com.my/news/nation/2014/06/14/isis-and-the-first-malaysian-suicide-bomber/.

Johnston, P. (2007). MI5: Al-Qaeda recruiting U.K. children for terror. *The Telegraph*. Retrieved from https://www.telegraph.co.uk/news/uknews/1568363/MI5-Al-Qaeda-recruiting-UK-children-for-terror.html.

Navarro, J. M. B., & Villaverde, J. C. (2014). The future of counter-terrorism in Europe. The need to be lost in the correct direction. *European Journal of Futures Research*, 2, 50. Retrieved from https://link-springer-com.ezlibproxy1.ntu.edu.sg/content/pdf/10.1007%2Fs40309-014-0050-9.pdf.

Samuel, T. K. (2012). Reaching the youth: Countering the terrorist narrative. Malaysia: Ministry of Foreign Affairs. Retrieved from http://www.searcct.gov.my/images/PDF_My/publication/Reaching_the_Youth_Countering_The_Terrorist_Narrative.pdf.

Samuel, T. K. (2016). Radicalisation in Southeast Asia: A selected case study of Daesh in Indonesia, Malaysia and the Philippines. Malaysia: Ministry of Foreign Affairs. Retrieved from https://www.unodc.org/documents/southeastasiaandpacific/Publications/2016/Radicalisation_SEA_2016.pdf.

Samuel, T. K. (2018). *Don't Lah-Wei: A Peer-to-Peer Resource Guide on Ensuring that your Kawan never becomes a Terrorist*. Malaysia: Ministry of Foreign Affairs.

Schmid, A. P. (2005). Terrorism as psychological warfare. *Democracy and Security*, *1*(2), 137–146.

Schmid, A. P. (2014). Al-Qaeda's single narrative and attempts to develop counter-narratives: The state of knowledge. *International Centre for Counter-Terrorism*. Retrieved from http://www.icct.nl/download/file/Schmid-Al-Qaeda's-Single-Narrative-and-Attempts-to-Develop-Counter-Narratives-January-2014.pdf.

Schmid, A. P., & Graaf, J. D. (1982). *Violence as Communication: Insurgent Terrorism and the Western News Media*. Beverly Hills, CA: Sage.

Singer, P. W. (2005). *Children at War*. New York: Pantheon Books.

Top Malaysian ISIL operative killed in Syria (2017, May 8). *Al-Jazeera*. Retrieved from http://www.aljazeera.com/news/2017/05/top-malaysian-isil-operative-killed-syria-170508182519182.html.

Underwood, J. (2016). Why we need to stop calling ISIL a death cult. *The Huffington Post*. Retrieved from https://www.huffingtonpost.co.uk/jon-underwood/why-we-need-to-stop-calli_b_8700968.html.

Williams, A., & Head, V. (2007). *Freedom Fighters*. England: Canary Press.

Section 4

Insights for Dealing with At-Risk Population

We will not see the last of Singaporeans being influenced by what they read and who they meet online. We will likely see more cases of foreign religious teachers preaching hate, or preachers exhorting followers to stay away from those who do not share the same faith.

MDM HALIMAH YACOB
PRESIDENT OF SINGAPORE

CHAPTER 13

At-Risk and Radicalised Singaporean Youths: Themes Observed and Considerations for a Youth-Centric Rehabilitation Framework

BRIDGET ROBERT

Ministry of Home Affairs, Singapore

While the recent terror attacks[1] around the world by the Islamic State of Iraq and Syria (ISIS) evince anger, disgust, and sadness at the unnecessary loss of lives, the fact that an increasing number of the perpetrators of these violent attacks are young people, gives pause

[1] One such example is the Manchester arena terror attack in 2017. The perpetrator of the suicide attack was Salman Abedi, who was 22 years old at the time of the attack. This terror attack resulted in the death of 22 people — many of them children — and 64 others who were injured.

for concern. The process of youth radicalisation is a complex one and certainly goes beyond the youth's exposure to radical rhetoric online. This chapter suggests the importance of situating the issue of youth radicalisation within the broader frame of the youth's cognitive and psychosocial development, and how these issues may increase the youth's vulnerability to ISIS's propaganda. This chapter further provides a sample of themes observed in at-risk and radicalised Singaporean youths and using the central argument of looking at both person-related and ecological contexts, suggests five rehabilitation principles that practitioners and policymakers can consider in developing a youth-centric rehabilitation framework.

Scope of the Chapter

The present chapter focuses on the process of youth[2] self-radicalisation in a Singaporean context and is based on local case studies. The concept of "self-radicalisation" is defined in this chapter as a process where an individual adopts radical ideology through self-learning and without a pre-existing physical affiliation with a terrorist group. These individuals become persuaded by the group's ideology and come to hold a sufficiently significant level of commitment to the group such that it manifests in the way they behave (e.g., open support online for ISIS, stating a desire to be physically part of the terror group, etc.). Through this process of self-radicalisation, the individual is likely to start seeking like-minded individuals for ideological support as well as to engage in the discourse, either in the virtual or physical world. This serves to further solidify his or her commitment to the group.

It is important to note that radicalisation is not peculiar to any specific religious or national group, but this chapter focuses solely on the current threat presented by ISIS and the youths who are inspired by their ideology. The present chapter also covers a range of youth cases — from individuals who are at the nascent stages of radicalisation to those who came to be fully committed to the ideology propagated by ISIS and as manifested in a willingness to use

[2]In Singapore, a youth is an individual between the ages of 15 and 35.

violence for a perceived religious cause. The scope of the present chapter is to provide an overview of some of the key processes involved in the youth's process of radicalisation — apart from sociopolitical factors — and articulates a youth-centric rehabilitation framework developed specifically to meet local needs.

The Internet as a Facilitator of the Radicalisation of Young People

The terrorism threat has evolved in significant ways in recent times — from structured, organisation-based groups guided by doctrines articulating clear recruitment, training, and ideological imperatives (i.e., principles) such as Al-Qaeda and the Jemaah Islamiyah (JI) to individuals who are "remotely" indoctrinated without being physically immersed in these groups. In large part, this evolution from a "traditional" method of indoctrination to a process of self-radicalisation, has been contributed by technological advancements. This has been clearly evidenced by the way with which ISIS has capitalised on the Internet and social media to expand their outreach efforts at a low cost, while targeting their key demographic group — youths — to join their cause.

It is important to note, however, that extremists and hate groups have long used the Internet for various reasons, going back more than a decade. Weimann (2004), for instance, identified eight such ways that terrorist groups use the Internet — "psychological warfare, publicity and propaganda, data mining, fundraising, recruitment and mobilisation, networking, information sharing and planning and coordination" (Weimann, 2004, pp. 5–11). The Internet, however, has experienced a sea change over the last decade, as observed from the move from static to rich visual graphics, from single to multiple web browsers, the introduction of various social media platforms, and the sheer speed of the Internet compared to a decade, ago ("The Internet: a decade of explosive growth and changes", n.d.).

Locally, as at January 2018, Singapore's Internet and active social media registered 4.83 million users (or 84% penetration rate) and 4.8 million users (or 83% penetration rate), respectively, with the largest demographic of users being within the age range of 18 and 34 (Kemp, 2018). The Global Digital Report also indicated that Singaporeans spend an average of 7 hours a day on the Internet and listed, in order of frequency of use, WhatsApp, YouTube, Facebook, Instagram, and Facebook Messenger as their top five platforms. Additionally, the study indicated that 68% of active Internet users watch online videos on a daily basis. Increasingly, much younger Singaporeans — those between the ages of eight and 12 — are demonstrating similar patterns (6.5 hours a day on digital devices) of use as the older age brackets in studies such as the Global Digital Report (Yang, 2017). As young consumers dominate social media platforms, they are naturally far more exposed to various types of extremist and hate materials online, thus increasing their risk of being persuaded by radical rhetoric.

The exposure to radical content online, however, represents one of the means by which an individual may potentially become radicalised. In Singapore's youth cases, there is a combination of factors that form the basis of their appeal for ISIS' narratives and contributed to their process of radicalisation. These are a mix of pre-existing factors such as those related to the developmental stage of the youth, his or her specific inter- and intrapersonal traits, as well as to situational factors that emerge in the youth's life that renders the youth vulnerable to becoming radicalised. Examples of situational factors include those related to familial conflict, difficulty coping in school, or the emergence of other life stressors.

The Role of Cognitive and Psychosocial Development in Adolescence and Young Adulthood and the Appeal of ISIS's Narratives

In considering the reasons for why a number of young persons have found resonance with ISIS's narratives, it is important to situate this question within the larger issue of adolescent development and to extend this to identity formation in young adulthood. Seminal works by developmental psychologists such as Erikson (1968) and Arnett (2000) have argued that there are specific stages that humans go through as part of life course development. Of specific relevance to this chapter is Erikson's argument that the main task in adolescence is the establishment of a strong sense of personal identity and a failure to do so, often leads to role confusion (i.e., poor sense of self) and manifests itself in a variety of ways — including adopting extreme positions such as behaving in risky or delinquent ways. However, more contemporary work in developmental psychology has focused on the transition between the period of adolescence and young adulthood in terms of identity formation. These studies have highlighted that, apart from the chronological age of the individual, sociocultural factors such as family processes and socioeconomic status also influence identity in young adulthood (Benson & Elder, 2011).

Specific to the process of cognitive development in middle adolescence[3] — between the ages of 15 and 17 — young people move from concrete thinking styles (i.e., here and now) to abstract thinking (i.e., ability to make connections between different timeframes). This is also a time where young people start to think in idealistic ways and this is often framed in terms of desiring to make the world a better place (e.g., wanting to eradicate suffering or poverty, to right the perceived injustices of the world). Added to this is the role that religion plays in the youth's identity formation. In particular, youths who perceive their religious identity as a salient aspect of who they are, tend to report meaning and purpose in their lives, which impacts decisions about their life goals; these individuals also tend to hold more pro-social concerns (Furrow *et al.*, 2004). Another feature at this stage of cognitive development is the adolescent's perception of omnipotence and infallibility; the idea that one is able to engage what would ordinarily be perceived as risky behaviours without believing that he or she is at risk of death. In terms of psychosocial development, middle stage adolescents begin to define their identities beyond their parents; friends become the key source of what defines their identity. Thus, one of the articulated characteristics that define the period of adolescence is the individual's

[3]Adolescence = 12–20 years; Early adolescence = 12–14 years; Middle adolescence = 15–17 years; and Late adolescence = 18–20 years.

"ambivalent view of adults as a helpful social resource" (Hanley *et al.*, 2013, p. 70).

In essence, some of the developmental characteristics include a young individual who is idealistic and seeks meaning and certitude in life; who perceives himself as infallible and where peer group membership becomes an important aspect in terms of how they view themselves and who are ambivalent towards adults and other figures of authority. These are characteristics that may make a young person vulnerable to engaging in maladaptive behaviours. An interesting issue therefore, would be to understand how these characteristics interact with the way a youth interprets the range of radical rhetoric that is purveyed online such that it results in his or her willingness to become involved in terrorism-related activities.

Various authors have analysed the range of narratives propagated by terrorist groups such as ISIS. Some examples include narratives aimed at creating a sense of urgency to act on a religious obligation, to fight the oppressors of fellow Muslims, and importantly, painting the Islamic caliphate as a utopian ideal. Other such narratives appeal to the nature of youth — such as framing the individual's participation as an adventure or narratives that underscore the idea that the individual will experience a sense of belonging and have a clear sense of identity being part of the Islamic caliphate (Gartenstein-Ross *et al.*, 2016). These are narratives that seem to have been crafted to capitalise on the developmental issues experienced by the youth and with an understanding of what would clearly resonate with this group.

Some Themes Observed in Local Youth Cases

Emotional Justification for Action

Some of these themes also seem to overlap with what has been observed in Singaporean youth cases. A common theme is the articulation of having experienced an emotional reaction to issues affecting fellow Muslims elsewhere in the world, which justified the need for action. Specifically, the youths identified emotional sensitivity to the suffering of fellow Muslims and oft-quoted examples include exposure to online information or imagery of individuals — in particular women and children — being killed in conflict areas. For some of these youths, this triggers a desire to help others who are perceived to be suffering (i.e., to right an injustice). While experiencing high empathic concern and wanting to help alleviate suffering, in and of itself, are not negative aspects of human functioning, the means with which the youth seeks to express these may become problematic — such as wanting to join ISIS or taking up arms as a means to help fellow Muslims who are suffering in conflict zones.

One such youth planned to engage in armed violence in a conflict zone after he came across content that highlighted the suffering of Muslims in such areas and developed a deep emotional reaction to their suffering. He believed that not helping them meant that he failed as a Muslim. He started looking at a range of jihadi websites to identify ways with which he could take action. He was soon convinced that the only way to help was to go to a conflict zone and take up arms to alleviate the suffering of fellow Muslims there.

Another youth was singularly focused on the suffering of Syrian children after viewing videos related to the Syrian conflict. He believed that he needed to go to Syria to help these children, even if it meant that he had to use violence. He was assured that, if he was killed in the process of helping, he would die as a martyr for having done a good deed.

Fulfilling a Sense of Purpose in Life and Legitimisation of Violence

Apart from wanting to champion the weak, a few of the youth cases also felt that joining ISIS would help them fulfil a sense of purpose, such as the revival of Islam to its "Golden Age" — even if it meant using violence. ISIS has framed the use of violence as a legitimate means with which to pursue a religious goal — the establishment of an Islamic caliphate. The terrorist group legitimises violence by liberally citing religious texts underscoring the idea that it is the obligation of Muslims to defend the Islamic caliphate and assuring the youth that his act of killing will be rewarded in the afterlife. Thus, the underlying motivation for the use of instrumental violence[4] is framed as necessary to achieve a superordinate goal — the establishment of a utopian Islamic state. Compounding the youth's acceptance of these violence-related beliefs is the general observation that the local youth cases do not hold deep religious knowledge but were persuaded by the simplistic narratives that were construed as compelling and true, but more importantly, had fit in with their new belief system.

One of the youths believed that violence was a legitimate and necessary means to fulfil God's obligation for all Muslims to be united within an Islamic caliphate. He reasoned that the violence against non-Muslims as well as Muslims who do not agree with this "mandate", is justified.

Desire to Belong and the Psychology of In-group Out-group Bias

The youth cases also demonstrated a desire to seek camaraderie and a sense of belonging with individuals who are perceived as the "in-group". The psychological need to belong to a group, as a way to socially connect with others, has been established as a fundamental human need. The corollary to belonging to an in-group is that there has to be an out-group. Research going back 50 years has found that people tend to attribute positive traits to members of their own group compared to individuals of the other group — even though individuals were assigned to the different groups in an arbitrary manner.

Pioneering research by social psychologists such as Muzafer Sherif and Henry Tajfel led to the development of social identity

[4]Instrumental violence is defined as goal-oriented aggression or violence that occurs as a by-product on an individual's attempt to achieve a superordinate goal. This is distinguished from expressive or reactive violence as defined as acts of violence that occur as a result of emotional states such as anger, frustration, or rage that are disproportionate to the situation that elicited the harm.

theory (Tajfel, 1982), which argues that apart from focusing on similarities or positive attributes of members in one's group, individuals also attribute negative traits to members in an out-group, thereby enhancing their self-image. A study by Johnson *et al.* (2012) on religiosity and intergroup bias illustrated that self-reported religiosity (i.e., Christian, heterosexuals) correlated positively with more negative attitudes towards perceived out-groups (i.e., atheists, Muslims, and homosexual men). Interestingly, the study also found that when the in-group was primed with religious concepts, it "increased intergroup bias, regardless of pre-existing levels of religiosity" in that the in-group showed significantly larger increases in negative attitudes toward the out-group compared to those primed with neutral words (Johnson *et al.*, 2012, p. 163).

A youth distinguished between believers, whom he felt would receive the gift of heaven, from non-believers, whom he believed would end up in hell. Thus, the individual felt that it was best not to associate with non-believers given his perception that doing so would classify as a sin (i.e., adoption of perceived immoral values) and that this would mean that he too would end up in hell.

Another youth felt that ISIS provides unity given that people of different races will be accepted in the Islamic caliphate as long as the individuals going there share the same beliefs. This provided the youth with a sense of belonging to what he felt was the "right group".

Poor Coping in the Face of Stressful Life Circumstances

The earlier section of this chapter articulated the importance of framing the issue of youth radicalisation within the individual's cognitive and psychosocial development. One of the key arguments posited by developmental psychologists is that the transition from childhood to young adulthood is defined by major life changes within the individual, as well as in terms of how they navigate the social environment and the expectations placed on them (Markova & Nikitskaya, 2017). Thus, the successful transition into young adulthood hinges on the ability of the individual to cope effectively with the various potential stressors during this stage.[5] While there are various theories of coping in the literature, this chapter focuses on Moos's (1993) conceptualisation of coping responses to stressful life circumstances. Specifically, Moos includes both the focus (problem or emotion-focused coping) and method (cognitive or behavioural) aspects of how individuals cope with stressful situations and further divides these components into either approach or avoidance responses (Moos, 1993). In broad terms, the primary process in avoidance coping tends to be emotion-focused and where the individual seeks to avoid thinking about the stressor and its implications. Approach coping, however, is problem-focused and the individual seeks to resolve life stressors (Moos, 1993).

In Singapore's youth cases, a pattern that was found suggested the utilisation of poor coping strategies in dealing with problems. Specifically, a number of the radicalised youths tended to adopt avoidance coping strategies more often than using approach coping strategies to deal with stressful events. Two common avoidance coping strategies observed in local radicalised youths are the tendency to engage in behavioural attempts to get involved in substitute activities as a way of either creating new sources of satisfaction in their lives or as a way to distract from the stressor. In addition, the youths also tended to utilise coping strategies that helped them avoid thinking realistically about a problem. One example that illustrates these strategies includes refocusing all of the individual's efforts on finding any and all information on ISIS, instead of dealing with interpersonal difficulties experienced at home or in school. Another such example would be the single-mindedness in making detailed plans to travel to Syria, including seeking and discussing with like-minded individuals online, to be part of ISIS as a way to escape from his or her current reality — based on the individual's subjective negative appraisal of the current reality. One other observation was that, in terms of approach strategies, local

[5]Stress-coping researchers have argued that the type of coping responses manifested by the individual is dependent on the interaction between person- and context-related factors, and examples include the availability of social resources, type, and frequency of the stressful event, the subjective appraisal of the stressor to the personality characteristics of the individual (Moos, 1993).

radicalised youths tended not to seek guidance or social support as strategies to deal with their problems.

One of the youths had gotten into a number of difficulties including relationship and financial problems. He felt that these issues were intractable and the way he chose to cope with these life stressors was to refocus his attention to what was happening in Syria. He started becoming fixated with information on the Syrian conflict and progressed by making specific plans to travel there to be a part of the armed conflict. Apart from becoming an effective distraction from his actual problems, it also started to provide him with a new purpose in life.

Another youth often fantasised about being a mujahideen (warriors for the faith) whenever he thought about the various problems present in his life, from doing poorly in school to the regular familial conflict at home. This fantasy of being an invincible fighter helped him to escape from his current reality.

Impact of ISIS's Extremist Narratives on Youth

The use of the concepts described in the preceding paragraphs is illustrated in ISIS's propaganda. Specifically, their anti-West, anti-democracy narratives argue that Muslims living in the West or in secular states are either not true Muslims, given that they are not practicing Islam in the way that should be practiced (i.e., strict adherence to Islamic law), that secular governments are deliberately oppressing Muslims, or that Islam is under attack by non-Muslims. In some of the youth cases, these narratives form the rationalisation that a return to Islam in its purest form will alleviate the various problems faced by Muslims as a global community — ranging from the disintegration of the *Ummah* (wider community of Muslims) to the social–moral decay of Muslims. Thus, specific beliefs that support these narratives include the belief that Islam is superior over all other religions (i.e., out-group consists of all other religions) and that Islamic rule is ideal compared to other forms of governance (i.e., out-group consists of all other forms of governance apart from an Islamic caliphate) or that living in a secular state facilitates un-Islamic practices in the Muslim community (i.e., out-group consists of all Muslims who live in secular states). ISIS's solution, therefore, is for Muslims to *hijrah*, or migrate to an Islamic caliphate. For the radicalised youth, this represents an opportunity to fulfil a religious obligation (i.e., being a good Muslim) and the need to belong to a perceived in-group.

Complexity of the Youth Radicalisation Process

The process of youth radicalisation is a complex one, in that it does not follow a set sequence of events but is the result of the interplay of psychosocial factors (i.e., behaviour resulting from person and environmental factors). Between individuals, the process is an idiosyncratic one — the combination of factors that contribute to the radicalisation of one youth may be fairly different from another youth. As discussed, these factors range from person-related psychological attributes such as a compromised ability to cope with stressors and factors related to the developmental needs of the youth, to situational or environmental factors such as the social influences in the form of exposure to radical narratives or presence of external stressors. Thus, it is important to conceptualise the various elements that have played a role in the radicalisation of the youth as areas to address in a youth-centric rehabilitation framework. Apart from understanding the radicalisation-specific factors, it would also be useful for practitioners to reference the vast literature on what works for young people who are in a rehabilitation setting.

Considerations for a Youth-specific Rehabilitation Framework

The present chapter suggests five points that practitioners and policymakers can consider when thinking about a youth-specific rehabilitation approach.

Rehabilitation Principle 1: A Whole-of-Community Approach to Deal With At-Risk Youth

The first principle proposed is that the whole of community approach needs to be adopted to be able to successfully deal with the issue of youth radicalisation. This means addressing the continuum — from at-risk youths to youths who were radicalised into violent extremism and where action was taken. The role that the community plays for at-risk youths compared to radicalised youths will necessarily differ in terms of objectives of engagement, types of activities, as well as intensity of intervention provided.

For at-risk youths, the key objective would be to ensure that the youth does not escalate in terms of his risk of radicalising into violent extremism and this can be done by working with community stakeholders as part of the wider outreach efforts of the relevant authorities. Schools, in particular, are important stakeholders given that young people spend a bulk of their time in schools. Thus, keeping schools up to date on the issues surrounding the threat of terrorism and highlighting the vulnerabilities that are specific to young people, are useful starting points. This ensures that where there is a possibility that the youth is susceptible to becoming radicalised, early intervention can be provided with the aim of mitigating this risk. In this instance, early intervention can be in the form of guidance from established religious clerics who can address faith-based questions that the youth might have. Where deemed relevant, early intervention strategies can also include non-religious aspects such as cyber-wellness or guiding the youth through coping with significant life stressors in an adaptive manner.

Rehabilitation Principle 2: Framework that Addresses Both Person-related and Ecological Factors that Contributed to Radicalisation

At the other end of the continuum is the group of youths who were radicalised and where actions were taken. Thus, another rehabilitation principle proposed is that the articulation of any rehabilitation framework for radicalised youths should take into account both the person-related issues as well as the wider ecological context that contributed to his or her process of radicalisation — as discussed in the first half of this chapter. The key objectives for this group would be to identify and address the various issues that had formed the basis for their radicalisation with the intent to mitigate their risk of the youth re-engaging in terrorism-related activities. For the youth, however, beyond ensuring that their risk is mitigated, an important additional objective is to cultivate more pro-social values and the ability to achieve their goals in an adaptive way without engaging in terrorism-related activities.

Rehabilitation Principle 3: Complement the use of Risk Management with Strengths-based Approaches in Rehabilitation of Youths

A useful rehabilitation principle to consider for youths is to extend the objective of rehabilitation beyond a risk management approach to including a strengths-based approach. These two objectives can be met through the use of established rehabilitation approaches — the traditional risk management approach through the Risk-Needs and Responsivity (RNR) model[6] (Andrews & Bonta, 2010) and strengths-based approach through the use of the Good Lives Model (GLM)[7] (Ward *et al.*, 2007). These are complementary approaches and would help address the range of issues presented by radicalised youths.

The risk management approach is critical in terms of ensuring that the various dynamic risk factors presented by the youth — such as the range of religious ideological beliefs and cognitive distortions that supported and perpetuated the terrorism-related behaviours — are

[6]The risk principle is concerned with the match between level of risk presented by the individual and the actual amount of treatment received (i.e., higher risk, higher intensity of treatment). The need principle states that programmes should address criminogenic needs (dynamic risk factors) which contribute to recidivism and which can be changed. The responsivity principle states the importance of tailoring interventions that would maximise the individual's ability to benefit from the programme (i.e., cognitive behavioural based approach, learning styles, motivation for change, etc.) based on the assumption that not all individuals are the same (Andrews & Bonta, 2010).

[7]The Good Lives Model (GLM) is a strengths-based approach to offender rehabilitation, and based on the idea that individuals need to build strengths and capabilities in order to reduce their risk of reoffending. Thus, the focus is on guiding "individuals to develop and implement meaningful life plans that are incompatible with future offending" (Willis *et al.*, 2013).

addressed, so that the youth does not pose a threat to society and his risk is mitigated. Other examples of dynamic risk factors include aspects such as poor interpersonal relationship with significant others (i.e., family, school peers). It is important to note that the articulation of the range of risk factors relevant to a radicalised youth is an area that requires further research to ensure that the factors are empirically derived.

The GLM approach to rehabilitation emphasises primarily on "approach goals" and these are in reference to desirable goals that the youth can work towards (e.g., building interpersonal competencies that would help the individual connect with pro-social peers) which is distinct from "avoidant goals" which are undesirable goals that the individual avoids (e.g., seeking sense of belonging and connectedness with extremists). For instance, one of the themes highlighted in this chapter was of youth who articulated the desire to help fellow Muslims who are perceived to be oppressed, by wanting to engage in armed conflict, is framed within GLM as the youth engaging in negative and harmful behaviour in order to fulfil a valued outcome — which was wanting to be part of a community that shares common values and goals (i.e., "brothers" who are fighting to alleviate suffering). Thus, in this scenario, the objective of intervention is to help the youth develop prosocial ways of being part of a community and contributing to the needs of others. The end goal is essentially to provide the youth with an opportunity to lead productive lives in the community.

Rehabilitation principle 4: Systematic and Comprehensive Approach to Assessment

Another useful rehabilitation principle is to articulate a systematic and comprehensive approach in assessing the youth. This is important as it will help practitioners identify and prioritise areas of intervention that will be most impactful in terms of rehabilitation outcomes. As indicated in the preceding paragraph, the assessment of youths should incorporate aspects from both a risk management (i.e., mitigating key risk factors) and strengths-based perspective (i.e., cultivating prosocial ways of seeking primary human goods). Thus, apart from identifying contributing factors to the radicalisation process, it would also be useful to think about how the individual gains from his participation in terrorism-related activities and the means with which he sought to fulfil a valued goal.

Rehabilitation Principle 5: Importance of Adopting Multiperspective Approach to Dealing with a Radicalised Youth

Given the argument that the youth is situated within a larger ecological framework — family, peers, school, and the wider community — it would be useful to approach rehabilitation from this perspective. This means that, where relevant, these various groups within the youth's ecosystem can be co-opted in the rehabilitation of the individual. For instance, working with the families of a radicalised youth is an important aspect within a youth-centric rehabilitation framework. This is based on the premise that the youth's family can serve as a central source of support for the youth, and thus strengthening the family system as a whole is likely to lead to better rehabilitation outcomes for the youth.

Families can also be strengthened by building their resilience in terms of navigating the challenges that may come with having a youth detained or placed on restriction order. Apart from ensuring that the youth who is detained continues his or her regular family visits, it would be useful for community stakeholders such as social workers to also provide guidance to family members in relevant areas of need — such as teaching general coping skills, guidance on dealing effectively with interpersonal conflicts, and so forth.

For radicalised youths, another key role that the community stakeholders can play will be to assist with the reintegration component of the rehabilitation programme. One useful component in this area is the implementation of a youth mentorship programme run by community volunteers. Mentoring as a form of intervention for young people has traditionally been used to prevent youths from engaging in unhealthy behaviour and, more recently, as a way to promote positive development in youths. A meta-analysis reviewing the effectiveness of mentoring programmes from research done between 1999 and 2010, concluded that mentoring programmes were effective in terms of positive outcomes in the areas of the youth's social, emotional, behavioural, and cognitive functioning (DuBois *et al.*, 2011). A mentoring programme for radicalised youths can serve various objectives. These can range from addressing the psychosocial aspects of the youth's functioning that are either under-developed or absent to functioning as an additional form of scaffolding for the youth as a prosocial source of support to facilitating the youth's engagement with the broader community.

Apart from promoting positive development in the youth in the area of social skills, another important aspect is to facilitate opportunities for the youth's educational upgrading. Educational upgrading provides the youth with the means to redirect his or her behaviour from negative goals (i.e., terrorism-related activities) to achievement-oriented goals (i.e., sense of personal mastery, goal-setting behaviour, inculcating perseverance, etc.). Educational upgrading can also facilitate the means by which the young person can reintegrate effectively into society and, beyond that, have the opportunity to contribute positively to the community.

Conclusion

The present chapter covered some of the key issues of youth radicalisation in the Singaporean context and, specifically, highlighted the complexity that underlies the process of radicalisation beyond the youth's exposure to extremist content online. Of note is the central idea, that to understand why a young person finds resonance with radical rhetoric, it is important to situate this within the larger frame of the cognitive and psychosocial development of a young person. This same principle of looking at both person-related and the wider ecological context is extended to thinking about useful principles that could guide practitioners and policymakers in articulating a youth-centric rehabilitation framework. These principles are meant to be useful broad strokes given the lack of available literature that specifically articulates effective components of intervention for radicalised youths. However, what remains an important aspect is that more work certainly needs to be done in terms of applying specific rehabilitation approaches such as the RNR and GLM approaches to this group and measuring the effectiveness of the various components of a youth-specific rehabilitation framework.

References

Andrews, D., & Bonta, J. (2010). Rehabilitating criminal justice policy and practice. *Psychology, Public Policy, and Law, 16*(1), 39–55.

Arnett, J. J. (2000). Emerging adulthood: A theory of development from the late teens through the twenties. *American Psychologist*, *55*(5), 469–480.

Benson, J. E., Elder, & G. H. (2011). Young adult identities and their pathways: A developmental and life course model. *Developmental Psychology*, *47*(6), 1,646–1,657.

DuBois, D. L., Portillo, N., Rhodes, J. E., Silverthorn, N., & Valentine, J. C. (2011). How effective are mentoring programs for youth? A systematic assessment of the evidence. *Psychological Science in the Public Interest*, 12, 57–91.

Erikson, E. H. (1968). *Identity, Youth and Crisis*. New York: W.W. Norton Company.

Furrow, J. L., King, P. E., & White, K. (2004). Religion and positive youth development: Identity, meaning and prosocial concerns. *Applied Developmental Science*, *8*(1), 17–26.

Gartenstein-Ross, D., Barr, N., & Moreng, B. (2016). *The Islamic State's Global Propaganda Strategy*. The International Centre for Counter-Terrorism — The Hague.

Hanley, T., Humphrey, N., & Lennie, C. (Eds.) (2013). *Adolescent Counselling Psychology: Theory, Research and Practice*. London: Routledge.

Johnson, M. K., Rowatt, W. C., & LaBouff, J. P. (2012). Religiosity and prejudice revisited: In-group favoritism, out-group derogation, or both? *Psychology of Religion and Spirituality*, *4*(2), 154–168.

Kemp, S. (2018). Digital in 2018: world's internet users pass the 4 billion mark. *We are social*. Retrieved from https://wearesocial.com/sg/blog/2018/01/global-digital-report-2018.

Markova, S. & Nikitskaya, E. (2017). Coping strategies of adolescents with deviant behaviour. *International Journal of Adolescence and Youth*, *22*(1), 36–46.

Moos, R. H. (1993). *Coping Responses Inventory: Adult Form (Professional Manual)*. Lutz, Florida: Psychological Assessment Resources (PAR), Inc.

Tajfel, H. (1982). Social psychology of intergroup relations. *Annual Review of Psychology*, *33*, 39.

The Internet: a decade of explosive growth and changes (n.d.) *i-Scoop*. Retrieved from https://www.i-scoop.eu/internet-decade-explosive-growth-changes/.

Ward, T., Mann, R. E., & Gannon, T. A. (2007). The Good Lives Model of offender rehabilitation: Clinical implications. *Aggression and Violent Behaviour*, 12, 87–107.

Weimann, G. (2004). www.terror.net: How modern terrorism uses the Internet. United States Institute of Peace Special Report.

Willis, G. M., Prescott, D. S., & Yates, P. M. (2013). The Good Lives Model (GLM) in theory and practice. *Sexual Abuse in Australia and New Zealand: An Interdisciplinary Journal*, 5(1), 3–9.

Yang, C. (2017). 12-year-olds in Singapore spend 6½ hours daily on electronic devices: Survey. *The Straits Times*. Retrieved from https://www.straitstimes.com/singapore/glued-to-screen-for-612-hours-digital-habits-in-singapore.

CHAPTER 14

Understanding Intergroup Contact on Terrorist Prisoners in Indonesia

MIRRA NOOR MILLA*,
AHMAD NAUFALUL UMAM†

**Faculty of Psychology,*
Universitas Indonesia, Indonesia
†*Faculty of Psychology,*
Mercu Buana University, Indonesia

Introduction

How can we disengage someone from his or her terrorist group? To answer this question, it is necessary to understand the underlying context of terrorism. The lack of empirical data in the literature has been a major problem in understanding the issue. This problem remains unsolved due to the covert nature of terrorist activities and national security concerns that prevent academics from mapping out the problem. Additionally, strict prison security procedures limit interaction with terrorist prisoners, which is considered a potential data source for studying terrorism. Some researchers, however, have managed to meet the prisoners and conduct systematic interviews with them. Nonetheless, even where access is granted, the terrorists' resistance and ideological restrain have made the data gathering process challenging. Therefore, primary data source is the most concerning problem in countering terrorism and de-radicalisation studies.

In-prison de-radicalisation programmes have allowed us to systematically gather primary data from terrorist groups. Government-sponsored de-radicalisation programmes provided the authorities access to the terrorists, so the routine interaction schedule could be assured, and a sustainable data source could be secured. This chapter will describe our experiences during the implementation of government-supported de-radicalisation programmes across Indonesia, involving more than 150 terrorists in 53 prisons.

Such de-radicalisation programmes have been conducted since 2006 (Abbas, 2017), but the systematic and supervised programmes only began by 2015 (Sukabdi, 2015). The later programmes ensured a proper evaluation of the programme's effectiveness through academic rigor by prominent scholars appointed by the National Counter Terrorism Agency, or also known as Badan Nasional Penanggulangan Terorisme (BNPT). Based on the de-radicalisation blueprint of BNPT, the de-radicalisation programme consists of identification, rehabilitation, re-education, and resocialisation (BNPT, 2017). The programme starts with identification assessment, which aims to categorise the terrorists into several classes of intervention groups. The programme that follows is rehabilitation. At this stage, terrorists are persuaded to evaluate their ideology and strategy in religion and daily life. Afterwards, the re-education programme helps terrorist prisoners explore alternative goals and identities. The main focus of this stage is to introduce them to non-violent ideologies in order to accommodate their great enthusiasm in implementing religious teachings. Finally, the resocialisation programme is offered to help prisoners reintegrate into society.

Reflecting on the evaluation of de-radicalisation programmes up to 2017, we identified several underlying factors and potential

Table 14.1. Description of the Prisoners of Terrorism.

	Mean (SD)		
Variable	2015	2016	2017
1. Age	34.26 (7.40)	35.27 (6.92)	33.03 (7.95)
2. Detention period	7.22 (5.14)	5.57 (3.55)	3.09 (1.84)
3. Support for jihad as war	5.09 (1.93)	7.46 (1.72)	6.82 (2.36)

Source: National Counter Terrorism Agency (2017).

strategies for future de-radicalisation programmes. Firstly, the demographic data showed that the newly detained terrorists were mostly youths with short sentences and more diverse cases compared to the older detainees (see Table 14.1). Secondly, we also found that prisoners' support for radical ideology, an idea of replacing Indonesian constitution with sharia law remained high over time. There is no indication that the idea of sharia sovereignty declined in conjunction with the length of time they served in custody.

Although the data shown in Table 14.1 is not exclusively a longitudinal investigation but rather yearly cross-sectional observation, it raises the question of whether the in-prison de-radicalisation programme was ineffective in shifting the terrorists' radical ideology. Certainly, it cannot be simply interpreted as failure, since radicalisation is a long process, established through a socialisation process including family, values reinforcement from surrounding community, and internalisation through identity consolidation process (Milla, 2010; Milla *et al.*, 2013). The process will be intensified by a religious belief-based self-concept that is constantly being evaluated and reinforced, thus the radical ideas tend to linger relentlessly (Kruglanski *et al.*, 2014). Therefore, people who shift their ideology are like fish out of water, where disturbances and restlessness await them in a new community with new rules. We believe these conditions cause strong resistance among the prisoners. However, intrinsic motivation, positive attitude, and willingness to participate in the programme have been found to contribute to the effectiveness of the programme (Milla *et al.*, 2018; Webber &

Kruglanski, 2017). For that reason, certain approaches to gain a positive attitude are needed to alleviate the resistance among terrorist prisoners.

One strategy we used to gain the prisoners' openness and acceptance towards the de-radicalisation programme was through the psychological approach. This approach was specifically designed to create psychological readiness and to introduce contra-ideology discussions that might follow. There are two focuses of this approach. Individual-focused approach is aimed at improving cognitive and affective capacity so that one will be able to self-evaluate their beliefs about themselves, their group, and their extreme ideology. Group-focused approach is aimed at interrupting group dynamics, which notably has been reported to strengthen the radicalisation process among terrorists in prison. After years of observation, we believe that dealing with the terrorist social network is a bigger concern than encouraging ideological discussions to break the cycle of radical ideology and allows them to liberate themselves from their group's cohesiveness. Aside from individual ideology, social ties and social relationships have been found to play an important role in keeping people within a terrorist group (Muluk *et al.*, 2013; Sageman, 2004). More specifically, positive intergroup contact has been firmly employed in the recent years with the main goal of endorsing inclusivity by breaking strong ties in small groups (cells), and developing weak ties in a more open and wider group.

Research has shown that positive intergroup interaction experiences tended to reduce prejudice and increased cooperation (Page-Gould *et al.*, 2008). In the process of radicalisation, many terrorist candidates have experienced selective exclusivism and strict isolation from the out-group. Terrorist ideologists control this isolation in order to prevent new members from experiencing dissonance; thus, they can safely hold on to their terrorist beliefs. In this chapter, we will describe how group exclusivity and competitiveness have become a challenge, and how positive intergroup experiences were selected as our aim to disengage terrorist prisoners from their preoccupying group and activities. However, intergroup contact was not the only programme in the entirety of the de-radicalisation programme. It served as an essential prelude that aimed to create suitable conditions for upcoming contra-ideology discussions by reducing destructive competitiveness and increasing acceptance for alternative social identity.

Drawing from the latest records on de-radicalisation programmes in prisons, we will first describe the challenges faced by the government and the agencies with respect to terrorist prisoner exclusivity and thought rigidity. Then, we will describe how we implemented the principal of positive intergroup contact in order to break the barrier of thoughts of "us versus them" and incorporating the practice of looking at multiple perspectives.

The Challenge of Exclusivism in Radicalisation

Radicalisation can be understood as a process that explains why someone is willing to join a terrorist group (Idris, 2016; Milla *et al.*, 2013). Kruglanski and Fishman (2009) explained that a radicalised person is an individual who adheres to only one worldview and goal, and constantly ignores and rejects the others. McCauley and Moskalenko (2010) explain radicalisation as a process of changing beliefs, feelings, and behaviours aimed at enhancing support during conflict. When someone internalises a radical ideology, his or her identification towards the particular radical group will strengthen his or her social identity and goal commitment (Webber *et al.*, 2018). In our field experience, the process of radicalisation manifested in terrorists who excluded themselves from their community and only committed themselves to one radical group.

Exclusivism

During the radicalisation process, as one's self-identification towards their group strengthens, they become more selective in their other social interactions. Common radical group prospective members usually experience social exclusivism prior to their engagement in extreme radical behaviour. They feel uncomfortable being in a community that does not share their worldview, thus they withdraw from the society in order to protect their beliefs from cognitive dissonance derived from opposing or varying worldviews by other people in the society. Moreover, the group is also actively reinforcing this process by providing repeated trainings, indoctrination, and isolation (Milla *et al.*, 2013). Group pressure and persuasion by terrorist ideologists pull the members even deeper into the group, making it even harder to leave the group. Families in this case will face two consequences, they will either play the role of a bonding agent to the radical group, serving as an important thing that one must protect, or the family is the first thing that radicalised individuals leave, followed by peers and their society.

Take Imam Samudra as an example for exclusivism (Aziz, 2004). The notorious Imam Samudra, the mastermind behind the Bali Bombing in 2002, went through an identity crisis as a teenager. He found refuge in religious narratives that gave him guidance for all aspects in his life; he gradually paid no heed to other worldviews due to their imperfections compared to Islamic teachings. Despite the fact that he was a keen reader, his reading materials were only limited to a small selection of Islamic books. His favourite book was *Allah's Miracle in Afghanistan* by Abdullah Azzam, the founding member of Al-Qaeda. The book gave him definite purpose, which was to stand with the Mujahedeen and be committed to the cause. Over time, he left his friends and only befriended those who identified themselves as Mujahedeen. At one point, only members of his group were considered as friends and righteous human beings. Numerous interviews reported his loathing for Western countries, infidels, and even Muslims who did not support his cause and ideology.

Hostility

Exclusivism is followed by hostility towards out-group members. One's exclusion from their previous peers and community also demands the feeling of hate towards other groups. A common dogmatic principle held by most radicals is to be fierce to infidels for they are the enemy of God, and radicals view themselves as God's soldiers who are responsible for defending God's religion.

Referring back to the example of Imam Samudra (Aziz, 2004), his journey to find meaning in his identity led him to manifest his generativity virtue through exterminating Westerners who were deemed to be threatening the Islamic community from practicing the religion. Both media and academic interviews consistently stated his belief that he was doing the right thing for *ummah* (Muslim community) and had no regrets in doing so (Milla, 2010).

If Imam Samudra got the story of suffering Palestinian and Afghan brothers from Abdullah Azzam's book, other terrorist group members got the story from ideologists such as Abdullah Sungkar's or Ali Ghufron's preaching materials. The two of them were known as the Jemaah Islamiyah leaders. Soon after, other stories relating to the oppression of Islamic groups in Indonesia were constructed along with Afghanistan's story to claim that it was the time for Muslims to defend and fight back against those who try to defy God's religion. One story that terrorists mention frequently is the Tanjung Priok incident in 1984, when Suharto's authoritarian regime killed locals and many protesters from community mosques. It was reported that the ruling regime at that time was extremely suspicious of any Islamic political activities and wanted to constrain them accordingly (Muluk, 2009). Usually, such stories are used to define the current ruling government as Islam's enemy and subsequently this is followed by scriptural justification to kill those enemies and to wage war (Ba'asyir, 2012a, 2012b). Terrorist members who are already excluded from general society will be further drawn to the idea when repeatedly consuming such violence-invoking material.

Isolation

Besides personal experiences of exclusivism, terrorist leaders intensively use isolation during the indoctrination process for their recruits. Usually, it begins when the new members receive their first assignment from the group. The assignment is intended to measure the individuals' commitment and effectiveness; it requires the member's clandestinity and loyalty so that he/she will only trust people from their network. During this isolation stage, members will have already committed themselves to a singular goal, uniformed way to reach that goal, and defined their existence with a single identity not giving any room for alternative option or the chance for critical evaluation of any of them. The members of radical groups tend to develop close-mindedness (which is distinguished by high need for closure) and view intergroup distinctiveness with derogatory mechanisms (Kruglanski, 2004; Kruglanski *et al.*, 2006; Kruglanski *et al.*, 2002; Webber & Kruglanski, 2017).

The isolation process can be seen in HD's story. He was a student of philosophy in a notable university in Indonesia, but he also described himself as deviant. He used to drink, gamble, and extort merchants in the market. Once, his friend abandoned him in a dangerous situation, but he was saved by a member of a terrorist group who later became his mentor. Feeling indebted to him, HD followed the footsteps of his new mentor even till he was tasked to plant a bomb. The mentor supported him in every way so that he could do the job successfully. HD admitted that he suppressed his own doubts about the assignment and placed his belief in his mentor and religion. Although the bomb missed the target, HD and his mentor were captured.

Commitment

Another challenge in shifting terrorist detainees' paradigm is their persistence to stay in their ideology and their ideological group. As Altier *et al.* (2014) demonstrated, by borrowing Rusbult's (1983) investment model, terrorist's commitment towards their group can be viewed through their satisfaction from being in the group, their investment in the group, and the availability of existing alternatives if they chose to leave the group.

In one discussion at a prison in a province in Central Java, observers reported that younger detainees tended to be more accepting towards de-radicalisation materials than older detainees, who in Rusbult's term can be considered to be members who have invested more in the terrorist group than their younger peers. Those who have plans for post-release also have been reported to talk more about their plans than about the importance of their old cause, compared to those who did not have plans. This confirms using alternatives as leverage points to lower detainees' preoccupation toward their ideological group.

Commitment to radical jihadist groups is sometimes expressed in *baiáh* pledges, which means to listen and obey. From the moment a person is committed to a group, he will obey the command of the leader and attach himself to the group's goals regardless of his interests in his personal life. A person, who has given a *baiáh*, is categorised as a trusted person and someone who is ready to be further involved in group activities. *Baiáh* does not allow differences of opinion within the group, which creates many obstacles for leaving the group. This was experienced by AI (Imron, 2007), who had given a *baiáh* commitment to Jemaah Islamiyah before leaving for Afghanistan. In the end, although he did not agree with the Bali Bombing plan, he has no option but to follow orders and help his friends prepare for the attack in Bali.

Positive Intergroup Contact as Proposed Solution in De-radicalisation

Social psychology literature suggests that positive intergroup contact has been known to reduce intergroup prejudice (Pettigrew & Tropp, 2006). However, there are certain prerequisite conditions that have to be met before the "contact" can have a positive effect. These conditions are: equal status of the interacting parties, personal interactions beyond formal group interactions, agreed norms that benefit all parties, and cooperation between the parties (Forsyth, 2010). Once the conditions have been met, the resulting positive interactions can be expected to lower intergroup bias, lower competitiveness, and enhance cooperation.

In our programme, the end goal of applying positive interaction with terrorist prisoners is to lower their commitment towards terrorist groups, and eventually lower their support towards the violence justifying ideology. The programme is specifically constructed to provoke multiple perspectives, empathy, and curiosity toward public affairs via discussions about daily life and mundane matters. Depending on the situation and acceptance by the group, different types of activities are implemented.

Instructors and facilitators were instructed to tailor the training materials for the prisoners (i.e., so that the prisoners can understand the content), and avoid any discrimination or name calling during the interactions. All of these programmes were administered before the ideological discussion the following day. Listed below are our insights from the experience of executing these programmes over the last four years.

Perspective Taking

In some prisons, terrorist prisoners who decided to hold onto their group identity but denounce their ideology were observed to have actively engaged in discussions about different points of view and their consequences on behavioural choices. They were involved in role-playing activities, book discussions, and film screenings with cross-cultural themes. They were also more willing to discuss the characters and plots with instructors and facilitators during the programme. Even during their leisure time, they were observed to have watched Western movies or Asian dramas together with other inmates. However, some terrorist prisoners refused to watch these movies because they perceived these movies to promote *maksiat*, or sinful acts such as promiscuity, alcohol consumption, and other hedonistic behaviours. The messages delivered in some movies were also believed to be harmful to the Muslim community. Terrorist prisoners mentioned that movies which portrayed Arabs or people with an Islamic identity as cold-blooded villains were hypocritical, because the filmmakers denied the involvement of Western countries in creating turmoil in the Middle East.

Instructors and facilitators noted that many terrorist prisoners did not like to talk about their family because they rarely considered family as their priority. However, some of them seemed very enthusiastic about discussing their family problems in individual sessions. Terrorist prisoners who were already willing to cooperate and embrace new points of view were usually more open to talking about their families and exchanging information on dealing with difficult children.

This was also seen during role-playing sessions. Terrorist prisoners were given different situations and assigned roles. We used the scenario of a family that sold street food, and incorporated roles of the father, mother, and children who could not agree on what to sell during the rainy season. This role-playing activity aimed to encourage perspective taking, and reminding participants of their duty as the respected breadwinner of the family. During the discussion session, the facilitator guided participants to examine the perspective of each character and their partisanship. They were asked to criticise their own views and encouraged to adopt different views. Some inmates started expressing remorse after talking about their families. For example, DN, a barber who joined a terrorist group in a province in Central Java, said: "All my life, I wanted to feel the pride of being useful. My life journey that brought me here made me realise that I should start being useful for my family first". For others who believed that the caliphate was the best governmental system also decided to leave political activities and discussions because they wanted to work and fulfil their duty as the provider for their families.

Reflective Thinking

Most terrorist prisoners enjoyed writing workshops. Those who expressed the intention to denounce violent acts were interested in doing *da'wah*, or delivering sermon. In our programme, religious narratives were used to guide the participants in engaging in reflective thinking rather than using it as material for radical propaganda. We frequently emphasised Quranic stories and teachings relating to interpersonal mannerisms in daily life as preferable sermon material. During the workshop, detainees were instructed to create a story about being kind and generous to others and to list several problems that might hinder people from doing good deeds towards others. Quranic stories of war and conflict were discussed more comprehensively from the historical perspective in contra-ideology sessions after the psychology session.

Detainees reported that the writing workshop helped them to think and speak systematically. Furthermore, several testimonies stated that terrorist prisoners learnt to express their feelings more freely through writing. Some of them admitted that their grudge towards authorities were there since they were teenagers because they always felt left out by their peers. Through the workshop, some of them began to realise the source of their angst and anger, and how they have wrongly associated and generalised their feelings to authority figures. These revelations were often shared with other detainees during the workshop. Observers reported that a small number of participants were inspired to write a book about their reflections on their lives and their growing understanding of religious teachings after finishing the workshop. Some detainees who started writing even consulted the instructors about their book during the workshop.

Alternative Social Identity

As mentioned previously, the most difficult challenge in applying positive intergroup contact was the individuals' prior social ties to terrorist groups. For them, the group members were like family and friends who supported them and gave them a sense of identity. Therefore, introducing detainees to an alternative social identity was a crucial strategy in promoting positive contact with others. Interactional experience inside the prison through strategic cell placement coupled with the diverse prison community contributed to positive contact. These positive outcomes were commonly seen in prisons at secluded areas, especially in far-east islands in Indonesia; regions in Indonesia where the majority of inhabitants are not Muslims, but are Christians or pagans. The terrorists who were placed in such regions were the ones who did not seclude themselves from others while in prison, unlike some of the notorious ideologists and group leaders.

Take AR, one of terrorist prisoners arrested for his involvement in the Poso conflict, as an example. AR was placed in a prison on an island where Muslims were the minority group; he previously lived in the neighbouring island where Muslims were the majority. During the session, AR surprisingly expressed his joy and awe towards the non-Muslim community inside the prison. He shared that he had never lived in a non-Muslim majority community and felt welcomed by members of that community. During his three months in solitary confinement, some Christian inmates took the chance to greet and chat with him through his closed door. "This novel experience should be shared with my friends back in my hometown!" said AR during the session. Other terrorist prisoners also reported similar experiences. Some even attempted to show other people that Islam is not violent by actively participating in social activities and befriending other inmates. This interaction signified an ideological shift of a terrorist. Many newly captured terrorists refused to participate in any kind of prison activities because they believed that the activities were intended to change their ideas and goals of establishing an Islamic state, therefore they viewed them as an act of abandoning God's order to establish Islam sovereignty in the country.

However, the capacity of prisons in secluded areas is limited, and many prisoners objected being incarcerated in prisons that were too far away from their families. Therefore, terrorist prisoners are mainly located in Java Island. It is common in many prisons to house several diverse groups of terrorists in the same cellblock. Interestingly, some terrorist prisoners became disillusioned as a result of this arrangement. Newly radicalised terrorist prisoners, who never met the famous ideologists like Ali Ghufron and Imam Samudra before, witnessed for themselves how the terrorist prisoners behaved in prison and became disillusioned by it. They subconsciously distanced themselves from terrorist groups and denounced their jihadist identity.

Intergroup Cooperation

Another aspect that strengthens detainees' social identity is the experience of intergroup cooperation inside prison. In several cases, the less violent group members were willing to interact with other prisoners not belonging to their group. Direct contact was implemented through planned activities, and terrorist prisoners were encouraged to engage in joint activities with other prisoners from various groups, religions, and tribes. They were also usually willing to meet journalists, academics, and representatives from non-government organisations. They tended to be more receptive and willing to engage in special programmes for terrorist prisoners while being in custody.

However, there were several prisoners who continued to maintain their group exclusivity and refused to make any contact with people outside of their group. They retained their radical ideology while in custody and maintained contact with their leader and fellow members of the group. The Islamic State of Iraq and Syria (ISIS) supporters belonged to this category. This sense of exclusivity also affected the way ISIS supporters interacted with other terrorist prisoners. Since ISIS supporters supported the use of indiscriminate violence, the terrorist prisoners became polarised into those who supported the use of indiscriminate violence and those who supported selective use of violence as a strategy. In the end, those who embraced the selective use of violence tended to abandon the justification of violence to maintain positive distinctiveness as compared to the ISIS supporter group. What happened next was that the former adopted a less violent form of ideology and started to resemble mainstream Muslims; they wanted to portray a good example of Islam. Usually, ISIS and non-ISIS groups were separated during the programme. The non-ISIS groups would share their aspirations of re-portraying the image of Islam that was misconstrued by ISIS. In other words, they started to cooperate with others in order to achieve their new goals. Our duties in the de-radicalisation programme were to facilitate the discussion about these relational dynamics within the prison setting, guide their thoughts on disillusionment, and embrace new perspectives of religious life.

In the meantime, ISIS supporters were encouraged to make contact with selected resource persons who were acceptable to them. There were also individual approaches initiated by prison officers who earned their trust. ISIS supporters usually refused to join group activities with other terrorist inmates, but they did not mind being involved in programmes with people from various backgrounds, but maintained limited interactions.

Alternative Goals

This brings us to another learning lesson: alternative goals have become the defining moment when terrorist prisoners start to renounce and leave their violent ways. Once detainees thought about other achievable goals (other than their previous religious or political cause), they became more relaxed in their daily interactions with others. In fact, some observers reported that these terrorist prisoners become more appreciative towards others. Those who began to change their behaviour toward others usually believed that it was the time for them to promote Islam peacefully and to start building good relationships with others in order to achieve that goal.

Numerous reports on the de-radicalisation programme stated that many terrorist prisoners expressed their gratitude for being able to participate in the programme. It was also common for some detainees to express their gratitude and astonishment at the opportunity to meet respected academics across the country. Some of them stated that despite their low status within the society (i.e., low-paying job), they were still able to meet and learn from these respected academics. "Who would expect that me, a food street vendor taught by top university professors and doctors in a class specially designed for us. It's such a great honour for me and my friends" said CH, one of the detainees who was charged with hiding explosive materials for a terrorist group.

Conclusion: The Challenge of Ideological Shift

The ultimate goal of the de-radicalisation programme is ideological shift, from violence to peace, from radical to moderate. Have intergroup contacts succeeded in supporting ideological shift in terrorist groups? The report from de-radicalisation programmes in 2016 showed that there were significant declines in terrorists' commitment towards their ideological group and a meaningful shift in interpretation of jihad (Milla *et al.*, 2018). Formerly, all terrorists held on to their notorious motto of "Live with dignity, or die as *syahid* (died by defending Islam)". Terrorists used to limit jihad and *syahid* in the context of holy war, whereas the Prophet Muhammad himself stated clearly that fighting one's desire is a greater jihad compared to physical war. Jihad literally means "struggle" or "effort", but terrorists usually used the term jihad only in specific meanings, such as jihad as war.

Therefore, the main objective of de-radicalisation is to open the interpretation of many things believed by terrorists, so that they can reconsider and re-evaluate their priorities. Besides jihad's alternative interpretation mentioned previously, the phrase "live with dignity" can also be viewed from different perspectives. Terrorists often interpret "live with dignity" as living with a duty to defend their religion; it can also be interpreted as living as Mujahedeen who stand firmly against anyone who rejects their ideology. However, the phrase can also be interpreted as being benevolent to others, giving the best out of us as a means of "live with dignity", so that we do not become a liability or threat to others (Idris, 2016). Reflecting on former terrorists' confessions, they interpret "live with dignity" as a means of being good Muslims who are always obedient and submissive to all of the God's commands without romanticising violent jihad.

The de-radicalisation programme showed more improvement regarding the concept of positive intergroup contact. It showed that the more positive their attitude was towards the programme, the lower their support for jihad as war (Milla *et al.*, 2018). Those who participated in writing workshops also showed stronger support towards democracy and Indonesia's constitution (Muluk *et al.*, 2018). Consequently, we might safely assume that our intergroup contact model contributed significantly to their improvement in perspective and knowledge.

Besides that, the successfulness of intergroup contact did not depend on the current execution of the programme. There are some factors that draw beyond the time of the terrorists' capture, such as history of the relation and narratives in making sense of intergroup relation (Muluk, 2009). The groups who experienced violent acts in their historical relation found it harder to reach ideal conditions to participate in positive contact. Even though some groups never experienced actual historical violence, they often got involved in out-group bias that made them feel like they were experiencing real violence, justified, and elevated by scriptural stories from the Holy Book, which is believed to be an inerrant literal command from God. All of the conditions mentioned above are obstacles in changing terrorists' perspective.

We can reflect on MB's case regarding historical violence. MB is a young man who sold the explosive material to blow up the Myanmar embassy. His family experienced persecution and state-initiated violence during the dictatorship era of the second president. MB, now an ISIS supporter, refuted every idea proposed by a scholar of Islamic studies when he talked about Pancasila (Indonesia's five pillars of ideological foundation) and the legitimacy of the state's constitution. The more the scholar persuaded him, the more he resisted. At the end of the discussion, the scholar concluded that MB did not show any willingness to receive new information, let alone willingness to change his perspective. However, the situation changed the following day. The other scholar who was a doctorate in law shared his story about various Islamic countries he visited, especially about how they dealt with regulation and prohibition. The scholar also shared stories on how Western countries' policies resembled classic Islamic values and how Indonesian scholars have started to try to implement this information for modern Muslim community. This time, the scholar did not talk about the Pancasila or the Indonesian constitution at all. MB and two other ISIS sympathisers did not reject the new information from the scholar, instead they asked for more stories or deeper explanations about the given stories.

Referring to AR's case mentioned previously, he was eager and happy to meet other group members. However, at the following religion and civic life discussion session, AR's opinion was completely in the opposite direction. When the cleric asked about AR's position on the Poso war, he expressed anger toward Christians whom he thought was putting Muslims in a very horrible situation. "We should take arms and fight those who oppress us, that's what The Prophet would do at his time," said AR to the cleric. AR had experienced benevolent contact with Christians, but he still needed the clarity of the political situation in the Poso conflict area. This is what the cleric actually did that day; he explained how the situation during the Prophet's era and the current situation were different. This example suggests that positive contact will help to condition open mindedness, and ultimately smooth the ideological shift.

We should emphasise that positive intergroup contact was not intended as a standalone programme. As mentioned earlier, this particular psychological intervention is a prelude to the counter ideology discussion in the following session. This is similar to the French's psychology programme for incarcerated ISIS supporters, which is also a prelude to the actual legal process (Bouzar & Martin, 2016). We also should note that intergroup contact alone did not sufficiently fulfil our main objective, which was to reduce the support towards jihad as war and increase support towards democracy and proper civic life. Ideological discussions with Islamic scholars and other related scholars are still a critical part in de-radicalisation programmes. At the end of the day, permanent change can only be expected if ideologies that justify the use of violence to achieve the group goals have truly been left behind.

References

Abbas, N. (2017). Rehabilitasi dan reedukasi narapidana dan mantan narapidana kasus teror. In M. A. Darraz (Ed.), *Jihad, Khilafah, dan Terorisme: Reformulasi Ajaran Islam* (pp. 289–303). Bandung: Mizan Media Utama.

Altier, M. B., Thoroughgood, C. N., & Horgan, J. G. (2014). Turning away from terrorism: Lessons from psychology, sociology, and criminology. *Journal of Peace Research*, *51*(5), 647–661.

Aziz, A. (2004). *Aku Melawan Teroris*. Solo: Jazera.

Ba'asyir, A. B. (2012a). *Hakikat Iman dan Murtad*. Jakarta: JAT Media Center.

Ba'asyir, A. B. (2012b). *Hakikat Tauhid dan Syirik*. Jakarta: JAT Media Center.

Badan Nasional Penanggulangan Terorisme (BNPT) (2017). National Counter Terrorism Agency Deradicalisation Annual Report 2017. Sentul, Indonesia: Indonesian Government.

Bouzar, D., & Martin, M. (2016). Méthode expérimentale de déradicalisation: Quelles stratégies émotionnelles et cognitives?. *Pouvoirs*, *158*(3), 83–96.

Forsyth, D. R. (2010). *Group Dynamics*. Belmont: Wadsworth Cengage Learning.

Idris, I. (2016). *Membumikan Deradikalisasi: Soft Approach Model Pembinaan Terorisme Dari Hulu Ke Hilir Secara Berkesinambungan*. Jakarta: Daulat Press.

Imron, A. (2007). *Ali Imron Sang Pengebom*. Jakarta: Penerbit Republika.

Kruglanski, A. W. (2004). *The Psychology of Closed Mindedness*. Hove: Psychology Press.

Kruglanski, A. W., & Fishman, S. (2009). Psychological factors in terrorism and counterterrorism: Individual, group, and organizational levels of analysis. *Social Issues and Policy Review*, *3*(1), 1–44.

Kruglanski, A. W., Gelfand, M. J., Bélanger, J. J., Sheveland, A., Hetiarachchi, M., & Gunaratna, R. (2014). The psychology of radicalisation and deradicalisation: How significance quest impacts violent extremism. *Advances in Political Psychology*, *35*(1), 69–93.

Kruglanski, A. W., Pierro, A., Mannetti, L., & De Grada, E. (2006). Group as epistemic providers: Need for closure and the unfolding of group centrism. *Psychological Review*, *113*(1), 84–100.

Kruglanski, A. W., Shah, J. Y., Pierro, A., & Mannetti, L. (2002). When similarity breeds content: Need for closure and the allure of homogeneous and self-resembling groups. *Journal of Personality and Social Psychology*, *83*(3), 648–662.

McCauley, C., & Moskalenko, S. (2010). Individual and group mechanisms of radicalization. In L. Fenstermacher, L. Kuznar, T. Rieger, & A. Speckhard (Eds.), *Protecting the Homeland from International and Domestic Security Threats: Current Multidisciplinary Perspectives on Root Causes, the Role of Ideology, and Programs for Counter-Radicalization and Disengagement*. Washington, D. C.: START.

Milla, M. N. (2010). *Mengapa Memilih Jalan Teror: Analisis Psikologis Pelaku Teror*. Yogyakarta: Gadjah Mada University Press.

Milla, M. N., Faturochman, & Ancok, D. (2013). The impact of leader–follower interactions on the radicalisation of terrorists: A case study of the Bali bombers. *Asian Journal of Social Psychology*, *16*, 92–100.

Milla, M. N., Hudiyana, J., & Arifin, H. H. (2018). Intrinsic motivation as key predictor for adoption of alternative identity in a deradicalisation

program: Investigation of terrorist detainees interview profiles. Manuscript submitted to publication (under review).
Muluk, H. (2009). Memory for sale: how groups "distort" their collective memory for reconciliation purposes and building peace. In C. J. Montiel, & N. M. Noor (Eds.), *Peace Psychology in Asia* (pp. 105–122). New York: Springer.
Muluk, H., Milla, M. N., & Cahyono, W. (2013). The dynamic of network trust on radical group in Indonesia. Research Report.
Muluk, H., Umam, N., & Milla, N. M. (2018). Beyond the Narratives: Insight from psychological support for contra-ideology in a deradicalisation program in Indonesian Prisons. Manuscript submitted to publication (under review).
Page-Gould, E., Mendoza-Denton, R., & Tropp, L. R. (2008). With a little help from my cross-group friend: Reducing anxiety in intergroup contexts through cross-group friendship. *Journal of Personality and Social Psychology*, *95*, 1,080–1,094.
Pettigrew, T. F., & Tropp, L. R. (2006). A meta-analytic test of intergroup contact theory. *Journal of Personality and Social Psychology*, *90*, 751–783.
Rusbult, C. E. (1983). A longitudinal test of the investment model: The development (and deterioration) of satisfaction and commitment in heterosexual involvements. *Journal of Personality and Social Psychology*, *45*(1), 101.
Sageman, M. (2004). *Understanding Terror Network*. Philladelphia: University of Pensylvania Press.
Sukabdi, Z. (2015). Terrorism in Indonesia: A review on rehabilitation and deradicalisation. *Journal of Terrorism Research*, *6*(2), 36–56.
Webber, D., Babush, M., Schori-Eyal, N., Vazeou-Nieuwenhuis, A., Hettiarachchi, M., Bélanger, J. J., Moyano, M., Trujillo, H. M., Gunaratna, R., Kruglanski, A. W., & Gelfand, M. J. (2018). The road to extremism: Field and experimental evidence that significance loss-induced need for closure fosters radicalisation. *Journal of Personality and Social Psychology*, *114*(2), 270–285.
Webber, D., & Kruglanski, A. W. (2017). The social psychological makings of a terrorist. *Current Opinions in Psychology*, *19*, 131–134.

CHAPTER 15

In the Search of Home: Tackling Support for ISIS Ideology Among Ordinary People

WHINDA YUSTISIA and
WAHYU CAHYONO

*Faculty of Psychology,
Universitas Indonesia, Indonesia*

Introduction

Islamic State in Iraq and Syria (ISIS) is a transnational phenomenon. More than a hundred groups have pledged allegiance to it, including groups in Indonesia. ISIS succeeded in becoming a prominent group with a large number of followers, resources, and more importantly controlling large areas of land in a relatively short period of time between 2014–2016. ISIS not only believed that the suffering of Muslims around the world, structural injustice, and oppression would be solved by establishing a Khilafah (Caliphate), but it would also fulfil Islamic end-of-times prophecies. ISIS worldview was appealing to radical figures in Indonesia such as Aman Abdurrahman and Abu Bakar Baasyir, who pledged their allegiance to ISIS. Subsequently, radical organisations, such as Jamaah Ansharut Tauhid, Jamaah Tauhid Wal Jihad, Darul Islam Ring Banten, Mujahidin East Indonesia, Bima Group, and other affiliated groups also followed suit.

Once it had control of territory, ISIS's first task was to create a conducive environment not only for fighters but also for non-combatants. They were also creating propaganda to recruit doctors, engineers, and other professionals to strengthen and legitimise their endeavour of creating a "global" caliphate. ISIS claimed that Islam required Muslims to live in an Islamic state that practiced Shari'ah law rather than in a territory governed by non-Muslims or by Muslims administering man-made laws. Hijrah or emigration became a religious duty or obligation for all Muslims. This led to an alarming trend where Muslims and their families travelled to Iraq and Syria hoping to establish themselves in ISIS-controlled territory. One noteworthy example was Iman Santosa (alias Abu Umarthe) who convinced his brother-in-law, Dwi Djoko Wiwoho, a former director of the Indonesia Investment Coordinating Board's licensing office on Batam island, to migrate to Syria with his 26 family members (Soeriaatmadja, 2018).

The large numbers of ISIS returnees raised international attention as there were concerns that returnees would spread their radical ideologies in their home countries. Moreover, it was possible that they might use their military capabilities (having trained in Syria) to carry out violent attacks.

Given these threats, it is essential to develop some strategies to prevent people from joining ISIS or radical groups in general in the future. This chapter attempts to address this issue. However, before discussing the issue in-depth, it is necessary to understand what challenges we face when tackling ISIS's appeal. We will use Santosa and his family members' experiences as a case study to provide some valuable insights on how extreme ideology can appeal to ordinary people.

By way of background, we will briefly introduce the context of the present case study by providing some information about Santosa and his family in the following section. Most of the information we have comes from interviews with his family members. The authors interviewed the family during their stay at the National Body for Counter-Terrorism (BNPT)'s compound during the first two weeks after they returned to Indonesia. The authors also had a chance to interview Santosa in person, and determined that the accounts from his family members matched his own.

Context to the Case Study

In November 2015, one year after ISIS declared the establishment of the Islamic State, 26 Indonesians took a challenging journey from Jakarta to Syria. The motivation for the trip resulted from a routine Islamic group discussion known as pengajian in Bahasa Indonesia. The 26 Indonesians were relatives of Iman Santosa.

Iman Santosa was a moderate Muslim initially. He began to learn more about Islam intensively from 2001. At one point, Santosa suffered a major financial set-back, and he was being blacklisted by all banks in Indonesia as he had accumulated a huge debt. Nevertheless, Santosa pursued his religious studies and began learning Islam from a *utaz* (religious teacher). He gained basic knowledge in *Tauhid* and then found a teacher to learn Arabic language from. After he felt confident with the knowledge he had, in 2009, he started a group of *pengajian* for his family members and his employees at the office.

Santosa continued to learn while teaching. However, he was no longer taught by a teacher. He found new information about Islam through the Internet instead and, through that, he gained access to fundamentalist content. He moved from teaching general concepts in Islam like *Tauhid* (i.e., the concept of oneness of God) and the process and the creation of the universe to *aqidah* (i.e., firm belief and strong conviction on Islam), with an emphasis on Al-Wala and Al-Bara, key concepts in Islamic fundamentalist ideology. Al-Wala means drawing the self closer to fellow Muslims by loving and helping them. Meanwhile, Al-Bara means disconnecting from the *kaffir* (non-believers).

Belief in this doctrine made Santosa and converted family members avoid others who did not subscribe to their beliefs. For instance, they did not eat any food from or pray in the house of such family members.

While actively searching for fundamentalist content on the Internet, Santosa eventually found ISIS websites. Since then, as told by one of his wives, he actively consumed ISIS propaganda material on the Internet. He shared information he obtained with his family members or staff in the *pengajian*. He convinced them about apocalyptic prophecies, which required all Muslim to move to Syria, and about the practical aspect that it would provide them life conveniences, such as, free education, free housing, free electricity, free healthcare, and many job opportunities. He also learnt through an ISIS recruiter that any outstanding debts of potential migrants to Syria would be fully paid by ISIS.

Building on that information, Santosa and his family members developed a very positive impression of ISIS. They felt that living in Syria under an ISIS government would help them realise their Islamic dream (i.e., to live under Islamic law and government and prosper). Some family members naturally expressed reservations, but Santosa was able to persuade others. He did this using tailored approaches, which proved successful. While most of the family members were attracted to his proposal due to health and economic motivations, Santosa persuaded one of his wealthy sisters through an ideological approach. Santosa convinced her that Muslims must live under Islamic laws as described in the Quran and Hadith.

Five Key Challenges

No Common Profile of Migrants to Syria

The large number of Foreign Terrorist Fighters (FTFs) has gained international attention. A report from the United Nation Office of Counter Terrorism (2017) revealed that there is no single profile of a FTF. This is also what we found within the present context. Unlike previous studies, ISIS supporters who travelled in the present case travelled as one family with Santosa at the centre of the network. Amongst the 26 people who travelled, two of them were children, five of them were teenagers aged between 11–16 years old, six of them aged between17–42 years old, and eight of them older than 42 years old. In terms of educational background, five of them had a bachelor's degree and one of them had a master's degree. In relation to social and economic status, they were generally doing well, at least till Santosa's failure in his business. One of Santosa's sister was married to a director in a governmental institution.

Migration Driven by Economic Factors Rather Than Religion

Inequality has repeatedly been found to cause social discontent (Song & Appleton, 2006), socio-political conflicts (Muller, 1985; Simpson, 1990), and even political violence (Blau & Blau, 1982). Such conditions form the basis for disadvantaged groups to engage in collective action as an attempt to voice their expectations and aspirations, and to solve their difficulties (Justino, 2016). Although some studies suggest that inequality could lead to political action, existing literature in the terrorism context revealed that the relationship of economic factors and involvement in radicalism and extremism varied. On the one hand, some studies provided evidence that some terrorist activities are conducted by those who have economic issues in their life (Blomberg & Hess, 2005; Freytag *et al.*, 2011). On the other hand, some studies suggest that there is negative or no association between the level of prosperity and involvement in terrorism (Benmelech *et al.*, 2012; Benmelech & Klor, 2017; Krueger & Laitin, 2007; Piazza, 2007).

In the present context, we also found similar mixed factors. Some individuals in our case study had economic difficulties, while others were wealthy. Those with financial difficulties included Santosa and his three wives, his older sister, and his brother. The difficulties stemmed from Santosa's business failure. The latter group of individuals did not have any major financial difficulties. Santosa's brother-in-law had a good career and educational background.

It is tempting to conclude that these individuals did not have economic reasons for supporting the move to Syria. However, it is important to note that they did have some strong feelings about relative deprivation. They believed that inequality was still pervasive in Indonesia, and while many non-Muslims led a wealthy lifestyle, the majority of Muslims were still financially disadvantaged. They believed that such inequalities would not exist if Indonesia implemented strict Islamic law. Taken together, it can be seen that although this group of individuals did not experience actual injustice, they had strong views of the inequalities experienced by fellow Muslims in Indonesia.[1]

The Role of Psychological Factors

Previous studies have repeatedly found that psychological factors play an important role in being able to encourage involvement or support for radical acts. Some socio-psychological factors that we identified in the present case as motivational factors for ISIS supporters are quest for significance, group identity, and ideology. These factors were introduced by Webber and Kruglanski (2017) as

---

[1]Some studies indicated that perceived injustice played a more important role than actual injustice as a factor for support for radicalisation (Borum, 2004; Krieger & Meierrieks, 2015), at least regarding extrapolated involvement (Koseli, 2007; Krueger & Maleckova, 2003). Borum (2003) explained that sense of dissatisfaction, caused by perceived deprivation, emerges at the initial process of drawing adherents to extremist groups. The process begins when candidates initially perceive deprivation that exists in their environment indicating that "something is not right". When they see the unpleasant condition in a comparative context, they will move onto the stage of "it's not fair". The perceived injustice would make them feel less loyal to the existing political system (Koseli, 2007). Afterwards, they start to blame others for their aversive condition. Lastly, when the hateful attitude is combined with a justification that their in-group is under threat, violent jihad would then be a justified means to achieve goals. In the context of FTFs, it was also found that economic prosperity (i.e., examined by GDP, level of inequality, job opportunities) does not necessarily lead to participation in ISIS (Benmelech & Klor, 2017). Benmelech and Klor (2017) explained that it was more likely to be caused by some frustration in life and lack of social and economic prospects.

a 3 'N' approach (i.e., need for significant, narrative, and network) in understanding radicalism.

Quest for significance

Humans have a fundamental need to feel significant. Maslow (1943) suggested that self-actualisation is the highest basic need of an individual. One way to meet such a need is to be useful in society, for instance, by pursuing a meaningful job for societal significance (Frankl, 2000). Kruglanski and others (2009, 2013, 2014) have repeatedly demonstrated that the need for significance is a fundamental factor that drives individuals' involvement in radicalism. The basic idea is that due to the feeling of insignificance, individuals will seek certain ways to restore it by doing something "useful". In the context of terrorism, Kruglanski and colleagues (2014) suggest that the sense of insignificance can be managed through in-group/out-group competition, particularly in terms of out-performing rival groups.

Alternatively, the sense of insignificance can be redeemed by adherence to authority. Such an action can make us feel like doing something useful for someone we love very much. In this case, the authority is the Prophet Muhammad. It is believed that Prophet Muhammad has said that there will be a conflict in "Dabiq or al-Amaq", which is at the border of Syria and Turkey, as a sign of the anticipated end of time. Some people believe that the current conflict in Syria is the conflict the Prophet warned of thousands of years ago. Is it said that, when that moment comes, Muslims have a duty to travel there to fight the evil for the final victory of Islam.

Membership of a fringe group can arguably restore a sense of significance; the question then is whether the individuals in this case study possessed such feelings? Previous studies have shown that FTFs in Syria were frustrated as a result of their minority status in Western countries. Many were second generation Muslims or new Muslim converts who had grown up in a relatively homogenous community and were minorities (Benmelech & Klor, 2017; Bergen *et al.*, 2015; Dawson & Amarasingam, 2017; Verwimp, 2016).

Similar to the phenomenon of FTF, most of the individuals in this case study were also found to possess feelings of insignificance. According to our data, there are at least six individuals who had such experiences, namely Santosa, his second and third wives, his brother, his sister, and his mother-in-law. Drawing on the significant loss' categorisations developed by Jasko *et al.* (2017), it was found that some of them had an achievement-related loss (i.e., failure in business, economic difficulties) and some others had relationship-related loss of significance (i.e., marriage failure). There might have been another type of significant loss, namely traumatic/abusive experience, but we did not find sufficient support for it.

In addition to the personal significant loss, Webber and Kruglanski (2017) suggest that support for radicalism might also be derived from group-based significant loss, potential loss of significance, and opportunity for significant gain. Individuals in this case study seem to have experienced such feelings. As explained earlier, most of them had a strong negative emotion towards out-groups who they perceived caused suffering to Muslims in their home country or in other countries (e.g., Palestine and Syria). Moreover, they also had perceived an opportunity for significant gains. Therefore, they believed that they could fulfil their life aspirations, the Islamic dream, by living a prosperous life under the caliphate.

Ideology

The preceding explanation has indicated that humans have a basic need to feel significant. The question is why should it be through radicalism rather than peaceful interactions? Before answering that question, it is important to first understand the definition of radicalism. Radicalism refers to the view in which individuals act in a way that is not typical to societal norms (Kruglanski *et al.*, 2014). Borum (2012) explained that to be radical meant to reject the *status quo*. However, it is important to note that the rejection of the *status quo* is not necessarily expressed through violence. It depends on several factors such as cultural values, belief in peaceful movements (Putra & Sukabdi, 2013), and the level of commitment to the focal goal (Kruglanski *et al.*, 2014).

One might argue that it does not make sense that personal significance can be restored by harming others or by doing something immoral. To some extent, that notion is true. However, it should be known that terrorists have strong moral justifications for the violence that they or their group perpetrate. A 2004 report on the Bali bombings (Aziz, 2004) revealed that Imam Samudra, one of the bombers, had dehumanised his victims to justify his actions. He said:

> How agonising is it to see the land of Muslims taken by the Monsters of Zion and the Crusades? How many Muslim states have been attacked and occupied by those envious parties? Look at the jihadist front of Palestine, Chechnya, Afghanistan, Kashmir, Philippines, Dagestan and Indonesia itself. Can't you see that lots of armed conflicts are occurring between Muslims and those infidel occupiers? And look at the litres of blood being poured out by those Dracula monsters. Those facts are more than enough to explain the fardhu'ain (foremost obligation) nature of jihad (Aziz, 2004).

Although the individuals in this case study did not engage in violence during their time in Syria, they could be categorised as supporters of radicalism. They were a family that wanted to travel to Syria to meet some of their basic needs, such as healthcare, jobs, and to be good Muslims who understood the commitment to the order of *hijrah* to Syam (it was believed to be in Syria). ISIS tried to force the male family members to join the fighters, but none of them were willing to do so. They claimed that they had moved to Syria not to be soldiers but normal citizens. When they refused to fight, all the men (including teen boys) were imprisoned for several weeks.

One factor that can explain why they did not want to participate in the fighting is that they did not fully commit to the focal goal of ISIS. As explained by Kruglanski and colleagues (2014), radical people are highly committed to the focal goal so that they can ignore other interests. The important aim for them is to achieve group goals, although it might cause harm to other groups. The individuals in this case study did not have such a strong commitment. It was indicated in some interviews that some of them felt very disappointed that ISIS were very cruel towards non-Muslims and even fellow Muslims. For example, a respondent expressed "...Subhanallah, we were very disappointed with ISIS. We were deceived a lot. We hope no more Indonesians experience the same thing as us". Such disappointment was the result of daily events, such as her elderly mother who was caught by ISIS for not covering her face, ISIS fighters taking advantage of women, and a very slow response from the ISIS officials regarding their concerns.

In the case of ISIS, ideologisation begins with end-time prophesies and the claim that the emergence of ISIS's caliphate had been predicted by the Prophet, and as such, all Muslims were duty-bound to support it (Daskin, 2016). ISIS supported this claim by referencing selective writings from the Hadith. ISIS also employed clever propaganda such as using the Black flag, claiming that the war in "Dabiq or al-Amaq" had begun, and pointing to signs that the end of days was approaching.

After being able to convince people that ISIS is legitimate, their acts could be justified as something permissible or even required by God and the Prophet. ISIS worldview attracted many people, who were prepared to perpetrate acts of violence for the cause. In this case study, ideology was not able to force the Indonesians to commit violence. Instead, they rejected ISIS's use of violence towards women and fellow Muslims with different views. However, it is important to note that it does not mean that they did not support the use of violence at all, as they fully supported the idea of ISIS's violent acts toward out-groups (e.g., Western targets) as the right thing to do.

Network

The final factor that we think significantly motivated the individuals in this case study to move to Syria was that they were all from the same family. This trend is common in terrorist networks where members are related to each other (Bjorgo & Horgan, 2009). What we know from de-radicalisation literature is that a family can be an important factor in encouraging disengagement from terrorism. Here, however, the family took on the role of a facilitator towards involvement in violent extremism. Previous literature indicates that Al-Qaeda and Jemaah Islamiyah specifically employed family-based recruitment strategies in developing their organisation (Bjorgo & Horgan, 2009). Moreover, they arrange marriages of family members to members of their organisations and other organisations to strengthen the kinship between the groups.

Why could family-based recruitment be an effective strategy in influencing people to join a radical group? Based on Webber and Kruglanski's research (2017), there are two possible explanations. First, it is a lot easier to influence people who have the same identities. Family members in the present case, and like most other families, have the same family and religious identities. Previous studies have indicated that influencing others on new ideas will be much more effective when the information is sourced from in-group members rather than the out-group (Neighbors *et al.*, 2008; Terry *et al.*, 1999). Second, social psychology literature suggests that discussions among like-minded individuals are more likely to produce group polarisation, in which the group members position becomes more extreme than before after influencing each other in the discussion (Keating *et al.*, 2016; McGarty *et al.*, 1992; Strandberg *et al.*, 2017). In the case of Santosa, all of the family members admitted that Santosa was the first who introduced ISIS ideology to them. However, they also admitted that they did not obtain information solely from Santosa. Some of them also attempted to find information on their own. They had obtained material that corroborated Santosa's opinions, rather than challenging his views.

The Appeal of ISIS's Ideology for Ordinary People

As it has been seen in the previous section, the ISIS ideology in the present case influenced a family. Contrary to common belief that the typical characteristics of ISIS combatants include low education, *madrasah/pesantren* education, poor, and originating from a suburban deprived area, members of Santosa's family had higher education, graduated from non-religious-based school, had a good socioeconomic status, and originated from an urban area. Santosa had searched for ISIS contacts in Indonesia to arrange for their departure to Syria, but he could not connect with any ISIS's affiliations in Indonesia. In other words, their family had characteristics of ordinary people who typically have moderate political aspirations.

One reason that could explain why ISIS's ideology attracts urban, well-educated, and middle-class people, is related to the role of the Internet. Previously, radical groups were restricted to spreading their ideology in closes/small groups. Due to the Internet and social media, radical groups can now disseminate their ideologies to a wider audience. This means people with different social/economic characteristics can now gain access to radical ideologies (Basit, 2017; el-Said & Barrett, 2017; Vidino & Hughes, 2015). The question this raises is what prompts ISIS supporters to access extremist content on the Internet? Some people might not have the intention of consuming such messages. They just want to learn about the religion. The Internet, however, gives them many resources to learn from. Due to the massive radical content that ISIS has, it is only a matter of time before individuals like Santosa find ISIS websites.

There are some adverse consequences of radical ideologies easily reaching ordinary people. Firstly, they can become easily persuaded by ISIS's interpretation of Islamic texts because they have a limited understanding of Islam and rely on Internet resources. In fact, several psychological studies have found that people are most likely to get trapped in confirmation bias during web-based searching (Knobloch-Westerwick *et al.*, 2014; del Vicario *et al.*, 2016). Secondly, it is much easier for them to take action. As in the present case as well as other cases, the individuals were able to plan the trip to Syria by themselves.

No Longer Supporting ISIS does not Mean no Longer Supporting the Caliphate

Information that we collected from individuals in this case study indicated that they were disillusioned with ISIS. This was mainly because ISIS was not like what they had imagined. They expected ISIS to function like an Islamic government that fully applied Islamic values such as ensuring equality, listening to the voices of its people, treating fellow Muslims with kindness, respecting women, and committing to justice. However, we should be aware that despite their deep disappointment with ISIS, their support for the caliphate remained unchanged.

This outcome is in line with el-Badawy *et al.* study (2015) that suggests that support for radical groups is premised on foundational identity, ideology, and narrative. With regard to the foundational identity, this is a prerequisite before individuals begin to get attracted to the ideology. In the case of Salafi-jihadist ideology, their ideology occupies their foundational identity. In another words, they are more focused on their Salafi-jihadi group goal (i.e., establishing the Caliphate) rather than Islam in general. ISIS, in this case, is only one such group that emerged to actualise the Salafi-jihad ideology. There are currently two other radical groups with a similar ideology, such as Al-Qaeda and Jabhat al-Nusra. If ISIS falls, there might be another group in the future that will replace it.

Five Key Strategies

Based on our research, we suggest five strategies that can help address the above-mentioned challenges.

Integrated Approach on De-radicalisation and Counter-radicalisation

One major insight we gained from the group of people we analysed here is that there is no common profile of ISIS supporters. Therefore, we suggest that governments expand the scope of anti-terrorism policies. The target of counter-terrorism programmes should not be limited to the primary group, but also consider the secondary and tertiary groups. It is very important to pay equal attention to groups at all levels. The first level consists of the target groups that include the perpetrators, former perpetrators, and their families. They have a high potential to spread radical ideologies and re-engage in terror networks. However, targeting the programme only at primary groups will not completely prevent the future threat of terrorism. The governments also need to target secondary level groups, that includes groups and organisations that have the potential to support radicalism and violent extremism. More importantly, the case study discussed above demonstrates the need for governments to reach the groups on the third level: ordinary people who might not have a direct connection to primary level or even secondary level groups, but are still vulnerable to radicalisation.

Development of Family-based Approach

The family has an important role in both the radicalisation and de-radicalisation process (Weine *et al.*, 2010; Williams *et al.*, 2015). They can be a prevention factor that might discourage someone from getting involved in radicalism. Being far away from parents and/or wife/husband/children might make someone reconsider participating in terrorism. On the other hand, families could play a big role in an individual's radicalisation process. In the case of Santosa, the move to Syria and the return from Syria to Indonesia, were both family decisions. The information from in-group members will be more effective in influencing people. Once people have been radicalised, the power of influence from in-group members becomes even stronger. They are less likely to be persuaded by counter-narratives from outside their group (Bertijan *et al.*, 2016).

Based on these considerations, we propose that it is important to place more emphasis on developing family-based approaches when designing counter-terrorism and de-radicalisation programmes. When Indonesian communities had a sense of urgency to combat the spread of drugs, families took on the responsibility to raise awareness and to warn their family members about the dangers of drugs. However, this has not been the case for issues regarding radicalism. Families should be the first agents to detect the risk of involvement in radical groups and prevent further involvement. This could be initiated by increasing the awareness of the threat of violent extremism and its impact on social, economic, and political conditions. Those who were previously involved in radicalism should not be stigmatised and discriminated. This will only create more negative experiences for them, making them more vulnerable to return to radical behaviour. It is important to provide a supportive environment while continuing to conduct ongoing monitoring efforts.

The Role of Negative Contact Experience

One main factor that caused Santosa and his family to withdraw their support for ISIS was the negative contact experience they had in Syria. It began during the first month of their arrival at Raqqa. At the shelter where they lived, the members did not pay attention to hygiene, fought among themselves, and the general rough behaviour made them feel that it was far from their ideal view of an Islamic society. It got stronger as they were preparing to leave the shelter. They felt that the ISIS fighters' behaviour was incompatible with Islamic values and they were quick to use violence as a punishment (e.g., beheadings and extreme forms of violence).

Fink and Hearne (2008), Garfinkel (2007), and Skonovd (1979) found that such negative experiences and disappointments raised doubts in former ISIS supporters and caused them to re-evaluate their membership in the organisation. Therefore, a strategy that can be used for de-radicalisation is exploring the negative experiences of individuals who have lived under ISIS. These negative experiences can be used as a starting point for them to evaluate their thoughts and intentions. These negative experiences can be shared through multichannels as a strategy to prevent or reduce the support for ISIS amongst the wider community.

The Role of Relative Deprivation

In the interviews with Santosa and his family, we found that they were disappointed and frustrated with social problems and policies that ignored Muslims. They believed that the solution to the problem was the implementation of Sharia law. They felt a sense of relative deprivation. Although this group of individuals did not experience direct instances of injustice, they had developed quite a strong perception of injustice that was built upon their understanding of fellow Muslims' socio-economic conditions in Indonesia. To reduce such perceived injustices, there are two possible strategies that can be adopted. First, the government needs to minimise the objective discrepancy between groups in Indonesia. Once the demands of disadvantaged groups (as perceived by the relevant groups) are fulfilled by the government, it would contribute to more stability. Second, it would also be useful to increase procedural justice (i.e., the perception of fairness that is derived from the process of resources allocations). Past studies have repeatedly shown that procedural justice would enhance public support and government legitimacy (Tyler, 2006; Ulbig, 2008). In this case, the government needs to ensure that all parties in the society have a channel to make their views known.

Web-based Counter-narratives

The final but probably the most potent strategy to counter radicalism is to optimise the Internet to spread counter narratives. Governments have attempted to actively produce moderate content on the Internet. However, it does not reach the wider population. Probably because the content is delivered through government websites that are rarely visited by people. Thus, it would be more effective if the content was created and shared by the larger community. Moreover, initiating a systematic media literacy campaign would be beneficial. Relying only on the government to handle radical content might not be that effective, and the government should encourage the individual to participate in this effort as well. One possible strategy is to educate people to be more critical when evaluating content that they find on the Internet.

References

Aziz, A. (2004). *Aku Melawan Teroris*. Solo: Jazera.

Basit, B. A. (2017). *The Urban and Educated Jihadists of South Asia*. Singapore: Nanyang Technological University.

Benmelech, E., & Klor, E. F. (2017). What explains the flow of foreign fighters to ISIS? Retrieved from https://scholars.huji.ac.il/sites/default/files/eklor/files/w22190.pdf.

Benmelech, E., Berrebi, C., & Klor, E. F. (2012). Economic conditions and the quality of suicide terrorism. *The Journal of Politics*, *74*(1), 113–128.

Bergen, P., Schuster, C., & Sterman, D. (2015). ISIS in the West: The new faces of extremism. Retrieved from https://static.newamerica.org/attachments/11813-isis-in-the-west-2/ISP-ISIS-In-The-West-Final-Nov-16-Final.66241afa9ddd4ea2be7afba9ec0a69e0.pdf.

Bertijan, D., Moghaddam, F. M., Kruglanski, A. W., Wolf, A., Mann, L., & Feddes, A. R. (2016). Terrorism, radicalisation and de-radicalisation. *Current Opinion in Psychology*, *11*, 79–84.

Bjorgo, T., & Horgan, J. (2009). *Leaving Terrorism Behind: Individual and Collective Disengagement.* UK: Routledge.

Blau, J. R., & Blau, P. M. (1982). The cost of inequality: Metropolitan structure and violence crime. *American Sociological Review*, *47*(1), 114–129.

Blomberg, S. B., & Hess, G. D. (2005). *The Lexus and the Olive Branch: Globalization, Democratization and Terrorism.* Washington, D.C.: World Bank Workshop on Security and Development.

Borum, R. (2003). Understanding the terrorist mind-set. *FBI Law Enforcement Bulletin*, 72(7), 7–10.

Borum, R. (2004). *Psychology of terrorism.* Tempa, FL: University of South Florida.

Borum, R. (2012). Radicalisation into violent extremism I: A review of social science theories. *Journal of Strategic Security*, 4(4), 7–36.

Daskin, E. (2016). Justification of violence by terrorist organisations: Comparing ISIS and PKK. *Journal of Intelligence and Terrorism Studies*, *1*, doi:10.22261/PLV6PE.

Dawson, L. L., & Amarasingam, A. (2017). Talking to foreign fighters: Insights into the motivations for Hijrah to Syria and Iraq. *Studies in Conflict and Terrorism*, *40*(3), 191–210.

del Vicario, M., Bessi, A., Zollo, F., Petroni, F., Scala, A., Caldarelli, G., Stanley, H. E., & Quattrociocchi, W. (2016). The spreading of misinformation online. *Proceedings of the National Academy of Sciences*, *113*(3), 554–559.

el-badawy, E., Comerford, M., & Welby, P. (2015). *Inside the Jihadi Mind Understanding Ideology and Propaganda.* UK: Tony Blaire Faith Foundation.

el-Said, H., & Barrett, R. (2017). Enhancing the Understanding of the Foreign Terrorist Fighters Phenomenon in Syria. Retrieved from http://www.un.org/en/counterterrorism/assets/img/Report_Final_20170727.pdf.

Fink, N. C., & Hearne, E. B. (2008). *Beyond Terrorism: De-radicalisation and Disengagement from Violent Extremism.* New York: International Peace Institute.

Frankl, V. E. (2000). *Man's Search for Ultimate Meaning.* New York: Basic Books.

Freytag, A., Krüger, J., Meierrieks, D., & Schneider, F. (2011). The origins of terrorism: Cross-country estimates of socio-economic determinants of terrorism. *European Journal of Political Economy*, *27*(1), 5–16.

Garfinkel, R. (2007). Personal transformations: Moving from violence to peace. Report No. 186. Washington, DC: United States Institute of Peace.

Jasko, K., LaFree, G., & Kruglanski, A. (2017). Quest for significance and violent extremism: The case of domestic radicalisation. *Political Psychology*, *38*(5), 815–831.

Justino, P. (2016). Supply and demand restrictions to education in conflict-affected countries: New research and future agendas. *International Journal of Education Development*, *47*, 76–85.

Keating, J., van Boven, L., & Judd, C. M. (2016). Partisan underestimation of the polarizing influence of group discussion. *Journal of Experimental Social Psychology*, *65*, 52–58.

Knobloch-Westerwick, S., Johnson, B. K., & Westerwick, A. (2014). Confirmation bias in online searches: Impacts of selective exposure before an election on political attitude strength and shifts. *Journal of Computer-Mediated Communication*, *20*(2), 171–187.

Koseli, M. (2007). The poverty, inequality and terrorism relationship: An empirical analysis of some root causes of terrorism. In S., Ozeren, I. D., Gunes, & D. M. Al-Badayneh (Eds.), *Understanding Terrorism: Analysis of Sociological and Psychological Aspects* (pp. 109–119). Netherlands: IOS Press.

Krieger, T., & Meierrieks, D. (2015). Does income inequality lead to terrorism? Evidence from the post-9/11 era. Germany: Universität Freiberg. Retrieved from https://www.researchgate.net/publication/278037634_Does_Income_Inequality_Lead_to_Terrorism_Evidence_from_the_Post-911_Era.

Krueger, A. B., & Laitin, D. D. (2007). Kto Kogo?: A cross-country study of the origins and targets of terrorism. Retrieved from https://krueger.princeton.edu/sites/default/files/akrueger/files/terrorism4.pdf.

Krueger, A. B., & Maleckova, J. (2003). Education, poverty and terrorism: Is there a causal connection? *Journal of Economic Perspectives*, *17*(4), 119–144.

Kruglanski, A. W., Bélanger, J. J., Gelfand, M., Gunaratna, R., Hettiarachchi, M., Orehek, E., Sasota, J., & Sharvit, K. (2013). Terrorism — A (self) love story: Redirecting the significance quest can end violence. *American Psychologist*, *68*(7), 559–575.

Kruglanski, A. W., Chen, X., Dechesne, M., Fishman, S., & Orehek, E. (2009). Fully committed: Suicide bombers' motivation and the quest for personal significance. *Political Psychology*, *30*(3), 331–557.

Kruglanski, A. W., Gelfand, M. J., Bélanger, J .J., Sheveland, A., Hetiarachchi, M., & Gunaratna, R. (2014). The psychology of radicalisation and de-radicalisation: How significance quest impacts violent extremism. *Political Psychology*, *35*(1), 69–93.

Maslow, A. (1943). A theory of human motivation. *Psychological review*, *50*, 370–396.

McGarty, C., Turner, J. C., Hogg, M. A., David, B., & Wetherell, M. S. (1992). Group polarization as conformity to the prototypical group member. *British Journal of Social Psychology*, *31*(1), 1–19.

Muller, E. N. (1985). Income inequality, regime repressiveness and political violence. *American Sociological Review*, *50*(1), 47–61.

Neighbors, C., O'Connor, R. M., Lewis, M. A., Chawla, N., Lee, C. M., & Fossos, N. (2008). The relative impact of injunctive norms on college student drinking: The role of reference group. *Psychology of Addictive Behaviors*, *22*(4), 576–581.

Piazza, J. A. (2007). Rooted in poverty?: Terrorism, poor economic development, and social cleavages. *Terrorism and political violence*, *18*(1), 159–177.

Putra, I. E., & Sukabdi, Z. A. (2013). Basic concepts and reasons behind the emergence of religious terror activities in Indonesia: An inside view. *Asian Journal of Social Psychology*, *16*(2).

Simpson, M. (1990). Political rights and income inequality: A cross-national test. *American Sociological Review*, *55*(5), 682–693.

Skonovd, L. N. (1979). Becoming apostate: A model of religious defection. *Paper presented at the Annual Meeting of the Pacific Sociological Association, Anahiem, CA*.

Soeriaatmadja, W. (2018). Ex-Batam official who joined ISIS faces life sentence. *The Straits Times*. Retrieved from https://www.straitstimes.com/asia/se-asia/trial-of-batam-official-who-joined-isis-set-to-start-in-indonesia.

Song, L., & Appleton, S. (2006). Inequality and Instability: An Empirical Investigation into Social Discontent in Urban China. Report No. 45. UK: The University of Nottingham.

Strandberg, K., Himmelroos, S., & Grönlund, K. (2017). Do discussions in like-minded groups necessarily lead to more extreme opinions? Deliberative democracy and group polarization. *International Political Science Review*, 1–17.

Terry, D. J., Hogg, M. A., & White, K. M. (1999). The theory of planned behaviour: Self-identity, social identity and group norms. *British Journal of Social Psychology*, *38*(3), 225–244.

Tyler, T. R. (2006). Psychological perspectives on legitimacy and legitimation. *Annual Review of Psychology*, *57*(1), 375–400.

Ulbig, S. G. (2008). Voice is not enough: The importance of influence in political trust and policy assessments. *The Public Opinion Quarterly*, *72*(3), 523–539.

United Nation Office of Counter-Terrorism. (2017). *Enchancing the understanding of the foreign terrorist fighters phenomenon in Syria*. Author: United Nations Office of Counter-Terrorism.

Verwimp, P. (2016). Foreign fighters in Syria and Iraq and the socio-economic environment they faced at home: A comparison of European countries. *Terrorism Research Initiative*, *10*(6).

Vidino, L., & Hughes, S. (2015). *ISIS in America from retweets to Raqqa*. Washington, DC: Program on Extremism.

Webber, D., & Kruglanski, A. W. (2017). Psychological factors in radicalisation. In G., LaFree, & J. D., Freilich (Eds.), *The handbook of the criminology of terrorism* (pp. 33–46). UK: John Wiley & Sons, Inc.

Weine, S., Horgan, J., Robertson, C., Loue, S., Mohamed, A., & Noor, S. (2010). Community and family approaches to combating the radicalization and recruitment of Somali-American youth and young adults: A psychosocial perspective. *Dynamics of Asymmetric Conflict*, *2*(3), 181–200.

Williams, M. J., Horgan, J. G., & Evans, W. P. (2015). Research summary: Lessons from a U.S. study revealing the critical role of "gatekeepers" in public safety networks for countering violent extremism. In S. Zeiger, & A. Aly (Eds.), *Countering Violent Extremism: Developing an Evidence-Base for Policy and Practice* (pp. 139–143). Australia: Curtin University.

LEARNING TO RESPOND TO VIOLENT EXTREMIST ATTACKS

Section 5

Strategies to Build Resilience

It is important to strengthen the resilience of the community and the nation to deal with crises that come our way.

MR MASAGOS ZULKIFLI
MINISTER FOR THE ENVIRONMENT AND WATER RESOURCES

CHAPTER 16

Preparing for the Day After Terror: Five Things to Do to Build National Resilience

JETHRO TAN, JANE QUEK, and GABRIEL ONG

Home Team Behavioural Sciences Centre, Ministry of Home Affairs, Singapore

Introduction

The recent spate of terror attacks across the world serves as a stark reminder that no country is truly safe from the reaches of terrorism. While it is necessary to invest in countering the advances of terrorists, societies and nations can no longer simply take on just a *prevention* strategy towards such threats. In fact, policymakers have also since adopted a *resilience* approach towards dealing with the threat of terrorism (Government of Singapore, 2018), which, in essence, assumes that a crisis (i.e., a terrorist attack) will eventually come to pass within one's nation, and policymakers must thus plan for resources to cope with its aftermath (Gomes *et al.*, 2015; Tan *et al.*,

2016). This ensures that when a terrorist attack comes to fruition, the nation can recover and resume day-to-day functioning quickly (i.e., being resilient).

Governments need to be prepared to cope with the day after a terrorist attack. Through the lens of *resilience*, a nation must "adapt and respond to crisis, with the goal of survival and continuity in her core structures and people, allowing the nation to thrive post-crisis" (Tan *et al.*, 2016, p. 309). To be resilient against attacks, nations need to first understand what can happen in the aftermath of such crises, and then plan for the whole of nation to cope with these consequences.

This chapter aims to provide strategies for nations to build resilience in the aftermath of a terrorist attack. This is done through a practical approach of (i) understanding what may potentially happen to a nation after an attack, and subsequently (ii) developing strategies that can be undertaken to address these consequences.

Five Consequences of a Terrorist Attack

There will be Deaths and Injuries

Terrorists often aim to promote their cause or ideology by causing deaths or damaging infrastructure within a society (Schmid, 2004). The 2001 September 11 attacks on the U.S. (i.e., 9/11 attacks) illustrated a highly devastating outcome of a terrorist attack, with an estimate of 3,000 deaths as a result of the event (9/11 attacks, 2010). More recent attacks suggested that the 9/11 attacks in actuality reflected an extreme scenario, in contrast to other terror attacks that resulted in substantially smaller number of causalities. Such examples include the 2014 Sydney Siege, 2016 Berlin truck attack, as well as the 2017 London Bridge attack.

Regardless of the extent of deaths and injuries in the aftermath of terror attacks, emergency response will be a key challenge. Emergency services will be required to conduct triaging and management of medical aid following an attack, and such mass causality incidents will naturally demand extensive use of emergency resources. Operations may extend beyond regular hours and team morale within the uniform services will be tested. Furthermore, emergency service providers must also be prepared for deaths within their own pool of emergency responders. For example, in the aftermath of the World Trade Centre plane crashes of the 9/11 attacks, 343 firefighters and paramedics died in their line of duty (Kean & Hamilton, 2004). Under these circumstances, emergency responses could be hindered by the sudden lack of manpower.

Prepare to deal with causalities during a major attack

The effectiveness of the emergency services' response towards an attack will be most integral in determining the success of dealing with deaths and casualties. In fact, emergency responses to the 2013 Boston Marathon bombing were found to be effective and arguably also the reason why the number of deaths could be minimised to three (Biddinger *et al.*, 2013; Gates *et al.*, 2014); post-attack analysis have also identified that the state's emergency responders' and agencies' frequent participation in exercises prior to the bomb attack had increased Boston's preparedness (Gates *et al.*, 2014). These exercises had involved the joint participation of multiple agencies, which further enhanced coordination between the public agencies and hospitals (Massachusetts Emergency Management Agency, 2014).

In essence, emergency services need to plan for the eventuality of a terror attack occurring and train responders accordingly. Additionally, it is integral to ensure that these planning and training involve the various critical agencies. In the Singapore context, this may mean joint exercises involving the police, civil defence, army, and hospitals to work out coordinated plans and procedures. Crisis leaders should then also consider how such plans will be carried out in the event of lower emergency responders' headcount because of death or injuries. Building spare capacities in terms of manpower and effective shift planning would be key in such instances.

From a cultural standpoint, the management of deaths should entail being cognisant of any cultural issues pertaining to funerals. A multiracial and religious society — like Singapore — will have to prepare for various funeral rituals of the various faith groups, and this is important because funerals provide meaning-making to the deceased's next-of-kin (NOK) (Giblin & Hug, 2006). Crisis managers and responders need to work out how post-crisis operations can accommodate or even facilitate the meaning-making for NOKs. In addition, as seen in the aftermath of previous terror attacks, victims may have to be declared as dead in absentia. This may cause considerable stress to NOKs. Thus, considerations must be taken on how to communicate the bad news of death in a culturally sensitive manner, so as not to aggravate the psychological trauma that will be experienced by NOKs.

There will be Short- and Long-term Health Consequences

Intelligence sources and historical records have indicated that biological and chemical forms of terrorist attacks are significant threats due to their propensity to cause widespread harm in urban cities (Kawana *et al.*, 2001; Okumura *et al.*, 2005). In the aftermath of the 1995 Tokyo Subway sarin gas attack, the release of the sarin toxicant had caused widespread immediate health implications to commuters in the subway (Pletcher, 2018). The Centres for Disease Control and Prevention (CDC) (2015a) reports that some examples of somatic symptoms of sarin contamination are weakness, drowsiness, and chest tightness. Additionally, some primary responders suffered from secondary contamination during the rescue and recovery efforts (Pangi, 2002).

The 2001 anthrax attacks in the U.S. illustrated how biological agents can, and will likely, be used as a means of terrorism. In the attack, anthrax spores were found to have been deliberately distributed through mail sent to media companies and political stakeholders, causing a total of five deaths and 17 infections ("Timeline: How the anthrax terror unfolded", 2011). While not contagious via person-to-person contact, anthrax infections can be transmitted through inhalation, ingestion, or skin absorption (CDC, 2015b; Riedel, 2005), causing somatic symptoms leading up to death after an incubation period of up to 19 days (Riedel, 2005). This makes such threats harder to detect, and also more difficult to allay fears that the public may have. Following the anthrax attacks, the U.S. CDC had to send out advisories to remind the public "that they need not fear opening letters and packages delivered to their homes" ("CDC: Don't worry, open mail happy", 2001, para. 6).

The effects of terror attacks can also be long-term. Studies conducted years after the 9/11 attacks have shown that asthma prevalence in the victims have risen to three times the national rate ("A message from the commissioner", 2018). This can be attributed to the air pollution caused by the plane crash at ground zero (Biello, 2011). Emergency workers who were responding to the crisis also experienced significant long-term health concerns due to the air pollution (Lippmann *et al.*, 2015).

Health concerns grow beyond the typical casualties and injuries familiar to us; both the sarin and anthrax attacks have highlighted how terrorists can utilise tools and weapons that can cause medical effects detrimental to individuals' health. These health consequences also have the propensity to be contagious, which makes the threat difficult to contain. The long-term health consequences of terrorist attacks are also often neglected in lieu of the immediate pressing concerns at the point of crisis.

Prepare for health consequences of terrorist attacks

Emergency plans for the aftermath of a biological or chemical attack will vary according to the destructive agent used. With that said, it is imperative for the government to prepare drawer plans to manage these novel threats. Given the nature of such "invisible" threats, it is then crucial to prepare the public to identify and know what to do in the event of such attacks. The SGSecure movement in Singapore, which aims to equip citizens with essential resources to cope with a terror attack, has already served as a platform to impart such knowledge to the citizens. Continued effort to train and update the public on the what-to-dos can mitigate the spread of biological and chemical attacks.

There must be plans to deal with the long-term health consequences of a terror attack. In fact, these health ramifications can add up to significant economic costs for both individuals and nations. Being prepared, in ways such as providing health coverage and ensuring ample resources to provide interventions, are crucial to the resiliency of the nation.

There will be Psychological Impact on Society

Terrorist attacks are designed to cause not only physical, but also psychological damage through inciting fear and uncertainty within the populace (Borum, 2004; Neo *et al.*, 2015). When one's sense of safety and security is breached, societal resilience is compromised. Psychological impact can disrupt the day-to-day functioning of societies even after the recovery phase of the crisis (Gomes *et al.*, 2015), and can manifest both at the individual and societal levels.

A study by Fetter (2005) showed that after a mass casualty event such as a terror attack, individuals will experience psychosocial responses such as anxiety, survivor guilt, grief, paranoia, and withdrawal. There exists conclusive evidence that this psychological distress will manifest in direct victims, indirect victims, emergency responders, and the general population at large after a terror attack (Salguero *et al.*, 2011; Tanielian & Stein, 2006). Psychosomatic symptoms such as being unable to sleep, loss of appetite, or even irritableness were reported in up to 44% of the population (Schuster *et al.*, 2001).

In further follow-up studies after terror attacks, researchers also found significant increase in the prevalence rates of mental disorders such as Post-Traumatic Stress Disorder (PTSD) (Neria *et al.*, 2011). While estimates suggested only about 10% of initial mental-health support seekers eventually developed PTSD, this long-term impact can do significant harm to the overall well-being of the nation.

Aside from the clinical manifestations, psychological impact can also linger in the populace. Research has espoused that societies that experienced a recent terror attack may experience fear, confusion, disbelief, shock, despair, and panic, and this may cause societies to no longer be able to maintain daily routines (Hobfoll *et al.*, 2007). Resuming normalcy is a key tenet of resilience (Gomes *et al.*, 2015;

Tan *et al.*, 2016), and a reluctance to return to day-to-day functioning constitutes a serious threat to the recovery efforts of a nation. Even more alarmingly, a nation like Singapore — who has not yet experienced a major terror incident — is likely to experience these psychological effects more intensely, due to the novelty of the event.

Deal with psychological trauma and plan for effective crisis communications

It is evident that planning a response for psychological interventions post-terror attack is integral. While therapy is required for severe diagnosis such as PTSD, many of the psychosomatic symptoms that prevail after terror attacks can be addressed by Psychological First Aid (PFA) (World Health Organization, War Trauma Foundation, & World Vision International, 2011). In essence, PFA is about providing timely social support to those who need it in the aftermath of a crisis (World Health Organization, War Trauma Foundation, & World Vision International, 2011); having a ready pool of PFA providers within the community will thus be useful to quickly address the psychological symptoms after a terror incident. Governments need to recognise that they have to go beyond simply addressing physical damages, and invest also in addressing the psychological trauma in the aftermath of terror. Thus, the SGSecure movement's deliberate focus on training PFA within the community (Government of Singapore, 2018) serves to highlight the importance of PFA as an emergency skill, supplementing other skills such as medical first aid, cardiopulmonary resuscitation (CPR), and use of the automated external defibrillator (AED).

From a societal perspective, there is a need for leaders to engage in effective crisis communications to address the psychological effects of terror attacks. By addressing the public's information needs quickly and effectively, it fills in the gap for the need for information by the public. This reduces the spread of rumours and its undesirable consequences (Fearn-Banks, 2007), and the feelings of "ambiguity" and confusion associated with the aftermath of an attack (Hobfoll *et al.*, 2007; Tan *et al.*, 2017). More importantly, it can instil a sense of hope within community by highlighting how the nation can move forward in terms of recovery efforts (Hobfoll *et al.*, 2007). A useful reference would be the SIR3 model of crisis communications[1] developed by the Home Team Behavioural Sciences Centre (Tan *et al.*, 2017), that provides a set of guidelines for effective crisis communication.

Trust in Authorities and Leaders Drops

During a terror attack, plans and recovery efforts are typically decided upon and communicated by national institutions. High levels of trust within a nation will therefore encourage cooperation in the populace, ultimately improving security results (Gomes *et al.*, 2015). However, a potential consequence of a terror attack in Singapore is the loss of trust in government leaders, particularly if the public perceives the crisis to be related to the government's mistake or lapse in judgement. Decline in public trust can create cynicism about the country's political system and upset the existing social order of the nation (Diamond, 2007). For example, after the 2016 Nice truck attack, it was found that the French had low trust in the French government (Goulard, 2016).

Psychological literature indicated that there is a natural tendency for people to look for culprits on whom they can pin the responsibility for crises (Penuel *et al.*, 2013), explaining why people tend to look for a "scapegoat" to blame during periods of uncertainty and confusion. Research has also indicated that people do so in order to preserve their self-esteem and to exert control over a helpless situation (Whitbourne, 2015), serving as a defence mechanism for the public to deal with the crisis. Individuals whom the public may put the blame on include authorities; in many instances, authorities and leaders have been targeted by the public,

---

[1]The SIR3 Model of Crisis Communications proposes that after a terror attack, crisis communicators can abide by five principles: (i) Show deterrence, (ii) Inform the public, (iii) Reassure the people, (iv) Rally the people, and (v) Communicate Resiliency.

regardless of whether it was a man-made crisis or natural disaster (e.g., Penuel *et al.*, 2013).

Engage the public pre- and post-terror

One strategy for authorities to restore trust with the public is matured governance and engagement after a terror attack; through engaging the public in a transparent and accountable manner to clear any doubts. Citizens should also be informed be of the threat in a straightforward manner such that they can understand the actions of the government (Diamond, 2007). Additionally, authorities need to be aware of and sensitive to the intergroup dynamics when managing intergroup tensions that may occur as a result of the terror attacks. Maintenance of an impartial stance towards potentially divisive issues, such as islamophobia, is essential for a multicultural and multiracial society like Singapore. In this aspect, the government's crisis communication, especially in showing deterrence and rallying the people, is crucial to the aftermath of a terror attack (see SIR3 model of crisis communications, and Tan *et al.*, 2017).

Social Trust and Harmony are Affected

Social trust and harmony between groups in a community can be affected after terror attacks. Recent terror attacks, such as the 2014 Sydney Siege and 2017 London Bridge attacks, saw tensions rising between anti-Muslims and anti-racism demonstrators; some of the hate was also directed towards the Muslims living in the country. Following the Sydney Siege, anti-Muslim protestors took to the streets to rally and protest against those in favour of multiculturalism. Violent clashes occurred between anti-Muslim protestors and anti-racism demonstrators in Melbourne, prompting riot police to intervene ("Anti-Islam rallies, counter-protests flare in Australia", 2015). Hate messages were posted on social media and Sydney faced increased islamophobia, mosques had been defaced (Aston, 2014), Muslims were abused and threatened in public places (Aston, 2014), and multiple food companies bearing the halal certification were also targeted by social media campaigns (Thomsen, 2014). Such conflicts are also transboundary. In aftermath of the 2015 Charlie Hebdo attacks, for example, the U.K. reported a surge in hate crimes against Muslims (Travis, 2017).

Principles from the social identity theory suggest that people have multiple social identities, and these different social identities facilitate the formation of an individual's perceived in-groups and out-groups (Tajfel & Turner, 2004). Comprehensive research has shown that there is a tendency for people to favour in-groups, i.e., groups with characteristics that are similar to oneself, and protect the in-group identity especially in the presence of threats (Cooper & Fazio, 1986; Duckitt & Mphuthing, 1998). In other words, it serves to describe why there is heightened distrust, suspicion, and aggression expressed towards other groups following terror attacks. For instance, islamophobic attacks had increased five-fold — from 25 to 139 incidents — in the week after the 2017 Manchester Arena bombing (Travis, 2017). The potential fragmentation of social tapestry is a significant issue to address because Singapore is a multiracial and multireligious society.

Building a collective identity within the community

A solution to address social distrust and disharmony is to foster trust[2] within the community before and after the attack. Creating a collective identity can help to overcome the boundaries of in-groups and out-groups. Widening identity boundaries helps to increase relatability to others and this has shown to be effective for racial and religious identities (Levine *et al.*, 2005). Following the Sydney Siege, the social media campaign and ground-up initiative #iwillridewithyou was meant to stand in solidarity with the Muslim community, by riding on the public transport with them and protecting them from possible anti-Muslim retaliation. The initiative serves to recognise

---

[2]This is in line with the SGSecure component of "Stay United" where there is a need to deepen mutual trust and respect between communities so that violent extremists will not succeed in weakening our social fabric.

the Muslims as fellow mates of the Australians, who were equally at the mercy of terrorism. In times of uncertainty and confusion, these behaviours signal acceptance and solidarity to the minority or target groups and help to foster unity and harmony. In Singapore, this means emphasising the collective identity of people in Singapore to overcome the multiethnic, multireligious, and multicultural identities of various groups.

Conclusion

In summary, five potential consequences of a terror attack were highlighted: (i) death and injuries, (ii) health consequences, (iii) psychological impact, (iv) decline in trust of leaders and authorities, and (v) decline in social trust. These five consequences serve to inform preparatory efforts that in turn contributes to enhancing recovery efforts within the nation. Various solutions were also discussed within this chapter, and they serve as some guiding principles on how nations can prepare and respond after a terror attack. However, it should be noted that building resilient nations remain a complex task that requires a multidisciplinary thinking, incorporating ideas and expertise from various branches of knowledge. It is hoped that this chapter has contributed to resilience-building through the behavioural sciences perspective.

Acknowledgement

The views expressed in this chapter are the authors' only and do not represent the official position or view of the Ministry of Home Affairs, Singapore.

References

9/11 attacks (2010). *History.com*. Retrieved from https://www.history.com/topics/9-11-attacks.

A message from the commissioner (2018). *NYC.gov*. Retrieved from https://www1.nyc.gov/site/911health/researchers/what-we-know.page.

Anti-Islam rallies, counter-protests flare in Australia (2015). *The Jarkarta Post*. Retrieved from http://www.thejakartapost.com/news/2015/07/19/anti-islam-rallies-counter-protests-flare-australia.html.

Aston, H. (2014). Dozens of anti-muslim attacks as Islamic leaders warn of community fear. *The Sydney Morning Herald*. Retrieved from http://www.smh.com.au/national/dozens-of-antimuslim-attacks-as-islamic-leaders-warn-of-community-fear-20141009-113tmk.html.

Biddinger, P. D., Baggish, A., Harrington, L., d'Hemecourt, P., Hooley, J., Jones, J., & Dyer, K. S. (2013). Be prepared — The Boston marathon and mass-casualty events. *New England Journal of Medicine*, *368*(21), 1958–1960.

Biello, D. (2011). What was in the World Trade Center plume? [interactive]. *Scientific American*. Retrieved from https://www.scientificamerican.com/article/what-was-in-the-world-trade-center-plume/.

Borum, R. (2004). *Psychology of Terrorism*. Tampa: University of South Florida.

CDC: Don't worry, open mail happy (2001). *Wired*. Retrieved from https://www.wired.com/2001/10/cdc-dont-worry-open-mail-happy/.

Centres for Disease Control and Prevention (CDC) (2015a). *Facts About Sarin*. Retrieved from https://emergency.cdc.gov/agent/sarin/basics/facts.asp.

Centres for Disease Control and Prevention (CDC). (2015b). *How People Are Infected*. Retrieved from https://www.cdc.gov/anthrax/basics/how-people-are-infected.html.

Cooper, J., & Fazio, R. H. (1986). The formation and persistence of attitudes that support intergroup conflict. In S. Worchel, & W. Austin (Eds.), *Psychology of Intergroup Relations* (pp. 183–195). Chicago: Nelson-Hall.

Diamond, L. (2007). Building trust in government by improving governance. *Paper Presented at the 7th Global Forum on Reinventing Government: Building Trust in Government, Vienna, Italy*. Retrieved from https://web.stanford.edu/~ldiamond/paperssd/BuildingTrustinGovernmentUNGLobalForum.pdf.

Duckitt, J., & Mphuthing, T. (1998). Group identification and intergroup attitudes: A longitudinal analysis in South Africa. *Journal of Personality and Social Psychology*, *74*(1), 80–85.

Fearn-Banks, K. (2007). *Crisis Communications: A Casebook Approach* (3rd edn.). Mahwah, NJ: Lawrence Erlbaum Associates.

Fetter, J. C. (2005). Psychosocial response to mass casualty terrorism: Guidelines for physicians. *Primary Care Companion to the Journal of Clinical Psychiatry*, *7*(2), 49–52.

Gates, J. D., Arabian, S., Biddinger, P., Blansfield, J., Burke, P., Chung, S., & Yaffe, M. B. (2014). The initial response to the Boston marathon bombing: Lessons learned to prepare for the next disaster. *Annals of Surgery*, *260*(6), 960.

Giblin, P., & Hug, A. (2006). The psychology of funeral rituals. *Liturgy*, *21*(1), 11–19.

Government of Singapore. (2018). *SGSecure*. Retrieved from https://www.sgsecure.sg/.

Gomes, D., Tan, J., Wang, Y., Neo, L. S., Ong, G., & Khader, M. (2015). National resilience: HTBSC Singapore's national resilience proposed framework. Research Report No. 3/2015. Singapore: Home Team Behavioural Sciences Centre.

Goulard, H. (2016). French don't trust government on terrorism: Poll. *Politico*. Retrieved from https://www.politico.eu/article/french-dont-trust-government-on-terrorism-poll/.

Hobfoll, S. E., Watson, P., Bell, C. C., Bryant, R. A., Brymer, M. J., Friedman, M. J., & Ursano, R. J. (2007). Five essential elements of immediate and mid-term mass trauma intervention: Empirical evidence. *Psychiatry: Interpersonal and Biological Processes*, *70*(4), 283–315.

Kawana, N., Ishimatsu, S. I., & Kanda, K. (2001). Psycho-physiological effects of the terrorist sarin attack on the Tokyo subway system. *Military Medicine*, *166*(12), 23–26.

Kean, T. H., & Hamilton, L. (2004). *The 9/11 Commission Report*. DC: National Commission on Terrorist Attacks upon the United States.

Levine, M., Prosser, A., Evans, D., & Reicher, S. (2005). Identity and emergency intervention: How social group membership and inclusiveness of group boundaries shape helping behaviour. *Personality and Social Psychology Bulletin*, *31*(4), 443–453.

Lippmann, M., Cohen, M. D., & Chen, L. C. (2015). Health effects of World Trade Center (WTC) dust: An unprecedented disaster with inadequate risk management. *Critical Reviews in Toxicology*, *45*(6), 492–530.

Massachusetts Emergency Management Agency (2014). After action report for the response to the 2013 Boston marathon bombings. Retrieved from http://www.mass.gov/eopss/docs/mema/after-action-report-for-the-response-to-the-2013-boston-marathon-bombings.pdf.

Neo, L. S., Khader, M., Shi, P., Dillon, L., & Ong, G. (2015). *Extremist Cyber Footprints: A Guide to Understanding and Countering Online Extremism*. Singapore: Home Team Behavioural Sciences Centre.

Neria, Y., DiGrande, L., & Adams, B. G. (2011). Posttraumatic stress disorder following the September 11, 2001, terrorist attacks: A review of the literature among highly exposed populations. *The American Psychologist*, *66*(6), 429–446.

Okumura, T., Hisaoka, T., Yamada, A., Naito, T., Isonuma, H., Okumura, S., & Suzuki, K. (2005). The Tokyo subway sarin attack — Lessons learned. *Toxicology and Applied Pharmacology*, *207*(2), 471–476.

Pangi, R. (2002). Consequence management in the 1995 sarin attacks on the Japanese subway system. *Studies in Conflict and Terrorism*, *25*(6), 421–448.

Penuel, K. B., Statler, M., & Hagen, R. (2013). *Encyclopedia of Crisis Management*. Thousand Oaks, CA: SAGE Publications.

Pletcher, K. (2018). Tokyo subway attack of 1995. *Encyclopædia Britannica*. Retrieved from https://www.britannica.com/event/Tokyo-subway-attack-of-1995.

Riedel, S. (2005). Anthrax: A continuing concern in the era of bioterrorism. *Proceedings (Baylor University Medical Center)*, *18*(3), 234–243.

Salguero, J. M., Fernández-Berrocal, P., Iruarrizaga, I., Cano-Vindel, A., & Galea, S. (2011). Major depressive disorder following terrorist attacks: A systematic review of prevalence, course and correlates. *BMC Psychiatry*, *11*(1), 96.

Schmid, P. A. (2004). Frameworks for conceptualising terrorism. *Terrorism and Political Violence*, *16*(2), 197–221.

Schuster, M. A., Stein, B. D., Jaycox, L. H., Collins, R. L., Marshall, G. N., Elliott, M. N., Zhou, A. J., & Berry, S. H. (2001). A national survey of stress reactions after the September 11, 2001, terrorist attacks. *New England Journal of Medicine*, *345*(20), 1507–1512.

Tajfel, H., & Turner, J. C. (2004). The social identity theory of intergroup behavior. In J. T. Jost, & J. Sidanius (Eds.), *Key Readings in Social Psychology. Political Psychology: Key Readings* (pp. 276–293). New York: Psychology Press.

Tan, J., Goh, P., Chen, X., Neo, L. S., Ong, G., & Khader, M. (2017). Crisis Communications in the Day after Terror: The SIR3 Model. Research Report 17/2017. Singapore: Home Team Behavioural Sciences Centre.

Tan, J., Wang, Y., & Gomes, D. (2016). Building national resilience in the digital era of violent extremism: Systems and people. In M. Khader, L. S. Neo, G. Ong, E. Tan, & J. Chin (Eds.), *Combating Violent Extremism and Radicalisation in the Digital Era* (pp. 402–420). Hershey, PA: IGI Global.

Tanielian, T. L., & Stein, B. D. (2006). Understanding and preparing for the psychological consequences of terrorism. In D. Kamien (Ed.), *The McGraw-Hill Homeland Security Handbook* (pp. 689–701). New York: McGraw-Hill.

Thomsen, S. (2014). An anti-muslim facebook group is targeting Australian companies for making halal food. *Business Insider Australia.* Retrieved from https://www.businessinsider.com.au/an-anti-muslim-facebook-group-is-targeting-australian-companies-for-making-halal-food-2014-10.

Timeline: How the anthrax terror unfolded (2011). *NPR.* Retrieved from https://www.npr.org/2011/02/15/93170200/timeline-how-the-anthrax-terror-unfolded.

Travis, A. (2017). Anti-Muslim hate crime surges after Manchester and London Bridge attacks. *The Guardian.* Retrieved from https://www.theguardian.com/society/2017/jun/20/anti-muslim-hate-surges-after-manchester-and-london-bridge-attacks.

Whitbourne, S. K. (2015). 5 reasons why we play the blame game. *Psychology Today.* Retrieved from https://www.psychologytoday.com/blog/fulfillment-any-age/201509/5-reasons-we-play-the-blame-game.

World Health Organization, War Trauma Foundation, & World Vision International (2011). *Psychological First Aid: Guide for Field Workers.* WHO: Geneva.

CHAPTER 17

Psychological First Aid: Addressing Worldwide Challenges for Implementation in an Asian Context

SHUKTIKA BOSE

Bond University, Australia

Introduction

Extensive literature exists, regarding the detrimental psychological impacts of trauma following terrorist attacks on individuals and populations (e.g., Neria *et al.*, 2011; Schuster *et al.*, 2001). In a world of increasing violent extremist attacks, which have the potential to cause widespread fear and panic, it is critical for individuals to be equipped with the necessary skills so that they can assist themselves and others in the event of a crisis. Alongside emergency first responders, vulnerable populations that were found to be more susceptible to psychological trauma following a terrorist attack are, namely, children, the elderly, those with physical and intellectual impairments, as well as those at risk of discrimination (Jaycox *et al.*, 2006; World Health Organization, War Trauma Foundation, & World Vision International, 2011).

The human response to a disaster is generally conceptualised as the survival response of fight, flight, or fright (freeze). These reactions are adaptive in the majority of instances, and usually dissipate following the restoration of safety and normalcy (Cloak & Edwards, 2004). Following the 9/11 terrorist attacks, for example, approximately 90% of New York citizens experienced a fear and distress response (e.g., concentration and sleep difficulties), with only 44% of these individuals experiencing a significant form of behaviour change (Schuster *et al.*, 2001). However, some reactions associated with trauma reminders or persistent triggers, such as bereavement, may precipitate and perpetuate the sensitisation of the fear response; two months after the 9/11 terrorist attacks, approximately 11.2% of New York citizens were experiencing post-traumatic stress disorder (PTSD) (Schelenger *et al.*, 2002). Social support and active coping strategies have been identified as critical protective factors of physiological stress responses.

Numerous terrorist attacks have taken place throughout the Asian subcontinent in the last five years, and the threat of an attack in countries such as Singapore remains imminent (Cheong *et al.*, 2016). Noting the significant negative impacts of such crises on the psychological well-being of individuals, the implementation of demographic-specific immediate interventions is essential to minimising long-term mental health effects. In Singapore, the SGSecure movement[1] introduced in 2016 was designed to encourage Singaporeans to become more aware of their surroundings in the potentiality of a terrorist attack, as well as to educate and train citizens on critical skills such as first aid and cardiopulmonary resuscitation. Given that the size of the psychological footprint will greatly exceed the medical footprint following a disaster or crisis (Schultz *et al.*, 2003), ensuring resilience, recovery, and functionality

---

[1]The SGSecure movement is an initiative that aims to "sensitise, train, and mobilise" Singaporeans to deal with a terror attack (Government of Singapore, 2018).

following a terrorist attack also involves the vital need to look after the psychological well-being of a nation's people. With that, the SGSecure movement also provides community training in critical psychological first aid (PFA) concepts following a crisis.

Psychological First Aid

Psychological first aid (PFA) is described by the Sphere Project (2004) as "a humane, supportive response to a human being who is suffering and may require support". It addresses the importance of a supportive approach in the provision of care for distressed individuals, and can be administered following natural or man-made disasters (e.g., flood, terrorist attack) and individual incidents (e.g., car accident, house fire). PFA can be provided by anyone to both individuals and groups as long as they are equipped with the necessary skills to do so; it can be administered to others at any time from immediately following the event, to several days or weeks afterwards depending on event duration and severity.

Individuals are likely to be distressed following a crisis, and PFA involves listening and providing comfort to the distressed in order to help them feel calm. PFA also advocates for the provision of practical care and support to individuals, through means such as assessing their needs and concerns (e.g., medical assistance, food, shelter), helping them connect to information, services, and social supports, protecting them from further harm by removing them from unsafe environments, or minimising risk of discrimination. In essence, five intervention principles form the foundation of PFA: sense of safety, calming, connectedness, sense of self- and community efficacy, and hope (Hobfoll *et al.*, 2007). These principles facilitate community awareness of and engagement with one another, alongside identifying coping skills and strengths to promote positive expectations.

Aims

The information in this chapter was compiled through a literature review of PFA models and cultural perspectives applicable for disasters and crises, as well as interviews with international subject matter experts. This chapter aims to address five major worldwide challenges associated with the investigating, understanding, and implementing of PFA — of which may be applicable within Asian communities — and subsequently provide five strategies to address these challenges in a systematic manner. Throughout this chapter, Singapore will be utilised as a case study for understanding the applicability of PFA within an Asian context. It is anticipated that the insights from this chapter will inform policymakers regarding best-practice interventions within their respective communities in the aftermath of a terrorist attack.

Challenge 1: The Criticisms of PFA

Schultz and Forbes (2014) reported that PFA models do not possess any empirical or quantitative support to provide for the highest level of evidence. In a comprehensive research analysis that looked into 20 years of peer-reviewed literature, Fox *et al.* (2012, p. 249) identified that while scientific evidence for PFA is lacking, it is, on the contrary, widely supported by "expert opinion and rational conjecture".

Although occurring on broad intervention aims, most PFA training programs have significant shortcomings including minimal standardisation and accountability for quality (McCabe *et al.*, 2014). Additionally, the scarcity of data examining the effectiveness of PFA in the post-disaster context has been deemed to be due to the lack of prioritisation, design, and implementation of robust evaluation strategies. This has created difficulties in the verification of PFA's effectiveness. However, other researchers have noted that decision-making should incorporate additional and inclusive forms of evidence such as qualitative studies, case reports, scientific principles, and expert opinion (Woodbury & Kuhnke, 2014). Subsequently, discussion ensues regarding the utility of PFA over the absence of interventions in the post-crisis stage.

Strategy 1: Engage in Action Over Inaction in Crisis

Many guidelines caution against inaction shortly after traumatic events, noting that supportive and practical input should be delivered in a non-intrusive, empathic manner (Inter-Agency Standing Committee, 2007). A comparison of brief and multisession interventions conducted on over 1,000 individuals one and two years following the September 11 attacks yielded two findings (Boscarino *et al.*, 2011). Firstly, psychological crisis intervention (or PFA) at a community level is superior to multisession psychotherapy post-disaster for reducing acute distress. Secondly, psychotherapy post-disaster may complicate psychological and behavioural recovery, due to differing needs and concerns between the crisis environment and therapeutic setting.

Upon examination of Hobfoll *et al.*'s (2007) five intervention principles (sense of safety, calming, connectedness, sense of self- and community efficacy, and hope), two characteristics were found to be specifically relevant for PFA: calmness and connectedness. Evidence suggested that extremely high levels of emotionality and heightened heart rate during immediate post-trauma periods may lead to panic attacks, dissociation, and long-term PTSD symptoms (Bryant *et al.*, 2003); promoting calmness is likely to alleviate these symptoms. In relation to connectedness, following the September 11 attacks, a common coping response was the identifying of and linking up with loved ones (Stein *et al.*, 2004). Comparatively, following the 2005 London Bombings, delays in facilitating these connections had been a major risk factor for long-term trauma symptoms (Rubin *et al.*, 2005). Recognised for its potential impact in these areas, PFA has been widely endorsed by disaster mental health experts (Forbes *et al.*, 2011), and many international treatment guidelines now recommend the use of PFA following a crisis (Inter-Agency Standing Committee, 2007; National Institute of Mental Health, 2002; North Atlantic Treaty Organization, 2009; Sphere Project, 2004).

Despite this, the lack of adequate scientific support for PFA continues to be a concern that should be addressed. While present-moment quantitative or qualitative data on the effectiveness of PFA is difficult to obtain — especially from real-life crises over controlled environments — providing support to crisis-related populations should remain the highest priority. Establishing markers of "effectiveness" itself is difficult, either for the objective or subjective determination of "feeling better after the interaction". Test-retest data (Time 1 = time of crisis, Time 2 = several weeks following the crisis, Time 3 = several months following the crisis) may also be difficult to obtain from individuals who have lost their home and possessions, or are unable or unwilling to engage in long-term research. In fact, such a test method may not align with the original PFA aims of providing immediate humane psychosocial support and helping people meet their basic needs.

A recent retrospective and qualitative exploration of the use and impact of PFA was undertaken in the 2014 Gaza conflict, that had resulted in 2,104 fatalities (Schafer *et al.*, 2016). PFA was offered to approximately 61,000 people by 300 previously trained individuals over the course of three months. The exploratory study involved eight PFA providers, 10 women, eight men, 11 children, and one lead PFA trainer. Although difficulties with generalisability were noted, focus group discussions and a key informant interview outlined that PFA was positively received and valued by those who received the service. Distress was reduced, people were taught calming strategies for themselves, their children, and others in their community, and greater social connections were created thereby promoting hopefulness during a crisis situation. This exploration offers scope for future empirical research protocols to systematically assess PFA's effectiveness through research design and examination of broad psychosocial impact of PFA, rather than clinical measurement outcomes.

Challenge 2: Identifying the Best PFA Model for Use

PFA training models have been developed for both professional and layperson audiences. There are numerous PFA models available for use throughout the world, with varying degrees of complexity in language and assumed knowledge in health and counselling skills. This section will describe three PFA models identified throughout the literature as major models that have been utilised cross-culturally, or have demonstrated a potential for use in a cross-cultural context. Please note that this list is by no means exhaustive and does not minimise the importance of other PFA models available; rather, the author aims to provide a greater understanding of PFA through demonstration of terminology used within specific models.

Critical Incident Stress Management (CISM) (Everly & Mitchell, 1999) is a short-term process that focuses on an immediate and identifiable problem, in which it guides the assessment of the incident and affected individuals' underlying psychological processes at every stage of a crisis (S. B. Samion, personal communication, July 24, 2017). The formulation incorporates the "SAFER-R" model of crisis intervention with individuals and describes five steps: Stabilise, Acknowledge, Facilitate Understanding/Normalise, Encourage Effective Coping, and Recovery/Referral. It is important to note that the "SAFER-R" model is a small component of CISM, which also provides services at three pivotal time periods: before a crisis, during a crisis (PFA begins here), and after a crisis (where defusing, debriefing, and follow-up services are introduced). Additionally, CISM was originally designed not for primary trauma victims but for first responders themselves who are involved in addressing trauma victims, due to the risk of secondary PTSD.

The World Health Organization model (World Health Organization, War Trauma Foundation, & World Vision International, 2011) was specifically developed for use in low to medium income countries and was a collaborative effort by the World Health Organisation, World Trauma Foundation, and World Vision International. The action principles of the WHO model are "Look, Listen, Link" — where "Look" indicates the observation for physical safety and people with urgent basic needs or serious distress reactions, thereby safely approaching these people who may require support; "Listen", which involves the asking and understanding of affected individuals' needs and concerns; and "Link", which involves the provision of coping strategies as well as connecting them with loved ones and social support.

The National Child Traumatic Stress Network (NCTSN) framework was developed as a form of basic grassroots psychological support for the general population following a crisis (Barbanel & Sternberg, 2005). This model focuses on eight key principles which by nature are similar to those identified within the WHO Model, but provide for more extensive information. These eight principles are: (1) Contact and Engagement, (2) Safety and Comfort, (3) Stabilisation, (4) Information Gathering: Current Needs and Concerns, (5) Practical Assistance, (6) Connection with Social Supports, (7) Information on Coping, and (8) Linkage with Collaborative Services.

With that, the question remains: which model should be chosen?

Strategy 2: Establish the Most Parsimonious Model for the Specific Context

Knowing which PFA model to use requires examination and understanding of the purpose of PFA within a set context. Who are the prospective or targeted students of this model — are they health professionals, first responders, or community volunteers? What is their grasp of the English language? Are the trainees able to maintain concentration for vast amounts of time, or do they require briefer pieces of information for ease of comprehension?

In Singapore, prospective trainees of PFA trainings are primarily grassroots community volunteers from various districts across the country. When examining for the PFA model that would be the most parsimonious with Singapore's needs, there were two major considerations. Firstly, Singapore faces a growing aging population, with many community volunteers aged 55 years old and above. Secondly, the current general Singaporean population has yet to come face to face with any large-scale traumatic incidents in Singapore. As such, the PFA model that Singapore should and has eventually adopted must ideally be easy to understand, remember, and disseminate to the community.

The WHO model, having been endorsed by 23 international agencies and translated into multiple languages and communities internationally, advocates that training information about PFA should be adapted appropriately to local and cultural contexts. In other words, the WHO model allows for a degree of cultural malleability in its framework. Research undertaken into the Philippines' adapted version of PFA following Typhoon Haiyan has identified positive perceived efficacy by responders, during their usage of the adapted model in supporting survivors (McPherson *et al.*, 2015).

It is clear that the WHO model is one of simplicity and adaptability. Likewise, the SGSecure movement has adopted the WHO model to be trained across community leaders within Singapore. The WHO model is also the chosen model for many other countries across Asia such as Malaysia, Philippines, Japan, and Sri Lanka.

Challenge 3: Managing Variability in Individuals Requiring PFA

The estimated 90% of New York citizens who experienced a fear and distress response following the 9/11 terrorist attacks (Schuster *et al.*, 2001) would have likely benefited from some form of PFA implementation. Extrapolating this data to major terrorist attacks throughout the world, it can be asserted that a staggering number of individuals following a terrorist attack would require some form of supportive response. But, does a blanket approach to providing supportive care work?

A major concept that has to be taken into consideration is the influence of culture, which essentially refers to the values, beliefs, behaviours, shared history, and the language of a group of people (Hall, 1976). At any given time, there is a high likelihood of multiple cultural groups being present in the same locale when a terrorist attack takes place. For example, the multitude of terrorist attacks which have occurred across the Philippines in public places such as street markets impacted not only the various indigenous ethnic groups present in the country, but also the tourist population. Culture and social setting have the capacity to significantly affect disaster management, and when that is disregarded or misjudged, cultural issues become more problematic (Hewitt, 2009).

Truong *et al.* (2014) stated that the ability to function competently within cultural contexts is essential for establishing rapport and maximising intervention outcomes. A significant negative impact is subsequently likely to transpire if first responders, officials, or professionals display a lack of cultural sensitivity by behaving inappropriately towards communities at risk. People respond differently to distressing events, dependent on multiple factors such as the nature and severity of the event experienced, personal and family history of mental health problems, age, as well as cultural background and traditions.

A blanket approach to implementing PFA might then be both unhelpful and significantly detrimental to all those whom PFA is being administered. In this case, how do we provide a supportive response to individuals of varying cultural and linguistic groups?

Strategy 3: Develop Cultural Competency in the Implementation of PFA

Serious consideration is required for cultural matters, particularly in the context of disaster prevention and preparedness. To be culturally appropriate and sensitive, PFA responders must be aware of how disasters can affect not only the vulnerable populations, but also the traumatic experiences of different individuals within a cultural context (Stebnicki, 2017). Major cultural norms, of which responders should be mindful of when implementing PFA to individuals within Asian communities, are outlined in Table 17.1.

In order to prevent potential discrimination against vulnerable groups following a crisis, encouraging social cohesion through proactive activities during peacetimes is recommended. Viewing one's identity as part of a broader categorisation, such as on a national rather than an individual level, would facilitate the creation of a sense of shared identity with others, thereby reducing "in-group" and "out-group" mentalities (Wang *et al.*, 2015). It is also important for PFA responders to recognise that their own age, gender, religion, schooling, and ethnicity may influence how they speak to individuals following a crisis. As such, seeking guidance about the cultural and social norms from others — such as community cultural leaders — may facilitate greater self-awareness regarding their own processes, in order to provide the best assistance to others.

Table 17.1. Cultural Norms for Consideration when Implementing PFA.

Norm	Note
Dress code	• Consider the necessity of dressing in a particular manner that is respectful in the crisis environment, and also whether people in need may require certain clothing items to maintain their dignity and customs (World Health Organization, War Trauma Foundation, & World Vision International, 2011).
Eye contact	• Cultural norms affect eye contact behaviours (Akechi *et al.*, 2013); individuals from Eastern cultures display less eye contact than individuals from Western cultures. It is possible to display listening skills in other ways, such as non-verbal cues like nodding. • When interacting with people with disabilities, address them directly rather than talking to their caregiver (unless direct communication is difficult).
Dietary restrictions	• Be respectful of food options provided to individuals during a crisis. If specific requirements such as halal/kosher/vegetarian/vegan cannot be catered for, consider alternatives to ensure that the individual's basic needs are met.
Body language	• Physical affection (e.g., hugging, touching shoulder), although considered necessary for displaying empathy, may not be appropriate. It is possible to display empathy in other ways, such as providing material assistance (e.g., a tissue or glass of water) to a distressed individual. • When interacting with children, sit or crouch in order to speak at their eye level.
Gender	• Individuals may feel more comfortable speaking with someone of the same gender. It is essential to clarify this information prior to providing support.
Language choice	• Consider the customary greeting that would initiate rapport, using colloquial terms. • Ensure that the information provided is tailored for individuals, i.e., age-appropriate, clear, and practical. • When working with older adults, be mindful that they may have acquired effective coping skills over a lifetime of managing adversities. Attempt to help them identify and utilise these coping skills.

(*Continued*)

Table 17.1. (*Continued*)

Norm	Note
	• There are multiple dialects spoken throughout regions. A translator, or another responder who speaks the dialect, may be required. • Some individuals may not display willingness to talk due to inappropriateness in some cultures to share information with people outside of family members. Be respectful of individuals' denial of services, whilst reminding them that the services are available should they be required at any stage.
Faith and spirituality	• Cultural differences have been identified in processes surrounding death, mourning, and grief. Assumption of an individual's faith is unhelpful; ask the individual regarding their coping skills, and encourage spiritual routines if mentioned. • Listen respectfully and without judgement to an individual's spiritual beliefs, and ensure that the responder's own beliefs or religious interpretations of the crisis are not imposed upon the individual.

Challenge 4: Lack of Awareness of Specialist Services Following an Attack

Cultural competency in the provision of PFA can and will go a long way towards providing a more supportive response in the immediate aftermath of a crisis. However, PFA is only a short-term response. Where do survivors turn to in the days, weeks, or months following an attack? How can continuity of support be ensured for those who require it?

PFA training in Australia places great emphasis on the "Link" component of the WHO model by connecting people back to their families or network, which is a critical follow-up action after offering empathic support and helping survivors to remain calm. Nonetheless, PFA training in Australia still faces some issues of identifying appropriate and adequate community resources for major areas in times of crisis. Although training individuals in PFA inherently improves their confidence in application, the perceived lack of information on what long-term support is available for survivors can instead result in perceived inadequacy, thereby reducing the confidence and willingness of trained personnel to apply PFA during crises. In fact, attempts to continue to administer PFA in spite of the reduced confidence and "mistakes" in the provision of PFA (e.g., pushing people to talk about their experiences, as evidenced in the 2014 Gaza conflict) defies the basic PFA principle of "do no harm", and has the capacity to be psychologically harmful for individuals.

Strategy 4: Compile a Culturally Relevant Set of Community Resources

Barriers in the access to and utilisation of mental health care are exacerbated following crises; individuals are often inherently more concerned with addressing their basic physiological needs than considering the impact of the incident on their mental wellbeing. It may not be until a long period of time following the incident that survivors identify the need for specialist services. To ensure continuity of support from PFA providers to community support staff, designated contact persons can play important roles in facilitating access to relevant mental health services (Reifels *et al.*, 2013).

It should be recognised that there is complexity in the compilation of community resources, particularly due to the breadth of organisations and institutions available within specific areas targeting specific demographics. Depending on the locale in which an attack has taken place, there may be unofficial community resources identified only through word-of-mouth, resulting in this service being known only at a local level. As such, a multifaceted approach is required, incorporating individuals from diversified districts as well as varying professional, cultural, linguistic, and personal backgrounds.

In collaboration with the government, mental health professionals, and volunteers, the author recommends for the compilation of a set of community resources pertaining to (but not limited to): individuals speaking different dialects who may act as voluntary translators, religious groups and religious leaders, and community organisations representing the interests of vulnerable groups. These groups may include individuals with physical or intellectual impairments, LGBTIPAQ[2] individuals, or even aged-care or child-care centres. Providing PFA volunteers with this resource list (or an abridged form) or creating a central website with information on available services — as was implemented following Japan's 2011 natural disaster (Kim, 2011) — is more likely to increase confidence in the application of PFA, ultimately facilitating public trust in the overall crisis response.

Challenge 5: Insufficient Established Training Guidelines for PFA Trainers

Due to minimal standardisation and quality control in PFA training programs throughout the world, a certain level of variability is expected in the implementation of PFA training programs. This is more likely for the WHO model training program which is readily available online for dissemination and implementation, and less likely in more stringent training programs like CISM, which involves a fee, multiple-day training, and exams for trainers to establish competency with content. Despite the difference, it is expected that the adherence to the facilitator manual for a specific PFA training program (accounting for adaptations due to cultural differences) should result in a similar quality output for students. Unfortunately, a lack of sufficient oversight into training programs based on freely available PFA models may result in training programs deviating from the recommended method, potentially impacting upon the efficacy of the model itself.

Strategy 5: Provide Extensive Established Training Guidelines to Trainers

Many non-Western countries such as Malaysia and Yemen are now implementing "Training of Trainers" workshops, with the purpose of

[2]It refers to lesbian, gay, bisexual, transgender, intersex, pansexual, asexual, queer, and questioning.

creating a team of "master-trainers" to conduct trainings for other colleagues and partners. This ensures the capacity to generate and expand the knowledge on providing PFA, which can ultimately be disseminated to volunteers in their respective communities. Such workshops are generally an extension of basic training workshops, and aim to provide comprehensive knowledge and principles of PFA, impart workshop facilitation skills, and enhance trainers' capacity in PFA. Trainers are taught to understand and utilise interactive and experiential delivery techniques properly, as research has highlighted the importance of interactive learning on retention of information (Roehl *et al.*, 2013). It is important to note that these workshop facilitators are experts in disaster mental health, and as subject matter experts, they are well equipped to provide adequate adaptations to PFA training programs whilst maintaining quality.

Although the output quality is unquantifiable due to the inability to establish the effectiveness of PFA (which circles back to Challenge 1), engaging in extensive training of trainers through established training guidelines has many benefits for both trainers and students. Alongside increasing the self-confidence of trainers to address difficult students and questions, trainers are equipped with the necessary facilitation skills to lead discussions and utilise appropriate verbal and non-verbal communication skills, as well as the knowledge base to speak confidently about PFA. There is a significant impact of training on the quality of first response provided during or after a crisis; improving the quality of trainers through established training guidelines is likely to significantly improve first response outcomes, and reduce the number of citizens displaying significant behaviour changes or enduring PTSD in the months following a crisis.

Conclusion

PFA is a fundamental crisis intervention skill taught throughout the world to health professionals and community first response teams. This chapter outlined the importance of PFA, selecting a model most parsimonious to the specific context, acting in a culturally-appropriate manner, compiling culturally relevant community resources, and providing extensive training to trainers. By addressing the multitude of challenges faced when incorporating a whole-of-society intervention, an empathic and supportive response may be provided to those in need during a crisis.

Editors' Note

It is important to note that PFA is not a standalone model or intervention *per se*. It is still early days with regard to the use of PFA, and more research is required.

References

Akechi, H., Senju, A., Uibo, H., Kikuchi, Y., Hasegawa, T., & Hietanen, J. K. (2013). Attention to eye contact in the west and east: Autonomic responses and evaluative ratings. *Public Library of Science One*, *8*(3), 1–10.

Barbanel, L., & Sternberg, R. J. (Eds.) (2005). *Psychological Interventions in Times of Crisis* (1st edn.). New York: Springer Publishing Company.

Boscarino, J. A., Adams, R. E., & Figley, C. R. (2011). Mental health service use after the World Trade Center disaster: Utilization trends and comparative effectiveness. *The Journal of Nervous and Mental Disease*, *199*(2), 91–99.

Bryant, R. A., Harvey, A. G., Guthrie, R. M., & Moulds, M. L. (2003). Acute psychophysiological arousal and posttraumatic stress disorder: A two–year prospective study. *Journal of Traumatic Stress*, *16*(5), 439–443.

Cheong, D., Tan, B., & Tan, H. Q. R. (2016). 3 in 4 Singaporeans believe terror strike here 'only a matter of time.' *The Straits Times*. Retrieved from http://www.straitstimes.com/singapore/3-in-4-singaporeans-believe-terror-strike-here-only-a-matter-of-time.

Cloak, N. L., & Edwards, P. (2004). Psychological first aid: Emergency care for terrorism and disaster survivors. *Current Psychiatry*, *3*(5), 12–23.

Everly, G. S., Jr., & Mitchell, J. T. (1999). *Critical Incident Stress Management (CISM): A New Era and Standard of Care in Crisis Intervention*. Ellicott City, MD: Chevron Publishing.

Forbes, D., Lewis, V., Varker, T., Phelps, A., O'Donnell, M., Wade, D. J., & Creamer, M. (2011). Psychological first aid following trauma:

Implementation and evaluation framework for high-risk organizations. *Psychiatry*, 74, 224–239.
Fox, J., Burkle, F., Bass, J., Pia, F., Epstein, J., & Markenson, D. (2012). The effectiveness of psychological first aid as a disaster intervention tool: Research analysis of peer-reviewed literature from 1990–2010. *Disaster Medicine and Public Health Preparedness*, 6(3), 247–252.
Government of Singapore. (2018). *SGSecure*. Retrieved from https://www.sgsecure.sg/
Hall, E. T. (1976). *Beyond Culture*. New York: Anchor Books/Doubleday.
Hewitt, K. (2009). Cultural and risk: Understanding the sociocultural settings that influence risk from natural hazards. Synthesis Report from a Global E-Conference organised by ICIMOD and facilitated by the Mountain Forum Kathmandu, ICIMOD: 14.
Hobfoll, S. E., Watson, P., Bell, C. C., Bryant, R. A., Brymer, M. J., Friedman, M. J., & Ursano, R. J. (2007). Five essential elements of immediate and mid–term mass trauma intervention: Empirical evidence. *Psychiatry: Interpersonal and Biological Processes*, *70*(4), 283–315.
Inter-Agency Standing Committee (2007). *IASC Guidelines on Mental Health and Psychosocial Support in Emergency Settings*. IASC: Geneva.
Jaycox, L. H., Morse, L. K., Tanielian, T., & Stein, B. D. (2006). How schools can help students recover from traumatic experiences: A tool-kit for supporting long-term recovery technical report. Retrieved from https://www.rand.org/pubs/technical_reports/TR413.html.
Kim, Y. (2011). Great East Japan earthquake and early mental-health-care response. *Psychiatry and Clinical Neurosciences*, *65*(6), 539–548.
McCabe, O. L., Everly, G. S., Jr., Brown, L. M., Wendelboe, A. M., Hamid, N. H. A., Tallchief, V. L., & Links, J. M. (2014). Psychological first aid: A consensus-derived, empirically supported, competency-based training model. *American Journal of Public Health*, *104*, 621–628.
McPherson, M., Counahan, M., & Hall, J. L. (2015). Responding to typhoon Haiyan in the Philippines. *Western Pacific Surveillance and Response Journal*, 6(1), 1–4.
National Institute of Mental Health (2002). *Mental Health and Mass Violence: Evidence-based Early Psychological Intervention for Victims/Survivors of Mass Violence. A Workshop to Reach Consensus on Best Practices*. NIH Publication No. 025138. Washington, D.C.: U.S. Government Printing Office.
Neria, Y., DiGrande, L., & Adams, B. G. (2011). Posttraumatic stress disorder following the September 11, 2001, terrorist attacks: A review

of the literature among highly exposed populations. *The American Psychologist*, *66*(6), 429–446.

North Atlantic Treaty Organization (2009). *Psychosocial Care for People Affected by Disasters and Major Incidents: A Model for Designing, Delivering and Managing Psychosocial Services for People Involved in Major Incidents, Conflict, Disasters and Terrorism.* Brussels: NATO.

Reifels, L., Pietrantoni, L., Prati, G., Kim, Y., Kilpatrick, D. G., Dyb, G., & O'Donnell, M. (2013). Lessons learned about psychosocial responses to disaster and mass trauma: An international perspective. *European Journal of Psychotraumatology*, *4*, 1–9.

Roehl, A., Reddy, S. L., & Shannon, G. J. (2013). The flipped classroom: An opportunity to engage millennial students through active learning strategies. *Journal of Family and Consumer Sciences*, *105*(2), 44–49.

Rubin, G. J., Brewin, C. R., Greenburg, N., Simpson, J., & Wessely, S. (2005). Psychological and behavioral reactions to the bombings in London on 7 July 2005: Cross-sectional survey of a representative sample of Londoners. *The British Medical Journal*, *331*, 606–612.

Schafer, A., Snider, L., & Sammour, R. (2016). A reflective learning report about the implementation and impacts of Psychological First Aid (PFA) in Gaza. *Disaster Health*, *3*, 1–10.

Schelenger, W. E., Caddell, J. M., Ebert, L., Jordan, B. K., Rourke, K. M., Wilson, D., Thalji, L., Dennis, J. M., Fairbank, J. A., & Kulka, R. A. (2002). Psychological reactions to terrorist attacks: findings from the National Study of Americans' Reactions to September 11. *JAMA*, *288(5)*, 581–588.

Schultz, J. M., Espinel, Z., Cohen, R., Shaw, J., & Flynn, B. (2003). *Behavioral Health Awareness Training for Terrorism and Disasters.* Miami, FL: Center for Disaster and Extreme Event Preparedness.

Schultz, J. M., & Forbes, D. (2014). Psychological first aid: Rapid proliferation and the search for evidence. *Disaster Health*, *2*(1), 3–12.

Schuster, M. A., Stein, B. D., Jaycox, L. H., Collins, R. L., Marshall, G. N., Elliott, M. C., & Berry, S. H. (2001). A national survey of stress reactions after the September 11, 2001, terrorist attacks. *The New England Journal of Medicine*, *345*, 1,507–1,512.

Sphere project (2004). Sphere handbook: Humanitarian charter and minimum standards in disaster response. Retrieved from http://www.refworld.org/docid/4ed8ae592.html.

Stebnicki, M. A. (Ed.) (2017). *Disaster Mental Health Counselling: Responding to Trauma in a Multicultural Context* (4th edn.). New York: Springer Publishing Company.

Stein, B. D., Elliott, M. N., Jaycox, L. H., Collins, R. L., Berry, S. H., Klein, D. J., & Schuster, M. A. (2004). A national longitudinal study of the psychological consequences of the September 11, 2001 terrorist attacks: Reactions, impairment, and help–seeking. *Psychiatry*, *67*(2), 105–117.

Truong, M., Paradies, Y., & Priest, N. (2014). Interventions to improve cultural competency in healthcare: A systematic review of reviews. *BMC Health Services Research*, *14*(99), 1–17.

Wang, Y., Gomes, D., Tan, J., Neo, L. S., Ong, G., & Khader, M. (2015). Day after terror: 9 strategies to sustaining Singapore's resilience. Research Report No. 18/2015. Singapore: Home Team Behavioural Sciences Centre.

Woodbury, M. G., & Kuhnke, J. L. (2014). Evidence-based practice vs evidence-informed practice: What's the difference? *Wound Care Canada*, *12*(1), 18–21. Retrieved from https://www.researchgate.net/publication/260793333.

World Health Organization, War Trauma Foundation, & World Vision International (2011). *Psychological First Aid: Guide for Field Workers.* WHO: Geneva.

CHAPTER 18

Responding to a Violent Extremist Attack: Insights from the 2016 Orlando Shooting Incident

SHI HUI TEE

Home Team Behavioural Sciences Centre, Ministry of Home Affairs, Singapore

Introduction

On 12 June 2016, a deadly active shooting which evolved into a hostage-taking situation took place between 2:02 a.m. and 5:15 a.m. at Pulse nightclub in Orlando, Florida. The shooting left 49 dead and 53 wounded. This violent extremist attack was regarded as both the worst mass shooting event in modern U.S. history (Zambelich & Hurt, 2016), as well as the most significant act of violence towards the Lesbian, Gay, Bisexual and Transgender (LGBT) community. Investigations revealed the perpetrator to be Omar Seddique Mateen, a 29-year-old U.S. citizen, who lived in Fort Pierce, Florida ("Orlando gay nightclub shooting: Who was Omar Mateen?", 2016). He worked as a licensed armed security guard for G4S, a security company

(Henderson *et al.*, 2016). It was speculated that he might have been a gay homophobe who targeted Pulse clubgoers as he hated his sexual orientation (Weaver & Ovalle, 2016). It is also possible that he might have been radicalised online through the consumption of radical propaganda such as that of radical preacher Anwar al-Awlaki (Ellis *et al.*, 2016), as he pledged allegiance to the Islamic State of Iraq and Syria (ISIS) leader in a 911 call (Ackerman, 2016b). Following the attack, ISIS claimed responsibility and praised Mateen as a soldier of God (Silverstein, 2016). However, no formal connections were found between Mateen and ISIS (Ackerman, 2016a).

Why are we Looking at the 2016 Orlando Shooting Incident?

While most of the researches chose to focus more on the perpetrator and his/her motivations, and the operational aspects of the attack, it is equally important to look at the community reaction and response in the aftermath of a violent extremist attack. To this end, the 2016 Orlando shooting incident provides a good illustration of how adequately facilitated community response can help to mitigate post-crisis damage and help the community recover from the attack. Following the Orlando shooting incident, a critical incident review on the response to the event was published by the U.S. Department of Justice, evaluating the event and its aftermath (Straub *et al.*, 2017). Information on reactions and behaviours of various groups of stakeholders (i.e., community, group, individual level) during and after the event surfaced as well. An analysis of the above could shed insights on what can be expected during and after a violent extremist attack, and provide several implications on responding to a violent extremist attack.

Five Responses and Insights from the 2016 Orlando Shooting

Response 1 — Usage of Smart Devices During the Three Hours of the Active Shooting Turned Hostage-taking Incident

Several victims, survivors, and members of the public utilised their smart devices to reach out to others during the shooting incident, relaying information through calling, text messaging, as well as social media sites such as Twitter and Facebook (Nielsen, 2016; Salinger, 2016). The information relayed ranged from last messages, situation inside the nightclub, to getting their loved ones to relay their hiding positions to the authorities (Salinger, 2016; Towner, 2016). These behaviours can be considered as instinctive human behaviours in the current technologically advanced world, with the good intention of seeking help for themselves and others. Notwithstanding these good intentions, it was revealed later that the perpetrator was also on Facebook, searching for keywords such as "Pulse Orlando" and "Shooting" in the midst of the shooting event (Alexander, 2016). Unknown to the hostages, their online postings stating their hiding positions, while intended as a plea for help, may have unintentionally compromised their own and others' safety. However, the behaviour of sharing information on social media may have been partially prompted by practical constraints, such as the need to maintain silence so as not to reveal their hiding positions to the perpetrator (Salinger, 2016), as well as the sharp rise in call volume to the 911 helpline, causing several calls to be unable to go through (McLaughlin & Campbell, 2016; Sanchez, 2016).

Insight 1: Importance of informing and educating the public on crisis behaviours

To ensure the safety of the public in the case of a crisis incident, there is a need for the government to inform and educate the public on how they should behave during a crisis situation. This includes the provision of guidelines[1] not only on encouraged behaviours, but also discouraged behaviours in times of a crisis. There are several behaviours that the public may be educated on.

Firstly, in the context of United States, there is a need to ensure that the public are informed and educated on the U.S. Department of

---

[1]In addition to guidelines, legislations such as the Singapore's Public Order and Safety (Special Powers) Act (POSSPA) can be implemented. In the case of POSSPA, it allows law enforcement to prohibit the public in the incident area from "making or communicating films or pictures ... and ... text or audio messages about ... ongoing security operations" (Ministry of Home Affairs, 2018, para. 10).

Homeland Security's (DHS) encouraged crisis behaviour of "Run, Hide, Fight, and Call 911" (Department of Homeland Security, 2017), and that they act accordingly in the event of a crisis. A majority of survivors managed to run out of the nightclub when the shooting first broke out (Holley & Achenbach, 2016). Several who were injured played dead while waiting for an opportunity to escape or be rescued (Buncombe, 2016; Miller, 2016). Several patrons hiding in the bathroom also attempted to collectively take down Mateen (i.e., fight; Healy & Eligon, 2016), while others called 911 to provide information on Mateen's actions and location (Sanchez, 2016; McLaughlin *et al.*, 2016).

Secondly, learning from the shooting incident, the public may be educated on the discouraged behaviours observed. Several patrons chose to run towards and hide in the bathrooms instead (Keneally, 2016; Healy & Eligon, 2016). Several victims who died were shot in the bathroom where they were hiding (Collman, 2016). The youngest victim, Akyra Murray, had initially ran out of the nightclub, but returned for a friend. She was eventually shot and bled to death in the bathroom (Platon, 2017). The patrons who attempted to collectively take down Mateen (i.e., fight) were unsuccessful, and many were shot instead (Healy & Eligon, 2016). It is hence important to inform and educate the public on encouraged and discouraged crisis behaviours.

Encouraged behaviours include adhering to the DHS's guidelines, and ensuring one's own and others' safety before reporting key details regarding the situation to the relevant authorities through proper channels (e.g., 911 hotline). Discouraged behaviours include publicising photos, videos, and police operations related to the crisis event on social media, and returning to the scene of the attack. The anticipative and preparatory nature of these guidelines can give rise to ideal crisis behaviour from the public, successfully mitigating the negative impacts of a violent extremist attack (e.g., reduced death rates, increased citizen support in the form of information provision).

However, it should be noted that the onus still lies with the public to be familiar with the guidelines. Finally, the government should also have in place sufficient and adequate systems that can support heavy public usage during a crisis.

Response 2: A Multi-Agency Operation and Response Involving 27 Local, Federal, and State Agencies was Kicked Into Action

A multi-agency operation took place for the event, where a total of 27 agencies from various jurisdictions responded to the Orlando shooting incident ("Report reveals dramatic new details from Orlando nightclub massacre", 2017). Involved agencies include local police departments such as the Orlando Police Department (OPD), federal agencies such as the Federal Bureau of Investigation (FBI), Bureau of Alcohol, Tobacco, Firearms and Explosives (ATF), and DHS, state agencies such as the Florida Department of Law Enforcement, as well as medical centres such as the Orlando Regional Medical Center (ORMC), and more ("List of Agencies involved", n.d.).

During the incident, the operations and response of the various agencies were coordinated via a unified command centre, where the "ability to immediately determine specific agency investigative roles and responsibilities is crucial to effective incident and investigative management" (Straub *et al.*, 2017, p. 98). However, the fire departments and emergency medical services were not included in the unified command centre, impeding communication and information flow to those departments ("Report reveals dramatic new details from Orlando nightclub massacre", 2017; Straub *et al.*, 2017). Despite that, a majority of the critically injured victims were rescued within 40 minutes and sent to the ORMC (Straub *et al.*, 2017).

Despite being caught off guard, the medical professionals at the ORMC were able to administer prompt medical help to those who were brought there, and most of the victims survived. This may be attributed to the active shooter emergency drill carried out by Orlando Health and the FBI three months prior to the shooting incident, where the training provided during the drill helped the medical professionals at the ORMC understand how to react in a crisis situation (Washington, 2016).

Insight 2: Importance of a whole-of-government approach in crisis response strategizing and training

The Orlando shooting incident highlighted the importance of employing a whole-of-government approach in the planning, rescue, and response phase of a crisis incident, where the various agencies should work together before, during, and after a crisis incident. Prior to the incident, relevant agencies should get together to discuss the assignment of responsibilities and agree on a crisis communication plan. A clear demarcation of responsibilities, together with crucial communication between agencies involved in the rescue operation could expedite rescue missions, reducing the loss of lives.

However, on top of having an all-encompassing crisis plan involving all relevant agencies, there is a need to conduct cooperative trainings and emergency drills involving these agencies, allowing agencies to familiarise themselves with how other agencies operate, and also to leverage on one another's expertise. More importantly, trainings and drills conducted have to be realistic and reflect both the physical and psychological demands during an actual crisis situation. As highlighted in the critical incident review, "your body can't go where your mind has never been" (Straub *et al.*, 2017, p. 68). Additionally, it would be beneficial to involve the public in some of the emergency drills, so as to promote awareness among the public and sensitise them to the threat of violent extremism.

Response 3: Some Survivors and Responders Continue to Experience Symptoms of Post-Traumatic Stress for a Long Time Following the Crisis Incident

Several survivors and responders experienced symptoms of post-traumatic stress after the Orlando shooting incident, some still experiencing these symptoms long after the incident despite having received psychological help (Capretto, 2017; Hadad, 2017). According to the American Psychiatric Association (2013), the symptoms range from feelings of distress, flashbacks of incident, avoidance of the incident and incident site, negative emotions such as fear, guilt, anger or shame, sleep disturbance, and more.

One survivor named Patience Carter suffers from feelings of guilt for having survived the Orlando shooting while she had watched her friend die from bleeding and had a stranger take a bullet for her (Zezima & Sullivan, 2016). She shared in an interview a year after the incident that she still struggles in dealing with her emotions, as she sometimes finds herself "falling into this dark place that I [Carter] don't want to go back to" ("A year after Pulse shooting, survivor reflects on recovery", 2017, para. 16). Survivor Ilka Reyes still feels unsafe and is trying to recover and get her life back together slowly (Williams & Mills, n.d.).

Several first responders experienced post-traumatic stress following the attack. Former police officers, Gerry Realin and Omar Delgado, were both diagnosed with PTSD following the incident (Luscombe, 2017; Schladebeck, 2017). Delgado still experiences recurring nightmares from what he had witnessed at the incident, is uncomfortable being in crowded and noisy places, and lives in constant state of fear that similar incidents will occur (Corey, 2017). He was dismissed from his job due to his PTSD diagnoses, the treatment for which is not covered under his workers' compensation insurance (Corey, 2017).

Insight 3: Importance of managing the psychological wellbeing of individuals in the vulnerable zone

Besides physical safety, the numerous reported cases of post-traumatic stress brings out the importance of managing survivors' and responders' psychological well-being after a violent extremist attack, on top of ensuring their physical safety and well-being. There are several ways of doing so. One way is through psychological first aid (PFA), which is an approach meant to help individuals reduce the psychological distress following a violent extremist attack (The National Child Traumatic Stress Network, n.d.). Another is to deploy trained mental health specialists, counsellors, and practitioners to the affected zones (Tanielian & Stein, 2016). Finally, psychological and critical incident debriefings may also be held in the aftermath of a violent extremist attack to care for the psychological wellbeing of responders.

In the case of the Orlando shooting incident, several counsellors and practitioners signed up voluntarily to provide psychological help, crisis counselling, and therapy for those who were affected and in need of support (e.g., victims, victims' families, general public) within the first 24 hours (Bray, 2016). There were also volunteers who offered support in the form of providing a listening ear (Bray, 2016).

In addition to providing psychological help to those in need, the Office for Victims of Crime (OVC) had set up a resource webpage for the victims of the shooting incident, providing information on the organisations which they may approach for assistance. The webpage of resources (e.g., related to coping with grief, distress, and recovery) provides a safe space for those who have not sought help immediately after the attack to approach the relevant organisations for help whenever they wish to do so (Office for Victims of Crime, n.d.), especially for those who may be experiencing a delayed onset of trauma (Bray, 2016).

However, it is important to ensure that the mental health specialists, counsellors, and practitioners deployed to the scene are adequately trained to handle the psychological reactions that occur as a result of a violent extremist attack, as the reactions are inherently different from other forms of psychological distress (Tanielian & Stein, 2016). Aside from that, the OPD have adequately ensured the mental wellbeing of their responders and officers through various measures (e.g., mandatory debriefings, employee assistance program), where "OPD leadership prioritized the mental health of all OPD personnel following the response to Pulse" (Straub *et al.*, 2017, p. 84). However, despite the measures, several officers still experienced psychological trauma after the shooting incident, which required further mental health support (Luscombe, 2017; Schladebeck, 2017).

Learning from the Orlando incident, the authorities can consider the inclusion of PTSD coverage in the insurance for first responders and emergency workers. This could serve to help the officers receive the support they need for treatment and recovery after a crisis event. Governments can also consider including paid time off and treatment for PTSD in the worker's compensation insurance, which can go a long way in showing support for emergency responders, and helping them recover faster from post-traumatic stress.

Response 4: Negative Behaviours from the General Public is to be Expected in the Aftermath of a Crisis Incident

Several negative behaviours were observed following the shooting incident. These behaviours include speculations of the tragedy, as well as homophobic and Islamophobic reactions. Following the shooting incident, messages dismissing the tragedy and speculating that it did not happen at all and was staged by the government, started making its round on Twitter (Mele, 2016). The insensitivity of these conspiracy theories had a negative impact on the families of victims and the survivors, who had been harassed at lengths by members of the public who believed in these theories (Wilson, 2018). Such behaviours can impede a community's post-crisis recovery and cause greater distress to the affected.

Additionally, as the Orlando shooting involved the LGBT community, the public engaged in homophobic behaviours. Several anti-LGBT individuals commended the shooter for killing LGBT people, and even religious leaders voiced homophobic remarks (Bogart, 2016; Brennan, 2016; Geers, 2016). Such public homophobic expressions led the LGBT community to question their progress in gaining acceptance in society (Vick, 2016; Wall, 2016). While the individuals who voiced these homophobic views were a minority, their hurtful remarks and actions have an adverse impact on the LGBT community. In a specific incident, a highly conservative anti-LGBT group from the Westboro Baptist Church held a rally at the funeral wake of two of the LGBT victims (Pleasance, 2016). Islamophobia was also observed after the Muslim identity of the shooter was revealed, where the public blamed the entire Muslim community for the attack, rather than on the perpetrator himself (Shahin, 2016). Such negative behaviours from the public may impede the community's recovery from the tragedy.

Insight 4: Importance of staying united against negative behaviours targeted at selected communities following the crisis incident

Negative behaviours after violent extremist attacks are to be expected. Hence, there is a need to be prepared to deal with such negative behaviours. As the Orlando shooting incident involved the LGBT community and a Muslim perpetrator, most negative public behaviours were targeted at these two communities of people in the community. However, despite the onslaught of negative public behaviours towards the targeted groups, the LGBT and Muslim community in Orlando responded differently. Several LGBT groups stood up together in solidarity for the LGBT victims. Stuart Milk, the founder and president of the Harvey Milk Foundation, a non-profit organisation seeking to celebrate diversity, took the lead in uniting the LGBT community to pay tribute to the victims, encouraging the LGBT community to stay united (Graaf, 2016). Support for the LGBT community also came in the form of members from the Orlando Shakespeare Theatre dressing up as angels to keep the members of the Westboro Baptist Church from interrupting the wakes of the LGBT victims (McNamara, 2016; Palm, 2016). Several religious leaders also publicly voiced their support for the LGBT community, reassuring them that they would not be discriminated against (Bogart, 2016). In dealing with Islamophobia, several Muslim organisations had been expecting the spike in Islamophobia and hence were well-prepared in handling the situation (Colson, 2016). Learning from the Orlando incident, the solidarity of the affected groups (LGBT and Muslim community), as well as the public support given to both communities have gone a long way in helping and enabling the communities to stay resilient in the face of discrimination.

Response 5: Individuals and Private Organisations May Step in to Lend a Helping Hand after a Crisis Incident

Other than negative public behaviours, pro-social public behaviours were also observed in the aftermath of the incident, where the public rendered help in the form of blood donation, fundraising, social media campaigns, and public memorials (Edwards, 2016; GoFundMe, 2016; Taylor, 2016). An individual, Greg Zanis, went the extra mile to deliver 49 hand-made crosses for the victims, placing these crosses outside ORMC for the public to write their last messages to the victims (Yam, 2016).

Businesses, non-profit organisations, and social groups also provided help in the form of food for blood donors, as well as monetary donations, lodgings, flights, and transportation for those who were affected (Bradley, 2016; Lee, 2016; Sieczkowski, 2016). Walt Disney Company donated a million dollars to the "OneOrlando Fund" for victims and their families, and also matched their employees' donations dollar-for-dollar (Smith, 2016).

Various celebrities took a stand against the shooting incident (Blakinger & Sblendorio, 2016), one of whom is Lady Gaga, who condemned the attack and lent support to the victims and their families ("Lady Gaga condemns 'hateful' Orlando shooting in candlelight vigil", 2016). These positive helping behaviours took place without governmental intervention, where individuals and organisations stepped in — their own capacity — to lend a helping hand to the victims and their families. Such positive behaviours can serve to negate the negative public behaviours and help the community recover from a crisis and become more resilient.

Insight 5: Importance of encouraging organisations and individuals in the community to take on responsibility following a crisis incident

After a crisis, it is important to encourage individuals and organisations to be more proactive in taking on responsibility and contributing to their community's recovery. Having individuals and organisations lend a helping hand to their community in need can go a long way in reducing the community's reliance on the government during a crisis. Such positive behaviours can also enhance communal bonds and build community resilience. Singularly, the government has limited capacity and would not be able to help a community recover as quickly without help from the local stakeholders. It is hence important for the government to involve private organisations in their crisis recovery plan. As the government makes plans on rebuilding a community after an attack, they can rope in and work with the private organisations in their community, who are usually well-equipped with resources and are more than willing to assist wherever required.

With a private organisation taking the lead in facilitating certain aspects of post-crisis recovery (e.g., rallying the crowd, crowdsourcing), the government can focus on core areas of recovery (e.g., structural rebuilding). The government can also encourage businesses and enterprises to start initiatives that can help build resilience and social cohesion in the community.

Additionally, pro-social behaviours from the community can be encouraged through commending instances of positive behaviours, as in Zanis's case, where Florida Governor Rick Scott posted a tweet on his Twitter account, commending Zanis for the 49 crosses that he made for the victims (Yam, 2016). Such commendations can increase the likelihood of positive behaviours occurring again as these behaviours are reinforced with positive outcomes. In conclusion, tapping into the resources of the community and private organisations can go a long way in helping a community recover faster.

Acknowledgement

The views expressed in this chapter are the author's only and do not represent the official position or view of the Ministry of Home Affairs, Singapore.

References

A year after Pulse shooting, survivor reflects on recovery (2017). *PBS News Hour.* Retrieved from https://www.pbs.org/newshour/show/year-pulse-shooting-survivor-reflects-recovery#transcript.

Ackerman, S. (2016a). CIA has not found any link between Orlando killer and Isis, says agency chief. *The Guardian.* Retrieved from https://www.

theguardian.com/us-news/2016/jun/16/cia-orlando-shooter-omar-mateen-isis-pulse-nightclub-attack.

Ackerman, S. (2016b). Omar Mateen described himself as 'Islamic soldier' in 911 calls to police. *The Guardian*. Retrieved from https://www.theguardian.com/us-news/2016/jun/20/omar-mateen-911-calls-orlando-shooting-fbi-release-isis.

Alexander, H. (2016). Omar Mateen searched for Facebook posts about Orlando shooting while he was carrying it out. *The Telegraph*. Retrieved from http://www.telegraph.co.uk/news/2016/06/16/omar-mateen-searched-for-facebook-posts-about-orlando-shooting-w/.

American Psychiatric Association (2013). *Diagnostic and Statistical Manual of Mental Disorders* (5th edn.). Arlington, VA: American Psychiatric Association.

Blakinger, K., & Sblendorio, P. (2016). Celebrities react after tragic mass shooting at Orlando gay club. *New York Daily News*. Retrieved from http://www.nydailynews.com/news/national/celebrities-react-tragic-mass-shooting-orlando-gay-club-article-1.2670637.

Bogart, N. (2016). 'The tragedy is that more of them didn't die': Pastor sparks outrage with hateful sermon following Orlando shooting. *Global News*. Retrieved from http://globalnews.ca/news/2763554/orlando-shooting-pastor-outrage-hateful-sermon/.

Bradley, L. (2016). Disney just donated $1 million to help Orlando's shooting victims. *Vanity Fair*. Retrieved from https://www.vanityfair.com/hollywood/2016/06/disney-donation-orlando-victims.

Bray, B. (2016). Counselors play part in Orlando crisis response. *Counseling today*. Retrieved from https://ct.counseling.org/2016/07/counselors-play-part-orlando-crisis-response/.

Brennan, C. (2016). Texas pastor says he prays those wounded in Orlando massacre die. *New York Daily News*. Retrieved from http://www.nydailynews.com/news/national/texas-pastor-prays-wounded-orlando-massacre-die-article-1.2684431.

Buncombe, A. (2016). Orlando attack: Survivor reveals how he 'played dead' among bodies to escape nightclub killer. *Independent*. Retrieved from http://www.independent.co.uk/news/world/americas/orlando-attack-survivor-reveals-how-he-played-dead-among-bodies-to-escape-nightclub-killer-a7080196.html.

Capretto, L. (2017). 5 survivors of the Pulse massacre return to the club together for the first time. *HuffPost*. Retrieved from https://www.

huffingtonpost.com/entry/pulse-shooting-survivors-return-to-the-club-together_us_5931b00de4b075bff0f323e5.

Collman, A. (2016). The youngest victim of Orlando massacre, 18, was celebrating her graduation when she bled to death in a bathroom stall after being shot in the arm and calling her mom for help. *Daily Mail*. Retrieved from http://www.dailymail.co.uk/news/article-3639838/Philadelphia-teen-killed-nightclub-attack-called-mom.html#ixzz5CuNU6sYh.

Colson, N. (2016). An act of hate. *Jacobin*. Retrieved from https://www.jacobinmag.com/2016/06/orlando-pulse-nightclub-shooting-mass-murder-mateen-islamophobia/.

Corey, D. (2017). Police officer with PTSD from Pulse massacre loses his job. *NBC News*. Retrieved from https://www.nbcnews.com/storyline/orlando-nightclub-massacre/police-officer-ptsd-pulse-massacre-loses-his-job-n827171.

Department of Homeland Security (2017). Active shooter: How to respond. Retrieved from https://www.dhs.gov/sites/default/files/publications/active-shooter-how-to-respond-508.pdf.

Edwards, V. (2016). Thousands flood to donate blood after Orlando club massacre — But scores are turned away because homosexuals are still banned from giving blood in the US. *DailyMail*. Retrieved from http://www.dailymail.co.uk/news/article-3637775/Hundreds-people-line-donate-blood-leaving-banks-overloaded-following-horrific-mass-shooting-Orlando-nightclub.html.

Ellis, R., Fantz, A., McLaughln, E. C., & Hume, T. (2016). Orlando shooting: What motivated a killer? *CNN*. Retrieved from https://edition.cnn.com/2016/06/13/us/orlando-nightclub-shooting/index.html.

Geers, J. (2016). Here are all the people applauding the Orlando gay club shooter. *ThoughtCatalog*. Retrieved from https://thoughtcatalog.com/jacob-geers/2016/06/here-are-all-the-people-applauding-the-orlando-gay-club-shooter/.

GoFundMe (2016). Support victims of Pulse shooting. Retrieved from https://www.gofundme.com/PulseVictimsFund.

Graaf, M. D. (2016). "These victims had their dreams stolen and their potential stolen from us all": Harvey Milk's family leads tributes as LGBTQ community rallies around Orlando club. *DailyMail*. Retrieved from http://www.dailymail.co.uk/news/article-3637776/Not-just-gay-club-Orlando-venue-founded-promote-LGBT-rights-memory-Florida-man-died-HIV.html.

Hadad, C. (2017). 5 faces of the Orlando Pulse attack, a year later. *CNN*. Retrieved from https://edition.cnn.com/2017/06/12/us/orlando-pulse-shooting-one-year-anniversary-five-faces/index.html.

Healy, J., & Eligon, J. (2016). Orlando survivors recall night of terror: 'Then he shoots me again'. *The New York Times*. Retrieved from http://www.nytimes.com/2016/06/18/us/pulse-nightclub-orlando-mass-shooting.html.

Henderson, B., Alexander, H., & Sherlock, R. (2016). Omar Mateen: Everything we know so far about Orlando gunman. *The Telegraph*. Retrieved from https://www.telegraph.co.uk/news/2016/06/12/omar-mateen-everything-we-know-so-far-about-orlando-gunman/.

Holley, P., & Achenbach, J. (2016). 'It was just complete chaos': Orlando massacre survivors on the desperate struggle to stay alive. *The Washington Post*. Retrieved from https://www.washingtonpost.com/news/post-nation/wp/2016/06/12/it-was-just-complete-chaos-survivors-of-orlando-massacre-recall-desperate-struggle-to-stay-alive/?noredirect=on&utm_term=.6545f44760c5.

Keneally, M. (2016). Video shows survivors hiding out in Orlando nightclub bathroom for hours. *ABC News*. Retrieved from http://abcnews.go.com/US/video-shows-people-hiding-orlando-nightclub-bathroom/story?id=39902907.

Lady Gaga condemns 'hateful' Orlando shooting in candlelight vigil (2016). *Telegraph*. Retrieved from http://www.telegraph.co.uk/news/2016/06/14/lady-gaga-condemns-hateful-orlando-shooting-in-candlelight-vigil/.

Lee, S. (2016). In tribute to Orlando victims, Uber provides free rides this weekend to local LGBT sites. *Newsweek*. Retrieved from http://www.newsweek.com/tribute-orlando-victims-uber-provides-free-rides-weekend-local-lgbt-sites-471738.

List of agencies involved (n.d.). City of Orlando. Retrieved from http://www.cityoforlando.net/cityclerk/wp-content/uploads/sites/12/2016/06/List-of-Agencies-Involved.pdf.

Luscombe, R. (2017). Orlando police officer who saved Pulse shooting victims fired from force. *The Guardian*. Retrieved from https://www.theguardian.com/us-news/2017/dec/07/orlando-shooting-pulse-nightclub-police-officer-omar-delgado.

McLaughlin, M., & Campbell, A. (2016). Heartbreaking 911 calls from Orlando nightclub shooting revealed. *The Huffington Post*. Retrieved from http://www.huffingtonpost.com/entry/orlando-nightclub-911-calls_us_579918e2e4b01180b5317eaf.

McLaughlin, M., Murdock, S., & Campbell, A. (2016). 911 calls shed light on what happened during Orlando nightclub shooting. *The Huffington Post*. Retrieved from http://www.huffingtonpost.com/entry/orlando-shooting-pulse-911-calls_us_57e2b6e9e4b0e80b1b9f978a.

McNamara, B. (2016). You need to see the angels showing up at the funerals of Orlando shooting victims. *TeenVogue*. Retrieved from http://www.teenvogue.com/story/orlando-shooting-victims-funerals-angels-westboro-baptist-church.

Mele, C. (2016). After Orlando shooting, 'false flag' and 'crisis actor' conspiracy theories surface. *The New York Times*. Retrieved from https://www.nytimes.com/2016/06/29/us/after-orlando-shooting-false-flag-and-crisis-actor-conspiracy-theories-surface.html.

Miller, Z. J. (2016). 'He's shooting everyone who's already dead:' Orlando shooting survivor recalls playing dead. *Time*. Retrieved from http://time.com/4368570/orlando-shooting-pulse-survivors/.

Ministry of Home Affairs (2018). Public Order and Safety (Special Powers) Bill 2018. Retrieved from https://www.mha.gov.sg/newsroom/press-releases/newsroom-detail-page?news=public-order-and-safety-(special-powers)-bill-2018.

Nielsen, K. (2016). Orlando shooting: Witnesses tell their stories on social media during attack. *Global News*. Retrieved from http://globalnews.ca/news/2757141/orlando-shooting-witnesses-tell-their-stories-on-social-media-during-attack/.

Office for Victims of Crime (n.d.). Support for mass shooting victims in Orlando, Florida. *Office of Justice Programs*. Retrieved from https://www.ovc.gov/news/orlando-florida.html.

Orlando gay nightclub shooting: Who was Omar Mateen? (2016). *BBC News*. Retrieved from http://www.bbc.com/news/world-us-canada-36513468.

Palm, M. J. (2016). Orlando Shakes creates 'angel wings' to block Westboro protesters. *Orlando Sentinel*. Retrieved from http://www.orlandosentinel.com/entertainment/arts-and-theater/os-orlando-shakespeare-theater-angel-wings-20160617-story.html.

Platon, A. (2017). Orlando nightclub shooting survivor Patience Carter recruits Nitty Scott, L'Shai & Iliana Eve for 'Lost Souls': Premiere. *Billboard*. Retrieved from https://www.billboard.com/articles/columns/hip-hop/7604470/orlando-pulse-nightclub-shooting-survivor-patience-carter-lost-souls.

Pleasance, C. (2016). Families of Orlando victims continue to honor their dead as some opt for open caskets to see their loved ones a final time.

DailyMail. Retrieved from http://www.dailymail.co.uk/news/article-3647380/Families-Orlando-victims-continue-honor-dead-opt-open-caskets-loved-ones-final-time.html.

Report reveals dramatic new details from Orlando nightclub massacre (2017). *CBS News*. Retrieved from https://www.cbsnews.com/news/orlando-nightclub-shooting-report-reveals-new-details-inside-pulse/.

Salinger, T. (2016). Orlando nightclub shooting 911 calls released. *New York Daily News*. Retrieved from http://www.nydailynews.com/news/crime/orlando-nightclub-shooting-911-calls-released-article-1.2771905.

Sanchez, R. (2016). Their night of terror. *CNN*. Retrieved from http://edition.cnn.com/2016/06/17/us/orlando-shooting-survivors-account/.

Schladebeck, J. (2017). Pulse responder with PTSD sues Orlando Police Department. *New York Daily News*. Retrieved from http://www.nydailynews.com/news/national/pulse-responder-ptsd-sues-orlando-police-department-article-1.3686032.

Shahin, S. (2016). After Orlando: Twitter recoils from Islamophobia, takes aim at gun laws. Foreign *Policy in Focus*. Retrieved from http://fpif.org/orlando-twitter-recoils-islamophobia-takes-aim-gun-laws/.

Sieczkowski, C. (2016). Chick-Fil-A opens on Sunday to give free food to Orlando shooting blood donors. *The Huffington Post*. Retrieved from https://www.huffingtonpost.com/entry/chick-fil-a-opens-on-sunday-to-give-free-food-to-orlando-shooting-blood-donors_us_576016fbe4b053d433064c87.

Silverstein, J. (2016). ISIS embraces Omar Mateen as one of its American 'soldiers'. *DailyNews*. Retrieved from http://www.nydailynews.com/news/national/isis-embraces-omar-mateen-american-soldiers-article-1.2671649.

Smith, T. (2016). Walt Disney Company Donates $1 Million to OneOrlando Fund. *Disney Parks Blog*. Retrieved from https://disneyparks.disney.go.com/blog/2016/06/walt-disney-company-donates-1-million-to-oneorlando-fund/.

Straub, F., Cambria, J., Castor, J., Gorban, B., Meade, B., Waltemeyer, D., & Zeunik, J. (2017). Rescue, response, and resilience: A critical incident review of the Orlando public safety response to the attack on the Pulse nightclub. *Office of Community Oriented Policing Services*. Retrieved from https://ric-zai-inc.com/Publications/cops-w0857-pub.pdf.

Tanielian, T. L., & Stein, B. D. (2016). Understanding and preparing for the psychological consequences of terrorism. *The RAND Corporation*. Retrieved from https://www.rand.org/content/dam/rand/pubs/reprints/2006/RAND_RP1217.pdf.

Taylor, A. (2016). Worldwide vigils and memorials for Orlando victims. *The Atlantic*. Retrieved from http://www.theatlantic.com/photo/2016/06/worldwide-vigils-and-memorials-for-orlando-victims/486782/.

The National Child Traumatic Stress Network (n.d.). About PFA. *NCTSN*. Retrieved from https://www.nctsn.org/treatments-and-practices/psychological-first-aid-and-skills-for-psychological-recovery/about-pfa.

Towner, M. (2016). 'Tell them I'm in the bathroom. He's coming. I'm gonna die': Terrified last text son sent to his mother as Orlando terror unfolded. *DailyMail*. Retrieved from http://www.dailymail.co.uk/news/article-3637576/Terrified-text-son-sent-mother-Orlando-terror-unfolded.html.

Vick, K. (2016). The surprising — and welcome — social advance embedded in the Orlando attacks. *Time*. Retrieved from http://time.com/4369974/orlando-shooting-gay-rights/.

Wall, S. (2016). Despite more acceptance, struggle and fear remain for gay Americans after Orlando shooting. *The Sun*. Retrieved from http://www.sbsun.com/lgbt/20160618/despite-more-acceptance-struggle-and-fear-remain-for-gay-americans-after-orlando-shooting.

Washington, E. (2016). Orlando Health, FBI held active shooter training response drill months before Pulse shooting. *News 6*. Retrieved from http://www.clickorlando.com/web/wkmg/news/orlando-health-fbi-held-active-shooter-training-response-drill-months-before-pulse-shooting.

Weaver, J., & Ovalle, D. (2016). What motivated Orlando killer? It was more than terrorism, experts say. *Mianmi Herald*. Retrieved from http://www.miamiherald.com/news/state/florida/article84511132.html.

Williams, A. B., & Mills, R. (n.d.). A year after Pulse nightclub shooting, a legacy of healing. *NewsPress*. Retrieved from https://www.news-press.com/story/news/2017/06/07/pulse-nightclub-orlando-one-year-later-mass-shooting-legacy-of-healing/350331001/.

Wilson, J. (2018). Crisis actors, deep state, false flag: The rise of conspiracy theory code words. *The Guardian*. Retrieved from https://www.theguardian.com/us-news/2018/feb/21/crisis-actors-deep-state-false-flag-the-rise-of-conspiracy-theory-code-words.

Yam, K. (2016). Man travels 1,200 miles to deliver 49 handmade crosses for Orlando victims. *The Huffington Post*. Retrieved from http://www.huffingtonpost.com/entry/greg-zanis-orlando-crosses_us_57617133e4b0df4d586eba62.

Zambelich, A., & Hurt, A. (2016). 3 hours in Orlando: Piecing together an attack and its aftermath. *The Two-Way*. Retrieved from http://www.npr.

org/2016/06/16/482322488/orlando-shooting-what-happened-update.

Zezima, K., & Sullivan, K. (2016). 'The guilt of being alive is heavy,' survivor of nightclub shooting says. *The Washington Post.* Retrieved from https://www.washingtonpost.com/politics/the-guilt-of-being-alive-is-heavy-survivor-of-nightclub-shooting-says/2016/06/14/ac366268-3251-11e6-8ff7-7b6c1998b7a0_story.html.

CHAPTER 19

Against the Norm: The Act of Helping During Violent Extremist Attacks

PAMELA GOH

Home Team Behavioural Sciences Centre, Ministry of Home Affairs, Singapore

Introduction

Violent extremist attacks have the capacity to produce a myriad of human reactions, evident in the crowd behaviours that transpired after these events occurred. The nature of responses varies, with general themes of crowd behaviour ranging from the behavioural manifestation of negative emotions (e.g., running and screaming) to the engagement of evacuation behaviours, and even the expression of solidarity for those affected (Ellis, 2015; Goh *et al.*, 2017; Mawson, 2005). A striking peculiarity among the range of behaviours is the prosocial act of helping people, often beyond one's personal safety and well-being.

The notion of helping others during a crisis is uncharacteristic. Yet, the understanding of the psychology of crowd behaviours in the context of violent extremist attacks has revealed that helping emerges naturally and at considerable levels. It is essential to, therefore, understand why and how people will help, and to subsequently account for these prosocial behaviours in emergency planning. Insights gained can facilitate response and recovery efforts, either through the development of plans that leverage on these helping behaviours, or to take active measures that ensure minimal disruption and hindrance on the overall emergency responses. In this chapter, the helping phenomenon resulting from an attack is explored and comprehended through five learning lessons.

Five Things We Need to Know about Helping during Attacks

Some People will Help

A violent extremist attack results not only in deaths and injuries, but also evokes powerful emotions of fear, terror, and helplessness in the society (Butler *et al.*, 2003; Smith, 2015). Consequently, it becomes rational for people to quickly run away and hide from the scene of danger to ensure their safety (Getz, 2014; Kehayan & Napoli, 2005). Research has shown that it is instinctive for people to prioritise the maintenance of one's personal survival over social responses during emergencies (Schultz, 1964; Strauss, 1944).

Contrary to this human tendency, many individuals across many violent extremist attacks had in fact readily rendered varying types of assistance to one another during and immediately after the crisis (Cocking, 2005; Drury *et al.*, 2009b). Some prosocial acts were efforts to subdue the attackers directly, often attempted by individuals who had disregarded their personal safety. A case in point is the 2016 Nice truck attack, where Franck Terrier and Alexandre Migues had jumped onto the driver's door — at different times while the vehicle was moving — to try and stop the attacker through the driver's window. Although they could not end the attack, they managed to slow the vehicle down substantially such that others had more time to run away from the path of danger[1] ("Nice attack: Hero motorcyclist 'punched driver again and again'", 2016). Further along the spectrum of helping behaviours were those that were less dangerous but still impactful, such as tending to the wounds of the injured despite the ongoing danger. Helping behaviours also took place under safer circumstances (Koebler, 2013), such as using the social media to facilitate helping after the attack has ended. For instance, many people had flocked to donate blood in the wake of attacks, as observed in cases such as the 2013 Boston Marathon bombing (Hartogs, 2013) and the 2017 Manchester attack ("Blood donor centres inundated with people helping any way they can after Manchester attack", 2017).

Violent extremist attacks are a form of psychological warfare that strives to tear a society apart, by inciting widespread fear and undermining citizens' sense of security and daily functioning (Ganor, 2004; Waxman, 2011). The organic helping behaviour among the affected henceforth contributes to the resilience of these individuals, as well as the community as a whole against violent extremism. Taking into account the positive impact of their potential contributions, people and the affected society could and should be seen as a part of the solution (Cole *et al.*, 2011; Drury *et al.*, 2009b). However, given that the presence and movement of people may affect official response efforts, these helping behaviours should be managed or directed whenever necessary to ensure utmost assistance to the affected community.

There are Different Forms of Helping Behaviours

Prosocial behaviours in the event of a violent extremist attack can largely be seen as acts of heroism and altruism. While both principally posit a certain degree of sacrifice or selflessness, the nature of these acts differs.

---

[1]Franck Terrier eventually fell off from the truck after being subjected to punches from the attacker, while Alexandre Migues was forced to let go of the door after being pointed at with a pistol ("Nice attack: Hero motorcyclist 'punched driver again and again'", 2016).

Altruism involves helping others directly, out of unselfishness and doing what is right (Franco *et al.*, 2011; Svoboda, 2013). These altruistic acts can manifest in different forms, evident in the themes of helping behaviours commonly observed in many attacks across the world. People had helped one another to hide or escape,[2] or tend to the injuries of victims.[3] Despite being caught in the same attack, there were individuals who had also provided emotional support to others who needed it.[4] Additionally, many affected communities offered free transport and physical refuge to anyone who requires them, in a bid to send them to safety, the hospital, or to even search for their loved ones.[5]

Heroism, conversely, is more sacrificial in nature and often transpires in extreme situations, such as saving someone's life (Franco *et al.*, 2011). Many individuals caught in attacks had placed themselves in the line of danger for others, either as an attempt to stop or slow down the attackers, or to protect others from danger.[6] Interestingly, research has also shown that such prosocial behaviours are often spontaneous (Drury *et al.*, 2009b; Franco *et al.*, 2011).

A noteworthy type of prosocial behaviour is online helping by the community at large, including those who did not experience the attack. Through the means of posting and reposting of posts by online users on various social media platforms, details of loved ones who went missing as a result of the attack were disseminated.

---

[2]Such as in the case of the 2016 JFK shooting scare (Sapone, 2016).

[3]Such as in the case of the 2016 Orlando Pulse nightclub shooting (Lentini, 2016), 2013 Boston Marathon bombing (Duke, 2013), and 2013 Lee Rigby killing (Allan, 2014).

[4]Such as in the case of the 2016 Nice truck attack ("There's something that's not right. Someone lost control of their truck", 2016) and 2016 Orlando Pulse nightclub shooting (Lentini, 2016).

[5]Such as in the case of the 2017 Manchester Arena bombing (McIntyre, 2017) and 2016 Nice truck attack (Kottasova, 2016).

[6]Such as in the case of the 2017 London Bridge attack (Fox, 2017; "London attack: Romanian baker and Spanish banker among heroes", 2017), 2016 Nice truck attack ("Nice attack: Hero motorcyclist 'punched driver again and again'", 2016), 2016 Orlando Pulse nightclub shooting (Gulledge *et al.*, 2016), and 2001 September 11 attacks (Campbell, 2001).

In addition, valuable information such as the availability of free transport and homes were shared.[7]

Different types and natures of prosocial behaviours are likely to transpire in the event of an attack. Additionally, although some acts of heroism and altruism will impose a threat to the individual's life, people have helped and are likely to still do so when the need arises. It may then be more imperative for authorities to prepare the public by reminding them the importance of prioritising personal survival. This should include the education of factors that people are encouraged to consider and apply, such as whether physical circumstances are ideal for helping and if the individuals are sufficiently equipped with the appropriate skills and knowledge (e.g., medical first aid, psychological first aid) to do so. Given the varied nature of heroism and altruism, more than one educational outreach message may also be required to prepare people for the different forms of helping that are likely to occur. In Singapore, for instance, the *Run, Hide, Tell* and *Improvised First Aid Skills*[8] (SGSecure, 2018) are separate advisories developed to guide people on what to note and do — to enhance the survival of the self and others — during a violent extremist attack.

People Help for Various Reasons

The kinship and reciprocity theories are reasons frequently used to explain why people go beyond self-interest and engage in prosocial behaviours that benefit others. While the kinship theory postulates that people do so because these "others" — also known as kin — are close relatives, the reciprocity theory suggests that people help because the receivers are likely to return the favour (Allison, 1992).

---

[7]Such social media postings were evident in various attacks, such as the 2017 Manchester Arena bombing (Samuels, 2017), 2016 Nice truck attack (O'Brien, 2016), and 2013 Boston Marathon bombing (Oremus, 2013).

[8]The "Run, Hide, Tell" advisory advocates for the appropriate life-saving behaviours that one should undertake to promote the survival of oneself and others during a violent extremist attack. The "Improvised First Aid Skills" advisory educates people on how to manage the bleeding wounds of the injured during such attacks (SGSecure, 2018).

However, there are many acts of helping in violent extremist attacks that cannot be appropriately explained by these two theories. These behaviours, in other words, are often directed towards strangers and those unlikely to reciprocate. Franck Terrier and Alexandre Migues in the 2016 Nice truck attack are classic examples of such helping behaviours. In the 2017 London Bridge attack, various individuals also engaged in a melee confrontation with the attackers in an effort to stop them, while other strangers remained at the scene of the attack so that they could tend to the injured (Nsubuga, 2017).

Other psychological concepts are able to capture the reasoning behind such prosocial behaviours. Crowd psychology research specifically relating to the helping context has discovered that people do so because individuals in the crowd see each another as "one" or "part of self" (i.e., the self-categorisation theory; Drury *et al.*, 2009b), and helping behaviours can spread and thus proliferate across the crowd (i.e., the contagion theory; le Bon, 2009).

The self-categorisation theory explores the humans' sense of identity. People are said to possess two identities in general, one as a unique individual and the other as a member of a group (Drury *et al.*, 2009b). When a violent extremist attack occurs, it creates the perception across those affected that everyone is in the dangerous situation together. A collective identity develops, whereby the experience of the common event leads to the transition of individuals' identity from "me" (i.e., as a distinctive individual) to "we" (i.e., everyone as a group or crowd; Drury, 2009a; Williams & Drury, 2009). The outcome of the collective identity is the increased likelihood of individuals acting in the interests of others who are involved in the same adversity, since others have become part of one's "self" (Drury *et al.*, 2009b). Researchers have proposed that this shared sense of identity was a reason for the cooperation and benevolence of the crowds in attacks like the 2005 London and 2016 Brussels bombings (Cocking, 2016).

The contagion theory posits that helping behaviours emerge and spread in a crowd as a result of observing what others are doing (le Bon, 2009). It states that the motives, sentiments, and actions of individuals within a crowd are contagious, and can influence others to perform similar behaviours (Snow, 2013). When this contagion effect becomes sufficiently pronounced, people may sacrifice their personal interest for the interest of the collective (le Bon, 2009).

Anecdotal accounts of individuals who put their lives forward have revealed additional reasons underlying their helping behaviours during attacks. Interestingly, not all acts of heroism and altruism were by the virtue of compassion (Seppälä *et al.*, 2017). Some prosocial acts had indeed stemmed from the genuine concern for the well-being of others, as observed in various accounts such as refusing to abandon victims until professional assistance was rendered[9] (Gulledge *et al.*, 2016). For many others, on the contrary, helping was the outcome of non-compassion reasons. Some prosocial behaviours were automatic and instinctive[10] (Chrisafis, 2015; Sengupta, 2016), largely driven by "intuitive decision-making" and minimal deliberation[11] (Rand, 2015, p. 3). Otherwise, it was about fulfilling one's job and responsibility to protect anyone affected,[12] as a result of the individual's military, law enforcement, or medical training (Fox, 2017; Koebler, 2013). In fact, studies have shown that people with prior first-responder training were more likely to intervene in split-second situations, while those without such training were more inclined to help later (Koebler, 2013). Helping behaviours might also be an emulation of helping behaviours of others during an attack.

Efforts to understand attributions of helping behaviours have highlighted that there is no definite profile of helpers which one can use to identify who will help, as well as how one will help. Different reasons have and will continue to motivate different people to act.

---

[9]Such as in the case of the 2016 Orlando Pulse nightclub shooting (Gulledge *et al.*, 2016).

[10]Such as in the case of the 2016 Nice truck attack (Sengupta, 2016) and 2015 Thalys train attack (Karimi, 2015).

[11]Also known as the danger of deliberation, it is suggested that people are less likely to help in any circumstance — regardless if it is low- or high-stake situation — if they had hesitated to think about helping (Rand, 2015).

[12]Such as in the case of the 2017 London Bridge attack (Fox, 2017).

A question of interest subsequently follows: can these various attributions of helping be employed to "train" people to help when the need arises? The answer is potentially yes. To illustrate, the provision of prior training has been observed to increase the prospect of helping because it facilitates the internalisation of the necessary skills and knowledge to do so (Kehayan & Napoli, 2005; Koebler, 2013). Based on the self-categorisation theory, emphasis on fostering a shared identity among people during peacetimes may encourage helping behaviours in times of crisis, since it helps people to perceive one another as part of the in-group (i.e., part of the same group). Additionally, it is with the expectation that widespread helping will occur, since others are likely to follow suite and render aid if others are already doing it.

Culture May Influence Helping

Different cultures emphasise different practices, and these practices can bear varying impacts on the likelihood and nature of helping. For instance, a meta-analysis conducted by Steblay (1987) has revealed that the tendency to which people are likely to receive help from strangers is inversely correlated with the population size of a city. In other studies, prosocial behaviour is also suggested to be inversely correlated with a country's economic health, whereby wealthy countries tend not to endorse the traditional value of helping others in the society (Inkeles, 1997; Levine *et al.*, 2001).

A common yet important way to explore the potential effects of culture is by adopting the individualism versus collectivism perspective (Levine *et al.*, 2001). Individualism advocates for the personal self over group allegiances, as typically observed in Western countries such as America and Europe (Darwish & Huber, 2003). Collectivism, on the other hand, emphasises group allegiances and others' social well-being — especially with their in-group — over one's personal interests, and is more commonly seen in Asian countries (Darwish & Huber, 2003). Naturally, it seems that collectivist societies should display greater prosocial behaviours than individualist societies, due to its emphasis on prioritising amiable social behaviours such as being concerned for and helping others.

The claim only holds true to a certain extent. A series of independent field experiments conducted in many cities across the world has discovered that there are helpful individualistic and unhelpful collectivist societies (Levine *et al.*, 2001). One possible reason that accounts for this phenomenon is the identity of the recipients of help rendered, and whether they belong to the in-group or out-group of the person providing the aid. According to Kassin *et al.* (2011), individuals with a collectivist inclination are more likely to help their in-group than out-group members, and those with an individualist inclination are more likely to help anyone in general regardless of their membership. Other researches on altruism have also revealed supporting results. In a study conducted by Oda and colleagues (2013), personality — measured in terms of the Big-Five personality traits[13] — was found to contribute to prosocial behaviour, and the extent to which each trait affects helping depends on who the recipients are. People who endorse a high sense of individualism tend to score higher on the Big-Five personality traits *Openness to Experience* and *Extraversion*[14] (McCrae *et al.*, 2005), and each trait is necessary for extending help to even strangers (Oda *et al.*, 2013).

Although specifications are unclear, culture generally seems to exert a certain level of influence on the potentiality of helping during attacks. Both individualists and collectivists can be expected to help others in need, but they differ in terms of who they are more willing to help.

Ground-up Helping Can Make a Difference to Response and Recovery Efforts

First-respondents are vital stakeholders to the response and recovery efforts after a violent extremist attack (Benedek *et al.*, 2007).

[13]The Big-Five personality traits are openness to experience, conscientiousness, extraversion, agreeableness, and neuroticism.

[14]Openness to experience is the personality trait in which an individual is curious, generally receptive of variety and novelty, and tends to be liberal in terms of beliefs, ideas, and values (Costa & McCrae, 2008). Extraversion is the personality trait in which an individual is sociable, and enjoys excitement, stimulation, and thrills (Costa & McCrae, 2008).

Nonetheless, it is important to recognise that there are boundaries to the effectiveness of first-respondents' involvement. Time is an essential consideration, particularly so when the injured require critical medical first-aid, and the attack has to be contained as soon as possible to prevent escalating casualty rates. The number of professionals who can be activated to respond to the attack will certainly be limited, as time is needed for them to travel to the scene of attack.

The organic contribution (i.e., ground-up helping) by any ordinary person (i.e., those without first-responder training) caught in or is near the attack can help in the response and recovery efforts. For one, spontaneous acts of heroism and altruism have shown to be potential "game-changers", by facilitating the containment of the attack or complementing response and recovery efforts. At the same time, the proximity of others to the scene of danger also allows them to reach and provide timely medical aid to victims. Above all else, organic helping is an important facet to building long-term resiliency (Williams & Drury, 2009), since it is seen as an act of empowerment and closure by allowing people to be part of the response and recovery process.

While valuable, however, the impact of ground-up helping can be negative and detrimental in nature. For instance, while pictures and video recordings of the attack will indeed function as useful evidence for law enforcers (Allan, 2014), these visual imageries can sometimes only be captured if individuals have placed themselves in the line of danger (Smith, 2017). In fact, according to Allan (2014, p. 8), many criticisms have been made towards the incessant capturing of these imageries as it did not "lend assistance" to the victims, and may have even fuelled "the perpetrators' narcissistic desire for notoriety, possibly even inviting "copy-cat responses". Alternatively, the dissemination of these imageries can spread fear and incite secondary traumatisation even in non-primary victims (Bilgen, 2012), or serve as a reminder of the attack for the community (Pfefferbaum *et al.*, 2001). As described by violent extremist expert Brian Jenkins, "Terrorism is aimed at the people watching, not at the actual victims. Terrorism is a theatre" (Paganini, 2016, p. 9).

The negative consequences of ground-up helping indicate the need to account for these behaviours while developing emergency plans for a potential violent extremist attack. One possible initiative is to consider the effects of such behaviours on recovery efforts and the development of relevant follow-up plans to manage the resulting consequences. Alternatively, providing specific directions during peacetimes as to how one can help is a practical solution to manage ineffective helping. In Singapore, the value of community helping is emphasised through the SGSecure movement (SGSecure, 2018). It is a nation-wide initiative in which public education and community exercises are conducted to inform how people can help and the significance of doing so. In order to effectively harness the public's helping responses, relevant trainings should also be made available, some of which are necessary to facilitate the provision of appropriate medical and psychological first aid.

Conclusion

Prosocial crowd behaviours have evidently manifested in violent extremist attacks across the world, despite the danger that these attacks present. Some forms of helping offered by individuals go beyond personal safety, while others occurred under safer circumstances and possibly even on the online platform. Regardless, the impact of prosocial behaviours must be understood for authorities to develop a holistic response towards violent extremist attacks.

Acknowledgement

The views expressed in this chapter are the author's only and do not represent the official position or view of the Ministry of Home Affairs, Singapore.

References

Allan, S. (2014). Witnessing in crisis: Photo-reportage of terror attacks in Boston and London. *Media, War & Conflict*, 7(2), 133–151.

Allison, P. D. (1992). How culture induces altruistic behaviour. *Paper Presented at Annual Meetings of the American Sociological Association*, Pittsburgh.

Benedek, D. M., Fullerton, C., & Ursano, R. J. (2007). First responders: Mental health consequences of natural and human-made disasters for public health and public safety workers. *Annual Review of Public Health*, 28, 55–68.

Bilgen, A. (2012). *Terrorism and the Media: A Dangerous Symbiosis*. Washington, DC: The George Washington University.

Blood donor centres inundated with people helping any way they can after Manchester attack (2017). *The Telegraph*. Retrieved from http://www.telegraph.co.uk/news/2017/05/23/blood-donor-centres-inundated-people-helping-way-can-manchester/.

Butler, A. S., Panzer, A. M., & Goldfrank, L. R. (Eds.) (2003). *Preparing for the Psychological Consequences of Terrorism: A Public Health Strategy*. Washington, DC: The National Academies Press.

Campbell, D. (2001). Passengers sacrificed their lives to avert even greater tragedy. *The Guardian*. Retrieved from https://www.theguardian.com/world/2001/sep/13/september11.usa15.

Chrisafis, A. (2015). France train attack heroes: 'It feels unreal — like a dream'. *The Guardian*. Retrieved from https://www.theguardian.com/world/2015/aug/23/france-train-attack-heroes-in-time-of-crisis-do-something.

Cocking, C. (2005). Don't panic! Crowd behaviour in emergencies [Powerpoint Slides]. Retrieved from http://www.sussex.ac.uk/affiliates/panic/Rotary%20presentation%20(CC).ppt.

Cocking, C. (2016). Brussels terror attack victims show how humans help each other in times of crisis. *The Conversation*. Retrieved from http://theconversation.com/brussels-terror-attack-victims-show-how-humans-help-each-other-in-times-of-crisis-56707.

Cole, J., Walters, M., & Lynch, M. (2011). Part of the solution, not the problem: The crowd's role in emergency response. *Contemporary Social Science*, 6(3), 361–375.

Costa, P. T., & McCrae, R. R. (2008). The revised NEO personality inventory (NEO-PI-R). *The SAGE Handbook of Personality Theory and Assessment*, 2, 179–198.

Darwish, A. F. E., & Huber, G. L. (2003). Individualism vs. collectivism in different cultures: A cross-cultural study. *Intercultural Education*, *14*(1), 47–56.

Drury, J., Cocking, C., & Reicher, S. (2009a). Everyone for themselves? A comparative study of crowd solidarity among emergency survivors. *British Journal of Social Psychology*, *48*(3), 487–506.

Drury, J., Cocking, C., & Reicher, S. (2009b). The nature of collective resilience: Survivor reactions to the 2005 London bombings. *International Journal of Mass Emergencies and Disasters*, *27*(1), 66–95.

Duke, A. (2013). Boston Marathon bombing heroes: Running to help. *CNN*. Retrieved from http://edition.cnn.com/2013/04/16/us/boston-heroes/index.html.

Ellis, B. (2015). A model for collecting and interpreting World Trade Center disaster jokes. *New Directions in Folklore, 5*.

Fox, A. (2017). Police officer describes how he took on all three London Bridge terrorists with just a baton. *Independent*. Retrieved from http://www.independent.co.uk/news/uk/home-news/london-bridge-attack-police-officer-btp-hero-baton-wayne-marques-a7813071.html.

Franco, Z. E., Blau, K., & Zimbardo, P. G. (2011). Heroism: A conceptual analysis and differentiation between heroic action and altruism. *Review of General Psychology*, *15*(2), 99–113.

Ganor, B. (2004). Terrorism as a Strategy of Psychological Warfare. *Journal of Aggression, Maltreatment & Trauma*, *9*(1-2), 33–43.

Getz, G. E. (2014). *Applied Biological Psychology*. New York: Springer Publishing Company.

Goh, P., Tan, J., Neo, L. S., & Khader, M. (2017). Understanding crowd behaviour during violent extremist attacks: Insights from the Nice truck attack 2016. HTBSC Research Report 16/2017. Singapore: Home Team Behavioural Sciences Centre.

Gulledge, J., Kann, D., & Lee, L. (2016). Orlando shooting: Heroes among us. *CNN*. Retrieved from http://edition.cnn.com/2016/06/13/health/iyw-pulse-nightclub-heroes-trnd/index.html.

Hartogs, J. (2013). Stories of kindness amid tragedy in Boston Marathon bombing. *CBSNews*. Retrieved from https://www.cbsnews.com/news/stories-of-kindness-amid-tragedy-in-boston-marathon-bombing/.

Inkeles, A. (1997). *National Character: A Psycho-Social Perspective*. New Brunswick, NJ: Transaction Books.

Karimi, F. (2015). Train shooting heroes: The men who helped avert a massacre in Europe. *CNN*. Retrieved from http://edition.cnn.com/2015/08/22/europe/france-train-shooting-heroes/index.html.

Kassin, S., Fein, S., & Markus, H. (2011). *Social Psychology*. Belmont, CA: Wadsworth.

Kehayan, V. A., & Napoli, J. C. (2005). *Resiliency in the Face of Disaster and Terrorism: 10 Things to Do to Survive*. Fawnskin, CA: Personhood Press.

Koebler, J. (2013). Why do people risk their lives to help others during emergencies such as the Boston Marathon bombing? *U.S.News*. Retrieved from https://www.usnews.com/news/articles/2013/04/19/why-do-people-risk-their-lives-to-help-others-during-emergencies-such-as-the-boston-marathon-bombing.

Kottasova, I. (2016). Weary taxi drivers work through the night to help Nice terror attack victims. *CNN Money*. Retrieved from http://money.cnn.com/2016/07/15/news/businesses-help-nice-terror-attack/index.html?iid=EL.

le Bon, G. (2009). *Psychology of Crowds*. United Kingdom: Sparkling Books Ltd.

Lentini, R. (2016). Orlando shooting: Stories of survival emerge as 15 people were trapped in a bathroom at Pulse Nightclub. *news.com.au*. Retrieved from http://www.news.com.au/world/orlando-shooting-stories-of-survival-emerge-as-15-people-were-trapped-in-a-bathroom-at-pulse-nightclub/news-story/078ae22313e6258c9dc25720a89c7ba7.

Levine, R. V., Norenzayan, A., & Philbrick, K. (2001). Cross-cultural differences in helping strangers. *Journal of Cross-Cultural Psychology*, *32*(5), 543–560.

London attack: Romanian baker and Spanish banker among heroes (2017). *BBC*. Retrieved from http://www.bbc.com/news/uk-40149836.

Mawson, A. R. (2005). Understanding mass panic and other collective responses to threat and disaster. *Psychiatry*, *68*(2), 95–113.

McCrae, R. R., Terracciano, A., & 79 Members of the Personality Profiles of Cultures Project (2005). Personality profiles of cultures: Aggregate personality traits. *Journal of Personality and Social Psychology*, *89*(3), 407–425.

McIntyre, N. (2017). Manchester Arena: Taxis drive people home for free as city unites after terror attack. *Independent*. Retrieved from http://www.independent.co.uk/news/uk/home-news/manchester-arena-taxi-free-drive-people-explosion-attack-home-city-unite-terror-attack-suicide-bomb-a7750651.html.

Nice attack: Hero motorcyclist 'punched driver again and again' (2016). *BBC*. Retrieved from http://www.bbc.com/news/world-europe-36860152.

Nsubuga, J. (2017). Police thank the heroes of London Bridge who risked their lives to help victims. *Metro*. Retrieved from http://metro.co.uk/2017/06/10/police-thank-london-bridge-attack-heroes-who-risked-lives-to-help-victims-6698988/.

O'Brien, S. A. (2016). Nice attack prompts desperate search for loved ones on Twitter. *CNN tech*. Retrieved from http://money.cnn.com/2016/07/15/technology/nice-france-terrorism-twitter/index.html.

Oda, R., Machii, W., Takagi, S., Kato, Y., Takeda, M., Kiyonari, T., Fukukawa, Y., & Hiraishi, K. (2013). Personality and altruism in daily life. *Personality and Individual Differences*, *56*, 206–209.

Oremus, W. (2013). Basically all of Boston is offering stranded runners a warm bed and a fuzzy dog. *Slate*. Retrieved from http://www.slate.com/blogs/future_tense/2013/04/16/boston_marathon_bombing_in_google_drive_doc_locals_offer_warm_beds_fuzzy.html.

Paganini, P. (2016). The role of technology in modern terrorism. *Infosec Institute*. Retrieved from http://resources.infosecinstitute.com/the-role-of-technology-in-modern-terrorism/.

Pfefferbaum, B., Nixon, S. J., Tivis, R. D., Doughty, D. E., Pynoos, R. S., Gurwitch, R. H., & Foy, D. W. (2001). Television exposure in children after a terrorist incident. *Psychiatry*, *64*(3), 202–211.

Rand, D. (2015). The key to being a hero: Don't think about it. *wbur.* Retrieved from http://www.wbur.org/hereandnow/2015/08/24/extreme-altruism-david-rand.

Samuels, G. (2017). Six practical ways you can help in the aftermath of the Manchester Arena bombing. *Independent*. Retrieved from http://www.independent.co.uk/news/uk/home-news/manchester-arena-bombing-six-ways-to-help-give-blood-safe-spaces-free-ride-missing-people-no-fake-a7750771.html.

Sapone, M. (2016). I was at JFK during the shooting scare, and I can't believe how easily we terrorized ourselves. *Qz.com*. Retrieved from https://qz.com/764954/i-was-at-jfk-during-the-shooting-scare-and-i-cant-believe-how-easily-we-terrorized-ourselves/.

Schultz, D. P. (1964). *Panic Behaviour: Discussions and Readings*. New York: Random House.

Sengupta, K. (2016). Nice attack: Hero motorcyclist reveals how he threw himself onto truck to try to stop killer. *Independent*. Retrieved from http://www.independent.co.uk/news/world/europe/nice-attack-hero-motorcyclist-reveals-how-he-threw-himself-onto-truck-to-try-to-stop-killer-a7144326.html.

Seppälä, E. M., Simon-Thomas, E., Brown, S. L., Worline, M. C., Cameron, C. D., & Doty, J. R. (2017). *The Oxford Handbook of Compassion Science*. New York: Oxford University Press.

SGSecure (2018). *Ministry of Home Affairs*. Retrieved from https://www.sgsecure.sg/Pages/default.aspx.

Smith, J. (2015). One of the purposes of terrorism is to magnify the terrorist. *Independent*. Retrieved from http://www.independent.co.uk/voices/one-of-the-purposes-of-terrorism-is-to-magnify-the-terrorist-10350362.html.

Smith, L. (2017). Police urge teenagers not to take photos if caught up in a terror attack. *Independent*. Retrieved from http://www.independent.co.uk/news/uk/home-news/police-terror-attack-warning-teenagers-not-take-photos-selfies-parsons-green-a7972301.html.

Snow, D. A. (2013). Contagion theory. *The Wiley-Blackwell Encyclopaedia of Social and Political Movements*. Retrieved from https://doi.org/10.1002/9780470674871.wbespm050.

Steblay, N. M. (1987). Helping behavior in rural and urban environments: A meta-analysis. *Psychological Bulletin*, *102*(3), 346–356.

Strauss, A. L. (1944). The literature on panic. *The Journal of Abnormal and Social Psychology*, *39*(3), 317–328.

Svoboda, E. (2013). *What Makes a Hero? The Surprising Science of Selflessness*. New York: Penguin Group.

There's something that's not right. Someone lost control of their truck (2016). *The New York Times*. Retrieved from https://www.nytimes.com/interactive/2016/07/15/world/europe/16survivors.html.

Waxman, D. (2011). Living with terror, not living in terror: The impact of chronic terrorism on Israeli society. *Perspectives on Terrorism*, *5*(5–6).

Williams, R., & Drury, J. (2009). Psychosocial resilience and its influence on managing mass emergencies and disasters. *Psychiatry*, *8*(8), 293–296.

Section 6

Strategies to Build Cyber Psychological Resilience

Now sometimes it's a matter of days. Prior to that, there is exposure to a line of thought, a type of religious teaching that predisposes one towards becoming radicalised. And the kind of people you come in contact with, the thoughts they convey to you. That's a problem all over the world, including Singapore.

MR K. SHANMUGAM
MINISTER FOR HOME AFFAIRS
AND MINISTER FOR LAW

CHAPTER 20

Managing Social Media in the Event of a Terror Attack

STEPHANIE NEUBRONNER

S. Rajaratnam School of International Studies, Nanyang Technological University, Singapore

Introduction

The year 2017 saw terrorist attacks occurring at places such as Las Ramblas in Barcelona, where a van plowed into crowds, killing 13 and injuring dozens ("Barcelona attack: 13 killed as van rams crowds in Las Ramblas", 2017); at the Manchester Arena, where an explosion during an Ariana Grande concert left 22 dead and over a hundred injured ("Manchester attack: What we know so far", 2017); in Stockholm, when a man rammed a truck through the Swedish capital's pedestrian only shopping street and a popular shopping centre, killing four and injuring at least 15 (Anderson, 2017); in New York, when a truck ran through a crowd of pedestrians and cyclists on a bike path near the World Trade Center in Manhattan, killing eight and injuring 11 (Mueller *et al.*, 2017); and in London, where seven were killed and dozens others injured when three assailants drove through pedestrians on London Bridge and stabbed revellers at Borough Market (Alexander, 2017).

While the West was the main target of these attacks, Singapore was not spared from the threat of such acts of terror. On 1 June 2017, the Ministry of Home Affairs (MHA) released its Singapore Terrorism Threat Assessment Report and emphasised the reality that terrorist groups have specifically named Singapore a target. Having plotted to carry out at least two terrorist attacks in Singapore in the past few years, ISIS, or the Islamic State in Iraq and Syria has been the most significant threat to the city-state. Coupled with continued threats from groups like Al-Qaeda (AQ) and the Jemaah Islamiyah (JI), the MHA report reiterated that the threat of terrorism Singapore faced remained at the highest level (Ministry of Home Affairs, 2017).

In an effort to counter such threats and prepare the public for the inevitability of a terrorist attack, Singapore has introduced and implemented initiatives such as SGSecure and the Total Defence campaign. These initiatives not only raise public awareness and encourage citizenry involvement, but also assure the Singaporean community that processes are in place to manage crisis situations should an attack occur.

The city-state's increasing acknowledgement and inclusion of social media as a legitimate communication and information platform have also created new, innovative, and useful methods that have been utilised in such initiatives. For instance, besides the dissemination of information and the facilitation of response and recovery strategies, accessible and easy-to-use apps that can be downloaded on mobile devices have been created and implemented to encourage vigilance, the public's reporting of suspicious activities, and also solidarity in times of crisis.

Research on social media usage during emergency situations have highlighted social media's significance in mediating response and recovery strategies, as well as its ability to enhance communication links in crisis scenarios. A 2011 report prepared for the members and committees of Congress, released by the United States Congressional Research Service, advocated the crucial role social media played in the event of emergencies and disasters. The report indicated individuals were increasingly utilising social media to "warn others of unsafe areas or situations, inform friends and family that someone is safe, and raise funds for disaster relief" (Lindsay, 2011). These findings correspond with the reactions observed in the aftermath of the Manchester Arena bombing that occurred six years after the report was published.

After the bomb exploded at the Manchester Arena on 22 May 2017, many caught in the midst of the chaos posted images and videos on social media, offering first-hand updates from the ground. Frantic parents and relatives turned to social media in an effort to locate their children who were at the concert. Social campaigns in the form of hashtags such as #PrayForManchester, #WeStandTogether, and #WeAreManchester were also started online, prompting extraordinary messages of defiance, expressions of love, as well as support and solidarity for the victims and their families of the attack (Harris, 2017).

This unity and outpouring of support observed on social media after the Manchester Arena bombing parallels the situation that occurred after the Charlie Hedbo massacre. On 7 January 2015, a pair of Islamist terrorists, brothers Saïd and Chérif Kouachi, claiming to act for Al Qaeda, stormed the offices of the French satirical weekly newspaper *Charlie Hedbo* and murdered 12 of its staff (Whitehead, 2015). This sparked a series of attacks that lasted three days, claiming the lives of 17 individuals.

In the aftermath of the attacks, the hashtag, #jesuischarlie or #iamcharlie emerged on social media. Created by Joachim Roncin, art director of the Paris magazine *Stylist*, the hashtag was born out of the urge to say something on Twitter, which was the platform carrying most of the early information about the attack (Groll, 2015). Roncin said that he wanted to honour those who were killed rather than simply repeat the facts of their murder (Groll, 2015).

Supporters of the freedom of expression and free speech united alongside the victims of the attack and showed their solidarity by retweeting the hashtag. The tag quickly became one of the most popular tags in the history of Twitter, trending at the top of Twitter hashtags worldwide. At its height, the tag was tweeted at a rate of

6,500 times a minute and was featured in 3.4 million tweets in just one 24-hour period (Whitehead, 2015). The hashtag was used about six million times over the following week on Twitter, Instagram, and Facebook (Devichand, 2016). The slogan was also used at demonstrations on printed and hand-made place cards, on mobile phones at vigils, as well as on many websites ("#JeSuisCharlie: Signs of solidarity after Paris terror attack", 2015).

Such hashtags and slogans demonstrate humankind's innate capacity and desire to work together and overcome unjust atrocities as a collective. Rejecting terrorist objectives, the creation and participation of online social capital validates social media's ability to inspire positive sentimentalities and community unity. Social media assisting recovery efforts and helping in the mitigation of chaos situations, further emphasises the importance of utilising new media technologies in the fight against terrorism. Yet, the advancement of social media use and technologies have created new kinds of challenges and issues that need to be addressed.

Ranging from ensuring the accuracy of information shared to the impact information circulating online will have on Singapore's social fabric, the challenges posed by new media's inclusion as a viable information and communication resource in the fight against terrorism cannot be taken lightly. The next two sections will discuss key challenges and response strategies that should be considered when deciphering ways to mitigate the issues brought about by the use of social media in an event of a terror attack.

Key Challenges Posed by Social Media

1. *Ensuring Information Reaches the Right Recipients*

The hours immediately following an attack are the most vital for authorities and especially emergency services. Coordinating response strategies and ensuring victims receive the right kind of help depend mainly on authorities obtaining accurate and timely information. Having to sieve through the mass of information online and decipher the truthfulness of materials circulating on social media not only takes time, but utilises resources that could otherwise be better deployed elsewhere.

As much as it has become an instinctive response to take to social media to post updates of trending news stories that are developing, it is vital that information is directed to authorities in the first instance, before they are shared on social media platforms. Ensuring the right information reaches the right groups of people that could actually help mitigate the chaos that was occurring, not only helps strategize recovery efforts, but also prevents unnecessary panic on the ground.

Furthermore, when an attack occurs, many families and friends take to social media in search of information about their loved ones. Their scouring the Internet for any information they can find about the location and safety of their loves ones could result in social media adding to the distress families and friends experience. Viewing disturbing footage online, or seeing gory images of victims that family members might be able to use to identify their loved ones before they are contacted by authorities will intensify the grief and despair felt by them.

The inappropriateness of media outlets and social media platforms overwhelming victims' families with unwanted attention adds to the anguish the families of victims' experience, making such unwelcome attention even more difficult to manage. Internet trolls have also used such information to subject victims and their families to vile and upsetting abuse. For instance, after the Manchester Arena bombing, Dan Hett, whose brother Martyn was a victim, said he was extremely overwhelmed by the flood of media attention directed at him and his family (Silver, 2017). He told the BBC that even before confirming his brother had died, when emotions were still very raw, he "had a couple of bad run-ins with people physically turning up at my [*sic*] house, my [his] parents' house and my [his] place of work" (Silver, 2017). The same scenario was observed to have played out after the London Bridge attacks, with media harassing victims' family members for comments and survivors being forced to relive the trauma they had just experienced through the many questions reporters asked of them.

2. *Ensuring the Public has Ready Access to Accurate and Updated Information*

The importance of authorities communicating directly with the public in times of crisis and especially in an event of a terrorist attack cannot be stressed enough. This is even more significant in the age of new media, where the need to verify facts and ensure precise updates of the situation on the ground are communicated accurately to the public is vital to the preservation of social stability and the promotion of recovery efforts.

The evolution of the Internet and the rise of social media have transformed the way news and media are circulated to the masses today. The speed at which content is spread, the type of content that can be distributed and the way content is created, is vastly different from the way print media was circulated after the invention of the printing press. Now, content is published instantly, does not need to be vetted, and can be created by anyone who has access to the Internet. If a clear line of communication is not established between authorities and the public, the public will find other ways of obtaining information online.

As seen in the fiasco that occurred in the aftermath of the Benghazi Attack on two U.S. government facilities in Libya, the lack of clarity of information distributed by the U.S. government amplified the confusion and anger the public felt. Feeling that the government was withholding facts and was not being transparent and honest in their press statements, the public assumed a cover-up was occurring. This lead to the development of many conspiracy theories, which resulted in the U.S. government being forced to clarify the actual details of the attack.

The ease at which netizens can create stories and speculate conspiracy theories on what was occurring when information from authorities and credible news sources was delayed or made unavailable, adds to the chaos and fear terror attacks inflict on societies. Moreover, the way messages and pieces of information observed on social media are interpreted will also affect the effectiveness of response and recovery strategies.

3. *The Spread of Misinformation Online*[1]

Social media have altered the dynamics of traditional information flows. Social media platforms have caused traditional news sources such as newspapers and government announcements to become just one of the many avenues netizens can access to obtain news and information. This technological advancement has also permitted two-way interactive communication and content creation, accentuating the significance of ensuring the validity and accuracy of the information that is circulated online.

Besides the presence of online trolls altering news stories to suit various agendas, emotional responses to acts of terror could result in eyewitnesses inflating, misjudging, or misconstruing information. The rush to deliver new information in today's hyper-competitive news environment can also lead to the reportage of unverified information leads. This not only confuses authorities and the public, but also increases disorder, promotes hysteria, and disrupts recovery processes.

For instance, in the wake of the London Bridge attack, the perpetrator was wrongly identified. Within hours of the attack, Twitter posts, Facebook messages, and a live British television news programme named Abu Izzadeen as the suspect (Scott, 2017). However, Izzadeen was not the assailant and was, in fact, in a British prison at the time of the attack (Scott, 2017). In the 1 October 2017 Las Vegas shooting, where a lone gunman opened fire on spectators at the Route 91 Harvest Music Festival leaving 58 people dead and another 546 injured, the perpetrator was also falsely identified (Ohlheiser, 2017). False reports of there being multiple shooters and misleading information that a nearby hospital, the county's most comprehensive trauma centre, University Medical Center (UMC)

---

[1] A high-level parliamentary committee had been formed to look at ways Singapore can thwart deliberate online falsehoods. Sixty-five individuals and organisations from diverse backgrounds appeared before the 10-member parliamentary committee to present their views. The participants included representatives from media companies and technology firms, members of civil society groups, local and overseas academics, as well as students.

was rejecting patients were also found to be spreading on Google and Facebook (Alvarez, 2017; Woods, 2017).

While the perpetrator's motive for the attack was not linked to any terrorist groups, the violence and horror elicited by such an attack, as well as the impact the misinformation that was spreading online had on the situation, was significant. The rumours that were being spread by unreliable sources online increased confusion, stirred emotions, and resulted in an uneven surge of patients being sent to various hospitals in the vicinity. The overcrowding at Sunrise Hospital and Medical Center in Las Vegas, the nearest hospital to the scene of the shooting, meant that medical and nursing staff were overwhelmed by the number of critically injured patients awaiting treatment, further adding to the chaos that ensued (Woods, 2017).

4. *Messages Unintentionally Supporting Terrorists' Agendas*

While the sharing of information on social media platforms is a natural response, such practices increase the disarray terrorists intend. Seeking to spread fear and mayhem, the attention accorded to such acts of violence and extremism amplifies the terrorist networks' use of social media to recruit, inspire, and connect.

Besides augmenting terrorist messaging through the spread of gory images on social media platforms, the reportage of such imagery on news and social media networks helps spread the impact of their atrocities to social networks the terrorists themselves are unable to reach. In addition, such imagery portrays the perpetrators as martyrs and serves as inspiration for copycats.

During the 2014 Sydney Lindt café hostage crisis, ISIS achieved its aim of getting the world to pay attention to the viciousness it supported. By having social media platforms and the world's media focus its attention on the ongoing hostage situation, which provoked fear the world over, ISIS got free publicity for its cause. In an attempt at manipulating the situation's outcome for his own ends, the hostage taker, Man Haron Monis, also forced one of the hostages, Marcia Mikhael, to post his demands on her Facebook page (Duffy, 2014).

New South Wales Deputy Police Commissioner Catherine Burn later confirmed that social media hampered authorities' ability to control information that was being circulated (Duffy, 2014). This made it problematic for authorities to operationalise their response strategies and heavily affected their tactical decisions.

Immediately after the Manchester Arena bombing incident, terrorists also utilised the app, Telegram, to spread the news that there were shooters all around the stadium (Dreyfuss, 2017). This was, however, not true. Still, the app's users swiftly picked up on this piece of information and started disseminating it. While some users tried to refute the false information that was being circulated, the social media posts contributed to the mayhem on the ground, instigating the swelling of disorder and panic at the scene of the bombing. Social media trolls also started spreading fake news about missing children on social media platforms like Facebook and Twitter (Titcomb, 2017). All this inevitably heightened the impact of the attack, further enabling the terrorists' goal of inciting widespread fear and panic.

5. *Impact on Social Cohesion and Multiracial Harmony*

The rush to report details in today's extremely competitive news environment, coupled with individuals' desire to attract attention and followers on social media platforms, have created the perfect breeding ground for confusion and hearsay to flourish. The overrunning of basic facts with fake news, hate speech, and unverified information alongside the ease at which information can be taken out of context online can result in the intensification of social fault lines.

In the wake of the 22 March 2017 London Westminster terror attack, an image of a woman wearing a hijab, walking past and seemingly ignoring a group of civilians attempting to assist a severely wounded victim was circulated on Twitter by @SouthLoneStar (see Figure 20.1). The tweet was recirculated widely by netizens and traditional media outlets, with far-right extremists and activists in the U.K. and the U.S. adding that the woman was indifferent for

Figure 20.1. Screen Capture of a Tweet Posted by @SouthLoneStar Depicting the Indifference of a Muslim Woman in the Aftermath of the London Westminster Terror Attack.
Source: Dixon (2017).

being more interested in her phone than helping nearby victims (Seidel, 2017).

@SouthLoneStar account's bio declared itself to be "Proud TEXAN and AMERICAN patriot" (Wills, 2017). Twitter later confirmed that elements of the tweet were false and that the account was in fact a Russian bot account (Wills, 2017). Twitter subsequently shut the account down. Still, the damage had already been done.

Jamie Lorriman, the photographer who took the picture, tried setting the record straight by explaining that he had actually distributed two pictures of the woman that day, in the immediate aftermath of the attack. One showed the woman looking terrified, while the other was of her glancing down at her phone (Seidel,

2017). Netizens also defended the woman, pointing out that she looked both distraught and distressed in the picture. Still, an innocent bystander was targeted with the aim of instigating racial hatred online.

Highlighting the selective use of one photo taken out of context to incite outrage and promote netizens jumping to conclusions was a despicable act, one with a clear intention of provoking hostile reactions from a multicultural community such as London's. Should no one have spoken up about the misappropriation in the use of the image, or supported the woman in publicising the statement she gave to TellMAMA UK, a charity monitoring attacks on Muslims (see Figure 20.2), the Russian bot account's attempt at diverting public opinion, encouraging xenophobic sentiments to

Figure 20.2. Screen Capture of the Tweet TellMAMA UK Circulated with a Statement from the Muslim Woman who was Photographed on Westminster Bridge in the Immediate Aftermath of the Westminster Terror Attack.
Source: Wills, 2017.

brew in a multicultural society, could have resulted in much public disharmony and hatred against Muslims. Such a situation would certainly have made it even harder for authorities to conduct their operations and restore order after the terrorist attack.

In Singapore's context, the city-state's unique multicultural make-up necessitates the maintenance of racial and religious harmony for Singapore's continued success. Yet, according to a study conducted by the Institute of Policy Studies in 2016, while the support for multiracialism is strong, racism is an issue many respondents said they still experienced (Mathews, 2016). Underscoring the influence fake news or exaggerated, unverified information can have in causing unnecessary cleavages in society, as well as in adding to the panic, distress and even unrest in times of crisis, the need to be responsible for comments and posts circulated online before, during, and after an attack, is crucial in maintaining the racial and religious harmony Singapore has worked so hard to maintain.

Spreading anti-Muslim messages, whether in the media or on social media platforms, and labelling an entire religion and its followers because of the actions of a few extremist individuals can cause severe misunderstandings and fractures within communities. Additionally, being impervious to the feelings of others through the articulation of indifferent remarks could damage social cohesion in Singapore.

Seib (2017) has suggested that the reportage of ISIS-inspired attacks in the West almost always, explicitly or implicitly, suggests a link to Islam. The association is also not usually clarified as many journalists shy away from commenting on religious topics. This creates a vacuum of public knowledge, which terrorists, anti-Muslim activists, and politicians can exploit. Although anti-Muslim activists and politicians in Singapore have not exploited this flaw in journalistic reportage, the examples observed in other parts of the world and the implications of such episodes, such as those expressed by Pauline Hanson and her Party against Muslims in Australia, should not be viewed lightly.

In addition to this, a 2017 Pew Research Centre study found that significant numbers of Americans viewed Muslims as anti-American and violent (Lipka, 2017). Based on the exposure to anti-Muslim messages spread by the media, this finding emphasises the pervasiveness of stereotypes and their accompanying tensions. The insinuations such labels produce could further result in Muslims all over the world adopting the view that their religion is under siege, making them susceptible to recruitment by terrorist groups who portray themselves as defenders of the religion.

The presence of such divisions within Singapore's social fabric will make it challenging for both authorities and citizens to trust social movements or feel like they will be able to rely on civic mindedness, social capital, and social defence approaches to combat the extremist ideologies terrorists employ. Allowing social divisions to multiply will make it harder for Singapore to safeguard its resilience capacities and bounce back after an attack.

What Can Be Done — Possible Responses and Strategies

1. *Educate the Public*

The purpose of rolling out the SGSecure initiative was to prepare Singaporeans for the inevitability of an attack on Singapore's shores. While it is aimed at educating the public on how to respond to crisis situations by being vigilant, staying united, and being resilient, it also advises the public on the appropriate procedure to follow should they find themselves in danger.

The "Run, Hide, Tell" approach the SGSecure initiative advocates is particularly pertinent in today's new media context. When safe, individuals should provide detailed information about attackers and also their location to the Police or by using the SGSecure App. Curbing the posting of gory images will not only prevent additional distress for victims' friends and families, but will also help authorities regain and maintain order after an attack.

Subsequent direction from authorities should be followed, so as to facilitate a smooth recovery operation. Assistance from individuals should also be rendered in coordination with authorities' instructions. This way, civic and social defence can be utilised appropriately and can help lessen the strain crisis situations place on resources.

While efforts have been made to reach out to various segments of the population, educating individuals about the importance of being vigilant, the need to learn basic first aid skills, and emphasising the significance of community cohesion and resilience through initiatives such as SGSecure and the Total Defence campaign, more can be done to educate the public on social media practices they should be practicing. For instance, public campaigns on social media etiquette could be initiated. The Media Literacy Council's 2018 Safer Internet Campaign, which is currently focused on youths and the issue of cyberbullying, can be further tailored to raise awareness about the impact of content spread during a crisis. Establishing a cyber-smart community through such public campaigns would help educate the public and act as a counter-narrative to the very real and tangible effects online posts can have in various situations.

2. *Be Transparent and Provide Timely Updates*

To prevent the perpetuation of mass panic, as well as the development of conspiracy theories and rumours online, authorities need to update the public at timely intervals. Even if no new information is available at the time, honest and precise reports should be made. This will assure the public that action was being taken to locate perpetrators and/or control the situation.

Such timely communication would have helped prevent the confusion that took place after the Las Vegas shooting. The overwhelming of medical resources at Sunrise Hospital and Medical Center because most of the injured were being sent there instead of UMC, which was located a bit further away, but was better equipped to manage a larger scale emergency, was due to authorities not being able to communicate to the public the emergency plans they had developed.

Transparency in government communications and in updates offered to the public is important, as trust is essential before the resilience of a society can be safeguarded. In order for everyone to play a part and accept the advice of authorities, the public needs reassurance that they are following the advice of stable and reliable authorities. Ensuring netizens trust the information authorities make available will also prevent the spread of inaccurate information on social media.

3. *Emphasise the Influence of Online Posts*

Fake news or exaggerated, unverified information can cause unnecessary panic, distress, chaos, and even unrest. While it is not possible to control social media and the content that is spread via its various platforms, it is possible to encourage the sharing of only credible news pieces.

Getting netizens to think twice about sharing information online will help reduce the noise that is prevalent online, making it easier for individuals who are using social media to make decisions about their own safety during an attack, allow news agencies and media personnel to provide the public with correct updates of the situation at hand, and ensure authorities are using accurate intelligence to inform their plans of action. While social media platforms like Facebook and Google have been trying to clamp down on the spread of misinformation online, netizens should take it upon themselves to stop the spread of unverified information. Any claim made online needs to be verified before it can be considered accurate.

Social media practices that promote tolerance, prevent the spread of rumours, and also ensure netizens are able to access the latest information and advisories from official sources need to be taught to all segments of the Singaporean population. It cannot be taken for granted that the younger, more social media savvy segment of the population, for instance, will be aware of the need for such practices, and hence, be overlooked in the plans put in place to prepare the rest of the population for the challenges brought about by the spread of misinformation online.

4. *Work Together to Prevent the Spread of Terrorist Ideologies*

Between June and December 2016, Twitter suspended close to 377,000 accounts for supporting terrorist activities ("Twitter shuts

377,000 'terrorism' accounts", 2017). Other social media platforms like Facebook and YouTube have also been working together to try and suspend the spread of terrorist messaging and propaganda online. Still, the attention terrorists get when news of the attacks they carry out are circulated online is unprecedented. This is amplified by the breadth of reach such social media posts get.

Guidelines need to be put in place to help social media users understand what is acceptable and what should not be shared online. Besides eradicating the spread of fake news, clear recommendations on where to direct specific information and the types of information deemed inappropriate or sensitive should be looked into. More importantly, explaining why such information has been classified as such needs to be openly elucidated and communicated directly to the public.

Another way to counter this challenge is to engage youths in the development of strategies that could be used to counter terrorist propaganda online. This would help facilitate the emergence of more relevant, relatable, and practical strategies that would result in netizens' adoption of more responsible social media practices. Engaging youths in the formulation of counter-ISIS messaging ideas in national and regional policy forums will contribute to the involvement of youth in the crafting of their own counter-narratives against the ISIS appeal. This method is especially useful as youths' vulnerability is currently the target of online terrorist propaganda.

5. *Go Beyond Mere Tolerance and Engage in Community Activities*

The fear that terrorists hope to incite through their violent and senseless acts of violence requires counter-narratives that emphasise community bonding and togetherness. These issues can be tackled by encouraging Singaporeans to participate more in social events organised by grassroots organisations. The organisation of events that cater to and interest all segments of the Singaporean population, and which, will allow intergenerational and interracial mixing and socialising, is needed if Singapore is to preserve the social cohesion and harmony it currently enjoys.

Engaging in community activities will also help build community ties and develop bonds between the different racial groups in Singapore. Investing in social relationships will deepen Singaporeans' sense of belonging and encourage them to partake in the five pillars of the Total Defence campaign, as well as ensure Singapore's resilience and ability to recover after an attack.

The media's portrayal of Islam, the public's understanding of the religion, and what it stands for also need to be considered if the meaning of multiculturalism in Singapore is to go beyond the mere tolerance of differences. Both the public's and authorities' responses to social media posts, as well as the acknowledgment and proper utilisation of two-way communication strategies are vital in today's new media context. Everyone has to chip in and plays a part in safeguarding Singapore's recovery should an attack occur. It is no longer possible to rely wholly on government intervention to regain peace and stability after a crisis.

Conclusion

The way social media is utilised, as well as the role it plays in furthering either public chaos or encouraging solidarity and unity in response to attacks is crucial in ensuring a community's ability to respond appropriately and bounce back after ruthless acts of violence. While social media have stimulated new and innovative ways the Singapore government has utilised in its fight against terror, more can be done to ensure Singapore's recovery and resilience.

Social media having elevated the public's role in crisis response indicates the importance of educating the public on how to appropriately participate on social media platforms before, during, and after an attack. This will help maximise the potential benefits of social media use and inculcate better online etiquette.

In summary, social media has surfaced new challenges that need to be addressed. The way social media is used before, during, and after an attack will have an impact on the degree of disarray senseless acts of violence will have on societies. Establishing positive social media practices in times of peace will benefit both authorities and the public in this regard. Such an approach will, however, require two-way communication, cooperation, and engagement from all parties. A solely top-down approach or bottom-up initiative will not be enough to adequately tackle such pressing issues.

References

#JeSuisCharlie: Signs of solidarity after Paris terror attack (2015). *CBS News*. Retrieved from https://www.cbsnews.com/news/jesuischarlie-sign-of-solidarity-after-paris-terror-attack-charlie-hebdo/.

Alexander, H. (2017). London Bridge attack — Everything we know. *The Telegraph*. Retrieved from http://www.telegraph.co.uk/news/2017/06/03/london-bridge-everything-know-far/.

Alvarez, E. (2017). After Las Vegas shooting, Facebook and Google get the news wrong again. *Engadget*. Retrieved from https://www.engadget.com/2017/10/02/facebook-google-fake-news-las-vegas-shooting/.

Anderson, C. (2017). Sweden mourns Stockholm attack victims; Suspect is formally identified. *The New York Times*. Retrieved from https://www.nytimes.com/2017/04/10/world/europe/sweden-terror-attack.html.

Barcelona attack: 13 killed as van rams crowds in Las Ramblas (2017, August 18). *BBC News*. Retrieved from http://www.bbc.com/news/world-europe-40965581.

Devichand, M. (2016). How the world was changed by the slogan 'Je Suis Charlie'. *BBC Trending*. Retrieved from http://www.bbc.com/news/blogs-trending-35108339.

Dixon, H. (2017). Russian bot behind false claim Muslim woman ignored victims of Westminster terror attack. *The Telegraph*. Retrieved from https://www.telegraph.co.uk/news/2017/11/13/russian-bot-behind-false-claim-muslim-woman-ignored-victims/.

Dreyfuss, E. (2017). After a terrorist attack, social media can cause more harm than good. *National Public Radio*. Retrieved from https://www.npr.org/2017/05/26/530257519/after-a-terrorist-attack-social-media-can-cause-more-harm-than-good.

Duffy, C. (2014). Sydney siege: Social media could hamper police operations, being exploited by modern terrorists, expert says. *ABC News*. Retrieved from http://www.abc.net.au/news/2014-12-16/sydney-siegesocial-media-a-liability-says-expert/5971622.

Groll, E. (2015). Meet the man who put the 'Je Suis' in the 'Je Suis Charlie'. *Foreign Policy*. Retrieved from http://foreignpolicy.com/2015/01/19/meet-the-man-who-put-the-je-suis-in-the-je-suis-charlie/.

Harris, S. (2017). Manchester Bombing prompts extraordinary messages of defiance. *Huffington Post UK*. Retrieved from http://www.huffingtonpost.co.uk/entry/manchester-bombing-mancunians-defiance-in-the-face-of-terror_uk_5923f5b2e4b034684b0f6874.

Lindsay, B. (2011). Social media and disasters: Current uses, future options and policy considerations. Retrieved from https://www.nisconsortium.org/portal/resources/bin/Social_Media_and_Dis_1423591240.pdf.

Lipka, M. (2017). Muslims and Islam: Key findings in the U.S. and around the world. *Pew Research Centre*. Retrieved from http://www.pewresearch.org/fact-tank/2017/08/09/muslims-and-islam-key-findings-in-the-u-s-and-around-the-world/.

Manchester attack: What we know so far (2017). *BBC news*. Retrieved from http://www.bbc.com/news/uk-england-manchester-40008389.

Mathews, M. (2016). Channel NewsAsia-Institute of Policy Studies (CNA-IPS) *Survey on Race Relations*. Retrieved from http://lkyspp2.nus.edu.sg/ips/wp-content/uploads/sites/2/2013/04/CNA-IPS-survey-on-race-relations_190816.pdf.

Ministry of Home Affairs. (2017). *Singapore Terrorism Threat Assessment Report 2017*. Retrieved from https://www.mha.gov.sg/newsroom/press-releases/Pages/Singapore-Terrorism-Threat-Assessment-Report-2017.aspx.

Mueller, B., Rashbaum, R., & Baker, A. (2017). Terror attack kills 8 and injures 11 in Manhattan. *The New York Times*. Retrieved from https://www.nytimes.com/2017/10/31/nyregion/police-shooting-lower-manhattan.html.

Ohlheiser, A. (2017). How far-right trolls named the wrong man as the Las Vegas shooter. *The Washington Post*. Retrieved from https://www.washingtonpost.com/news/the-intersect/wp/2017/10/02/how-far-right-trolls-named-the-wrong-man-as-the-las-vegas-shooter/?utm_term=.7bdac5cea6d2.

Scott, M. (2017). Fake sleuths: Web gets it wrong on London attacker. *The New York Times*. Retrieved from https://www.nytimes.com/2017/03/24/technology/london-terror-attack-suspect-social-media.html.

Seib, P (2017). Mainstream media outlets are dropping the ball with terrorism coverage. *The Conversation*. Retrieved from https://theconversation.com/mainstream-media-outlets-are-dropping-the-ball-with-terrorism-coverage-78442.

Seidel, J. (2017). US Congress told how Russia 'weaponised' this photo of a 'Muslim woman'. *News Corp Australia Network*. Retrieved from http://www.news.com.au/technology/online/social/us-congress-told-how-russia-weaponised-this-photo/news-story/8135ca050976761ab476c04c32d44fd2.

Silver, K. (2017). Beware of social media during terror events, NHS guidelines warn. *BBC*. Retrieved from http://www.bbc.com/news/health-41203920.

Titcomb, J. (2017). Manchester attack: Social media trolls spread fake posts about missing children. *The Telegraph*. Retrieved from http://www.telegraph.co.uk/technology/2017/05/23/manchester-attack-social-media-trolls-spread-fake-posts-missing/.

Twitter shuts 377,000 'terrorism' accounts. (2017, March 22). *BBC News*. Retrieved from http://www.bbc.com/news/technology-39351212.

Whitehead, T. (2015). Paris Charlie Hebdo attack: Je Suis Charlie hashtag one of most popular in Twitter history. *The Telegraph*. Retrieved from http://www.telegraph.co.uk/news/worldnews/europe/france/11336879/Paris-Charlie-Hebdo-attack-Je-Suis-Charlie-hashtag-one-of-most-popular-in-Twitter-history.html.

Wills, E. (2017). Muslim woman pictured 'ignoring victims of London terror attack' was fake news Tweet created by Russians. *Evening Standard*. Retrieved from https://www.standard.co.uk/news/world/russian-bot-account-claimed-muslim-woman-ignored-westminster-attack-victims-a3689751.html.

Woods, A. (2017). Las Vegas shooting: Patients went to wrong hospital as misinformation spread. *The (Arizona) Republic, Part of the USA Today Network*. Retrieved from http://www.rgj.com/story/news/2017/12/05/las-vegas-shooting-patients-went-wrong-hospital-misinformation-spread/922474001/.

CHAPTER 21

Media Effects within the Context of Violent Extremism in the Post-9/11 Era

LEEVIA DILLON*, JOSHUA D. FREILICH*, and STEVEN M. CHERMAK†

*Criminal Justice Department, John Jay College of Criminal Justice, USA
†School of Criminal Justice, Michigan State University, USA

Introduction

Media coverage of violent extremist attacks play an important role in shaping public views on violent extremism. As research suggests, the media helps to facilitate public opinion by informing the public, formulating public opinion, and scrutinising issues (Overholser & Jamieson, 2005). Within the context of violent extremism, the central event that changed media reporting is the September 11 attacks and its continuing effects on the public, social, cultural, and legal issues

(Chermak & Gruenewald, 2006). Since 9/11, media accounts about violent extremism in the media have risen exponentially (Segalla, 2017), with some events being highly sensationalised. According to Held (2012), media has a tendency to "over-label" violent acts as "violent extremism" which provokes negative reactions within many people, based on the way and the degree of exposure on how they view violent extremism. Manjoo (2008) drew heavily from psychological research, in particular selective exposure and selective perception, to inform the interaction between media and their consumers.

Prior to 9/11, Duyvesteyn (2004) found the media's stereotypical image of violent extremism and a violent extremist included small-group activity and middle-class males aged between 22 to 25, holding anarchist/Marxist ideologies. Similarly, prior to 9/11, the violent extremism label was used to define certain acts of political violence (e.g., left-wing extremist acts), as compared to those committed by other groups (Nagar, 2010). This is in stark contrast to the post-9/11 era. This could be due to the shock and destruction that was caused by these attacks, leaving a deep physical and emotional impression (Keinan *et al.*, 2003; Shoshani & Slone, 2008; Wicks, 2006). The current era saw an expansion of those who are labelled an extremist. The term extremist is used loosely, almost carelessly, and there is an inclination to focus on radical Islamic groups more often due to the demographic characteristics of the 9/11 attackers (Nagar, 2010).

Another associated issue is that the post-9/11 era highlighted the contrasting agendas of various claim-makers. First, the U.S. administration used the media to promote their military objectives in the 2003 Iraq war and to gain support for its policy response to violent extremism domestically and abroad (Kellner, 2006). Next, the unintended consequence of magnifying the impact of violent extremism promotes the designs of these violent extremist organisations by providing them publicity and thus spreading fear and panic (Bassiouni, 1981; Schmid, 1989). Lastly, there is the media's interest in the pursuit of events deemed to be newsworthy (Allan, 2004). Previous coverage of crime generally and violent extremism specifically provided a useful foundation for the presentation. Investigation and research on post-9/11 violent extremism coverage found that reporters defined a description of a violent extremist event and understood that an infamous individual was probably the instigator responsible for the deviant action (Chermak & Gruenewald, 2006).

This chapter includes the following five main points. First, the chapter introduces the media coverage on violent extremism in the post-9/11 era. Second, the chapter will review media influence on public perception. The third and fourth points include the exploration into the specifics of media framing and the usage of the 2009 Fort Hood shooting. We use this case study to contextualise the media coverage of extremism. The chapter concludes by discussing the implications for policy and research.

Media Coverage and Violent Extremism in the Post-9/11 Era

As outlined, the importance behind understanding the decision-making processes of the media, specifically the selection and saliency of presentation of violent extremist incidents, have significant consequences on public opinion, agenda setting, and policymaking, and the agendas and activities of violent extremist organisations.

The advent of the Internet and related technological advancements aggravated the fragmented nature of society (Manjoo, 2008), exemplified by the events following the 9/11 attacks. Noting Americans' reactions to the 9/11 attacks, Osama bin Laden said with palpable contentment: "There is America, full of fear from north to south, from west to east. Thank God for that!" Since then, bin Laden and other violent extremist leaders have threatened more disturbing internal and external attacks on the United States. Familiar with fear psychology, violent extremists know that violence and the mere threat of such acts in the aftermath of major attacks accomplish one of their primary goals — to intimidate the public and force governments, more often than not, to overreact (Nacos *et al.*, 2007). Regardless of whether or not these threats are carried out, violent extremists win instantaneous access to media publicity. With this, government officials in charge of counter-violent extremism response will be in an excellent position to exploit the available "window of opportunity" by utilising the media to win public support for their policies and military response. However, this easy access to media publicity has a drawback. Coverage of an unfolding violent extremist attack may inadvertently endanger security forces and public safety and hinder counter-terrorism efforts by disclosing key information (e.g., strategies and status of law enforcement). One example was the 2013 Westgate Mall attack in Kenya. The use of unsynchronised accounts by the Kenyan authorities made it difficult to track and stem the flow of information that was disseminated in real-time. This prolonged the siege and hindered the government's response (Simon *et al.*, 2014).

Public Perception and the Media

A phrase by Thomas and Thomas (1928, p. 572) captures the essence of public perception and the importance of examining the media influence on public opinion: "If men [or women] define situations as real, they are real in their consequences".

Following this line of thought, Manjoo (2008, p. 66) highlights the uncertainty in the contemporary fragmented era:

> [With] more cameras, tape recorders and better systems to broadcast...you make it easier for people to capture and disseminate documentary evidence from any event's ground zero — you don't necessarily bolster agreement about what's actually happening around us. In other words, you don't always strengthen the truths...more recordings lead to greater uncertainty.

Although scholars disagree about the degree of influence of the media on public attitudes, there is a consensus that the media plays some role and increases public's attention to it as a social problem (Slone, 2000; Wanta & Hu, 1993). Thus, the media has the potential in shaping public opinion on social issues like violent extremism.

Public Perception and Moral Panic

Cohen-Almagor (2005) explains that there are many instances where media coverage of violent extremist events was problematic and this subsequently evoked flak (Herman & Chomsky, 1988), a negative response towards the media, stemming from public criticism. As highlighted above, violent extremism coverage tends to incite negative emotions (e.g., anger, hostility, fear, uncertainty, anxiety) within individuals despite their lack of proximity to the attack (Strozier, 2011). Examples of flak include the bombardment of detail and images related to the violent extremist event (Keinan *et al.*, 2003) and insensitive portrayal of religious violent extremism (Wicks, 2006). As Garland (2008) puts it, the contemporary era is an age of "exaggeration", where the mass media often flock towards a single emotional issue and exploit it, which in this case would be violent extremism.

Violent extremism events often generate negative emotions within the audience (despite them not being victims of a violent extremist attack) most often through vicarious experience from the media coverage linking the act itself to a larger problem (e.g., breakdown of societal moral fabric, lack of community integration, economic and immigration problems), and the portrayal of violent extremists taking centre stage with associated stereotypical images, specifically in religious radical Islamist violence (e.g., Muslim, Arab-descent, immigrant, male, and unemployed). The role of media in generating moral panic has been documented in research, in which the coverage stimulates fear of deviance and promotes a public outcry for sanctions that may or may not be justified (Altheide, 2006; Cohen, 2004), which creates a "window of opportunity" for policymakers and politicians to further their own agendas. Chermak (2002) documents this process when exploring media coverage of the 1990s militia movement in the United States. After Timothy McVeigh destroyed the Murrah building in Oklahoma City, the media intensely examined the characteristics of this movement and its members. The media framed the movement as a significant threat, and policymakers and law enforcement then prioritised responding to this threat.

Public Interest, Elite Interest, and Expertise

According to Entman (1993), framing appears to be a central power in the democratic process for political elites to control the framing of issues and guide public opinion. Coverage of violent extremist acts are most commonly framed in two ways (Edy & Meirick, 2007): (i) context of an act of war and (ii) context of an act of crime. Interestingly, research finds that viewers adopted a mixed frame — victims of violent extremist acts were murder victims and not war victims and perpetrators should be killed during the event. The categorisation of this mixed-frame involves the perception that victims are individuals and perpetrators are group associated with strong military response as compared to viewing the act in the context of a war.

Within the context of elite interest, one argument is that political leaders use the media to garner support by campaigning on issues on crime and punishment, and help to increase their legitimacy in the public's eye by priming the audience to judge them based on their actions/stances on criminal justice issues. Green (2008) claims one such factor of legitimacy are expert views expressed as a legitimate and trustworthy authority (e.g., evidence-based and prestige of sources). To push for a legitimate elite agenda, Green's (2009) concepts of "quiet high-roading" and "loud low-roading" come into play. Quiet high-roading is the inconspicuous pursuit of progressive aims as insulated from public scrutiny at the cost of jeopardising legitimacy once exposed. Loud low-roading entailed the employment of tough-on-crime rhetoric but not always following through/enforcing this rhetoric. Both share the core assumption of tried-and-true patterns of tough-on-crime talk, strengthening the legitimacy of the traditional narratives by reiteration and proliferation. Within the context of the post-9/11 era, counter-violent extremism rose to the top of the public policy agenda in America. This led the Bush administration to boost expenditure on police, firefighters, and emergency medical teams, create the Department of Homeland Security, improve airport and border security, intelligence gathering, and protect medicine reserves (Norris *et al.*, 2003).

Media Framing

Journalism often attracts controversy especially when news coverage becomes part of the contest to define the social meaning of events (Norris *et al.*, 2003). There are three common types of journalistic reporting, which are: (i) descriptive reporting, (ii) opinionated reporting, and (iii) highly perspective reporting (Overholser & Jamieson, 2005). Entman (1993), similarly highlights the concept of journalistic objectivity where journalists follow rules for "objective" reporting, and yet they still tend to convey a dominant framing of the news text. Selection of dominant frames by journalists are defined as "persistent patterns of cognition, interpretation, and presentation of selection, emphasis, and exclusion [to] routinely organise discourse whether verbal or visual" (Gitlin, 1980, p. 12). The selection, emphasis, and exclusion of frames provide preferred social meanings, structures, and understandings to specific events. As a result, this prevents most audience members from making a balanced assessment of a situation which highlights the importance of media framing and agenda setting.

Framing involves the selection of some aspects of a perceived reality and makes them more salient in communicating text and results in three consequences: (i) forming opinions, (ii) priming opinions, and (iii) shaping opinions (Overholser & Jamieson, 2005). Green (2009) adds that the increased competition that has accompanied media proliferation has caused media outlets to shape their messages to fit the preferences of niche consumers. This suggests that the public utilises mass media information to fortify and sustain existing views.

Beale (2006) explored a variety of media framing mechanisms within the context of crime salience and increased punitiveness, including: (i) episodic frames versus thematic frames, in which journalists tend to focus on episodic framing rather than thematic ones and can influence punitiveness and policy preferences and (ii) stock stories which influence punitive attitudes and invoke racial stereotypes, which prompt individual selection of matching stories, illustrating "selective exposure" (i.e., an individual's preference for information that strengthen his/her pre-existing views over opposing information) and "selective perception" (i.e., a process in which individuals perceive what they want in media content and ignoring opposing ones) (Manjoo, 2008). The mechanism that increases crime salience highlights the significance of priming and agenda setting which make issues salient. Priming rests on cognitive accessibility theory where people make judgements using subconscious shortcuts by relying on accessible information (e.g., stock stories, recently acquired information — highlights the recency effect). Agenda setting refers to the media's capability to capture public's attention and focus on certain issue (which will be further explored in the next section). The mechanism that produces increased punitiveness (attributed to episodic framing and stock stories) is sensationalising the increasing fear of crime which may provoke an affective response. This in turn plays a role in moral panics and in reinforcing links between race and crime where the coverage of crime triggers racism (portrayal of crime as a minority phenomenon).

Agenda Setting

How important events are constituted as "news" is subjected to different judgements/biases of not only the journalist's, but the media's agenda setting as well. Agenda setting refers to the association between how much the media emphasises an issue and the importance placed on it by the public and policymakers. Media focus on a topic enhances the saliency by priming its audience, thus increasing its role in the shaping of political attitudes and judgments. Similarly, Overholser and Jamieson (2005) posited that the influence of agenda setting can successfully shape what and how to think about a certain issue.

Agenda setting is attributed to many factors such as newsworthiness of events, public and elite preferences, and newsroom culture. According to Chermak (1995, p. 24), journalists tend to "rely on sources that are easily established and accessible and abide by...organisational policy." In other words, organisational policies and protocols of media outlets play a role in shaping journalists' media framing preference. The goal of media outlets is the efficient production of news where journalists "routinise" media coverage of events with the development of relationships with sources that provide them with reliable information about events (Chermak, 1995; Gans, 1979). With these close contacts, "windows of opportunity" can be created in media coverage of events. In other words, these relationships not only serve the interest of media outlets but those of the elites' as well (Chermak & Weiss, 2005). For instance, Birkland (2004) found that though the 9/11 events provided the impetus for change (and it being a newsworthy event), the threat of violent extremism was already well-grounded in the policy process and these attacks created a window of opportunity for changes.

Newsworthiness of Violent Extremism

Within the context of violent extremism, it is a recognisable social problem, but not all events are presented to the public, and the media does not cover all approaches to responding to violent extremism (Chermak & Gruenewald, 2006). In other words, some events are ignored, and others are prominently displayed as significant events. The differential media coverage for certain events highlights the issue of newsworthiness (i.e., news values) of a violent extremist event. Hall *et al.* (1978) outlined the process by which news becomes "news", which is the end product of a complex process. The process begins with systematic organisation and selection of events and topics according to a pre-set criterion, which can be further expounded upon by Chibnall's (1977) and Jewkes's (2004) concept of news values: structural and content, respectively.

Chibnall (1977) identified eight structural news values including: (1) immediacy (i.e., news is about what is new and what just happened), (2) dramatisation (i.e., event-orientation of news is reinforced by an emphasis on the dramatic and over-sensationalised violent extremist events), (3) personalisation (i.e., personalities like infamous charismatic clerics, leaders of violent extremist organisations), (4) simplification (i.e., oversimplification of reality — making reality dichotomous and eliminating the grey area — "us-versus-them" theme), (5) titillation (e.g., simultaneous portrayal and condemnation of the more exotic/

lurid forms of deviance — extreme torture of prisoners such as beheadings and women/children conducting extreme acts of violence such as suicide bombings), (6) conventionalism (i.e., situating emergent phenomena in existing structures of meaning — homegrown violent extremists, online violent extremism, and radicalisation), (7) structured access (i.e., ensures that newspaper accounts and representations are "structured in dominance" — objectivity paradigm is based on the dominant frames of interpretations of the world), and (8) novelty (i.e., element of randomness — violent extremist events may occur without warning despite security overhauls).

Jewkes (2004) posits there are six content news values: (1) risk (i.e., the idea that we are all at risk of being a victim of terror — perceived vulnerability versus actual victimisation), (2) sex (i.e., tendency to highlight strict gender roles within violent extremist organisations — women as jihadi brides, raising the next generation of violent extremists), (3) proximity (i.e., spatial proximity — geographical nearness of events, cultural proximity — relevance of an event to an audience), (4) violence, (5) spectacle and graphic imagery (i.e., violence and deaths), and (6) children (i.e., highly vulnerable to radicalisation and seen as potential new recruits). As such, media coverage of violent extremism contains the characteristics of news values outlined by Chibnall (1977) and Jewkes (2004), which may account for differential reporting of certain violent extremist events receiving more attention than others.

Thus, it is clear that the media framing of violent extremism contributes to the fear resulting from these attacks. This in turn influences policy and advances the violent extremists' cause. For this reason, it is vital to understand the specifics of the media frame.

Media Frame Specificity — Social Problem Framing of Violent Extremism

Loseke (2003) maintains that there are three parts to social problem framing — diagnostic, motivational, and prognostic framing. Diagnostic frames refer to statements on causes of the incident. Prognostic frames are statements about solutions (e.g., policy responses/changes) to address these problems. Motivational frames refer to statements about why the audience should take care of these problems. To engage in what Loseke calls "social problem work", claim-makers (i.e., a segment of the population that is involved in the production and management in resolving social problems which include scientists, politicians, and the mass media) engage in claim-making strategies. The credibility, legitimacy, and prestige of such claim-makers hinges on wealth, authority, and expertise (Green, 2008; Herman & Chomsky, 1988; Manjoo, 2008). As Schlesinger *et al.* (1991, p. 260) explain "...the different patterns of emphasis in coverage have important implications for our understanding of audience perceptions..."

Diagnostic and Prognostic Frames

Sasson's (1995) five themes of crime and justice inform the diagnostic and prognostic social problem frame. These themes include: (1) faulty criminal justice system (i.e., regard crime as a consequence of impunity), (2) blocked opportunities (i.e., crime as a consequence of inequality and discrimination), (3) social breakdown (i.e., crime as a consequence of family and community disintegration), (4) racist system (i.e., depiction of the criminal justice system rather than an attribution of the responsibility for crime), and (5) violent media (i.e., crime as a consequence of violence on television, in the movies and popular music). Since these themes overlap with examples of depictions of crime, they are easily applied to the media coverage of violent extremism.

Faulty criminal justice system

Lack of law and order as well as too much leniency are the descriptive angles that reflect the diagnostic frame. Being tough on violent extremism and violent extremists is the descriptive angle that reflects the prognostic frame.

Blocked opportunities

Acts of violent extremism resulting from societal discrimination against vulnerable populations would be a descriptive angle that reflects the diagnostic frame. Social integration and employment and educational opportunities are descriptive angles that reflect the prognostic frame.

Social breakdown

Immigration issues, identity loss, and community disintegration are some examples of descriptive angles that reflect the diagnostic frame. Community integration and immigration policy changes are descriptive angles that reflect the prognostic frame.

Racist system

Political correctness, misinformation, and intelligence turf wars are some examples of descriptive angles that reflect the diagnostic frame. Tighter security and recommendations for transparency would be the descriptive angles that reflect the prognostic frame.

Violent media

Violent/extreme/radical content leading to radicalisation would be a descriptive angle that reflects the diagnostic frame. Content censorship is a descriptive angle that reflects the prognostic frame.

Motivational Frame

To inform the motivational social problem frame, audience persuasion would be done through appeals involving cultural themes such as emotion and logic (Loseke, 2003). For instance, by drawing on unique cultural themes such as patriotism and religion within the context of violent extremism, such narratives will resonate with the public. In terms of patriotism, victims of a violent extremist-related event can be portrayed for their heroic actions (e.g., helping others or taking down the attacker) during the event. In terms of religion, politicians and community leaders make declarations denouncing these acts and not being part of any faith-related teachings.

Next, there are many strategies that claim-makers may use to persuade their audience. Both logical and emotional strategies are usually employed.

Logical strategies can include: (1) focus on familiarity where construction of a new problem as a different instance of an existing problem (i.e., piggybacking) or contents of previously accepted social problem category are expanded (i.e., domain expansion), (2) focus on simplifying complex issues, and (3) focus on social structure (e.g., organisation of families, schools, community) or social forces (e.g., ageism, sexism, racism).

Emotional strategies can include how victims and perpetrators are portrayed within the narrative and in the mass media. There is a deep contrast between the portrayals of victims and perpetrators. In other words, "culturally feeling rules" will guide the emotional reactions to victims (i.e., generating compassion and sympathy) as compared to villains (i.e., generating moral outrage and anger). On one hand, victims will be typified based on their horrible suffering and their innocence. On the other hand, villains will be typified as dangerous and medicalising their deviance, emphasising mental health disturbances and violent propensities.

Case Study: 2009 Fort Hood Shooting

For illustration purposes of social problem framing, we purposefully selected the 2009 case study of the Fort Hood shooting incident (see Table 21.1 for a summary). We extracted media coverage of the incident from the *New York Times*[1] articles. The sample of articles was taken from the website archive within the 2009–2016 period. The initial search of the event coverage yielded 53 items. To ensure standardisation of the sample, the authors manually screened the items and included only news articles for the coding process while excluding the rest which consisted of interview transcripts, opinion

[1] *The New York Times* is chosen because of its national media coverage (Winter & Eval, 1981), and being a reliable indicator of agenda setting (Chermak & Weiss, 1998).

Table 21.1. Dominant Frames, Themes, and Angles Utilised During News Coverage of the Shooting.

Frames	Themes	Angles
	Diagnostic — Assignment of blame and responsibility	
Perpetrator	• Violent media • Social breakdown	• Radicalisation • Emotional turmoil
Authorities	• Faulty criminal justice • Racist system	• Political correctness • Information-sharing
	Motivational — Narrative construction using cultural and emotional themes	
Perpetrator	• Medicalisation of mental state	• Vulnerable individual
Victims	• Patriotism	• Officer heroism • Victims' strength • Forgiveness
	Prognostic — Construction of solutions	
Perpetrator		• Murder and attempted murder charges • Death penalty
Authorities		• Investigations and changes implemented to prevent future attacks • Mass shooting/workplace violence incident classification • Blame/responsibility on 9 Fort Hood officers
Victims		• Memorial services • Nawal foundation

pieces (which may contain biased language), and other unrelated content (i.e., 2014 Fort Hood shooting incident) which resulted in 13 news articles.

The 2009 mass shooting incident at Fort Hood occurred on November 9 in Texas and was perpetrated by Major Nidal Hasan, 39, an Army psychiatrist. The attack claimed 13 lives and wounded more than 30 others (Rubin & Smith, 2013). At 1:34 p.m., Hasan entered the Soldier Readiness Processing Center, where military personnel receive routine medical check-ups prior to and on return from deployment where he opened fire using a modified pistol (Thomas & Ryan, 2009). On 23 August 2013, Hasan was found guilty on 13 counts of premediated murder and 32 counts of attempted premediated murder and was sentenced to death on 28 August 2013. This case has been surrounded by intense controversial debates in terms of its classification — workplace violence, mass shooting, or terrorism (Fernandez & Blinder, 2014).

The diagnostic frame deals with the assignment of blame and responsibility to both the individual perpetrator and the authorities. The perpetrator acted in that manner because of a cumulative number of factors such as emotional and ideological turmoil, psychological stress over his counselling activities, and unhappiness over his deployment to Afghanistan (Johnston & Schmitt, 2009). Next, the authorities were implicated as highlighted by the culture of "political correctness" which prevented officials from taking precautionary measures before the fruition of this shooting. This was attributed to the fear of impinging upon his free speech rights as well as concerns over ruining Hasan's career as a military psychiatrist. Subsequently, this impacted information sharing and coordination between intelligence agencies.

The motivational frame integrates both cultural ideas (i.e., patriotism) and emotional themes (i.e., portrayal of perpetrator and victims). In terms of the construction of the perpetrator narrative, Nidal Hasan was portrayed as not only a "murderer" but also as a "vulnerable individual who acted out" due to a number of factors (i.e., emotional turmoil, psychological stress, unhappiness, attempt to medicalise his mental state) and not a "terrorist" by underplaying the link to terrorism (i.e., because of the lack of evidence that he was part of an organised plot and the e-mail communication with Awlaki was deemed insignificant). In terms of the construction of the victim narrative, the articles underscored their bravery and heroism in helping others who were injured as well as painting a positive account of the aftermath by highlighting forgiveness and the strength to move past this incident. In addition, there was a patriotic portrayal of the female police officer, Kimberly Denise Munley, who responded to a call on a gunfire report and engaged the shooter before bringing him down and stopping the attack (Mckinley, 2009).

The prognostic frame deals with the construction of solutions with regard to the shooting incident and the entities involved: (1) perpetrator, (2) authorities, and (3) victims. With reference to the shooting incident, the unclear link to terrorism (i.e., lack of evidence that Hasan had ties to terrorist organisations) subsequently resulted in classifications of the incident as "workplace violence" and "mass shooting". Hasan was charged with 13 counts of premediated murder and 32 counts of attempted premediated murder and was sent to death row in 2013 (Fernandez, 2013). Next, in terms of the authorities, investigations and reviews (both internal and external) were conducted to determine errors, assign blame/responsibility to various entities, and prevent future attacks. Interestingly, there was a detailed account of a similar incident of a failed plot involving an active shooter at the Pentagon in an attempt to illustrate the complexity of such incidents and the evolution of security operations (Barry, 2010). With regard to the victims, memorial services for the fallen victims were held, which President Obama attended, as well as the establishment of the "Nawal Foundation" where family members from both sides (i.e., perpetrator and victim) were involved (Kovaleski, 2012) in an attempt to illustrate forgiveness and strength to move on despite the difficulties.

Implications for Policy and Research

This chapter explored the media effects within the context of violent extremism by highlighting the importance of media framing and its potential to shape public support and inform public policies targeted towards counter-terrorism efforts. There are several key conclusions from this chapter that have policy and research implications. The policy implications include: (1) development of a dynamic database to capture media portrayals (i.e., media frame specificity) of violent extremist events which is similar to the U.S.

Extremist Crime Database (ECDB) (Freilich *et al.*, 2014), which also uses media information to track the incident, victim, and perpetrator characteristics, and (2) emphasis on highlighting the positive contributions of the media and good practices of news reporting. Research implications include: (1) calls for future media effects research with a specific focus on labelling and its impact on the public and policy and (2) calls for interdisciplinary social sciences research (i.e., psychology, criminology, sociology, political science) with a specific focus on media framing of violent extremism.

References

Allan, S. (2004). Making news: Truth, ideology and newswork. In S. Allan (Ed.), *News Culture* (pp. 46–76). New York: McGraw Hill.

Altheide, D. L. (2006). Terrorism and the politics of fear. *Cultural Studies*, 6(4), 415–439.

Barry, D. (2010). A quiet evening, waiting for the next angry man. *The New York Times*. Retrieved from http://www.nytimes.com/2010/03/15/us/15land.html.

Bassiouni, M. C. (1981). Terrorism, law enforcement, and the mass media: Perspectives, problems, proposals. *The Journal of Criminal Law and Criminology*, 72(1), 1–51.

Beale, S. S. (2006). The news media's influence on criminal justice policy: How market-driven news promotes punitiveness. *William and Mary Law Review*, 48(2), 397–481.

Birkland, T. A. (2004). The world changed today: Agenda-setting and policy change in the wake of the September 11 terrorist attacks. *Review of Policy Research*, 21(2), 179–200.

Chermak, S. M. (1995). *Victims in the news: Crime in American news media*. Boulder, CO: Westview Press.

Chermak, S. M. (2002). *Searching for a Demon: The Media Construction of the Militia Movement*. Boston, MA: Northeastern University Press.

Chermak, S. M., & Gruenewald, J. (2006). The media's coverage of domestic terrorism. *Justice Quarterly*, 23(4), 428–461.

Chermak, S. M., & Weiss, A. (1998). The news value of African American victims: An examination of the media's presentation of homicide. *Journal of Crime and Justice*, 21(2), 71–88.

Chermak, S. M., & Weiss, A. (2005). Maintaining legitimacy using external communication strategies: An analysis of police-media relations. *Journal of Criminal Justice*, *33*(5), 501–512.

Chibnall, S. (1977). Press ideology: The politics of professionalism. In C. Greer (Ed.), *Crime and Media: A Reader* (pp. 201–214). London: Routledge.

Cohen, S. (2004). *Folk Devils and Moral Panics* (3rd edn.). London: Routledge.

Cohen-Almagor, R. (2005). Media coverage of acts of terrorism: Troubling episodes and suggested guidelines. *Canadian Journal of Communication*, *30*(3), 383–409.

Duyvesteyn, I. (2004). How new is the new terrorism? *Studies in Conflict & Terrorism*, *27*(5), 439–454.

Edy, J. A., & Meirick, P. C. (2007). Wanted, dead or alive: Media frames, frame adoption, and support for the war in Afghanistan. *Journal of Communication*, *57*(1), 119–141.

Entman, R. M. (1993). Framing: Towards clarification of a fractured paradigm. *Journal of Communication*, *43*(3), 51–58.

Fernandez, M. (2013). Defendant in Fort Hood shooting case admits being gunman. *The New York Times*. Retrieved from http://www.nytimes.com/2013/08/07/us/court-martial-begins-in-fort-hood-killings.html.

Fernandez, M., & Blinder, A. (2014). At Fort Hood, wrestling with label of terrorism. *The New York Times*. Retrieved from https://www.nytimes.com/2014/04/09/us/at-fort-hood-wrestling-with-label-of-terrorism.html.

Freilich, J. D., Chermak, S., Belli, R., Gruenewald, J., & Parkin, W. S. (2014). Introducing the United States Extremist Crime Database (ECDB). *Terrorism and Political Violence*, *26*(2), 372–384.

Gans, H. (1979). *Deciding What's News: A Study of CBS Evening News, Newsweek and Time*. New York: Patheon Books.

Garland, D. (2008). On the concept of moral panic. *Crime, Media & Culture*, *4*(1), 9–30.

Gitlin, T. (1980). *The Whole World is Watching: Mass Media in the Making and Unmaking of the New Left*. Berkeley, CA: University of California Press.

Green, D. A. (2008). Suitable vehicles: Framing blame and justice when children kill a child. *Crime, Media, Culture*, *4*(2), 197–220.

Green, D. A. (2009). Feeding wolves: Punitiveness and culture. *European Journal of Criminology*, *6*(6), 517–536.

Hall, S., Critcher, C., Jefferson, T., Clarke, J., & Roberts, B. (1978). The social production of news. In C. Greer (Ed.), *Crime and Media: A Reader* (pp. 237–250). London: Routledge.

Held, V. (2012). *How Terrorism is Wrong: Morality and Political Violence*. New York: Oxford University Press.

Herman, E. S., & Chomsky, N. (1988). A propaganda model. In C. Greer (Ed.), *Crime and Media: A Reader* (pp. 32–43). London: Routledge.

Jewkes, Y. (2004). The construction of news. In C. Greer (Ed.), *Crime and Media: A Reader* (pp. 213–227). London: Routledge.

Johnston, D., & Schmitt, E. (2009). Little evidence of terror plot in base killings. *The New York Times*. Retrieved from http://www.nytimes.com/2009/11/08/us/08investigate.html.

Keinan, G., Sadeh, A., & Rosen, S. (2003). Attitudes and reactions to media coverage of terrorist acts. *Journal of Community Psychology*, *31*(2), 149–165.

Kellner, D. (2006). 9/11, spectacles of terror, and media manipulation: A critique of Jihadist and Bush media politics. *Critical Discourse Studies*, *1*(1), 41–64.

Kovaleski, S. F. (2012). Killers' families left to confront fear and shame. *The New York Times*. Retrieved from http://www.nytimes.com/2012/02/05/us/killers-families-left-to-confront-fear-and-shame.html.

Loseke, D. R. (2003). *Thinking about Social Problems: An Introduction to Constructionist Perspectives* (2nd edn.). New York: Aldine de Gruyter.

Manjoo, F. (2008). *True Enough: Learning to Live in a Post-Fact Society*. Hoboken, NJ: Wiley.

McKinley, J. C. (2009). She ran to gunfire, and ended it. *The New York Times*. Retrieved from http://www.nytimes.com/2009/11/07/us/07police.html.

Nacos, B. L., Bloch-Elkon, Y., & Shapiro, R. Y. (2007). Post-9/11 terrorism threats, news coverage, and public perceptions in the United States. *International Journal of Conflict and Violence*, *1*(2), 105–126.

Nagar, N. (2010). Who is afraid of the T-word? Labeling terror in the media coverage of political violence before and after 9/11. *Studies in Conflict & Terrorism*, *33*(6), 533–547.

Norris, P., Kern, M., & Just, M. (2003). Framing terrorism. In P. Norris, M. Kern, & M. Just (Eds.), *Framing Terrorism: The News Media, the Government and the Public* (pp. 3–23). New York: Routledge.

Overholser, G., & Jamieson, K. H. (2005). *The Press*. New York: Oxford University Press.

Rubin, J., & Smith, M. (2013). 'I am the shooter', Nidal Hasan tells Fort Hood court-martial. *CNN*. Retrieved from http://www.cnn.com/2013/08/06/justice/hasan-court-martial/index.html?hpt=hp_t2.

Sasson, T. (1995). Frame analysis. In C. Greer (Ed.), *Crime and Media: A Reader* (pp. 153–164). London: Routledge.

Schlesinger, P., Tumber, H., & Murdock, G. (1991). The media politics of crime and criminal justice. In C. Greer (Ed.), *Crime and Media: A Reader* (pp. 251–263). London: Routledge.

Schmid, A. P. (1989). Terrorism and the media: The ethics of publicity. *Terrorism and Political Violence, 1*(4), 539–565.

Segalla, M. (2017). Five decades of reporting terrorism: Has there been too little or too much coverage? *The Conversation.* Retrieved from https://theconversation.com/five-decades-of-reporting-terrorism-has-there-been-too-little-or-too-much-coverage-73882.

Shoshani, A., & Slone, M. (2008). The drama of media coverage of terrorism: Emotional and attitudinal impact on the audience. *Studies in Conflict & Terrorism, 31*(7), 627–640.

Simon, T., Goldberg, A., Aharonson-Daniel, L., Leykin, D., & Adini, B. (2014). Twitter in the cross fire — The use of social media in the Westgate Mall terror attack in Kenya. *PLOSOne, 9*(8). Retrieved from http://journals.plos.org/plosone/article/file?id=10.1371/journal.pone.0104136&type=printable.

Slone, M. (2000). Responses to media coverage of terrorism. *Journal of Conflict Resolution, 44*(4), 508–522.

Strozier, C. (2011). *Until the Fires Stopped Burning: 9/11 and New York City in the Words and Experiences of Survivors and Witnesses.* New York: Columbia University Press.

Thomas, P., & Ryan, J. (2009). Alleged Fort Hood shooter bought gun, despite ongoing terrorism investigation. *abcNews.* Retrieved from http://abcnews.go.com/Politics/fort-hood-shooter-obtained-weapon-ongoing-terrorism-investigation/story?id=9058803.

Thomas, W. I., & Thomas, D. S. (1928). *The Child in America.* UK: Knopf.

Wanta, W., & Hu, Y. (1993). The agenda-setting effects of international news coverage: An examination of differing news frames. *International Journal of Public Opinion Research, 5*(3), 250–264.

Wicks, R. H. (2006). Emotional response to collective action media frames about Islam and terrorism. *Journal of Media and Religion, 5*(4), 245–263.

Winter, J. P., & Eyal, C. H. (1981). Agenda-setting for the civil rights issue. In D. L. Protess, & M. L. McCombs (Eds.), *Agenda setting: Readings on Media, Public Opinion, and Policymaking* (pp. 101–107). Hillsdale, NJ: Erlbaum.

CHAPTER 22

Social Media Response after an Attack: Perspectives from the Jakarta Bombings

JONY EKO YULIANTO and JESSIE JANNY THENARIANTO

School of Psychology,
Universitas Ciputra, Indonesia

Introduction

24 May 2017 was a frightening day for Jakarta citizens. Two bombs exploded at Kampung Melayu Station in East Jakarta. The first explosion occurred at 9:00 p.m. Western Indonesian Time near a toilet, and the second explosion took place right in front of the Kampung Melayu bus terminal approximately five minutes later. The attack came two days after the explosion in Manchester and a day after the Indonesian government voiced their support towards the attack on the Islamic State of Iraq and Syria (ISIS) militants in Marawi, sparking the notion that the 2017 Jakarta bombing was related to ISIS.

Figure 22.1. The Brave Jakarta (ariefbhpy, 2016).

The 2017 Jakarta bombing was also characterised by the complexity of post-terror events on social media. Photographs of mutilated limbs spread across Twitter. This information went viral quickly, triggering a reaction of fear among social media users. However, a number of users brought up the hashtag #KamiTidakTakut (#WearenotAfraid), #JakartaBerani (#BraveJakarta) (see Figure 22.1), and #PrayforJakarta. President Joko Widodo also asked for the people to stay calm.

Similar pattern of netizen behaviour was seen in 2016 when a bomb exploded at Thamrin, Jakarta. Twitter users, for example, used the #PrayforJakarta hashtag after that attack. It was similar to the #PrayforParis hashtag used by netizens in France as a response to the Paris bombing, and the #PrayforBrussels hashtag that appeared after the explosions in Belgium. Twitter has become a popular choice for netizens because of its hashtag feature that allows similar information to be accessed through a single click. In addition, Twitter is a real-time social media platform (Hermida, 2013), which allows users to access the latest information.

Empirical studies of terrorism have expanded beyond the focus on pre- and during attacks, with post-attack situations being studied as well. For example, results from a recent study conducted by Colin *et al.* (2017) affirmed that social media is a platform that allows social interaction between its users during post-terror events. Experts also agree that social media posts can be used to predict people's psychological condition after an attack (for the case of Boko Haram, see Chiluwa & Adegoke, 2013).

What do Twitter users do in response to terror attacks? In a recent study that examined the Lee Rigby's murder in London in 2013, Innes *et al.* (2018) found that netizens exhibit the 10-Rs of post-attack social reaction in cyberspace, which consist of Reporting, Requesting, Responding, Recruiting, Risking, Retaliating, Rumoring, Remembering, Reheating, and Resiliencing. These 10 social reactions show that netizens interact and exchange information intensely.

The complexity of the online activities indicates that besides curative measures at the attack site, post-terror social media situation should also receive serious attention. This is essential considering that some groups, especially the younger generation, tend to depend on social media as their first reference when searching for news (Chew *et al.*, 2011). So far, media coverage tends to focus more on the situation at the attack location. Even though there have been news reports about the situation in social media, these reports tend to focus more on the hashtags that have emerged as trending topics. Although the situation on social media has been recognised as an important area that should be observed after attacks, further discussion on how practitioners and policymakers can respond to the developments on social media has not yet been extensively studied.

Using the events of the 2017 Jakarta bombing, this chapter seeks to highlight the challenges and opportunities that authorities may have to address in terms of the behaviour of social media users, especially after an attack. The key points in this chapter are not intended to be generalised to attacks in other locations, but rather as material for discussion that practitioners and policymakers should pay attention to.

Five Key Points/Challenges Practitioners and Policymakers Need to Be Aware of

(1) *Netizens' Act of Resistance Towards Terrorism*

In the last two years, each time a terrorist attack happens in Indonesia, #KamiTidakTakut immediately becomes a trending topic on social media. In the 2017 Jakarta bombing, it was used by approximately 100,000 netizens and appeared on the trending topic list on Twitter ("#PrayForJakarta, #KamiTidakTakut trend worldwide following bomb blast", 2017). Previously, in the 2016 Jakarta bombing, the same hashtag was also used by a large number of netizens. On the day of the attack, 14 January 2016, from 10:38 a.m. to 23:59 a.m. alone, there were around 180,000 tweets containing the hashtag (Brajawidagda *et al.*, 2016). In the same year, the hashtag also went viral after the suicide bombings in Solo, a city in Central Java province.

Each time #KamiTidakTakut becomes popular on social media, local and national news agencies rush to report it through their channels. Several times, major international news agencies also covered the hashtag's popularity in addition to news concerning the attack. However, the reports were only descriptive in nature. They only described the hashtag, how much it was tweeted, and that it was a defiant message from the citizens to the terrorists. The questions about why netizens post such defiant messages through social media or what purpose does it serves, have not been addressed.

Below are several tweets containing #kamitidaktakut posted online:

> *Oppose all forms of terrorism. We are not afraid because we are INDONESIA. #KamiTidakTakut* (Mustahid Anis, 2017).

> *Let's show those pathetic human beings responsible for the current terror in Jakarta that we are not afraid. Stay safe.* (@VVYND, 2016).

From the messages accompanying the hashtag, netizens directed defiant messages towards the terrorists even though they were not directly involved in the attack. In the 2016 Jakarta bombing, several tweets, which went viral after the attack, contained pictures that intended to show the terrorists that they have failed to scare Indonesians. One of the pictures showed a satay seller continuing making satay at the time of the attack, and not running away from it.

The netizens use the word "us" to show that they stand together and support each other. They form a collective voice online that they are not afraid of terrorist attacks. People refuse to be a victim of fear, and use #KamiTidakTakut to showcase an act of collective resistance and solidarity. This will build resilience within the community.

When a critical incident happens, there tends to be a focus on the direct loss, such as injured victims at the scene. What is often overlooked is the fact that besides the people at the scene of the incident, there is an online community who is affected as well. They also feel sad and angry about what has happened. Social media users are not just account usernames, but also individuals, civilians, human beings that have emotions. Previous studies have found that social media and blogs have been used to share emotions in disaster situations (Macias *et al.*, 2009; Neubaum *et al.*, 2014). For this reason, in times of crisis, such as terrorist attacks, more attention should be paid to the online community by communicating with them through their preferred channel: social media.

(2) *Hashtags are Not Enough*

#KamiTidakTakut and #PrayforJakarta were meant to show sympathy and courage in the face of terror. The #KamiTidakTakut hashtag was used by approximately 100,000 people and became a trending topic just hours after the explosion in Kampung Melayu. This shows that Twitter users in Indonesia had participated actively in reacting and showing solidarity towards a national incident. Up to this point, this online behavioural pattern has been found to be similar to the behaviour of users in other countries when an attack occurs. Paris, Brussels, and other cities that have experienced terrorist bombings saw voices of solidarity emerging from Twitter users around the world. This brings up the question: is the usage of hashtags effective in combatting terrorism?

The use of collective hashtags is a potential way to mobilise netizens online. However, it is hard to imagine that these digital movements will have the same effect in the real world. It is essential to note that the population of internet users in Indonesia is dominated by middle-class urban citizens (Puskakom, 2015). These individuals tend to engage in many conversations, moving from one topic to another very quickly. Hence, expressing support for such hashtags may not be reflective of how committed they are in terms of showing solidarity and support; what Twitter users show through their social media posts do not always represent what they think about the real world. This phenomenon is known as slacktivism.

Another observation is the shift in the use of the hashtag, which has taken on a "comedic" tone. After the hashtags #KamiTidakTakut and #PrayforJakarta, the next hashtags that appeared as a trending topic were #KamiNaksir ("We have a crush") and #PolisiGanteng (#HandsomePolice). This phenomenon emerged after several users uploaded photos of some handsome police officers helping the victims of the 2016 Jakarta attack.

The emergence of #KamiNaksir and #PolisiGanteng can be interpreted in two ways. First, netizens demonstrate the ability to manage a fearful situation by using comedy. Tense situations that suddenly become humorous are not a new phenomenon in the Indonesian Twitter community. Previously, there were several national criminal cases that were also imbued with a sense of humour, such as the House of Representatives (DPR) speaker Setya Novanto's corruption case. This shows that Twitter users in Indonesia have a tendency to look at a phenomenon with a different perspective. It also suggests that follow-up mechanisms are needed so that it does not turn into meaningless social movements.

Second, the online community did not empathise with the grief and suffering experienced by the victims. In other words, contrary to the findings of Eichstaedt *et al.* (2015), the empathetic narratives shown by Twitter users when responding to terror incidents cannot be entirely regarded as acts of resistance towards terrorism.

(3) *Beware of Misattribution*

Humans basically have the tendency to find out the causes of an event. In social psychology, this process is called attribution (Sahar, 2014). Through the process of attribution, humans may attempt to overcome the perceived uncertainty using heuristics.

The urgency of addressing misattribution is growing since patterns of misattribution has been found to be occurring on social media. Subasic and Berendts (2011) claimed that Twitter is a platform for citizen journalism. On Twitter, users not only create news, but also extend it with their own comments and interpretations. Misattribution may occur when Twitter users have a certain belief related to terrorist attacks, such as Islamophobia. In terrorism cases, simplifications and overgeneralisations of information on social media can easily occur, as Netizens began to formulate various possible explanations. The 2017 blast at Kampung Melayu took place only two days after the Manchester bombing and one day after the ISIS attack in the Philippines. As a result, people began to associate the few events as related; the attack was thought to be carried out by the same group — i.e., ISIS. In addition, the retweet button acted as a tool to spread the unverified information rapidly.

As Innes *et al.* (2018) found, both policymakers and practitioners should be concerned of netizens' inference-making reaction. The process of attribution by netizens can be very misleading and chaotic. In some cases, attribution contains stereotypical views that may trigger intergroup conflict in cyberspace. This is understandable considering that, in recent incidents, terrorism cases have been linked to the issue of religion and, as a result, the discourse that develops in society is not only related to the moral issues of terrorism itself, but also the association of a particular religion with terrorism.

Conway (2017) argued that this tendency of misattribution will not only happen to civilian netizens, but also to netizens who are law enforcement practitioners and policymakers. Thus, practitioners and policymakers are expected not to be caught in the cognitive tendency to overgeneralise and oversimplify a terrorist attack by linking one incident to another. An approach that can counteract this problem of misattribution is needed.

(4) *Unclear Division of Roles*

In Indonesia, the Indonesian National Police (POLRI) has the legal authority to deal with and combat terrorism. The agency has created a special task force known as Detachment 88. Since its establishment in 2003, Detachment 88 has played a significant role in countering terrorism in Indonesia. Several notable cases include the killing of

Noordin M. Top (one of the masterminds behind a number of attacks in Indonesia).

The Indonesian government also has other anti-terror units. The Indonesian National Police has the Satuan I Gegana, which performs counter-terrorism duties. The Indonesian Army, Indonesian Navy, and Indonesian Air Force all have their own respective anti-terror units. In addition to those already mentioned, the Indonesian government has established the National Counterterrorism Agency (BNPT) and National Intelligence Agency (BIN). However, the roles held by each of the agencies have not been clearly articulated to the public. The public may know the names of these agencies, heard of their activities in the media, but not the difference between them; especially in terms of role and authority. There is also the possibility that the units have overlapping responsibilities when it comes to combating terrorism. As a result, when a terrorist attack occurs, the lack of knowledge, combined with situations of high tension and anxiety, can make members of public confused as to which agencies should they turn to in order to obtain the information they are looking for.

In the case of the 2017 Jakarta bombing, several government agencies tweeted about the attack. The Jakarta Metropolitan Police Traffic Management Center's twitter account (TMCPoldaMetro, 2017) posted updates related to the situation at Kampung Melayu bus station, the location of the attack, stating that it started from 21:59 p.m. and ended at 01:41 a.m. the following day. At about 23:30 p.m., the Indonesian National Police Public Relations Division (@DivHumasPolri) posted a picture about what had happened. The National Counterterrorism Agency (BNPT) only came forth the next day, to ask netizens not to share "horrible content" from the explosion. A question then arises as to which agency is responsible to share information to netizens after terrorist attacks.

Just like the Indonesian National Police, BNPT also has the legal authority to conduct activities related to counter-terrorism, as stated in the Presidential Regulation No. 46/2010 on National Counterterrorism Agency. BNPT has the specific responsibility to develop counter-terrorism policies and coordinate other agencies to implement these policies. In other words, it can be argued that BNPT is the key agency in combating terrorism in Indonesia. Since BNPT is the spearhead of counter-terrorism, it is essential for the agency to create a strong presence on social media and address issues related to terrorism, especially attacks that have just happened.

(5) *Lack of Information Control*

Another point worth noting is the lack of information control on social media. During and after a terrorist attack, netizens who are at the location of the attack may go on social media to report what has happened. In the case of the 2017 Jakarta terror attack, Indonesian netizens posted about the situation and uploaded pictures of the attack. Other people who were not at the location could therefore get an overview about what was happening, including journalists who were then able to relay the information to the mass media. However, at the same time, photographs of the victims' scattered human body parts also went viral, spreading terror across the whole country. Hours after the major terrorist attack in Jakarta the previous year, false information about bombs at other locations have also spread across social media, causing panic and fear (Maulana, 2016). There was also information that the Indonesian police and military had engineered the attack (Adyatama, 2016).

False and inaccurate information tend to spread fast and easily during terrorist attacks. This is evident in other terrorist attacks, such as the Nairobi Westgate Mall attack and the murder of Lee Rigby in 2013. In a case study on the use of social media during the Westgate Mall attack, two tweets that claimed to contain photographs of the attackers were retweeted 106 times. However, the researchers found that the photographs were incorrect and depicted the Kenyan armed forces instead. The tweets were not removed until two days later (Simon *et al.*, 2014). In a case study on the social media responses after Lee Rigby's murder, netizens did what the researchers called "rumouring" — i.e., biased and inaccurate information from unknown sources was posted online. For example, details, such as the number of victims and the type of attack were found to be incorrect. In addition, the identity of the alleged killers appeared on social media before the information surfaced in the press (Innes *et al.*, 2018).

Netizens may accidentally disclose sensitive information during the attack by posting live updates since terrorists may have access to the media. Researchers who studied the 2008 Mumbai terrorist attack found that a proportion of the tweets posted contained crucial information about the authorities' movement that was potentially useful for the terrorist group to make decisions on their next moves and achieve their specific political agenda (Oh *et al.*, 2011). If this occurs during terrorist attacks, it may compromise the government's operational activity, and endanger hostages (if any) and civilians.

It is important to note that the government in Indonesia cannot control information on social media using advanced methods, such as tracking. These methods may impair the freedom of speech and generate low public accountability, resulting in low public trust (Oh *et al.*, 2011). Controlling information to make it work to the government's advantage while ensuring freedom of speech therefore presents itself as a challenge.

Key Approaches and Strategies that Practitioners and Policymakers Can Adopt

(1) *Hire Social Media Analysts*

If Indonesian people, especially the younger generation, like to use social media to express themselves, the government should be responsive by paying more attention to developments on social media. One of the strategies the government can adopt is to create "social media analyst" positions within their agencies.

Social media analyst is a job position that did not exist a decade ago. It appeared and grew in popularity along with the growth of social media. Social media analysts are responsible for maintaining and enhancing an organisation's presence on social media (Sponder, 2011); social media analysts in government agencies will work to create and maintain a strong social media presence of their agencies. For example, they can handle online communications between the agency and netizens. According to Kavanaugh *et al.* (2012), in order to use social media effectively, the government should determine what platform they should use to communicate effectively with netizens. They should also think of how messages can be effectively delivered to netizens, and what content would be suitable for the netizens.

Social media analysts should also work to monitor trends that are relevant to the agency on social media. If a certain anti-terror issue is found to be gaining prominence rapidly, social media analysts should design ways to make use of the issue in the favour of the agency's mission. For example, if the agency has the mission to protect citizens and there is a heated subject on safety during terrorist attacks, they can educate the public about ways to stay safe during such crises. They can create informative and catchy social media posts that contain simple steps to stay safe.

(2) *Importance of the National Leader's Presence*

President Joko Widodo is known for visiting problematic or critical locations to directly inspect the situation. Widely known as *blusukan* (an impromptu visit), these visits allow him to understand the problem straight from the grassroots. Shortly after the explosion in Kampung Melayu, Jokowi visited the explosion site (Hidayat, 2017). However, Jokowi does not only interact with the citizens on-site. During the initial press conference, Joko Widodo told his citizens not to be afraid and intimidated by the terrorists (Saputro, 2017). At the time of the attack in Kampung Melayu, for example, Jokowi through the State Secretariat also reportedly tweeted several messages in order to calm his followers.

Through his actions, President Joko Widodo illustrates how influential national figures can "connect" the hashtag used in cyberspace to the real world. The actions of these influential national figures provide a straightforward means of denouncing terrorism both in the real and virtual worlds. In addition, the Head of State can use his official Twitter account as a way to address the public as well as reassure them about their safety concerns. National leaders may also cooperate with the relevant authorities to simultaneously declare resistance against terrorism by denouncing the attack.

Thus, the leader and his officials can act as a social reference for Twitter users to follow in showing their negative stances towards attacks in their country. Leaders will also be able to quickly clarify hoaxes or rumours that are likely to spread in the aftermath of the attack. However, in order to create a conducive culture for members of public to follow, the government has to first build relationships with the public way before an attack happens so that the people trust them, and will be more likely to listen to what they say during an attack.

(3) *The Importance of Mastering the Ethnographical View*

Several studies have found that terrorism is a topic that is easily linked to religious motives. Furthermore, some people implicitly think that terrorism is strongly related to a certain religious affiliation. Such views promote overgeneralisation and the tendency to exhibit cognitive bias. To tackle this issue, Conway (2017) suggested that practitioners should use a virtual ethnographic approach in order to be able to assess situations, which are observed on the Internet, in a broad and cautious fashion. The implementation of this virtual ethnographic approach can be carried out in the following ways.

- *Widen.* That is, expanding beyond the view that the threat of terrorism is always associated with the concept of jihad. Although jihad has been viewed as the primary driver that determines one's choice to become a terrorist (Milla, 2009), it should be noted that not all terrorist acts are solely motivated by the concept of jihad. In recent literature on the study of terrorism in Indonesia, it has been found that terrorist acts can also be caused by the need to "exist", economic reasons, and so on (Harb & Fisher, 2013; Kruglanski, 2013; Milla *et al.*, 2013; Putra & Sukabdi, 2013). The ability to specifically recognise an antecedent of a terror incident (such as environmental factors, personal factors) will help practitioners to clarify and understand the incident. On the contrary, misidentifying antecedents may render social interventions done by practitioners and policymakers ineffective. Another advantage of knowing the antecedents of a terror incident is that it allows practitioners and policymakers to formulate contextual strategies. For example, the Indonesian government's knowledge of Telegram, an instant messaging app, as a platform used by terrorists to spread radical views, led to the decision to block the app.

- *Compare*. Practitioners and policymakers need to conduct various comparative studies, not only on ideologies, but also groups, countries, languages, and other social media platforms. By expanding the focus and study of terrorism in various areas, we will be able to have a deeper understanding of context. The advantage of comparing is that policymakers and practitioners will not be hasty in making strategic and pragmatic decisions.
- *Deepen*. That is, the need to deepen analyses by using online-based interview methods. These methods will enable practitioners to understand the specific context of an event by getting directly in touch with Twitter users and treating them as the main subject in the generation of scientific knowledge.
- *Upscale*. Stakeholders should seek to collect large amounts of data. The era of technology and information allows for access to big data. Moreover, terrorism cases have always captured the world's attention and never escaped the watchful eye of the world's major media. Related tweets can be regarded as a database, and analysed as raw data that reflects social behaviour of netizens.
- *Outreach*. That is, collaborate with other related fields of study. The field of terrorism is not only studied by political science or sociology, but also social psychology, computer science, literature, cultural sciences, and even mathematics. The collaboration of multidisciplinary practitioners will enable a more comprehensive process of generating knowledge.

(4) *Increasing Information Control During Terrorist Attacks*

The Indonesian government cannot prevent and resist public post-attack social media participation. However, a strategy should be implemented to manage the public's social media participation as well as ensure information control at the same time. The government agency, which is directly involved with the issue, should actively monitor social media posts related to the attack, during and after the incident. The agency can monitor posts by searching for relevant keywords, hashtags, and posts originating from a certain radius of the attack. This will allow them to know and understand public opinions, gain information about the attack, and detect circulating rumours. In Indonesia, there is an institution responsible for communication and information affairs, the Ministry of Communication and Information, which plays the role of detecting hoaxes related to terrorist attacks.

The government should educate the public through all communication channels, especially official social media accounts, about the risks of sharing sensitive information and spreading rumours related to terrorist attacks. During an attack, the counter-terrorism government agency should identify and analyse the terrorist's agenda, as soon as possible, based on available intelligence and social media reports. By identifying the agenda, the government may know what kind of information would be sensitive (e.g., information related to the ongoing attack), and persuade the netizens not to post such information publicly. Through these education efforts, it will then raise awareness in netizens about the etiquettes of sharing information on social media during and after terrorist attacks.

Updates about the attack should be shared as soon as possible in order to address rumours that might be circulating. Credible information published through official accounts will be able to manage the public's anxiety in times of crisis. Netizens should also be notified to proactively check and compare information regarding the terrorist attack that they may come across on social media with the official social media posts from the government. If a certain account is posting or questioning unverified information, the government should verify and publicly reply them, so that other netizens may learn about the actual facts. This practice has already been done by Airmin, the Indonesian Air Force Twitter admin, who engages followers by replying questions in a friendly but informative manner. Authorities should also ask netizens to repost or retweet their official posts by simply adding "Please repost/retweet" at the end of the post, in order to reach more people other than their direct followers.

Conclusion

As discussed within the chapter, it can be concluded that practitioners and policymakers need to pay attention to the social media responses after an attack. Taking two attacks in Indonesia as references, this chapter showcases the complex dynamics of information sharing among Indonesian netizens on Twitter. It is worth mentioning that policymakers and practitioners should also pay attention to other social media platforms.

References

#PrayForJakarta, #KamiTidakTakut trend worldwide following bomb blast (2017). *The Jakarta Post*. Retrieved from http://www.thejakartapost.com/news/2017/05/25/prayforjakarta-kamitidaktakut-trend-worldwide-following-bomb-blast.html.

Adyatama, E. (2016). Polri buru penyebar berita bohong terorisme di media social. *Tempo*. Retrieved from https://nasional.tempo.co/read/736773/polri-buru-penyebar-berita-bohong-terorisme-di-media-sosial.

ariefbhpy (2016). *JAKARTA BERANI #KamiTidakTakut* [Digital image]. Retrieved from https://twitter.com/ariefbhpy/status/687536506303463424.

Brajawidagda, U., Reddick, C. G., & Chatfield, A. T. (2016). Social media and urban resilience: A case study of the 2016 Jakarta terror attack. In *Proceedings of the 17th International Digital Government Research Conference on Digital Government Research* (pp. 445–454). New York: ACM.

Chew, H. E., LaRose, R., Steinfeld, C., & Velasquez, A. (2011). The use of online social media networking by rural youth and its effect on community attachment. *Information, Communication, & Society*, *14*(5), 726–747.

Chiluwa, I., & Adegoke, A. (2013). Twittering Boko Haram uprising in Nigeria: Investigating pragmatics acts in the social media. *Africa Today*, *59*(3), 83–102.

Colin, R., Innes, M., Preece, A., & Rogers, D. (2017). After Woolwich: Analyzing open source communications to understand the interactive and multipolar dynamics of the arc of conflict. *British Journal of Criminology*, *58*(2), 434–454.

Conway, M. (2017). Determining the role of the internet in violent extremism and terrorism: Six suggestions for progressing research, *Studies in Conflict and Terrorism, 40*(1), 77–98.

DivHumasPolri (2017). *Breaking News. Tlh trjd ledakan pd hari Rabu, 24 Mei 2017 di Kamp. Melayu, Jak-Tim pd pukul 21.00 dan pukul 21.05. ... https://t.co/thThAaNHr4* [Tweet]. Retrieved from https://twitter.com/DivHumasPolri/status/867417647381479424.

Eichstaedt, J. C., Schwartz, H. A., Kern, M. L., Park, G., Labarthe, D. R., Merchant, R. M., *et al.* (2015). Psychological language on Twitter predicts county-level heart disease mortality. *Psychological Science*, *26*(2), 159–169.

Harb, C., & Fischer, R. (2013). Terrorism and jihad in Indonesia: Questions and possible ways forward. *Asian Journal of Social Psychology*, *16*(2), 117–122.

Hermida, A. (2013). #JOURNALISM: Reconfiguring journalism research about Twitter, one tweet at a time. *Digital Journalism*, *1*(3), 295–313.

Hidayat, A. (2017). Raut sedih nampak di wajah Jokowi-JK saat kunjungi TKP bom Kampung Melayu. *Oke Zone News*. Retrieved from https://news.okezone.com/read/2017/05/25/337/1700003/raut-sedih-nampak-di-wajah-jokowi-jk-saat-kunjungi-tkp-bom-kampung-melayu.

Innes, M., Roberts, C., Preece, A., & Rogers, D. (2018). Ten "Rs" of social reaction: Using social media to analyse the "post-event" impacts of the murder of Lee Rigby. *Terrorism and Political Violence*, *30*(3), 454–474.

Kavanaugh, A. L., Fox, E. A., Sheetz, S. D., Yang, S., Li, L. T., Shoemaker, D. J., & Xie, L. (2012). Social media use by government: From the routine to the critical. *Government Information Quarterly*, *29*(4), 480–491.

Kruglanski, A. W. (2013). Psychological insight into Indonesian Islamic terrorism: The what, the how, and the why of violent extremism. *Asian Journal of Social Psychology*, *16*(2), 112–116.

Macias, W., Hilyard, K., & Freimuth, V. (2009). Blog functions as risk and crisis communication during Hurricane Katrina. *Journal of Computer-Mediated Communication*, *15*(1), 1–31.

Maulana, A. (2016). Pasca ledakan bom Sarinah, waspadai pesan hoax berantai. *CNN Indonesia*. Retrieved from https://www.cnnindonesia.

com/teknologi/20160114150903-185-104329/pasca-ledakan-bom-sarinah-waspadai-pesan-hoax-berantai.

Milla, M. N. (2009). Dinamika psikologis perilaku terorisme: Identitas dan pengambilan keputusan jihad di luar wilayah konflik pada terpidana kasus bom Bali di Indonesia. Doctoral Dissertation. Indonesia: Universitas Gadjah Mada.

Milla, M. N., Faturochman, & Ancok, D. (2013). The impact of leader-follower interactions on the radicalization of terrorist: A case study of the Bali bombers. *Asian Journal of Social Psychology*, 16(2), 92–100.

MustahidAnis (2017). Lawan segala bentuk terorisme. Kami tidak takut karena kami INDONESIA. *#KamiTidakTakut* [Tweet]. Retrieved from https://twitter.com/MustahidAnis/status/867530054812581888.

Neubaum, G., Rösner, L., Rosenthal-von der Pütten, A. M., & Krämer, N. C. (2014). Psychosocial functions of social media usage in a disaster situation: A multi-methodological approach. *Computers in Human Behaviour*, *34*, 28–38.

Oh, O., Agrawal, M., & Rao, H. R. (2011). Information control and terrorism: Tracking the Mumbai terrorist attack through twitter. *Information Systems Frontiers*, *13*(1), 33–43.

Polisi Indonesia (2016). #PrayForJakarta #KamiTidakTakut mari bersatu lawan terorisme, berikan informasi Anda ke kantor kepolisian terdekat [Digital image]. Retrieved from https://twitter.com/Polisi_R1/status/687514716608987137.

Puskakom (2015). Profil pengguna internet Indonesia 2014. Jakarta: Asosiasi Penyelenggara Jasa Internet.

Putra, I. E., & Sukabdi, Z. A. (2013). Basic concepts and reasons behind the emergence of religious terror activities in Indonesia: An inside view. *Asian Journal of Social Psychology*, *16*(2), 83–91.

Sahar, G. (2014). On the importance of Attribution Theory in Political Psychology. *Social and Personality Psychology Compass*, *8*(5), 229–249.

Saputro, I. (2017). Ini pernyataan resmi presiden Jokowi terkait bom bunuh diri di Kampung Melayu. *Tribun News*. Retrieved from http://www.tribunnews.com/nasional/2017/05/25/ini-pernyataan-resmi-presiden-jokowi-terkait-bom-bunuh-diri-di-kampung-melayu.

Simon, T., Goldberg, A., Aharonson-Daniel, L., Leykin, D., & Adini, B. (2014). Twitter in the cross fire — The use of social media in the Westgate Mall terror attack in Kenya. *PLOS ONE*, *9*(8).

Sponder, M. (2011). *Social Media Analytics: Effective Tools for Building, Interpreting, and Using Metrics*. New York: McGraw Hills.

Subasic, I., & Berendt, B. (2011). Peddling or creating?: Investigating the role of Twitter in news reporting. Retrieved from http://people.cs.kuleuven.be/~bettina.berendt/Papers/subasic_berendt_2011.pdf.

TMCPoldaMetro (2017). 21:59 Imbas penanganan ledakan di Kampung Melayu, Casablanca arah ke Pondok Bambu lalin padat [Tweet]. Retrieved from https://twitter.com/TMCPoldaMetro/status/867395045241966592.

VVYND (2016). #KamiTidakTakut Let's show those pathetic human beings responsible for the current terror in Jakarta that we are not afraid. Stay safe [Tweet]. Retrieved from https://twitter.com/VVYND/status/687511542129033216.

CHAPTER 23

Fake News After a Terror Attack: Psychological Vulnerabilities Exploited by Fake News Creators

KEN CHEN XINGYU

Home Team Behavioural Sciences Centre, Ministry of Home Affairs, Singapore

Introduction

Fake news became a prominent topic following the Las Vegas shooting on 1 October 2017. Before the authorities identified the shooter as Stephen Paddock, there was a surge in fake news and false claims about the incident online. Fake news creators were able to manipulate Facebook and Google's algorithms into promoting fake stories which claimed that the shooter was a Democrat linked to the Antifa[1] (Levin, 2017). Even the Islamic State of Iraq and Syria (ISIS) claimed that Paddock had converted to Islam and that he was a soldier of the caliphate, a claim which investigators found no

[1]Antifa is short for anti-fascists, this term is used to define a broad group of people with left/far-left beliefs. Groups associated with this movement are known to incite violence during their protests.

evidence for (Moore, 2017). While the shooter's motivations have remained unknown as of the writing of this chapter, these claims can be considered as fake news especially when there was no evidence available at that time for anyone to link the shooter to either ISIS or the Antifa movement.

The Las Vegas shooting reflected a grim trend of fake news creators hijacking tragedies to spread fake news to support their agendas. Such actions by fake news creators, especially after a terror attack, often result in real-world consequences, sowing discord in society or in some cases, causing financial losses. "Fake news" has been used as a broad term to describe the entire phenomenon of problematic information, with competing definitions coined by different scholars. As a result, it is often heavily misused. However, for this chapter, fake news will be used to refer to inaccurate, misleading, inappropriately attributed, or altogether fabricated information that is presented as accurate information.

This chapter will identify five psychological vulnerabilities exploited by fake news creators in the aftermath of a violent extremist attack, and discuss ways to disrupt such tactics. The psychological vulnerabilities discussed are: arousal of high emotional states, perceptions of ingroup-outgroup hostility, perceived homophily, availability heuristic, and prosocial behaviour.

Psychological Vulnerabilities

High-arousal Emotional States

One common tactic used by fake news creators to garner attention is to induce high-arousal emotional states such as anger or fear in their readers. Making use of situations such as wars and terror attacks which often result in strong negative feelings (Khaldarova & Pantti, 2016; Sunstein, 2014) and high-arousal emotional states such as fear, fake news creators can induce people to believe in the stories that they fabricated (Fessler *et al.*, 2014; Sunstein, 2014). In a separate study, emotional arousal has also been shown to boost the sharing of news content (Berger, 2011). These studies lend support to the link between emotion-laden information and virality.

It is also suggested that knowing how to agitate emotions is an easy way to propagate fake news and encourage desired behaviours

(Gneezy & Imas, 2014; Holiday, 2013). If fake news creators know about the fears and hopes of their target audiences, it would be simpler to spread propaganda or misinformation through messages designed to elicit a strong emotional reaction.

The Westminster attack[2] demonstrated that fake news can go viral by riding on outrage. After the attack, an image of a Muslim woman on the phone was circulated with a false claim that she was callously ignoring the victims on the bridge. As a result, the photo received thousands of retweets and fuelled an Islamophobic backlash by many from the far-right, many of whom used that image to support their rhetoric against Muslims (Mezzofiore, 2017). However, in reality, the picture was actually taken out of context, and there were other photos which showed that she was visibly distressed.

To understand the dynamics behind this tactic, studying the virality of online content is relevant. It is found that content that evokes high-arousal emotions such as anger, awe, and anxiety are more likely to go viral as compared to low-arousal emotions such as sadness or contentment (Berger & Milkman, 2012; Guerini & Staiano, 2015; Heimbach & Hinz, 2016). Emotions have also been known to play a role in triggering a set of responses in individuals, enabling them to decide how to address the problems that they encounter (Lerner *et al.*, 2015). It follows that creating stories that arouse fear or anger can trigger people to change their attitudes towards certain policies (Lerner *et al.*, 2003), and increase the sharing of content (Berger, 2011). Therefore, arousal of heightened emotions in people could lead to widespread circulation of fake news and increasingly polarised attitudes in society after an attack.

Perception of Existing Ingroup–Outgroup Hostilities

There is a trend that fake news tends to highlight certain attributes of the assailant's social identity such as race, religion, political affiliation, or ideology after a terror attack. One of the reasons for

[2]On 22 March 2017, a terrorist attack took place in the vicinity of the Palace of Westminster in London. The assailant, Khalid Masood, drove a car into pedestrians, resulting in six dead (including the perpetrator) and more than 50 injured.

doing so is to reinforce existing ingroup–outgroup hostilities in societies, as they serve as fertile grounds for fake news to spread. As such, fake news creators are able to attract the attention of hostile groups, as they would be more motivated to believe in the negative portrayals of their outgroup, regardless of the authenticity of the information.

The Las Vegas shooting illustrated how fake news creators leveraged on the incident to demonise their outgroups by alleging that the shooter was linked to liberals. Far-right websites such as Infowars and YourNewsWire.com claimed that the shooter, Stephen Paddock, was connected to the Antifa or liberals (Spencer, 2017). YourNewsWire.com published pictures of a Facebook page pretending to be Antifa as proof that the shooter was connected to Antifa. The fake Facebook page claimed responsibility for the attack, stating the shooter's intention was to murder supporters of the Trump administration (Levin, 2017). While there was no evidence for such claims, it reflected how different parties can stir up tensions due to trumped-up charges and disseminate their messages to a wider audience.

From an intergroup threat theory perspective, one common response by people who perceived that their social identity is threatened is to engage in hostility towards the group related to the source of the threat (Stephan *et al.*, 2009). After a terror attack, it is common to witness hostility being generated online through spreading false rumours, expressing hate and calling for tougher policies to be enacted against a group. This hostility can be exacerbated by existing ingroup–outgroup biases in a society which can further drive the transmission of false information.

Perceived Homophily

In the fields of advertising, marketers have long recognised that people are more likely to be influenced by a message coming from someone whom they feel a strong sense of similarity to (Belch & Belch, 2009). For example, regular-looking people are often portrayed using the advertised products in commercials that attempt to connect with the average consumers. This perceived homophily, or how similar the targeted audience is to the source in terms of age, gender, education, and social status, reduces the need to engage in greater cognitive deliberation on the messages presented (Boutyline & Willer, 2017; Nekmat, 2012). It follows that a message source tends to be more persuasive if it is perceived to share common values or experiences with the recipient.

Knowing that an audience is receptive to messages from sources with perceived homophily provides a means to exploit it. Recent trends indicate that fake news creators tend to mislead people about their identity (Berghel, 2017). It is achieved by fabricating personal details such as nationality or political affiliation on their social media accounts which are used to share fake news.

This was demonstrated in the aftermath of the Westminster attack, in which a Twitter bot linked to a Russian-based Internet Research Agency[3] was responsible for misrepresenting the photo of the Muslim woman, as mentioned in the previous example. The account, known as @SouthLoneStar, posed as an American conservative, with a profile picture of a bearded man in a cowboy hat and a biography claiming that the user was a "proud TEXAN and AMERICAN patriot" (Hern, 2017). After the attack, the account tweeted: "Muslim woman pays no mind to the terror attack, casually walks by a dying man while checking phone #PrayForLondon #Westminster #BanIslam", and it was later discovered that the account had been tweeting anti-Islam posts on multiple occasions, including the Manchester arena attack before it was shut down by Twitter (Burgess, 2017).

Researchers studying how individuals process persuasive messages pointed out that displaying certain features regarding the source of message can alter attitudes by increasing the audience's confidence in the information presented. Simple cues creating a sense of perceived similarity are more likely to convince people as they

---

[3]The Internet Research Agency is a Russian company based in Saint Petersburg. It was known for employing trolls to create pro-Kremlin propaganda using fake identities in order to create the illusion of an army of supporters (Chen, 2015).

function as pieces of evidence that are relevant to the topic they are concerned with (Brinol & Petty, 2009). In this case, conservative Americans might perceive the Russian-based @SouthLoneStar account to be familiar, and in turn believe the tweets posed by the account, simply because it had the appearance of an account belonging to an American with conservative values.

Availability Heuristic

A recent development in the dissemination of fake news is the emergence of social bots or networks of social media accounts that are partially or fully automated, capable of pushing fake news into prominence by tweeting or sharing the same content at a volume and frequency beyond what is humanly possible. There are many instances where the usage of social bots have been effective in shaping public opinion by drowning out the opposition (Ferrara *et al.*, 2016).

The usage of social bots to incite anti-Islam sentiments has been observed in the context of terror attacks. One example is the Quebec mosque shooting on 29 January 2017, where an army of bots and right-wing commentators managed to distort the incident and spin an anti-Muslim narrative out of this attack. The Daily Dot reported that bots were involved in promoting fabricated details about the attacker, claiming that he was a Syrian refugee (Cameron, 2017). The spread of fake news was worsened when right-wing commentators such as Pamela Geller and Richard Spencer also became involved in parroting false claims that the attacker was Muslim, further pushing the false information into greater prominence (Cameron, 2017).

Moreover, there are indications that prior and repeated exposure to fake news can create an illusion of truth in which repetition of the same piece of information increases its perceived level of accuracy (Pennycook *et al.*, 2017). In fact, in the 2016 U.S. elections, researchers have found that over half of those who recalled seeing fake news stories believed that those fake news stories were accurate (Allcott & Gentzkow, 2017).

One psychological explanation for the efficacy of this tactic is the availability heuristic which refers to a cognitive mental shortcut that relies on immediate examples surfaced in an individual's mind when they evaluate a topic (Tversky & Kahneman, 1973). Given that people may attend to information that is immediate and easily accessible to them, it creates an opening for fake news creators to leverage on this effect by pushing their messages into prominence to their audience using sheer computational force.

Prosocial Behaviour

After a crisis, there is usually an outpouring of altruism which is facilitated by social media. People on social media engage in prosocial behaviours such as helping families and friends find missing persons or organising donations. However, there have been cases of opportunistic fake news creators exploiting such prosocial behaviours for their own gains.

For example, fraudsters took advantage of the recent attacks like the Manchester arena attack, London Bridge attack, and Westminster attack to create fake donation appeals on JustGiving, an online fundraising platform (Baynes, 2017; "Manchester attack: Ensuring donations get to victims", 2017; Moyes, 2017). In the case of the Westminster attack, donors became suspicious of a JustGiving fundraising page as the administrator of the page shared the same name as another person who was convicted of fraud in 2013 (Moyes, 2017). The administrator later changed his username many times after questions were raised, which then prompted owners of the website to intervene, so as to ensure that money donated to the victims did not end up in the wrong hands (Diebelius, 2017; Moyes, 2017). There have been fake fundraising campaigns popping out after various terror attacks, which indicates that fake news creators are making use of the wave of generosity to their benefit.

The motivation to create fake news can also be non-monetary. While social media has been used to help people find their loved ones in the aftermath of attacks or disasters, trolls have been found to post fake missing persons information on social media platforms after an attack (i.e., the 2017 Manchester arena attack) for their own satisfaction or to seek attention (Titcomb, 2017). While the intentions of such antics are contestable, it can definitely hinder search and rescue efforts after an attack.

Implications

In the previous section, the purpose of understanding the psychological vulnerabilities is to frame our understanding of how societies can best counter the pernicious effects of fake news in the aftermath of a terror attack. This section will look at solutions to reduce the psychological vulnerabilities of individuals to fake news.

Emotional Scepticism

In light of the recent trend of fake news, Craig Silverman, a media editor for Buzzfeed and fake news researcher, argued that the public need to practice emotional scepticism ("The Rise and Fall of Fake News", 2017; Waldrop, 2017). For Singapore, the Media Literacy Council has been reaching out to communities to promote cyber-wellness such as sharing tips with the public on how they can better navigate the online space. Some tips include stopping and thinking about the implications of posting what one intends to post, especially when one is experiencing strong emotions (Media Literacy Council, n.d.). The rationale is that urging people to slow down and be sceptical of their emotional reactions to the news could help reduce the spread of fake news (Waldrop, 2017).

There are some techniques to dissipate emotions; the public can be educated to either pause and wait for more information or be aware of their response and think about the news from a different angle. These techniques are supported by a strong weight of evidence in psychology which indicates that humans revert to baseline emotional states over time and that a 10-minute delay can lessen the effect of emotions on decision-making (Gneezy & Imas, 2014; Lerner *et al.*, 2015).

Using reappraisal techniques such as thinking about a topic in a cold and detached manner has shown promising results in terms of its effects on decision-making. Halperin *et al.* (2013) studied the responses of Israelis to a Palestinian bid for United Nations recognition and found that participants trained in cognitive reappraisal showed greater support for conciliatory policies and lesser support for aggressive policies towards Palestinians, as compared to participants in a control condition. It follows that practising behaviours which can reduce emotional arousal could act as a defence against the influence of emotionally-charged fake news.

Building Intergroup Contact

Given that existing ingroup–outgroup hostilities in society can fuel the spread of fake news, efforts to pre-empt and mitigate potential communal tensions can act as a protective factor to buffer the effects of fake news on social cohesion after a terror attack. In Singapore, the Inter-Racial and Religious Confidence Circles (IRCCs) is one avenue through which networks of trust are formed between people of different races and religious groups (Latif, 2011). The IRCCs help to promote racial and religious harmony at the local level and promote social cohesion. Given that fake news has the potential to weaken social cohesion after a terror attack, building and deepening of intergroup contact are instrumental in preventing terrorists and those who seek to polarise society through fake news from reaching their objectives.

Furthermore, there is evidence showing that positive experiences with outgroup members can help with not just improving attitudes towards the outgroups but also act as a buffer against hostility towards them. An experiment on the effects of news about terrorism perpetrated by ISIS showed that these news increased participants' fear of terrorism and resulted in hostile perceptions toward Muslims in general (von Sikorski *et al.*, 2017). However, the researchers found no such relationship between fear of terrorism and hostile perceptions towards Muslims for people with positive prior experiences with Muslims. This suggests that people with positive prior experiences with Muslims are capable of differentiating between Muslims and jihadi terrorists. Therefore, fostering positive intergroup contact acts as a strong protective factor against fake news that seeks to exarcebate existing social tensions.

Priming Scepticism

Inducing a state of healthy scepticism in individuals can counter the effects of misinformation (Chan *et al.*, 2017). Given that fake news creators are constantly devising techniques to disguise their identity, it might not be possible or effective to educate the public about all the techniques used. However, if people are encouraged to be sceptical and fact-check information, it could help them to better detect fake news.

There are a variety of ways to promote healthy scepticism. One method is through behavioural nudging. The rationale for a behavioural approach is that the main transmission mechanism of fake news is through people's behaviours online. In a collaboration between Reddit and the Massachusetts Institute of Technology, researchers encourage users to fact-check by using a series of behavioural nudges such as posting a sticky comment telling people to fact-check news stories they encounter (Matias, 2017). They found that prompting people to fact-check potentially misleading or sensationalist stories has led to the posts being pushed down the page. In addition, people engaged in fact-checking behaviour by posting evidence to debunk the news in the comments sections. It has appeared that if people are primed to be sceptical of incoming information, they would be more likely to engage in fact-checking behaviour.

Building Credible Sources of Information

Fake news tends to spread when certain groups of people do not trust the media (Guess *et al.*, 2017), creating an audience for fake news creators to spread their messages to. The cases of the Quebec shooting and the Las Vegas shooting showed how far-right commentators were able to tap on polarisations in society to hijack the narrative. They can dominate the conversation by creating and spreading false information before the relevant authorities release the truth.

Combatting the spread of fake news means that there is a need to look for ways to maintain a healthy information ecosystem. Hence, building credible sources of information that people can turn to during a terror attack is one way to defend against the spread of fake news. This means that governments should be ready during peacetime to plan and prepare for crisis communications which is a critical and necessary step to fulfil the informational needs of the public as well as to combat fake news (Tan *et al.*, 2017).

During a crisis, consistent messages are more likely to be noticed, heard, and trusted over inconsistent messages (Chess & Clarke, 2007; Robinson & Newstetter, 2003). Hence, being prepared to respond to fake news after an attack entails training, preparing messages, and coordinating national leaders, public institutions, religious leaders, and experts in sending out consistent messages of solidarity after an attack.

Additionally, media agencies should practise extra caution in their reporting of news on terrorism, as it might further escalate intergroup tensions if one is not careful enough. For example, news coverage on terror attacks should refrain from sensationalising the attack especially along the lines of religion, race, or ethnicity as it could create unnecessary fear, hostility, or panic in the public (Tan *et al.*, 2017; von Sikorski *et al.*, 2017).

Eliminating Abuses of Technology by Fake News Creators

Creating a healthy information ecosystem also involves weeding out fake news creators. Given the fact that there is a trend of spreading fake news through automated means such as social bots or by manipulating search algorithms, it is important to prevent fake news creators from abusing these technologies either through legal or technological means.

Many countries have been considering the use of legislation to combat fake news. One of them is Germany who had recently passed a law which entails fining social media companies if they fail to remove any illegal content such as hate speech or disinformation posted by users within 24 hours (Evans, 2017).

For technological means, one approach of preventing fake news creators from abusing technology is through spam detection. For example, Facebook has developed ways to identify repeated posting of the same content, enabling them to take action against more than 30,000 fake accounts in France during the recent French elections (Weedon *et al.*, 2017). Similarly, Twitter has been employing machine learning to scan tweets for spam-like patterns (Dwoskin, 2017).

Another approach is through detecting and weeding out fake websites. For example, Google has cut off advertising revenue to websites with clearly spoofed domains (e.g., FoxNews123.au) that have posed as an official website. Google was even more motivated to undertake such measures when their business interests were compromised after brands started pulling out their advertising money when they discovered that the Google algorithms had placed them on extremist sites (Rath, 2017).

It should be noted that neither laws nor technology can be a silver bullet for combating fake news. Fake news creators will adapt and improvise new ways to spread fake news. Nevertheless, solutions that can reduce exposure to unreliable or suspicious sources of information should be put in place as they can lessen the menace of the repercussions of fake news.

Conclusion

This chapter has endeavoured to outline five psychological vulnerabilities that fake news creators exploit to propagate their messages after a terror attack. The implications for practitioners and policymakers have been explored. In the future, fake news creators will be more creative at spreading misinformation after an attack, and they would use new technologies to deceive people. Nevertheless, there is still reason to be hopeful; societies are not entirely at the mercy of fake news creators, as they can take steps to mitigate the effects of fake news. A healthy scepticism in media consumers combined with the efforts by governments, technology companies, and media outlets, can diminish the worst effects of fake news and prevent it from escalating social tensions.

Acknowledgement

The views expressed in this chapter are the author's only and do not represent the official position or view of the Ministry of Home Affairs, Singapore.

References

Allcott, H., & Gentzkow, M. (2017). Social media and fake news in the 2016 election. *Journal of Economic Perspectives*, *31*(2), 211–236.

Baynes, C. (2017). London Bridge terror attack: Crooks set up fake JustGiving funds in sick bid for cash. *London Evening Standard*. Retrieved from https://www.standard.co.uk/news/london/london-bridge-terror-attack-crooks-set-up-fake-funds-in-sick-bid-for-cash-a3558836.html.

Belch, G. E., & Belch, M. A. (2009). Source, message, and channel factors. In G. E. Belch, & M. A. Belch (Eds.), *Advertising and Promotion: An Integrated Marketing Communications Perspective* (pp. 174–205). New York: McGraw-Hill/Irwin.

Berger, J. (2011). Arousal increases social transmission of information. *Psychological Science*, *22*(7), 891–893.

Berger, J., & Milkman, K. L. (2012). What makes online content viral? *Journal of Marketing Research*, *49*(2), 192–205.

Berghel, H. (2017). Lies, damn lies, and fake news. *Computer*, *50*(2), 80–85.

Boutyline, A., & Willer, R. (2017). The social structure of political echo chambers: Variation in ideological homophily in online networks. *Political Psychology*, *38*(3), 551–569.

Brinol, P., & Petty, R. E. (2009). Source factors in persuasion: A self-validation approach. *European Review of Social Psychology*, *20*(1), 49–96.

Burgess, M. (2017). Russian trolls live-tweeted Manchester and London attacks. *Wired*. Retrieved from http://www.wired.co.uk/article/russian-twitter-troll-westminster-bridge-manchester-southlonestar.

Cameron, D. (2017). After Quebec mosque shooting, Fox News, Twitter bots, racists spread "fake news". *The Daily Dot*. Retrieved from https://www.dailydot.com/layer8/quebec-shooter-muslim-mosque-fox-news-white-nationalists-misinformation/.

Chan, M. S., Jones, C. R., Hall Jamieson, K., & Albarracín, D. (2017). Debunking: A meta-analysis of the psychological efficacy of messages countering misinformation. *Psychological Science*, *28*(11), 1,531–1,546.

Chen, A. (2015). The Agency. *The New York Times*. Retrieved from https://www.nytimes.com/2015/06/07/magazine/the-agency.html.

Chess, C., & Clarke, L. (2007). Facilitation of risk communication during the anthrax attacks of 2001: The organizational backstory. *American Journal of Public Health*, *97*(9), 1,578–1,583.

Diebelius, G. (2017). JustGiving take over London terror attack victim fundraising page amid fraud fears. *Metro*. Retrieved from http://metro.co.uk/2017/03/25/justgiving-take-over-london-terror-attack-victim-fundraising-page-amid-fraud-fears-6533665/.

Dwoskin, E. (2017). Twitter is looking for ways to let users flag fake news, offensive content. *Washington Post*. Retrieved from https://www.washingtonpost.com/news/the-switch/wp/2017/06/29/twitter-is-looking-for-ways-to-let-users-flag-fake-news/.

Evans, P. (2017). Will Germany's new law kill free speech online? *BBC News*. Retrieved from http://www.bbc.com/news/blogs-trending-41042266.

Ferrara, E., Varol, O., Davis, C., Menczer, F., & Flammini, A. (2016). The rise of social bots. *Communications of the ACM*, *59*(7), 96–104.

Fessler, D. M., Pisor, A. C., & Navarrete, C. D. (2014). Negatively-biased credulity and the cultural evolution of beliefs. *PloS One*, *9*(4), 1–8.

Gneezy, U., & Imas, A. (2014). Materazzi effect and the strategic use of anger in competitive interactions. *Proceedings of the National Academy of Sciences*, *111*(4), 1,334–1,337.

Guerini, M., & Staiano, J. (2015). Deep feelings: A massive cross-lingual study on the relation between emotions and virality. In *Proceedings of the 24th International Conference on World Wide Web* (pp. 299–305), New York: Association for Computing Machinery.

Guess, A., Nyhan, B., & Reifler, J. (2017). *"You're Fake News!": The 2017 Poynter Media Trust Survey*. St. Petersburg, FL: The Poynter Institute.

Halperin, E., Porat, R., Tamir, M., & Gross, J. J. (2013). Can emotion regulation change political attitudes in intractable conflicts? From the laboratory to the field. *Psychological Science*, *24*(1), 106–111.

Heimbach, I., & Hinz, O. (2016). The impact of content sentiment and emotionality on content virality. *International Journal of Research in Marketing*, *33*(3), 695–701.

Hern, A. (2017). How a Russian "troll soldier" stirred anger after the Westminster attack. *The Guardian*. Retrieved from http://www.

theguardian.com/uk-news/2017/nov/14/how-a-russian-troll-soldier-stirred-anger-after-the-westminster-attack.

Holiday, R. (2013). *Trust Me, I'm Lying: Confessions of a Media Manipulator*. UK: Penguin Books.

Khaldarova, I., & Pantti, M. (2016). Fake news: The narrative battle over the Ukrainian conflict. *Journalism Practice*, *10*(7), 891–901.

Latif, A. I. (2011). Religious and other groups. In A. I. Latif (Ed.), *Hearts of Resilience: Singapore's Community Engagement Programme* (pp. 28–30). Singapore: Institute of Southeast Asian Studies.

Lerner, J. S., Gonzalez, R. M., Small, D. A., & Fischhoff, B. (2003). Effects of fear and anger on perceived risks of terrorism: A national field experiment. *Psychological Science*, *14*(2), 144–150.

Lerner, J. S., Li, Y., Valdesolo, P., & Kassam, K. S. (2015). Emotion and decision making. *Annual Review of Psychology*, *66*, 799–823.

Levin, S. (2017). Facebook and Google promote politicized fake news about Las Vegas shooter. *The Guardian*. Retrieved from http://www.theguardian.com/us-news/2017/oct/02/las-vegas-shooting-facebook-google-fake-news-shooter.

Manchester attack: Ensuring donations get to victims (2017). *BBC News*. Retrieved from http://www.bbc.com/news/uk-england-manchester-40046196.

Matias, J. N. (2017). Persuading algorithms with an AI nudge. *Medium*. Retrieved from https://medium.com/mit-media-lab/persuading-algorithms-with-an-ai-nudge-25c92293df1d.

Media Literacy Council (n.d.). Values and social norms. Retrieved from https://www.medialiteracycouncil.sg/Best-Practices/Values-and-Social-Norms.

Mezzofiore, G. (2017). That tweet trolling a Muslim woman during the Westminster attack was actually by a Russian bot. *Mashable*. Retrieved from http://mashable.com/2017/11/14/troll-fake-muslim-picture-westminster-attack-russian-bot/.

Moore, J. (2017). ISIS claims Las Vegas shooting, says Stephen Paddock "converted" to Islam. *Newsweek*. Retrieved from http://www.newsweek.com/isis-claims-las-vegas-shooting-says-stephen-paddock-converted-islam-675504.

Moyes, S. (2017). JustGiving bosses investigate page for London terror victim over fraudster fears. *The Sun*. Retrieved from https://www.thesun.co.uk/news/3175429/justgiving-bosses-investigate-funds-for-westminster-terror-attack-victim-over-fears-it-was-set-up-by-convicted-fraudster/.

Nekmat, E. (2012). Message expression effects in online social communication. *Journal of Broadcasting & Electronic Media*, *56*(2), 203–224.

Pennycook, G., Cannon, T. D., & Rand, D. G. (2017). Prior exposure increases perceived accuracy of fake news. *SSRN*. Retrieved from https://ssrn.com/abstract=2958246.

Rath, J. (2017). Here are the biggest brands that have pulled their advertising from YouTube over extremist videos. *Business Insider Singapore*. Retrieved from http://www.businessinsider.sg/these-brands-pulled-ads-from-youtube-and-google-over-extremist-content-2017-3/?r=US&IR=T.

Robinson, S. J., & Newstetter, W. C. (2003). Uncertain science and certain deadlines: CDC responses to the media during the anthrax attacks of 2001. *Journal of Health Communication*, *8*(S1), 17–34.

Spencer, S. H. (2017). No evidence linking Vegas shooter to Antifa. *FactCheck.org*. Retrieved from https://www.factcheck.org/2017/10/no-evidence-linking-vegas-shooter-antifa/.

Stephan, W. G., Ybarra, O., & Morrison, K. R. (2009). Intergroup threat theory. In T. D. Nelson (Ed.), *Handbook of Prejudice, Stereotyping, and Discrimination* (pp. 43–59). Mahwah, NJ: Lawrence Erlbaum Associates.

Sunstein, C. R. (2014). *On Rumors: How Falsehoods Spread, Why We Believe Them, and What Can be Done*. NJ: Princeton University Press.

Tan, J., Goh, P., Chen, X., Neo, L. S., Ong, G., & Khader, M. (2017). Crisis Communications in the Day After Terror: The SIR3 Model. HTBSC Research Report 17/2017. Singapore: Home Team Behavioural Sciences Centre.

The rise and fall of fake news (2017). WNYC Studios. Retrieved from http://www.wnyc.org/story/rise-and-fall-fake-news/.

Titcomb, J. (2017). Manchester attack: Social media trolls spread fake posts about missing children. *The Telegraph*. Retrieved from http://www.telegraph.co.uk/technology/2017/05/23/manchester-attack-social-media-trolls-spread-fake-posts-missing/.

Tversky, A., & Kahneman, D. (1973). Availability: A heuristic for judging frequency and probability. *Cognitive Psychology*, *5*(2), 207–232.

von Sikorski, C., Schmuck, D., Matthes, J., & Binder, A. (2017). "Muslims are not terrorists": Islamic state coverage, journalistic differentiation between terrorism and Islam, fear reactions, and attitudes toward Muslims. *Mass Communication and Society*, *20*(6), 825–848.

Waldrop, M. M. (2017). News feature: The genuine problem of fake news. *Proceedings of the National Academy of Sciences*, *114*(48), 12,631–12,634.

Weedon, J., Nuland, W., & Stamos, A. (2017). Information operations and Facebook. Retrieved from https://www.mm.dk/wp-content/uploads/2017/05/facebook-and-information-operations-v1.pdf.

Section 7

Strategies to Build Emergency Preparedness

When a terror attack occurs, there will be injuries and precious lives lost. But that is not the only thing that the terrorists will try to do. They will also try to destroy our social harmony, strike fear amongst our population and prevent us from carrying on with our daily lives. If we are not prepared for an attack, it can disrupt our way of life and cause widespread damage to our social harmony.

MR TEO CHEE HEAN
DEPUTY PRIME MINISTER AND
COORDINATING MINISTER FOR
NATIONAL SECURITY

CHAPTER 24

Emergency Preparedness Towards Terror Attacks in Singapore

SIEW MAAN DIONG, WEI JIE TAN, and RAYMOND LEE

Singapore Civil Defence Force, Ministry of Home Affairs, Singapore

Introduction

In light of the terrorist attacks that have occurred across the globe in the past decade, the spotlight has been casted on how governments or authorities would react to such incidents. As such, governments across the world have been focusing their efforts on preparing their countries for any potential terrorist incidents. Emergency preparedness for countries can take place at many levels, and is generally defined as a state of readiness to react constructively (through protective and precautionary activities) to threats in a manner that minimises the negative consequences on the safety and health of individuals (Perry & Lindell, 2003), as well as to promote resilience after the incident (Norris *et al.*, 2008). The authors acknowledged that there are several ongoing initiatives and preparations that have been put in place by the emergency response agencies within Singapore. Hence, this chapter aims to outline some of the challenges that would affect emergency preparedness at various levels, and to provide some recommendations to emergency management practitioners, authorities, and policymakers.

Challenge 1: Getting Emergency Responders to be Prepared and Ready to Respond to Terrorist Incidents

In this chapter, emergency responders refer to the police, fire service, and those providing emergency medical services (EMS). In Singapore, one of the main challenges that influences the preparedness of emergency responders is the limited amount of exposure to disasters — both natural and man-made — which can affect responders' familiarity with such incidents. For example, emergency responders[1] in Singapore may not be familiar with the nature and varying types of terrorist scenarios such as mass casualty incidents which could lead to a surge in demand for emergency response, active shooter incidents, secondary attacks, utilisation of secondary explosive devices, or even the use of biological or chemical weapons (Autrey *et al.*, 2014; Smith, 2008).

The various stressors that could be experienced during a terrorist incident is another challenge that emergency responders have. Specifically, such stressors involved having to work under immense time pressure, facing uncertainty in dynamic scenarios, facing immediate threats to personal safety, and experiencing fatigue during long hours of operations (Thompson *et al.*, 2014). In fact, the experience of the post-incident sequalae is also another key concern that emergency responders face, and research has established that emergency responders could experience many types of negative physical (e.g., injuries, respiratory complications) and mental health

[1] While emergency responders in Singapore may not be familiar with the nature and varying types of terrorist scenarios (due to the lack of attacks in Singapore), it is important to note that they do receive realistic training and visit their counterparts from other countries to learn from their experiences.

consequences (e.g., depression, anxiety, post-traumatic stress disorder) after terrorist-related incidents (Beinecke, 2014; Benedek *et al.*, 2007; Berninger *et al.*, 2010; Misra *et al.*, 2009).

Ensure that Emergency Responders are Prepared and Ready to Respond to Terrorist Incidents

Some studies have been done to identify the factors associated with the preparedness of emergency responders. In a study conducted among 805 Swedish emergency responders (i.e., police, rescue, ambulance services), it was reported that the level of emergency preparedness was influenced by factors such as terrorism-related management training, table-top exercises, functional field exercises, and access to personal protective equipment (PPE) (Holgersson *et al.*, 2016). Pedersen and colleagues (2016) found — in their sample of 1,213 healthcare providers, police officers, and firefighters — that being sufficiently alert and perceiving previous rescue efforts as successful were significantly associated with preparedness for future terrorist incidents. To ensure that emergency responders are ready to respond, emergency response authorities in Singapore have put into place plans and preparations to address preparedness from the physical, tactical, and psychological angles.

Physical preparations

Similar to routine emergency response work, response to terrorist incidents is also physiologically strenuous. To ensure that frontline responders are physically prepared for long hours of operations, practitioners and emergency response authorities in Singapore need to plan for simulations that are designed to mimic the physiologically challenging nature of such terrorism-related incidents.

Tactical preparations

Before any form of training or exercise is conducted, authorities and agencies in Singapore will have to formulate Standard Operating

Procedures (SOPs) for a variety of terrorist incidents that can potentially occur within their boundaries. For example, drawer plans would be in place for terrorist incidents that include but are not limited to: vehicle collisions into crowds, active shooter incidents, chemical or biological explosive situations, secondary devices dedicated to injuring responders. Formulation of drawer plans have to account for and draw reference from the various emergency response operations to similar incidents in other parts of the world. Once the plans and procedures have been crafted, it is essential for emergency responders to be familiarised with it. Responders in Singapore would also have to be notified that rigid adherence to the SOP is discouraged, since terrorist incidents are dynamic in nature. This would encourage responders to utilise their situational awareness skills before making critical decisions on the field. Besides the formulation of response plans, it is also vital for the responders to be tested both at table-top exercises as well as ground deployment exercises (Perry, 2004). Several authors have suggested that table-top exercises and ground deployment exercises could cover realistic simulations of homemade explosive devices or active shooter/hostile events, where medical service responders or firefighters are increasingly required to respond to (Abir & Nelson, 2017; Jones *et al.*, 2014; Molloy, 2017). These simulations could enhance operations in terms of factors such as communication lines used (i.e., use of dedicated radio frequency or text messaging if voice communication networks are down), staging practices used (i.e., having to set up in the warm zone, scene safety, bystander management, field triage), provision of adequate PPE (i.e., ballistic vests and helmets), and the type of medical care required (i.e., effective application of tourniquets, focus on aggressive haemorrhage control, and attending to shrapnel-related injuries).

Psychological preparations

For emergency responders to be comprehensively prepared, practitioners and emergency response commanders in Singapore would need to address the psychological component as well. Firstly, the potential stressors that responders would face (e.g., exposure to high levels of risk, severe injuries to fellow crew and team, death of children) and the possible reactions — both psychological and behavioural — that they may encounter could be highlighted during pre-mission briefings (Alexander & Klein, 2009). Secondly, the preparation briefings could include elements of practical coping strategies (e.g., use of tactical deep breathing, positive imagery) that responders can employ to regulate their stress levels. Thirdly, the types of psychological interventions and mental health support services available (e.g., Critical Incident Stress Debriefing or Psychological First Aid) could also be made known to the responders so as to provide assurance that their mental well-being is taken care of (Mansdorf, 2008). Lastly, psychological preparations could also include briefings to remind responders to adequately prepare their families should an activation occur (e.g., informing spouse/partner of prolonged absence, sourcing for alternative childcare arrangements, medical care arrangements for the elderly, setting aside money for emergencies, managing insurance policies in the event of injury or death).

Challenge 2: Coordination Between Agencies

As terrorist attacks aim to cause confusion, chaos, and fear, a coordinated response involving multiple agencies becomes extremely challenging. Chen and colleagues (2008) listed several challenges that could surface during terror attacks, and these challenges included: unexpected occurrence of the event, possible mass casualty, increased time pressure and urgency, disruption of infrastructure support, multi-agency involvement, and an increased demand for timely information. The importance of coordination between agencies has consistently been highlighted in several post-action reviews of terrorist-related incidents across the world. In the United States, post-action reviews of the Orlando Pulse nightclub mass-shooting (Straub *et al.*, 2017), and San Bernardino terrorist shooting at the Inland Regional Center (Braziel *et al.*, 2016) revealed that communications between first responder agencies (i.e., law enforcement, fire services, the EMS) should have been better coordinated as they had affected incident response processes (e.g., location of staging and assembly areas for responders, or access/traffic routes towards the incident site). In France, a post-incident review of the attacks on Stade De France and Bataclan Concert Hall (Homeland Security Advisory Council, 2016) suggested that communication between first responders was hampered, due to the lack of a centralised incident command system as well as a dedicated tactical radio frequency during the operations.

Ensure a Coordinated Response from Agencies Towards Terrorist Incidents

Several studies in the extant literature on crisis management have attempted to identify the factors that facilitate multi-agency coordinated responses to terrorist attacks. Emergency management authorities and policymakers in Singapore could consider enhancing the communication systems for a multi-agency approach towards responding to terrorist incidents, and to hold regular joint exercises between these agencies that are required to respond.

Integrated communication systems with effective information exchange

In their extensive interviews with professionals who work for homeland security in the United States (e.g., directors of offices of emergency management, captains and chiefs of city-level police and fire departments, mid- to senior-ranking officers from the United States military), Hocevar *et al.* (2006) identified several factors that affect interorganisational collaboration and coordination when reacting to terrorist incidents. Specifically, the interviews conducted by Hocevar and colleagues (2006) suggested that in order for effective multi-agency collaboration to occur, the following conditions were necessary: having a formalised coordination committee to ensure representation from each responding agency, putting in place information exchange processes which encourage sharing of best practices and post-incident reviews, introducing prerequisites such as multi-agency collaboration for project funding, and cross-agency interactions and exposure so as to increase familiarity in each other's work. In another study on the World Trade Centre 9/11 attacks, Kapucu (2005) highlighted the importance of establishing and integrating communication systems (e.g., centralised incident command information system) between agencies (e.g., government, law enforcement, emergency management offices, hospitals, traffic authorities) as well as extensive information sharing (e.g., intelligence reports, analysis of threats, SOPs) before terrorist attacks occur, so as to establish proper contact points and to communicate effectively during emergencies.

Joint exercises

Policymakers or crisis response authorities in Singapore could also consider continuing regular joint exercises (both table-top and actual ground deployment) between various agencies to identify potential gaps, develop new capabilities, and enhance multi-agency coordination. The table-top exercises could be used by leaders and authorities for the purpose of identifying gaps in capabilities to respond to terrorist events, simulating the effects of the attack on society and the business community, and examining the issue of resource prioritisation based on risk estimates (Meade & Molander, 2006). Ground deployment exercises with realistic terrorist attack scenarios could help to reinforce and improve multi-agency coordination during crises. For example, the London Metropolitan Police Service hosts regular joint exercises known as the Hanover Series (Strom & Eyerman, 2008) to practice their responses to major incidents, while the German police and military conduct joint exercises to identify gaps in both crisis response plans and coordination procedures (Knight, 2016). In line with this recommendation, counter-terrorism exercises are regularly held in Singapore where multiple agencies (such as law enforcement, search and rescue, emergency medical services (EMS), and transport) work together to identify gaps in both crisis response plans and coordination procedures (Cheong & Lim, 2016).

Challenge 3: Getting the Community to be Prepared and Ready to Respond to Terrorist Incidents

Engaging the community to address terrorism is not a novel concept, however, getting the community to be prepared to respond to terrorist incidents is an arduous task and its difficulty is compounded by a myriad of factors. For example, factors such as the lack of saliency (Levac *et al.*, 2012) if the community has not been exposed to acts of terrorism as well as common psychological reactions to the event (panic, confusion, disbelief, etc.) may act as barriers to effective community preparedness (Kehayan & Napoli, 2005). Furthermore, phenomena such as the bystander effect and the diffusion of social responsibility (i.e., individuals are less likely to offer help to a victim when other people are present) could also affect the response of the community (Staub, 2012; Williams *et al.*, 2015). Nonetheless, through incidents such as the Boston Marathon bombings, it has also been observed that the community has the potential to mitigate the consequences of a terror attack — most noticeably where members of public helped to apply first aid and tied tourniquets for the victims of the explosion, thereby saving lives (Massachusetts Emergency Management Agency, 2014).

Ensure that the Community is Prepared and Ready to Respond to Terrorist Incidents

Research in the area of preparation for terrorist incidents has highlighted the increasing need for effective community engagement, and several practitioners have proposed for various programmes that focus on reinforcing the bonds within a community and enhancing its resilience towards terror attacks (Briggs, 2010; Ellis & Abdi, 2017). These efforts need to be geared towards strengthening a country's social fabric, as well as to encourage communities to be proactive in their response to an attack instead of relying entirely on government agencies (Neumann, 2017; Organisation for Security and Co-operation in Europe, 2014). Special attention, in addition, has to be paid to the way community engagement programmes are framed in order to avoid misconception by the public. For instance, public engagement programmes could be framed as initiatives to strengthen the community's ability to respond to terror attacks, and to empower individuals to assist others in times of crises. This could help to prevent situations where the public perceives: (i) community engagement initiatives as tools to "spy" or gather intelligence on certain communities or ethnic groups or (ii) that the selective engagement of certain ethnic communities is an act of stigmatisation (Thomas, 2010).

In Singapore, the SGSecure initiative launched by the government is aligned with the findings from the literature on community engagement to counter terrorism. Under the SGSecure umbrella, a series of initiatives were rolled out to both prepare the general public to respond to terror attacks as well as to strengthen the social fabric of Singapore. Specifically, practical training on emergency preparedness skills and psychological first aid skills have been organised for community volunteers (Lim, 2017), aimed at equipping the community with essential knowledge and skills to perform first aid, CPR, and basic psychological support. The importance of equipping citizens with emergency preparedness skills is reinforced by the lessons learned from the Boston Marathon bombings, where the immediate life-saving actions (e.g., CPR, compression of wounds, tying of tourniquets) by the bystanders were credited as one of the factors that have helped to save lives on scene (Gates *et al.*, 2014). In addition, the SGSecure initiative deliberately sets out to guard the local community against extremist ideologies, where religious leaders and the community have been reminded to stand united against views that could undermine the peace of the country (Ramakrishna, 2017).

Emergency management practitioners or policymakers could also consider utilising technology to facilitate communication between the authorities and the public during a terror attack. For instance, the CitizenAID mobile phone application that was released in the United Kingdom serves as a platform to guide the public on what immediate and straightforward actions they can undertake during a terrorist incident, such as the numbers to call upon discovering a suspected bomb or how to apply first aid to victims of a stabbing, shooting, or bomb blast (U.K. National Counter Terrorism Security Office, 2017).

Challenge 4: The Untapped Potential of Businesses/ Non-profit Agencies

As the role of the authorities in preparing and responding to terror attacks takes centre stage, less attention has been paid towards the potential contributions that businesses or non-profit agencies have to offer. It has to be noted that there are several inherent challenges when engaging businesses to help in the event of a terror attack, due to the profit-driven nature of businesses or the politically sensitive context of terrorism. As pointed out by Cunningham and Koser (2016), private businesses are predominantly accountable to their shareholders for profits, and corporate boards might be less interested in extensive community-related engagements. Cunningham and Koser (2016) also suggested that private businesses and non-profit agencies might not be keen to be associated with counter-terrorism-related initiatives for fear of offending or being misconstrued by certain ethnic communities, which could represent a significant portion of their clientele.

Despite this, there were several instances when businesses have come forward to help after disasters or major incidents. In the wake of the attacks in Paris on 13 November 2015, businesses were temporarily foregoing profits in an effort to help those affected (Canal, 2015). Specifically, Airbnb urged hosts to offer free housing for victims and anyone stranded by delays, while Skype and Google Hangouts dropped fees for phone calls to France. On a similar note, there were several occasions in the United States where businesses have proactively rendered help after major emergencies. After the 9/11 attacks, for example, several businesses and non-profit agencies had stepped forward to offer their help and services. These businesses offered assistance in: mental health, employment, healthcare, finances, and childcare (Kapucu, 2007). In the aftermath of Hurricane Katrina in 2005, Walmart utilised its extensive network of logistics and its supply chain to deliver vital commodities to stranded citizens, while Home Depot delivered equipment and materials to affected citizens so that they could repair and rebuild their homes (U.S. Chamber of Commerce Foundation, 2012).

Engage Businesses and Non-profit Agencies to be Prepared for Terrorist Incidents

Traditionally, the responsibility of preparing for and responding to terrorist incidents lies within the boundaries of law enforcement and emergency management agencies. With communities being increasingly integrated, however, it is recognised that businesses and non-profit agencies do not act as sole entities and that they have an important role to play in major incidents. In fact, various researchers have proposed plausible strategies (e.g., establishing formal information-sharing mechanisms for private businesses to report suspicious activities, government agencies to be more transparent about the nature and specific character of terrorism threats, certifying volunteers to help in security for events with large crowds) through which governments can engage with the private sector and help them to build preparedness against terrorist attacks (Gregory, 2007; Neal, 2008).

Practitioners and policymakers in Singapore could similarly consider introducing programmes aimed at developing partnerships between the private and public sector, ultimately enhancing the safety and security of the community. For instance, these programmes could entail helping private business operators to develop plans for the protection of employees. In the United States, the Department of Homeland Security has introduced the Hometown Security Programme that aims to encourage businesses to do the following: develop relationships in the community with local law enforcement and customers, develop various plans (emergency response, security, business continuity, evacuation, protection, etc.) for major emergencies, train employees in crisis management, such as identifying and reporting suspicious activities to the local law enforcement, as well as to carry out emergency response plans.

Another example of developing partnerships between the private and public sector can be found in the United Kingdom, where the National Counter Terrorism Security Office has been helping businesses — through simulated exercises — to prevent, manage, and recover from terrorist incidents. Specifically, both Project Argus (U.K. National Counter Terrorism Security Office, 2016a) and Project Griffin (U.K. National Counter Terrorism Security Office, 2016b) aim to guide business owners and communities to recognise and report suspicious activities, develop adequate plans to safeguard staff, visitors, and assets, and implement measures to protect staff and clients during an attack.

Challenge 5: The Sustainability of a Continual State of High Alert

With significant increases in spending on counter-terrorism and other related initiatives over the past 10 years by Western Countries (European Union, 2016), one challenge that may arise would be the economic sustainability (e.g., cost effectiveness, returns-on-investment (ROI)) of such spending, and this is directly relevant to a financially prudent country such as Singapore. To compound matters, budgetary spending remains a highly debated topic in Singapore as public opinion polls in 2017 (Reaching Everyone for Active Citizenry Singapore, 2017) revealed that Singaporeans were primarily concerned about the high cost of living and job security amidst an economic slowdown, suggesting that there were other social issues to grapple with other than counter-terrorism. The physical-cognitive dimension of sustainability could also be called into play as some authors have opined that emergency responders and even the community could suffer from vigilance fatigue, which is a phenomenon of being continuously on high alert for terror attacks thereby leading to stress and strain (Evans, 2016). Nickerson (2011) and Krause (2012) proposed that vigilance fatigue could set in due to factors such as extended exposure to ambiguous threat information and excessive pressure to maintain performance that is error free.

Sustain a Continual State of High Alert

There is currently a lack of evidence to evaluate the economic justification of continual spending on counter-terrorism efforts. However, some researchers have suggested that this could be addressed through systematic cost–benefit evaluations that assess counter-terrorism expenditure against variables such as consequences of a successful terrorist attack, likelihood of a successful attack, degree to which the security measure reduces risk, and the cost of the security measure (Keeney & von Winterfeldt, 2011; Mueller & Stewart, 2014). Following this notion, policymakers in Singapore may also conduct studies to evaluate the economic sustainability of the various counter-terrorism efforts. To address the physical dimension of sustaining a continual state of high alert, emergency management authorities could implement fatigue management processes for their crew. Based on Clarke's (2011) compilation of resources on fatigue management for emergency responders, for example, authorities in Singapore could introduce fatigue–risk assessments during state of high alerts or introduce scenario-based exercises in which responders' vigilance fatigue would be addressed by the players. To address the cognitive dimension of vigilance fatigue, possible strategies could include keeping the message of terrorism fresh by contextualising international examples of terrorist incidents to Singapore, and sharing the latest information on threats in digestible forms (Spadanuta, 2013).

Conclusion

Although there are several ongoing initiatives and preparations that have been put in place by the emergency response authorities and policymakers within Singapore, this chapter sets out to identify challenges towards effective emergency preparedness at various levels and to recommend some tangible strategies for practitioners and policymakers to consider.

The first challenge would be getting frontline responders to be ready to respond to terrorist incidents. To address this, emergency response managers or policymakers in Singapore could consider having a system in place to ensure that responders are physically, operationally, and psychologically prepared.

The second challenge in terms of emergency preparedness towards a terrorist attack would be ensuring that a multi-agency coordinated response towards any incident exists. As such, some of the suggested interventions include establishing integrated communication systems with effective information exchange between all of the agencies, and to conduct joint exercises (both table-top and fully functional ground deployment) between the relevant agencies.

With terrorist attacks occurring in public spaces more frequently, the third challenge would involve getting the community at large to be ready and prepared for such incidents. In response to this challenge, policymakers and authorities in Singapore could look towards implementing community engagement programmes, with a focus on equipping the public with practical emergency response skills and to strengthen the social fabric through establishing a firm stand against extremist ideology. In addition, technology (i.e., through mobile phone apps) could be utilised to facilitate emergency-related communication between the authorities and the public, and to provide direct instructions to the public during terror incidents.

The fourth challenge towards effective emergency preparedness revolves around the untapped potential of businesses and non-profit agencies. To effectively harness the potential of these bodies, policymakers and the authorities in Singapore could consider introducing programmes aimed at fostering partnerships with these private businesses, as well as running joint-exercises with them to enhance their crisis response plans.

The last challenge towards emergency preparedness would entail the ability to sustain a continual state of high alert, economically, physically, and cognitively. To address the economic sustainability, authorities and emergency management practitioners could consider evaluating the returns-on-investment (ROI) on counter-terrorism expenditure. With regard to managing physical sustainability, authorities and policymakers could also consider introducing processes to circumvent vigilance fatigue in emergency responders. On the other hand, addressing the cognitive dimension of vigilance fatigue could include keeping the message of terrorism fresh by relating examples of terrorist incidents to the local context, and sharing the latest information on threats in digestible forms.

Acknowledgement

The authors would like to thank the following individuals for their ideas and contributions toward the chapter: Stephanie Lim; Raymond Choo, and Jasmine Tan. The views expressed in this chapter are the authors' only and do not represent the official position or view of the Ministry of Home Affairs, Singapore.

References

Abir, M., & Nelson, C. (2017). Lessons for first responders on the front lines of terrorism. Retrieved from https://www.rand.org/blog/2017/07/lessons-for-first-responders-on-the-front-lines-of.html.

Alexander, D., & Klein, S. (2009). First responders after disasters: A review of stress reactions, at-risk, vulnerability and resilience factors. *Prehospital and Disaster Medicine*, *24*, 87–94.

Autrey, A., Hick, J., Bramer, K., Brendt, J., & Bundt, J. (2014). 3 Echo: Concept of operations for early care and evacuation of victims of mass violence. *Prehospital and Disaster Medicine*, *29*, 1–8.

Beinecke, R. (2014). Addressing the mental health needs of victims and responders to the Boston Marathon Bombings. *International Journal of Mental Health*, *43*, 17–34.

Benedek, D. M., Fullerton, C., & Ursano, R. J. (2007). First responders: Mental health consequences of natural and human-made disasters for public health and public safety workers. *Annual Review of Public Health*, *28*, 55–68.

Berninger, A., Webber, M. P., Niles, J. K., Gustave, J., Lee, R., Cohen, H. W., Kelly, K., Corrigan, M., & Prezant, D. J. (2010). Longitudinal study of probable post-traumatic stress disorder in firefighters exposed to the World Trade Center disaster. *American Journal of Industrial Medicine*, *53*, 1,177–1,185.

Braziel, R., Straub, F., Watson, G., & Hoops, R. (2016). *Bringing Calm to Chaos: A Critical Incident Review of the San Bernardino Public Safety Response to the December 2, 2015, Terrorist Shooting Incident at the Inland Regional Center (Critical Response Initiative)*. Washington, DC: Office of Community Oriented Policing Services.

Briggs, R. (2010). Community engagement for counterterrorism: Lessons from the United Kingdom. *International Affairs*, *86*, 971–981.

Canal, E. (2015). How Businesses Are Helping After Paris Terrorist Attacks. *Forbes*. Retrieved from https://www.forbes.com/sites/emilycanal/2015/11/16/how-businesses-are-helping-after-paris-terrorst-attacks/#41c7880d76d3.

Chen, R., Sharman, R., Rao, R., & Upadhyaya, S. (2008). An exploration of coordination in emergency response management. *Communications of the ACM*, *51*, 66–73.

Cheong, D., & Lim, Y. L. (2016). Singapore stages biggest islandwide counter-terrorism exercise. *The Straits Times*. Retrieved from www.straitstimes.com/singapore/singapore-stages-its-biggest-counter-terrorism-exercise.

Clarke, J. L. (2011). Addressing emergency response provider fatigue in emergency response preparedness, management, policy making, and research. *Journal of Emergency Management*, *9*, 19–29.

Cunningham, A. E., & Koser, K. (2016). *Why preventing violent extremism is the private sector's business*. Retrieved from https://www.economicsandpeace.org/wp-content/uploads/2016/11/Global-Terrorism-Index-2016.2.pdf.

Ellis, B. H., & Abid, S. (2017). Building community resilience to violent extremism through genuine partnerships. *American Psychologist*, *72*, 289–300.

European Union (2016). Counter-terrorism funding in the EU budget. Retrieved from https://www.europarl.europa.eu/RegData/etudes/BRIE/2016/580904/EPRS_BRI(2016)580904_EN.pdf.

Evans, M. (2016). Terror alerts leave public prone to 'vigilance fatigue', warns police chief. *Telegraph*. Retrieved from https://www.telegraph.co.uk/news/2016/04/15/terror-alerts-leave-public-prone-to-vigilance-fatigue-warns-poli.

Gates, J. D., Arabian, S., Biddinger, P., Blansfield, J., Burke, P., Chung, S., Fischer, J., Friedman, F., Gervasini, A., Goralnick, E., Gupta, A., Larentzakis, A., McMahon, M., Mella, J., Michaud, Y., Mooney, D., Rabinovici, R., Sweet, D., Ulrich, A., Velhamos, G., Weber, C., & Yaffe, M. B. (2014). The Initial Response to the Boston Marathon Bombing:

Lessons Learned to Prepare for the Next Disaster. *Annals of Surgery, 260*, 960–966.

Gregory, F. (2007). Private sector roles in counter-terrorism. In P. Wilkinson (Ed.), *Homeland Security in the UK: Future Preparedness for Terrorist Attack since 9/11* (pp. 321–331). Oxford: Routledge.

Hocevar, S. P., Thomas, G. F., & Jansen, E. (2006). Building collaborative capacity: An innovative strategy for homeland security preparedness. In M. M. Beyerlein, S. T. Beyerlein, & F. A. Kennedy (Eds.), *Innovation through Collaboration: Advances in Interdisciplinary Studies of Work Teams* (pp. 255–274). UK: Emerald Group Publishing Limited.

Holgersson, A., Sahovic, D., Saveman, B-I., & Bjornstig, U. (2016). Factors influencing responders' perceptions of preparedness for terrorism. *Disaster Prevention and Management, 25*, 520–533.

Homeland Security Advisory Council (2016). The attacks on Paris: Lessons learned: White paper. Retrieved from https://static1.squarespace.com/static/5782ad8f9de4bb114784a8fe/t/5783fec9d482e95d4e0b79bf.

Jones, J., Kue, R., Mitchell, P., Eblan, G., & Dyer, K. (2014). Emergency medical services response to active shooter incidents: Provider comfort level and attitudes before and after participation in a focused response training program. *Prehospital and Disaster Medicine, 29*, 350–357.

Kapucu, N. (2005). Interagency communication networks during emergencies: Boundary spanners in multiagency coordination. *American Review of Public Administration, 36*, 207–225.

Kapucu, N. (2007). Non-profit response to catastrophic disasters. *Disaster Prevention and Management, 16*, 551–561.

Keeney, R. L., & von Winderfeldt, D. (2011). A value model for evaluating homeland security decisions. *Risk Analysis, 31*, 1,470–1,487.

Kehayan, V. A., & Napoli, J. C. (2005). *Resiliency in the Face of Disaster and Terrorism: 10 Things to Do to Survive.* Fawnskin, California: Personhood Press.

Knight, B. (2016). Bundeswehr joins police for anti-terror exercises. *DW*. Retrieved from www.dw.com/en/bundeswehr-join-police-for-anti-terror-exercises/a-37843161.

Krause, M. (2012). Vigilance fatigue in policing: A critical threat to public safety and officer well-being. Retrieved from https://leb.fbi.gov/articles/featured-articles/vigilance-fatigue-in-policing-a-critical-threat-to-public-safety-and-officer-well-being.

Levac, J., Toal-Sullivan, D., & O'Sullivan, T. L. (2012). Household emergency preparedness: A literature review. *Journal of Community Health, 37*, 725–733.

Lim, K. (2017). Grassroots leaders to get training on helping residents deal with terror attacks. *Channel News Asia*. Retrieved from www.channelnewsasia.com/news/singapore/grassroots-leaders-to-get-training-pon-helping-residents-deal-wit-8577470.

Mansdorf, I. J. (2008). Psychological interventions following terrorist attacks. *British Medical Bulletin*, *88*, 7–22.

Massachusetts Emergency Management Agency (2014). After action report for the response to the 2013 Boston Marathon bombings. Retrieved from https://www.mass.gov/eopss/docs/mema/after-action-report-for-the-response-to-the-2013-boston-marathon-bombings.pdf.

Meade, C., & Molander, R. C. (2006). Considering the Effects of a Catastrophic Terrorist Attack. *RAND Corporation Technical Report*. Retrieved from https://www.rand.org./pubs/technical_reports/TR391/html.

Misra, M., Greenberg, N., Hutchinson, C., Brian, A., & Glozier, N. (2009). Psychological impact upon London ambulance service of the 2005 bombings. *Occupational Medicine*, *59*, 428–433.

Molloy, D. (2017). Preparing for active shooter and hostile events. Retrieved from https://www.emsworld.com/article/12305042/preparing-for-active-shooter-and-hostile-events.

Mueller, J., & Stewart, M. G. (2014). Evaluating Counterterrorism Spending. *Journal of Economic Perspectives*, *28*, 237–248.

Neal, S. R. (2008). Business as usual? Leveraging the private sector to combat terrorism. *Perspectives on Terrorism*, *2*(3).

Neumann, P. R. (2017). Countering violent extremism and radicalisation that lead to terrorism: Ideas, recommendations, and good practices from the OSCE Region. Retrieved from https://www.osce.org/charirmanship/346841?download=true.

Nickerson, R. S. (2011). Roles of human factors and ergonomics in meeting the challenge of terrorism. *American Psychologist*, *66*, 555–566.

Norris, F. H., Stevens, S. P., Pfefferbaum, B., Wyche, K. F., & Pfefferbaum, R. L. (2008). *American Journal of Community Psychology*, *51*, 127–150.

Organisation for Security and Co-operation in Europe (2014). Preventing and countering violent extremism and radicalization that lead to terrorism: A community-policing approach. Retrieved from https://www.osce,.org/atu/111438?download=true.

Pedersen, M. J. B., Gjerland, A., Rund, B. R., Ekeberg, O., & Skogstand, L. (2016). Emergency preparedness and role clarity among rescue workers during the terror attacks in Norway, July 22, 2011. *PLoS One*, *11*, 1–12.

Perry, R. W., & Lindell, M. K. (2003). Preparedness for Emergency Response: Guidelines for the Emergency Planning Process. *Disasters*, *27*, 336–350.

Perry, R. (2004). Disaster exercise outcomes for professional emergency personnel and citizen volunteers. *Journal of Contingencies and Crisis Management*, *12*, 64–75.

Ramakrishna, K. (2017). The threat of terrorism and extremism: "A Matter of 'When', and Not 'If'". *Southeast Asian Affairs*, 335–350.

Reaching Everyone for Active Citizenry Singapore (2017). Top concerns in pre-budget 2017 feedback. Retrieved from https://www.reach.gov.sg/participate/discussion-forum/2017/02/13/top-concerns-in-prebudget-2017-feedback.

Spadanuta, L. (2013). Vigilance fatigue. *Asian Online*. Retrieved from https://sm.asisonline.org/Pages/Vigilance-Fatigue.aspx.

Staub, E. (2012). The psychology of morality in genocide and violent conflict: perpetrators, passive bystanders, rescuers. In M. Mikulincer, & P. Shaver (Eds.), *The Social Psychology of Morality*. Washington, DC: American Psychological Association Press.

Straub, F., Cambria, J., Castor, J., Gorban, B., Meade, B., Waltemeyer, D., & Zeunik, J. (2017). *Rescue, Response, and Resilience: A Critical Incident Review of the Orlando Public Safety Response to the Attack on the Pulse Nightclub. Critical Response Initiative*. Washington, DC: Office of Community Oriented Policing Services.

Strom, K. J., & Eyerman, J. (2008). Interagency coordination: A case study of the 2005 London train bombings. *International Journal of Comparative and Applied Criminal Justice*, *32*, 89–110.

Smith, E. (2008). Willingness to work during a terrorist attack: A case-study of first responders during the 9/11 World Trade Centre terrorist attacks. *Journal of Emergency Primary Health Care*, *6*, 1–11.

Thomas, P. (2010). Failed and friendless: The UK's 'Preventing Violent Extremism' programme. *The British Journal of Politics and International Relations*, *12*, 442–458.

Thompson, J., Rehn, M., Lossius, H. M., & Lockey, D. (2014). Risks to emergency medical responders at terrorist incidents: A narrative review of the medical literature. *Critical Care*, *18*, 521.

U.K. National Counter Terrorism Security Office (2016a). Guidance: Project Argus. Retrieved from https://www.gov.uk/government/publications/project-argus/project-argus.

U.K. National Counter Terrorism Security Office (2016b). Guidance: Project Griffin. Retrieved from https://www.gov.uk/government/publications/project-griffin/project-griffin.

U.K. National Counter Terrorism Security Office (2017). CitizenAid advice supports Run Hide Tell. Retrieved from https://www.gov.uk/government/news./citizenaid-advice-supports-run-hide-tell.

U.S. Chamber of Commerce Foundation (2012). The role of business in disaster response report. Retrieved from https://www.uschamberfoundation.org/promising-practice/role-business-disaster-response-report.

Williams, M. J., Horgan, J. G., & Evans, W. P. (2015). Research summary: Lessons from a U.S. study revealing the critical role of "gatekeepers" in public safety networks for countering violent extremism. In A. Zeiger, & A. Aly (Eds.), *Countering Violent Extremism: Developing an Evidence-Base for Policy and Practice* (pp. 139–144). Perth, Western Australia, Australia: Curtin University.

CHAPTER 25

The Looming, the Creeping, and the Black Swan: Modern Crises and Recommendations for Building Resilience

SHERYL CHUA HWEE CHIN, MAJEED KHADER, and EUNICE TAN

Home Team Behavioural Sciences Centre, Ministry of Home Affairs, Singapore

Introduction

The increased occurrence of novel crises we have witnessed over the last decade reflects a new characteristic of the world we are living in — a *fat tail* world. Contrary to a standard normal distribution, a fat tail distribution indicates that the probability of extreme events occurring is higher than expected (Bremmer & Keat, 2009). Unfortunately, the perception that extreme events are occurring more frequently is not simply anecdotal (Mitroff, 2004).

Some of the extreme events seen over the last decade include natural disasters and pandemics of massive risks to human lives. For example, the 2011 Great East Japan earthquake and tsunami caused the meltdown in the nuclear reactors at Fukushima and subsequent radioactive leakage. The 2009 H1N1 influenza pandemic was considered unusual, with the emergence of the new strain resulting from the reassortment of four different viruses, and the transmissibility of the virus among humans was unexpected (Centers for Disease Control and Prevention, 2009). Political instability and violent conflicts have become more rampant over the last decade (von Einsiedel *et al.*, 2014). For instance, political upheaval in the Middle East has intensified in recent years. Consequently, the world is also facing the worst refugee crisis since World War II, where close to 60 million refugees from Afghanistan, Iraq, Libya, Syria, and Yemen are fleeing violence and conflicts in their countries (UN High Commissioner for Refugees, 2015). Also, since the September 11 terrorist attacks in 2001, the threat of violent extremism has been on the rise and there have been notable acts of terrorism in Europe as well as in Southeast Asia. The terror threat has become more imminent as the Islamic State of Iraq and Syria (ISIS) has turned to Asia to establish an Islamic caliphate (Chan, 2016). The global power transition from West to East is also likely to create new international challenges (Boin, 2009; Hoge Jr., 2004).

These extreme events that had happened over the last decade revealed the rapidly changing array of threats that the world is facing. Be it natural disasters, pandemics, terrorism, armed conflicts, or financial crises, the crises the world is facing today possess characteristics that are distinct from conventional crises. Hence, unlike crises that occurred decades ago, these trends and occurrences witnessed across the globe or what this chapter terms as *modern crises*, are more complex, dynamic, transboundary, and have cascading effects that point to new challenges of today's world (Ansell *et al.*, 2010; The Organisation for Economic Co-operation and Development (OECD), 2015). These modern crises often attract worldwide attention and create transitory shocks that have strong impact on the economy, politics, and social functioning (OECD, 2015). In light of the heavy-weight expectations on leaders, it is imperative to be familiar with issues of the fat tail world, the best practices and strategies to not just cope with, but also prepare for and to potentially better manage these modern crises.

Five Key Points about Managing Modern Crises

Key Point #1: Understand the Complexity of Today's World and its Impact on Crisis Management

According to the Future Global Shocks (OECD, 2011), three key characteristics of today's world include globalisation, heightened mobility, and centralised systems. A financial crisis faced by one country can impact the world economy such as affecting commodity prices and financial assets. Similarly, as the world becomes denser and urbanised, it also creates crisis hotspots for the transmission of diseases. Heightened mobility of people due to ease of travel also allows terrorists to cross borders and facilitates proliferation of terrorist groups. Additionally, in today's age of high-speed mass communication, online radicalisation has been increasingly common (Alarid, 2016).

Rapid flow of data elevates the risk for cyber-attacks and compromises national security (Lagadec & Topper, 2012). The rise of new technologies or what some has called the arrival of the "Fourth Industrial Revolution" also transforms the management and governance of both the physical world and the cyber realm (Schwab, 2016). For instance, the connectivity among everyday devices, systems, services through data, cloud, analytics, and technology (i.e., Internet of Things (IoT) ecosystem) introduces new cybersecurity threats (U.S. Department of Homeland Security, 2016). The emergence of new cyber weapons that attack critical infrastructures poses serious security implications. In August 2010, it was noticed that the centrifuges used to enrich uranium gas at Iran's Natanz nuclear facility were failing. Months later, it was found that the SCADA control systems were infected with *Stuxnet*, a malicious computer worm, designed to sabotage the Iranian nuclear programme (Collins & McCombie, 2012). More recently, an assessment report jointly released by the Central Intelligence Agency (CIA), The Federal Bureau of Investigation (FBI), and The National Security Agency (NSA), revealed Russia's efforts in influencing the 2016 U.S. Presidential election (National Intelligence Council, 2017). Systems have also become more centralised and hubs are established to improve efficiency. Systems that are tightly coupled, i.e., higher interdependency, increase the likelihood that any disruptions would ripple through the systems, resulting in multiple failures (OECD, 2011). Thus, any trivial incidents can cascade and spiral out of control.

The characteristics of today's world change how crises manifest themselves, and new approaches in crisis management are warranted. Modern crises not only necessitate immediate responses but also require crisis leaders to anticipate and mitigate the adverse effects that may unfold in diverse trajectories. Crisis leaders would also need to develop new capabilities to collaborate with different groups of stakeholders to manage their interests, priorities, agendas, and values (OECD, 2015). The transboundary nature may also contribute to fragmentation of responses (Ansell *et al.*, 2010). Hence, crisis leaders would need to formulate strategies to orchestrate the response efforts by multiple agencies. The involvement of multiple agencies would also increase the chances of contradicting messages that may increase uncertainty and hamper cooperation from the public. Crisis that crosses temporal boundaries can create enduring uncertainty and fear, which tests a society's resilience (Ansell *et al.*, 2010). Thus, modern crises change the way crises should be managed.

Key Point #2: Identify Potential Ripple Effect During Pre-crisis Stage

The changing characteristics of today's world contribute to the transboundary nature of modern crises. Crises are considered to be transboundary when they transcend through: (i) geographical boundaries, (ii) functional boundaries, and/or (iii) temporal boundaries.

Some crises are not confined within a nation's boundaries; they have repercussions on multiple cities, regions, countries, or continents (Ansell *et al.*, 2010). For instance, pandemics such as the 2009 H1N1 outbreak started with few sporadic cases in the United States. Less than three months from the first emergence of H1N1, 30,000 cases were reported across 74 countries and the World Health Organisation (WHO) raised the pandemic alert (Chan, 2009).

Modern crises can originate from a specific system and influence or snowball to affect other systems, functions, or infrastructures

(Ansell *et al.*, 2010). The Great East Japan earthquake was not just a natural disaster that required immediate emergency responses. It also induced fear of radiation that affected a drastic drop in the number of tourists visiting Japan (Wu & Hayashi, 2013), and disrupted international trade and global supply chain (Carvalho *et al.*, 2014). The aftermath of this crisis required collaboration with stakeholders from different functions and systems.

Lastly, modern crises are not one-off single episodes that can be demarcated by a clear starting and ending point (Ansell *et al.*, 2010; Boin *et al.*, 2008). The impact of a crisis can unfold over time and has long-lasting effects. For example, many countries such as Iceland, Ireland, and the United Kingdom are still recovering from the global financial crisis that happened in 2008. These countries are still dealing with high unemployment rates, growth slowdown, and deficits in the government's budget (Faola, 2016).

The transboundary nature of modern crises poses unique challenges to leaders such as the call for more integrated crisis response (Boin *et al.*, 2009). Identifying potential ripple effect during the pre-crisis stage is important; coordinated networks of stakeholders, multi-disciplinary experts, and international partnerships could be mapped out and knowledge sharing could be facilitated before a crisis hits (Boin *et al.*, 2009; OECD, 2013).

Key Point #3: Incorporate Unpredictable Elements in Crisis Simulation Exercises

Crises such as the imminent threats of violent extremism are considered to be manageable, given the wealth of knowledge on the threat and the know-how on how to respond to such crises. However, these crises have low predictability in terms of spatial and/or temporal context. Hence, these forms of crises are termed as *looming crises;* being aware that the threat is out there, but unable to predict where and when it will happen. For example, since the September 11 attacks, much has been learnt about terror attacks and the world has called for a "war on terror". Countries have also stepped up on strategies in counter-terrorism such as strengthening border security, improving surveillance in public areas and transport systems, and enhancing intelligence sharing. Emergency response teams are also trained and equipped with skills relevant for counter-terrorism. While preventive and mitigating measures are put in place, it is difficult to predict where and when an attack will happen. A shift in the *modus operandi* of terrorist groups since the September 11 terrorist attacks has also been observed, from elaborated acts of terrorism to high-profile, lone-wolf attacks that were executed by local, self-radicalised individuals (e.g., 2011 Norway attacks, 2016 Orlando nightclub shooting); this poses new challenges for national security.

Another example of looming crises would be public health outbreaks or pandemics. While healthcare providers are equipped with the resources to monitor and manage outbreaks, the pattern of entry of the virus to the country is unpredictable. Increased global transportation of animals and people not only increases the risk of infectious transmission but also makes it harder to anticipate and track the transmissibility. Furthermore, some viruses such as the Zika virus are contagious before the symptoms manifest. Some infectious diseases (e.g., Ebola virus) are less likely to spread globally because they are transmitted through close contact (Kim, 2016). Hence, the outbreaks are localised and confined to a few countries (Foley Jr., 2012). However, there are other infectious diseases (e.g., BSE, commonly known as mad cow disease) that do not confine themselves to national borders and could be transmitted to other parts of the world causing a pandemic. A pandemic is "an epidemic of an infectious disease that has spread through human populations across geographical regions globally" (Ministry of Health, 2014, p. 1). Not all epidemics lead to a pandemic. Examples of diseases with pandemic potential include Severe Acute Respiratory Syndrome-associated Coronavirus (SARS-CoV) and Middle East Respiratory Syndrome Coronavirus (MERS-CoV). The first case of SARS was reported in Guangdong province in China in November 2002 and, within months, it spread rapidly to 37 other countries such as Singapore, Hong Kong, Taiwan, and Canada. Pandemics not only is a major public health concern but can also cause ripple effect on social and economic functioning.

While knowledge on the threats and know-hows of managing these looming crises are useful in crisis preparation, its unpredictable nature cannot be ignored. Looming crises can still come as a surprise and leaders may be caught off guard, especially if one is overconfident in one's crisis response plans. Therefore, crisis simulation exercises may consider incorporating unpredictable elements for leaders to practise their responses to surprises.

Key Point #4: Recognise and Mitigate Creeping Crises Early

Creeping crises, as the name suggests, creep up and may even take years to be resolved rather than having an abrupt occurrence. Creeping crisis can be predicted sufficiently; it is easy to identify the sources and implications are well-known. However, this form of crises are often shrouded by emerging acute crises ('t Hart & Boin, 2001). Existing researches on crisis management have also largely focused on acute or fast-burning crises (Porfiriev, 2000). One example of creeping crises would be the on-going climate crisis. Despite scientific consensus that the global temperature has increased over the past decades, there were debates over the authenticity of the climate crisis (Volcovici, 2017). The climate crisis controversies and the uncertainties over which countries should be involved in signing a climate agreement, defer coordinated efforts to tackle and implement effective mitigation strategies (Bosetti *et al.*, 2008).

Although creeping crises may be intractable or take years to be resolved, it is important for leaders to identify these crises and call for actions before it snowball, resulting in irreversible damages. However, the need for involvement of multiple organisations and nations may make interference almost impossible (Gundel, 2005). Often, conflicts of interest and polarised opinions could impede countermeasures for these creeping crises. Take the Singapore's ageing crisis as an example. If the crisis is not dealt with, it can have multiple repercussions. First, public spending would increase and strain national budget as more public monies are directed to provide support for older people. Second, the crisis could undermine economic growth as the working-age population would cease to grow or even decrease, which can subsequently lead to global financial instability (Jackson *et al.*, 2008).

Key Point #5: Think of the Unthinkables

Black Swan is a metaphor to describe an unexpected outlier event that has low probability of occurrence, has catastrophic ramification, and is perceived to be explainable and predictable in retrospect (Taleb, 2007). At the 2017 Institute of Policy Studies-Nathan Lecture, former Head of Civil Service, Mr. Peter Ho, warned of increasing frequency of Black Swan events especially in an uncertain and complex world (Ho, 2017). Early warning signals of Black Swan events may be weak, random, and incomprehensible. Black Swan events are increasingly becoming the norm, and it is essential for crisis leaders to develop new knowledge to detect and deal with these Black Swan events (Lagadec & Topper, 2012).

According to Taleb (2007), Black Swan events are the most dangerous. Although Black Swan events are unprecedented and unpredictable, it is not entirely impossible to prepare for them (Ahlqvist *et al.*, 2015). Preparing for the unknown is a great challenge to crisis management (Weick & Sutcliffe, 2007). Even though some modern crises may be unforeseeable and unimaginable, leaders are still held accountable for their failure in anticipating as leaders are expected "to have seen it coming" by thinking about the "unthinkable" and to develop contingency plans to minimise catastrophic losses (Gowing & Langdon, 2015).

Five Key Approaches to Managing Modern Crises

The transboundary nature of modern crises poses new challenges for crisis leaders and there is a need to adopt new approaches and processes to anticipate and mitigate these modern crises. It is hard to identify where the crisis originates, how it propagates, and the types of knock-on effects it produces (OECD, 2011). Modern crises not only necessitate immediate responses but also require crisis leaders to anticipate and mitigate the adverse effects that may unfold in diverse trajectories. Thus, modern crises change the way how crises should be managed and there is also rising need for developing resilience to cope with the uncertain, unimaginable, and unforeseeable threats (Comfort *et al.*, 2010).

Recommendation 1: Be Mindful of Cognitive Traps

Cognitive biases can affect rational thinking and good judgment. Crisis leaders not only need to understand these cognitive biases but also be mindful and minimise these biases during crisis planning and management (Gowing & Langdon, 2015). While cognitive biases are innate and natural, crisis leaders should identify and challenge the assumptions underpinning their analyses and decisions (Leigh, 2015). Table 25.1 summarises the different types of cognitive biases and their implications on crisis management.

Recommendation 2: Develop a Crisis-ready Mindset and Understand how Culture May Influence the Mindset

A crisis-ready mindset refers to "psychological preparedness regarding how to process and react to a crisis" (Wang *et al.*, 2015, p. 6). The National Resilience Division, which was developed in the Ministry of Communications and Information in 2002, highlighted the importance of increasing psychological resilience of Singaporeans to manage crises effectively, and crisis readiness is one of the measurements of psychological resilience (Menon, 2005). Ang *et al.* (2017) proposed six dimensions that make up the crisis-ready mindset: (1) recognition of potential crises, (2) adequate crises preparation, (3) capacity to act swiftly, (4) adaptive emotional reactions, (5) systematic thought processes, and (6) effective coping resources.

Using Japan as an example, the concept of crisis-ready mindset can be further understood. Japan is known to be disaster-prone as its location along the Pacific Ring of Fire makes it vulnerable to tsunamis and earthquakes. Japan has experienced several tragedies over the years. However, Japan's recovery responses were efficient

Table 25.1. Summary of Cognitive Biases in Crisis Management.

Cognitive Biases	Definitions and Implications
Black elephant	**Definition:** The tendency to ignore, discount, or bypass a visible problem (elephant in the room), yet react in surprise as though it is a Black Swan event when it occurs (Ho, 2017). **Implication on crisis management:** Failure to recognise the threat and mobilise resources to mitigate the crisis (Ho, 2017).
False sense of inevitability	**Definition:** The assumption that the organisation would be able to safeguard all forms of crises (Boin, 2008). **Implication on crisis management:** Undermines effective crisis response as it increases vulnerability to surprises (Boin, 2008).
Positive illusion	**Definition:** Unrealistic optimism that leads individuals to perceive the world and future to be more positive than the facts reflect it to be (Catino, 2013). **Implication on crisis management:** Diminishes the ability to identify or even deny unfavourable signs such as early warning signals and affects evaluation and judgment to mobilise resources to address the issue (Catino, 2013).
Confirmation bias	**Definition:** Tendency to prioritise information that confirms existing beliefs and to ignore or underestimate those that contradict (Catino, 2013). **Implication on crisis management:** Possibility of gathering selective information that may not provide the big picture of the crisis (Catino, 2013).
Self-serving bias	**Definition:** Tendency to attribute success to internal factors while attributing failures to external factors (Catino, 2013). **Implication on crisis management:** Impedes effective learning from past crises or near-misses (Catino, 2013).
Discounting the future	**Definition:** Tendency to prefer short-term options to medium-to-long-term options (Catino, 2013). **Implication on crisis management:** Signals from creeping crisis may be ignored or discounted and the crisis may snowball (Catino, 2013).

and swift. For instance, during the Great East Japan earthquake and tsunami, there was a mass evacuation of 465,000 people and citizens actively helped each other tide through the crisis through their strong volunteerism culture (Ferris & Solis, 2013). This shows how Japan displayed a composed reaction towards the unexpected crisis, managed emotions in dire times, and coped well with circumstances. Japan also has various safety and disaster management measures put in place to improve the crisis readiness and crisis management of its citizens such as a Tsunami Warning Service, distribution of emergency kits, back-up power systems, earthquake drills in schools, and tsunami shelters in high-rise buildings (Fogarty, 2011). Japan clearly displays a crisis-ready mindset as it prepares its citizens annually for earthquakes and has a myriad of measures in place to help its citizens manage the situation better. It is also evident that the Japanese possess crisis readiness as they do not panic and wallow in pessimism, but instead, continually prepare themselves for future crises and rise up to the situation to help one another out in dire times.

There are several ways to develop a crisis-ready mindset. For instance, developing foresight capacities has become increasingly crucial to deal with novel crises (OECD, 2015); organisations would need to proactively identify threats that are beginning to emerge and act before the crisis escalates. Leaders would have to "think of the unthinkable" instead of shoving the issue under the rug (Gowing & Langdon, 2015). Employees should also be encouraged to think about inconceivable threats and to develop innovative strategies and contingency plans.

Scenario planning, a technique to envision future events (Petty, 2011), can be an enabler for foresight capacities (Masys, 2012). Through scenario planning, leaders can generate all possible risk scenarios, identify the threats, assess the probability of occurrence, and analyse the vulnerabilities in the existing crisis management strategies (Petty, 2011). Worst-case scenarios may also be considered to ensure preparedness during pre-crisis and develop resilience (Lagadec, 1993). The goal of scenario planning is to strengthen the organisation's ability to identify potential Black Swan events and to minimise the uncertainty and surprises. *Back casting* is another method used in scenario planning where a future event is imagined (e.g., a cyberattack on telecommunication networks after a terrorist attack); stakeholders then work together to examine whether the existing policies, contingency plans, and systems are robust in managing the crises. Anticipatory backwards scenarios can help to identify the precursors that allowed a future crisis or a failed system to unravel (Aven, 2015). The information gathered could help to identify weaknesses where failures may follow. Similarly, the *premortem technique* focuses on prospective hindsight, which involves generating explanations and reasons for a future event by imagining that the event had occurred already (Mitchell *et al.*, 1989). Individuals have to think of possibilities for the event by focusing on what went wrong, instead of what could go wrong. One study found that by using the premortem technique instead of conventional brainstorming, individuals were able to spot more black swans by neutralising deliberate ignorance (Gallop *et al.*, 2016). This may be due to the certainty of the outcome which enables deeper processing, thus, heightening the ability to come up with more efficient and concrete reasons (Mitchell *et al.*, 1989).

Culture can also play a role in influencing the crisis-ready mindset. For instance, *kiasuism* (from the Hokkien term, *kiasu* (怕输), which is literally translated as fear of losing out) is an entrenched feature of Singaporean society (Kirby & Ross, 2007; van de Vijver & Tanzer, 2004). Bedford and Chua (2017) explored the kiasuism construct and found that *kiasu* behaviours are motivated by different beliefs that entail comparison with others and the use of others as a standard to assess own needs and goals. Additionally, it is the motivation that determines whether kiasuism is present and not *kiasu* behaviours *per se*. Chua (2017) developed and validated a questionnaire to measure kiasuism and found that kiasuism is a multidimensional construct consisting of *getting ahead*, *not to lose out*, and *pursuit of self-interest*. The findings revealed that not being worse than others and getting ahead are related but are not exactly the same; a *kiasu* person may be motivated to not lose out to others but this may not mean that he/she aims to perform better than others. *Getting ahead* and *pursuit of self-interest* focus on outperforming others and demonstration of one's ability while *not to lose out* is concerned with not being judged as inferior. The difference between *getting ahead* and *pursuit of self-interest* is that *pursuit of self-interest* involves elements of selfishness and goal achievement at the expense of others.

Kiasuism, particularly the *pursuit of self-interest*, may result in self-serving *kiasu* behaviours observed during a crisis. For instance, stockpiling and profiteering of N95 masks were observed during 2013 Southeast Asian haze crisis (Wee, 2013). Such *kiasu* behaviours can potentially result in others not having sufficient resources to be crisis ready, or delay society's recovery from the crisis as society is unable to unite as one and display communal resilience. In an effort to examine how culture may influence the crisis-ready mindset, Ang *et al.* (2017) examined the relationship between kiasuism and crisis-ready mindset and the results showed an inverse relationship. One of the explanations for such observed relationship could be due to the close association of kiasuism and fear of failure (Chua, 2017). Due to ambiguity in the unthinkables, individuals may perceive such crises to be events with a high likelihood of failure and this fear may impede preparation for the crises. This finding also suggests that *kiasu* behaviours observed during a crisis may not be translated from having a crisis-ready mindset but instead could be due to irrational fear.

Recommendation 3: Avoid a Silo Mentality

Having a silo mentality can make it harder to see systemwide failures and is a barrier to effective crisis management (Weick & Sutcliffe, 2007). A silo mentality not only disperses information but also undermines an organisation's resilience (Fenwick *et al.*, 2009). For instance, the CIA and other intelligence agencies were criticised for not sharing information among themselves, which resulted in failure to prevent the September 11 terrorist attacks (Kean & Lee, 2004).

One of the ways to prepare for novel and complex crises is to engage with multidisciplinary stakeholders to ensure accessibility of information (OECD, 2015) and also ensure seamless coordination and cooperation during a crisis (Fenwick *et al.*, 2009). This is consistent with David Snowden's recommendation in dealing with complicated contexts in the Cynefin framework (Snowden & Boone, 2007). Crisis leaders should consider engaging international agencies, academics, public–private partnerships, NGOs, religious leaders, and even the whole community during the pre-crisis stage and to mobilise these stakeholders during crisis responses and recovery. During the pre-crisis stage, these stakeholders must be trained regularly to work together to resolve various simulated crises. Additionally, an actor map, indicating the interrelations between the stakeholders (e.g., Ministries, public, NGOs, communities), can be utilised to create an awareness of who should be involved and consulted in handling the crisis (Tveiten *et al.*, 2012).

Engaging with multidisciplinary stakeholders during the pre-crisis stage helps to build trust and rapport, ensure common understanding of the technical or scientific languages, train experts to simplify professional jargons and technical data that can be easily understood by layman, develop a shared mental model, identify integrated, specialised solutions, and strengthen crisis responses through learning the good practices across agencies (OECD, 2015). Additionally, rapid pooling of *ad hoc* networks would be swift to provide knowledge and expertise to unforeseen crises (Weick & Sutcliffe, 2007).

Recommendation 4: Adopt the Resilience-by-design Approach

Stephen Flynn, a leading security expert, advocates the importance of building resilience as a strategic response to the unthinkables (Flynn, 2007, 2011). Instead of reviewing why the existing structures and crisis response plans are unable to withstand major disruptions in times of crises, crisis leaders should adopt the *resilience-by-design* approach that proactively builds and engineers resilience directly in infrastructures, critical systems, crisis response plans, and even in the organisational culture. In view of the importance of resilience in a disruptive environment, five recommendations that aim to develop resilience in people and also in systems are made.

Leaders should work closely with experts and system designers to improve and expand the crisis management systems. Some characteristics of resilient systems include *redundancy* and *loose coupling*. Redundancy, or buffering, is a state where reserves and alternative options are available when an individual unit fails (Fink, 1986; Longstaff *et al.*, 2010). Systems with no redundancy are vulnerable to system failures, which can impede crisis response (Streeter, 1992). The most cost-effective form of redundancy is reserve backup. Reserve backup redundancies are designed such that if a core system fails, a replacement would be called into action as a substitute (Streeter, 1992). Redundant channels of communication systems can also ensure that communication is not blocked or overloaded in times of crisis (Streeter, 1992). Redundancies may also be designed in jobs and functions; employees can be trained in more than one job and develop multiple skills so that in the event of a crisis and a member is unable to perform his/her job, these functional redundancies may ensure effective crisis response. For instance, are frontline responders ready to take up non-traditional roles such as providing psychological first aid to distressed victims before social workers arrive?

Next, loosely coupled systems are more resilient than tightly coupled systems (Longstaff *et al.*, 2010). In tightly coupled systems, a single failure can result in large-scale catastrophic consequences (Hovden *et al.*, 2010). Modular designs can be adopted in systems such that the individual components are less connected and more independent; the loose coupling between the components reduces the risks that if an individual component fails, the effect would ripple through the whole system. Modularity also increases the flexibility of adding new components or replacing individual components of a system.

Aside from developing crisis management plans, testing the robustness of these plans is also critical. Red teaming, similar to the concept of devil's advocate, is a valuable tool for crisis management (Ministry of Defense, 2013). A red team is "a team that is formed with the objective of subjecting an organisation's plans, programmes, ideas and assumptions to rigorous analysis and challenge" (Ministry of Defense, 2013, pp. 1–2). A red team may take the perspective of an adversary, challenge established assumptions, test the robustness of the existing protocol, identify the weaknesses, and explore alternative solutions (Boin *et al.*, 2004; Masys, 2012). For example, a red team could be set up to test whether countermeasures against terrorist attacks or cyberattacks put in place are effective, and to identify the possible cascading effects or unforeseen consequences.

Recommendation 5: Use of Data Analytics for Sense-making

Taleb (2007) argued that not all extreme events are Black Swans. There are also rare events that are somewhat predictable. Detecting and analysing early warning signals is the key to anticipating changes and avoiding surprises (Hiltunen, 2006). Predictable surprises are known threats where prior information or early warning signals are ignored, discounted, or bypassed (Gowing & Langdon, 2015), and leaders fail to respond with necessary preventive actions (Watkins & Bazerman, 2003).

Krupa and Cameron (2013) recommended policymakers to build resilient and robust systems. To improve organisation's crisis sense-making, organisations should develop and invest in early warning systems. Early warning system is an integrated system that not only collects and analyses multidisciplinary data on the phenomenon, but also monitors adverse trends, detects potential risks, disseminates warning information to policymakers, and supports the timely activation of emergency measures (OECD, 2015). In fact, early warning systems have helped in reducing casualties and limiting damages caused by various crises (OECD, 2015). Horizon scanning tools and location-based inventories are important systems to identify risks and assess damages of potential crises. For example, in Mexico, the System for the Analysis and Visualization of Risk Scenarios (SAVER) was developed for emergency preparedness. SAVER integrates risk maps and georeferencing to provide information on the damages and populations affected by potential disaster based on the systems' location data (OECD, 2015).

While new technologies may challenge our current practices, it also creates new opportunities that we could tap on. For instance, information and communication technology (ICT) such as crowdsourcing and Big Data analytics can be used as early warning systems. Big Data analytics refer to the gathering of large-scale data from social media, sensors, geotagging, and other databases. Sensors are used to detect physical quantities such as sound, chemical, and vibration; these data are then converted to digital signal. Web crawlers are common tools used to gather data from web search engines and web caches (Emmanouil & Nikolaos, 2015). Recently, a group of researchers developed LITMUS, a landslide detection system that integrates data from various social media (e.g., Twitter, Instagram, YouTube) with physical sensors that detect rainfall and seismic activity (Musaev *et al.*, 2015). Another way of gathering information is through crowdsourcing, which utilises the general public as eyes and ears on the ground to identify and monitor potential risks (OECD, 2015). For instance, an online website, HealthMap, utilised multiple sources such as online news, WHO reports, experts-curated discussions, official reports, and eyewitness reports, to provide real-time surveillance of disease outbreak and monitor for emerging public health threats (Boston Children's Hospital, 2007).

Although crowdsourcing and Big Data analytics are valuable for crisis management, crisis leaders need to be aware that they are dealing with large amount of data from multiple sources and some of these data may be irrelevant, inaccurate, or lack credibility. For instance, Google Flu Tracker failed to identify the first wave of 2009 H1N1 pandemic and miscalculated the severity of the 2013 flu epidemic (Olson *et al.*, 2013). The rapid flow of unstructured data in Big Data analytics can also derail effective crisis management especially if there is no robust ICT infrastructure to organise and make sense of the data. One possible solution is to have a central information hub to consolidate, verify, and disseminate all information of an emerging threat or near-crisis from different agencies and sources (Mitroff & Pearson, 1993).

Conclusion

The fat tail world is characterised by disruptions and catastrophic shocks. While prevention and preparation are effective strategies for crisis management, these strategies are useful for known threats (Comfort *et al.*, 2010). Crisis leaders not only need to be prepared for conventional crises, but new skills and capacities are also required. Anticipation and resilience are key strategies to manage modern crises, apart from the ability of organisations to plan for shocks and be able to rebound after disruptions (Fink, 1986). Crisis leaders should engage in future thinking and develop contingency plans for different possible futures to mitigate and minimise damages. New technologies can also be used for crisis sense-making and anticipation of novel crises. Additionally, systems need to be resilient against disruptions and new systems need to be mobilised to detect weak signals as well as to identify and assess emerging issues ahead of time. These systems can be utilised to complement on prevailing systems and build on existing capacities (OECD, 2015).

Acknowledgement

The views expressed in this chapter are the authors' only and do not represent the official position or view of the Ministry of Home Affairs, Singapore.

References

Ahlqvist, T., Uotila, T., & Hietanen, O. (2015). Chasing black swans through science fiction: Surprising future events in the stories of a Finnish writing competition. *Journal of Futures Studies*, *20*(2), 47–66.

Alarid, M. (2016). Recruitment and radicalization: The role of social media and new technology. Retrieved from: http://cco.ndu.edu/Publications/Books/Impunity/Article/780274/chapter-13-recruitment-and-radicalization-the-role-of-social-media-and-new-tech/.

Ang, D., Chua, H. S., & Khader, M. (2017). *Gearing Up for Crises: Developing a Crisis Readiness Questionnaire*. Singapore: Home Team Behavioural Sciences Centre.

Ansell, C., Boin, A., & Keller, A. (2010). Managing transboundary crises: Identifying the building blocks of an effective response system. *Journal of Contingencies and Crisis Management*, *18*(4), 195–207.

Aven, T. (2015). Implications of Black Swans to the foundations and practice of risk assessment and management. *Reliability Engineering and System Safety*, *134*, 83–91.

Bedford, O., & Chua, H. S. (2017). Everything also I want: An exploratory study of Singaporean kiasuism (fear of losing out). *Culture & Psychology.* Advance Online Publication:http://doi: 10.1177/1354067X17693831.

Boin, A. (2008). Managing transboundary crises: What role for the European Union? *International Studies Review, 10*, 1–26.

Boin, A. (2009). The new world of crises and crisis management: Implications for policymaking and research. *Review of Policy Research, 26*(4), 367–377.

Boin, A., Ekengren, M., Myrdal, S., & Rhinard, M. (2009). Preparing for transboundary threats: What role for the next Commission? *European Policy Centre.* Retrieved from: http://www.epc.eu/documents/uploads/970080380_Preparing%20for%20transboundary%20threats.pdf.

Boin, A., Kofman-Bos, C., & Overdijk, W. I. E. (2004). Crisis simulations: Exploring tomorrow's vulnerabilities and threats. *Simulation and Gaming: An International Journal of Theory, Practice and Research, 35*, 378–393.

Boin, A., McConnell, A., & 't Hart, P. (2008). *Governing After Crisis: The Politics of Investigation, Accountability and Learning.* US: Cambridge University Press.

Bosetti, V., Carraro, C., Sgobbi, A., & Tavoni, M. (2008). Delay action and uncertain targets. How much will climate policy cost? Retrieved from http://ageconsearch.umn.edu/bitstream/44219/2/69-08.pdf.

Boston Children's Hospital (2007). *Healthmap.* Retrieved from http://www.healthmap.org/print_materials/brochure.pdf.

Bremmer, I., & Keat, P. (2009). *The Fat Tail: The Power of Political Knowledge in an Uncertain World.* New York: Oxford University Press.

Carvalho, V. M., Nirei, M., & Saito, Y. U. (2014). Supply chain disruptions: Evidence from the Great East Japan Earthquake. Research Report No. 1/2017. USA: Becker Friedman Institute for Research in Economics.

Centers for Disease Control and Prevention (2009). Origin of 2009 H1N1 Flu (Swine Flu): Questions and Answers. Retrieved from http://www.cdc.gov/h1n1flu/information_h1n1_virus_qa.htm — d.

Catino, M. (2013). *Organisational Myopia: Problems of Rationality and Foresight in Organisations.* Cambridge, UK: Cambridge University Press.

Chan, F. (2016). ISIS may set up caliphate in South-east Asia. *The Straits Times.* Retrieved from http://www.straitstimes.com/asia/isis-may-set-up-caliphate-in-south-east-asia.

Chan, M. (2009). World now at the start of 2009 influenza pandemic [Press release]. Retrieved from http://www.who.int/mediacentre/news/statements/2009/h1n1_pandemic_phase6_20090611/en/.

Chua, H. S. (2017). Influence of failure and kiasuism on entrepreneurial intention. Unpublished Doctoral Dissertation. Singapore: Nanyang Technological University.

Collins, S., & McCombie, S. (2012). Stuxnet: The emergence of a new cyber weapon and its implications. *Journal of Policing, Intelligence, and Counter Terrorism*, 7(1), 80–91.

Comfort, L. K., Boin, A., & Demchak, C. (2010). *Designing Resilience: Preparing for Extreme Events*. Pittsburg, PA: University of Pittsburgh Press.

Emmanouil, D., & Nikolaos, D. (2015). Big data analytics in prevention, preparedness, response and recovery in crisis and disaster management. *Recent Advances in Computer Science*, 476–482.

Faola, D. (2016). The causes and aftermath of the 2007–2008 financial crisis. Retrieved from http://themarketmogul.com/causes-aftermath-2007-2008-financial-crisis/.

Fenwick, T., Seville, E., & Brunsdon, D. (2009). Reducing the impact of organisational silos on resilience. Retrieved from https://ir.canterbury.ac.nz./bitstream/handle/10092/9468/12619818_silos.pdf?sequence=1&isAllowed=y.

Ferris, E., & Solís, M. (2013). Earthquake, tsunami, meltdown — The triple disaster's impact on Japan, impact on the world. *Brookings Institution*. Retrieved from https://www.brookings.edu/blog/up-front/2013/03/11/earthquake-tsunami-meltdown-the-triple-disasters-impact-on-japan-impact-on-the-world/.

Fink, S. (1986). *Crisis Management: Planning for the Inevitable*. New York: American Management Association.

Flynn, S. (2007). *The Edge of Disaster: Rebuilding a Resilient Nation*. US: Random House.

Flynn, S. (2011). A national security perspective on resilience. *Resilience: Interdisciplinary on Science and Humanitatianism*, 2, i–ii.

Foley Jr., W. A. (2012). Developing a systematic pandemic influenza program for preparing a state. In J. Eric Dietz & D.R. Black (Eds.), *Pandemic Planning* (pp. 65–94). Boca Raton, FL: CRC Press.

Fogarty, P. (2011). How Japan tackles its quake challenge. *BBC*. Retrieved from http://www.bbc.com/news/world-asia-pacific-12709793.

Gallop, D., Willy, C., & Bischoff, J. (2016). How to catch a black swan: Measuring the benefits of the premortem technique for risk identification. *Journal of Enterprise Transformation*, 6(2), 87–106.

Gowing, N., & Langdon, C. (2015). Thinking the unthinkable: A new imperative for leadership in the digital age. Retrieved from https://www.cimaglobal.com/Documents/Thought-leadership_docs/Enterprise_governance/Thinking-the-Unthinkable-cima-report.pdf.

Gundel, S. (2005). Towards a new typology of crises. *Journal of Contingencies and Crisis Management*, *13*(3), 106–115.

Hiltunen, E. (2006). Was it a wild card or just our blindness to gradual change? *Journal of Futures Studies*, *11*(2), 61–74.

Ho, P. (2017). The black elephant challenge for governments. *The Straits Times*. Retrieved from http://www.straitstime.com/opinion/the-black-elephant-challenge-for-governments.

Hoge Jr., J. F. (2004). A global power shift in the making. Retrieved from http://www.foreignaffairs.com/articles/united-states/2004-07-01/global-power-shift-making.

Hovden, J., Albrechtsen, E., & Herrera, I. A. (2010). Is there a need for new theories, models, and approaches to occupational accident prevention? *Safety Science*, *48*, 950–956.

Jackson, R., Howe, N., Strauss, R., & Nakashima, K. (2008). *The Graying of the Great Powers: Demography and Geopolitics in the 21st Century*. Washington, DC: Center for Strategic and International Studies.

Kean, T. H., & Lee, H. H. (2004). Release of 9/11 commission report. Retrieved from govinfo.library.unt.edu/911/report/911Report_Statement.pdf.

Kim, J. Y. (2016). Are we prepared for the next global epidemic? The public doesn't think so. *Huffington Post*. Retrieved from http://www.huffingtonpost.com/jim-yong-kim/are-we-prepared-for-the-n_b_7939812.html.

Kirby, E. G., & Ross, J.K. (2007). Kiasu tendency and tactics: A study of their impact on task performance. *Journal of Behavioral and Applied Management*, *8*(2), 108–121.

Krupa, J., & Cameron, J. (2013). Black swan theory: Applications to energy market histories and technologies. *Energy Strategy Reviews*, *1*(4), 286–290.

Lagadec, P. (1993). *Preventing Chaos in a Crisis: Strategies for Prevention, Control, and Damage Limitation* (J. M. Phelps, Translation). New York: McGraw-Hill.

Lagadec, P., & Topper, B. (2012). How crises model the modern world. *Journal of Risk Analysis and Crisis Response*, *2*(1), 21–33.

Leigh, M. (2015). Critical thinking in crisis management. Retrieved from https://www.epcresilience.com/EPC/media/Images/Knowledge Centre/Occaionals/Occ15-Paper-DEC-2015.pdf.

Longstaff, P. H., Armstrong, N. J., Perrin, K., Parker, W. M., & Hidek, M. A. (2010). Building resilient communities. *Homeland Security Affairs*, *6*(3), 1–23.

Masys, A. J. (2012). Black swans to grey swans: Revealing the uncertainty. *Disaster Prevention and Management: An International Journal*, *21*(3), 320–335.

Menon, K. U. (2005). National resilience: From bouncing back to prevention. *Ethos: Journal of the Society for Psychological Anthropology*, *11*(1), 14–17. Retrieved from https://www.cscollege.gov.sg/knowledge/ethos/ethos%20january%202005/Pages/National%20Resilience%20From%20Bouncing%20Back%20to%20Prevention.aspx.

Ministry of Defense (2013). *Red Teaming Guide*. London: Ministry of Defense.

Ministry of Health (2014). MOH pandemic readiness and response plan for influenza and other acute respiratory diseases. Retrieved from http://www.moh.gov.sg/content/dam/moh_web/Diseases and Conditions/DORSCON 2013/Interim Pandemic Plan Public Ver _April 2014.pdf.

Mitchell, D. J., Russo, J. E., & Pennington, N. (1989). Back to the future: Temporal perspective in the explanation of events. *Journal of Behavioral Decision Making*, *2*(1), 25–38.

Mitroff, I. I. (2004). *Crisis Leadership: Planning for the Unthinkable*. Hoboken, NJ: Wiley.

Mitroff, I. I., & Pearson, C. M. (1993). *Crisis Management: A Diagnostic Guide for Improving your Organisation's Crisis-Preparedness*. San Francisco, CA: Jossey-Bass Publishers.

Musaev, A., Wang, D., & Pu, C. (2015). LITMUS: A multi-service composition system for landslide detection. *IEEE Transactions on Services Computing, 8*(5), 715–726.

National Intelligence Council (2017). Assessing Russian activities and intentions in recent US elections. Retrieved from https://www.dni.gov/files/documents/ICA_2017_01.pdf.

't Hart, P., & Boin, A. (2001). Between crisis and normalcy: The long shadow of post-crisis politics. In U. Rosenthal, A. Boin & L. K. Comfort (Eds.), *Managing Crisis: Threats, Dilemmas, Opportunities*. US: Charles C Thomas.

Taleb, N. N. (2007). *The Black Swan*. US: Random House.

Taleb, N. N. (2007). *The Black Swan: The Impact of the Highly Improbable*. New York: Random House.

The Organisation for Economic Co-operation and Development (OECD) (2011). Future global shocks: Improving risk governance. Retrieved from www.oecd.org/governance/48329024.

The Organisation for Economic Co-operation and Development (OECD) (2013). OECD risk management: Strategic crisis management. Retrieved from www.oecd.org/gov/risk/crisis-management.htm.

The Organisation for Economic Co-operation and Development (OECD) (2015). The changing face of strategic crisis management. Retrieved from www.oecd.org/publications/the-changing-face-of-strategic-crisis-management-9789264249127-en.htm.

Tveiten, C. K., Albrechtsen, E., Wærø, I., & Marit Wahl, A. (2012). Building resilience into emergency management. *Safety Science*, *50*, 1,960–1,966.

Olson, D. R., Konty, K. J., Paladini, M., Viboud, C., & Simonsen, L. (2013). Reassessing google flu trends data for detection of seasonal and pandemic influenza: A comparative epidemiological study at three geographic scales. *PLOS Computational Biology*, *9*(10), 1–11.

Petty, M. (2011). The dark side of leadership: Catastrophic failure. *Strategic Leadership Review*, *1*(1), 20–29.

Porfiriev, B. (2000). Preparing for creeping crises: The case of the Samara region. *Journal of Contingencies and Crisis Management*, *8*(4), 218–222.

Schwab, K. (2016). The fourth industrial revolution: What it means, how to respond. *World Economic Forum*. Retrieved from http://www.weforum.org/agenda/2016/01/the-fourth-industrial-revolution-what-it-means-and-how-to-respond/.

Snowden, D. J., & Boone, M. E. (2007). A leader's framework for decision making. *Havard Business Review*, *85*(11), 68–76.

Streeter, C. L. (1992). Redundancy in organisational systems. *Social Service Review*, *66*(1), 97–111.

UN High Commissioner for Refugees (2015). UNHCR global trends: Forced displacement in 2014. *Reliefweb*. Retrieved from https://reliefweb.int/report/world/unhcr-global-trends-forced-displacement-2014.

U.S. Department of Homeland Security (2016). Strategic principles for securing the internet of things (IoT). Retrieved from https://http://www.dhs.gov/sites/default/files/publications/Strategic_Principles_for_Securing_the_Internet_of_Things-2016-1115-FINAL_v2-dg11.pdf.

van de Vijver, F., & Tanzer, N. K. (2004). Bias and equivalence in cross-cultural assessment: An overview. *European Review of Applied Psychology*, *54*(2), 119–135.

Volcovici, V. (2017). EPA Chief wants scientists to debate climate on TV. *Reuters*. Retrieved from https://www.reuters.com/article/us-usa-epa-pruitt/epa-chief-wants-scientists-to-debate-climate-on-tv-idUSKBN19W2D0.

von Einsiedel, S., Bosetti, L., Chandran, R., Cockayne, J., de Boer, J., & Wan, W. (2014). Major recent trends in violent conflict. Retrieved from https//i.unu/media/cpr.unu.edu/attachment/1558/OC_01-MajorRecentTrendsinViolentConflict.pdf.

Wang, Y., Tan, J., Gomes, D., Neo, L., Ong, G., & Khader, M. (2015). National resilience factor: Developing and sustaining a crisis ready mindset. Research Report: 09/2015. Singapore: Home Team Behavioural Sciences Centre.

Watkins, M. D., & Bazerman, M. H. (2003). Predictable surprises: The disasters you should have seen coming. *Havard Business Review*, *81*(3), 72–80.

Wee, W. (2013). Scalping of sought-after goods getting worse. *The Straits Times*. Retrieved from: http://www.asiaone.com/print/News/Latest%2BNews/Singapore/Story/A1Story20130702-433861.html.

Weick, K. E., & Sutcliffe, K. M. (2007). *Managing the Unexpected* (2nd edn.). USA: Jossey-Bass.

Wu, L. H., & Hayashi, H. (2013). The impact of the great east Japan earthquake on inbound tourism demand in Japan. *Journal of Institute of Social Safety Science*, *21*, 109–117.

CHAPTER 26

Striking the Right Balance in Relation to Target Hardening

DAMIEN D. CHEONG

S. Rajaratnam School of International Studies, Nanyang Technological University, Singapore

Introduction

In 2017, several terrorist-related incidents in Barcelona, Berlin, Paris, and London underscored that public places were extremely vulnerable to vehicular attacks. Lone individuals inspired by the Islamic State of Iraq and Syria's (ISIS) violent extremist ideology, drove into crowds killing and injuring many. The change in offensive tactics whereby ordinary vehicles are "weaponised" and used for nefarious purposes makes target hardening or infrastructure protection enhancement a necessary response to mitigate such threats.

The U.K. Government's Centre for the Protection of National Infrastructure (CPNI) (2018b) argues that target hardening in the contemporary sense involves three key measures:

a. Deter: Stop or displace the attack.
b. Detect: Verify an attack, initiate the response.

c. Delay: Prevent the attacker from reaching the asset — including measures to minimise the consequences of an attack.

Target hardening therefore involves more than simply erecting bollards, gantries, and/or other protective measures around buildings or public venues. It also involves taking steps to deter, and in the wake of the attack, help post-incident investigation. The incorporation of CCTVs and, increasingly, SMART CCTVs, as part of an infrastructure protection enhancement package is useful in this regard. As technology improves and these cameras become even more advanced, their dual-purpose utility to combat both terrorist and criminal threats will become more apparent.

Despite a clear rationale for target hardening, adoption and implementation are not always forthcoming. This is due primarily to the concerns of the different stakeholders that, at times, conflict with one another. Ultimately, infrastructure protection enhancement will require striking a balance between costs, aesthetics, security, efficiency, and privacy (Cheong & Ramakrishna, 2017). This chapter identifies the challenges in each of the above-mentioned domains and suggests approaches to mitigate these challenges.

Challenges

Costly Infrastructure Protection Enhancements Dissuade Acceptance

According to the Centre for the Protection of National Infrastructure (CPNI) (2018a, para. 1), target hardening is a complicated process as:

> [E]ach layer of security may be comprised of different elements, including, for example:
>
> a. Measures to assist in the detection of threat weapons, including for example explosives, knives, firearms, chemical/biological/radiological material, etc.
> b. Measures to assist in the detection, tracking, and monitoring of intruders and other threats such as unmanned aerial vehicles.

c. Access control and locking systems.
d. Physical and active barriers to deny or delay the progress of adversaries.
e. Measures to protect people or assets from the effect of blast or ballistic attack.
f. Measures to protect against or limit the spread of chemical, biological, or radiological material.
g. Measures to protect sensitive (e.g., classified) material or assets.
h. Command and control.
i. The response to an incident.
j. Security personnel (covered within the Personnel and People Security).

Installing some or all of these features inevitably add to the costs of owners of both new and old buildings. During a parliamentary debate in October 2017, Singapore's Second Home Affairs Minister Josephine Teo estimated that total construction costs of new buildings could go up by "0.2 to 3 percent" as a result of incorporating enhanced infrastructure protection measures (Cheong, 2017). For older buildings, costs could also be significant as such buildings may require structural changes or reinforcements to accommodate the new protective feature(s) (e.g., new electrical wiring system for CCTVs or new window frames to hold heavier reinforced glass panels). The "total assets lifecycle cost", which is essentially the cost of operating/maintaining the asset throughout its lifecycle and applies to all buildings, needs to be taken into account as well (Yusof, 2017).

Expectedly, the prospects of these add-on costs make some building owners less enthusiastic about enhancing infrastructure protection (Toh, 2017).

Target Hardening is Perceived to Ruin Aesthetics

Despite a rise in vehicular terrorist attacks in Europe in recent times, many European cities seem hesitant to beef up infrastructure citing, among other concerns (which will be discussed later), that it would adversely affect the city's overall aesthetics (Bergin, 2017). In

Australia, the erection of bollards in Melbourne's city-centre has also elicited some negative sentiment. "Absolutely hideous" remarked Jean, a city worker. "What next — barbed wire? It doesn't look good at all" (Ham, 2017; Pearlman, 2017).

In addition, some researchers have maintained that enhanced infrastructure protection can increase "fearfulness, suspicion, paranoia, exclusion and ultimately insecurity" (Coaffee *et al.*, 2009). Some critics have even gone so far as to argue that such "security measures ... is not to protect citizens, but ... to control them through a manipulation of threat perceptions — by creating and exploiting fear to legitimise government control, counterterrorism measures, and spending" (Coaffee *et al.*, 2009; Dalgaard-Nielsen *et al.*, 2016; Sorkin, 2008).

In any case, negative *perceptions* invariably give rise to apprehensions about enhanced infrastructure protection.

Target Hardening can Negatively Impact Businesses

As mentioned earlier, one of the more common arguments made, at least in Europe, against enhanced infrastructure protection is that it creates inefficiencies and inconvenience especially for businesses. For example, hotels and eateries that rely on the free and easy movement of customers and delivery personnel will be affected by additional security features that disrupt this flow. "You cannot block every street. You have to live and shops need to have deliveries. We have to have a compromise between security and still living in the city" said Els Ampe, Deputy Mayor of Brussels (Bergin, 2017).

For transport hubs such as terminals, train stations, airports, and seaports, the efficient and expedited movement of foot traffic is integral from an operation, logistics, customer service, and, ultimately, economic perspective. Enhanced security measures can create inefficiencies that negatively impact operators. "The more security you put in place the more you slow things down" remarked Professor Clive Williams from the Australian National University (Brook, 2016).

Target Hardening does Not Prevent Attacks

Critics often point out that target hardening including the installation and use of CCTVs does not prevent terrorist attacks. For instance, Kade Crockford, a privacy-rights coordinator with the Massachusetts American Civil Liberties Union (ACLU), argued that "Dragnet surveillance ... doesn't stop terrorism, nor does CCTV monitoring. That has been shown time and time again after the Charlie Hebdo and Bataclan attacks" (Joseph, 2016). Robert Draper, writer-at-large for *The New York Times Magazine* observed that "there is really no evidence that all of these CCTVs [in London] prevent crimes of any kind, much less terrorist attacks" (Gross, 2018). Critics have therefore argued that target hardening may not be worth the investment.

Privacy Challenges vis-à-vis CCTVs

According to Muhammad Faizal, Research Fellow at RSIS, debates over "privacy concerns with respect to surveillance technology" often focus on "whether the reliability and accuracy (rate of false positives and negatives) of CCTVs could justify the perceived loss of privacy". He notes that in future, "privacy concerns may arise from the linking of (Artificial Intelligence Enabled) SMART CCTVs with privately-owned CCTVs as such initiatives would extend the surveillance gaze of law enforcement agencies beyond public spaces and into privately owned (or semi-public) spaces" (Abdul Rahman, 2017, p. 32).

A related challenge is whether CCTV footage should be shared on social media to help in the identification of suspects. A major concern is vigilante justice perpetrated against individuals who are mistaken for suspects — as in the case of Sunil Tripathi, who was mistaken as the Boston Bomber in 2013 (Lee, 2013). "Now, people take videos of others all the time — on the train, for instance" observed Singaporean lawyer Nicholas Aw. "It is true that posting CCTV footage [on social media] has value because the culprit gets identified, but the concern that I have is abuse, when vigilante justice occurs or if people find the wrong person" he said. Aw also noted "that there are no laws [in Singapore] that prohibit such videos from being uploaded online ... so people should be careful and be clear of the effect before posting such videos" (Tan, 2017, paras. 15–17).

Despite such issues, many in Singapore, seem supportive of the expansion of CCTV networks, and prioritise "national security and public safety" above individual privacy (Toh, 2016). However, such sentiments cannot be taken for granted as mindsets could change in the future.

Potential Mitigating Approaches

Communicating Indirect Costs from Terrorism to Building Owners and Providing some Financial Assistance for Security Enhancement

The costs of a terrorist attack are not limited simply to direct costs. There are also indirect costs such as loss of life, tourism, reputational damage, public confidence, and so on. These are not easily quantifiable, and may be significantly greater than direct costs in the long run. For example, the New York City comptroller's office estimated that the cost of replacing destroyed and damaged property from the 9/11 attacks was about US$26 billion. However, the estimates for indirect costs such as value of life (US$24 billion), loss of revenue from airline and other travel (US$100 billion), as well as loss of revenue from business interruption (US$22 billion), were significantly higher (Carter & Cox, 2011).

In Europe, many countries are experiencing a decline in tourist revenue as a result of terrorism. For example, Belgium (where the Brussels airport and subway were attacked) reported that "the economy has already suffered a nearly €1 billion loss in business and tax revenue" with "hotels, restaurants ... tourism [and the] entertainment industry" enduring the "biggest hits" (Alderman, 2016).

When considering the significant indirect costs of terrorism, target hardening should be seen more as a long-term investment rather than a short-term cost. Authorities could consider several options to help owners with the costs of security enhancements, which would encourage acceptance. These include: (a) one-off grants or subsidies, (b) subsidised security enhancement packages, (c) corporate tax relief, (d) subsidised security audits and/or consultancy, and (e) discounts on building insurance premiums.

Incorporating Security-by-Design in Target Hardening and "Hardening" Society

Security-By-Design is essentially "the idea that architecture and aesthetics can be built from the get-go to facilitate security efforts" (Loke, 2016, para. 2). Singapore's Sports Hub is a good example of how security-by-design has resulted in a secure set of buildings that do not resemble "unwelcoming fortresses" (Loke, 2016).

The CPNI argues that for new buildings, "considering the physical security requirements at the outset, as part of the building or facility design, will often result in more effective and lower cost security" (CPNI, 2018a, para. 4). It also suggests that:

> [F]or new builds, high level security requirements should be incorporated into the original brief. Physical security requirements should also be considered during the construction phase of new builds or the modification of existing facilities, as these are likely to be subject to different risks and issues. Consideration should be given to: (a) Identification and assessment of existing and new security risks; (b) Identification of security requirements for both the construction works and any changes to the security of the facility itself (this will depend on whether the construction works are adjacent to or within the facility); and (c) Determination of the transition of the security measures from 'construction phase' into normal operations. (CPNI, 2018a, paras. 4–5).

Existing/old buildings will, however, require some creative interventions to ensure that the added security features blend in with the aesthetics. In 2017, the Australian Government produced a publication known as *Hostile Vehicle Guidelines for Crowded Places*, which aimed:

> [T]o provide those responsible for crowded places with knowledge to inform security design considerations and decisions. It is intended to be a starting point to the development of effective and aesthetically complementary designs that help protect crowded places from hostile vehicles Commonwealth of Australia (2017, p. 5).

Some of the suggestions include using trees, planter boxes, sculptures, and retractable bollards as less unsightly countermeasures. Other useful insights include "the variety of traffic management options, including different forms of vehicle approaches" (Commonwealth of Australia, 2017, p. 19). The report notes that:

> [E]ven a small reduction in the velocity of a hostile vehicle will have a significant decrease in the amount of energy that vehicle is carrying, thus reducing its impact and permitting less intrusive Hostile Vehicle Mitigation (HVM) devices, which may reduce costs (Commonwealth of Australia, 2017, p. 20).

In the Singapore context, security-by-design approaches and creative interventions to make enhanced security features aesthetically-acceptable help to ensure that feelings of "fearfulness, suspicion, paranoia, exclusion and ultimately insecurity" do not take root among residents — both Singaporeans and residents alike (Cheong & Ramakrishna, 2017).

In addition, the government has been trying to: (a) instil "a security consciousness [awareness]" in the population (Toh, 2016), (b) emphasise that a terror attack affects *everyone*, and (c) focus increasingly on preparedness (Cheow, 2017). To that end, it has provided solutions (e.g., SGSecure App) and training (e.g., first-aid, mental-health) to help individuals respond collaboratively and effectively in the event of a terror attack (Lim, 2017). Such initiatives are designed in part to minimise feelings of fear and helplessness.

Furthermore, Singaporean pragmatism in relation to national security (in terms of prioritising public safety above other considerations such as privacy) (Toh, 2016), and the "extraordinary level of faith and trust Singaporeans have in" law enforcement

(Seow, 2017), help negate potential negative sentiment towards enhanced security features.

Leveraging SMART CCTVs

An inherent limitation of traditional CCTVs is that captured footage "cannot be efficiently processed and analysed" due in part to the volume and complexity of the footage and the limited manpower available (Abdul Rahman, 2017; Tang, 2017).

Developments in Artificial Intelligence (AI) and Machine Learning (ML) technologies have enabled the creation of SMART CCTVs that comprise:

> [V]arious digital cameras that are web-connected (IP-enabled) or connected over a wireless mesh network. The in-built AI technology automates real-time monitoring and improves analytics of recorded footage. The system is linked to other types of databases, which help facilitate the identification of individuals and objects. Among the key features of SMART CCTVs are: (i) facial recognition (physical biometrics); (ii) detection of anomalous behaviour and gait (behavioural biometrics); (iii) detection of unattended objects; (iv) vehicle license plate recognition; (v) crowd and directional flow detection; and (vi) tracking of persons and objects (Abdul Rahman, 2017, p. 5).

Muhamamd Faizal, Research Fellow at RSIS, argues that:

> [...] the AI technology driving SMART CCTVs enhances the camera's ability to better scrutinise the landscape for anomalies, which makes it extremely useful for threat detection. Of significance is the facial recognition feature that can identify persons of interest with greater speed and accuracy. Regarded as a form of 'silent technology', facial recognition is less intrusive as compared to other forms (i.e., fingerprints and iris recognition) of biometric recognition. The technology is versatile, and can be integrated into existing CCTV systems, immigration clearance systems and law enforcement photo databases (Abdul Rahman, 2017, p. 7).

Singapore, according to Minister of Home Affairs and Minister for Law, K. Shanmugam, is developing "deep data analytical capabilities to allow real-time monitoring and analysis of the CCTV data" ("Enhancing Singapore's response to terrorism", 2016). It is also planning to "set up the network infrastructure to allow CCTV data in more areas to be accessible to the Police, on-demand. These include CCTVs monitoring the public transportation system, commercial buildings with high footfall and Government buildings" ("Enhancing Singapore's response to terrorism", 2016). Such measures are envisaged to improve planning and overall responses of law enforcement.

As with all CCTV and SMART CCTV systems, attention must be paid to attempts by adversaries to disable the cameras, either by tampering with the wiring, power, and/or launching a cyberattack on the system (Abdul Rahman, 2017; Flaherty, 2015). A 52-year-old man was recently arrested in Singapore for setting fire to several police CCTV cameras ("Man arrested for burning police cameras in Jurong West", 2017). While the damage was not that severe, the incident underscores the possibility that adversaries could attempt to disrupt CCTV networks by targeting the cameras and/or other physical components.

Improving Risk Management with Target Hardening

While an unfortunate reality, target hardening's ultimate aim is to minimise risks by deterring adversaries from attempting the attack in the first place (Hsu & McDowall, 2017). The United Kingdom's Ring of Steel ("New 'ring of steel' planned for London Square Mile", 2016) and Israel's Separation Barrier in the West Bank[1] are some examples where target hardening has shown to be an effective deterrent.

If target hardening fails to deter and the attack is carried out, security enhancements help minimise the number of casualties/fatalities resulting from the attack, which would expectedly increase

[1] "The Barrier together with associated security activities was effective in preventing suicide bombings and other attacks and fatalities with little if any apparent displacement. Changes in terrorist behaviour likely resulted from the construction of the Barrier, not from other external factors or events" (Perry *et al.*, 2017).

if enhanced security measures were absent. Dominic Casciani, a BBC journalist writing about The United Kingdom's target hardening measures observed:

> [D]epending on the specific location, many of the barriers increasingly built into our landscape have been tested to see if they can withstand a head-on impact from a seven-tonne lorry driven at 50mph (80 kmh). The most well-known example of that kind of planning in action can be found at Arsenal's Emirates' Stadium, where giant letters spelling out the club name are, in fact, also a massive shield. If a Berlin-like lorry attack were attempted at the stadium, the letters would absorb the energy of the collision. In all likelihood, the lorry would simply smash itself to pieces (Casciani, 2016, paras. 16–18).

Finally, the use of SMART CCTVs can deter potential adversaries by increasing their risks of getting caught (if the attack is not a suicide attack) via post-attack analysis of CCTV footage (Gross, 2018). On this point, to ensure that the CCTV footage is usable, it is useful to ensure that all newly-installed or existing CCTVs meet industry standards.

Addressing Privacy Concerns

Muhammad Faizal, Research Fellow at RSIS, argues that "privacy concerns should not be allowed to demonise the adoption of SMART CCTVs given its pivotal role in law enforcement, to ensure safety and security" (Abdul Rahman, 2017, p. 30). He notes that "advances in SMART CCTV technology" will ultimately "enhance the accuracy of CCTVs" making "the process of surveillance ... smart" rather than "mass". He believes that "privacy would be better preserved as the footage is processed by AI instead of human operators" and

> [H]uman operators would be alerted only if: (a) anomalous behaviour or objects are detected; and (b) persons with criminal records are detected through facial recognition. Hence, only the privacy of persons with criminal records or those behaving suspiciously would be affected (Abdul Rahman, 2017, p. 30).

Faizal also believes that:

> [P]eople may be more amenable to CCTVs if there are safeguards to ensure responsible use of CCTVs and to prevent abuse. For example, legislation such as the Data Protection Act in the United Kingdom and the Personal Data Protection Act in Singapore help to regulate the responsible use of CCTVs. In the U.S., privacy guidelines regulate the responsible use of the New York Police Department's Domain Awareness System (Abdul Rahman, 2017, p. 31).

As law enforcement may need to access privately owned CCTVs, Faizal suggests that related privacy concerns can be addressed by:

(a) limiting access only to privately owned CCTV cameras that are placed outdoors and along public thoroughfares where people expect minimal or zero privacy;
(b) eschewing audio surveillance;
(c) maintaining a tight access control of the CCTV monitoring centre.

These policies, for example, underpin the initiative in Grand Rapids, Michigan, the United States, which enables law enforcement agencies to access privately owned CCTVs in real-time (Abdul Rahman, 2017, p. 32).

Also,

> [P]olicies that regulate the responsible use of CCTVs in public spaces should be reviewed for its possible impact on the rights and responsibilities of both owners and operators of private CCTVs who collaborate with law enforcement. For example, Western Australia's State CCTV strategy stipulates that existing legislation which regulates the use of surveillance devices will be reviewed given the involvement of the privately-owned CCTVs. Reviews should include public consultations in order to maintain trust by meaningfully engaging all stakeholders for their views. (Abdul Rahman, 2017, p. 32).

Conclusion

Target hardening is often contemplated after an attack. However, for countries that have yet to experience a hostile vehicle attack or a terrorist attack on infrastructure, the experience of other countries underscores the necessity to treat target hardening as a pre-emptive rather than reactive approach.

Singapore recently introduced the Infrastructure Protection Act, which essentially: (a) requires selected new buildings to integrate security measures within their design before they are built, and selected existing buildings to do so when they are about to be renovated; and (b) allows the Ministry of Home Affairs (MHA) to direct selected buildings to put in place security measures to protect against terrorist attacks (Infrastructure Protection Act, 2017). This law provides the necessary legal framework to operationalise target hardening in the city-state. Other countries such as Australia have also introduced creative initiatives to improve infrastructure protection.[2]

In addition, countries could look at improving "inclusivity, strong civic mindedness and rule of law". A 2011 Danish study argued that these were "just as important in reinforcing feelings of safety" (Dalgaard-Nielsen *et al.*, 2016). This is because these attributes enhance societal resilience and enable communities to cope better in the wake of a terror attack. Ultimately, effective responses in the wake of any terrorist attack will have to include both hard and soft measures.

References

Abdul Rahman, M. F. (2017). Smart CCTVs for secure cities: Potential and challenges. *RSIS Policy Report*. July. Retrieved https://www.rsis.edu.sg/wp-content/uploads/2017/08/PR170815_Smart-CCTVs_WEB.pdf.

Alderman, L. (2016). Terrorism scares away the tourists Europe was counting on. *New York Times*. Retrieved from https://www.nytimes.

[2]It is important to adopt the resilience-by-design approach (refer to Chapter 25).

com/2016/07/30/business/international/europe-economy-gdp-terrorism.html.

Bergin, T. (2017). Europe wary of Security Infrastructure despite Vehicle Attacks. *Reuters*. Retrieved from https://www.reuters.com/article/us-spain-security-streetscapes/europe-wary-of-security-infrastructure-despite-vehicle-attacks-idUSKCN1B11OJ.

Brook, B. (2016). Questions raised about Security at Airports and Railway Stations following Brussels Attack. *News.com.au*. Retrieved from http://www.news.com.au/travel/travel-updates/incidents/questions-raised-about-security-at-airports-and-railway-stations-following-brussels-attacks/news-story/f3f9d82350ede7855140ceaaba2183d7.

Carter, S., & Cox, A. (2011). One 9/11 Tally: $3.3 Trillion. *New York Times*. Retrieved from http://www.nytimes.com/interactive/2011/09/08/us/sept-11-reckoning/cost-graphic.html.

Casciani, D. (2016). Can a lorry attack ever be stopped? *BBC*. Retrieved from http://www.bbc.com/news/uk-36806691.

Centre for the Protection of National Infrastructure (CPNI) (2018a). Physical security. Retrieved from https://www.cpni.gov.uk/physical-security.

Centre for the Protection of National Infrastructure (CPNI) (2018b). Protecting my asset. Retrieved from https://www.cpni.gov.uk/protecting-my-asset.

Cheong, D. (2017). New Law to Shield Buildings, Key Installations from Attacks. *The Straits Times*. Retrieved from http://www.straitstimes.com/politics/new-law-to-shield-buildings-key-installations-from-attacks.

Cheong, D. D., & Ramakrishna, K. (2017). Making a CASE for enhancing security of infrastructure. *TODAY*. Retrieved from https://www.todayonline.com/commentary/making-case-enhancing-security-instructure.

Cheow, S. (2017). SGSecure will Shift focus to Lifting Levels of Preparedness. *The Straits Times*. Retrieved from http://www.straitstimes.com/singapore/sgsecure-will-shift-focus-to-lifting-levels-of-preparedness.

Coaffee, J., O'Hare, P., & Hawkesworth, M. (2009). The visibility of (in) security: The aesthetics of planning urban defences against terrorism. *Security Dialogue*, *40*(4-5), 489–511.

Commonwealth of Australia (2017). *Hostile Vehicle Guidelines for Crowded Places: Guide for Owners, Operators and Designers*. Retrieved from https://www.nationalsecurity.gov.au/Media-and-publications/Publications/Documents/hostile-vehicle-guidelines-crowded-places.pdf.

Dalgaard-Nielsen, A., Laisen, J., & Wandorf, C. (2016). Visible counterterrorism measures in urban spaces — fear-inducing or not? *Terrorism and Political Violence*, *28*(4), 692–712.

Enhancing Singapore's response to terrorism (2016). *The Straits Times*. Retrieved from https://www.straitstimes.com/opinion/enhancing-singapores-response-to-terrorism.

Flaherty, C. (2015). The role of CCTV in terrorist TTPs: Camera system avoidance and targeting. *Small Wars Journal*. Retrieved from http://smallwarsjournal.com/jrnl/art/the-role-of-cctv-in-terrorist-ttps-camera-system-avoidance-and-targeting.

Gross, T. (2018). With closed-circuit TV, satellites and phones, millions of cameras are watching. *Fresh Air*. Retrieved from https://www.npr.org/2018/02/08/584243140/with-closed-circuit-tv-satellites-and-phones-millions-of-cameras-are-watching.

Ham, L. (2017). 'What next — barbed wire?' Anti-terror Bollards installed across Melbourne's CBD. *The Age*. Retrieved from https://www.theage.com.au/national/victoria/what-next--barbed-wire-antiterror-bollards-installed-across-melbournes-cbd-20170623-gwwu0y.html.

Hsu, H. Y., & McDowall, D. (2017). Does target-hardening result in deadlier terrorist attacks against protected targets? An examination of unintended harmful consequences. *Journal of Research in Crime and Delinquency*, *54*(6), 930–957.

Infrastructure Protection Act (2017). Government of Singapore. Retrieved from https://sso.agc.gov.sg/Acts-Supp/41-2017/Published/20171031?DocDate=20171031.

Joseph, G. (2016). One reason Nice's surveillance culture didn't stop terror attacks. *CityLab*. Retrieved from https://www.citylab.com/equity/2016/07/one-reason-nices-surveillance-culture-didnt-stop-terror-attacks/491555/.

Lee, D. (2013). Boston bombing: How internet detectives got it very wrong. *BBC*. Retrieved from http://www.bbc.com/news/technology-22214511.

Lim, K. (2017). Grassroots leaders to get training on helping residents deal with terror attacks. *Channel News Asia*. Retrieved from https://www.channelnewsasia.com/news/singapore/grassroots-leaders-to-get-training-on-helping-residents-deal-wit-8577470.

Loke, K. (2016). Tackling Singapore building security in early stages of design, construction. *Channel News Asia*. Retrieved from https://www.channelnewsasia.com/news/singapore/tackling-singapore-building-security-in-early-stages-of-design-c-8192746.

Man arrested for burning police cameras in Jurong West (2017). *Channel News Asia*. Retrieved from https://www.channelnewsasia.com/news/singapore/man-arrested-for-burning-police-cameras-in-jurong-west-9447338.

New 'ring of steel' planned for London Square Mile (2016). *BBC*. Retrieved from http://www.bbc.com/news/uk-england-london-38418877.

Pearlman, J. (2017). Anti-terror barriers go up in Australia. *The Straits Times*. Retrieved from http://www.straitstimes.com/asia/australianz/anti-terror-barriers-go-up-in-australia.

Seow, B. (2017). Parliament: 87% of public view police as world-class crime-fighting Organisation, says Survey. *The Straits Times*. Retrieved from http://www.straitstimes.com/politics/87-per-cent-of-public-view-police-as-world-class-crime-fighting-organisation-survey.

Sorkin, M. (2008). Introduction: The fear factor. In M. Sorkin (Ed.), *Indefensible Space: The Architecture of the National Insecurity State*. Abingdon, Oxon, England: Routledge.

Tan, S. (2017). OK to share CCTV footage online to nab culprits? *The Straits Times*. Retrieved from http://www.straitstimes.com/singapore/ok-to-share-cctv-footage-online-to-nab-culprits.

Tang, S. (2017). Long hours, thankless job: Singapore's security sector struggles to secure talent. *Channel News Asia*. Retrieved from http://www.channelnewsasia.com/news/singapore/long-hours-thankless-job-singapore-s-security-sector-struggles/3422890.html.

Toh, E. (2016). Public security 'more important than privacy'. *TODAY*. Retrieved from http://www.todayonline.com/singapore/public-security-more-important-privacy.

Toh, W. L. (2017). Building security bill timely but firms say cost a concern. *The Straits Times*. Retrieved from http://www.straitstimes.com/singapore/building-security-bill-timely-but-firms-say-cost-a-concern.

Yusof, Z. M. (2017). Industry welcomes new law to protect buildings against attacks. *The Straits Times*. Retrieved from http://www.straitstimes.com/singapore/courts-crime/industry-welcomes-new-law-to-protect-buildings-against-attacks.

CHAPTER 27

Risk and Crisis Management during a Major Terror Attack: Singapore's Approach

DAMIEN D. CHEONG

S. Rajaratnam School of International Studies, Nanyang Technological University, Singapore

Introduction

Crisis and risk management during a major terrorist attack is highly complex. Although managing the unfolding crisis is the main priority, and is itself extremely challenging, law enforcement agencies can find themselves dragged into unanticipated minor crises that are manufactured by cunning adversaries or by miscommunication or misinformation spread on social media.

Given also that new and emerging technologies like unmanned aerial vehicles (UAVs) (i.e., drones) are growing in popularity, managing the crisis and communications has become extremely challenging. In May 2018, for instance, a criminal gang reportedly used a drone swarm to disrupt an FBI operation as well as conduct surveillance of the entire operation. Footage from the drones were live streamed so that the "wider group could keep tabs on the FBI's movements" (Rigg, 2018, para. 2).

This chapter discusses five key challenges *vis-à-vis* crisis and risk management during a major terrorist attack, as well as five potential mitigating responses. It suggests that a pre-emptive and holistic approach, as adopted by Singapore, may be the most effective way to deal with the problem.

Challenges

Communications during Major Security Incidents can Compromise Operations

Several incidents over the last decade underscore the severity of live streaming and communicating the positions of law enforcement officers during ongoing operations.

First, in the 2008 Mumbai attacks, "live media broadcast of security forces preparing to storm the Taj Mahal Palace Hotel allowed the gunmen within to anticipate the actions of the security forces" (Ministry of Home Affairs, 2018, para. 9).

Second, the Ottawa Police had to remind the public not to tweet or post photos of where officers and snipers were stationed during the attack at Parliament Hill in 2014 (Bogart, 2014).

Third, the terrorist who was holding several hostages in the 2015 Hyper Cacher Deli attack, "was able to watch live television broadcasts showing the location of officers preparing to storm the deli" (Ministry of Home Affairs, 2018, para. 9). Live broadcasts also put the lives of the hostages at risk. In the aftermath of the attack, six hostages who hid in the supermarket freezer during the attack, sued the French media for broadcasting their location live during the siege (Tomlinson, 2015).

In the above-mentioned examples, "the information available to the terrorists made the ... operation more difficult, reduced the chances of a successful operation, and put the safety of the officers and ... [those involved] at greater risk" (Ministry of Home Affairs, 2018, para. 9). Furthermore, videos/images of police tactical operations/methodologies (e.g., response times, movements) could be studied by adversaries to help them strategise and plan future attacks as well as plan escape routes and/or avoid police cordons and road blocks.

Misinformation Creation and Spread are Likely due to High Demand for Information[1]

During any major crises, especially a major security incident like a terror attack, demand for information will expectedly be high. People want to find out if their loved ones are affected/involved, and if they are, whether they are safe. People directly affected want to know how to evacuate and respond. People may also want to help by providing ground intelligence and information that can be used by law enforcement. The organisation or entity involved will be put under immense pressure to put information out quickly.

In an unfolding crisis, information may not be available, and even when it does become available, needs to be verified before being released. When the demand for speedy information is not met, it is natural for some individuals to fill in the gap(s) by pushing out a story/tweet that may be factually inaccurate or incorrect.

As smartphones enable users to be both information creators and broadcasters, and because such individuals often do not need to verify their posts, misinformation can inevitably be generated and disseminated (Beckett, 2016).

Creation of Smaller Crises to Distract and Undermine Current Operations

The dissemination of misinformation through online channels (e.g., social media) can adversely affect how law enforcement manages the ongoing crisis/terrorist incident.

First, misinformation could spark smaller crises that require a diversion of resources from the main incident to the smaller one, which could undermine recovery efforts. In an extreme case, the

---

[1]For a more detailed discussion, see Department of Homeland Security (2018).

diversion could result in an ambush of law enforcement and first responders. As a 2011 United States Congressional Research Service report titled *Social Media and Disasters: Current Uses, Future Options, and Policy Considerations* warns:

> [S]ome individuals or organisations might intentionally provide inaccurate information [to law enforcement] to confuse, disrupt, or otherwise thwart response efforts ... One tactic that has been used by terrorists involves the use of a secondary attack after an initial attack to kill and injure first responders. Social media could be used as a tool for such purposes by issuing calls for assistance to an area, or notifying officials of a false hazard or threat that requires a response (Lindsay, 2011, p. 7).

In December 2017, rumours circulated via social media that London's West End was the target of a terror attack, resulting in a major stampede as people panicked and attempted to rush out of the area. Law enforcement were activated and deployed to various locations as there were "reports" of gunshots. Investigations revealed that an altercation between two men had actually sparked off the chaos (Gregory, 2017). In this scenario, adversaries could had easily exploited both the bedlam and the fact that law enforcement was preoccupied with dealing with the crises to carry out attacks in other locations.

In November 2016, Ms Sun Xueling, a Singaporean Member of Parliament (MP), cited how police and civil defence forces were mobilised to respond to an apparent roof collapse of a high-rise apartment block that turned out to be a hoax. This "caused a wastage of public resources which could have been used in other areas where they are needed more" (Sin, 2018, para. 17).

Creation of Crises that can Undermine Social Cohesion

Ethnic and/or religious groups can become targets of hate crimes following a terrorist incident due in part to existing prejudice and/or misinformation.

With regard to the former, in 2017, it was reported that Greater Manchester experienced a 500% increase in the number of Islamophobic attacks following the suicide bombing at the Ariana Grande concert (Halliday, 2017). Rob Potts, assistant Chief Constable, observed:

> When a major tragedy occurs such as the attacks in Manchester and London, it is sadly not unusual for there to be a spike in the amount of hate crimes, specifically against race and religion, but thankfully they do decrease again quickly (Halliday, 2017, para. 7).

In relation to the latter, following the 2015 Paris attacks, a photo of Veerender Jubbal, a Canadian of Sikh heritage, was doctored and miscaptioned to portray him as one of the terrorists involved. The photo was seemingly so convincing that even a Spanish newspaper ran the story (Rawlinson, 2015). Jubbal is still reportedly treated suspiciously even though it was proven that the story was inaccurate and the photo, a hoax (Jubbal, 2016).

Vigilantism/Lawlessness Based on Misinformation

In 2013, a Brown university student, Sunil Tripathi, was misidentified as one of the Boston Marathon bombers. This resulted in a manhunt for the wrong individual, as well as resulted in the harassment of his family (Bidgood, 2013).

In 2012, Muslims in Bangladesh burned down at least four Buddhist temples and 15 homes of Buddhist Bangladeshis, following rumours that a local Buddhist boy had posted a derogatory image of the Quran on his Facebook page ("Muslim protesters torch Buddhist temples, homes in Bangladesh", 2012). Investigations revealed that the boy "had only been tagged in the photo. He had not destroyed a Quran himself, and was not the person who posted the picture" ("Battle against fake news: Rise of the truth-seekers", 2017). Misinformation dissemination especially during a time when emotions run high, can increase vigilantism involving physical attacks against individuals, and/or lawlessness.

Potential Mitigating Approaches

Employing a Communications Stop Order during Major Security Incidents

Singapore recently passed the Public Order and Safety (Special Powers) Act (POSSPA), which contains a Communications Stop Order (CSO) provision that allows law enforcement to prohibit the public in the incident area from "making or communicating films or pictures ... and ... text or audio messages about ... ongoing security operations" (Ministry of Home Affairs, 2018, para. 10). The broad aim of the CSO is to "minimise terrorists' access to information, which could compromise" both ongoing and future "law enforcement operations" (Ong, 2018, para. 2).

While POSSPA grants extraordinary powers to the police, there are safeguards to prevent potential abuse and ensure accountability. First, POSSPA would only be activated under special conditions:

> The Minister for Home Affairs must first issue an order to authorise the use of the powers. To do so, the Minister must be of the opinion that (a) a serious incident has occurred or is occurring in Singapore, or there is a threat of such a serious incident occurring, and (b) that the special powers are necessary to prevent the occurrence of the incident, reduce its impact, or control, restore or maintain public order (Ministry of Home Affairs, 2018, para. 6).

Second, the CSO does not "automatically come into force" and must be "specifically unlocked" by the Police Commissioner "as and when deemed necessary" (Seow, 2018, para. 16).

Dealing with New/Emerging Surveillance Technologies

Related to the above-mentioned point is the fact that images and videos from an ongoing operation can be captured by commercial unmanned aerial vehicles (UAVs) or drones. UAVs have grown in popularity over the last few years and are relatively cheap to obtain. They are often fitted with cameras that can take high-quality audio and video.

The security risks associated with UAVs have been well-documented (Beaumont, 2017; Bergen *et al.*, 2017), and, in particular, how violent non-state actors and/or individuals with nefarious intentions can exploit the technology. For example, *New America*, a U.S. think-tank, cited an example of how this could occur:

> On August 14, 2017, a drone hobbyist posted video footage recorded from his DJI Phantom drone, a popular consumer brand, flying close to the HMS Queen Elizabeth. The freshly minted warship, which was docked in Scotland, is the United Kingdom's largest aircraft carrier. Following the flyover, the drone enthusiast landed his remote-controlled plane on the carrier without detection, demonstrating how a tech-savvy group such as ISIS could potentially exploit gaps in security around significant military targets (Bergen *et al.*, 2017, p. 45).

In September 2017, Israel reportedly shot down "an Iranian-supplied Hezbollah reconnaissance drone over the Syrian border" (Beaumont, 2017, para. 1), which suggests that violent non-state actors are already using UAVs for surveillance.

In light of these risks, Singapore through POSSPA empowers law enforcement "to take down or disable any unmanned aircraft and autonomous vehicles and vessels in and around the incident area, regardless of their intention and activity" (Ministry of Home Affairs, 2018, para. 11). This is envisaged to account for new devices/methods of obtaining images and video footage of the incident.

Becoming the Source of Information

Crisis communication practitioners often suggest that an official communication channel/source needs to be established to ensure that accurate and regularly updated information is disseminated to the public. For example, the U.S. Centres for Disease Control and Prevention's (CDC) *Crisis and Emergency Risk Communication Handbook*, advises organisations to:

> (a) Be First: Crises are time-sensitive. Communicating information quickly is almost always important. For members of the public, the

> first source of information often becomes the preferred source; (b) Be Right: Accuracy establishes credibility. Information can include what is known, what is not known, and what is being done to fill in the gaps; and (c) Be Credible: Honesty and truthfulness should not be compromised during crises" (U.S. Department of Health and Human Services, Centers for Disease Control and Prevention (CDC) 2014, p. 2).

Such principles apply to public communications via social media as well. For example, during the 2011 floods, the Queensland Police (QPS):

> [T]urned to social media as the vehicle to reach the public and the media in the shortest timeframe. Given the majority of the information the QPS released was factual and in the interests of public safety it could be released immediately and without a clearance process. The team was trusted to use their judgement. If there was an issue that needed further verification or was potentially contentious then a more stringent approval process would be applied. There was no directive or policy decision to escalate the use of social media during the disasters. The team instinctively gravitated towards the social media channels because they were clearly the fastest and best way to distribute important public safety information. Within days, not only were the media relying on the QPS social media accounts as their key source of information but they were actively referring the public to our social media channels. QPS tweets would appear in national TV networks news tickers and would be read out by radio station announcers within moments of the media team publishing them (Queensland Police Service, 2011, pp. iv–v).

In Singapore, the Singapore Civil Defence Force (SCDF) has developed and continually honed its public communications on social media as well:

> Col Razak [Col Abdul Razak Raheem, Director, Public Affairs Department, SCDF] recalled an incident … where a fire engine got stuck in front of VivoCity shopping mall on a weekday. The SCDF issued a statement as soon as the team had a good grasp of the

> facts. "You need to be upfront and honest in this age. We rather people hear the news from us. And sharing things that are perceived as damaging to you also helps your credibility," he said. Another incident ... arose when a video captured an SCDF paramedic's [seeming] lack of urgency in attending to a patient who collapsed while jogging ... It [turned] out that the patient was already being attended to by an off-duty paramedic who happened to be a colleague of the paramedic on duty. "We clarified the whole thing within six hours. I told the team this was a race against time" said Col Razak" (Chin, 2016, paras. 22–26).

By becoming *the* source of information, agencies are able to minimise the spread of misinformation during crises.

Active Mythbusting Online

Active "mythbusting" on social media channels is useful to manage misinformation generation/spread. Unfortunately, studies have shown that people are inclined to believe misinformation even if presented with correct information due in part to cognitive biases (Resnick, 2018). Hence, realistically, agencies can only manage as opposed to eliminate misinformation even with active mythbusting.

The daunting task of mythbusting has to be done primarily by the organisation/agency, even though the public can be roped in to help (a point explored below). This is because firstly, it reduces confusion since the correction is being put out by an official source (e.g., law enforcement agency's official social media account). Secondly, it enables the organisation to build credibility as the source of information, which enables it to better manage information flow. For instance, during the Boston Marathon bombing in 2013,

> [M]isinformation, spread by professional media outlets and social media itself, was quickly corrected by the BPD ... It didn't take long for the media to realise that the most accurate information about the bombing was coming from the official BPD Twitter account (Newcombe, 2014, para. 2).

Enlisting the Public's Help

The public can be enlisted to help in two ways: (a) provide information and intelligence useful to the authorities and (b) mythbust.

Singapore has developed two apps that allow members of the public to provide information to the police: SGSecure App (Ministry of Home Affairs, 2016) and the Police@SG App (Singapore Police Force, 2017). Each has features that use the camera on mobile devices to allow individuals to send pictures and videos (anonymously or not) to the authorities (Ng, 2016). The challenge for agencies is that they may receive too much information. Sifting through the voluminous information and determining what information is accurate and/or relevant within a short period of time, requires significant processing power. The use of and investment in Artificial Intelligence (AI) will be useful in this regard as it can significantly speed up the analysis (Pan & Koh, 2018).

The public can help mythbusting efforts by correcting misinformation and misperceptions by complementing/supporting mythbusting efforts by the authorities on their social media channels. Individuals can also help manage misinformation and misperceptions on their personal social media pages or through messaging-apps. They can help prevent the spread of misinformation by being discerning about what they receive via messaging apps ("WhatsApp: Mark Zuckerberg's other headache", 2018) and refusing to share information that seems dubious.

Apart from these online efforts, it is important to mobilise people on the ground to help manage possible ethnic/religious tensions that could arise from a major security incident. Singapore introduced the SGSecure Pledge as part of the overall SGSecure movement to help prepare Singaporeans for a terrorist attack:

> Under the initiative, residents are encouraged to pledge to support the SGSecure movement in a number of ways, such as staying alert and reporting suspicious activity or behaviour to the police, helping to maintain social cohesion and harmony, learning life-saving skills, or volunteering as a first-aider or counsellor during a crisis (Seow, 2017, para. 7).

The broad "aim is to get people thinking about what they can do immediately after a terrorist attack, whether it is through spreading positive messages of harmony or looking after a neighbour who is afraid" (Seow, 2017, para. 11).

National unity and social cohesion can be adversely affected following a major security incident. Singapore believes that racial and religious harmony is not a given and efforts must be made to maintain this positive state of affairs. It enlists the help of the public through various organisations such as OnePeople.sg (OPSG). OPSG was established as "the ground-up national body championing racial and religious harmony in Singapore".[2] Its programmes and initiatives "aim to create an environment that facilitates deeper interaction and better understanding between individuals and communities, fostering a stronger sense of identity and building a more resilient social fabric" (Ask Me Anything, 2018). A recent community-led initiative supported by OPSG is the "Ask Me Anything" dialogue, which is a series of "interfaith discussions to educate, clarify misconceptions, engage on sensitive religious issues, and deepen...understanding of one another" (Ask Me Anything, 2018). Mobilising the public prior to a crisis prepares them for the possibility that relations between different ethnic or religious groups may be sorely tested as a result of the incident.

Conclusion

Terrorist organisations are learning entities that evolve and adapt their strategies and tactics according to the changing circumstances (Mumford, 2015). They have access to new and emerging technologies, and can exploit them to advance their agenda. As such, countries need to stay ahead of the curve to handle this challenge. This may not always be possible given respective constraints. However, empowering law enforcement through legislation to do their jobs effectively may be a useful first step.

---

[2]Refer to the link for more information: https://www.onepeople.sg/.

Singapore has done this through POSSPA. POSSPA was enacted due in part because: (a) law enforcement are often constrained/disadvantaged in terms of how they operate and respond as a consequence of legislation not keeping pace with rapid technological advancements (Schaub & West, 2014), (b) managing operations and communications in an ongoing terror attack is highly complex, and (c) other unintended crises can be triggered in the immediate aftermath of an attack. POSSPA enables law enforcement to manage both the ongoing crisis and the potential risks that can stem from it (e.g., vigilantism, threats from UAVs). Singapore has also focused on managing communications via POSSPA as this has become more important in the era of deliberate online falsehoods aka fake news.

Finally, the city-state is mindful that a whole-of-society approach is key to dealing with terrorism-related crises given the adverse effects on social cohesion and national unity. As such, it continues to adopt a pre-emptive and persistent approach to foster racial and religious harmony across all sectors and strata of Singapore society. As race and religious issues are, by nature, highly sensitive, this approach is high risk, and has no perfect solutions. But, as many global examples have demonstrated, states that shy away from tackling these issues may experience unexpected challenges in the aftermath of terrorism-related incidents.

References

Ask Me Anything (website) (2018). Retrieved from https://askmeanything.sg/about/.

Battle against fake news: Rise of the truth-seekers (2017). *The Straits Times*. Retrieved from https://www.straitstimes.com/opinion/battle-against-fake-news-rise-of-the-truth-seekers.

Beaumont, P. (2017). Israel: 'We have shot down Iranian-supplied Hezbollah drone'. *The Guardian*. Retrieved from https://www.theguardian.com/world/2017/sep/19/israel-we-have-shot-down-iranian-supplied-hezbollah-drone.

Beckett, C. (2016). Fanning the flames: Reporting on terror in a networked world. Tow Center for Digital Journalism, Graduate School of Journalism, Columbia University. Retrieved from https://www.cjr.org/tow_center_reports/coverage_terrorism_social_media.php.

Bergen, P., Sterman, D., Ford, A., & Sims, A. (2017). The Jihadist terrorism 16 years after 9/11: A Threat Assessment. *New America.* Retrieved from https://na-production.s3.amazonaws.com/documents/Terrorism_9-11_2017.pdf.

Bidgood, J. (2013). Body of missing student at Brown is discovered. *New York Times*. Retrieved from https://www.nytimes.com/2013/04/26/us/sunil-tripathi-student-at-brown-is-found-dead.html.

Bogart, N. (2014). The power of social media: How citizen reporting may impede active police investigations. *Global News*. Retrieved from https://globalnews.ca/news/1631615/the-power-of-social-media-how-citizen-reporting-may-impede-active-police-investigations/.

Chin, D. (2016). SCDF wins fans with its Social Media Persona. *The Straits Times*. Retrieved from http://www.straitstimes.com/singapore/scdf-wins-fans-with-its-social-media-persona.

Gregory, J. (2017). Panic on Oxford street as armed police respond to reports of gunshots. *The Guardian*. Retrieved from https://www.theguardian.com/uk-news/2017/dec/26/panic-on-oxford-street-as-armed-police-respond-to-reports-of-gunshots.

Halliday, J. (2017). Islamophobic attacks in Manchester surge by 500% after Arena Attack'. *The Guardian*. Retrieved from https://www.theguardian.com/uk-news/2017/jun/22/islamophobic-attacks-manchester-increase-arena-attack.

Jubbal, V. (2016). Experience: I was accused of carrying out the Paris attacks. *The Guardian*. Retrieved from https://www.theguardian.com/lifeandstyle/2016/jul/01/experience-i-was-accused-of-carrying-out-the-paris-attacks.

Lindsay, B. (2011). Social media and disasters: Current uses, future options, and policy considerations. U.S. Congressional Research Service, 7-5700, R41987. Retrieved from https://www.nisconsortium.org/portal/resources/bin/Social_Media_and_Dis_1423591240.pdf.

Ministry of Home Affairs (2016). SGSecure (Version 1.2.3) (Mobile application software). Retrieved from https://itunes.apple.com/sg/app/sgsecure/id1095191664?mt=8.

Ministry of Home Affairs (2018). Public Order and Safety (Special Powers) Bill 2018. Retrieved from https://www.mha.gov.sg/newsroom/press-releases/newsroom-detail-page?news=public-order-and-safety-(special-powers)-bill-2018.

Mumford, A. (2015). How terrorist groups 'learn': Innovation and adaptation in political violence. *British Academy Conference*. Retrieved from https://www.britac.ac.uk/sites/default/files/BAR26-08-Mumford.pdf.

Muslim protesters torch Buddhist temples, homes in Bangladesh (2012). *Reuters*. Retrieved from https://www.reuters.com/article/us-bangladesh-temples/muslim-protesters-torch-buddhist-temples-homes-in-bangladesh-idUSBRE88T03I20120930.

Newcombe, T. (2014). Social media: Big lessons from the Boston Marathon bombing. *Government Technology*. Retrieved from http://www.govtech.com/public-safety/social-media-big-lessons-from-the-boston-marathon-bombing.html.

Ng, H. (2016). In an emergency, alert police via i-Witness. *The Straits Times*. Retrieved from http://www.straitstimes.com/singapore/in-an-emergency-alert-police-via-i-witness.

Ong, J. (2018). Parliament passes law banning photos, videos of security operations during a terror attack. *Channel News Asia*. Retrieved from https://www.channelnewsasia.com/news/singapore/ban-photos-videos-messages-terrorist-posspa-10062836.

Pan, J., & Koh, G. (2018). Use of Artificial Intelligence in the Home Team. *Home Team Journal*, 7, 18–24.

Queensland Police Service (2011). Disaster management and social media — A case study. Retrieved from https://www.police.qld.gov.au/corporatedocs/reportsPublications/other/Documents/QPSSocialMediaCaseStudy.pdf.

Rawlinson, K. (2015). Canadian pictured as Paris terrorist in suspected Gamergate smear. *The Guardian*. Retrieved from https://www.theguardian.com/world/2015/nov/16/canadian-pictured-as-paris-terrorist-in-suspected-gamergate-smear.

Resnick, B. (2018). False news stories travel faster and farther on Twitter than the truth. *VOX*. Retrieved from https://www.vox.com/science-and-health/2018/3/8/17085928/fake-news-study-mit-science.

Rigg, J. (2018). Criminals used a drone swarm to disrupt an FBI hostage rescue. *Engadget*. Retrieved from https://www.engadget.com/2018/05/04/drone-swarm-fbi-hostage-rescue/.

Schaub, H., & West, D. M. (2014). How emerging technology affects law enforcement. *Brookings*. Retrieved from https://www.brookings.edu/blog/techtank/2014/10/28/how-emerging-technology-affects-law-enforcement/.

Seow, B. (2018). Parliament: Communications stop order in public order Bill not an information blackout, says Josephine Teo. *The Straits Times*. Retrieved from http://www.straitstimes.com/politics/parliament-communications-stop-order-in-public-order-bill-not-an-information-blackout-says.

Seow, J. (2017). Commit to maintaining cohesion and normalcy after an attack: Chan Chun Sing. *The Straits Times*. Retrieved from http://www.straitstimes.com/politics/commit-to-maintaining-cohesion-and-normalcy-after-an-attack-chan-chun-sing.

Sin, Y. (2018). Parliament: Ministers, MPs give examples of deliberate falsehoods in Singapore and beyond. *The Straits Times*. Retrieved from http://www.straitstimes.com/politics/singapolitics/ministers-mps-give-examples-of-deliberate-falsehoods-in-singapore-and-beyond.

Singapore Police Force (2017). *Police@SG* (Version 3.14) (Mobile application software). Retrieved from https://itunes.apple.com/sg/app/police-sg/id472603758?mt=8.

Tomlinson, S. (2015). Paris supermarket hostages who hid in freezer sue French media for broadcasting their location live during the siege. *Daily Mail*. Retrieved from http://www.dailymail.co.uk/news/article-3024231/Paris-supermarket-hostages-hid-Islamist-gunman-freezer-sue-French-media-broadcasting-location-live-siege.html.

U.S. Department of Health and Human Services, Centers for Disease Control and Prevention (CDC) (2014). Crisis and emergency risk communication handbook. Retrieved from https://emergency.cdc.gov/cerc/resources/pdf/cerc_2014edition.pdf.

WhatsApp: Mark Zuckerberg's other headache (2018). The Economist. Retrieved from https://www.economist.com/news/business/21735623-popular-messaging-service-shows-facebooks-efforts-fight-fake-news-may-fail-whatsapp.

Section 8

Strategies to Build Communal Harmony

If you try to strengthen trust after an attack, it is too late. We need to strengthen our cohesiveness and our unity now.

DR YAACOB IBRAHIM
FORMER MINISTER-IN-CHARGE OF MUSLIM AFFAIRS

CHAPTER 28

The Effects of Religious Fundamentalism on Communal Harmony

VERITY ER

Home Team Behavioural Sciences Centre, Ministry of Home Affairs, Singapore

Introduction

In Karl Marx's theory of modernisation, he argued that as societies become more developed, higher educational levels, increasing affluence, and changing cultural norms will ultimately allow men to be less primordial and more rational, therefore diminishing the influence of religion in the public sphere (Avineri, 1969). Yet, the present-day world has proved otherwise; religion and spiritual beliefs have not faded but remain salient and influential in the way people interact with one another and how they perceive the world (Inglehart & Baker, 2000). The 21st century, in particular, saw the rise of religious fundamentalism; a term once used specifically to describe the practices of conservative evangelical Protestants in the early 1900s (Almond *et al.*, 2002). However, the upsurge in conflicts involving religions in the world today, often precipitated from the fear that one's faith could be obliterated by the forces of secularisation or other religions, affirmed the fact that religious fundamentalist tendencies exist beyond the faith of Christianity.

According to Emerson and Hartman (2006), religious fundamentalism[1] rides on a perceived fear that one's religion is losing ground in a progressively secularised world. They described this fear as a response to a perceived marginalisation of one's religion, upholding the "absolutism and inerrancy" of one's faith (Emerson & Hartman, 2006, p. 134). Faced with an increasingly globalised world which may threaten their existence, some proponents of religion choose to compromise, adapt, or assimilate, while others respond by eliminating those they perceive to be "in the wrong" (Almond *et al.*, 2002). The Buddhist 969 movement, Jewish militant Zionism, and the long-lasting conflict between the Sunni and Shia sects of Islam in several Muslim-dominated countries are a few out of the many examples of aggression that religious fundamentalists engaged in to get rid of the so-called traitors of their faith (Tan, 2008). Indeed, a religious fundamentalist's perspective reinforces differences and encourages an uncompromising defence of one's beliefs, rendering one to be psychologically susceptible to destructive violent extremist ideologies that can create tensions and disrupt communal harmony within the society. Hence, this chapter aims to consolidate five key things about religious fundamentalism that law enforcers, policymakers, religious and community leaders should know, as well as suggest ways that could potentially address this phenomenon.

---

[1]It is important to note that religious fundamentalists can exist in all religions.

Five Things to Know about Religious Fundamentalism

Religious Fundamentalism is Different from Being Devout or Conservative

Religious fundamentalism[2] is not considered a novel phenomenon but the interpretations of it are often ambiguous and protean. However, while the literature has avoided providing absolute definitions for religious fundamentalism, it is largely understood that religious fundamentalism is different from being devout or conservative (Stroizer & Boyd, 2010). Religious fundamentalism is also not simply the preference of an orthodox or traditional form of one's religion, as often misunderstood in popular discourse (Jones, 2010). Rather, Stroizer and Boyd (2010) emphasised the need to understand the psychological underpinnings of the fundamentalist mindset, which may involve an apocalyptic version of religion, dualistic thinking, paranoia, and humiliation. Almond *et al.* (2002) also highlighted that the crux of a fundamentalist mindset is that of reactivity; religious fundamentalism is a *reaction* towards a perceived marginalisation of one's religion resulting in an act of defending one's faith. For example, religious fundamentalists would attempt to form political parties or interest groups to lobby the government in implementing policies that would preserve certain practices of their religion (Garvey, 1993). For instance, the Hamas, a Palestinian Sunni-Islamic fundamentalist organization, pushed for resistance movements by interfering in the Palestinian political process; it was the first Islamist group in the Arab world to win an election through democratic voting ("Profile: Hamas Palestinian movement", 2017).

A study comparing the three major religions in the world — Judaism, Christianity, and Islam — by Lawrence (1989) suggested

[2]In Singapore, Islamic Religious Council of Singapore (MUIS) President Mohammad Alami Musa has called for interfaith dialogue to deepen and go beyond sharing of meals, as religious fundamentalism continues to rise elsewhere (Vijayan, 2017). He said the worst thing that can happen is when religion becomes politicised and politics, in turn, is theologised: "Everything is about God, and you have to take a certain position as you want to seek the pleasure of God — there is no compromise".

five traits that could distinguish fundamentalists from their conservative and religious counterparts; among Protestant Christians, quasi-Hasidim and Haredim (also known as ultra-Orthodox Jews), as well as Sunni and Shia Muslims, religious fundamentalists are postulated to typically exhibit these five traits: (1) has historical antecedents but no ideological precursors, (2) perceive and project themselves as a minority, (3) confront secular people, (4) mediated through exclusively male interpreters, and (5) generate their own technical vocabulary (Lawrence, 1989). A religious fundamentalist also tends to be prejudiced against others who do not share the same faith due to the perception that his/her religious beliefs are absolute, essential, and inerrant, setting them apart from those who are merely devout or conservative (Altemeyer, 2003).

Fundamentalism Exists in Every Religion

It is absolutely vital to recognise that fundamentalism is not limited to any one faith — it can exist in every religion. Based on "The Fundamentalism Project",[3] Marty and Appleby (1991) observed that religious fundamentalist movements neither occur at specific geographical locations nor involve any particular host religion. Fundamentalist tendencies span across various religions, from Christianity, Judaism, Sunni and Shia Islam, Hinduism, Sikhism, Buddhism, to neo-Confucianism. Despite the differences in doctrines, cosmologies, social composition, sizes, organisational structures, political settings, and scope of influence, most religious fundamentalist movements were found to share similar traits (Marty & Appleby, 1991). In other words, almost all the fundamentalist movements that were studied revolve around the separation from the mainstream community, and set themselves as an opposition to both non-believers and "lukewarm" believers. A common

[3]The Fundamentalist Project is a well-known multiyear study directed by Martin Marty and R. Scott Appleby from 1991–1995 under the American Academy of Arts and Sciences, and funded by the John D. and Catherine T. MacArthur Foundation. The study produced five encyclopaedic volumes on world fundamentalisms, all of which were edited by Marty and Scott Appleby and published by The University of Chicago Press (Marty, 1996).

belief of religious fundamentalists from different religions is that a conspiracy was made between secularists and liberal religionists to adopt strategies to fight a perceived oppression (Marty & Appleby, 1991).

In light of rising jihadist attacks after 9/11, one might be misled into thinking that fundamentalism is only applicable to the faith of Islam. However, it is important to note that it is not the type of religion *per se*, but the unyielding, inflexible, and intolerant nature of the mindset developed in the name of religion that is problematic (Ramakrishna, 2005). Besides Islam, other religions like Christianity, Judaism, Buddhism, and Hinduism have also seen followers engaging in the manifestations of religious fundamentalism (Genia, 1996; Tan, 2008). The massacre of Rohingya Muslims by Buddhist fundamentalists in the Rakhine state of Myanmar (Smith, 2017) and anti-Muslims riots by Hindu fundamentalists in Gujarat, India (Barry, 2016), are just some notable examples of incidents involving aggression by other faiths. It is, therefore, crucial to recognise that religious fundamentalism is not exclusive to certain religions or people who receive certain religious teachings. Instead, anyone can potentially develop religious fundamentalist mindsets.

Religious Fundamentalism has been Associated with Prejudice and Discrimination

Religious fundamentalists ascribed to the dichotomy of a world with two opposing camps: the pure and righteous in-group whom one identifies with versus the demonic and evil out-group who is responsible for the suffering one has experienced (Strozier & Boyd, 2010). Establishing such clear distinction from others, particularly those of a different faith or even within the same faith but diverged on the opinion of what constitutes the "correct" practices of their religion, can lead to acts of prejudice and discrimination (Altemeyer & Hunsberger, 1997). Altemeyer (2003) further observed that religion *per se* does not particularly associate with prejudice, but "the attitude that one's beliefs are the fundamentally correct, essential, inerrant ones is associated with bigotry" (p. 19). He went on to suggest that the development of a religious fundamentalist mindset during youth may open up a person to adopting other kinds of prejudice in later years. In his study, it was showed that religious fundamentalism "correlates about 0.70 with university students' responses to a 16-item Religious Emphasis scale that asks how much the family religion was stressed as they were growing up" (Altemeyer & Hunsberger, 1997, pp. 22–23). Given the amount of emphasis on religion within the family, parents — playing a major role in their children's development — are postulated to be able to "plant the seeds for prejudice" in adulthood.

A study conducted by Kirkpatrick (1993) also discovered that Christian fundamentalism, along with intrinsic religious orientation and Christian orthodoxy, are positive predictors of discrimination, specifically against blacks and homosexuals (as cited in Layth *et al.*,2001). Hunsberger (1995) posited that Christian fundamentalism is frequently found to be associated with right-wing groups, such as neo-Nazis and "skinheads" groups, as they often utilise the bible as a justification for racial prejudice and discrimination (Hunsberger, 1996; Rowatt & Franklin, 2004). In another study, Brandt and Van Tongeren (2017, p. 76) suggested that "religious fundamentalist may be especially susceptible to expressing prejudice toward 'dissimilar others', whereas people who are less religious and fundamentalist do not show the same effect". The authors highlighted that attempts to vigorously "defend the validity and vitality of their religious beliefs" have resulted in religious fundamentalists to be more prone to prejudice (Brandt & Van Tongeren, 2017, p. 76).

Religious Fundamentalism may Encourage Social Isolation

Fundamentalists may isolate and withdraw themselves from the mainstream society if they perceive that society is not in line with their beliefs (Salzman, 2008). This creates cognitive dissonance, wherein religious fundamentalists tend to establish clear boundaries with those of different faiths, for fear of being "contaminated" (Ramakrishna, 2016). As Lott and Maluso (1995) have aptly pointed out, discrimination of a perceived "out-group" does not only manifest through extreme and destructive actions, it may also take the form of day-to-day distancing and avoidance.

The desire to avoid interacting with people of other faiths, also known as "social distancing" can definitely affect the harmony and cohesion within the society. Besides removing opportunities for deeper understanding, it also reinforces the "obsession with differences" by members of the same faith rather than focusing on the things in common with non-believers (Ruthven, 2004). It was reported that as high as 23% of British Muslims are supportive of the implementation of Sharia law over secular law in Muslim dominant areas within the country, causing the authorities to worry that this might signal the beginning of the formation of a "separate nation within nation" in Britain (Kern, 2016, para. 2). For example, followers of radical preacher Anjem Choudary have established "Sharia controlled zones" in London where people, regardless of Muslims or non-Muslims, would be harassed, threatened or abused if they did not adhere to the so-called Islamic rules and regulations imposed in those areas (Kennedy, 2013).

Religious fundamentalism is also ubiquitous for its rigid, sometimes literal, adherence to a set of behaviours which is claimed to have been derived from religious teachings or sacred texts (Savage, 2011). These are "rules" that determine how one should behave, including who one is allowed to interact with (Emerson & Hartman, 2006). The fact that questions like "Can Muslims wish Christians Merry Christmas?" or "Can Christians/Catholics hold joss sticks when paying respects to the deceased?" abound across websites and forums on the Internet further attest to the uncomfortable truth that many are still uncertain of the practices that might "contradict" their loyalty to their faith. As such, while some fundamentalists may be actively involved in pushing for reforms within their countries, others may withdraw into enclaves where they can safely practice their religious beliefs (Ramakrishna, 2016). Thus, these behaviours may result in individuals becoming socially distant from the mainstream community.

Coupled with Certain Factors, Religious Fundamentalism can Accelerate the Adoption of Violence

While religious fundamentalism generally does not involve the use of violence, it has the potential of becoming so, especially when the violence is often justified in the name of god (Rogers *et al.*, 2007). A religious fundamentalist perspective becomes problematic when it imbues an uneasiness to live with people who do not believe in the same god or practices, resulting in a desire to conform others to their ideas (Raush, 2015). According to Pech and Slade (2006), religion — among other forces such as history, tradition, and a cultural need for revenge — is perceived to provide a legitimate justification for using violence to attain a sense of presence and control over the value of one's religion.

Religious fundamentalism is also found to be closely associated with violent extremism as religious fundamentalists and violent extremists often share similar motivations (Rausch, 2015). However, it is necessary to note that fundamentalists are essentially different from violent extremists. As compared to violent extremists who resort to violence to reach their agendas, those with fundamentalist inclinations primarily push for reforms in the political arena to achieve their agendas (Khosrokhavar, 2010). In a comparison between jihadists and fundamentalists, Khosrokhavar (2010, p. 1) eloquently pointed out that fundamentalists "consider a peaceful road to Islamic society one in which the political realm will be gradually Islamicised" while Jihadists tend to reject the peaceful, democracy-friendly fashion of attaining this goal and propose the recourse to jihad in the most violent manner so as to restore Islam to its former glory. While they might carry similar attitudes, most notably with regard to the humiliation by and rejection of the overwhelming presence of Western values, there is still a "large gap" between the desire of seeking violence between the two groups (Khosrokhavar, 2010). However, fundamentalist mindsets can escalate into violent extremism, as seen from the justification that Ashin Wirathu, the leader of the 969 movement, made of the killings of the Rohingya Muslims: "If we do not protect our own people we will become weak, and we will face more mass killings of this kind (the Muslims) when they grow to outnumber us." (Kaplan, 2015). In such scenarios, fundamentalists resorted to violence as it was perceived as a reasonable means to defend one's religion. As such, even though religious fundamentalists are not innately violent people, their perspective may predispose them to it.

Religious fundamentalism is also a group phenomenon rather than an individual one, wherein the utmost interest lies in preserving the "group's history, values, and goals" (Jones, 2010, p. 2). Therefore, any threat to these aspects are deemed to be an infringement on the self-esteem and identity of individual members, motivating them to protect these characteristics of their religion, to an extent where they are willing to use violence to do so (Terman, 2010). This was demonstrated by the members of the Armed Islamic Group (GIA), an Algerian Islamic fundamentalist group, who indiscriminately massacred innocent people in retaliation to the opposing secular policies put forth by the Algerian government (Kornblet, 2011).

Implications

Create and Establish a Common Understanding on what Religious Fundamentalism is

The lack of a concrete definition of religious fundamentalism, and its associated behaviours might actually be a hindrance to managing the issue at hand. Without a clear understanding of what constitutes religious fundamentalism, the community may not be able to know what to look out for as it is challenging to pinpoint a certain behaviour as merely uncooperative, fundamentalist, or extremist in nature, simply because these behaviours exist on a spectrum (Stroizer & Boyd, 2010). Besides, when policymakers and the community are on the same page with regard to religious fundamentalism, it would be easier to demarcate practices which are acceptable and those which are not. Educational institutions should also start to raise awareness about religious fundamentalism, as the trajectory of forming a fundamentalist mindset may start from a young age (i.e., how family can plant the seeds of prejudice). For a start, discussion about the characteristics of what defines religious fundamentalism is advised to be carried out in controlled and guided platforms such as a closed-door dialogue, where the terminology can be safely debated among players of society — government, social media influencers, academics, religious groups, etc. (K. Ramakrishna, personal communication, 2017).

Religious Leaders and Educators to Debunk Misconceptions About one's Religion

Religious leaders and educators play an important role in debunking misconceptions about one's religion, and can potentially identify early signs of a fundamentalist perspective. Particularly so in secular states where modernity is perceived to be fast taking over traditions and culture, religious leaders might be one of the few sources of authority that people can turn to for questions regarding their faith. Being in this position and through their interactions with the community, religious leaders would probably be the first to pick up any signs of injustice about one's religion being forgotten or not given due respect. Even if religious leaders are not able to resolve any grievances at the point in time, simply being aware of such emotions is helpful in preventing them from developing skewed religious worldviews.

It is also vital for religious educators to be equipped with skills to delegitimise any divisive teachings promptly, especially so as youths today rely heavily on social media or the Internet for information, putting them in a vulnerable position to dangerous propaganda put forth by radical preachers online. The recent decision to make the Asatizah Recognition Scheme (ARS) compulsory in Singapore is an example of how policymakers can take steps to ensure that local Islamic religious teachers are equipped with the ability to educate and debunk misconceptions (Chia, 2016). The scheme ensures that the applicant is sufficiently trained to "preach and teach Islamic religious knowledge" at an Islamic education center and "meet the standards and training requirements set by the Asatizah Recognition Board (ARB)" (Chia, 2016, para. 2–4). With this, religious leaders are in a better position to educate the dangers of stereotyping which can widen the distance among the different faiths, feed into existing misunderstandings, and diminish any motivation to build trust.

Encourage Moderation in Religious Practices and Foster Integration

Most religious fundamentalists wish to uphold the true meaning of their religion but have been indoctrinated with the incorrect approaches to achieve their agenda, many of which are purveyed by radical preachers active on the Internet (Barzilai-Nahon, & Barzilai, 2005). As such, encouraging moderation in religious practises based on nation's values (e.g., multiculturalism and inclusiveness) can remind people of the need to consider contextual factors even in the practise of one's faith. It is essential to adapt and implement only what is relevant and compatible with the local context, and reinforce the fact that all religions advocate building harmonious relationships with people of other faiths.[4] On top of that, since a fundamentalist mindset is tied to one's identity and thus gives meaning to one's life, it is necessary to remind people that religious identity is just one out of the many identities of a person; besides religious duties, one still has to fulfil the responsibilities of their other identities (K. Ramakrishna, personal communication, 2017). Ensuring continuous effort in fostering integration can also help minimise the potential of developing prejudices and create opportunities to know people from other religions. This is necessary as one is indeed most vulnerable to adopting a fundamentalist mindset when support from the wider community is lacking. Therefore, garnering such a support system will be effective in discouraging social distancing/isolation.

Conclusion

Religious fundamentalism is no doubt a complicated phenomenon. While acts of bigotry, regardless of religion, may increase the "social distance" between various religious groups and be detrimental to communal harmony, it should also be acknowledged that religious fundamentalism is intrinsically a psychological state and a defence mechanism for people who have the perceptions of being marginalised (Terman, 2010). Therefore, it is essential to understand the underpinnings of a religious fundamentalist mindset in order to prevent it from snowballing into violent extremism, and avoid

---

[4]There have been attempts at moderation in other countries. For example, in Indonesia, a major Islamic non-governmental organisation, Muhammadiyah, emphasises the doctrine of moderation in Islam in Indonesia, by promoting socio-economic development to counter radical ideas in the country.

potential strains on the harmony in our community — something that is much needed in our ongoing fight against violent extremism.

Acknowledgement

The views expressed in this chapter are the author's only and do not represent the official position or view of the Ministry of Home Affairs, Singapore.

References

Almond, G. A., Appleby, R. S., & Sivan, E. (2002). *Strong Religion: The Rise of Fundamentalisms around the World.* London: University of Chicago Press.

Altemeyer, B. (2003). Research: Why do religious fundamentalists tend to be prejudiced? *The International Journal for the Psychology of Religion, 13*(1), 17–28.

Altemeyer, B., & Hunsberger, B. (1997). *Amazing Conversions: Why Some Turn to Faith and Others Abandon Religion.* Amherst, NY: Prometheus.

Avineri, S. (1969). Marx and modernization. *The Review of Politics*, *31*(2), 172–188.

Barry, E. (2016). 24 convicted in massacre of Muslims during Gujarat Riots in India. *The New York Times.* Retrieved from https://www.nytimes.com/2016/06/03/world/asia/gujarat-riots-massacre-india-verdict.html.

Barzilai-Nahon, K., & Barzilai, G. (2005). Cultured technology: The Internet and religious fundamentalism. *The Information Society, 21*(1), 25–40.

Brandt, M. J., & Van Tongeren, D. R. (2017). People both high and low on religious fundamentalism are prejudiced toward dissimilar groups. *Journal of Personality and Social Psychology*, *112*(1), 76–79.

Chia, L. (2016). Asztizah Recognition Scheme to become compulsory from January 2017: Yaacob. *Channel News Asia.* Retrieved from http://www.channelnewsasia.com/news/singapore/asatizah-recognition-scheme-to-become-compulsory-from-january/3122772.html.

Emerson, M. O., & Hartman, D. (2006). The rise of religious fundamentalism. *Annual Review of Sociology*, *32*, 127–144.

Garvey, J. H. (1993). Introduction: Fundamentalism and politics. In M.E. Marty, & R.S. Appleby (Eds.), *Fundamentalisms and the State:*

Remaking Polities, Economies, and Militance (pp. 1–10). Chicago, IL: University of Chicago Press.

Genia, V. (1996). I, E, quest, and fundamentalism as predictors of psychological and spiritual well-being. *Journal for the scientific study of Religion*, *35*(1), 56–64.

Hunsberger, B. (1995). Religion and prejudice: The role of religious fundamentalism, quest and right-wing authoritarianism. *Journal of Social Issues*, *51*(2), 11–39.

Hunsberger, B. (1996). Religious fundamentalism, right-wing authoritarianism, and hostility toward homosexuals in non-Christian religious groups. *The International Journal for the Psychology of Religion*, *6*(1), 39–49.

Inglehart, R., & Baker, W. (2000). Modernization, cultural change, and the persistence of traditional values. *American Sociological Review*, *65*(1), 19–51.

Jones, J. W. (2010). Conclusion. In C. B. Strozier, D. M. Terman, J. W. Jones, & K. A. Boyd (Eds.), *The Fundamentalist Mindset: Psychological Perspectives on Religion, Violence, and History*. New York: Oxford University Press, Inc.

Kaplan, S. (2015). The serene-looking Buddhist monk accused of inciting Burma's sectarian violence. *The Washington Post*. Retrieved from https://www.washingtonpost.com/news/morning-mix/wp/2015/05/27/the-burmese-bin-laden-fueling-the-rohingya-migrant-crisis-in-southeast-asia/?utm_term=.ddee7e9916e9.

Kennedy, D. (2013). Muslim 'street patrol' attacked drinkers near London mosque. *The Times*. Retrieved from http://go.galegroup.com.gate.lib.buffalo.edu/ps/i.do?p=AONE&u=sunybuff_main&id=GALE|A349328709&v=2.1&it=r&sid=summon&authCount=1.

Kern, S. (2016). UK: What British Muslims really think. *Gatestone Institute*. Retrieved from https://www.gatestoneinstitute.org/7861/british-muslims-survey.

Khosrokhavar, F. (2010). The psychology of the global Jihadists. In C.B. Strozier, D. M. Terman, J. W. Jones, & K. A. Boyd (Eds.), *The Fundamentalist Mindset: Psychological Perspectives on Religion, Violence, and History* (pp. 145–146). Oxford: Oxford University Press.

Kirkpatrick, L. A. (1993). Fundamentalism, Christian orthodoxy, and intrinsic religious orientation as predictors of discriminatory attitudes. *Journal for the Scientific Study of Religion*, *32*(3), 256–268.

Kornblet, S. (2011). Armed Islamic group: A case study. *Encyclopedia of Bioterrorism Defense.*

Lawrence, B. B. (1989). *Defenders of God: The Fundamentalist Revolt against the Modern Age*. San Francisco: Harper & Row.

Layth, B., Finkel, D., & Kirkpatrick, L. A. (2001). Predicting prejudice from religious fundamentalism and right-wing authoritarianism: A multiple-regression approach. *Journal for the Scientific Study of Religion*, *40*(1), 1–10.

Lott, B. E., & Maluso, D. E. (1995). *The Social Psychology of Interpersonal Discrimination*. New York: Guilford Press.

Marty, M. E. (1996). Too bad we're so relevant: The fundamentalism project projected. *Bulletin of the American Academy of Arts and Sciences*, *49*(6), 22–38.

Marty, M. E., & Appleby, R. S. (Eds.) (1991). *Fundamentalisms Observed.* Chicago, IL: University of Chicago Press.

Pech, R. J., & Slade, B. W. (2006). Religious fundamentalism and terrorism: Why do they do it and what do they want? *Foresight*, *8*(1), 8–20.

Profile: Hamas Palestinian movement (2017). *BBC News*. Retrieved from http://www.bbc.com/news/world-middle-east-13331522.

Ramakrishna, K. (2005). Religion, terror and the fundamentalist mentality. *IDSS Commentaries* (29/2005). Retrieved from https://www.rsis.edu.sg/rsis-publication/cens/690-religion-terror-and-the-funda/#.Wkjee9-WY2w.

Ramakrishna, K. (2016). Religious fundamentalism and social distancing: Cause for concern? *RSIS Commentary No. 023*. Singapore: National Technological University.

Rausch, C. C. (2015). Fundamentalism and terrorism. *Journal of Terrorism Research*, *6*(2), 28–35.

Rogers, M. B., Loewenthal, K. M., Lewis, C. A., Amlôt, R., Cinnirella, M., & Ansari, H. (2007). The role of religious fundamentalism in terrorist violence: A social psychological analysis. *International Review of Psychiatry*, *19*(3), 253–262.

Rowatt, W. C., & Franklin, L. M. (2004). Christian orthodoxy, religious fundamentalism, and right-wing authoritarianism as predictors of implicit racial prejudice. *The International Journal for the Psychology of Religion*, *14*(2), 125–138.

Ruthven, M. (2004). *Fundamentalism: The Search for Meaning*. New York: Oxford University Press.

Salzman, M. B. (2008). Globalization, religious fundamentalism and the need for meaning. *International Journal of Intercultural Relations*, *32*, 318–327.

Savage, S. (2011). Four lessons from the study of fundamentalism and psychology of religion. *Journal of Strategic Security*, *4*(4), 131–150.

Smith, M. (2017). Myanmar's attempt to destroy Rohingya Muslims. *Time*. Retrieved from http://time.com/4994524/myanmar-rohingya-fortify-rights-genocide/.

Strozier, C. B., & Boyd, K. A. (2010). Definitions and dualisms. In C. B. Strozier, D. M. Terman, J. W. Jones, & K. A. Boyd (Eds.), *The Fundamentalist Mindset: Psychological Perspectives on Religion, Violence, and History* (pp. 11–15). New York: Oxford University Press, Inc.

Tan, A. T. H. (2008). Terrorism, insurgency and religious fundamentalism in Southeast Asia. *Defence Studies*, *8*(3), 311–325.

Terman, D. M. (2010). Theories of group psychology, paranoia, and rage. In C. B. Strozier, D. M. Terman, J. W. Jones, & K. A. Boyd (Eds.), *The Fundamentalist Mindset: Psychological Perspectives on Religion, Violence, and History* (pp. 16–28). Oxford: Oxford University Press.

Vijayan, K. C. (2017). Interfaith dialogue 'needs to go beyond sharing of meals'. *The Straits Times*. Retrieved from https://www.straitstimes.com/singapore/interfaith-dialogue-needs-to-go-beyond-sharing-of-meals.

CHAPTER 29

How Can Right-Wing Extremism Exacerbate Islamophobia After a Jihadi Attack? Insights from Europe

NUR AISYAH ABDUL RAHMAN

Home Team Behavioural Sciences Centre, Ministry of Home Affairs, Singapore

Introduction

Right-wing (RW) extremism[1] has been a persistent threat in Western countries for many decades (Koehler, 2016). However, it is often overshadowed by the threat of Islamist violent extremism, especially after the events of September 11 (Koehler, 2016). With the increasing number of Islamist-related attacks in recent years, RW extremism that manifests in the form of Islamophobic attacks, has been rising too.

---

[1]Extremism is an ideological position that does not allow for and undermines alternative points of view; imposing these views on others using violence may also be perceived as justified (Davies, 2008).

What is RW Extremism?

RW extremism does not have one specific definition but its main ideology revolves around ethnocentrism and an intolerance towards certain groups (Mudde, 2000). It has evolved over the years; beginning with fascism, Nazism, and White supremacism, it has evolved to become more anti-immigrant, xenophobic, and Islamophobic over the years (Baysinger, 2006; Hafez, 2014). For example, French right-wing political group Front National (FN), used to be strongly anti-Semitic in the 1980s but has now become more Islamophobic (Mondon, 2015).

RW extremism is also expressed differently in different countries, due in part to the different socio-political contexts. For example, British skinheads in the 1960s advocated white supremacy and fascist ideals, and were anti-Semitic and strongly opposed to homosexuality. This was arguably a response to the permissive culture that was characteristic of Britain during that era (Pollard, 2016). On the other hand, the currently active English Defence League (EDL) presents itself as the defender of Western democracy against radical Islam and also champion of gay rights. This is in line with contemporary socio-political trends where Islamic violent extremism is prominent and there is greater mainstream acceptance of homosexuality (Garland & Treadwell, 2010).

For the purposes of this chapter, right-wing extremism will be defined as an ideology that is intolerant of other cultures and religions.

What Drives RW Extremism?

In the current socio-political climate, Islamist violent extremism has become a dominant global problem, thrusting the Islamic faith and its followers to centre stage. With the prevalence of Islamist violent extremism, it is unsurprising that RW extremism has evolved to incorporate Islamophobia. RW extremists and groups often cite various reasons to justify their Islamophobic sentiments.[2] Due to the scope of this chapter, only the following themes will be discussed.

[2]Others include anti-government (RW extremists perceive their constitutional rights to be violated by the government).

Anti-immigrant Theme

The crux of RW anti-immigrant rhetoric revolves around how immigrants do not belong and are taxing the country. They are perceived as competitors for jobs, government aid, and other limited economic resources (Ciftci, 2012). With different cultures and values, immigrants pose a threat to the host country's own culture and values (Ciftci, 2012). In many Western countries, Muslims tend to be immigrants or descended from immigrants. In countries, such as France, Muslims tend to be of lower socio-economic status and are often associated with crime. Moreover, by continuing to practice their own religion and culture, Muslims are perceived as unwilling to integrate into local society (The Brookings Institute, 2006). Such perceptions are also prevalent in other EU countries like Germany, Spain, France, etc. Hence, the general perception of Muslims is highly negative.

With the increasing rates of Muslim immigration to Europe in the past 20 years (Croucher, 2013), and an influx of refugees from conflict regions such as Syria ("Migrant Crisis: Migration to Europe explained in seven charts", 2016), Muslim immigrants present physical (e.g., crime), economic, and symbolic (i.e., the expression of a religion that is different from the predominantly Judaeo-Christian ones in Western societies) threats. A more protectionist and anti-immigrant stance espoused by RW extremists thus becomes more appealing to those who feel threatened by immigrants' presence.

Racial and Religious Theme

Another feature of RW extremism rhetoric is the utilisation of religious ideas as justification for their intolerance towards certain groups (Baysinger, 2006). For these RW groups, their behaviour and worldview revolve around their religious identity as Christians. In this context, Jews are depicted as the offspring of the Devil and Eve, and the children of Adam and Eve are the "true Israelites" or Aryans and described "to be fair" (Baysinger, 2006; Smith-Christopher & Warner, 2011). This in turn contributes to the belief that Caucasians, who have fair complexions, are "God's Chosen people", while non-Whites are considered as "beasts in the fields". Thus, individuals who subscribe to these beliefs may use them to justify aggression and violence against other ethnic groups (Baysinger, 2006). These beliefs may then lay the foundation for RW extremists' negative attitudes towards non-Whites. Some RW extremists, emphasise their Christian identity, equating it with Western ideals and contrasting it against the threat of what they perceive to be creeping Islamisation (Goodwin, 2013).

Islamist Violent Extremism Theme

In the post-9/11 era, there was an added dimension to RW groups' anti-Muslim stance: Muslims were not only seen as a threat due to their immigrant status but were also an existential threat because of violent terrorism (Githens-Mazer & Lambert, 2010). With the rise of attacks perpetrated by locally born Muslims, such as the terror incident at Westminster Bridge[3] in 2017 and November 2015 Paris[4] attacks, it is not surprising that Islamophobic themes is gaining traction. Islam is painted as incongruent with Western ideals, with some RW extremists arguing that such acts of violent extremism are due to the incompatible nature of the religion and culture (Hafez, 2014). For example, after the Charlie Hebdo shootings[5] in 2015, Patriotic Europeans Against the Islamisation of the West (Pegida), a RW group based in Germany, held regular demonstrations purporting that "Germany was overcrowded with Muslims, refugees, and asylum seekers, and warning against the 'Islamization' of the West" (Machtans, 2016, p. 91).

---

[3]On 22 March 2017, a British-born Muslim convert, mowed down a crowd on the Westminster Bridge, with a car and proceeded to fatally stab an unarmed police officer (Allen & Henderson, 2017). Four people were killed, with 50 others injured.
[4]On 13 November 2015, multiple jihadi assailants, both local and migrant, conducted a series of coordinated attacks that killed 130 people and injured more than 400 others ("Paris attacks: What happened in the night", 2015).
[5]On 7 January 2015, two French jihadis attacked Charlie Hebdo, a satirical magazine, offices in Paris, killing 12 and injuring 11 ("Charlie Hebdo Attack: Three days of terror", 2015).

What is the Significance of Understanding RW Extremism?

RW rhetoric and Islamophobia tend to intensify after a jihadi terror attack as exemplified by the spike of hate crimes. For example, based on FBI records, hate crimes against Muslims in the United States spiked in 2001, from 20 to 30 cases annually to 481 cases in 2001 after the September 11 attacks (Ingraham, 2015). In Britain, Humans Rights First reported that hate crimes targeting individuals who were perceived to be Muslims, increased by about 600% in London after the 2005 bombings (Moten, 2012). The impact of such attacks is also not limited to the above-mentioned countries. For example, after the 2015 Paris attacks, Islamophobic incidents in London tripled (Gani, 2015). Hate crimes against Muslims in the United Kingdom also rose by 18% from the previous year (Gani, 2015).

Moreover, there is greater prominence of Islamophobic sentiments in the public discourse, especially with RW groups linking the attack(s) to local Muslim communities (Hafez, 2014). From social movements such as Pegida in Germany and the EDL in Britain, to the rise of far-right political groups, such as the Party for Freedom in the Netherlands and the FN in France, there has been increasing support for RW extremist rhetoric. For example, the FN garnered 28% of the national votes three weeks after the November 2015 Paris attacks. Utilising strong anti-immigrant and Islamophobic rhetoric, the FN was the only party to achieve monumental gains after the attack (Chrisafis, 2015).

RW extremism is a threat to communal harmony. The recent expression of RW extremism in Europe, as intolerance of immigrants and Islam, is problematic and a possible threat to Singapore even though it may not be explicitly labelled as "RW extremism". In the past decade, there have been recorded incidents of Islamophobia and intolerance of immigrants in Singapore (Salleh, 2017). For example, a Muslim woman tweeted how a man verbally abused her a day after the November 2015 Paris attacks happened ("Islamophobia moves from subtle whispers to outward displays in Singapore", 2015).

Given that these themes overlap with those that characterise RW extremism and the cross-pollination of ideas on the Internet, it is possible for RW extremism to take root in Singapore. It is thus prudent to know more about RW extremism and how it can worsen Islamophobia, as well as what measures to adopt to prevent or alleviate RW extremism's consequences.

Five Key Points and Tips

Point 1: RW's "Other-ing" of Muslims

One of the ways that RW extremist groups attract support is to use culturally relevant information (e.g., race, religion, cultural practices) to emphasise the differences between Muslims and the RW extremists' perceived in-group (Atton, 2006). For example, safeguarding Christianity and traditional British culture against Muslims are the core themes that Britain's First used to garner support among like-minded people (Palmer, 2014). In fact, the group has created Christian Patrols to "fight against" the perceived Islamisation of Britain (Palmer, 2014). Similarly, the EDL in Britain and Marine Le Pen in France argue that Islam's values are not congruent with Western ones. Even if they were locally born Muslims, their religion makes them "foreign". Such arguments are used to elicit fear that Islam may replace the current secular values and lifestyle. Thus, resulting in Islamophobia.

Tip 1: Encourage an inclusive national identity

While it is natural for people to have multiple identities, it is also important for there to be a common identity that everyone can relate to in the face of adversity. Research has found that highlighting a superordinate (i.e., a larger umbrella group) identity that emphasises similarities instead of differences is useful (Wenzel *et al.*, 2007). An example of such a superordinate identity is national identity. After the 2017 Westminster attack, Britons and Londoners, in particular, emphasised their national identity as a diverse and inclusive Britain.

Within days, there were vigils, interfaith dialogues, and prayers (Bashir, 2017; Bowden, 2017). There was the "Love for all, hatred for none" interfaith vigil and march, attended by the police and diverse members of the public (Addley, 2017). Organised by the Women's March of London group, women of diverse backgrounds stood on the Westminster Bridge, holding hands in "silent resistance against fear and division" ("London Attack: What we know so far", 2017, para. 22). Online, there were hashtags such as #WeStandTogether, #WeAreNotAfraid, and #LondonStrong ("London Attack: What we know so far", 2017; Hunt, 2017). These acts of unity were demonstrations of a superordinate identity that people were able to relate to and come together under.

However, for it to work, the national identity must be inclusive and relatable to everyone. If the national identity is homogenous and not reflective of the diversity in the country, people are more likely to see certain groups of people as different to the archetypal in-group. Britain is a good example where their national identity has evolved over the years to reflect the increasingly inclusive and multicultural society (Shi, 2008). Having an inclusive superordinate identity allows for empowerment, closure, and social support.

Point 2: RW Extremists' Prejudicial Narratives on Islam

RW extremists tend to perpetuate prejudiced narratives of Islam and Muslims (Hafez, 2014). Some RW extremists use flawed arguments and generalisations to highlight Islam as a threat. One of the tropes used included painting Islam as an inherently violent religion (Goodwin, 2013). For instance, in response to the Cologne Police inclusion of Arabic in its multilanguage new year wishes tweet, Alternative for Germany (Afd)[6] member Beatrix von Storch accused them of trying to "appease the barbaric, gang-raping Muslim hordes of men" (Huggler, 2018). They also tend to selectively use information and statistics to support certain claims. For example, RW extremist and English Defence League co-founder Tommy Robinson tweeted

[6] A right-wing political party in Germany.

the following after the Westminster attack: "Muslims make up only 4% of the U.K. population, look at the continued chaos & destruction they cause, what do u think it will be like with 20%". Through the use of statistics, the claims are made to seem more evidence-based and convincing.

Such narratives are also meant to evoke emotional responses. According to Matsumoto *et al.* (2015), powerful group leaders set the tone for the interpretation of critical events to their in-group members. The use of certain emotion-laden words, metaphors, images, and non-verbal behaviours communicate leaders' interpretation of the event and can affect in-group members' response to the event (Matsumoto *et al.*, 2015). Words and behaviour that evoke anger, contempt, and disgust can elicit intergroup hostility and political violence (Matsumoto *et al.*, 2015). Hence, how in-group members react to terror attacks can be based on the emotion communicated in their leader's narrative. After a terror attack, narratives that evoke these negative emotions may exacerbate existing tension and increase the likelihood of Islamophobia.

When the Westminster attack happened, Tommy Robinson,[7] along with his own media crew, went down to the scene of the attack while the emergency responders were still there (Oppenheim, 2017). In the resulting video,[8] neither Caolan Robertson — Robinson's colleague — nor Robinson distinguished Islamic terrorists from the general British Muslim population; they were generalising acts of terrorism to all Muslims. Robinson later declared, "We are at war", suggesting that Muslims have brought war to the streets of London. This statement served to incite anger towards Muslims for violating Britons' well-being, safety, and way of life. Robertson and Robinson were also quick to assume that the perpetrator was a foreign fighter. Robinson went on to say that "They've [foreign fighters] gone and fought for ISIS. They've been in training camps, they've been beheading people. They've been raping people and they're walking

[7]Tommy Robinson is a rather prominent RW figure in Britain. According to advocacy group, Hope Not Hate, he is eight on the list of most prominent RW figures (Collins, 2017).

[8]Retrieved from https://www.youtube.com/watch?v=CWykfEtDL8E.

the streets of our capital city. They're living with us". With the use of such violent imagery, he was suggesting that Muslims are morally inferior to the British thus provoking feelings of contempt towards them. Robertson also referred to Islam as an imported culture of "violence, destruction, and terrorism". This would evoke a sense of disgust towards Muslims for bringing in an inferior culture that harms Britons and needs to be kept away from British society.

According to the comments' section of the video, there were numerous people who echoed similar Islamophobic sentiments shared in the video. For example, one commenter said "I am sick and tired of all the [politically correct] crap and accusations of bigotry and racism coming from the liberal left ... There are a lot of dangerous people on the loose in Europe who hate us and want to impose Shariah on us". Another commenter went a step further and suggested indiscriminate violence with, "All Muslims should be sent to the gas chambers, sorted!".

Tip 2: Improve knowledge of RW extremism and Islam

To foster intergroup understanding, people need information. To begin with, there should be more education on the different types of extremism in an attempt to raise awareness. According to Tell MAMA[9] (Measuring anti-Muslim Attacks) app founder, Fiyaz Mughal, the British government's focus has been on countering Islamist violent extremism and not on RW extremism (Mughal, 2014). This, as Pasha-Robinson (2017, para. 12) argued, can be seen as a "systemic failure" in identifying the RW extremism threat in Britain. As such, providing more insight on RW extremism can be useful for both the public and the authorities. This can include learning to identify the logos, groups, and rhetoric that are associated with RW extremism.

Another useful way would be to debunk myths that people have about Muslims and the Islamic faith. For example, one myth that

[9]'Tell MAMA' (Measuring anti-Muslim Attacks) is a national project in Britain that records and measures Islamophobic attacks.

could be debunked is, "all terrorist acts are done by Muslims, so all Muslims are terrorists". People need to understand that there are other forms of terrorism (i.e., not all terrorist acts are by Muslims), and that most Muslims are mainstream moderates and do not express themselves violently (i.e., not all Muslims are terrorists).

Point 3: Negative Interactions with Muslims may Increase Susceptibility to RW Extremist Rhetoric

Intergroup interactions can influence prejudice; negative interaction has been found to be a consistent predictor of intergroup attitudes and prejudice while positive interactions can reduce prejudice (Techakesari *et al.*, 2015). More meaningful and quality interactions are negatively correlated with prejudice towards an out-group member; researchers found that non-Muslims with sustained relationships with Muslims are less likely to hold strong prejudicial attitudes of Islam and Muslims, as compared to participants who do not have such sustained relationships with Muslims (Croucher, 2013; González *et al.*, 2008). In other words, a lack of positive intergroup contact may increase susceptibility to prejudice towards outgroup members.

According to Treadwell and Garland (2011), RW strongholds in Britain are in areas with large Asian and Muslim communities (e.g., Luton). Despite close proximity, there is a lack of meaningful interaction, thus leading to mutual suspicion and fear between the communities (Treadwell & Garland, 2011).

Tip 3: Encourage meaningful interfaith relations

Meaningful interactions between people of different faiths take effort and have to be encouraged. According to Aberson (2015), negative intergroup interactions overwhelm the effects of positive intergroup contact because group identity is more salient during negative interactions. In order to enhance the effects of positive intergroup interaction, social group identity needs to be salient and intergroup threats need to be addressed (Aberson, 2015).

Community leaders can create opportunities and encourage the public to participate in meaningful interactions in formal or informal settings. For example, platforms[10] such as the Building Bridges Seminar in Singapore (Tan, 2015) provide formal opportunities for religious leaders to gather and have discussions on their respective religions. The Harmony Centre[11] is also a great place for members of the public to have such discussions (Mohamad Salleh, 2014). People need to have a safe space where they can ask questions, challenge ideas, and encourage tolerance.

There can also be gatherings and meals at different places of worship. For example, a Thai Buddhist Temple in Tennessee in the United States, has an annual interfaith lunch where people of various backgrounds are encouraged to come together and talk about their religious beliefs (Wilson, 2016). Through such efforts, people are placed in situations where their group identity is highlighted and are given a chance to dispel any perceptions of intergroup threat.

Point 4: RW's Quick Divisive Messages and Responses to Attacks

RW extremists are very responsive and are able to spread their divisive narratives quickly after an attack. Within hours of the Westminster attack, the RW extremist groups in the U.K. reacted with their own take on the attack and issued a call for Britons to unite against Muslims ("London Terror Attack — The Far-Right Response", 2017). Most of these messages appeared quickly on the Internet, often with speculations about the nature of the attack and characteristics of perpetrator(s).

---

[10] Another example is the Religious Rehabilitation Group (RRG) Resource and Counselling Centre (RCC), which is located on the premises of Khadijah Mosque. The Centre serves members of the public who wish to seek clarification on radical ideology and violent extremism as well as provide counselling services.

[11] The Harmony Centre is a space to enhance inter-faith dialogue and engagement via inter-faith exhibitions, training, and outreach programmes (Mohamad Salleh, 2014).

A picture of a Muslim woman walking past a victim on the Westminster Bridge became widely circulated by another RW extremist group in the U.K., the British National Party ("London Terror Attack — The Far-Right Response", 2017). The picture was captioned "London Terror Attack: A picture says a thousand words. LIKE and SHARE if you agree", suggesting that Muslims are indifferent towards the suffering of the victims. The picture was taken out of context, disregarding the fact that she was a distressed victim who had already offered her assistance (England & Pasha-Robinson, 2017). Such messages reinforce an "us-versus-them" mentality and Islamophobia within the online RW community.

Another RW extremist group, Britain First, also posted an event invite on their Facebook page within hours of the Westminster Bridge attack. The event was a "London March Against Terrorism", co-planned with another U.K. RW group, the EDL, in the upcoming weeks ("London Terror Attack — The Far-Right Response", 2017). According to the Britain First Facebook page, more than 1,900 people indicated their interest to attend the event, with 762 reporting their attendance at the event.

Tip 4: Ensure prompt crisis communications

In the event of an attack, swift crisis communication by the authorities and religious leaders is imperative to set a tone of unity. Providing current information, acknowledging the concerns of the public, and communicating what they can do are important aspects of crisis communication (Seeger, 2006). Crisis communication is integral in assuring the public, debunking rumours, and correcting misinformation that is propagated by RW groups, especially after an attack. In the immediate aftermath of the Westminster attack, the Metropolitan Police communicated regular updates of the incident over social media (Griggs, 2017). The police also took part in vigils and reiterated their "We Stand Together"[12] resilience campaign

[12] 'We Stand Together' is a resilience campaign started by British police and religious leaders in 2015 in response to terror attacks in Europe (Rucki, 2015).

(Griggs, 2017). Such communications from the authorities helped build the public's trust in them while communicating unity. With members of the public using #WeStandTogether on social media (West, 2017), it was evident that such communications were making an impact.

Religious leaders also condemned the attack, and interfaith gatherings and prayers were organised in the next few days following the Westminster attack (Chandler, 2017). In his speech at one of the interfaith gatherings, Justin Welby, Archbishop of Canterbury, said "That [anger] is appropriate when the innocent are killed. It is not appropriate to be angry at a whole category of people but simply at one person" (Al Jazeera English, 2017). Through this, he not only acknowledged the anger that people may be feeling, but also advised them against generalising the actions of one individual to a community. Such messages of unity are important after a crisis. As the acting Commissioner Craig Mackey noted, the rates of Islamophobic incidents would have likely been higher if the faith leaders did not act quickly to calm and rally the different religious communities together (Mortimer, 2017).

Point 5: Cycle of Discrimination and Violence Between Islamic Extremists and RW Extremists

There is a cycle of hate, violence, and retaliation between Islamic extremists and RW extremists. These groups and their supporters often utilise attacks to justify their own beliefs and rhetoric, highlighting their grievances, attracting sympathisers, and calling for more attacks from fellow supporters.

For instance, many RW extremist groups had spread Islamophobic narratives after the London Bridge attack[13] in 2017 ("After London Terror Attack, right-wing media react with predictable Islamophobia", 2017). Katie McHugh, a writer for a RW publication, tweeted, "There

[13]On 3 June 2017, three jihadi attackers drove a van into pedestrians on the London Bridge, followed by a knife attack in Borough Market ("London attack: What we know so far", 2017). Eight people were killed, with 48 others injured.

would be no deadly terror attacks in the U.K. if the Muslims didn't live here. #London Bridge" ("After London Terror Attack, right-wing media react with predictable Islamophobia", 2017). She had generalised blame to all Muslims for the attack. All Muslims are thus perceived to be the enemy that should be eradicated to keep Britons safe. For some, these claims may be interpreted as calls for action. One example is Darren Osborne, the perpetrator of the Finsbury Park Mosque attack.[14] Osborne had allegedly claimed that his attack was an act of revenge for the London Bridge attack (Evans *et al.*, 2017). Following the Finsbury Park Mosque attack, ISIS supporters reportedly used the attack to demonstrate that Muslims were being attacked and called for a retaliation against non-Muslims (Leo *et al.*, 2017). Thus, at a community level, such responses breed mistrust and division.

Tip 5: Encourage non-incendiary responses

To prevent or minimise hate, members of the public are encouraged not to respond in a similarly negative manner towards the perceived opposing community. People have to be reminded that they share a common identity and be encouraged to respond compassionately to alleviate intergroup tension (Motyl *et al.*, 2009).

Online material. On social media and other commonly used online platforms (e.g., forums), it is important for people to not respond to incendiary comments or posts. Trolling[15] is common online and can disrupt a civil conversation (Prier, 2017). Some troll accounts are bot accounts, which are programmed to work as part of a network that garners greater online exposure (Prier, 2017). For example, Twitter personality Jenna Abrams was popular among RW circles, but was later found to be a bot account (Tornoe, 2017). It had garnered 70,000 followers and was even featured in numerous news articles for its provocative tweets on immigration and racial segregation

[14]Darren Osborne drove a van into a crowd of worshippers who were leaving the Finsbury Park mosque. One person died and 11 were injured (Evans *et al.*, 2017).
[15]Deliberately disseminate provocative posts in a discussion forum which disrupts and angers other participants.

(Tornoe, 2017). While it is possible to ignore, taking action to remove or report these accounts and posts would be more ideal, ensuring that the spread of such messages can be stopped. On many social media platforms, there are "Report" buttons that users can click to flag a particular post for review and removal.

Offline or face-to-face interactions. However, there may be challenging situations, where one could be confronted by another person with strong extremist beliefs. A photo of Muslim girl Safiyyah Khan staring bemusedly at an EDL protester as he hurled verbal insults, went viral as people applauded her brave and nonviolent response (Perraudin, 2017). In Luton, the birthplace of the EDL, faith and community leaders created a guide of Dos (e.g., report all crime) and Don'ts (e.g., do not make physical contact) for people who are confronted by extremists. Such guides can aid people in preventing the situation from escalating in order to ensure their safety at that moment in time. Encouraging such responses at the community level will also help alleviate Islamophobia and reduce divisions between different communities (Motyl *et al*., 2009).

Acknowledgement

The views expressed in this chapter are the author's only and do not represent the official position or view of the Ministry of Home Affairs, Singapore.

References

Aberson, C. L. (2015). Positive intergroup contact, negative intergroup contact, and threat as predictors of cognitive and affective dimensions of prejudice. *Group Processes & Intergroup Relations*, *18*(6), 743–760.

Addley, E. (2017). 'Love for all, hatred for none': Hundreds gather for Westminster vigil. *The Guardian*. Retrieved from https://www.theguardian.com/uk-news/2017/mar/29/love-for-all-hatred-for-none-hundreds-gather-for-westminster-attack-vigil.

After London terror attack, right-wing media react with predictable Islamophobia (2017). *Media Matters*. Retrieved from https://www.

mediamatters.org/research/2017/06/04/after-london-terror-attack-right-wing-media-react-predictable-islamophobia/216775.

Al Jazeera English (2017). UK: Religious leaders call for unity after London attack (video file). Retrieved from https://www.youtube.com/watch?v=3NkB1iy0hTI.

Allen, E., & Henderson, B. (2017). Westminster attack: Everything we know so far about the events in London. *The Telegraph*. Retrieved from http://www.telegraph.co.uk/news/2017/03/22/westminster-terror-attack-everything-know-far/.

Atton, C. (2006). Far-right media on the internet: Culture, discourse and power. *New Media & Society*, *8*(4), 573–587.

Bashir, M. (2017). Dialogue marks faiths' response to the Westminster attacks. *BBC News*. Retrieved from http://www.bbc.com/news/uk-39482705.

Baysinger, T. G. (2006). Right-wing group characteristics and ideology. *Homeland Security Affairs*, *2*(2), 1–19.

Bowden, G. (2017). Expected hate crime increase after 2017 Westminster attack hasn't materialised, campaigners say. *Huffington Post*. Retrieved from http://www.huffingtonpost.co.uk/entry/hate-crime-after-2017-westminster-attack_uk_58e3b44ee4b03a26a3664b38.

Chandler, M. (2017). Muslim leaders unite with other faiths at Westminster Abbey to condemn 'appalling' attack. *Evening Standard*. Retrieved from https://www.standard.co.uk/news/london/muslim-leaders-unite-with-other-faiths-to-condemn-appalling-westminster-attack-a3498836.html.

Charlie Hebdo attack: Three days of terror (2015). *BBC News*. Retrieved from http://www.bbc.com/news/world-europe-30708237.

Chrisafis, A. (2015). Front National wins opening round in France's regional elections. *The Guardian*. Retrieved from https://www.theguardian.com/world/2015/dec/06/front-national-wins-opening-round-in-frances-regional-elections.

Ciftci, S. (2012). Islamophobia and threat perceptions: Explaining anti-Muslim sentiment in the West. *Journal of Muslim Minority Affairs*, *32*(3), 293–309.

Collins, M. (2017). The dirty dozen. *Hope not hate*. Retrieved from http://hopenothate.org.uk/2017/02/15/the-dirty-dozen/.

Croucher, S. M. (2013). Integrated threat theory and acceptance of immigrant assimilation: An analysis of Muslim immigration in Western Europe. *Communication Monographs*, *80*(1), 46–62.

Davies, L. (2008). *Education Against Extremism*. Stoke on Trent, UK: Trentham Books.

England, C., & Pasha-Robinson, L. (2017). London attack: Muslim woman photographed on Westminster Bridge during error incident speaks out. *The Independent*. Retrieved from http://www.independent.co.uk/news/uk/home-news/london-terror-attack-muslim-woman-photographed-westminster-bridge-help-tell-mama-a7648711.html.

Evans, M., Furness, H., & Ward, V. (2017). Finsbury Park suspect 'turned against Muslims' after London Bridge attack. *The Telegraph*. Retrieved from http://www.telegraph.co.uk/news/2017/06/19/finsbury-park-suspect-had-abused-muslim-neighbour/.

Gani, A. (2015). Targeting of London Muslims triples after Paris attacks. *The Guardian*. Retrieved from https://www.theguardian.com/uk-news/2015/dec/04/attacks-against-london-muslims-triple-in-wake-of-paris-attacks.

Garland, J., & Treadwell, J. (2010). 'No surrender to the Taliban!' Football hooliganism, Islamophobia and the rise of the English Defence League. Retrieved from http://epubs.surrey.ac.uk/772919/3/Garland%20 2012%20No%20surrender%20to%20the%20Taliban.pdf.

Githens-Mazer, J., & Lambert, R. (2010). Islamophobia and anti-Muslim hate crime: A London case study. Retrieved from https://lemosandcrane.co.uk/resources/Islamophobia_and_Anti-Muslim_Hate_Crime.pdf.

González, K., Verkuyten, M., Weesie, J., & Poppe, E. (2008). Prejudice towards Muslims in the Netherlands: Testing integrated threat theory. *British Journal of Social Psychology*, *47*(4), 667–685.

Goodwin, M. (2013). *The Roots of Extremism: The English Defence League and the Counter-Jihad Challenge*. London: Chatham House.

Griggs, I. (2017). Inside the Met Police comms response to Westminster attacks. *PR Week*. Retrieved from https://www.prweek.com/article/1432250/inside-met-police-comms-response-westminster-attacks.

Hafez, F. (2014). Shifting borders: Islamophobia as common ground for building pan-European right-wing unity. *Patterns of Prejudice*, *48*(5), 479–499.

Huggler, J. (2018). AfD politician faces criminal investigation over 'barbarian Muslim gang-raping hordes' tweet. *The Telegraph*. Retrieved from http://www.telegraph.co.uk/news/2018/01/02/afd-politician-faces-criminal-investigation-barbarian-muslim/.

Hunt, E. (2017). #WeAreNotAfraid: Londoners send out message after terror attack. *The Guardian*. Retrieved from https://www.theguardian.com/uk-news/2017/mar/23/wearenotafraid-londoners-send-out-message-after-terror-attack.

Ingraham, C. (2015). Anti-Muslim hate crimes are still five times more common today than before 9/11. *The Washington Post.* Retrieved from https://www.washingtonpost.com/news/wonk/wp/2015/02/11/anti-muslim-hate-crimes-are-still-five-times-more-common-today-than-before-911/.

Islamophobia moves from subtle whispers to outward displays in Singapore. (2015). Coconuts Singapore. Retrieved from http://singapore.coconuts.co/2015/11/20/islamophobia-moves-subtle-whispers-outward-displays-singapore.

Koehler, D. (2016). Right-wing extremism and terrorism in Europe: Current developments and issues for the future. *Prism: A Journal of the Center for Complex Operations*, *6*(2), 84–104.

Leo, B., Mullin, G., Loveridge-Greene, O., & Warnes, I. (2017). 'Wake up to the war' ISIS supporters use Finsbury Park mosque attack to make twisted call for more atrocities against the West. *The Sun.* Retrieved from https://www.thesun.co.uk/news/3829975/isis-supporters-use-finsbury-park-terror-attack-to-make-twisted-call-for-more-atrocities-against-the-west/.

London attack: What we know so far (2017). *BBC News.* Retrieved from http://www.bbc.com/news/uk-england-london-40147164.

London Terror Attack — The Far Right Response (2017). International Report Bigotry and Fascism. Retrieved from http://irbf.org.uk/london-terror-attack-the-far-right-response/.

Machtans, K. (2016). "Racism is not an opinion" Muslim responses on Pegida and Islamophobia in Germany. *German Politics and Society*, *121*(34), 87–100.

Matsumoto, D., Frank, M. G., & Hwang, H. C. (2015). The role of intergroup emotions in political violence. *Current Directions n Psychological Science*, *24*(5), 369–373.

Migrant crisis: Migration to Europe explained in seven charts (2016). *BBC News.* Retrieved from http://www.bbc.com/news/world-europe-34131911.

Mohamad Salleh, N. A. (2014). Muis' Harmony Centre drawing interest from abroad. *The Straits Times.* Retrieved from http://www.asiaone.com/singapore/muis-harmony-centre-drawing-interest-abroad

Mohamed Salleh, N. A. (2017). Singapore must safeguard position of minorities id growing polarisation abroad: Shanmugam. *The Straits Times.* Retrieved from http://www.straitstimes.com/singapore/singapore-must-safeguard-position-of-minorities-amid-growing-polarisation-abroad-shanmugam.

Mondon, A. (2015). The French secular hypocrisy: The extreme right. The Republic and the battle for hegemony. *Patterns of Prejudice*, *49*(4), 392–413.

Mortimer, C. (2017). Islamophobic crimes rose after Westminster attacks, police reveal. *Independent*. Retrieved from http://www.independent.co.uk/news/uk/crime/islamophobic-crime-numbers-rise-london-terror-attack-westminster-racism-anti-muslim-a7655971.html.

Moten, A. R., (2012). Understanding and ameliorating Islamophobia. *International Journal of Philosophy of Culture and Axiology*, *9*(1), 155–178.

Motyl, M., Rothschild, Z., & Pyszczynski, T. (2009). The cycle of violence and pathways to peace. *Journal of Organisational Transformation & Social Change*, 6(2), 153–170.

Mudde, C. (2000). *The Ideology of the Extreme Right*. Oxford: Manchester University Press.

Mughal, F. (2014). Coalition needs to reform penny-pinching anti-radicalisation policies, says Fiyaz Mughal. *Daily Express*. Retrieved from http://www.express.co.uk/comment/expresscomment/503984/ISIS-will-see-new-recruits-after-James-Foley-death-if-Coalition-Prevent-policy-unchanged.

Oppenheim, M. (2017). Tommy Robinson condemned for ranting about Islamic extremism at scene of London terror attack. *The Independent*. Retrieved from http://www.independent.co.uk/news/uk/home-news/tommy-robinson-london-terror-attack-islamic-extremism-westminster-bridge-a7644676.html.

Palmer, E. (2014). Who are Britain First? The Far-right party 'invading' mosques. *International Business Times*. Retrieved from http://www.ibtimes.co.uk/who-are-britain-first-far-right-party-invading-mosques-1449289.

Paris attacks: What happened in the night (2015). *BBC News*. Retrieved from http://www.bbc.com/news/world-europe-34818994.

Pasha-Robinson, L. (2017). Number of far-right extremists flagged to Government terror unit soars 30% in a year. *The Independent*. Retrieved from http://www.independent.co.uk/news/uk/home-news/finsbury-park-attack-far-right-extremist-rise-year-statistics-prevent-terrorism-scheme-referrals-a7798231.html.

Perraudin, F. (2017). Photo of Saffiyah Khan defying EDL protester in Birmingham goes viral. *The Guardian*. Retrieved from https://www.theguardian.com/uk-news/2017/apr/09/birmingham-woman-standing-in-defiance-of-edl-protester-goes-viral.

Pollard, J. (2016). Skinhead culture: The ideologies, mythologies, religions and conspiracy theories of racist skinheads. *Patterns of Prejudice*, *50*(4–5), 398–419.

Prier, J. (2017). Commanding the trend: Social media information warfare. *Strategic Studies Quarterly*, *11*(4), 50–85.

Rucki, A. (2015). We Stand Together campaign urges London communities to unite in wake of Europe terror attacks. *Evening Standard*. Retrieved from https://www.standard.co.uk/news/london/we-stand-together-campaign-urges-london-communities-to-unite-in-wake-of-europe-terror-attacks-10094292.html.

Seeger, M. W. (2006). Best practices in crisis communication: An expert panel process. *Journal of Applied Communication Research*, *34*(3), 232–244.

Shi, T. (2008). British national identity in the 21st century. *Intercultural Communications Studies*, *17*(1), 102–114.

Smith-Christopher, D. L., & Warner, J. A. (2011). Right-wing extremism. In M. Shally-Jensen (Ed.), *Encyclopedia of Contemporary American Social Issues* (Vol. 2, pp. 652–660). Santa Barbara, CA: ABC-CLIO.

Tan, S. (2015). Sharing the importance of inter-faith understanding. *Ministry of Culture, Community and Youth*. Retrieved from https://www.mccy.gov.sg/en/news/speeches/2015/May/Building_Bridges_Seminar.aspx.

Techakesari, P., Barlow, F. K., Hornsey, M. J., Sung, B., Thai, M., & Chak, J. L. (2015). An investigation of positive and negative contact as predictors of intergroup attitudes in the United States, Hong Kong, and Thailand. *Journal of Cross-Cultural Psychology*, *46*(3), 454–468.

The Brookings Institute (2006). The steady integration of France's most recent and largest minority. Retrieved from https://www.brookings.edu/wp-content/uploads/2016/07/integratingislam_chapter.pdf.

Tornoe, R. (2017), Two popular conservative Twitter personalities were just outed as Russian trolls. *The Inquirer*. Retrieved from http://www.philly.com/philly/news/politics/presidential/russia-fake-twitter-facebook-posts-accounts-trump-election-jenna-abrams-20171103.html.

Treadwell, J., & Garland, J. (2011). Masculinity, marginalization, & violence: A case study of the English Defence League. *The British Journal of Criminology*, *51*(4), 621–634.

Wenzel, M., Mummendey, A., & Waldzus, S. (2007). Superordinate identities and intergroup conflict: The ingroup projection model. *European review of social psychology*, *18*(1), 331–372.

West, M. (2017). #WeStandTogether: London unites after Westminster attack. *BBC News*. Retrieved from http://www.bbc.com/news/uk-england-london-39365398.

Wilson, B. (2016). Interfaith lunch bridges cultures. *Daily News Journal*. Retrieved from http://www.dnj.com/story/news/2016/01/15/interfaith-lunch-bridges-cultures/78739266/.

CHAPTER 30

Islamophobia and its Aftermath: Strategies to Manage Islamophobia

NUR ELISSA RUZZI'EANNE BTE RAFI'EE

Home Team Behavioural Sciences Centre, Ministry of Home Affairs, Singapore

Introduction

Incidences of jihadi extremist attacks in recent years have led to increasing occurrences of Islamophobic incidents after these attacks (Abdelkader, 2016). After the Paris attacks[1] on 13 November 2015, for example, Collective Against Islamophobia in France (CCIF) reported a rise in the number of Islamophobic incidents in France, particularly in places such as mosques and Muslim restaurants (Gopalakrishnan, 2015). In fact, the occurrence of Islamophobic incidents after the Paris attack was not limited to France but had

[1]The Paris attacks were a series of coordinated attacks that happened in Paris and France. Claimed by the Islamic State of Iraq and Syria (ISIS), the attacks included suicide bombings, mass shootings, as well as hostage taking (Almasy *et al.*, 2015).

spilled over to other countries as well, where such incidents were similarly recorded in the United Kingdom by TellMAMA UK[2] (Wright, 2015) as well as in Germany as reported by the Central Council of Muslims (Gopalakrishnan, 2015).

Islamophobic incidents directed at Muslims are diversified, and can range from hostile reactions to hate crimes, or even deliberate efforts aimed at preventing Muslims from integrating into mainstream communities (McClintock & LeGendre, 2007). In France, for instance, the implementation of the burkini ban was seen as Islamophobic (Vulliamy, 2016). In Manchester, Naveed Yasin was being racially discriminated against and was called a "terrorist" despite helping to save lives after the May 2017 Manchester Arena bombing (Travis, 2017). A week after the November 2015 Paris attacks, the words "Islam murderers" were found scribbled at a bus stop in a suburban neighbourhood in Singapore (Sim, 2016).

These examples of Islamophobic incidents highlighted the real threat of Islamophobia in creating divisions between different communities, where such divisions may generate a "Us versus Them" mentality[3] between the non-Muslims and Muslims. Having such a mentality may lead to discrimination and intolerance, ultimately fuelling further conflict between the two communities. This has been observed in countries such as the United Kingdom and France, where Muslims migrants were seen as being unable to assimilate into Western societies (Strabac *et al.*, 2014).

What is Islamophobia?

The Runnymede Trust (1997) defined Islamophobia as "the dread, hatred, and hostility towards Islam and Muslims perpetrated by a series of closed views that imply and attribute negative and

[2]TellMAMA UK is a Britain-based non-governmental organisation (NGO) that tracks hate crimes against Muslims.

[3]The "Us versus Them" mentality refers to how people come to see themselves as members of a group (i.e., the in-group) in comparison with another group (i.e., the out-group) (McLeod, 2008; Stets & Burke, 2000; Turner *et al.*, 1987).

derogatory stereotypes and beliefs to Muslims". These closed views included seeing Islam as a religion that does not integrate well into the Western society, which can lead to the creation of divisions between Muslims and the rest of the Western society. Throughout the years, the definition provided by the Runnymede Report has expanded, and Islamophobia[4] can now be broadly defined in two ways: (i) an irrational fear of Islam and Muslims (Gottschalk & Greenberg, 2008) and (ii) anti-Muslim hostility and negative stereotypes (Halliday, 1999). With the perception that Islam is different from other cultures and religions, individuals may develop a sense of fear — or Islamophobia — towards Islam and Muslims, possibly eventually distancing themselves or discriminate against Muslims. In fact, as opposed to other cultures and religions, Wilkins-Laflamme (2018) reported that Islam is perceived to be:

1. separated from the society;
2. a religion with no values in common with Westerners and is not influenced by Western culture in any way;
3. a violent religion and political ideology, where Muslims are religious radicals or fanatics;
4. a religion that is traditionalist and mistreats women.

In this chapter, the above-mentioned definition was adopted because it helps to explain the occurrence of Islamophobic incidents happening in the world today.

Five Key Points to Know About Islamophobia

To facilitate a better understanding of Islamophobia and its consequences, this chapter has highlighted five key points.

[4]There are some definitions of Islamophobia: (1) Abbas (2004) defined it as fear or dread of Islam or Muslims, (2) Zuquete (2008) defined Islamophobia as the widespread mindset and fear in which people make blanket judgments of Islam as the enemy, and that it is the subject of hostility from the Western society, and (3) Islam is seen to have few or no similarities with other cultures in terms of shared concepts and moral values (The Runnymede Trust, 1997).

Negative Media Portrayal Contributing to the Misconceptions of Muslims and Islam

One of the ways that the general public can develop misconceptions about the Muslim community is through the media, where Islam and Muslims are portrayed as fundamentalist and violent, and that they perpetrate acts of terrorism (Akbarzadeh & Smith, 2005). For example, the Times magazine published a photograph of Muslims soldiers performing their prayers with guns and had captioned it as "Guns and prayer go together in the fundamentalist battle" (Haque & Hossain, n.d.). However, the magazine failed to report that the Muslim soldiers were in actuality praying on a battlefield in Afghanistan, with which the lack of explanation of the picture's context can fuel current public opinion of Islam as a religion of violence.

Lack of Contact Between Muslims and Non-Muslims

Other than being portrayed negatively by the media, the lack of contact between Muslims and non-Muslims might lead to a situation whereby negative stereotypes and fear can fester (Ata *et al.*, 2009). For example, the districts of British cities such as Slough, Birmingham, and Bradford are becoming racially segregated as white populations are moving out and ethnic minorities are moving into those districts. The segregation drew divisions in areas such as education, employment, places of worship, language, as well as networks which do not encourage any meaningful contact between the different communities (Cantle *et al.*, 2016). The segregation also encourages communities to lead parallel lives with little or no contact with other communities (Pidd & Halliday, 2015). The little or no contact with other communities, coupled with news coverage of Muslims as terrorists, may result in the fostering of negative stereotypes.

Tendency for Victims of Islamophobia to not Report

Evidence from the British Crime Survey suggested that over 50% of hate crime incidents tend to go unreported (Flatley *et al.*, 2010).

Victims were not likely to report due to various factors such as believing that no action will be taken if they report such incidents, mistrust or fear of the police, fear of retaliation, lack of knowledge of hate crime laws, feeling shameful, denial, and fear of disclosing their ethnic, religious, or political affiliation (OSCE, 2009). Consequently, these victims may not get access to the assistance that they need.

"Hotspots" of Islamophobic Incidents

Knowing where Islamophobic incidents happen frequently can help authorities and community leaders implement interventions to keep the affected communities safe. These hotspots — both online and offline — can be identified by tracking the frequencies and locations of Islamophobic incidents, especially those that occurred after an attack. In the online sphere, hashtags were created to attract like-minded individuals and promote anti-Muslim sentiments. After the Charlie Hebdo attacks, for example, the #KillAllMuslims hashtag was used to reinforce provocative and racists comments towards Muslims and Islam (Awan & Zempi, 2015). Hotspots for Islamophobic incidents in the offline sphere included locations such as mosques and Muslim faith-based establishments (Bajekal, 2015). This was indeed seen in the aftermath of the Charlie Hebdo attacks, where armed guards were stationed outside several mosques across France (Stone, 2015).

Understanding the Motivations for Committing Islamophobic Incidents

Individuals who committed Islamophobic incidents may be motivated by various factors. By understanding these motivations that drive the desire to commit Islamophobic incidents, it can help guide law enforcement practitioners or policymakers in the implementation of strategies against Islamophobia. Currently, however, there is a lack of research that directly outlines the motivations for committing such incidents. Instead, previous research tends to examine motivations for committing hate crimes.

Levin and McDevitt (1993) argued that hate crime offenders could be divided into three major categories based on the motivations of such offenders. The three primary motivations were offenders who either commit their crimes for the sense of thrill, saw themselves as defenders of their turfs, or whose life's mission was to eliminate groups they saw as evil or inferior (Levin & McDevitt, 1993). Following Levin and McDevitt's research, McDevitt *et al.* (2002) analysed 169 hate crime cases which led to the identification of four main motivations: (i) thrill seeking, (ii) defenders of their turfs, (iii) mission offenders, and (iv) retaliatory.

Firstly, the main goal of the thrill-seeking individual is to seek excitement by attacking or discriminating a particular victim because of his or her identity (Walters *et al.*, 2016). Secondly, individuals will defend against certain groups that are being seen as a threat or invading their territory (Gadd *et al.*, 2005). Thirdly, Islamophobic individuals who make it their mission in life to cleanse the world of Muslims. These individuals are often members of anti-Muslim groups who organise protest and attacks against Muslims (Dunbar *et al.*, 2005). Lastly, individuals who feel that their group is directly under attack by another group may retaliate by committing hate incidents (Walters *et al.*, 2016). This can be seen in the aftermath of September 11 attacks, where there were retaliatory attacks towards Muslims. In order to further understand these motivations, one of the methods is to interview individuals with anti-Muslim sentiments, which can abet in learning and understanding more about them. During these interviews, details to look out for in order to understand their behaviours and motivations are the way these individuals speak, any slangs or slurs that they use, any display of any anti-Muslim ideologies, and how they express anti-Muslim sentiments online (McDevitt *et al.*, 2002).

Five Strategies to Manage the Effects of Islamophobia on Social Cohesion

In order to manage the effects of Islamophobia on social cohesion, the chapter also proposes five strategies, as explained in the following section.

Ground-up Public Education

To combat the misconceptions about Islam as portrayed in the media, educating the general public about Islam and the misconceptions would be useful. This can be done by encouraging civil society organisations[5] (CSOs) to actively disseminate information, organise awareness raising programs for the public, and improve relations between different communities through social events (Singam, 2015). As CSOs work with various communities, they have a wider network to reach out and educate the public about the misconceptions of Islam. For example, the Centre for Islamic Studies, a CSO in Sri Lanka, organised an "Open Mosque Day" to promote a greater understanding of Islam and diversity amongst non-Muslim and Muslim communities (Dipananda, 2017). The first public "Open Mosque Day" in Sri Lanka was held on 26 March 2017 and 100 participants attended. After the event, several participants who were Buddhist and Catholics commented that they had wrong ideas about Muslim customs on women and marriage. However, the visit to the mosque and engaging with the guides during the tour helped participants understand Islam better (Perera, 2017). The feedback and the number of participants indicate the need for the Centre for Islamic Studies' to continue its effort in providing people of various faiths opportunities to understand Islam better (Perera, 2017). These events should be held periodically to foster better relations and continue to educate people regarding misconceptions about Islam.

Increasing Contact Between Muslims and Non-Muslims

A research study with 916 participating students from 19 schools in Australia was conducted to examine attitudes towards Muslims and Islam, and its findings suggested that by having a Muslim friend or regular contact with a Muslim helps to reduce prejudice towards Muslims in general (Ata *et al.*, 2009). The results from the study are

---

[5]CSOs are organisations within the civil society that can come in many forms such as NGOs, faith-based organisations and community-based organisations (Moeti, 2012). They may also contribute to public policy, democratic practice, and effective governance (Singam, 2015).

consistent with previous literature which indicates that having direct intergroup contact is associated with improved attitudes towards the out-group (Pettigrew & Troop, 2006). Allport's (1954) intergroup contact theory argued that the prejudice-reducing effects of contact with specific members tend to generalise to the out-group as a whole, therefore impacting on intergroup relations. This hypothesis was further supported by a meta-analysis of 515 studies which involved a quarter of a million participants in 38 nations. The results showed that 94% of these studies support the statement that greater intergroup contact is associated with lower levels of intergroup prejudice (Pettigrew & Troop, 2006). This can be seen in the example of 'A Seat at the Table', a programme organised by the Faith and Culture Center in Nashville to encourage both Christians and Muslims to host small dinners and invite others of various faiths to attend (Hall, 2015). The success of the program can be seen in the example of Mark Saline, a participant of the A Seat at the Table program, who did not have any Muslim friends prior to the program and, with the program, Saline has gained two Muslim friends and learnt more about the religion and its culture (Hall, 2015). Furthermore, maintaining these positive relationships over time might help to reduce the occurrence of prejudices or discriminatory behaviours towards a particular group (Kieffer, 2016). For example, religious and community leaders may encourage religious congregations to come together through social events to maintain these relationships. These social events provide a platform for people of different faiths to come together and learn more about each other's culture (Wilson, 2015). In Singapore, the establishment of the Harmony Centre[6] provides an avenue for people of different faiths to visit and understand more about Islam. It includes having mosque open houses and collaborative initiatives between mosques, grassroots, and community organisations such as the Harmony

---

[6]The Harmony Centre is an integrated hub to promote greater understanding and engagement of all faith communities. It also aims to bring a greater understanding of Islam and Muslims amongst the multiracial and multireligious society of Singapore.

Games, which is an annual community effort to strengthen ties among Singaporeans of various backgrounds (Kiran, 2017).

Encourage the Reporting of Islamophobic Incidents

By encouraging both the victims and witnesses to report Islamophobic incidents, assistance may be rendered to the victims and other interventions can be put in place by relevant authorities to manage these incidents. Based on the factors identified for the lack of reporting, educating the public about the process of reporting and handling by the relevant authorities of hate crimes may help in encouraging victims to take the first step in reporting. This can be seen in the example of the Metropolitan Police in the United Kingdom whereby they have dedicated information online on reporting hate crimes. The information includes the different reporting platforms, useful links which may render assistance to the victims, and how the authorities will handle the case once it is reported ("How to report hate crime", 2018). In the event that the victims mistrust or fear the police, non-governmental organisations (NGOs) can help by encouraging the victims to report to them so that relevant assistance can be rendered. For example, the Council on American–Islamic Relations (CAIR) developed a mobile app that allow users to report if they are victims of, or if they witness any Islamophobic incident. Users would be required to fill in the details of the Islamophobic incident which will be investigated by the CAIR staff (Alkousaa, 2017). Other than being a reporting platform, the app serves as an online resource hub whereby users can get information about one's civil rights, receive notifications if there is a crisis in the community (e.g., terror attack), and assistance for those who are victims of an Islamophobic incident (Alkousaa, 2017). By having such resources provided by both relevant authorities and NGOs, it may encourage victims to come forward to report hate crimes.

Managing "Hotspots" of Islamophobic Incidents

Knowing where the "hotspots" of Islamophobic incidents can help authorities and community leaders in managing these incidents.

In the online sphere, social media platforms can be used to combat these anti-Muslim sentiments by directly engaging users who are espousing these sentiments or educating them about Islam by using hashtags. Through the use of hashtags, individuals espousing anti-Muslim sentiments can be engaged directly, creating an opportunity to engage them in a deeper discussion regarding their sentiments. In the long run, having these conversations online may help individuals with anti-Muslim sentiments to understand and be educated about Islam and Muslims. Furthermore, tracking the individuals with anti-Muslim sentiments can help authorities to understand the network that propagate such sentiments. Messages that promote unity and the importance of racial and religious harmony may be directed towards such networks to help reduce anti-Muslim sentiments and maintain cohesion in the society which is needed during and after a violent extremist attack. In the offline "hotspots", security measures such as increasing the presence of police patrols around these areas can be implemented to keep the Muslim communities safe and prevent more Islamophobic incidents from happening. Additionally, implementing security protocols in these establishments in the event of an Islamophobic incident may help in managing these incidents. The security protocol may guide the staff on what to do — i.e., what to look out for regarding Islamophobic incidents, which relevant authorities to report to, what information has to be communicated to the Muslims and the general public. By doing so, it may help in minimising the impact of the incident on the Muslim community, allowing the establishment to gain control of the situation, and aiding both the establishment and Muslims in the process of recovery.

Knowing the Motivations for Committing Islamophobic Incidents to Prevent Future Islamophobic Incidents

As there is limited research on understanding the motivations behind Islamophobic incidents and their implications, this chapter hopes to encourage more in-depth research in this area. By knowing the different motivations for committing Islamophobic incidents, authorities can better understand Islamophobic incidents and the perpetrators. For example, if the Islamophobic incident was committed by an offender who was defending his/her territory, he would target specific victims and justify their crimes as essential in order to keep these threats at bay (Burke, 2017). This can be seen in the event whereby a Muslim family moves into a predominately white neighbourhood and the offender might feel that his territory might be threatened by this. With a better understanding of the motivations underlying Islamophobia, authorities and community leaders can employ strategies to foster better relations between the victims and other members of the community.

Conclusion

Knowing these points highlighted in this chapter can help to better understand Islamophobia and its effects on social cohesion, and five strategies have been proposed in this chapter to counter these effects. However, it is important to note that these five strategies are not exhaustive and there is a need to update these strategies when the trends of Islamophobia change.

Acknowledgement

The views expressed in this chapter are the author's only and do not represent the official position or view of the Ministry of Home Affairs, Singapore.

References

Abbas, T. (2004). After 9/11: British South Asian Muslims, Islamophobia, multiculturalism, and the state. *American Journal of Islamic Social Sciences*, *21*(3), 26–38.

Abdelkader, E. (2016). When Islamophobia turns violent: The 2016 U.S presidential elections. Retrieved from http://bridge.georgetown.edu/wp-content/uploads/2016/05/When-Islamophobia-Turns-Violent.pdf.

Akbarzadeh, D. S. & Smith, D. B. (2005). The representation of Islam and Muslims in the media. *The age and Herald Sun Newspapers*. Retrieved from http://www.academia.edu/8645594/The_Representation_of_Islam_and_Muslims_in_the_Media.

Alkousaa, R. (2017). U.S. Muslim group launches cellphone app to report hate crimes. *Reuters*. Retrieved from https://www.reuters.com/article/us-usa-islam-technology/u-s-muslim-group-launches-cellphone-app-to-report-hate-crimes-idUSKBN19E2E4.

Allport, G. W. (1954). *The Nature of Prejudice*. Cambridge, MA: Addison-Wesley Publishing Company.

Almasy, S., Mellhan, P., & Bittermann, J. (2015). Paris massacre: At least 128 die in attacks. Retrieved from http://edition.cnn.com/2015/11/13/world/paris-shooting/.

Ata, A., Bastian, B., & Lusher, D. (2009). Intergroup contact in context: The mediating role of social norms and group-based perceptions on the contact-prejudice link. *International Journal of Intercultural Relations*, *33*(6), 498–506.

Awan, I. & Zempi, I. (2015). We fear for our lives: Offline and online experiences of anti-Muslim hostility. Retrieved from https://www.tellmamauk.org/wp-content/uploads/resources/We%20Fear%20For%20Our%20Lives.pdf.

Bajekal, N. (2015). Mosques attacked in France following Charlie Hebdo attack. *Time*. Retrieved from http://time.com/3659177/attacks-mosques-charlie-hebdo/.

Burke, D. (2017). The four reasons people commit hate crimes. Retrieved from https://edition.cnn.com/2017/06/02/us/who-commits-hate-crimes/index.html.

Cantle, T., Rowe, A., Uddin, B., Purkiss, B., Singh, D., Taj, M., Khan, H., Kaur, D., Abberley, B., Hey, D., & Ali, A. (2016). Community cohesion: A report of the independent review team. Retrieved from tedcantle.co.uk/pdf/communitycohesion%20cantlereport.pdf

Dipananda, B. D. (2017). Sri Lanka's centre for Islamic studies hosts open mosque day. *Buddhistdoor Global*. Retrieved from https://www.buddhistdoor.net/news/sri-lankars-centre-for-islamic-studies-hosts-open-mosque-day.

Dunbar, E., Quinones, J., & Crevecoeur, D. A. (2005). Assessment of hate crime perpetrators: The role of bias intent in examining violence risk. *Journal of Forensic Psychology Practice*, *5*(1), 1–19.

Flatley, J., Kershaw, C., Smith, K., Chaplin, R., & Moon, D. (2010). Crime in England and Wales 2009/10. Retrieved from https://www.gov.uk/government/uploads/system/uploads/attachment_data/file/116347/hosb1210.pdf.

Gadd, D., Dixon, B., & Jefferson, T. (2005). Why did they do it? Racial harassment in North Staffordshire. Retrieved from https://www.escholar.manchester.ac.uk/api/datastream?publicationPid=uk-ac-man-scw:122961&datastreamId=FULL-TEXT.PDF.

Gopalakrishnan, M. (2015). Attacks against Muslims on the rise after Paris strikes. *DW News*. Retrieved from http://www.dw.com/en/attacks-against-muslims-on-the-rise-after-paris-strikes/a-18878424.

Gottschalk, P., & Greenberg, G. (2008). *Islamophobia: Making Muslims the Enemy*. New York: Rowman & Littlefield.

Hall, H. (2015). Area Christians, Muslims come together as survey confirms divide. *Tennessean*. Retrieved from https://www.tennessean.com/story/news/2015/06/26/area-christians-muslims-come-together-survey-confirms-divide/29330965/.

Halliday, F. (1999). Islamophobia reconsidered. *Ethnic and Racial Studies*, *22*(5), 892–901.

Haque, F., & Hossain, M. K. (n.d.). Global media, Islamophobia, and its impact on conflict resolution. Retrieved from http://ihmsaw.org/resourcefiles/1260034024.pdf.

How to report hate crime (2018). *Metropolitan Police*. Retrieved from https://www.met.police.uk/advice-and-information/hate-crime/how-to-report-hate-crime/.

Kieffer, P. (2016). Faiths come together to combat Islamophobia through awareness and discussion in Wayzata. *Sun Sailor*. Retrieved from http://sailor.mnsun.com/2016/02/10/faiths-come-together-to-combat-islamophobia-through-awareness-and-discussion-in-wayzata/.

Kiran, S. (2017). Harmony Games: Minister stresses on religious harmony in Singapore. *IB Times*. Retrieved from http://www.ibtimes.sg/harmony-games-minister-stresses-religious-harmony-singapore-12942.

Levin, J., & McDevitt, J. (1993). *Hate Crimes: The Rising Tide of Bigotry and Bloodshed*. New York: Plenum.

McClintock, M., & LeGendre, P. (2007). Islamophobia: 2007 hate crime survey. Retrieved from https://www.humanrightsfirst.org/wp-content/uploads/pdf/07601-discrim-hc-islamophobia-web.pdf.

McDevitt, J., Levin, J., & Bennett, S. (2002). Hate crime perpetrators: An expanded typology. *Journal of Social Issues*, *58*(2), 303–317.

McLeod, S. A. (2008). Social identity theory. Retrieved from http://www.simplypsychology.org/social-identity-theory.html.

Moeti, K. (2012). Understanding the differences between civil society and civil society organisations. Retrieved from http://www.ngopulse.org/

blogs/understanding-differences-between-civil-society-and-civil-society-organisations.

OSCE (2009). Preventing and responding to hate crimes: A resource guide for NGOs in the OSCE region. Retrieved from http://www.osce.org/odihr/39821?download=true.

Perera, M. M. (2017). 'Open Mosque Day' in Colombo to bridge gap between Muslims and others. *Asia News*. Retrieved from http://www.asianews.it/news-en/'Open-Mosque-Day'-in-Colombo-to-bridge-gap-between-Muslims-and-others-41812.html.

Pettigrew, T. F., & Troop, L. R. (2006). A meta-analytic test of intergroup contact theory. *Journal of Personality and Social Psychology*, *90*, 751–786.

Pidd, H., & Halliday, J. (2015). One city, two cultures: Bradford's communities lead parallel lives. *The Guardian*. Retrieved from https://www.theguardian.com/uk-news/2015/jun/19/bradford-one-city-two-cultures-communities-lead-parallel-lives.

Stets, J. E., & Burke, P. J. (2000). Identity theory and social identity theory. *Social Psychology Quarterly*, *63*(3), 224–237.

Sim, W. (2016). Collective effort needed to safeguard racial, religious harmony in Singapore: Shanmugam. *Straits Times*. Retrieved from http://www.straitstimes.com/singapore/collective-effort-needed-to-safeguard-racial-religious-harmony-in-singapore-shanmugam.

Singam, C. (2015). Your say: Singapore civil society is a work in progress. *Yahoo News*. Retrieved from https://sg.news.yahoo./singapore-civil-society---a-work-in-progress--thoughts-on-saa-2015-053854341.html.

Stone, J. (2015). Firebombs and pigs heads thrown into mosques as anti-Muslim attacks increase after Paris shootings. *Independent*. Retrieved from http://www.independent.co.uk/news/world/europe/firebombs-and-pigs-heads-thrown-into-mosques-as-anti-muslim-attacks-increase-after-paris-shootings-9977423.html.

Strabac, Z., Aalberg, T., & Marko, V. (2014). Attitudes towards Muslim Immigrants: Evidence from survey experiments across four countries. *Journal of Ethnic and Migration Studies*, *40*(1), 343–354.

The Runnymede Trust. (1997). *Islamophobia: A challenge for us all*. Retrieved from https://www.runnymedetrust.org/companies/17/74/Islamophobia-A-Challenge-for-Us-All.html.

Travis, A. (2017). Anti-Muslim hate crime surges after Manchester and London Bridge attacks. *The Guardian*. Retrieved from https://www.

theguardian.com/society/2017/jun/20/anti-muslim-hate-surges-after-manchester-and-london-bridge-attacks.

Turner, J. C., Hogg, M.A, Oakes, P.K, Reicher, S.D., & Wetherell, M.S. (1987). *Rediscovering the Social Group: A Self-Categorization Theory.* New York: Basil Blackwell.

Vulliamy, E. (2016). They want us to be invisible: How the ban on burkinis is dividing the Cote d'Azur'. *The Guardian.* Retrieved from https://www.theguardian.com/world/2016/aug/20/burkini-ban-cote-d-azur-spreads-france-divide.

Walters, M. A., Brown, R., & Wiedlitzka, S. (2016). Causes and motivations of hate crime. Retrieved from https://www.equalityhumanrights.com/sites/default/files/research-report-102-causes-and-motivations-of-hate-crime.pdf.

Wilkins-Laflamme, S. (2018). Islamophobia in Canada: Measuring the realities of negative attitudes toward Muslims and religious discrimination. *Canadian Review of Sociology, 55*(1), 86–110.

Wilson, L. (2015). What I discovered from interviewing imprisoned ISIS fighters. *The Nation.* Retrieved from https://www.thenation.com/article/what-i-discovered-from-interviewing-isis-prisoners/.

Wright, O. (2015). Paris attacks: Women targeted as hate crimes against British Muslims soars following terrorist atrocity. *Independent.* Retrieved from http://www.independent.co.uk/news/uk/home-news/paris-attacks-british-muslims-face-300-spike-in-racial-attacks-in-week-following-terror-a6744376.html.

Zuquete, J. P. (2008). The European extreme-right and Islam: New directions. *Journal of Political Ideologies, 13*(3), 321–344.

CPSIA information can be obtained
at www.ICGtesting.com
Printed in the USA
BVHW080326040119
536871BV00005B/10/P

9 789813 275430